This volume has emerged from a collaboration among:

The NWO Research Council for the Humanities (GW),
The NWO Research Council for Social Sciences (MaGW), and
The Netherlands Foundation for the Advancement of Tropical Research (WOTRO).

Netherlands Organisation for Scientific Research

THE FUTURE OF THE RELIGIOUS PAST

Hent de Vries, General Editor

In what sense are the legacies of religion—its powers, words, things, and gestures—disarticulating and reconstellating themselves as the elementary forms of life in the twenty-first century? This sequence of five volumes publishes work drawn from an international research project that seeks to answer this question.

Things

RELIGION AND THE QUESTION OF MATERIALITY

Edited by **DICK HOUTMAN**

and **BIRGIT MEYER**

FORDHAM UNIVERSITY PRESS   NEW YORK   2012

Fordham University Press has no responsibility for the persistence or accuracy of URLs for external or third-party Internet websites referred to in this publication and does not guarantee that any content on such websites is, or will remain, accurate or appropriate.

Fordham University Press also publishes its books in a variety of electronic formats. Some content that appears in print may not be available in electronic books.

Library of Congress Cataloging-in-Publication Data is available from the publisher.

Printed in the United States of America
15 14 13   5 4 3 2 1
First edition

Contents

Illustrations

Frontispiece, illustration facing p. 1, and illustrations on opening pages for Parts II and IV: courtesy of Neil Hertz.

Illustration opening Part I: courtesy of Anna Niedźwiedź.

Illustrations opening Parts III and VI: courtesy of Birgit Meyer.

Illustration opening Part V: courtesy of Jojada Verrips.

Preface

This book has grown out of the international conference Things: Material Religion and the Topography of Divine Spaces, organized in Amsterdam on June 11 and 12, 2007, on behalf of the research program The Future of the Religious Past, funded by the Netherlands Organization for Scientific Research (NWO). Most of the contributions are based on papers presented during the conference, but we have added a number of essays to enable an even richer and more profound discussion of the topic than the conference already allowed. This topic is the relationship between religion and materiality: more specifically, the flawed notion that the relation between religion and "things" is inherently antagonistic. This notion, which has long informed the modern study of religion, has recently begun to be questioned, giving rise to a timely turn to matter and materiality in the humanities and social sciences. Religion cannot persist, let alone thrive, without the material things that serve to make it present—visible and tangible—in the world. The image of the Basilica of the Sacred Heart of Paris—Sacré Coeur, built as an embodiment of a conservative moral order in the aftermath of the Commune—on the cover of this book powerfully evokes the politico-religious use of material registers.

Even a simple comparison of our own disciplines, sociology (Houtman) and cultural anthropology (Meyer), suffices to reveal that this material turn is, nonetheless, not occurring everywhere equally. Whereas anthropology of religion is one of the major driving forces behind it, sociology of religion has remained by and large untouched until the present day. One can even argue that sociology has moved in precisely the opposite direction, becoming increasingly interested in "interior" aspects of religion that it had traditionally neglected. Due to this change in perspective, sociology's long-standing focus on religion's "external" institutional manifestations (the churches, in particular), an emphasis Thomas Luckmann influentially critiqued as early as the 1960s, is now waning, with attention shifting from "religious belonging" to "religious believing," from "churched religion" to "unchurched spirituality," and from "religious belief" to "religious experience."

Nonetheless, in most other academic fields, matter and materiality are now increasingly given their due, and the antagonism between spirit and matter is no longer simply taken for granted. We hope that this book will contribute to further unsettling this modern divide. We owe a well-deserved word of thanks to Marry Kooy, who has assisted us in a wonderfully accurate, careful, and cheerful manner throughout this book project. Without her help, the process would have taken us much longer and would have been much less smooth, too. We are also grateful to Helen Tartar, of Fordham University Press, whose experience as a humanities editor has been very helpful in making decisions about the book's composition and no less vital in the final editing of the individual contributions. It has been a privilege and a pleasure to work with her.

Dick Houtman and Birgit Meyer
Rotterdam and Berlin/Amsterdam
August 2011

Things

Introduction

Material Religion—How Things Matter

Birgit Meyer and Dick Houtman

This volume addresses the relation between religion and things. That relation has long been conceived in antagonistic terms, as if things could not matter for religion in any fundamental way. This antagonism resonates with a set of related oppositions that privilege spirit above matter, belief above ritual, content above form, mind above body, and inward contemplation above "mere" outward action, producing an understanding of religion in terms, basically, of an interior spiritual experience. And indeed, wasn't the opposition between spirituality and materiality the defining characteristic of religion, understood as geared to a transcendental "beyond" that was "immaterial" by definition? Grounded in the rise of religion as a modern category, with Protestantism as its main exponent, this conceptualization entails the devaluation of religious material culture—and materiality at large—as lacking serious empirical, let alone theoretical interest.

This stance has long informed the study of religion, yielding a focus on beliefs and questions of meaning as privileged domains of inquiry. Although it has been challenged in recent decades, it still lingers on in everyday parlance about religion in Western societies. Believers and (atheist) opponents alike speak of spirit and matter as being mutually exclusive. They hold true and sincere religiosity to be decidedly "anti-materialist" and, by the same token, "interior" and "spiritual." The current fascination with spirituality and New Age expresses a search for this kind of religiosity, while more outward-oriented, ritualistic religions are branded as inferior, superficial, or even insincere.[1] In turn, atheist critics mobilize materialism—referring, for instance, to evolutionary biology—in their crusades against religion, arguing that matter is all there is.[2] Both positions are two sides of the same coin: the presumed antagonism of religion and materiality.

Echoing post-Enlightenment debates in Northern Europe about religion in relation to matter and materialism, the antagonism between religion and things, spirituality and materiality, is a legacy of the "religious past" that demands our careful attention. This antagonism is sustained by a definition, largely taken for granted, of religion as a system of, to invoke E. B. Tylor's famous phrasing, "belief in spiritual beings."[3] Over the past twenty years, a sustained critique of "belief" as the guiding concept in the study of religion has evolved, on the grounds that this privileges a concern with interiority, meaning, and consciousness—with the mind, coded as "immaterial"—at the expense of issues of power, practice, and materiality, making us blind to how religion appears and becomes tangible in the world. Many scholars now agree that "belief" is part and parcel of a typically Protestant and hence historically situated religiosity (see Peter Pels and Matthew Engelke in this volume),[4] but they inherit a discipline that universalized "belief" at the core of the notion of "world religions," founding and enabling the comparative study of religion in the nineteenth century.[5] However, as Donald Lopez puts it succinctly: "Belief appears as a universal category because of the universalist claims of the tradition in which it was most central, Christianity."[6] Instead of being a universal disposition that, as it were, naturally forms the defining characteristic of religion, "belief" has been "universalized" through scientific, religious, and political practices, such as evolutionary schemes, Christian missionization, and colonial governance.

Far from operating as a politically neutral concept, "belief" has been shown to resonate with a broader secularist idea of religion as interiorized and private, according to which religion is ideally located outside of the public sphere.[7] In recent years, in Europe and beyond, the secularist truce that kept (Christian) religion more or less out of the public sphere has been broken. In part because of transnational migration, Western societies have become more culturally and religiously diverse. The rise of "political Islam," in particular, has sparked heated debates among scholars and in society generally about the place and role of religion in our "post-secular" time.[8] Intriguingly, these debates often are about the (vexing) public presence of "things"—such as headscarves or mosques—that are felt to erode the supposed neutrality of the public sphere (as Annelies Moors argues in this volume). As Michiel Leezenberg shows in his essay, a public sphere of this kind is usually attributed exclusively to the West, thereby ignoring the rise of such secular public spheres for literary and political discussion as the early modern Ottoman coffee-house. Indeed, debates about the shape of the public sphere often assume as a normative requirement that the private interior of individual subjectivity is the proper location for modern religiosity, revealing that "belief" is a powerful notion at the core of secularism. Precisely for that reason, it is problematic as a scholarly concept. Conversely, the concern with religious "things" that are perceived as disturbing reveals the gap between normative understandings of belief as interior and the actual material presence and tangibility of religion.

In short, the critique and rejection of "belief" or, more broadly, an interior spiritualized religiosity as a guiding scholarly concept raises major issues for the study of religion at large, which we have only begun to explore. How are we to approach, study, and speak about religion in new, critical ways, from a position beyond worn-out concepts such as "belief"?

Moving beyond "belief" as a guiding concept does not mean abandoning any interest in interior, spiritualized religiosity, such as Protestant faith, New Age spirituality, or Buddhist contemplation as an object of study. On the contrary, the point is to examine, as David Morgan puts it, "the conditions that shape the feelings, senses, spaces, and performances of belief, that is, the material coordinates or forms of religious practice."[9] Given that conceptualization itself is historically situated and political, shaping and shaped by debates about and policies concerning religion,[10] we must be alert to the politics of the use of religious concepts and of concepts of religion, in the past and the present. Although we agree on the need to question the universal definability of religion, we find it necessary to resist one possible consequence of this endeavor: the dissolution and rejection of the term *religion*. As a legacy from the past, religion is with us as a "second-order" term that features in scholarly and public debates and that needs to be addressed rather than simply abandoned. As the expression "the future of the religious past," the title of the research program on which this volume is based, indicates, we approach religion as being historically constituted—religion "as we know it"—and at the same time as hinting at something we have yet to know.

In the inaugural volume of the book series The Future of the Religious Past,[11] Hent de Vries calls for a "deeply pragmatic" attitude that, at least for the time being, would suspend the conceptualization of religion on a general level: "Speaking of 'Religion: Beyond a Concept' might simply mean that a concept or set of concepts is *not yet* available for its phenomenon, for its set(s) of phenomena, and hence stands in need of being invented or reinvented, created or revived, coined or rearticulated."[12] As the terms for the study of religion "stand in need of constant redescription and rethinking,"[13] de Vries's invocation of the "not yet" does not, in our view, betray a striving for a final, universal concept of religion but rather expresses a productive tension between conceptualization and empirical study that exists "ad infinitum." "Religion," here, is a negative category, not definable as something we already know but instead remaining elusive, resisting conceptualization yet present as a kind of "extra" in the ordinary, tangible world. Instead of starting out from one or another concept, de Vries calls for a "bottom-up" approach that would take "the singular" or "the particular" as a methodological entry point into the study of religion:

Words, things, gestures and powers—like sounds, silences, smells, touches, shapes, colors, affects, and effects—might be seen as instances and instantiations of the "everyday," of the "extraordinariness of the ordinary," of the "ordinariness of the extraordinary," of the "common," the "low." . . . They are the visible and tangible, the living and enabling conditions of "the religious," just as they typify its supposed counterpart, "the secular," including all the varieties of modern experience in between.[14]

Religion, in this understanding, mobilizes a sense of a "beyond" that is impossible to capture fully via any concept or definition—a sphere of possibilities, rather than a fixed subject matter or, to invoke Mattijs van de Port's felicitous phrasing—"the rest of what is."[15] Whether in invoking this "beyond" we are indebted to Protestant theology and its notion of God as wholly Other, and thus smuggling a typically Christian understanding into our inquiries,[16] is a question open for further debate. De Vries's basic idea, that we can "know" religion only, though not completely, through its past and present manifestations, opens up a fruitful potential for dialogue across the social sciences, humanities, religious studies, and theology. His call to explore the particular forms and elements through which "religion" is instantiated—or, as we would put it, *materializes*—in the world as part of a pragmatic approach of religion, understood to be as yet unknown, situates us well beyond the positions of either metaphysics or empiricism, as well as related dualisms such as idealism versus materialism. Our volume takes this approach as its starting point.

Religion and the Question of Materiality

Things are one of the "singulars"—together with powers, gestures, and words—used as nodes to crystallize our research program.[17] This interest in "things" echoes the current concern with materiality in the study of religion that, in turn, has been stimulated by broader debates in the aftermath of the "material turn."

Materiality has become an almost magical term in current scholarship in the social sciences and humanities. In German, the term *materiality* can be further unfolded as *Stofflichkeit* ("substantiality"), *Dinglichkeit* ("thingliness"), *Körperlichkeit* ("bodiliness"), and *Wesentlichkeit* (referring to what is essential, substantial, important). In one way or another, championing materiality signals the need to pay urgent attention to a real, material world of objects and a texture of lived, embodied experience. The importance of doing so is often stressed by invoking "matter" as a substantive (as in "the *matter* of belief"[18]) or as a verb (as in the subtitle of our Introduction, "How Things *Matter*"). And yet a gap exists between the promise of concreteness that makes the turn to "things" and the notion of "materiality" appear so attractive, on the one hand, and our still rather meager understanding of and lack of agreement about what we mean by "matter" and "materiality," on the other.[19]

4

This unclarity stems from the fact that "matter" itself, though hinting at the existence of a prediscursive, given material "something" that does not, however, exist in a fixed form, is a historically situated concept. As a concept, matter is part of different conceptual dualisms, from a counter-pole to "form," as in classical Greek philosophy, to the "transcendental," as in German Idealist philosophy; from a counter-pole to "God," as in Christian theology, to "Spirit" and "spirits," in Theosophy and modern spiritualism. In other words, matter and materiality are terms that have, as Peter Pels explains in his essay, a "relational character," implying that their meanings change "depending on how the relation is conceptualized." Therefore, rather than offering a shortcut to the tangible and concrete, the terms *matter* and *materiality* invoke complex conceptual issues that run through the entire history of philosophy.

If matter and materiality are—and only make sense as—relational terms that thrive on contrast, what contrasts to matter and materiality are invoked in the framework of the "material turn" that has been manifest in the humanities and social sciences since the mid 1980s? What are those who take the "material turn" *against*? The "material turn" affects a diverse field: its different strands include the reappraisal of material culture in anthropology from a perspective of Marxian dialectical materialism, as proposed by Daniel Miller;[20] critical analysis of the microphysics of power from a Foucauldian perspective; feminist work on "body matters" inspired by Judith Butler;[21] the concern with pictures and other artworks as "bodies" or "things" that act upon beholders, as developed by Hans Belting, David Freedberg, Alfred Gell, and W. J. T. Mitchell;[22] Bruno Latour's "actor-network-theory";[23] or recent work in the neurosciences that unmasks as material what was long held to be immaterial—the mind.[24] Major debates ensue within and between these different strands, particularly with regard to the implications of the argument, made by neuroscientists, that mind *is* matter.[25]

The turn to matter and materiality in the humanities and social sciences came about through a nagging dissatisfaction with approaches that take ideas, concepts, ideologies, or values as immaterial abstractions that are regarded as prime movers of history. Privileging the abstract above the concrete reduces material culture (as well as words and gestures) to expressions of an underlying meaning or to the status of "mere" signs. The current, lingering dissatisfaction with constructivism is particularly important in the call to place materiality at the center of scholarly research. Though an emphasis on constructedness has been important in unmasking essentializing ideologies and the naturalization of categories such as gender and other identities, it implies a misleading sense of fictionality (i.e., the construction is understood as being "made up" and hence interchangeable with other fictions) and even arbitrariness. In this manner, the concrete, tangible nature of construction can be passed over all too easily.[26] As Bruno Latour points out, construction needs to be understood as a more solid endeavor than a conceptual operation that creates "mere" fictions with no material existence.[27] Materiality, Judith Butler argues, is not a primal, given essence but an effect of power that shapes bodies and the material world.

Given that materiality is organized through form, one should focus on how processes of social and political formation *create* a tangible, material world.[28] Therefore, sociocultural constructions should be understood as world-making practices that vest what they construe with an intrinsic power and reality. The world is not "out there" or a point of reference that is represented through signification (as in Saussurian approaches); rather, signification itself achieves its own tangible and concrete reality effects.

In the study of religion, the turn to matter and materiality raises fundamental questions because religion has so long been imagined to stand in radical opposition to matter and materiality, while oriented toward the immaterial. Arising alongside the natural sciences in Europe starting in the seventeenth century, in a process through which theology lost its privileged position in explaining the world, "materialism" circumscribed a stance that was polemical rather than strictly philosophical. Initially used as a dismissive expression for the attitude of those who foolishly denied the existence of God in favor of sheer matter, in the nineteenth century materialism came to express a clearly antireligious position (as, for instance, with Feuerbach). Excluding the possibility of belief in God and the soul, materialism was mobilized against religion, while, in turn, religious worldviews and Christian theology opposed materialism.[29] Although this "vulgar" understanding of materialism is still invoked in debates about the supposed irrationality of religious belief, in philosophy it has long been surpassed by Hegelian dialectics and Marxian dialectical materialism.

In 2000, David Chidester signaled "an emergent horizon for the study of religion that might be called a new materialism."[30] Though he did not state which "old" materialism he had in mind, we take it that he referred to the nineteenth-century attacks on idealist philosophy and theology. By contrast, the "new" materialism is not a critique of religion in the name of sheer matter but rather a critique of the study of religion *from within* that advocates coming to terms with materiality as part of (the study of) religion. The point is not to simply unmask entities such as God, gods, and spirits as fictions but to grasp how practices of religious mediation effect the presence of these entities in the world through bodily sensations, texts, buildings, pictures, objects, and other material forms that involve bodies and things. When Chidester launched the term, he found this "new materialism" to be still largely implicit in scholarly work that explored how religion is implemented in concrete, material domains, such as the body and the senses, objects and exchange relations, or things and spaces.[31] But just a bit later, *materiality* and *material culture* became key terms in the study of religion,[32] generating new empirical questions about how religions shape the world in a concrete manner.

These terms are now prominent in a host of publications,[33] including the interdisciplinary journal *Material Religion* (of which Meyer is a co-editor), launched in 2005. Work in this new field shows that, to invoke a much-used expression, "taking materiality seriously" not only produces empirically rich studies of phenomena that have hitherto been sidelined but above all offers a productive starting point for new approaches to the complex relation between religion and things in the past, at present, and, possibly, in the future. As the editors of *Material Religion* stated recently: "Materializing the study of religion means asking how religion happens materially, which is not to be confused with asking the much less helpful question of how religion is expressed in material form. A materialized study of religion begins with the assumption that things, their use, their valuation, and their appeal are not something added to a religion, but rather inextricable from it."[34]

In the light of the traditional antagonism between religion and things, taking things to be "inextricable" from religion brings us up against an intriguing paradox. Indeed, once one's sensibility to the importance of materiality is awakened, one can only agree that "the idea of religion itself is largely unintelligible outside its incarnation in material expressions," as Elizabeth Arweck and William Keenan put it in one of the first works explicitly devoted to exploring the materiality of religion.[35] Conjoining spirit and matter, "incarnation" (whether understood as "the word become flesh," "transubstantiation," or, in a broader sense, the "icon" or "spirit possession") describes the process through which the "beyond" to which religion refers (call it the transcendental, spiritual, or invisible) is rendered tangible and becomes present in the world. And yet, if material stuff is indispensable—if, as Webb Keane puts it, "ideas must take material form at some stage"[36]—one can only wonder why it is so hard to acknowledge this, so that we need so many efforts—such as running the journal *Material Religion* or assembling a volume entitled *Things*—to (re)materialize the study of religion.

Indeed, despite being inextricable from religion, "things" can be heavily contested. The use of "icons" and other material means in addressing God was a key bone of contention between Catholics and Protestants (especially Calvinists) after the Reformation. The Protestant rejection of sacred objects as "idols" or "fetishes" went along with a heavy emotional investment—Bruno Latour coined the term *iconoclash* to capture this ambiguity—and spread all over the world in the course of missionization.[37] In a similar vein, the role of material objects in bringing about "true" faith has been downplayed. In our time, in an ever more determined quest for immediacy and immateriality, New Age movements, as Stef Aupers shows in his essay, claim to move "beyond belief"— understood as a critique of authorized Christian teachings—toward what they regard as a pure spiritual experience. In other words, "material" and "immaterial" are not *given* categories that echo a commonsense definition of matter and things. Instead, what features as material or immaterial depends on socially shared, authorized discourses or, to invoke Keane's felicitous expression, "semiotic ideologies."

Therefore, to state that religion, including even the most allegedly "immaterial" and even "antimaterialistic" version of New Age spirituality, necessarily involves some degree of materiality can only be the beginning of our inquiries. More is at stake than simply reconciling religion and materiality by directing attention to religious material culture.

The point is to explore how, notwithstanding the indispensability of material means—things, but also images, bodies, and words—for religion to be tangible and present, religion got and gets dematerialized both in religious practice and in the theoretical conceptualization of religion by scholars. Even though the example of charges of idolatry and iconoclasms (see the essays by W. J. T. Mitchell, Birgit Meyer, and Maria José A. de Abreu), the assault by Islamic reform movements on the use of prayer beads (see the essay by José van Santen), or the celebration of New Age spirituality (see the essays by Stef Aupers and Dorien Zandbergen) are about the radical rejection of things, clearly this rejection does not describe an actual process of doing away with materiality. Above all, "dematerialization" refers to a semiotic operation that downplays or overlooks (usually one's own) materiality, placing it in opposition to spirituality and establishing the antagonism between religion and things. In turn, rematerializing the study of religion means that scholars resist taking for granted and uncritically reproducing internal "emic" categories and ideologies as scholarly concepts.

For scholars, moving beyond the antagonism between religion and materiality demands a critical review of how this antagonism has shaped the modern study of religion. While in doing so it is important to explore how scholarly approaches to religion got dematerialized, we need to avoid reinscribing the opposition between spirit (or immateriality) and matter that underpins dematerialized conceptualizations of religion into our intellectual endeavors by simplistically embracing matter. This would leave us trapped in the opposition between religion and materiality and even revive "old" and "vulgar" versions of materialism that have long become obsolete. In other words, shifting from a process of demateralization to rematerialization is not simply a question of bringing "things" back in, but requires a critical, reflexive endeavor that rescripts the meaning of materiality itself on the basis of detailed historical and ethnographic research—indeed, through what de Vries calls a "deeply pragmatic" approach.[38]

Therefore, the key concern of this volume is to place the study of religious material culture within a broader reflection about the conditions under which materiality got sidelined conceptually, both among scholars and in the sphere of religious traditions, as well as to point out the empirical and conceptual possibilities and questions that open up as materiality moves back into the study of religion. Some of our contributors reflect explicitly on how paying close empirical attention to "things" opens up fresh new perspectives, for instance, with regard to Islamic prayer (José van Santen), the Jewish festival of Sukkoth (Galit Hasan-Rokem), or metonymic signs, such as the "blood of Jesus," that have thing-like qualities in the Pentecostal imagination (Miranda Klaver). In a similar vein, Donald Lopez shows how a dematerialized, modern understanding of religion produced an outsiders' description of Buddhism remarkably different from those prior to the eighteenth century. He indicates a shift from written accounts of Buddhism in which "the focus was not on the man or his teachings, but on the thing, the statue, and . . . on the hair" to an increasingly textualized view in which things were marginalized, feeding into current

Western understandings of Buddhism as "immaterial" and "spiritual." The limitations of such a view of Buddhism become apparent in Irene Stengs's essay, in which she explores the power attributed to portraits of King Chulalongkorn in the setting of a popular cult rooted in Theravada Buddhism.

Protestant Legacies

Protestantism is usually regarded as the prototype of modern religion, grounded in the iconoclasm of the Reformation and therefore regarded as distinct from more thing-friendly religious traditions, such as Catholicism. As Max Weber famously argued, Protestantism, with its emphasis on "faith" or "belief," a "methodical way of life" that requires constant self-evaluation, and "innerworldly ascesis," gave birth to modern capitalism.[39] Note the intriguing paradox that exists between the Protestant practice of more or less deliberately overlooking the importance of materiality, with regard to both religious experience and consumption,[40] and the crucial role of the resulting perspective in the rise of consumer capitalism, which cherishes materiality in a historically unprecedented manner. According to Weber, once it was in place, capitalism could do without the "Protestant ethic" that had initially sustained it. He held that modern people are locked in a secular and materialistic "casing of steel," yearning for a new spirituality yet hopelessly mired in a "disenchanted" world. In Weber's scenario, with the evaporation of the "spirit of capitalism," the possibility that any other spirit might take its place disappeared. As it brings about disenchantment, Protestantism itself, as the ultimate modern religion, is thoroughly rationalized. This implies not only the end of religion but, as Stef Aupers points out in his essay, ultimately the end of the possibility for creating meaning: "In a totally 'disenchanted world,' Weber argues, 'the world's processes simply are . . . and happen but no longer signify anything.'[41] Contesting Weber's thesis about the end of religion, Aupers argues that the nihilist limbo in which modern people find themselves generates the New Age, with its self-centered spirituality, emphasis on personal experience, fascination with Wicca, Buddhist mediation, fantasy figures, a techno-spiritual cyber-world, and the like.

As Meyer has recently argued,[42] Max Weber's analysis of Protestantism as a salvation religion that moved beyond reliance on concrete material forms has served as a distorting lens even in the study of Protestantism. In his essay "Religious Rejections of the World and Their Directions," Weber sketches an evolutionary scheme according to which salvation religions—epitomized by Protestantism—are on the highest level.[43] Mentioning key dimensions of religion—artifacts, music, dance, buildings—Weber stresses that religion was the cradle of art. However, he contrasts the synthesis of art and religion, which was dominant throughout most of the history of religion and still characterizes Catholicism, with an alternative, higher religiosity that is severed from art: the "religious ethic of brotherliness" characteristic of salvation religions. Valuing religious bonds with fellow believers

9

higher than blood ties and faith more than earthly pleasures, this ethic endorses a distancing attitude toward the "world." Therefore, Weber argues, "all sublimated religions of salvation have focused on the meaning alone, not upon the form, of the things and actions relevant for salvation. Salvation religions have devalued form as contingent, as something creaturely and distracting from meaning."[44]

Weber's dismissive stance with regard to religious material culture, by contrast to a focus on meaning, is also evident in his essay on the sociology of religion,[45] where he suggests a parallel between the religious devaluation of art and the devaluation of magical, orgiastic, ecstatic, and ritual elements of religiosity in favor of ascetic and spiritual or mystical elements.[46] The higher religion develops, the less it depends on material forms. Obviously this view echoes typically Protestant criticisms of Catholicism and, for that matter, "paganism" as "idol worship," as being steeped in a magical attitude that falsely attributes a spirit to inanimate matter.

Weber's evolutionary scheme differs from the one proposed by E. B. Tylor. In the latter's intellectualist approach, "belief" is at the core of religion. The human inclination to imagine matter as "animated" by spirits declines with the evolution of the mind, and so ultimately religion is replaced by rational thinking and science. As Peter Pels points out below, Tylor's view of the "fetish" as animated (and thus as referring to a spirit, rather than being taken to be a sheer thing) "can be read as marking a certain transcendence of the sociocultural over the material." While Weber notes a declining centrality of material forms in favor of a meaning-centered religiosity,[47] Tylor postulates that, even in its earliest expressions, religion already was a matter of the mind, to which material objects were secondary. Tylor's emphasis on animism, Pels argues, implies a reductive understanding of matter as a material for the higher purpose of human signification. Downplaying materiality itself, Tylor stands for a dematerializing approach not only to religion but also to society. The point of studying religion and society is to get beyond matter to higher levels of abstraction and signification. This stance, as Pels observes, prefigures the twentieth-century Saussurian split between arbitrary signifiers and an abstract signified that has come under siege with the "material turn."[48]

Notwithstanding the differences that exist between the evolutionary models of Tylor and Weber, both scholars reproduced a typically Protestant inclination, which had developed since the eighteenth century, to regard matter as secondary and signification as primary. As Webb Keane points out, from a Protestant perspective, the value of the human lies in "its distinctiveness from, and superiority to, the material world."[49] Whether this superiority is present from the outset (as for Tylor) or generated through the rise of rational salvation religions (as for Weber), both scholars work within a dematerializing approach to religion. Their mode of analysis burdens the study of religion with a pejorative attitude toward things and ritualized practice, which has as its flip side a strong emphasis on making meaning.[50] Although more historical research needs to be done to grasp the genealogy of struggles with materiality within Christianity since the Middle

Ages,[51] paying attention to transformations with Protestantism, there are good reasons to state that, with the rise of religion as a modern category, scholars tended to overlook—or perhaps better, look *through*—religion's material forms. As this volume seeks to point out, looking through such forms—for instance, by reducing them to carriers of meaning—is utterly problematic both for Protestantism itself and for other religious traditions.

The problem with a "Protestant" Weberian lens is that it prevents us from getting a more realistic picture of how things matter in Protestant practice. Such a picture emerges more clearly in "frontier zones," into which Western Protestant missionaries exported the old "iconoclash" with Catholic imagery in the course of Western colonial expansion.[52] In such settings, as Keane shows in his formidable study of Dutch Calvinist missionaries among the Sumbanese (Indonesia), local potential converts were not ready to accept the dismissal of materiality that is at the core of Protestant preachings. Thick with misunderstandings and contestations, such a frontier setting lays bare competing "semiotic ideologies." Based on Peirce's theory of a distinction between types of signs implying different relations to reality (such as icon, index, and symbol), the notion of "semiotic ideology" refers to a meta-level of statements about the status and value attributed to words, things, or images, from the perspective of a particular, historically situated religious tradition.[53] What were *marapu* (invisible, yet materially present spirits) for the Sumbanese were qualified as "fetishes" or "idols" by the missionaries, who found that the Sumbanese erroneously ascribed agency to inanimate matter. The invocation of notions such as "fetish" and "idol" by Protestant missionaries not only distorted and dismissed local religious practices as being predicated on a confusion of the proper (for a Protestant) distinction between things and spirits. Paradoxically, this dismissal also sustained a logic of animation that recast "fetishes" and "idols" as powerful instances of a "heathendom" that was, so to speak, alive and kicking.[54]

Matthew Engelke's analysis of the Masowe "Friday apostolics" is another remarkable study of a "frontier zone"—the local negotiation of Protestantism in Zimbabwe—in which the question of religion and materiality is placed center stage.[55] Engelke shows how the Friday apostolics negotiate between an ultra-iconoclastic semiotic ideology that regards things as problematic because of their thingliness, on the one hand, and the necessity that God somehow be present in the world, on the other. Pointing to the dual character of God as both material and immaterial, Engelke analyzes the struggle of the apostolics in terms of a broader "problem of presence," which he identifies as being characteristic of Protestantism in general: How can a God who is stated to be beyond human understanding and imagination be present for believers? In his essay in this volume, Engelke invokes the intriguing example of "sticky honey," which apostolics code as an immaterial substance. By virtue of this semiotic operation, honey belongs to a category different from, for instance, the Bible, which is dismissed as a dangerous object through which people are led away from God. However, even "honey," if not used in the proper manner, can transform into a "dangerous object." Instead of taking believers' claims about imma- teriality at face value, Engelke argues that both materiality and immateriality are not given but produced. Similarly, inspired by Keane's and Engelke's research, Miranda Klaver shows how Dutch Pentecostals, notwithstanding the strong claims they make about the immediacy and immateriality of spiritual experience, appreciate the "blood of Christ as a substance." She points out that these Pentecostals mobilize a "semiotic ideology" in which words and modes of speaking have tangible, material effects.[56]

One of the most important lessons that can be drawn from studies of Protestant missions in nineteenth- and early-twentieth-century "frontier zones" is that it is necessary to distinguish between internal self-representations and actual religious practices. Instead of taking as real an ideal and ahistorical version of Protestantism as antagonistic or opposed to materiality, it is necessary to conduct research on the level of actual Protestant practices.[57] A theoretically important and refreshing angle that is highly sensitive to mate- rial culture concerns the place and role of pictures in popular Protestant lived religion. In such studies as his pathbreaking research on the use of images of Jesus in America, David Morgan has been one of the first scholars to correct facile views of Protestantism that take for granted the usual Protestant lens.[58] Far from being rejected in line with a supposed Protestant iconophobia, pictures of Jesus, though not worshiped as such, are focal mate- rial nodes in private Protestant prayer and worship through which believers experience the presence of God. Exploring contestations that arise around Jesus pictures in Ghana, Birgit Meyer's essay shows that these pictures are not only embraced and employed in popular Christian devotion but also rejected as dangerous by staunch Pentecostal believ- ers. By virtue of their materiality, even representations of Jesus are held to be prone to be "hijacked" by the devil, who casts beholders under his spell through a chiastic visual encounter. Through such contestations, Jesus pictures are coded as "idols"—a typical instance of iconoclash, through which the image gains power by virtue of being opposed.

Even on the high level of theology, as Ernst van den Hemel points out in his essay, one needs to avoid simplifying Protestantism's presumed immateriality. Exploring Cal- vin's writings on the Eucharist, van den Hemel corrects the notion that Protestantism holds a merely symbolist stance with regard to the question of transubstantiation, that is, the question of the incarnation of divine presence in the host. Positing that in Calvin's writings "a problematic comes together that ties a nascent notion of modern interaction with materiality, with the divine presence of the divine in the ritual of the Supper," van den Hemel shows that these writings "offer an original but undervalued theory, in which material presence and divine truth are combined." A symptom of the dematerialization of religion in modern times, this "undervaluation" is a fruitful starting point for envisag- ing what a "future of the religious past" that takes materiality seriously might look like.

In sum, on closer investigation, even Protestantism, which is usually taken to be an iconophobic and antimaterial religion, proves to attribute considerable importance to material stuff, simply because some degree of materiality is indispensable for religion to be present in the world. Moreover, it is important to realize that Protestantism encompasses a variety of strands, including Lutheranism, which conceptualize and use material stuff in diverse ways, calling to be unpacked in future research. Questioning facile understandings of Protestantism that are enshrined in what we call the "Protestant legacy" in the study of religion, the ultimate concern of this volume is to critique the limitations of symbolist and meaning-centered approaches that look through and sideline "things." In order to undo dematerializing approaches in the study of religion at large so as to envisage alternative perspectives and understandings, a critical discussion of the "Protestant legacy" is of central importance. What is needed is a fresh look at the history of understandings and use of materiality in all varieties of Protestantism, but also in other religious traditions, and in other mappings of the spirit-matter dichotomy (as by Christians onto Jews in late antiquity, for example). One case in point is, of course Judaism, which (as Galit Hasan-Rokem shows) embraces a deeply embodied and materialized code of religious worship. Her analysis of the *Sukkah*—a temporary booth erected during the week-long holiday of Sukkoth—as a temporary construction that envelops its inhabitants into a topography of divine space powerfully shows the centrality of practices around things. Another intriguing case is Catholicism. While it would be too simple to call for a "re-Catholicization" of the study of Christianity, much can be learned about the question of religion and materiality by paying attention to Catholic repertoires of dealing with images, artifacts, and bodily fluids, as a number of essays in our volume also show. That such repertoires may also be mobilized outside the sphere of religion in a more narrow sense is shown evocatively in Elizabeth Castelli's analysis of the use of blood in a political act of protest by Catholic activists against the U.S. attack on Iraq in 2003.

How Things Matter

In his essay, David Morgan analyzes the transformation of the understanding of the Sacred Heart of Jesus for Catholic devotion between the mid seventeenth and the twentieth centuries: from a living organ (not unlike a "fetish") to a pictorial presence (an "icon" of Jesus), to a "symbol" that signifies theological meaning. Tied to shifts in devotional practices—from requiring a strong visceral engagement with the wounded heart to a symbolic reading—this transformation can be viewed as a successive process of dematerialization in a Catholic setting. Similarly, in her essay on the Brazilian Catholic Charismatic Renewal, Maria José A. de Abreu explores how "electronic media are affecting the status of traditional icons within their midst." Although icons are nodes in a complex spiritual encounter within the framework of pneumatic theology, Abreu discerns among Charismatics a constant concern about the danger of freezing them into mere objects. She points out how, struggling to remain within Catholicism, the Charismatic Renewal seeks to "reformulate the traditional status of the image as an item of mediation—in favor of a more direct and unmediated experience with the divine." In this process, electronic media are employed as replacements for statues, producing a new kind of "living icon," for instance, in the televised performance of popular Charismatic priest Marcello Rossi. Both examples show that, within a religious tradition such as Catholicism, how things matter is subject to transformation, entailing a constant redefinition of the relation between persons, objects, and the divine.

Dematerialization notwithstanding, the study of religion provides us with a long-standing repertoire of categories of what W. J. T. Mitchell poignantly calls "bad object-hood."[59] Terms such as *totem*, *idol*, and *fetish* refer not simply to distinct types of material objects but rather to particular human attitudes toward and modes of using "things." Far from simply denoting a neutral religious use of objects by others, these terms entail fixed presuppositions and value judgments by those who use them. All three terms signal a relation to objects that appears problematic from a modern perspective, which insists on a clear separation and hierarchical relation between people and things. In practice, *totem* is the least offensive. In the wake of Durkheim's *The Elementary Forms of Religious Life*, "totems" are analyzed as symbols that stand for the abstract norms and values enshrined in collective representations. Coded as symbols through which a group defines and worships itself through a logic of distinction from other groups, totems are placed outside the question of materiality—above all, to invoke Claude Lévi-Strauss's famous dictum, they are "good to think with."

By contrast, *idol* and *fetish* point to a scandalous materiality. Formerly, these terms were used in a pejorative manner to identify a mode of worship that is false from a Christian—particularly, a Protestant—perspective. These terms are ideological constructs that constitute objects in a particular, dismissive manner. As Mitchell argues in his essay, a concern with "idolatry" and "iconoclasm" has been central to Judaism and Christianity from the outset. The Second Commandment not only rejects the making and worshipping of "idols," but also introduces God as jealous, punishing idol worshippers through a sweeping, violent act of iconoclasm. The tension between the interdiction on making images and their apparent indispensability runs through the history of Christianity, over and over again generating both devotional practices around icons and relics *and* their often violent dismissal as "idols" (or, as de Abreu evocatively shows, a struggle to keep alive the icon as a medium of spirit, rather than allowing it to freeze and become a static object). The charge of "idolatry" clashes with the religious practices of those who are branded as "idol-worshippers," for whom the representation of a divine force through an image is a normal part of their devotion. Crystallizing the tension between the love for and rejection of images, the issue of idolatry also forms a central dilemma in art history.[60] Far from being a relic of a primitive past, the concern with idolatry has persisted and been reenergized in modern times, for instance, in the work of Nietzsche, William Blake, and Marx. Reflecting on Poussin's *The Adoration of the Golden Calf* (1633–36) and *The Plague at Ashdod* (1630–31), Mitchell explains that idolatry and iconoclasm form an "evil twin" because, far from erasing the idol, acts of iconoclasm load it with power through negative affection. This logic still underpins the politics of visual representation in our time, as acts like the terroristic attacks on the Twin Towers and the subsequent "War on Terror," the destruction of the Buddha figures at Bamiyan, the commotion around the so-called Muhammad cartoons, or the complicated management of images of Osama Bin Laden after his assassination by American elite troops indicate. Indeed, the fact that the fight against "idols" tends to enhance rather than destroy their power and efficacy shows that the notion of the idol implicates in its logic even those who mobilize it against others.

Unlike the notions of the idol and idolatry, which have long been intrinsic to Judaism, Christianity, and Islam, the term *fetish* emerged around 1470 in the context of the Portuguese presence in West Africa.[61] Deriving from the pidgin term *fetisso*, the notion of the "fetish" was born out of African-European encounters and exchange.[62] Right from the beginning, as Bruno Latour points out, "the word's etymology refused, like the Blacks [when questioned about their sacred objects by the Portuguese] to choose between what is shaped by work and what is artificial; this refusal, this hesitation, induced fascination and brought on spells."[63] As has been well documented, the term *fetish* and the discourse on "fetishism" was adopted into European languages and mobilized to mark the difference between those who falsely mistake a mere thing as being imbued with power and agency, on the one hand, and those who are able to distinguish persons from objects (and to use the latter adequately), on the other. As Hartmut Böhme stresses, the term *fetish* was initially used interchangeably with *idol*, and Protestants employed it to point out the convergence of paganism and the Catholic devotion to saints and icons, which they coded as "idol worship" or "fetishism."[64] Thus, *fetish* came to refer to an illicit use of things in a religious context—another important index of Protestantism's dematerializing inclination. The partly overlapping discourses of the fetish and the idol are a symptom of the fear of matter, spotlighted by Peter Pels, that has long haunted the study of religion.

Until today, the notion of the fetish has been invoked to identify an irrational attitude toward a "thing," whether by a neurotic, to be cured through psychoanalysis, or by workers, who are to transcend their "false consciousness" and realize that commodities are the products of their own work. Describing the commodity as "in reality, a very queer thing, abounding in metaphysical subtleties and theological niceties,"[65] Marx took *fetish* to be the term adequate to describe how commodities fool people into vesting inanimate things with a spirit and will: "forces beyond human making."[66] In this sense, capitalism produces its own mystifications and modes of enchantment. Walter Benjamin, in "Capitalism as Religion," famously suggests that capitalist consumer culture has developed into a new kind of undogmatic cult, worshipping the "secret God of debt."[67] Invoked in this framework, the term *fetish* no longer describes a false attitude toward things by some primitive other but is situated in the midst of modernity, pointing toward the seductive lure of the things under whose spell we find ourselves.[68] Commodities shape desire within a logic of enchantment, through which consumers generate personal authenticity by consuming things.[69] Exploring the spiritual economy of New Age products that promise to convey personal "authentic" experiences, Stef Aupers notes a remarkable "spiritualization of commodities," which index the inexhaustibility of "commodity fetishism"—now in a "new style" of attributing spirit to matter. Therefore, Aupers contends, it is high time for scholars to turn attention "to this spiritualization of commodities rather than endlessly debating the commodification of spirituality as evidence for secularization." If capitalism produces its own enchantments, the notion of the fetish—read against the grain of the demystifying way in which the notion has normally been invoked—is a fruitful starting point for grasping how enchantment works.

While working on this volume, we became ever more aware of the extent to which the study of religion itself has inherited the Enlightenment project of the evolution of religion toward interiority, transcendence, and reason, indeed, toward religion's evaporation.[70] By contrast to the tremendous attention paid to concepts of "bad objecthood," in the study of religion (at least until the recent interest in "material religion") there has been comparatively little work on more "positive" categories for religious "things." For this reason, scholars of religion still seem ill equipped to understand how things matter in ways that recognize the valuation, animation, and role of "things" within a given religious setting. With this volume, we seek to initiate new lines of inquiry to explore how things matter in religion. The point is not only critically to deconstruct the genealogy and politics of terms such as *totem*, *idol*, or *fetish* but also to trace alternative semiotic ideologies according to which "things," and the structures of animation in which they operate, can appear in another light.[71]

We invoke the term *things*, and take it as the title for our volume, because it signals indeterminacy—something that cannot be clearly circumscribed and that creates some degree of nervousness or anxiety, as in the line from Shakespeare's *Hamlet* "Has this thing appeared again tonight?" The "thing" referred to here, as Freddie Rokem points out in his essay, is not only the appearance of the ghost of the recently buried king of Denmark but also the theatrical performance itself, facing the task of making the supernatural appear in a materially concrete form. More than the term *object*, which is usually invoked in the framework of a subject-object relation, in which the former supposedly wields control over the latter, *thing* suggests an extra dimension that expands the realm of rationality and utility. Here we follow Bill Brown's suggestion that we imagine things "as what is excessive in objects, as what exceeds their mere materialization as objects in their mere utilization as objects—their force as a sensuous presence, the magic by which objects become values, fetishes, idols, and totems" (see also the essay by Birgit Meyer).[72]

Calling attention to "things" (rather than simply to "objects") in the field of religion, this volume shows, opens up a broad field of inquiry. Instead of taking at face value how certain objects are employed (or despised) in religious practices, taking "things" as a starting point requires studying the processes through which the spiritual and the material—animation at work—are conjoined in religious forms. Counter to the categories of fetishes, idols, and totems mentioned by Brown, which refer to an illicit (from the perspective of outsiders) understanding and use of things, there exist more positive valuations of "things," imbuing them with a spiritual presence and power. This can be seen in the *extra calvinisticum*, which retains some degree of the materiality of the Eucharist (see Ernst van den Hemel's essay), portraits of the Thai King Chulalongkorn, which render him spiritually present (see Irene Stengs's essay), the icon of the Sacred Heart of Jesus (see David Morgan's essay), the miniatures and stones that "serve as tangible mediators" in a spiritual economy that links Bolivian pilgrims and Mary (see the essay by Sanne Derks, Willy Jansen, and Catrien Notermans), the sacralization of bodily fluids as blood and milk (see the essays by Willy Jansen and Grietje Presen and by Miranda Klaver), the "spilling of one's own blood" as an act of protest (see Elizabeth Castelli's essay), a Catholic theology of pneuma and the living icon that encompasses new digital technologies (see Maria José A. de Abreu's essay), or the vesting of digital technologies with spiritual power in a New Age context (see the essays by Stef Aupers, Dorien Zandbergen, and Ineke Noomen, Stef Aupers, and Dick Houtman). Obviously, such uses of "things" are prone to invoke counter reactions, whether in the logic of iconoclasm and other dismissals of thingliness (see the contributions by W. J. T. Mitchell, Matthew Engelke, and Birgit Meyer) or in the name of a neutral public sphere, cleansed of disturbing objects such as Muslim headscarves (see the essay by Annelies Moors).

We employ "things" in a broad sense, encompassing images, artifacts, bodies, and bodily fluids, as well as spaces and technologies. A focus on such religious "things"—and religious attitudes toward them—is a fascinating and promising point of departure in the study of religion, because it invites us to take seriously the often downplayed material dimension of religion, which is indispensable to the making of religious beliefs, identities, and communities. Addressing this issue more or less explicitly, the essays in this volume share a pragmatic approach in which the following questions are raised: How do things matter (or not) in religious discourses and practices? How is the value or devaluation, the appraisal or contestation, of things accounted for within particular religious perspectives? How does the current concern with "things" and "material religion" transform scholarly approaches and understandings of religion?

Composition of the Volume

To address these questions, we start with a predominantly theoretical discussion of the Protestant ambition to dematerialize religion and the "problem of presence" this inevitably sparks (Part I, "Anxieties about Things"). The subsequent parts of the book then address in more detail how things and spaces do actually matter to religion, that is, how they act to make the sacred present in the world. Part II, "Images and Incarnations," discusses the things that most obviously make the sacred present, in virtually all religions:

the statues and images that arouse so much anxiety among Protestants. In Part III, "Sacred Artifacts," we then move to a more heterogeneous category of things, ranging from huts to stones and miniature representations of cars or houses, to prayer beads. In Part IV, "Bodily Fluids," we then continue with a set of contributions about the human body and its fluids, particularly blood and milk—things that cannot be made to go away and thus need to be dealt with symbolically through often complex cultural codings, which reflect religious ideals as much as relations of power and privilege. Part V, "Public Space," then shifts attention from material "things" to public space, addressing how it makes religion visible and how religion's public presence may become a source of contestation in debates about the boundaries between the "private" and "public" realms. Part VI, "Digital Technologies," finally features a set of contributions that interrogate the role of advanced digital computer technology in religious mediation. Needless to say, because of the emphasis in "modernist" discourse on technology's radical "thingliness" and alleged incompatibility with religion, digital media constitute a theoretically special and vital category of "things." While at first sight digital media technologies may appear to be quite distinct from explicitly religiously charged objects, such as rosaries or Buddha images, this final section shows that these media, too, are subject to sacralization.

Part I, "Anxieties about Things," features essays—by Peter Pels, Matthew Engelke, and Ernst van den Hemel—that all address the problematic Protestant stance with regard to materiality. Pels demonstrates the historical construction and situatedness of notions of "matter" and "materiality," emphasizing their profoundly relational character: materiality may be understood as either "concrete" in opposition to "abstract," "material" in opposition to "spiritual," "objective" in opposition to "subjective," or "natural" in opposition to "cultural." Discussing the role of the Protestant "fear of matter" in nineteenth-century Victorian science, he traces shifts in all four oppositions, driven by a Calvinist combination of contempt for and fear of materiality and giving shape to a "dematerialization" of anthropology and the other social sciences that came to privilege the "immaterial" over the "material."

Informed by fieldwork conducted in Zimbabwe, Engelke discusses the logic of materiality among the Friday apostolics, who are deeply committed to a semiotic ideology of immateriality, understanding even the Bible as obstructing a direct connection to God. The "problem of presence" entailed by this semiotic ideology is solved by a semiotic coding of the "material" stuff of "sticky honey" as basically "immaterial." This proves to be an awkward, unstable, and vulnerable code, however, which underscores that "materiality" and "immateriality" are not simply given but actively produced and constructed.

In a different way, Van den Hemel also points out the impossibility of a religion that completely does away with matter. He does so by critiquing the widespread interpretation of Calvin's writings on the Eucharist as entailing merely a strictly symbolic and stereotypically Protestant understanding of transubstantiation. If we look closer and more critically, he argues, we find that Calvin understood divine presence as being simultaneously immanent and transcendent, and he thus avoided both the dangers of a veneration of matter and a strictly metaphorical interpretation of Christ's presence.

Part II, "Images and Incarnations," opens with a chapter by Donald Lopez, who traces the origins of the Buddha as we know him today: the friendly, peaceful, and wise embodiment of a "pure" spirituality who represents not a religion but rather a philosophy, or even a morality or way of life. This dematerialized and textualized Buddha is only a recent construction, Lopez demonstrates. It owes much to the publication in 1844 of Sanskrit scholar Eugène Burnouf's book *Introduction to the History of Indian Buddhism* and has since been popularized in the West and even in Buddhist Asia itself. This contemporary Buddha is remarkably different from the various figures known before, when Western understandings of Buddhism were principally informed by "things": his images, understood as "idols" by Western travelers and missionaries.

David Morgan then addresses modern Catholic devotion to the Sacred Heart of Jesus, originating in the appearances of Jesus experienced by nun Margaret-Mary Alacoque (1647–90). Since the seventeenth century, understandings of the Heart of Jesus have shifted from visceral to symbolic registers: from a fetish (a concealing object standing in for something else) to an icon (an image) and, finally, to a mere symbol (a sign). Yet from the eighteenth century up to the present day, the status of the Sacred Heart has remained a source of theological contestation between Jesuits and orthodox Catholics, who emphasize its viscerality, and Jansenist Protestants and Catholic reformers, who treat it as a symbol. W. J. T. Mitchell addresses the difficult relationship between words and images, as religiously encoded in the Second Commandment ("You shall not make for yourself a graven image") and as inscribed at the heart of art history as the clash between logos and icon, meaning and image. Discussing two paintings by Nicholas Poussin (1594–1665) that depict scenes of idolatry, he argues that Poussin's dilemma exemplifies the central problem of art history: How are we to make use of visual representation without lapsing into meaningless idolatry? Poussin's solution, he suggests, is to focus not merely on what idolaters and iconoclasts *believe* (or are believed to believe by their adversaries) but also on what they actually *do* to one another—particularly acts of violence inflicted on alleged idol worshippers.

Freddie Rokem then discusses the appearance of the supernatural on the theatrical stage and the movie screen. In the form of the deus ex machina, but also those of ghosts or dybbuks, the supernatural is still a frequent phenomenon in modern and contemporary art, even after the declaration of God's death. The stage can be seen as a utopian site, an aesthetic "no place," where the supernatural can appear, even if the audience does not necessarily subscribe to the religious belief systems this appearance implies. This creates a discursive encounter where religious things (alluding to the ghost in Shakespeare's *Hamlet*, referred to as a thing that appears again tonight) enter and even invade the aesthetic sphere of the performance. Finally, Irene Stengs addresses the role of mass-produced portraits of the Siamese King Chulalongkorn (Rama V, r. 1868–1910) in a personality cult that emerged in the 1990s among the urban Thai middle class in response to hopes and anxieties about Thai identity in a globalizing world. The portraits are understood as having sought out their owners themselves, even though they are typically obtained as gifts or bought from door-to-door venders, and as capable of exerting agency and providing support and security.

Part III, "Sacred Artifacts," contains contributions by Galit Hasan-Rokem, José van Santen, and Sanne Derks, Willy Jansen, and Catrien Notermans. Hasan-Rokem discusses the meaning of the Jewish *Sukkah* as it has been transformed throughout history. For a week every year, she argues, the *Sukkah* expresses an understanding of Jerusalem as a religious center as much as it represents the temporary huts of the biblical Israelite wanderers in the desert. This dialectic of the *Sukkah* destabilizes and unsettles the Jewish concept of the territorial centrality of Jerusalem in religious cosmology, producing changing constellations in different historical situations. Religious language and habitus associated with the *Sukkah* have historically carried associations of mobility and stability that deconstruct the very idea of an earthly place as center.

Drawing on her fieldwork among the Fulbe in northern Cameroon, Van Santen uses the *tasbirwol* as a material point of entry into the contested and submerged mystical Islamic brotherhoods. The *tasbirwol* is a string of ninety-nine prayer beads, corresponding to the ninety-nine beautiful names of Allah. It is used for *tashbugo*, "counting one's beads," a practice historically associated with mystical Sufism. Even though the Sufi brotherhoods have been banned for political reasons since the 1960s, their sympathizers can still be recognized by this practice of *tashbugo*, currently under attack by Islamic reform movements, who consider it an improper "pagan" influence.

Sanne Derks, Willy Jansen, and Catrien Notermans discuss the role of stones and *alasitas* (miniature representations of desired objects, such as cars, houses, or money) in the "spiritual economy" built around the pilgrimage to the Virgin of Urkupiña at Calvary Hill in Quillacollo, Bolivia. The event is informed by the precolonial goddess of fertility Pachamama (Mother Earth) and the cult of the Virgin Mary, deliberately conflated in Spanish colonial efforts to convert the locals to Catholicism. During the annual fiesta of the Virgin of Urkupiña, pilgrims buy *alasitas* to seek Mary's blessings for their (typically materialistic) requests, dislodge stones to take home as tangible reminders to Mary and themselves in the new year, and get rid of last year's stones and miniatures. If last year's requests have remained unmet, pilgrims blame themselves, holding that *alasitas* will work only if one has sufficient faith and makes reasonable requests.

Opening Part IV, "Bodily Fluids," Willy Jansen and Grietje Dresen discuss the religious meanings of blood and milk in Christianity and Islam. They demonstrate that these meanings matter in the construction of men and women as differently and hierarchically placed religious and social subjects. Whereas male blood, as in the passion of Christ or

Islamic blood sacrifices, has historically been valued as holy, female blood, in particular that of menstruation and childbirth, was considered impure and polluting; it was used as an argument to exclude women from religious leadership or certain religious practices. Milk, another bodily and quintessentially female fluid, mattered differently. In early Christianity, Mary's milk was sacralized as a symbol of passing on the Word of God and adored in the Maria Lactans. But whereas the religious values attached to blood only increased in Christian history, that of milk declined. In Islam, however, the high value attached to mothers' milk still can be seen in ideas of milk kinship.

Elizabeth Castelli analyzes the religious mobilization of materiality for political signification in a case study of a protest action by four Catholic activists, associated with the pacifist Catholic Worker movement, founded in New York City in the 1930s. Drawing upon their Catholic tradition, the activists poured their blood at an army recruiting center in upstate New York, just days before the U.S. attack on Iraq in March 2003. Contestations over the status of their blood were central to the trial that followed. Whereas the defendants emphasized the symbolic, sacrificial, and sacramental character of their blood, as well as its purifying qualities, the prosecutor conceived it as "matter out of place" (Mary Douglas)—as a "weapon," a "biohazard," and a "threat"—thus framing the symbolic pouring of blood as a violent, even terrorist act.

Miranda Klaver's essay is based on her ethnographic fieldwork in a Dutch Pentecostal church, a denomination that is typically taken to privilege the immediacy of experience over material and visual mediation. In this church, however, mostly because of the influence of Mel Gibson's blockbuster movie *The Passion of the Christ* (2004), much attention is paid to the blood and suffering of Christ, in a way traditionally associated with Catholicism. This is because Pentecostal biblical literalism resonates well with the movie's hyperrealism and Gibson's claims about its historical authenticity. In this Pentecostal context, then, the blood of Christ has come to be understood as an embodied source of material power.

Part V, "Public Space," features contributions by Michiel Leezenberg, Annelies Moors, Birgit Meyer, and Maria José A. de Abreu. Leezenberg discusses the Ottoman coffee house against the backdrop of the understanding that the emergence of the coffeehouse in seventeenth- and eighteenth-century Western and Central Europe indicates the rise of a modern liberal and secular public sphere. The new institution of the coffeehouse (just like coffee itself) had, after all, been imported from the early modern Ottoman Empire, where it had emerged as early as the sixteenth century, thus well before any substantial European influence. The Ottoman coffeehouse, Leezenberg argues, operated as a Foucauldian "heterotopia," constituting a public and secular counterpart to the mosque. The absence of the outspoken anticlericalism featured by its European counterpart reveals, however, the Eurocentrism of Habermas's rationalist conceptualization of the public sphere.

Moors delves into the feelings of discomfort, disgust, and fear evoked by the Islamic face veil in the Netherlands, negative affects that are discursively triggered in a cultural and political climate that insists on Muslims' cultural assimilation. Even though Islamic women in the Netherlands wear *niqabs* rather than *burqas*, the latter has become the preferred label in public debate. This has created an association with Afghanistan, the Taliban, radical Islam, and the oppression of women, even though such an interpretation is at odds with the motivations of those who actually choose to wear the face veil. At the same time, in popular visual imagery (government campaigns, film posters, etc.) the veil is used not to signify Muslim women's suppression but rather to draw attention to seductive and exotic Oriental bodies or (e.g., in cartoons) to mock the asexual public presence at which the wearing of the face veil aims.

Meyer addresses Pentecostal ambivalence toward and contestation of Jesus pictures in southern Ghana. These are massively present in public space, entailing a "pentecostalization" of Ghana's public sphere. Misgivings about these pictures can be traced back to the anti-iconic semiotic ideology of nineteenth-century Protestant missionaries, who drew strict boundaries between subject and object, spirit and matter, attacking indigenous religion as "heathendom," "idolatry," and "Devil worship." The pictures are considered harmless "symbols" for the pious, which publicly display their Christian identity, yet they are seen as liable to slip into "icons" that may be hijacked by the Devil—a radical reversal through which what is meant to display visually the outreach of Christianity may actually be subverted.

Maria José A. de Abreu's essay examines the role of traditional imagery in an age of electronic media through the example of the popularity of St. Expeditus among Catholic Charismatics in São Paulo, Brazil. Known for the expedient delivery of petitions, St. Expeditus, the "saint against procrastination" or "FedEx Saint," occupies a dual position. On the one hand, he allows Catholic Charismatics in Brazil to balance a desire for liveliness and movement with a theology of pneuma (as breath or spirit). On the other, he allows them to reestablish that principle of liveliness within a Catholic tradition of engagement with religious images. Given that the material properties of electronic media technologies allow devotees to structure the image of St. Expeditus within a "regime of passage," Abreu argues, he can embody the paradox of stillness in motion upon which liveliness ultimately depends.

Part VI, "Digital Technologies," features three essays about how advanced media technology shapes and is shaped by religion. Stef Aupers discusses the popular genre of online computer games rooted in the "fantasy" genre (Tolkien in particular) and exemplified by *World of Warcraft*. His analysis, as we have seen, leads to a critique of Weber's theory of the "disenchantment of the world," according to which religious belief increasingly evaporates as a viable option, so that enchantment is progressively relegated to the realm of fiction (the worlds of poetry, literature, television, and, more recently, computer games). Now that a massive epistemological shift has taken place from "religious belief" to "spiritual experience," Aupers maintains, this theory no longer holds: these computer games open up opportunities for spiritual engagement with fantasy fiction that go well beyond Coleridge's notion of a "willing suspension of disbelief."

Drawing on ethnographic fieldwork in the San Francisco Bay Area, Dorien Zandbergen writes about "New Edge," a brand of "New Age" spirituality featuring the belief that the New Age can be realized through advanced technologies of the type pioneered in Silicon Valley. Rooted in a network of artists, computer engineers, scientists, journalists, and entrepreneurs, most employed in corporate and academic settings, New Edge originated in the California countercultural movements of the 1960s and 1970s and continues to define itself as countercultural. It understands technology to be sacred, even though its "true potential" (i.e., extending people's senses by helping them to "see more," "become aware," "bring out their true selves," etc.) may remain unfulfilled due to corporate incorporation and commodification. Much like understandings of the Internet by scholars of "cyber-religion" back in the 1990s, then, and despite its keen awareness of the socially constructed nature of things, New Edge is still informed by the technologically deterministic notion that technology has a "true essence."

Ineke Noomen, Stef Aupers, and Dick Houtman finally discuss how the particularities of religious heritages, especially their understandings of the opportunities offered and constraints imposed by the Internet, matter in the new medium's religious appropriation. Catholic web designers face the dilemma of either creating the room for dialogue, debate, and diversity invited by the medium or following Roman orthodoxy. Their Protestant counterparts find themselves caught between their predominantly text-centered legacy and the visual opportunities of web design, a problem further aggravated by the sensitivities of and contestations among competing Dutch Protestant churches. Those active in the institutionally fragmented field of holistic spirituality, finally, experience neither of these problems and appropriate the Internet as their allegedly "natural" habitat for spiritual sharing and connecting.

PART I

Anxieties about Things

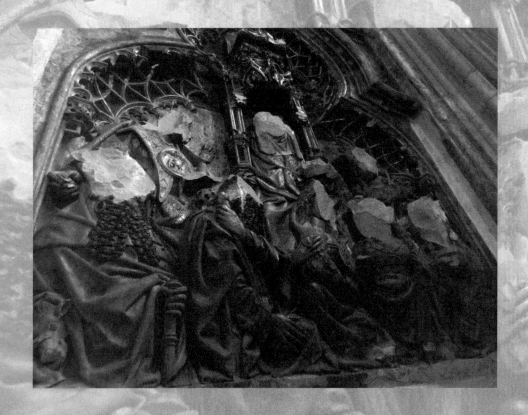

The Modern Fear of Matter

Reflections on the Protestantism of Victorian Science

Peter Pels

A certain confusion besets scientists, modernist thinkers, and other participants in Occidental[1] culture when they start to use notions like "fact," "fetish," "matter," or "material object." I believe that the confusion of modern people who assume the autonomy of fact and matter arises at least in part from the paradox that, despite their inclination to associate the material with the concrete, their focus on the material is part of a sociohistorical process of abstraction. A genealogy of the modern fact shows that it cannot be understood as a *Ding an sich* without also recognizing that it is always a "fact for" or "evidence of" some larger system. Moreover, the history of the isolated, seemingly concrete and material "modern" fact seems to end in the mid-nineteenth century, at the time that the aggregate fact of statistics becomes dominant.[2] Likewise, a genealogy of the notion of "fetish" shows that, like the "fact" and the "rarity," these understandings of matter also emerge, in the early modern period, on the basis of a form of abstraction—the alienation of objects from their contexts of use through global capitalism. During a later, nineteenth-century phase, however, they are further transformed by colonialism, modern aesthetics, and anthropology.[3] The subsumption of the "fetish" under "animism" in the work of Edward Tylor can be read as marking a certain transcendence of the sociocultural over the material,[4] so that, despite the evolutionists' heavy focus on the museum object, their "dematerializing" thought can also be seen as having prepared the way for the marginalization of material culture studies in early-twentieth-century anthropology.[5]

This Victorian moment in the history of understandings of materiality seems, therefore, to be important. I want to return to it because, when thinking about it earlier,[6] I failed to spell out the religious dimensions of these developments—religious developments that, summarized

27

in the concepts of prophecy and iconoclasm, will help to explain modern anthropology's dematerializing bias. As Webb Keane has argued, Protestant ontology defines the value of the human as "its distinctiveness from, and superiority to the material world."[7] It thereby seems to define this materiality, by implication, as a *Ding an sich*, something that cannot but resist, and yet get its meaning from, human traffic. It seems no coincidence that the "modern fact" of early modern science is characterized by a similar juxtaposition of a material isolate to the systems of evidence that give it meaning.[8] But what does the Protestant fear of matter (as evident from its different forms of iconoclasm[9]) do for Victorians, caught as they are between the icons of Protestant worship and the contemporary idols of "materialism"?

First, this fear of matter shows that Victorian science's opposition to religion should not be mistaken for a lack of continuity with its religious background. Second, it shows that Victorian "materialism" is opposed to "spiritualism" rather than being part of a secularist opposition to idealism. However, this shift in conceptual relations raises another set of questions: How specific is the conception of materiality in Victorian science, and how can we relate it to our own? If we are to study a situation in which scientists lambast Protestant theologians (as Tylor and his fellows did in their dealings with the Oxbridge establishment), how can the icons of the former iconoclasts, now smashed by a new breed of critics, be understood? Beyond the observation that the smashing of images will result in their proliferation and in uncertainty about what the human hand may or may not achieve,[10] can one also analyze the different ways in which images do, or do not, objectify "material" truths? Is, in other words, the "materialism" opposed by Victorian Christians similar to the materiality that Victorian scientists claimed as the basis of evidence, or is it something different? What understanding of "materiality" can grasp the contests played out in the Victorian era and their relevance for our present? I do not claim to be able to answer those questions in any definite sense, but I do need to clarify my position first by a digression on the relational character of "materiality" and by suggesting that this relational character implies that "materiality" will change in meaning depending on how the relation is conceptualized. Thus, "materiality" or "materialism" may be significantly different to a scholarly audience for whom religious valuations are crucial (such as the Victorian scientists), by contrast to an audience that has undergone various twentieth-century attempts at self-secularization. Yet the latter may also learn from the former what latent religious meanings their understandings of materiality may still carry. Therefore, this essay will adopt the same pattern as my earlier discussion of "fetish":[11] I use a more analytic section to clarify some of the meanings that I feel we need to understand a second, more fundamental genealogy of the concepts under study. It is only right and proper that, in an inquiry into how abstraction works in practice, history contextualizes theory rather than the other way around.

The Relationality of the Material

As Daniel Miller argued in 1987, the materiality of an artifact "is always an element in cultural transformation" and a bridge between processes of abstraction and concrete specification.[12] Although the physicality of the object can be a symbol sui generis, there is always a danger of "fetishizing" the object as an object *an sich*, for that would deny the essential location of the object in a relationship of objectification—that is, a relationship in which subject and object mutually constitute each other. Pierre Bourdieu reminded us that this relationship is one of objectification and embodiment—that is, a relationship between different types of matter, between (among other things) artifacts and bodies.[13] Alfred Gell has argued that, in this relationship, objects ("indexes") have agency,[14] something to which our discourses on "fetish" also point.[15] As Karl Marx put it when reflecting on the moment when human beings sense the materiality of their relationship with their objective surroundings, "to be sensuous is to suffer"[16]—at the same time, he criticized the false consciousness of people who let themselves be *suffered by* the commodity fetish. It takes two to tango: just as, in everyday life, one finds that people abhor becoming dependent on the objects that they cannot but desire to consume, just so one finds scholars of material culture stressing, on the one hand, that humans are the final cause of the social life of things and recognizing, on the other, that things act on humans with a life of their own.[17]

I have argued elsewhere that it may be useful to distinguish between an animistic "spirit in matter" (where, as in Tylor's view, the object is animated by some kind of intelligence modeled on the human or the divine) and a fetishistic "spirit of matter" (an untranscended materiality that makes human beings suffer the object's agency, from whatever source it derived[18]). Whatever the merit of such an argument, it seems to suggest at least two qualitatively different conceptions of materiality. I argued that this plurality of notions of materiality emerged from a historical layering of seventeenth-, eighteenth-, and nineteenth-century discourses deriving from different and historically particular engagements.[19] If, in a certain relationship, some material exchanges look like rational "matter" or merchandise and other, simultaneous and corresponding exchanges appear as "fetish," from the viewpoint of an early modern Protestant merchant like Willem Bosman (writing about West Africa), we can say that material exchange is at the bottom of both, but that the relationship comes to be abstracted into certain material and spiritual "essences"—in this case, European "rationality" juxtaposed to African "superstition."[20] To put this differently, if nothing can be recognized *as* matter except within a relationship, the sociocultural inequalities in the relationship determine what is going to be abstracted as a material essence and what is not. The Dutch merchant on the West African coast had procedures by which to determine what counted as "real" matter—procedures that were, in many cases, different from those of his African trade partners. At the same time, Dutch merchants and African traders *did* exchange material goods—systematically, continuously, and in some form of relational (mis-)understanding. In another colonial situation, the Dutch Protestant missionaries on Sumba related ideas about the valuation of material goods that were incommensurable with the ideas of Sumbanese, who heavily invested in ceremonial exchange, but they eventually came to share discursive, if antagonistic, elements of a critique of materialism and fetishism.[21] Likewise, "spiritualism" and "materialism" in Victorian public discourse do not point to any particular essential position but to a relativity of values arising from a specific historical and material relationship.

To recognize this tangle of relationships of mutually antagonistic statements about materiality does not merely point to a relativistic argument, as it might for a functionalist anthropologist who wants to downplay his own description of something as "material" that the people studied do not recognize as such or not in the same way. Even if the *churinga* of Australian indigenous society, for example, appeared as a painted piece of wood to a classical anthropological observer and as a manifestation of the spirits to native Australians, it is the historical analysis of the unequal material relationship between these views that gives us the ethnography to understand these material objects, and more importantly, the way their materiality was experienced by the different parties in contestation.[22] More pertinent to the subject of this essay, the material "facts" about which Victorian intellectuals disagreed around 1870—Bible texts, spiritual séances, fossil bones, geological strata, collections of artifacts, folklore stories, or ethnographic accounts— exerted a different "material" agency depending on the relationship in which they were produced. The value and possible meanings of objects are underdetermined, so the determination of their relationship with humans calls for speech, interpretation, and politics; yet the very materiality of objects means that they are not merely arbitrary signs and that the relationship cannot be determined by just any sociocultural convention.[23]

The underdetermined nature of material facts, coupled with the fact that they are indexes of something—whatever it may be[24]—leads to the necessity of conjecture and abduction.[25] However, conjecture is not an operation that can be conducted without anxiety: if Victorian theologians derived a historical account (flawed or not) from certain Bible texts, some of their Scientist opponents perceived the same material only in terms of primitive superstition hiding an original moral code. Similarly, the spirit manifestations of the Victorian séance were the material "facts" of a higher intelligence to a Spiritualist like Alfred Wallace but appeared like manifestations of female hysteria or working-class fraud to Edward Tylor.[26] Certain pieces of stone were, to Victorian scientists, the material signs of "evolution"; to contemporary Theosophists, the same stones were mere illusions or botched reflections—that is, deceptive material images—of a spiritual, eternal reality; and both scientists and Theosophists poured scorn on nineteenth-century creationists who regarded these stones as *lusus naturae*, intellectual traps and tricks built into the material world by God's creation. To belabor the obvious: what is material to some is spectral illusion to others. What is perhaps less obvious is that the uncertainties of conjecture make the impossibility of a final determination of what is "material"—for the Victorians of the 1870s, the Sumbanese of the 1980s, and, I wager, a large number of other "moderns" besides—a source of fear. Improper determinations of the material trigger not only contempt from the properly converted but also the fear that their subject position might not be as unassailable as their conversion seemed to signify.[27] Iconoclasts, in other words, frequently fear that the hammer of the righteous may descend on their own idols as well. The fear of matter haunts the modern world of anti-iconic abstraction.

Some Vectors of Contest over Materiality

This suggests that we can profitably try to locate the modern contempt, as well as fear, of "materiality" and "materialism" within different types of relationship, as a way of preparing for the diversity of contests in which we can find these terms embedded—both on the analytical and on the empirical level. I would like to briefly indicate four conceptual relationships in which materiality and materialism gain different meanings and work toward different outcomes: *abstraction* as opposed to *concreteness*, the *spiritual* as opposed to the *material*, the *subjective* as opposed to the *objective*, and the *cultural* as opposed to the *natural*. Materiality acquires different meanings and locations in each relationship— let alone when several of these relationships apply simultaneously to the social action under study. The same goes for "materialism," except that the addition of the *–ism* signifies that the abstraction of "materiality" now serves as a prescription as well as a description.[28] Occidental culture's invocations of "materialism" rarely explicate what *kind* of materiality it prescribes (although one might have to make an exception for Marx in this regard[29]), despite the fact that such invocations have become a global phenomenon since the 1870s.

Let me discuss some implications of these oppositions without pretending to be exhaustive or systematic. Regarding materiality or materialism as an aspect of a relation between the abstract and the concrete, it is necessary to point out that three of the main terms that Occidental culture used to talk about an untranscended materiality—*the fetish, the rarity,* and *the fact*—all emerged within a historical process marked by abstraction and are located in relation to the abstract spaces of the global market, of statistical enumeration and bookkeeping, and of early museum displays.[30] It seems, therefore, that it is impossible to think such radically concrete forms of materiality without the conditions created by this process of abstraction—that is, without capitalist calculation, mathesis, and (scientific) taxonomy. Thus, it seems necessary to stress that radical materiality emerges in Occidental discourses at least in part by neglecting the ways in which such abstract frames have been materialized in everyday practice and how these abstract frames produce untranscended materiality in contrast.[31]

We encounter something quite different when we discuss materiality in relation to the spiritual: here, the emphasis lies on the (im)possibility of discerning the invisible structures or causes of the human or natural world with the human eye or its prostheses. The spiritual is a supersensory entity that can only emerge as a "fact" by conjecture, that is, by treating the material as a mere *effect* of something invisible yet more fundamental.[32] The opposition between spirituality and materiality, therefore, always implies the possibility of *gnosis*: a mode of reasoning from the data of everyday experience toward a hidden or esoteric realm in which materialism is impossible and materiality never really real. This is the mode of reasoning of the Theosophist mentioned above (among many others), who says that fossil bones may not be *lusus naturae* but that their true reality lies several planes of existence above our sense perception. This is a globally popular mode of reasoning: it was not restricted to nineteenth-century occultists or their Indian nationalist counterparts but spread into twentieth-century forms of nationalism and "New Age religion" as well.[33] As we shall see, Victorian "agnosticism"—Thomas Huxley's attempt to escape the accusation of being an atheist and materialist—uses conjectures in some ways similar to modern gnosis when it invokes "statistical returns" and its patterns of "culture."

The modern gnostic perceives *all* reality as a contrived "fact," as something that forms a barrier to understanding the virtual reality of the spiritual. This shows that the opposition between subject and object—one of the ways to think the process of "objectification" referred to by Daniel Miller,[34] as well as my third conceptualization of the relationships in which materiality takes place—cannot determine the location of materiality, either. In the modern occultist's world of "spiritual" reality, the subject is fettered by flesh and convention, an individual who confronts an objective world that has no material reality except as an effect—something that seems to be diametrically opposed to the scientific notion of a transparently cogitating subject (usually generated by calculation and mathesis) that processes the "real" sensory data of the modern "fact." As Mary Poovey has argued, the modern fact is composed of Francis Bacon's notion of deracinated particulars (which brings it quite close to the rarity and/or fetish[35]), coupled to the idea that the fact should be "evidence for" some theory.[36] This view (which many argue was basic to the so-called Scientific Revolution) opposes a material isolate to an autonomous theoretical subject.[37] The modern gnostic, however, opposes a material subject, which is not autonomous but bound by its own incarnation and socialization, to the immaterial, transcendent, and spiritual object of hidden wisdom—only through the latter can he or she reach autonomous subjecthood. This has crucial consequences for our understanding of materiality, for in the scientific confrontation between subject and object, matter and morality have been separated from each other, while in the modern occultists' view, matter is inherently moral, that is, evil.[38]

Modern occultists, therefore, point to another, more phenomenological understanding of objectification, in which the autonomous theoretical subject has been replaced by an embedded perceiving subject that is itself material, and that may become the object of (or "suffer") an object with agency—a process more akin to Bourdieu's dialectic of objectification and embodiment. This materiality of the perceiving subject is more sharply articulated by the opposition between culture and nature. One needs to distinguish two dominant views here: one, fundamental to Victorian science and positivism in general, in which the cultured human being confronts objective nature "out there"; and the other, more common among Romantic forms of humanism, in which "human nature" confronts objectifications of culture and the social in a mostly threatening way. In the former view, "nature" (or even the supernatural) is a material truth (a "fact") if one can be certain that it is not man-made (that it is not culture in disguise)—for if truth were a cultural construction, rather than a reflection of nature or divinity, it would become subject to the iconoclastic action of critique.[39] The second view builds on this suspicion of man-made matter, since it regards the human subject as a natural organism that has difficulties in coming to terms with the alienating objectifications of culture. This subject fears to become enslaved to the machines of industry and bureaucracy, or to be turned into a mere effect of commodified desires—in short, to succumb to what many Romantics, modern Gnostics, and psychotherapists depict as the "materialism" of the modern world, which threatens our authentic spiritual development. These two views point to a peculiar modern conundrum. In the former, materiality is positively valued—as natural fact, a source of certainty on which to build human knowledge—as long as it is not man-made. However, it is not moral in itself—unless, of course, the fact turns out to be of divine origin, something that mere matter, in this view, can never prove. In the latter view, materiality is always moral, but *only* if man-made, and in that case, it is either of a lower order—as matter under control by human agency—or regarded with suspicion, as potentially agentive, alienating, and evil.

This attitude to materiality has been identified as typically "Calvinist": the combination of contempt for inferior, that is, man-made, signs and the fear that these material signs will nevertheless reduce human autonomy.[40] The modern fear of matter arises from this combination, which says that the visible and material can never be social agents unless animated by human or divine intention. This view thereby can "dematerialize exchange and treat material objects as merely signs of some immaterial value."[41] If we suppose—following Max Weber—that Calvinism had an important influence on the development of capitalist conceptions of rational calculation, we can expect this combination of contempt and fear of materiality to play an important role in Victorian science and inform much of the content of contemporary "materialism." At the same time, one may wonder how such fear of matter can be reconciled with the reliance of Victorian scientists on material evidence as a source of certainty—the positivist vector of culture and nature discussed above. All of the vectors of contest over materiality that I have discussed—in a very sketchy and unsystematic fashion—play a role in understanding the complexity of this situation, to which we now turn.

Late Victorian "Materialism"

The dominant Victorian use of *materialism* before Karl Marx does not rely on an opposition between materialism and idealism—that is a nineteenth-century philosophical innovation, which space does not allow me to deal with here. "Materialism" emerges in the late seventeenth and early eighteenth centuries as an accusation, a Protestant critique of a way of thinking that, since the early Christian patriarchs, was identified with Epicurean philosophy and its perceived tendency to liberate human lust and gluttony—a tendency that John Stuart Mill still had to counter when explaining the meaning of utilitarianism.[42] If "materialism" was, in Victorian intellectual circles, opposed to anything, that was "spiritualism" rather than idealism. Materialism was seen as a denial of the divinity of the soul, of God's natural plan, and of the divine provenance of morality—never mind that those who explicitly adhered to these propositions were scarce and rarely labeled themselves as "materialist" until well into the nineteenth century.[43] This does not, of course, deny that an increasing number of scientists and philosophers maintained a certain primacy of material evidence in order to reach conclusions about the order of things, but they understood materiality predominantly as "fact"—as *evidence for* an as yet insufficiently understood system. Rather than a denial of the moral heritage of Christianity, such a Scientific treatment of material evidence became subsumed under the prophecies of a "New Reformation," which, despite its huge differences, strongly resonated in tone as well as content with its Protestant predecessor.[44]

The ideas of the arguably most prominent exponent of this secularizing movement, the "Pope of Agnosticism," Thomas Henry Huxley, can illustrate this. Huxley consistently refused to accept the accusation of being a "materialist," arguing that the doctrine that matter was the all-determining instance of life and mind was just as metaphysical as the position that everything has to be explained by divine intervention. Unlike the physical determinism of his friend and colleague John Tyndall (whose position Huxley caricaturized by saying, "Given the molecular forces in a mutton chop, deduce Hamlet or Faust therefrom"), Huxley told his Christian interlocutor Charles Kingsley:

> I know nothing of Necessity, abominate the word Law. I don't know whether Matter is anything distinct from Force. I don't know that atoms are anything but pure myths. Cogito, ergo sum is to my mind a ridiculous piece of bad logic[,] all I can say at any time being 'Cogito.' The Latin form I hold to be preferable to the English "I think" because the latter asserts the existence of an Ego—about which the bundle of phenomena at present addressing you knows nothing.

To Huxley, the only sensible axiom was that "materialism and spiritualism are opposite poles of the same absurdity."[45] To escape the accusation of being a "materialist," therefore, Huxley invented the word *agnostic*, as a way of saying that he did not yet have the evidence required to prefer one metaphysical position over the other, assuming such evidence could ever become available. Agnosticism was the ideal middle ground between the Spiritualism of someone like Alfred Wallace (about whom more below) and the German Darwinian Ernst Haeckel's materialism—provided it was regarded as a method rather than a creed.[46] Thus, to Huxley, materiality was ideally meant to appear as a "fact" of nature—that is, a necessary methodological category that was destined to be subsumed under some system, at present still unknown or hypothetical. At the same time, Huxley—a true admirer of Thomas Carlyle—was a Romantic in his refusal to adopt a Cartesian subject position (and, in addition, a Protestant interiority and autonomy of the "soul") by seeing himself as a merely material "bundle of phenomena." Note that Huxley's agnosticism retains *both* the positivist materiality of objective fact *and* the Romantic materiality of the fettered and limited subject.

However, Huxley's "New Reformation" could never do without conjecture about an encompassing and enduring system of knowledge to be reached in the future, and his agnosticism therefore retained an aspect of modern gnosis. When countering Christians who argued that "agnostic" was merely a euphemism for "infidel," that is, someone who does not believe in the authority of Jesus Christ, Huxley said that either the evidence of the Bible shows that the authority of Christ was (partly) based on the primitive "survivals" of spirit possession and witchcraft (a position that he felt could not be defended) or it suggests that Christ's moral doctrine had been covered up by the superstitions of the evangelists.[47] This conjecture turned a large part of the texts of Scripture into merely man-made and mistaken matter that, in a gnostic fashion, betrayed the true spiritual causes of the success of Christianity: its morality—thus bypassing the theologians by reducing religion to moral philosophy. Despite criticizing the "gnostic" tendency in Auguste Comte's prediction that Science would become the religion of humanity, Huxley, too, divined that such a "new idol" could not endure and that religion as theology would die (whereas religion as morality would live). Huxley's prophecies were, as Adrian Desmond has brought out so well, the apotheosis of Dissent, the iconoclastic "last act of the Protestant Reformation," which, by shifting the emphasis of reform from dog-collar to white-collar experts, proclaimed the liberation of the industrial and professional classes (with a heavy emphasis on the primacy of the latter[48]). In such prophecies, material evidence was reduced to a sign of the new Scientific expertise embodied by a rising "intellectual aristocracy," of which Huxley was the most prominent advocate.[49]

Victorian "Spiritualism"

Huxley's paradoxical opposition to gnosis was informed not only by his attempts to counter the authority of Christian theologians, or the adherents of "Comtism," but also by his aversion to his contemporaries, the "Spiritualists"—those who believed in the possibility of communicating with the spirits of the dead through a sensitive medium. The main representative of this group was Huxley's former colleague Alfred Russel Wallace, who was famous for co-inventing "natural selection" together with Charles Darwin around 1860. Wallace described his conversion to Spiritualism as follows:

> Up to the time when I first became acquainted with the facts of Spiritualism, . . . I was so thorough and confirmed a materialist that I could not at that time find a place in my mind for the conception of spiritual existence, or for any other agencies in the universe than matter and force. Facts, however, are stubborn things. My curiosity was at first excited by some slight but inexplicable phenomena occurring in a friend's family, and my desire for knowledge and love of truth forced me to continue the inquiry. The facts became more and more assured, more and more varied, more and more removed from anything that modern science taught or modern philosophy speculated upon. The facts beat me.[50]

Here, the "fact's" materiality—the events that Wallace experienced during séances held at his house and at others'—is allowed to subvert "materialism" (as an abstract system associated with "modern science and philosophy"). As I have argued elsewhere, Wallace's "spiritual facts" mark a moment at which a more Baconian emphasis on the democratic epistemology of domestic experiment was superseded by a conception of "fact" founded on statistics and laboratory experiment, adopted by the recently triumphant intellectual aristocracy of John Tyndall, Thomas Huxley, John Lubbock, and Edward Tylor.[51] Statistics and the laboratory made public science increasingly inaccessible to lay audiences, and this new conception of expertise pushed the Baconian image of the "humble and self-taught" scientist and the field of domestic experiment into the margins—among other things, into the modern occultism of the Theosophical Society, founded in 1875 by Madame Blavatasky and Colonel Olcott.[52]

Blavatsky's modern gnosis tried to make this field of domestic experiment inviolable to Scientific critique by arguing that, although the methods of the "psycho-spiritual" and "natural and physical sciences" did not differ, "our fields of research are on two different planes, and our instruments are *made by no human hands*, for which reason perchance they are only the more reliable."[53] Similarly, Wallace—whose plea for spiritualism stood halfway between triumphant Science and emerging occultism—thought that "spirit-photography" was a method untainted by human manipulation.[54] By contrast, Scientific opponents such as Edward Tylor described the materiality of the séance as a human construction: as the result of either fraud or hysteria, as voluntary or involuntary deception.[55] Both Scientists and their plebeian and popular opponents, therefore, valued their subject matter the more it shed the taint of human hands. However, if both display a fear of matter that is inherited from Protestantism, it can be argued that the Scientists were more responsible for the process of dematerialization that occurred in social science as a result. Edward Tylor's understanding of "spiritualism" can clarify this.

Tylor shared, of course, Huxley's suspicion of theologians, and he was the probable source of Huxley's classification of biblical stories of spirit possession and trance states as superstitious "survivals." But even though Tylor distanced himself from the séance of the Spiritualists by inserting it in the same "allochronic" slot, he was much more coevally involved with Spiritualism than that suggests.[56] Not only did Tylor feel compelled to research Spiritualist phenomena himself—most likely because a debate with Alfred Wallace in 1872 pushed him to do so—but their emergence robbed Tylor of the chance to apply the term *spiritualism* to the field that he wanted to describe in *Primitive Culture*. I cannot go into this entanglement here,[57] except to note that Tylor's historically contingent decision to choose "animism" over "spiritualism" and "fetishism" for his antitheological description of "primitive culture" is highly significant for our understanding of Victorian "materialism."

Tylor's decision to define the earliest religion of humanity as "spiritualism"—and when this turned out to be uncomfortably contemporary, as "animism"—contrasts sharply with the similar use of "fetishism" by his teacher, Auguste Comte. With Huxley, Tylor confronted theologians who could heartily agree with a Romantic like Samuel Taylor Coleridge in saying that: "From the fetisch of the imbruted African to the soul-debasing errors of the proud fact-hunting materialist we may trace the various ceremonials of the same idolatry."[58] For theorists of fetishism from Charles De Brosses to Comte and Marx, the fetish's untranscended materiality provided a way to critique Christian monotheism, but to Victorian anthropologists like Tylor and Huxley, such materialism was a hindrance to achieving respectability in competition with, and in the eyes of, the contemporary Christian establishment.[59] The choice of "animism" over "fetishism" as a critique of the theological establishment was partly motivated by the fact that "fetishism" was too close to "materialism" and hence to immorality.[60] Even if Huxley openly dissociated himself from materialism as a form of metaphysics, he was still subject to the suspicion of attaching more value to material evidence than to morality and was continually anxious about it.[61] Likewise, Tylor tried to avoid being associated with a materialist "idolatry," and in retrospect, his consequent psychologization of the fetish in terms of animism stands (together with John McLennan's socialization of the fetish in terms of totemism and kinship[62]) as one of the more important steps in the dematerialization of culture that would characterize anthropology at least until the last decades of the twentieth century.

Such dematerialization seems the more paradoxical because Tylor was employed by an institution with firm roots in the Baconian reverence for material rarity and fact: the Pitt-Rivers Museum, holding the ethnographic collection from the Tradescant family's cabinet of wonders and the Ashmolean museum.[63] However, if Tylor, like Lubbock and Huxley, measured human progress at least in part on the basis of the evolution of artifacts or technology, one should be careful not to confuse this interest in material objects with an interest in their materiality as such. As any visitor to the Pitt-Rivers Museum will notice, objects take place there only as part of a classificatory *system*: in particular, the *series* that was a staple of the nineteenth-century exhibitionary complex.[64] The minimal abstraction of such classificatory acts consisted of the distinction between "survivals" and living examples of human construction, and Alfred Wallace unsuccessfully attacked their arbitrariness when opposing the material facts of the séance to the materialist classifications of "modern science and philosophy."[65] *Primitive Culture* shows that it was not *material* culture that interested Tylor. "Culture," that "complex whole,"[66] was presented as an effect of the scientist's expert operations modelled on "the statistician's returns":

> The fact is that a stone arrow-head, a carved club, an idol, a grave-mound where slaves and property have been buried for the use of the dead, an account of a sorcerer's rites in making rain, a table of numerals, the conjugation of a verb, are things which each express the state of a people as to one particular point of culture, as truly as the tabulated numbers of deaths by poison, and of chests of tea imported, express in a different way other partial results of the general life of a whole community.[67]

In other words, Tylor was looking for the *abstract* categories that tools and idols expressed, at the same level of, and thought analogously to, the abstracted facts of statistics and political arithmetic that, as Mary Poovey argues, were replacing the Baconian "modern fact" at around the same time.[68] Thus, the dematerialization of anthropological objects was reinforced by the implicit frame of abstraction and mathesis that was about to push ethnography into the margins of science.[69] This prophecy (of, among other things, ridding ourselves of present "survivals") identifies Tylor as a descendant of the same Dissenting stock as Huxley, and both as representatives of a secularized Protestantism that—adopting the frame of mind of its theological enemy—regarded materiality with both contempt and fear. In this frame of mind, both "culture" and statistical "returns" were immaterial, occult entities—but they derived from an ideology that regarded them as more real than the matters that met its eye.

Conclusion

One can conclude that at least some of the forms of materialism that emerge in the nineteenth century are—paradoxically—major steps in a process of social and natural abstraction.[70] One might even say that the gnostic move toward the spiritual made by Alfred Wallace in his assessment of spiritual séances employs a more "material" (because phenomenological) sense of "fact"—one that was marginalized in the decades to follow.[71] Prophetic dematerialization played a central role in the emergence of social science— through, for instance, the reification and deification of "Society" and "State" by, among others, early sociologists like Emile Durkheim.[72] That declaration of independence of the social expert (or the priest of the secular welfare state) legitimized his project by reifying its object, supported by a repetition of iconoclastic gestures that, in Durkheim's case, include the attempt to destroy his predecessors' "materialistic naturalism" in order to prophecy that "social life is defined by its *hyperspirituality*."[73] Similar processes of dematerialization can be said to constitute the objects of the "State" and the "economy," and thus to legitimize the rule of the social-scientific expert,[74] confirming that social science is, in many ways, the heir of the abstractions of Protestant dissent.

Early on in this intellectual process, when reflecting on the Protestant roots of rationality and capitalism, Weber equated prophecy with rationality, studying the combination of rationalization and disenchantment in theodicies that explained why the morally corrupt were usually materially better off and that proclaimed, through the prophet, a lower-class ethical mission of renouncing the material means of salvation.[75] He also said that the spiritual motivation supporting this ethical mission has long since evaporated from the iron cage of calculation.[76] Coupled to my examples, this suggests that the voice of reason may now merely be prophetic *because of* its opposition to materiality—understood here as the relationship of objectification and embodiment—and conversely, that the modern fear, or contempt, of matter, is a this-worldly materialization of a desire for an other-worldly existence. Putting this differently, one might say that Huxley's or Tylor's prophetic reduction of material evidence to a sign of an encompassing (future, immaterial) system announces the twentieth-century's Saussurian temptation to collapse the problem of the fetish (that is, the question, not if, but how and why things act on human beings) into the problem of ideology (that is, the question of how and why systems of signification act on human beings) thus eliding the question about the material existence of these systems.[77] Anthropology, like the other social sciences, was from the outset a "reformer's science,"[78] and any reformer needs an immaterial future—an ideology—to be able to disregard the material contingencies of his existing relationships—or "mark them out for destruction."[79] It may, therefore, be time to reverse Weber's identification of dematerialization and disenchantment, and recognize that in current social science, the abstractions of culture and the social produce a magic, or a fetish, of their own, and that we need a non-Protestant sense of materiality to counter such enchantments.

Dangerous Things

One African Genealogy

Matthew Engelke

To what extent can religion be given over to a project of immateriality? In 2003, the Victoria and Albert Museum in London mounted an exhibit called "Gothic: Art for England," which provided something of an answer. One of the pieces in the show was a defaced church panel. Sometime in the sixteenth century, the image on the panel had been scratched out. A verse from the Bible had been written in its place. The panel was an artifact of the Reformation: the Word had been used to destroy evidence of Catholic idolatry. But if some English iconoclast had purged the panel of its idolatrous nature, it was still, to the casual observer, an object. Whether or not its defacement was motivated by the idea that "nothing spiritual can be present when there is anything material and physical,"[1] it could still be hung on the wall. Stripped of its theological and social dimensions (in a manner perhaps only museum exhibits can accomplish), the materiality of the panel remained. The destruction of Christian art in Gothic England suggests something of greater importance to the study of materiality in religious modes of signification. In a "vulgar" sense,[2] it reminds us that a project of imma-teriality—of presenting the spiritual without the material and physi-cal—is difficult to accomplish. The repudiation of the material is a selective process. What sustains projects of immateriality in religious practice is always the definition of what counts as materially dangerous. Indeed, religion cannot do without material culture.[3] The question posed at the outset of this chapter then becomes:[4] In what *sense* can religion be given over to a project of immateriality?

Daniel Miller has recently suggested that we can approach the com-mitment to immateriality best through "the messy terrain of ethnogra-phy."[5] What matters in a museum exhibit documenting one strain of sixteenth-century iconoclasm is not the irreducible materiality of a church panel but how its defacement expresses a logic of spiritual transcendence. Within any semiotic ideology, we cannot assume that all material culture is valued in the same way. The task then becomes the recognition of how "relative" or "plural" materialities gain expression in practice.[6]

In this chapter I focus on the logic of materiality in the Masowe weChishanu (or "Friday") Church, an apostolic church with large followings throughout Zimbabwe. As I hope to make clear, the "Friday apostolics" are committed to a project of immateriality. They want a religion in which things do not matter. For them, as I have explained in more detail elsewhere,[7] material culture in its various forms constitutes the single most important obstacle in developing a spiritual relationship with God. But, as we might expect, the commitment to immateriality makes what things the apostolics do use in religious life all the more important. Here, I focus primarily on the stuff of their healing—the objects and substances that Friday prophets employ to cure people of their afflictions. Healing is of central importance in Zimbabwe to both African Christian and "traditional" religious practitioners. Because apostolic prophets and traditional healers use material things (and often the *same* things), how the authority of objects was defined as part of a Christian project of transcendence was a subject of some importance in the Church.

Spiritual healing in Zimbabwe is big business, literally and figuratively. The Friday prophets have staked out a significant corner in this market, but it is hardly theirs to control. One of the major concerns in the Friday churches is the relationship between the circulation of therapeutic materiel (i.e., the objects and substances that prophets use in healing) and the meanings people associate with that materiel. This concern stems from the fact that Friday prophets and "traditional healers" both use material things, and often the *same* things, in their healing practices. Defining the authority of objects in accordance with the terms of the Friday message is therefore a task of some importance. The commitment to immateriality makes what things the apostolics do use in religious life all the more important—not least when other healers want to define the qualities of those things in a different way. Within the realm of healing, I argue, keeping the commitment to immateriality depends on the ability to define the significance and authority of objects. It depends on the ability to assert, through the elaboration of a semiotic ideology, that "some things are more material than others."[8] There is a semiotics to therapeutics that tells us something important about how the Friday apostolics conceive of what they call a "live and direct faith," that is, one not mediated by things.

A Sticky Subject

Like many anthropologists, I found that my field research was punctuated by a number of ailments, both real and imagined. I was fortunate in that the Friday apostolics always took a polite interest in my well being. In an effort to maintain some critical distance from the churches, however, I tried to be careful about what I shared regarding my health, and also about what I took from the prophets when they did manage to extract a complaint or observe a symptom. This was not always easy, and on one occasion, at the congregation I most often attended, Juranifiri Santa ("the place of healing"), I found myself the recipient of one of their more significant preparations. It is called "holy honey," and, as far as the Masowe are concerned, it is the most effective spiritual medicine. Although the honey is primarily used to fight the ill effects of witchcraft, it was thought it might also relieve my this-worldly ailments.

Holy honey is not simply honey. Knowledge of the exact ingredients is guarded by the church's elders, but as I worked my way through two jars of the stuff over the course of several weeks, I could detect in it hints of cooking oil and lemon juice. The honey is dark brown and viscous. It is sticky-sweet and has a tangy aftertaste (the lemons), with hints of smoke. Regardless of the ingredients or their preparation, however, I was told that what mattered was the blessing conferred upon it by the Holy Spirit. Indeed, holy honey, like all apostolic medicines, is understood to be powerful because of its spiritual properties. As a substance, it does not matter.

The apostolics' honey, perhaps like an Azande's *benge* or a Thai Buddhist amulet, derives its importance from what is considered an immaterial quality.[9] Apostolics would always insist to me that the Holy Spirit can cure someone's afflictions without the benefit of any medicine or blessed object. Nevertheless, holy honey occupies a privileged position in their religious imagination. By contrast to the other medicines they might receive, honey is characterized as something like a smart drug: it just makes you feel good. It gives you more energy throughout the day. It helps you think clearly. Some men told me it increased their sexual stamina. All things considered, and dutiful statements about the power of the Holy Spirit aside, if apostolics could have any healing treatment, it would be honey.

Yet there was something about holy honey that unsettled the apostolics. While its properties were understood to be the result of a spiritual blessing, in practice they sometimes treated it as if these properties were inherent. It was as if holy honey, qua honey, could do things. I got a clear sense of this the day I received a second jar in the course of my own "treatment." It was immediately after one of the Wednesday early-morning church services at Juranifiri, and I had promised to give a friend in the congregation a ride to his office in Harare. He knew I had the honey in the car, and he talked about it all the way into town, reminding me of its beneficial side effects and remarking on the fact that he was about to face a long and tiring day at work. As we pulled into the parking lot of his office he lingered for a moment. "Ah," he said. "Just one sip of that stuff might do me good." The prospect of a miserable day at work does not constitute an illness, as far as the Masowe are concerned. Moreover, apostolics claim that their medicines are only ever intended and effective for the persons to whom they are "prescribed." Nevertheless, by asking for a sip of the honey my friend made it clear in that moment how easy it is to slip from the principle of the immaterial to the lure of the material.

One of the lessons in this awkward exchange is that material culture can play an important role in "spiritual" healing. In a sense, however, this point is so obvious that we might not think it warrants discussion. There has been a good deal of literature on medicines, witchcraft substances, and tools of divination in Africa—not least Evans-Pritchard's work on the Azande.[10] What is notable in the case with my friend is how his request for a sip of the honey undercut the more general claim that apostolics make about healing substances. If God's blessing is what makes honey a powerful spiritual medicine, and if its use is inspired for individual cases, then for my friend it ought to have been just an ordinary thing, mere honey. Clearly, it was not. Its materiality mattered.

I want to use this vignette to frame a more general discussion of the apostolic disposition toward therapeutic things, because it brings out so well the specificities of the relationship between material culture and immateriality in their "live and direct semiotics." What makes my friend's request for honey interesting is the extent to which it highlights an emphasis on the immateriality of religious practice. Apostolics are wary of spiritual materiel; religious things are dangerous things, and often betray shortcomings of faith. The manipulation of material culture is therefore a delicate matter in the church, and how the material and immaterial worlds are reconciled is a process fraught with pitfalls. As I hope to make clear later in this chapter, honey both challenges and confirms this logic in a poignant way. That morning in the car, it was a sticky subject for my friend. It made him feel awkward, even embarrassed, given his religious commitments. By treating the honey as a thing, he was undermining an important aspect of the semiotic ideology that, as an apostolic, he was supposed to uphold. Before explaining this further, however, it is necessary to say something about how the apostolics develop a systematic repudiation of the material. The discussion of healing allows us to bring these ways together into sharp focus.

Doing Without

Within the context of this chapter, I want to highlight two aspects of the apostolics' repudiation of material culture. The first has to do with the media of religious authority and experience. The Friday apostolics say the Bible is unnecessary because they have a live and direct connection with God. They trace this connection to the coming of their inspirational founder, Johane, in 1932. It is marked, in part, by stories of Johane burning the Bible and certain things he said during the initial days of his divinely inspired work.[11] The point I want to reinforce here is that rejection of the Bible is an indication of the apostolics' concern with material things—about what they can and cannot do. Books, in their view, cannot provide a personal relationship with God and often serve to stand in the way.

Following Colleen McDannell, we might say that apostolics consider themselves "strong" Christians, because they claim to "grasp spiritual truths directly."[12] In fact, even more than some of their Protestant forebears, the Masowe mean to do without things. Inasmuch as European iconoclasts moved away from images, they replaced those images—as evidenced in the V&A "Gothic" exhibit—with the book (what Ernst Troeltsch, as I will discuss in the conclusion to this chapter, would later call the "Lutheran Pope"). This practice of replacing objects with one another is widespread in the history of Protestantism. In the United States, for example, McDannell tells us how "Protestants turned words into objects. During the nineteenth century, family Bibles became so lavish and encyclopedic that they functioned more like religious furniture than biblical texts."[13] In the mission fields of southern Africa, missionaries also often spoke about the Bible as a thing in itself, something that had agency.[14] Today, the legacy of this ideology still shapes evangelism, and from the apostolics' point of view, a Protestant's Bible is no less a material impediment to faith than a Catholic's icon. The apostolics see evidence of this throughout Zimbabwe, where people in other churches treat the Bible as an end in itself. Elsewhere, the Bible will be wrapped in expensive leather bindings and displayed prominently in church services: the apostolics have no time for such "religious furniture."

The second aspect of the apostolics' concern with material culture brings us back to a consideration of apostolic etiology. The anthropological literature on healing in central and southern Africa often stresses that healing is "fundamentally concerned with the reconstitution of physical, social, and spiritual order."[15] For the apostolics these social orders must be reconstituted as Christian, and thus purged of the dangers of "African custom" or "culture." It is not that the apostolics deny the realities of witchcraft, then, or the sway of the ancestors. As Matthew Schoffeleers writes, most African Independent churches in southern Africa "take belief in the power of witches, evil spirits and other mystical agents seriously and are for that reason, in the eyes of a large section of the public, able to provide help in cases where such agents are thought to be involved."[16] Indeed, healing is what draws most people to the Friday churches.

Johane himself is remembered as a powerful healer—perhaps the most powerful of all, at least during the first few years of his mission. I was given several accounts of Johane's abilities. In each, the power of African Christian healing lay in its superiority to both Western biomedicine and traditional curative practices (spiritual and nonspiritual). One elder of the church, whom I call Marcus, once told me the story of how his grandmother came to Johane:

> when she joined Johane Masowe [in the early 1930s], one of her sons was very sick. And when she went to consult Johane, her son got better within three days. Yet she had moved around—she had gone to hospital and to other spiritual healers and to

the *n'anga* ["witch doctor"] without any joy, until in three days' time Johane Masowe prayed for him and the boy was up and running.

What made Johane such an effective healer, and what has fueled the success of Friday prophets since his time, was, in the opinion of Marcus and others, his focus on ridding the world of witchcraft medicines. In a November 1932 statement to the British South Africa Police, Johane states that the voice of God commanded him: "Tell the natives to throw away their witchcraft medicines."[17] Whether they had been given these medicines or whether they employed them to the benefit or detriment of others, the first step in the process of healing was to rid oneself of these *things*.

There is no exact term for "witchcraft medicines" in Shona (the language spoken by the majority of Friday apostolics in Zimbabwe), and we cannot be sure what word Johane used in his native chiManyika dialect. *Muti* is the most common word for "medicine" (it also means "tree"); another common term is *mushonga*. In Shona, however, *muti* and *mushonga* can have either positive or negative connotations. In other words, they can be used to signify what in English would be a difference between medicine and poison (Shona: *chepfu*). But Shona speakers (and Zimbabweans more generally) do not often describe what witches use as "medicines" at all; if anything, they would be said to use poisons—or perhaps *bwanga*, "'black' medicine." What witches use is *uroyi*, although this term refers both to an essence ("witchcraftness," as it were) and to the objects and substances that witches employ. These objects and substances are usually organic matter: the blood and organs of humans or animals, for example, and the thorns and leaves from certain kinds of plants. Witches also use inorganic things in their "black medicines," like coins and shards of glass.

Several of the "creatures" or "familiars" that witches use (in addition to snakes, hyenas, and owls) are constructed out of body parts and other things they can collect or steal. No one I met in Zimbabwe claimed to know exactly how this is done; witches keep their knowledge to themselves. "It's a mystery," my friend Shimmer said. "Because the people who create those things, they never reveal. They never say *tinogadzira so-so-so* ["we assemble (them) like so"]. It's top secret." Despite this, most of the people I knew in Zimbabwe agreed upon the general characteristics of the creatures in a witch's bestiary. A *chidhoma* (pl. *zvidhoma*), for example, is a dwarflike creature that feeds on the blood of humans. Shimmer told me that he'd heard about one *chidhoma* that was constructed out of bits of skin sewn together into a humanlike form, which was then stuffed with paper money. It was made for a man who wanted to succeed in business, and he had to give the *chidhoma* the blood of his relatives in yearly installments in exchange. A *chikwambo* (pl. *zvikwambo*) or *tokoloshi* (a Ndebele-language term that Shona speakers often use) can be made by witches but is more often a "real" creature—more like a goblin, in other words, than a homunculus.

Blair Rutherford has pointed out that "European colonizers [in Zimbabwe] often lumped together diverse practices, moral concepts and person categories under the rubric of witchcraft and sorcery, drawing on their own European categories and history for these terms."[18] This often meant that spirit mediums and *n'angas* were spoken about as witches or "witch doctors," even though they had nothing to do with the "occult." The Friday apostolics make similar lumpings. As far as they are concerned, the term *witchcraft medicines* should cover more than the substances and creatures manufactured by witches. Anything a spirit medium or traditional healer uses ought to be thought of in the same way. In theory, then, to an apostolic *muti* is more or less the same thing as *uroyi*.

In theory. According to Macheka Gombera, the apostolics have not always been so strict on this point. Gombera was a well-known healer, who helped formed the African N'angas Herbalist Association in the 1950s. His *sekuru* ("grandfather") taught him how to mix several kinds of medicine in a series of dreams. Gombera also traveled throughout Mount Darwin and Chiweshe in the mid-1930s, collecting mixtures from other spiritual healers. It was in that period that he ran into Johane's followers. "The climax of my knowledge came when it was announced that Johane had come and that he had ordered people to burn all the *n'anga* medicines," Gombera has told the oral historian Dawson Munjeri. According to Gombera, some of Johane's followers agreed to sell "all the *muti* that was of medicinal value" to him, rather than burn it, as they had been instructed. Gombera "hated the Church" for calling for "a halt to *n'anga* belief." He saw his work as a benefit to the people and resented the all-or-nothing militancy of Johane's principles. But the betrayal of those principles, as Gombera makes clear to Munjeri, was both a hopeful sign that *n'angas* might continue and a telling indication that some apostolics might have a price, no matter how strong their rhetoric.[19]

The rejection of traditional curative and occult practices is one way in which the Masowe seek to differentiate themselves in a crowded field of practitioners. This difference is still represented in Johane's forceful image of the witchcraft medicines. Indeed, driven as it is by the desire for accumulation,[20] "witchcraft" is an apostolic's catch-all phrase of scorn, shorthand for the dangerous things produced by practitioners of spirit outside Christianity. As Gombera's experience suggests, however, it is not always easy to control the circulation of things, much less their meanings or the ways in which they are exchanged.

The Places, Attires, and Practice of Healing

The principles of healing resemble the places in which it is performed. The sacred spaces of apostolic worship—clearings in the wilderness, which are not marked by any man-made constructions—are both everywhere and nowhere, a struggle against the fixed form.[21] While some of the major prophets now operate "hospital wards," these are built spaces in which to house patients during the course of their treatment. The increasing influence of architecture on the dynamics of church life is, to be sure, unmistakable. For all of the ways in which the apostolics' "innovations in space" are becoming grounded in the physical world, however, it is telling that no prophets in the Friday churches have advocated holding church services or healing sessions under a roof.[22] Resistance to the lure of the material is, in this sense, still quite strong. Healing takes place in a place that is, in principle, no place at all.

In the absence of church buildings, the white robes of the apostolics form a kind of phantom wall that defines the perimeters of the ritual space. These robes are important, because they are material evidence of commitment to the faith. And yet the robes also mark a paradox: they are the material evidence of the apostolic commitment to immateriality. What makes them special is their simplicity—their leveling effect. By contrast to the expensive suits and dresses one might see in other churches or the elaborate dress of a spirit medium or *n'anga*, apostolic fashion is an antifashion. The robes are another statement about why things should not matter in the religious life. They are supposed to be "insignificant in their materiality."[23]

Apart from the robes, the staffs (*tsvimbo*) that some men carry are the only other everyday artifacts of faith. However, not all prophets in the Friday churches ask the men in their congregations to keep staffs; some, in fact, forbid them.[24] Like robes, staffs give the men who carry them a sense of "having" faith, because they carry them only after becoming 'full-fledged' members. Staffs are made of bamboo, which in Zimbabwe often grows by the banks of rivers and streams.[25] They are whittled down at either end to smooth them out, but are not carved with elaborate heads, as are the staffs carried by men in other apostolic churches. This is, of course, because they must be "plain" and "not special."

Even with these places and ritual attires in mind, the ritual and social life of a Friday apostolic is, without question, less materially saturated than in most other churches in Zimbabwe. The apostolics have no houses of worship, no elaborate altars, and only simple robes. They do not even have the scripture of their scriptural religion. What is more, while prophets do not want to see their congregations live in poverty, being a successful and faithful Christian does not, in their view, require the accumulation of commodities and material riches. As strong Christians, those "who use objects or images in their devotional lives or who feel that certain places are imbued with special power are seen as needing spiritual help or crutches."[26]

With these points in mind, I want to move on to a more detailed description of the healing rituals that take place in the church. Healing sessions vary in style from one congregation to the next, but there is a general pattern. In most congregations healing sessions are held after the main services on Fridays and Sundays. The more influential prophets, such as Nzira, with whom I worked closely in the 1990s, would hold separate meetings on Saturday afternoons to accommodate the large numbers of people in attendance. When everyone has gathered in a grove or field, seated in a large circle with men and women facing each other, the "chorus" (Shona: *vaimbi*, "singers") begin to sing. Their voices help soothe the congregation's afflictions. The sounds are the call to, and of, the Holy Spirit. The singing may continue for an hour, interspersed with short monologues from a prophet about the power of God and the seriousness of the "battle" taking place. Other verses may be used to reinforce the overriding message that the spiritual war is "not of this world."

Eventually a prophet will ask those who have come for healing to stand up, in accordance with their particular illness. Can they not conceive a child? Are they estranged from their families? Have they lost their jobs? Do they have stomach pains? Are they "mentally ill"? When the sick have been accounted for, church elders call them off to one side of the main gathering. In many congregations, as the patients move off, they shuffle past the prophet, who touches their foreheads. The chorus stands around the prophet, so that the patients move between them. I asked one member of a chorus about the importance of the arrangement: "You see, even a doctor has got his consultation room. So that is [the prophet's] consultation room. So each and every sick person has got to pass through that. And if [some]one has got *zvikwambos* and so forth, [that person] will not be able to pass through that consultation room without that *chikwambo* talking [i.e., making itself known to the prophet]. That place is serious. It's so serious." That place, of course, in no place at all. The walls of a "consultation room" are the robes of the *vaimbi*, and the room thus created is insulated by the sound of voices in song.

After patients pass through the consultation room, the elders arrange them into long rows. The people bend down on their knees, and, over the course of the next hour or so, they are given holy water and other blessings from God in the form of medicines. It is in these sessions that one could expect to receive holy honey. More commonly, however, each person is given a sip of holy water and something else—some object or substance—that has been blessed and that he or she takes away as part of a prescribed treatment.

When apostolics talk about the stuff they receive for healing, they often refer to it, as I have, as "medicine." Indeed, the language of a healing session mirrors the language of a biomedical system. People come as "patients," they are treated in weekly "clinics" and "consultation rooms," and, if necessary, they are watched over by church elders in "hospital wards." Not much is made of this mirroring; they do not see it as a threat to the specificities of their own practices. And today, at least, the Friday apostolics see no reason not to take advantage of medical science. Medicine is, in fact, considered a blessing from God of another kind; it can supplement the more important work of spiritual healing. This is not to say that the apostolics think of aspirin as a spiritual treatment. They see it as entirely "natural." Medical doctors present no problems, theologically speaking, because they do not claim their authority from the spiritual world. In the apostolics' view, this is the key difference between a medical doctor and a *n'anga* or medium. Medical doctors present no cause for alarm because their material things carry no immaterial pretensions. And so, when someone is suffering from witchcraft or because of an angered ancestral spirit, biomedicine may help relieve his or her symptoms. There is nothing inherently wrong with giving aspirin to a bewitched person. All the same, biomedicine will never get to the root of the problem. It will never provide a cure. For that, spiritual intervention is required.

Pebbles and Prayers

Apostolics do not consider holy honey and aspirin to be substances of the same kind. The specific ways in which they refer to their spiritual medicines helps make this differentiation clear. For apostolics, indeed, "the relation between material things and immaterial meanings . . . must be effected through speech."[27] This is especially important when those material things might ambiguate the immaterial meanings. Calling their spiritual medicines *muteuro* is a move against the dangers of materiality in no uncertain terms. The word *muteuro* means "prayer." In the context of this chapter the force of this signification becomes clear. Holy medicines are not identified primarily as "things"; they are, rather, "words." Holy medicine is unlike other therapeutic substances because it is understood to have this languagelike quality.

The most common type of *muteuro* are pebbles.[28] Any pebble or stone about the size of a marble (or smaller) will suit the purposes of the church. I saw elders collect pebbles in the dirt around the *sowe* (place of worship) in preparation for healing sessions. What patients are meant to do with the pebbles can vary. Each case is handled individually, and so when one receives *muteuro* in this form, one also receives instructions for its use. For example, if a patient is suffering from stomach pains, he or she may be asked to place the pebble in a glass of drinking water. The pebble conveys its spiritual blessing to the water, in effect creating holy water "on the spot," without the burden of providing someone with a week's supply of it. Similarly, someone might be asked to place the pebble in the tub or a bucket of water with which one bathes each morning. The *muteuro* helps the water cleanse the body of any spiritual impurities or afflictions. But not every such spiritual remedy involves the manufacture of holy water. If someone has lost his job or is looking for a job, he might be asked to place the *muteuro* in his wallet (although it should never touch money directly). When taking a school exam or test at work, apostolics will keep the pebbles in their pockets, which can help them remember what they have studied. In one of the more unusual testimonies I collected, a man was made redundant from a factory job in Bulawayo. Subsequently, he came to Harare to consult a particular Masowe prophet. The prophet gave him a pebble and told him to mail it to a friend back in Bulawayo. On instruction, this friend then took the pebble and threw it over the perimeter wall of the factory site. Within a few weeks, the man was reinstated in his job.

What makes pebbles and small stones special is the fact that they are not special. Pebbles are free, easy to gather, and do not inspire envy or want—sentiments associated with witchcraft. Pebbles are also very practical. I was told water is an effective medium for healing, but it is difficult to carry, especially in large quantities. It can also be hard to come by for congregations that do not have easy access to a river, borehole, or tap. For this reason, water is used sparingly, and only in the course of an actual healing session, where one five-liter jug might last several weeks if doled out to the patients a sip at a time. Pebbles, on the other hand, are much easier to circulate. In most cases, elders will pass them out during a healing session immediately after the sharing of the water. They are durable, too. While no material thing is foolproof, pebbles come close. If you drop a pebble, you can pick it up. If you drop a cup of holy water, it might be gone forever— dissolving into the ground or spilling into a crack in the floor. Pebbles do not break or split easily. They maintain their integrity in the face of regular use (even as, in geological terms, they represent a process of gradual dissolution). Cloth and wood—long used in other Christian churches and in other healing rituals—might tear or splinter or break. And pebbles are easy for patients to keep track of. This is not always the case with other *muteuro*: think of how difficult it was for me to keep my honey to myself; that friend of mine put the pressure on for a sip. I doubt he would have been interested in my *muteuro* if it had been a pebble instead. In another incident, a friend of mine in the church was given *muteuro* in the form of a mango paste. He made the mistake of leaving it in the kitchen, and his brother used it as chutney for an evening meal.

Pebbles also have the distinct advantage of not sparking association with traditional African healing (either spiritual or medicinal).[29] The Friday apostolics might be comfortable using the language of biomedicine to describe their healing practices, but in their effort to break with African custom they would never use the language of a *n'anga* or spirit medium. *N'angas* and spirit mediums in Zimbabwe use a variety of objects and substances in their healing practices, but pebbles are not among them. The weChishanu have therefore made something significant out of something that had no prior meaning in the local social field of African therapeutics.

The paradox of the pebble is its being special because it is not. In this context the pebble is, to borrow a description from Roland Barthes, the paradigmatic "mere signifier."[30] As a key symbol of Christianity, it expresses the apostolics' systematic repudiation of the potential for religious representation through objects. At the same time, it is the thing through which the value of the material might be saved. In many respects, the pebble is the most important thing in the Friday churches. Some might argue that an apostolic's white robes are the best representation of faith; robes are indeed valued by their wearers as a sign of commitment to the church. But a *muteuro*, especially the pebble, is an index of the spiritual power of God; it is what makes donning the robes significant. Pebbles are the tools of evangelization. Whereas most Christians place the Bible at the center of their faith, the Masowe would want to stress their *muteuro* as evidence of Christian success. Having rejected the Bible, the apostolics objectify their faith in something that in and of itself should have no social or cultural value. What better way to undercut the importance of material culture than to hold up as its archetype something you find in the dirt? Indeed, as I suggested at the beginning of this section, the very word apostolics use to signify their ritual medicines is meant to shift attention away from the question of materiality. A pebble is a prayer. It is part of the live and direct relationship with God that strong Christians ought to possess, a claim that "signification offers the subject an escape from materiality."[31]

Immaterial Distinctions

The emphasis on live and direct faith and the rejection of the Bible can lead apostolics to be dismissive of other Christian churches. When pressed, or in certain moods, they might indeed claim that they are the only "true" Christians because they have seen past the false security of the Book. But in practice they are not always concerned with Christian objects other than the Bible, and it would be an overstatement to say they spend most of their time deriding other Christians, even as they insist on the correctness of their own live and direct approach. Rather, as I have already alluded to in discussing witchcraft medicines, the apostolics direct their concern with objects toward traditional healers and spirit mediums. *Muti* is bothersome and dangerous, and the Masowe take pleasure in talking about it as such. What healers and mediums use in their practices always evokes dismissal, as much as the stuff of witchcraft. But *muti* also sparks anxiety, because the apostolics are concerned that people might think prophets are simply another kind of spirit medium. The arguments of spirit mediums (such as Gombera) make them nervous, because they are not so easy to dismiss.

As I have said, traditional healers and spirit mediums occupy distinct roles in the social field of Zimbabwean therapeutics. *N'angas* may or may not have relationships with spirits that help them in their vocation.[32] Most, in any case, undergo training for the collection and preparation of flora and fauna used as *muti* in treatments for patients.[33] These healers are neither good nor bad per se; some have reputations as being helpful, others are said to be open to using their skills for malevolent purposes. Mediums, by contrast, are normally viewed in a positive light and are, moreover, figures with duties to their communities.[34] Indeed, the interventions of the ancestral spirits that speak through mediums are considered necessary for the maintenance of social order: "The most important quality of ancestral spirits is that they have the welfare of the people who live within their provinces at heart."[35] This is not to say the authority of mediums goes uncontested. (Or that ancestral spirits will not reprimand the people who live in their provinces, when necessary.) Both during and after Zimbabwe's Liberation War, for example, a number of mediums got caught up in politicized struggles concerning their authority and authenticity. In at least one high-profile case, involving the *mhondoro* ("tribal spirit") Chaminuka, the medium ended up being shot to death.[36] Whether in spite of or because of these contestations, mediums are prominent players in local and sometimes national politics.

The Friday apostolics have never denied that healers can use their skills to help alleviate people's ills, and they are well aware of the important role that mediums have played in the past. The problem is that these figures are not Christian: whatever ends they achieve, the means are unacceptable. And because the "means" in most cases involve the significant use of ritual objects and substances, the apostolics make an effort to distinguish their *muteuro* from the *n'anga* or medium's *muti*. If pebbles were the only *muteuro*, there might be little more to discuss on this point. But set against this normative "spiritual medicine" are, as I have already noted, a number of more specialized substances that do not have the benefit of being "mere signifiers." Many of the things prophets use are already meaningful. Of these, water and honey are two of the most important. Water and honey each highlight, in different ways, how apostolics try to differentiate the immateriality of *muti* and *muteuro* at the material level.

Water, Water Everywhere

The studies of "traditional" healing in Zimbabwe have documented hundreds of plant and animal extracts used in the production of *muti* and practice of divination.[37] Alongside these extracts water is probably the most prominent substance in the therapeutic imagination. Many healers claim to learn their skills underwater, at the bottom of rivers, and the most powerful healing spirits are the mermaids (*njuzu*).[38] More generally, rain is a key symbol of life and the social order; the significance of rain and the extent to which it defines idioms of the spirit has been the subject of important studies on both mediums and the Mwari cults.[39] In my own research with mediums and *n'angas*, the importance of fluid substances in healing practices was particularly evident: millet beer, water, and liquids produced by adding water to botanical poultices, the ashes from fires, and other substances were commonly employed. The literature on Zimbabwe lends support to Christopher Taylor's argument, based on his research into healing in Rwanda, that in many Bantu cosmologies fluids mediate "notions of causality."[40] To control the proper flow of fluids (water, humors) is to control the course of life and social well-being.

Water then, is not a substance that Masowe apostolics can claim as their own, despite its longstanding centrality in Christian symbolisms.[41] Almost any religious figure in Zimbabwe might claim to benefit from water's properties; there is nothing necessarily Christian about it. This made one medium I knew particularly angry over apostolic claims to have privileged access to the spiritual world. She uses mermaids to help cure the afflictions of the people who come to her, and she did not see why her reliance on these water spirits was any different from an apostolic prophet's reliance on holy water. The apostolics' answers to such criticisms suggested that water in and of itself did not have intrinsic qualities—that its meaning is imbued. This is the logic behind *muteuro*.

At the same time, however, I would argue that it is precisely because water is such a common element in religious symbolisms that the apostolics did not get too worked up over the accusations of their duplicity. Water is meaningful in so many different religious contexts that the apostolics were able to resolve their anxieties over any parallel between their use of it and that of a traditional healer or medium. In other words, the apostolics seemed to accept that water *did* have something of an intrinsic value, and so it hardly made sense to try to control the meanings people associated with it. Water's universal appeal made it both a lost cause and nothing to worry about. It is also worth pointing out how, above and beyond water's ubiquity in symbolic schemes, its material properties might be understood to inform its significative potentials. Water is in some respects like smoke (and even the human voice). Its materiality is—quite literally—difficult to pin down. Water does not offer much resistance; you can move through it. And it is, in a sense, highly unstable; it tends to seep away, evaporate, and condense. In its materiality, then, it is not always very "material"—at least not like a book or a brick wall. But just as such, it can be dangerous. Like smoke, its not-very-material properties can become powerfully so, as, for example, when they fill one's lungs. At that point, their not-very-material properties are beside the point.

So, from the apostolic point of view, the symbolic and material meanings of water are the opposite of the pebble. This difference is what makes them similarly unproblematic and begins to suggest how apostolics understand some things as "more material than others." Both are safe because both are mundane. As poles in a spectrum of material culture, they anchor the constellation of value in therapeutic things. But as is often the case, it is not the extreme things that elicit the most interest and concern. Extremes are predictable, because their associations are easier to control. That which lies between the poles is more disconcerting, because it embodies the potential problems in the substance of healing. For the apostolics, honey is the substance that best characterizes this tension, and so I return to it here by way of conclusion.

A Sticky Object

My friend who stressed the merits of honey on the way to work that Wednesday morning might have been the most enthusiastic proponent of its use, but he was not alone. Honey has been an important substance since the early days of Johane's mission. During his transformative illness, for example, through which he received revelatory dreams on Marimba Hill, Johane claims to have survived on wild honey.[42] Much was made of this point when I collected oral histories from the church's old-timers. Today, when describing the groves and fields in which they pray, apostolics often refer to them as their lands of milk and honey. In the *masowe* (church sites), apostolics can be heard to sing a verse whose simplicity and directedness is difficult to miss:

Uchi, uchi
uchi, uchi, uchi

Honey, honey
honey, honey, honey

This verse is used to soothe people when they are possessed by ancestral spirits, avenging spirits, or witchcraft familiars. Apostolics also use honey as a simile to describe any place that is particularly prosperous. After a good rainy season, for example, one apostolic from Chiweshe District said the farms looked like a land of milk and honey. Once, even, a friend of mine in the church jokingly referred to a Mercedes Benz as a "honey car" (*motokari weuchi*).

Within the wider socioreligious field, however, the holiness of honey breaks down. Honey produces comfort, but it also produces anxiety. Its positive qualities, which are linked to explicitly Christian imageries, are balanced out by more troublesome associations. Unlike pebbles (which the apostolics can claim as their own) and water (which is so obviously salubrious), honey occupies a more ambiguous therapeutic role. Part of the problem is that mediums and *n'angas* also use honey, so the apostolics cannot claim it as their own. But honey does not have the common currency of water, either. It is not so meaningful, in other words, that it becomes meaningless. Unlike water, a case has to be made for honey's meaning, because the apostolics do not want to cede the value of honey as something open to interpretation. While it is clear to them that the substance lends itself to Christian uses, there is nothing to stop a medium from mounting a convincing case that it lends itself equally well to African "customary" uses. This state of affairs is exacerbated by the properties of honey as a substance, chiefly, that it can be fermented. In fact, the process of fermentation is dependent upon its dilution, which is precisely what prophets and elders do to make it "holy." Yet honey wine is one of the last things the apostolics would want to make: along with millet beer, it is one of the worst kinds of alcohol because it is used to propitiate and honor the ancestors—practices the apostolics hope to end. In their appropriation of this substance as a powerful channel for spiritual healing, the apostolics seem to be playing with fire.

The positive potentials of honey help explain what drove my friend to ask for a sip of mine in the car that day. The negative potentials should give us a sense of why his request for some was a sticky subject. My friend was talking himself into temptation. He was allowing for the possibility that the honey carried inherent properties. In the car, the honey did not represent a live and direct connection with God. What it represented—

what it *was*—was a way of dealing with a long day in the office. The taste of honey was the hope for relief. In this instance my friend was treating it like aspirin or, worse yet, *muti*—not *muteuro*. He was suggesting that its materiality mattered in a way that cut against the grain of his faith.

From honey as a sticky subject of conversation, then, we come to see honey as a sticky object. Within the realm of healing, it becomes the practical channel through which the apostolics articulate an exception to the rule that a Friday faith should be immaterial. As a sticky object, it represents the realization that even "strong" Christians cannot divorce themselves from the material. Holy honey is both the testament and the test of faith. As I hope to have shown in this ethnographic discussion, the extent to which religious communities objectify their authority through the use of things deserves attention as much for what it tells us about the immaterial world as for what it says about the persistence of the material one. Apostolic religious practice is driven by a desire for immateriality, but this will always involve a process of objectification. More than this, however, what we add to our understanding of live and direct faith is that, within any semiotic ideology, specific forms of objectification become the processes through which immateriality can be both demonstrated and lost. How the apostolics talk about and use the substances of healing suggest that materiality is a matter of degree and kind.

Back to the V&A

It is important not to relegate this case study of a small church in a faraway place (far away, that is, from most readers in possession of this book) to any sort of "margin." Indeed, in moving toward a conclusion, I want to situate the concern with holy honey in relation to some of the broader themes raised out the outset of this chapter—to take us back to the issues that first struck me in the V&A's "Gothic" show.

The way in which the Word's materiality was reinforced through the display of a defaced church panel in "Gothic" is a good indication of how divine presence can be indexed in and through physical objects. Here, I want to focus on how this dual character of Scripture (material/immaterial) has been articulated within certain trends in Protestantism. I begin with a brief consideration of the sixteenth-century iconoclasm that produced such defaced church panels. I then move on to sketch the gradual differentiation between "liberal" and "conservative" Protestant theologies, which, I will argue, can help us make sense of how the Bible has been understood in the colonial and postcolonial African case study. My aim is to suggest how these trends can help us situate the apostolics' live and direct faith, at the formal level, as an engagement with how Christians apprehend God's presence.

As Hans Belting remarks, because the Word is paramount in any Christian theology, this begs an important question about presence through other representations: "the question of whether God has established other means of encountering him besides the word."[43] For the most extreme Protestant Reformers—those driven by iconoclasm—the answer is no:

> The Reformation taught the dominion of the word, which suppressed all the other religious signs. Christianity had always been a revelation through the word but now the word took on an unprecedented monopoly and aura. After all, the new preachers had only the word of Holy Scripture and no other authority in practicing a religion without the institution of the church. They wanted, as it were, to rediscover the primal sound of the word, free of all the dross and errors of papism, and to teach it to the congregations. "For on words rests all our ground, protection, and defense against all errors and temptation," as Luther says in his Large Catechism. "The kingdom of God is a kingdom of hearing, not of seeing," he announces in another place.[44]

As in any religious movement, the iconoclasm that sprang up in early Reformation Europe was not always a coherent project: it was driven sometimes by theologians, and sometimes by congregations; sometimes it was carried out with a kind of moderation, and sometimes to the point of an incoherent and unwitting hypocrisy.[45] But in general, the destruction of religious images in sixteenth-century Europe was driven by a concern with what they could legitimately represent and by the dangers inherent in their misrepresentation. Once again, "nothing spiritual can be present when there is anything material and physical."

This is an extreme articulation because it demands the impossible. It rests upon a differentiation of the spiritual and material that would have to deny the existence of the physical world as God's creation. (Because the world is God's creation, surely it stands as a sign of "the spiritual"?) But as an impossible statement, it tells us something important about how the categories of "the spiritual" and "the material" come into play. In the semiotic ideology of an iconoclast, in other words, the Bible is not significant in its materiality. As the Word, it is that against which "mere things" like images are pitched. The Bible is different from a crucifix or religious painting because language does not share their material qualities. The Word does not engender illusions, and the Bible, as a providential presence, is properly "spiritual" and not "material" or "physical." What Protestantism brought about was an increased emphasis on Scripture, and with it language, as a kind of immaterial presence.

One effect of the increasingly positive disposition toward language was a shift in attention away from the figure of Christ and toward Scripture. "And symmetrical with the thinning of Christocentricity," as John Milbank tells us, "was the loss of ecclesial mediation. When the individual 'directly' confronted the text, the text's finite and self-sufficient denotation (*sola scriptura*) found its equivalent in the internalisation of meaning within the private conscience."[46] In this context, then, a qualitative difference between letter and spirit became unfixed. The immaterial qualities of the written word have helped shape debates over the nature and authority of Scripture ever since. This is not the kind of live and direct relationship with God that the Friday apostolics are advocating, but it is a kind of "live and direct" faith nonetheless—a return to the kingdom of hearing.

Immateriality, however, is an inherently unstable lure. As the Reformation settled in the wake of its iconoclastic purges, for example, images regained a foothold—if not as signs of presence, then at least as *not* signs of absence or obfuscation. In England, where some of the most destructive purges took place, Henry VIII tempered his church's position by calling for a distinction between "abused" and "unabused" images.[47] Luther also recognized that religious images as such were not the problem: the problem was their misuse. Images became dangerous when they were understood to be something other than what the Reformers claimed. As the art historian Joseph Koerner reports, this middle ground on their significance was eventually recognized as the only viable position: "the supreme irrationality is not to venerate images but to imagine that it is the images that cause their own abuse."[48] Iconoclasm ironically created the objects of its own scorn. Nothing could draw more attention to mere things than to assault their thingness. "How material was materiality shown to be when, as sometimes occurred, a saint's effigy was decapitated by the town's executioner?"[49]

After the sixteenth century, Protestant theologies moved in what might be recognized as two directions. Both have been marked by concerns with materiality as a quality that can matter, and both have tackled these concerns through engagement with the Bible. But the conclusions drawn have been distinctly different. For "liberal" theologies, the Bible became an important guide, yet only that. In some of the more radical liberal theologies, there are even hints that in an ideal faith it is a guide one could do without. In liberal theology, the materiality of the Bible became recognition of its historicity, which signals both its human crafting and, in this era of suspicion, the limits of human understanding. For "conservative" theologians, on the other hand, the Bible often became not only a guide but the destination. The Bible is the unshakable bedrock of faith and something that, as the Word, cannot be separated out from God. In the most stringent of these faiths, the materiality of the Bible became the presence of the divine—not representation, but presence; not sign, but actuality. In the remainder of this subsection, I sketch more aspects these two trends.

A defining feature of liberal Protestant theologies is an emphasis on the role of interpretation in the understanding of Scripture. In these traditions the meaning of the Word is not self-evident; it has to be discerned by the reader. This hermeneutic approach reached full flower in the work of Friedrich Schleiermacher. His starting point was that understanding is not possible without interpretation; meaning does not assert itself. Moreover, the meaning of a text becomes "estranged" outside the original context of its creation. Interpretation, in other words, is defined by the tension between distance and proximity and is motivated by the effort to relieve it. Hans-Georg Gadamer puts it thus: "everything that is no longer immediately situated in a world—that is, all tradition, whether art or the other spiritual creations of the past: law, religion, philosophy, and so forth—is estranged from its original meaning and depends on the unlocking and mediating spirit that we, like the Greeks, name after Hermes: the messenger of the Gods."[50] Schleiermacher wanted nothing less than to understand the intention of an author and the world in which that author's work had been produced. His hermeneutics is based on "an apprehension of the 'inner origin' of the composition of a work, a re-creation of the creative act. Thus understanding is a reproduction of an original production."[51] Notice the tension between distance and proximity here. What Schleiermacher wants to do is close the distance through the act of interpretation and therefore regain, inasmuch as it is possible, that which is original. As Vincent Crapanzano points out, however, the implication of Schleiermacher's position is that a text "can never be understood immediately."[52] It is only through interpretation—that "mediating spirit"—that we can reach understanding. There is, then, no transparent relationship between truth and Scripture that makes itself known. In hermeneutics, reading is a historical project that can be marked by an unsettling distance and absence.

Where liberal theologians place an emphasis on interpretation, conservatives tend to emphasize revelation. In many conservative theologies, the meaning of the Word is considered self-evident; it does not have to be discerned by the reader (that is to say, its meaning does not depend on the reader). In such "Bible-based" Christianities, the divine is often considered present in the book. This position on the Bible has its roots in Luther's idea of *sola scriptura*, although it developed not in Germany but in the United Kingdom and, especially, the United States, where the Californian businessmen Lyman and Milton Stewart spearheaded a group of "Fundamentalists."

As one might expect, fundamentalist, or "literalist," churches can cover a significant patch of theological ground. Conservative Protestantism is not a coherent whole, and literalism is not a fixed idea.[53] Generally, however, Christians in these conservative churches "are committed to the inerrancy of Scripture and they resist, often passionately, any theology that departs in their eyes from the teachings of Scripture."[54] The fundamentalists take Luther's idea of *sola scriptura* to its most radical conclusion: in their vision of faith, the Bible offers the "internal affirmation of its own authority."[55]

It is interesting to note how conservative Protestants often stress the materiality of the Bible. The fundamentalist churches, for example, acknowledge and embrace this materiality by putting it to theological work. Actual bibles can matter to actual people. For the fundamentalists with whom Crapanzano worked in southern California, carrying the Bible around with them and taking pride in its physical condition (ideally worn from reading) "marked their total commitment to it and the truths, the stability, the guidance, and the discipline it gave them."[56] For the conservative Christian, the Bible is often as much presence as representation. In semiological terms, it is a sign without a divide—"the coalescence" of signifier and signified, in which the "Bible as book is to biblical truth as God's word in its materiality is to God's truth."[57]

While the Bible is central to liberal theologies as well, there is an important sense in which Schleiermacher and others have tried to push beyond Scripture. They have done this in part, I want to argue, by suggesting that the materiality of the Bible can be a barrier to reaching Christian truths. Consider this excerpt from Schleiermacher's second speech in *On Religion*, which captures this point:

> Every sacred writing is in itself a glorious production, a speaking monument from the heroic time of religion, but, through servile reverence, it would become merely a mausoleum, a monument that a great spirit was once there, but is now no more. Did this spirit still live and work, he would look with love, and with a feeling of equality upon his work which yet could only be a weaker impress of himself. Not every person has religion who believes in a sacred writing, but only the man who has a lively and immediate understanding of it, and who, therefore, so far as he himself is concerned, could most easily do without it.[58]

"Having religion" is not measured by knowing the Book, still less by material possession of it. Having religion is having that which lies beyond the object, that of which the object is a "weaker impress." As Ernst Troeltsch characterizes it, "Schleiermacher locates the essence of religion in the basic human disposition toward the divine, and the presence of the divine in the human. On the human side, this presence takes the form of absolute dependence, which is also a feeling of divine, sustaining power."[59] Religion, then, is a feeling, and in that sense not a thing. It is not objectlike—produced by cold reasoning—but a "lively and immediate" understanding. For Schleiermacher, "the barrier to reason and understanding . . . is to be overcome by *feeling*, by an immediate, sympathetic, and con-genial understanding."[60] His suggestion is that authentic Christianity is experienced, not grasped, either cognitively or physically—that its qualities are immaterial in the sense that they cannot be located outside of that experience as an object of knowledge. The opposition in play here is between sensation and apprehension, in which the former is superior because insignificant in its materiality. It is not that feelings are not material, but that they are not so in the way a book is.

Troeltsch, who was one of Schleiermacher's most influential supporters, developed more views along this line. In Troeltsch's work, the Bible is significant but not plenary. It should not be understood as "the insuperable limit to Christianity."[61] What I want to emphasize here is how, in making these remarks, Troeltsch evaluates the Bible according to its material qualities. He calls the Bible "the Lutheran Pope," and he faults both Catholics and Protestants for a wayward emphasis on things: "One side turns to the pope and the church, the other to the Bible, but both sides turn to a clearly circumscribed object."[62]

Troeltsch's vision of Christianity is a striving toward the lively and immediate understanding of the divine, an understanding that is "beyond the Bible."[63] He wants to develop a faith in which the written word is only ever a point of departure. In this regard Troeltsch looks positively upon Catholicism, which he sees as "much more practical and realistic than Protestantism" because it "recognizes that the gospel is only a germ from which everything else has sprung."[64] This is not to suggest that Troeltsch points to any given church as more realized than any other. Indeed, in his view the history of Christianity "has not been a process of adulteration, but of becoming."[65] And when religion is cast as a process of becoming, it is resisting the pull of the clearly circumscribed object, of rendering the spirit a mere thing.

Conclusion: On Thingification

The concept of immateriality is a useful one for liberal theologies because of the extent to which it bolsters a resistance to what I will call "thingification." This is an awkward term, but I am using it in an effort to distinguish it from the more expected term, *objectification*, and, in the process, to disentangle the latter from the conceptual weeds to which it has long been attached. As Hegel might have used the term, for instance, *objectification* is something that liberal theologians could actually endorse. And as both Schleiermacher and Troeltsch acknowledge debts to Hegel, this should indeed be borne in mind. While objectification has primarily been understood as a negative experience of separation, especially after Marx, in Hegel's work it was "used to describe a dual process by means of which a subject externalizes itself in a creative act of differentiation, and in turn appropriates this externalization through an act which Hegel terms sublation (*aufhebung*)."[66] In Christian theology, this kind of objectification becomes a way in which God manifests his presence. For liberal theologians this is a positive experience. So, "objectification" is not the best word to describe that which liberal theologians want to guard against.

What they want to guard against is, in fact, the more commonplace understanding of objectification—the one characterized by "a lack of agency and even motion, a distancing from the world, a lack of self-recognition, [or] an abuse of others."[67] While this is what most academics mean when they use the word, doing so tends to crowd out its other potentials and functions. As Daniel Miller and Webb Keane have argued, we cannot (or, at least, should not) rest our understanding of the concept of objectification wholly on this negative base.[68] Even without taking Hegel or theology on board, it is important to recognize that objectification can be a positive experience, or, at least, not a negative experience. "Objectification"—simply—"describes the inevitable process by which all expression, conscious or unconscious, social or individual, takes specific form."[69]

By rechristening the negative understanding of objectification as thingification, I want to shift attention away from the subject-object relationship in the most general sense and toward a particular understanding of that relationship in which the object in question gets recognized as problematic. In this I am following Bill Brown, who (after Heidegger and others) emphasizes that one function of the concept "thing" is to account for what does not fit into a coherent ordering of objects. A thing is often "the entifiable that is unspecifiable."[70] If we know what an object is, we name it; if not, it becomes a thing and, as such, dangerous. In other words, we are forced "to confront the thingness of objects when they stop working for us."[71] I want to suggest this is a useful distinction for understanding how the material gets configured within the Christian imaginations being discussed here. What is dangerous in these imaginations is not the object per se but the possibility of its becoming a mere thing—an object that "stops working," or never did so in the first place. When the qualities of immateriality are present in an object—as marked by the Spirit, or a particular power, or a kind of feeling—it cannot become clearly circumscribed, or merely a mausoleum. Thingification, then, is the process through which the object is divested of an "immateriality." Thingification makes dangerous things.

The two trends in Protestant theology sketched here are supposed to serve, at the formal level, as yardsticks for the accompanying ethnography. Throughout this chapter, I have argued that the Friday apostolics articulate a vision of Christianity that fits within the liberal traditions. The concept of immateriality is central to their notion of live and direct faith because of the work it does in helping them to distinguish material things from one another. Emphasizing what is immaterial and what is not is their way of claiming that "some things are more material than others."[72] To say that the apostolics want a faith in which things do not matter (whether books or honey) is not to say they are renouncing the world. It is, rather, to suggest that they are making specific claims about how God becomes present through words, objects, and actions that exist within a hierarchy of significative and expressive forms. The semiotics of live and direct faith hinges on the assertion of immateriality (that which is insignificant in its materiality).

Things That Matter

The *Extra Calvinisticum*, the Eucharist, and John Calvin's Unstable Materiality

Ernst van den Hemel

Standing on the fluid brink between the modern age and a medieval worldview, Reformer John Calvin developed his theology in a period during which "the material culture of the text" was buckling under a "general crisis of meaning."[1] In the light of a larger framework of the disenchantment of the world and inner-worldly asceticism, Calvin's theology has often been associated with the rise of capitalism,[2] a modern notion of the self, developed under the influence of a vision of the everyday life world as divinely ordained,[3] and/or a vision of creation as inherently flawed.[4] In this larger framework, the sphere of everyday materiality is seen as a world devoid of grace, with which one interacts in a hard-working, stick-to-your-calling mode. In a narrower, theological framework, Calvin's views on materiality, as evidenced in the debate on the divine presence in the Eucharist, are often characterized by a complicated stance on real presence. In Calvin's theology, it is stated, the real, affirmative presence of the Eucharist becomes problematic: present-day critics of Calvin's writings on the Eucharist have seen in them either an unholy combination of philosophy and theology or a problematic notion that threatens the totality of Calvin's theological system.[5] Calvin's writings on the Eucharist seem at first glance to be marginal. In the final edition of his magnum opus, *Institutio Christianae religionis*, he devotes one chapter to it, and on the whole Calvin does not seem to be as preoccupied with the Eucharist as, say, Zwingli and Luther. This has led commentators to state that Calvin's stance on the Eucharist was crafted as a necessary compromise, and not because it played a structural role in his theology. However, when viewed as not just a compromise but an integral part of Calvin's theology, his stance on the Eucharist reveals a deep concern with materiality. In the sixteenth-century world, which has been described as a disenchantment of natural creation, Calvin's writings on the Eucharist walk a tightrope: they deny unwarranted "miraculous" presence yet retain the reality of the presence of Christ. His thoughts on the Eucharist thus are an intriguing example of early modern negotiations with divine presence in the material world. An investigation into the relationship between the Eucharist and the created material world can shed light not only on the status of materiality in Calvin's theology but also on how the divine presence is tied up with early modern interaction with the created world in general.

In this chapter, I will show that Calvin's writings on the Eucharist offer an original but undervalued theory in which material presence and divine truth are combined. Calvin's theology negotiates a way between the crisis of interpretation that resulted from the Reformation and a truth claim regarding "real presence" (*presentia realis*) in the Eucharist. To do so, Calvin resorts to a theory of signs in which the signifier is unable to signify in a stable manner. Instead, as I will show, the semiotic presence Calvin constructs leads not to stable accessible knowledge but to an active rethinking of materiality.

Calvin's solution to the apparent stalemate at which sixteenth-century debates over the Eucharist had arrived was later called the *extra calvinisticum*. It is this *extra*, signifying both immanent and transcendent presence, that leads the believer away from the dangers of venerating matter, on the one hand, while avoiding a purely metaphorical interpretation of the presence of Christ, on the other. Far from being a political compromise combining the dominant but exclusive positions of fellow Reformers Luther and Zwingli, this solution was integral to Calvin's broader theology. His view of the Eucharist led him to develop a dynamic reflection on the present but indescribable divine reality that underlies all materiality. In his writings, the theory of the *extra* leads the way to a view of the material world as inviting direct human interaction, rather than being governed purely by principles accessible to reason, like the laws of physics and systematic theology. An examination of Calvin's stance on the Eucharist thus can contribute to an understanding of the idiosyncratic combination of solidity and the ungraspable in his theology.

The Eucharist Debate in the Sixteenth Century

Over the course of the sixteenth century, the debate over the Eucharist was probably what most fiercely divided the various Reformers. In 1529, at the Marburg colloquy, Luther and Zwingli, in particular, attempted to come to an understanding concerning the Lord's Supper. Although they did succeed in defining some common ground, one point remained unresolved at the end of the meeting: "And although we have not reached an agreement as to whether the true body and blood of Christ are bodily present in the bread and wine, nevertheless each side should show such Christian love to the other as their conscience will allow, and both sides should pray diligently to almighty God that, through his spirit, he might confirm us in the right understanding."[6]

The "is" of "This is my body" and "This is my blood"—Christ's words during the Last Supper, performatively enacted in the ritual of the Eucharist—was the focal point of the difference between Luther and Zwingli. Luther resisted allowing any role for the human imagination, tradition, or sensibilities in the meaning of Scripture.[7] For Luther, Christ clearly was really present in the Eucharist, and he maintained that any recourse to interpreting the relation between "this" and "body" as a sign or a representation amounted to subsuming the Word of God under human understanding. By contrast, Zwingli held that this presence was of a symbolic nature: Christ could not be corporeally present in every host and remain really bodily (meaning confined to flesh, to the same physical confinements as a human body) incarnate at the same time. The bread must therefore function as kind of sign, and the presence of Christ must be of a spiritual and not a material nature. To insist on the corporeal presence of Christ in the Eucharist would, for Zwingli, amount to denying the truth and singularity of the incarnation.[8]

At the time of the Marburg colloquy, it was plain to see that grave and divisive differences in interpretation could hinge on a single word. Yet the debate over the Eucharist illustrated a larger crisis of meaning and interpretation that was sweeping Europe. Brian Cummings, in *The Literary Culture of the Reformation*, emphasizes that the sixteenth century, with its comparative studies of sacred texts and their different languages "raised a . . . profoundly disturbing question of whether texts written in Hebrew and Latin could ever mean exactly the same thing." According to Cummings, this had a "destabilizing effect throughout Europe on the unity of literature culture."[9] "Luther," Cummings continues, "tried to end all doubt by subscription to the one word of God."[10] However, in criticizing the artificiality of man-made meanings and interpretations, Luther found himself caught in a self-defeating formula: By what criteria could one distinguish the Word of God from artificial, man-made perversities? Thomas More, in his *Responsio ad Lutherum*, effectively expresses the linguistic tension opened up by Luther: "And who will be the judge as to which is that word: Luther, or the catholic church?"[11] Cummings sums it up decisively: "Luther expressed absolute faith in language, when Luther himself made such faith in language impossible."[12]

Indeed, at the end of the century, Michel de Montaigne would look back and pass judgment on his time as an era in which a war was fought over words: "I note that Luther has left behind in Germany as many—indeed more—discords and disagreements because of doubts about his opinions than he himself ever raised about holy scripture. Our controversies are verbal ones. I ask what is nature, pleasure, circle or substitution. The question is about words: it is paid in the same coin."[13]

Calvin and the Semiotics of the Eucharist

The French Reformer John Calvin was twenty years old when the colloquy in Marburg failed to reach common ground on the words of institution. He therefore developed his theology at a time when it was clear how dangerously irreconcilable interpretations of even a single word could be. His theory should therefore be read against the backdrop of the impossible task of determining the single true meaning of Scripture and with the crisis of meaning postulated by Cummings in mind.

Calvin's own theory of the Eucharist, it has often been suggested, is characterized by an attempt to find a middle ground. Indeed, it has been described as a politically inspired compromise between Luther's and Zwingli's positions.[14] Although Calvin's theory does indeed embody aspects of both sides of Reformed thinking about the Eucharist—he emphasizes both its semiotic nature and its "real" presence—it would be a mistake to dismiss it as merely an attempted synthesis of Luther's and Zwingli's positions. To do so would be to overlook how Calvin's stance on the Eucharist, the sacraments, and, in a broader sense, his views on materiality are intimately connected to his epistemology. This connection between the presence of the divine and everyday reality is at the core of the Calvinist universe. In fact, Calvin's definition of presence in the Eucharist aims less at determining the meaning of the Eucharist than at ascertaining its ongoing effect; his goal is not to put an end to the ongoing process of interpretation by offering a clear and accessible definition but rather to put interpretation and human cognition in general in their right place.

Let us begin with Calvin's own definition of the sacraments:

> First, we must consider what a sacrament is. It seems to me that a simple and proper definition would be to say that it is an outward sign by which the Lord seals on our consciences the promises of his good will toward us in order to sustain the weakness of our faith . . . one may call it a testimony of divine grace toward us, confirmed by an outward sign, with mutual attestation of our piety toward him.[15]

The semiotic nature of the sacrament, the sacrament as a sign, is essential for Calvin. The sacrament is a signifier, but what it signifies remains unclear for the moment. Calvin does not offer solace to those who wonder what the content of the sign is. Elsewhere, he states that the content of the outward sign with which God's good will toward us is sealed should not be disputed too much: "believers ought to live by this rule: whenever they see symbols appointed by the Lord, to think and be convinced that the truth of the thing signified is surely present there."[16] What the sign signifies, first of all, is that there is no secret of the sign. It has no descriptive depth; the truth of the thing is simply there. Calvin emphasizes that it is not a symbol, nor is it a metaphor. The sign signifies a simple presence and not a standard meaning that could be unfolded, as in "the sign of the Eucharist symbolizes the historical fact of Christ's past incarnation," or even "the sign of the Eucharist is the miraculous transubstantiation of the essence of the host." This would amount to inquiring too deeply into matters that are not to be found at such analytical depth. But we are left guessing as to the nature of this presence. In clarification, Calvin offers a rather dense statement: "The sacred mystery of the Lord's Supper consists in two things: *physical* signs, which, when placed in front of our eyes, represent to us (according to our feeble capacity) invisible things; and spiritual truth, which is *at the same time* represented and displayed through the symbols themselves."[17] This point is of great importance for Calvin: the sacrament is a process in which matter becomes a sign that simultaneously "represents" and "displays" spiritual truth. One can see how easy it is to confuse Calvin's doctrine with a political compromise between Luther's and Zwingli's positions. By combining the representational nature of the sign with the real presence of the spiritual in symbols themselves, Calvin could be seen as trying to steer between the Scylla of overemphasizing metaphorical theories of the Eucharist and the Charybdis of the problematic material presence of the Lutherans.

Here Calvin's idiosyncratic epistemology comes into play: whereas for Zwingli Christ's incarnation had been a moment in time (and because of this historicity, Christ's presence in the Eucharist could therefore be only of a metaphorical nature), for Calvin, incarnation is a *process* that enables an ongoing understanding of the world as a timeless display of our failure to truly grasp divine presence. Calvin speaks of the natural world as follows: "This magnificent *theater* of heaven and earth, crammed with innumerable miracles. We *ought* in wisdom to have known God. But because we have profited so little by it, he calls us to the faith of Christ."[18]

The combination of displaying and representing real presence, far from being a compromise between two positions, is tied up with his view of the world. It is not that the whole of creation is constructed out of an easily perceived materiality; rather, one needs constant faith to see the world as it really is: a perpetual exercise of God's power. The project of Calvin's *Institutes* is to train his readers to recognize the trace of the divine in all earthly matters. The book as a whole is intended to enforce a habit on the human mind: to endow the outward sign with its right significance.

For Calvin, the idea that the real substance of Christ is to be venerated in the Eucharist entails the danger of confusing the everyday presence of matter with the divine mystery underlying it. Yet if one takes the presence to be only mental, metaphorical, one runs the risk of forgetting the way in which matter testifies to divine presence. Calvin's theory of the Eucharist therefore can be seen as an attempt to construct a third term between signification and material presence, combining immanence and transcendence. This third term is a presence that is both real and immanent, yet does not bring Christ down to our everyday understanding of matter.

The *extra calvinisticum* is proposed as this third term. In brief, Calvin argues that, in the incarnation, Christ retained divine properties, such as immensity and omnipresence, and that therefore He was not physically confined within the limits of a human person. The Incarnation thus expresses the divine essence without exhaustively revealing it. Calvin states this most clearly in the following passage from the *Institutes*:

Another absurdity which they obtrude upon us, viz. that if the Word of God became incarnate, it must have been enclosed in the narrow tenement of an earthly body, is sheer petulance. For although the boundless essence of the Word was united with human nature into one person, we have no idea of any enclosing. The Son of God descended miraculously from heaven, yet without abandoning heaven; was pleased to be conceived miraculously in the Virgin's womb, to live on the earth, and hang upon the cross, and yet always filled the world as from the beginning.[19]

The presence of Christ in the Eucharist then signifies not just the material presence of the divine but also its divine nature, which lies beyond the grasp of the human mind. The Eucharist signifies the inability of our conceptions of matter to sustain the presence of the divine. Therefore, the sign of the Eucharist signifies not only materiality but an *extra*, a sign that communicates to us not only the fullness of divine presence but also the lack in normal interaction with creation—*yet always filled the world as from the beginning*. The *extra calvinisticum* accounts for a presence that is "really there," yet that is also beyond the enclosing of the flesh. The presence of Christ in the Eucharist then both reveals the presence of the divine in the host and points to the limits of this presence: a "real" and immanent presence of the divine that retains a transcendent dimension.

From its conception, this stance has generated criticism and confusion. The expression *extra calvinisticum* was coined in the sixteenth century by Lutheran opponents: "that calvinistic beyond."[20] In its insistence that the material presence of Christ remains located at the right hand of God, *ad dexteriam dei*, yet that in the Eucharist a real presence is presented, opponents have seen a serious flaw: by separating the two natures, the *extra calvinisticum* in effect denies the hypostatic union of the two natures in Christ; even more seriously, this separation is inspired by a misuse of logic, of rational philosophical categories. By the seventeenth century, Calvin's critics were arguing that his position on the Eucharist amounted to blasphemously applying the philosophical principle *finitum non capax infiniti*, the finite is incapable of the infinite. Therefore, it was said, the Calvinist theology of the Eucharist remains too much focused on logic to incorporate the divine mystery of incarnation and transubstantiation. This accusation of philosophical austerity and logical complication of a theological issue has stuck to the *extra calvinisticum* ever since. Though the *finitum non capax infiniti* principle is mentioned nowhere in Calvin's work and its supposed centrality to Calvinist doctrine is unclear at best, the charge that Calvin maintains with iron persistence that earthly, limited matter cannot sustain the infinite can still be found in Calvin scholarship. In a recent article by the American philosopher David Andersen, "A Critique of John Calvin's Philosophical Axiom *finitum non capax infiniti*," Calvin's position on the Eucharist is criticized for being incapable of sustaining a fixed account of the meaning of Christ:

Specifically, I will argue that Calvin's application of the principle finitum non capax infiniti serves as a synthetic a priori within his thought that determines the limitations of Christ's human nature. With the principle at the heart of his Christology he denies the material presence of Christ in the Eucharist, and it becomes the basis of his opposition to Luther's understanding of the words of institution. . . . although Calvin wants to insist that there is a logical necessity in his definition, the fact stands that because such a description cannot be delimited in all possible directions, it cannot claim a priori status.[21]

Andersen, interpreting Calvin's stance on the Eucharist as a reshaping of the dogma *finitum non capax infiniti*, states that, in order for Calvin's theory to fly, one must succeed in interpreting his views on matter as an a priori status of being. Flesh, being a priori incapable of sustaining the divine, is cut off from receiving divine presence. Andersen concludes that, because Calvin's theory does not allow for such a closed view of man, any a priori status is impossible to defend, and Calvin's theory thus harbors a contradiction: "Calvin's Christological position, and therefore his Eucharistic position, presupposes an axiom that lacks philosophical meaningfulness."[22] Already in the title of his article, we see that Andersen applies a question that says more about the author of the article than about the sixteenth-century Reformer: the "critique of the *philosophical* axiom *finitum non capax infiniti*" implies that: (1) Calvin's theology harbors such a philosophical axiom (even though this axiom is nowhere named in Calvin's theology), and (2) that it points to an overemphasis on logic and philosophy in his theology. In what follows below, I will depart from the search for the logical and philosophical Calvin, arguing that "philosophical meaningfulness," if by this is meant the prerequisite for providing knowledge, might not be the most satisfying approach for reaching the kernel of Calvin's thought.

Indeed, according to Calvin, the uncomfortable status of the divine presence cannot easily be fitted into schemes of possible logical knowledge. However, Calvin does not deny or overlook this problem. On the contrary, a tense relationship to logic is an inherent element of the divine presence in the Eucharist. And, to push the point further, it is not that material presence in the Eucharist is downplayed in Calvin's epistemology, but *material presence in general* becomes unhinged by the Eucharist. An interpretation of Calvin's writings on the Eucharist that takes the failing of logic and language seriously will end up with a wholly different view of materiality and Calvinism in general.

The *Extra* as the Fallible Backdrop of Meaning

With this approach to the Eucharist, the *extra* can be conceived as an element of Calvin's conceptualizations of matter in general. As we will see, for Calvin, dealing with material creation is a matter not of static reflection but of dynamic interaction with materiality. We have already seen that Calvin describes the world as "God's theater," on the basis of which we "ought to have known God." Unfortunately, because we are not able to sustain this understanding of the physical world, we cannot build any solid knowledge on it. Therefore God granted man, through the incarnation, the presence of the divine in the flesh. Christ's presence is tied to the presence of the divine in the whole of creation, which became possible through the incarnation: "The sacrament, therefore, does not make Christ become for the first time the bread of life; but while it calls to remembrance that Christ was made the bread of life that we may constantly eat him, it gives us a taste and relish for that bread, and makes us feel its efficacy."[23] In the Eucharist we are reminded of the mysterious presence of the divine in creation. This does not put an end to our sinful perception, however. Precisely because we are too deeply embedded, conditioned by sin, we constantly fail to realize that our conceptions of matter are inadequate to sustain the divine mystery that is so central to them. The Eucharist is, for Calvin, the most important way of countering this tendency. The Eucharist offers, through its singular and divine nature, a basis for an interpretation of the world in general. It can be seen, then, as the interpretative act par excellence, offering a realization that should not stop with the ritual but that, ideally, would extend its scope to the whole of creation.

In order to escape any instrumental conception of this effect, Calvin, like most Reformers, upheld the notion that a sacrament is ineffectual when executed wrongly or insincerely: "Just as rain falling upon a hard rock flows off because no entrance opens into the stone, the wicked by their hardness repel God's grace so that it does not reach them. Besides, to say that Christ may be received without faith is as inappropriate as to say that a seed may germinate in fire."[24] In the material world, the divine is always present. The sinful, however, are unable to perceive or experience it. The Eucharist is one of the ways in which this insight can be communicated. To limit the effect of the Eucharist to signification alone would be to deny its disruptive effect. One needs something more to make it work; the words of institution need to be charged with something more than just signification to render the divine mystery present. As Lee Palmer Wandel formulates it: "the signs had meaning, flesh and blood, only within God's episteme."[25]

The signs Calvin refers to when describing the Eucharist are not a stable reference to divine/bodily presence. Rather, signification is an active, ongoing process. As Andersen observes, these signs are limited to their face-value meaning, confined to "human," and thus imperfect, conceptualizations such as space and time. Indeed, their "extra" signification exceeds these confinements. However, instead of seeing this as a flaw in Calvin's theology, we can begin to construct an interpretation in which this refusal to delimit material presence is not a mere inconsistency in his thinking about the Eucharist, but, on the contrary, an important and central point in his theology.

The Accommodated Statement: A Staging of the *Extra*

Calvin's theology contains a second famous theme in which a meaning is theorized that is both contained within earthly limits yet exceeds them. It should be kept in mind when interpreting these signs: the accommodation (*accommodatio*).

The accommodated statement is probably the most extensively discussed theme in Calvin's theology, in which signs take on more than descriptive content. Furthermore, it functions not only as an explanatory mechanism, helpful for understanding problematic parts of Scripture, but also as an ethical demand placed on the believer. Calvin cites Acts 20:28, for example, where Paul states that "God purchased the Church with his own blood" and that the "Lord of Glory was crucified." Of course, Calvin says, God does not suffer, has no blood, and does not die. But a property of his humanity is used to communicate an aspect of his divine nature. Calvin describes this as *communicatio idiomatum*. Even though the Scripture states that God laid down his life for us, what is meant is that the material, historical presence of the divine Christ has been laid down. Calvin states that the accommodated statement is, in a descriptive sense, improper; it does not describe what it is really like. Instead, we should understand these statements as expressions of God for our benefit. Their security lies not in their descriptive content but in their rhetorical function: "Such modes of expression are *accommodated* to our capacity, that we may the better understand how miserable and calamitous our condition is without Christ."[26]

The present-day theologian Paul Helm, in *Calvin's Ideas*,[27] compares the accommodated statement to the transformation of a stereo signal into mono sound: the true nature of God would be communicated in stereo sound, but mankind, only capable of receiving mono signal, is forever shut off from listening to stereo. That which is communicated in the accommodated statement, then, should not be taken at face value. To confuse the accommodated statements in Scripture with their actual meaning would amount to denying the existence of something like stereo sound, to bringing God down to our imperfect human level. In fact, the accommodated statement paradoxically tries to describe, in mono, that there is such a thing as stereo. Accordingly, there is a sort of roughness in the accommodated expression, which should not be confused with describable, accessible truth (nor, for that matter, with falsity), yet at the same time retains its truth claim: the word of God remains powerfully and eternally true. David C. Steinmetz describes the accommodated expression as follows: "Calvin suggested that when God spoke to the prophets and apostles, he lisped." He further explains the demand placed on anyone reading accommodated phrases: "the interpreter of Scripture needs to bear in mind . . . that behind such accommodation there remains an inexhaustible and impenetrable mystery." Accommodated expression happens in space and time, "under the conditions of sin and finitude."[28] Correct interaction with the accommodated statement would then be not to philosophize but to recognize the fallible backdrop of all acts of meaning.

Real Presence of Spiritual Truth

If one rereads Calvin's remarks on the Eucharist according to this model, it becomes possible to see how the miracle in the Eucharist is not a metamorphosis of the essence of the host, as in Lutheran theories. Instead, Calvin's theology allows a presence of material signs that become endowed with an *extra* charge, representing to us (according to our feeble capacity) both invisible things and "spiritual truth" at the same time. As we have seen, this "spiritual truth" is, according to Calvin, both represented and displayed "through the symbols themselves."

Calvin naturally remains reluctant to specify what this signifier signifies. That which underlies all understanding is and remains inherently mysterious. He emphasizes this link between the Eucharist and mystery by repeating an etymological claim concerning the word *sacrament*: "It is well known, that what the Latins call *sacramenta* the Greeks call *mysteries*."[29] A linguistic space is thus created that presents (renders present) and yet keeps open the indescribable mystery.

Heiko Oberman emphasizes that the *extra calvinisticum* should not be seen as an isolated phenomenon applied to descriptions of Christ or the Eucharist but "is rather like the top of an iceberg, only the most controversial aspect of a whole '*extra* dimension' in Calvin's theology."[30] Indeed, our bridge between the Eucharist and accommodation seems warranted by the fact that Calvin reminds the reader of our imperfect knowledge of the natural world:

> Bright however, as is the manifestation which God gives both of himself and his immortal kingdom in the mirror of his works, so great is our stupidity, so dull are we in regard to these bright manifestations, that we derive no benefit from them. For in regard to the fabric and admirable arrangement of the universe, how few of us are there who, in lifting our eyes to the heavens, or looking abroad on the various regions of the earth, ever think of the Creator? Do we not rather overlook Him, and sluggishly content ourselves with a view of his works?[31]

The importance of this failure of ours to interpret the material world is only intensified by Calvin's surprisingly medieval cosmology. He notes in his commentary on Genesis, for example, that the whole world is actively sustained by God's will:

> For even philosophers allow that the natural position of the waters was to cover the whole earth, as Moses declares they did in the beginning; first, because being an element, it must be circular, and because this element is heavier than the air, and lighter than the earth, it ought cover the latter in its whole circumference. But that the seas, being gathered together as on heaps, should give place for man, is seemingly *preternatural*. Let us, therefore, know that we are dwelling on dry ground, because

God, by his command, removes the waters that they should not overflow the whole earth.[32]

The natural world does not merely obey laws put in place by God at the beginning of time. Instead, a true reflection on the material world would recognize the divine mystery as an active force, present inside matter and upholding it. Therefore the correct way to interact with all matter, with the physical world, is to see it as a theater of God's glory. This means that to confuse cause and effect with the core of the issue would amount to committing the same sort of sin as believing that Christ's presence is confined in the host: it would be to deny the limits of our knowledge. These limits, and the mystery that lies beyond them, are present and knowable for those who know how to interpret. There is no de- or prescriptive law helping the believer to locate these limits. But they are omnipresent, and our constant task is to realize this.

Calvin thus constructs a third point, a third way that emphasizes not only physical presence, nor mere metaphor, but the presence of an act of interpretation. Connected though it may be to mystery, this third point becomes for Calvin a constitutive and even binding factor for Christianity. Those who accomplish the "testimony of divine grace toward us, confirmed by an outward sign, with mutual attestation of our piety toward him" constitute the community of Christians: the true Church. This church is not confined by buildings, doctrine, language, or location but is unified by the mystery of presence, executed in an important way in the Eucharist:

> As the whole kingdom of Christ is spiritual, so whatever he does in his Church is not to be tested by the wisdom of this world. . . . To use the words of Augustine, "this mystery is performed *by man* like the others, *but in a divine manner*, and *on earth, but in a heavenly manner*." Such I say is the corporeal presence which the nature of the sacrament requires, and which we say is here displayed such power and efficacy, that it not only gives our minds undoubted assurance of eternal life, but also secures the immortality of our flesh.[33]

The mystery is performed by man, but in a divine manner; it is performed on earth, but in a heavenly manner. This is, for Calvin, the corporeal presence of the Eucharist. The *extra calvinisticum* can now be conceived as a unique conflation in which earthly and divine signs, the singular and the universal, are mysteriously taken up in one foundational movement. This foundational moment combines a secure and truthful presence of material signs with a resistance to literal or confined interpretation. Materiality, then, becomes not a stumbling block but an immanent sign laden with grace. The *extra* offers a certainty that combines both the descriptive realm of quasi-accessible materiality and the detached realm of divine transcendence. Instead of logic and definitions, the mystery behind all creation becomes the foundation. This is how security and certainty are retained in the realm of material presence, while avoiding the pitfall of placing belief in matter and not in God. It is through the effective working of the Eucharist, the mediation of incarnation, that the everyday material world is opened up to a recognition of divine presence.

Andersen's suggestion that Calvin's thoughts concerning the Eucharist amount to an incomplete and unsuccessful application of a philosophical axiom cannot explain the presence of that which exceeds our normal, fixed ways of perception. For Andersen, Calvin's writings on the Eucharist are flawed because they are unable to account for "philosophical meaningfulness." Cummings emphasizes that it was precisely the criteria for "meaningfulness" of Scripture that had become unstable during the Reformation. For Calvin, the *extra calvinisticum* offers a truthful presence that combines everyday ways of interaction, such as matter and signification, with the mysterious. In this way Calvin negotiaties and works through the crisis of meaning that Cummings describes as the inherent problem of the Reformation, without relinquishing the truth claim of the Eucharist.

Concluding: The *Extra* as Interpretative Center

Reading the *extra calvinisticum* through the prism of the "crisis of meaning," we can construe in Calvinist theology a notion of materiality that functions as a mediation between the divine and the material, that can account for a presence yet does not confine the divine to material dimensions. Thus, Calvin acknowledges the modern problematics of space yet does not relinquish theology to rationalism or biblicism. Instead, materiality becomes the ground for a reflection of the *extra*, the beyond; the *extra* aims at retaining the truth claim of the real divine presence of Christ, without departing from the inherent limits of human understanding. Christ both is present at the right hand of God (*ad dexteram Dei*) and "rules the earth as from the beginning": this dual theological motif is present in Calvin's reflections on creation and history as well as his reflections on the divine presence in the Eucharist. It offers quite a promising basis for interpretations of Calvin's theology. It could, for instance, yield interesting grounds for studying the role of the believer in creation or the specific poetics of the *extra*: What is the basis from which Calvin speaks? And, to fold back this analysis onto the language Calvin himself deploys, how is this experience of the *extra* as present yet transcendent tied up with more "literary" uses of language? Better put, can Calvin's rhetoric be read in the light of this foundational presence of indescribable security?

Although I cannot answer these questions here, I hope I may have succeeded in pointing toward a conceptualization of matter and materiality that holds as a guiding principle the crisis of meaning and the absence of accessible descriptive truth that we have seen characterized by thinkers such as Cummings, Weber, and Taylor, yet that also seeks to formulate a notion of divine presence that retains the "reality" of this presence. We can thus see in Calvin's theorization of real presence interesting connections to notions of modernity. The emphasis on the "reality" of the presence, as well as a distrust of the descriptive content of language, generates an interaction with materiality that tries to combine immanence and transcendence. We have also seen in what way this presence calls, not for philosophical meaningfulness, but for an investigation into the linguistic, accommodated status of divine presence. In conclusion, we can see how a discussion of the materiality of the Eucharist can be a valuable contribution to discussions of notions of early modernity. In his *Passage to Modernity*, philosopher of religion and historiographer of modernity Louis Dupré emphasizes that Calvin was inherently aware of the problem of modernity: "Calvin understood the religious problem of modernity because he experienced it within himself. Once converted, he single-mindedly focused on the issue that concerned religious humanists most seriously, namely, the radical incompleteness of a nature that requires a transcendent dimension yet somehow appears to be deprived of it."[34] By examining the discussion of the Eucharist and the status of materiality in Calvin's theology, we have seen how, for Calvin, "radical incompleteness" can nonetheless harbor "real" presence. This material, real presence is at the same time "beyond" (*extra*) normal understanding and thus opens up an affirmative aspect of Calvin's theology and early modern thought on materiality in general.

To name only a few possible venues of further research, the question of affirmation in language can be seen to influence early modern thinking about literature. Sir Philip Sidney's remarks on the capacity of language to move in his *Defense of Poesy* can be seen as tapping into the limited trust in human capacities, yet locating affirmation in movement. Another promising venue of research would lie in connecting the linguistic dimension with current narratives about religious political agency—about, in short, what believers can do on the basis of earthly affirmation. Weber's analysis of Calvinist-inspired capitalism centers on the disenchantment of the early modern world (which, in turn, is connected to notions of secularization). The affirmative dimension I have uncovered above could add a complication to the oft-repeated bifurcation between modernity inspired by Calvinist disenchantment, on the one hand, and fundamentalism, on the other. This elusive affirmative dimension in early modern theology potentially problematizes current narratives of the interaction of religion and politics. It can do so because it retains an affirmative dimension, yet combines it with a distrust in logic or descriptive truth, thus enabling a modern affirmation that is sometimes forgotten in narratives of early modern secularization. But that analysis will have to wait.

PART II

Images and Incarnations

From Stone to Flesh

The Case of the Buddha

Donald S. Lopez, Jr.

Among the great religions of the world, Buddhism is widely regarded as
the most pleasant. Its teachings appear to be profound yet accessible. It
seems free of complicated rituals to perform or dogmas to believe. In
fact, for some it is such a pleasant religion that it might not be a religion
at all; it might be more accurate to call it a philosophy, or just a way of
life. The credit for creating Buddhism, of course, goes to the Buddha,
certainly the most pleasant of the founders of the world religions. He
never turned rivers of water into rivers of blood or caused a hail of
toads; he never ordered the execution of his enemies; he never even
overturned the tables of moneylenders. He just sat under trees and
talked to those who happened to be passing by. The image of the Buddha is also pleasing to the European eye. He is not depicted carrying
stone tablets, or wielding a sword, or nailed to a cross. He sits on the
ground with his legs crossed, his hands folded in his lap, his eyes cast
down. Everyone knows this.

This knowledge, however, if we can call it that, has been rather
recently acquired, little more than a hundred and fifty years ago. Yet the
Buddha lived twenty-five hundred years ago, and European references
to him go back to Clement of Alexandria in the third century c.e. How
did Europeans understand the Buddha, and his image, between around
200 and around 1850, before he became the pacific and positive figure
known and loved today? And what happened a century and a half ago
to make him that man? These are the questions I will try to address
briefly here. Although the narrative I provide will be my own, many of
the words will come from figures of the past, expressed in a quaint
language beloved by antiquarians. From those words, it will become
clear that for much of the period of the European encounter with the
Buddha, the Buddha was an idol, a thing, and an idol known by many

names. When the conclusion was eventually drawn that that these idols represented not a god but a historical figure, speculation about his place of origin ranged widely, from Egypt, to Scandinavia, to Siam.

In describing the Indian gymnosophists, Clement of Alexandria writes, "Some of the Indians obey the precepts of Boutta; whom, on account of his extraordinary sanctity, they have raised to divine honors."[1] After Clement, little is heard about the Buddha in Greek or Latin until the eighth century, when, in the works of St. John of Damascus, we find the story of Barlaam and Josaphat.[2] Although the connection was not recognized for many centuries, this story is clearly based on the life of the Buddha (the name *Josaphat* derives from the Sanskrit term *bodhisattva*). References to the Buddha—although not by that name—in European languages begin to appear with more frequency in the thirteenth century, when emissaries and missionaries come into contact, not always by choice, with the westward-advancing Mongol horde. King Het'um I of Armenia spent the years 1253 to 1255 at the court of the Mongol khan Möngke at Karakorum. In the description of his time there, we find the following:

> There is also a country with many idolators who worship very large clay idols called Šakmonia; and they say [this is] a god three thousand and forty years old. And there are also another thirty-five *tumans* of years, one *tuman* being ten thousand, and then he will be deprived of his divinity by another god called Matrin, of whom they have made clay images of immense size, in a beautiful temple.
>
> And the whole nation, including the women and the children are priests and are called *toyins*. They shave both the hair of the head and the beard; they wear yellow cloaks like Christians, but they wear them from the breast and not from the shoulders. And they are temperate in their food and in their marriages. They take a wife at twenty, and up to thirty approach her three times a week, and up to forty three times a month, and up to fifty, three times a year; and when they have passed fifty, they no longer go near her.
>
> The learned king related many other things regarding the barbarous nations which we have omitted lest they might appear superfluous.[3]

Four decades later, returning to Venice after seventeen years in the service of a different Mongol khan, Marco Polo's ship made port on the island of Sri Lanka, probably in 1292. He writes:

> Furthermore you must know that in the Island of Seilan there is an exceeding high mountain; it rises right up so steep and precipitous that no one could ascend it, were it not that they have taken and fixed to it several great and massive iron chains, so disposed that by help of these men are able to mount to the top. And I tell you they say that on this mountain is the sepulchre of Adam our first parent; at least that is

what the Saracens say. But the Idolaters say that it is the sepulchre of SAGAMONI BORCAN, before whose time there were no idols. They hold him to have been the best of men, a great saint in fact, according to their fashion, and the first in whose name idols were made.[4]

On January 29, 1552, Francis Xavier wrote a letter from Kochi on the southwest coast of India to his companions in Europe:

All the Japanese, both the bonzes and the common people, recite prayers with the help of rosaries that have more than one hundred and eighty beads. While they are reciting them, they continuously repeat at each bead the name of the founder of their sect. Some are devoted to frequently reciting their beads, but others less so. All of these sects, as I have said above, have two main founders, namely, Xaca and Ameda. . . .

I tried to learn if these two, Ameda and Xaca, had been men dedicated to philosophy. I asked the Christians to make an accurate translation of their lives. I discovered from what was written in their books that they were not men, since it was written that they had lived for a thousand and two thousand years, and that Xaca will be born eight thousand times, and many other absurdities. They were thus not men, but pure inventions of the demons.[5]

In 1660, a young Englishman named Robert Knox (1641–1720) was among a crew of sailors taken prisoner by Rājasiṃha II, the king of Sri Lanka, after their ship lost its mast in a storm. Knox spent more than nineteen years living in Sri Lanka, escaping eventually to a Dutch settlement on the island. On his long voyage home, he drafted a volume entitled *An Historical Relation of the Island Ceylon in the East-Indies; Together, With an Account of the Detaining in Captivity the Author and divers other Englishmen now Living there, and of the Author's Miraculous Escape.* It was published in 1681 and was read widely, serving as one of Defoe's inspirations for Robinson Crusoe. Describing pagodas, Knox writes:

In them are Idols and Images most monstrous to behold, some of silver, some of brass and other metals: and also painted sticks, and Targets, and most strange kind of Arms, as Bills, Arrows, Spears and Swords. But these Arms are not in the Buddou's Temples, he being for Peace: therefore there are in his Temples only Images of men cross-legged with yellow coats on like the Gonni-Priests, their hair frisled, and their hands before them like women. And these they say are the spirits of holy men departed. Their Temples are adorned with such things as peoples ability and poverty can afford; accounting it the highest point of Devotion, bountifully to dedicate such things unto their Gods, which in their estimation are most precious.[6]

Daniel Defoe was an ardent student of religion, and in 1704, he published his *Diction-arium Sacrum Seu Religiosum: A Dictionary of All Religions, Ancient and Modern, Whether Jewish, Pagan, Christian, or Mahometan*. This is a passage from his entry on "Confucius" from the expanded 1723 edition:

> [Confucius] openly declar'd he was not the Inventor of this [i.e., "Confucian"] Doc-trine; that he only collected it out of his Predecessors Writings, and used to say, there was a very Holy Man in the Western Lands, that he was called, by some *Zeuximgim*, but said no more of him. In the Year 66, after the Incarnation of our Blessed Saviour, the Emperor *Thinti* sent Ambassadors towards the *West*, to seek this Holy Man, but they stopped in an Island near the *Red Sea*, to consider a famous Idol named *Fe*, representing a Philosopher that lived 500 years before *Confucius*; this Idol they carried back along with them, with Instructions concerning the Worship paid to it and so introduced a Superstition, that in several things abolish'd the Maxims of *Confucius*, who always condemned Atheism and idolatry.[7]

We have here accounts from an Armenian, a Venetian, a Spaniard, and two Englishmen, from lands in the east, south, and west of Europe, accounts spanning some four centuries, describing Mongolia, Sri Lanka, Japan, and China—lands in the west, south, and east of Buddhist Asia. They describe five idols, named Šakmonia, Xaca, Sagamoni Borcan, Buddou, and Fe (or Fo). Travelers to these and other Asian lands would encounter gods named Sommona Kodom, Mahamoonie, Gouton, Daybot, and Budso.

Defoe's dictionary sought to encompass "All Religions, Ancient and Modern, Whether Jewish, Pagan, Christian, or Mahometan." And, indeed, until long into the nineteenth century, European writers divided the peoples of the world into four nations (in the old sense of the term): Christians, Jews, Mahometans, and Idolaters (or Pagans).[8] What we think of today as Buddhists were described by this last term, Idolaters, a word that we regard today, still feeling the power of St. Thomas Aquinas, as a term of abuse. And in some sense, what we think of today as the academic study of religion has, over the past two centuries, been devoted to the process of separating out various groups of these idolaters and giving them their own religions, each ending in *-ism*: Hinduism, Sikhism, Daoism, Confucianism, Shintoism, Buddhism, and, according to some, yet another idolatrous sect, Roman Catholicism. Thus Marco Polo, like the travelers who preceded and followed him, never identified the religion he encountered with the name "Buddhism" (or some rough Chinese or Mongol equivalent) or its priests as "Buddhists." Instead, he referred to the monks he encountered at the court of the great khan and in his travels through Asia simply as idolaters and the statues that they worshipped as idols.

From our perspective, it is clear that the statues that those intrepid travelers describe are not idols, and that what they term idols are statues not of different gods but of a single man, a historical figure and the founder of a great religion, whom we know simply as the

Buddha. But how could they have known that? Each of the Buddhist cultures of Asia developed its own artistic conventions for representing the Buddha. Not all images of the Buddha look alike. And in the centuries before photography, it was necessary to rely on artists' renderings, renderings not always made in situ, but based on a written account. Thus, for most of the long history of European contact with Buddhism, the Buddha was an idol, and he was known by many names. These various names are, in fact, for the most part various garbled versions of just four names by which he was commonly known across the Buddhist world: his epithet Śākyamuni, the "sage of the Śākya clan"; his family name Gautama; śramaṇa Gautama, "the ascetic Gautama"; and his title, Buddha. The Chinese character pronounced in the eighteenth century as *fo* was, in the Tang Dynasty, pronounced *budh*.

But none of this was known with what we would regard as historical accuracy until the early nineteenth century. The identification of these various names with a single god became widely known only in the early eighteenth century, and only then with a strange detour into Africa. Up until the middle of the eighteenth century and beyond, the focus was not simply on the man or his teachings but on the thing, the statue, and, as we shall see, on the hair. Again and again, travelers are not particularly interested in who or what the statue might represent; they are fascinated by the size of the statue and what it is made of.

In 1685, a noted memoirist and notorious transvestite, the Abbé de Choisy, was a member of the French delegation to the court of Siam. There he visited one of the most famous Buddhist temples in Southeast Asia, Wat Phra Sri Sanphet, today in ruins, known for its magnificent statue of the Buddha. But the Catholic cleric shows little interest in the figure depicted. In his diary entry of October 30, 1685, all he can talk about is the gold:

> Then, after having walked a lot, we arrived at the King's pagoda. When I went in I thought I was in a church. The nave is supported by tall thick columns, without architectural decoration. . . . The choir is small and very dark; there are at least fifty lamps continually lit there. But what will surprise you is that at the end of the choir is an image in solid gold, that is to say gold poured into a mould. It may be forty-two feet high by thirteen or fourteen feet wide, and three inches in thickness. It is said there is 12,400,000 *livres* of gold here. We also saw in other parts of the pagoda seventeen or eighteen figures in solid gold, as high as a man, most having diamonds on their fingers, emeralds and some rubies on their foreheads and their navels. These images are without doubt of gold; we touched and handled them, and although we only got to within five or six feet of the big statue, without touching it, I think it is made of gold like the others; to the eye it seemed the same metal. In addition to these there were more than thirty idols with golden vestments.[9]

Other missionaries, however, began to collect stories about the idols. The Portuguese Jesuit missionary to China Alvaro Semedo (1585–1658) spent twenty-two years in China. His account of China was published in Portuguese in Madrid in 1642 as *Relação da propagação da fé no reyno da China e outros adjacentes* and was translated into English and published in 1655 as *The history of that great and renowned monarchy of China wherein all the particular provinces are accurately described, as also the dispositions, manners, learning, lawes, militia, government, and religion of the people: together with the traffick and commodities of that countrey*. He writes:

> The third *Sect* is of the *Pagods* [idolaters], from *India,* from the part of *Indostan;* which Sect they call *Xaca,* from the Authour of it: concerning whom, they fable; that he was conceived by his Mother *Maia,* only upon the sight of a white Elephant, which she saw in her sleep; and for the more puritie she brought him forth at one of her flancks, and then presently died, being but nineteen yeares of age. And that, considering the death of his Mother, the cause whereof he was by his Birth, he resolved to leave the world, and to do pennance; the which he did in a Mountain called the Snowy Mountaine, where he had fower Masters, with whom he studied twelve yeares; so that by that time he was thirty yeares of age, he was accomplished in the Science of the first principle. He took the name of *Xekia,* or *Xaca:* he taught his doctrine for the space of 49 yeares; he had many Scholars, who, after his death collected his papers, and spread his doctrine through the greater part of Asia.[10]

Here, Father Semedo describes the birth of the Buddha. According to the traditional accounts, his mother, named Queen Māyā, dreamed of a white elephant on the night that he entered her womb; after ten lunar months, the future Buddha emerged from her right side; and she died shortly after his birth. But it was not her death that caused him to renounce the world; he practiced asceticism for six years rather than twelve; and he achieved enlightenment at the age of thirty-five, becoming known as Śākyamuni (hence, "Xaca" here). He taught the dharma for forty-five years, and after his death his disciples gathered his words, rather than his papers. Still, one clearly discerns European exposure to the traditional biography here.

A French Jesuit missionary to Siam, Nicolas Gervaise, recognized that, in some sense, both the Siamese and the Chinese practiced the same religion, and he sought to determine its origin:

> The era of this religion is very vague, and one cannot tell very exactly when it began nor in what manner it was established. Common opinion says it is about two thousand years old, and the Siamese would like to believe that it originated in their country. Those who have voyaged along the Coromandel coast think that this religion came from the Brahmins by reason of the great similarity that exists between them

and the Siamese in religion. The Chinese maintain that the glory is due to their country. It is seen in their books, which are exceedingly old, that Sommonokodom was Chinese. An emperor of China, they say, had sent his ambassador to Siam, and he acquitted himself so well that the King of Siam gave him his daughter in marriage and made him his successor. After having reigned several years to the people's liking, this ambassador voluntarily abdicated his sovereign power and retired to the woods, where the austerity of his life did not, however, prevent his being followed by a great number of people who placed themselves under his guidance. He taught them, not only by his own example, but also by means of precepts full of admirable wisdom. After his death his disciples spread his teaching, and, in order to immortalize their gratitude and his memory, they built temples in his honour and erected statues to him. As century followed century these statues served to cast the Siamese into the practice of idolatry, and led them to look upon Sommonokodom as a God, and, finally, in order to justify their worship of him and to legalize their errors, they invented those stories which their unfortunate posterity have received as fixed truths and articles of faith.[11]

Finally, late in the seventeenth century, a missionary to Sri Lanka speculated on the referent of the many names of the god encountered in Asia. In 1687, the Portuguese Jesuit Fernaõ de Queyroz completed *The Temporal and Spiritual Conquest of Ceylon*, which contained the most detailed life of the Buddha (referred to as Fô) yet to appear in a European language. It had been compiled from Chinese sources by the great Jesuit scholar Tomás Pereira, advisor to the Kangxi Emperor and director of the imperial observatory in Beijing. At the end of Father Pereira's account, Queyroz writes:

And as it has been observed that the Ganezes of Ceylon, the Talpoys of Arracan, Pegu, Siam and other neighbouring Realms, as well as the Lamazes of Tartary agree with the Bonzes of China and Japan in the essentials of their sect and profession, it is easy to understand that the Buddum of Ceylon, the Fô of China, the Xaka of Japan is the same as the Xekia of India, for the word Buddum is only an adapted name, and in Ceylon it means Saint by antonomasia. And if those who had read the documents of Ceylon had been more curious and had not been weary of giving us more detailed information, we could have shown more clearly from what they relate of his life the additions made by Chinese malice.

If intelligent Europeans wonder, considering what it is that such intelligent people embrace as true, let them remember what heathen Europe so pertinaciously believed and worshipped. The fact is the Devil has forestalled everything. When we preach to the heathens of hither India, they reply that they also have a Trinity, and that their Vixnu incarnated himself times out of number; if we preach to those of farther India and of Ceylon (for this Sect has disappeared from many parts of India wherein it began), they reply that their Buddum or their Fô or their Xaka also took the shape of a man, though he was an eternal being.[12]

Here, Father Queyroz correctly identifies the various idols of Asia as the same person. And he bemoans the difficulties of the Christian missions in converting his worshippers to the Gospel, blaming these difficulties on the Devil, who has forestalled, that is, anticipated everything they would preach, installing sham versions of the Trinity and the incarnation of God in heathen lands, waiting to mock the missionaries when they arrived.[13]

For a more sustained engagement with the question of the identity of this god, we must turn to a Dutch scholar, or at least to a Westphalian physician in the employ of the Dutch East India Company, who visited Siam just five years after the Abbé de Choisy. He is Engelbert Kaempfer (1651–1716), who sailed from Batavia (Jakarta) in May 1690, stopping in Siam before proceeding to Japan, where he would spend the next two years. Having seen statues of the local god in both Thailand and Japan, he offered the following account of their origin:

The Religion of these People is the Pagan Doctrine of the *Brahmans*, which ever since many Centuries hath been profess'd amongst all the Nations from the River Indus to the extremity of the East, except that at the Court of the Grand Mogul, and in his great Cities, as also in *Summatra*, *Java*, *Celebes*, and other neighbouring Islands the Mahometism has gain'd so much ground, that it seems to prevail above it. This general Paganism, (which is to be distinguish'd from the Religion of the old Persians worshipping the Sun, now almost extinct) tho' branch'd out into several Sects and Opinions, according to the various Customs, Languages, and Interpretations, yet is of one and the same Origine. The Siamites represent the first Teacher of their Paganism in their Temples, in the figure of a Negro sitting, of a prodigious size, his hair curl'd, the skin black, but as it were out of respect gilt over, accompanied on each side by one of his chief Companions, as also before and around him by the rest of his Apostles and Disciples, all of the same colour and most in the same posture. They believe according to the Brahmans, that the Deity dwelt in him, which he prov'd by his Doctrine, Way of Life, and Revelation. . . . The Ceylanese call him *Budhum*, the Chinese and Japanese *Sacka*, or *Siaka*, or plainly *Fotoge*, that is, the Idol, and with an honourable Epithet *Si Tsun*, the great Saint.

About his origine and native Country, I find the account of those Heathens do not agree. . . . But the Siamites, and other Nations lying further East, have whole Books full of the birth, life and miracles of this God *Prah*, or *Siaka*. I am at a loss how to reconcile these various and opposite accounts, which I have gather'd in the abovesaid Countries, unless by supposing, what I really think to be the true opinion, *viz.* that the Siamites and other Nations lying more Easterly have confounded a younger Teacher with *Budha'* and mistaken the former for the latter, which confusion of the Gods and their names is very frequent in the Histories of the Greeks and Egyptians; so that *Prah* or *Siaka*, is not the same with *Budha*, much less with *Ram*, or *Rama*, as he is call'd by Father Kircher in his *Sina Illustrata*, the latter having appear'd many hundred thousand years before, but that he was some new Impostor who set up but about five hundred years before Christ's nativity. Besides this, many circumstances make it probable, that the *Prah*, or *Siaka*, was no Asiatick, or Indian, but some Egyptian Priest of note, probably of *Memphis*, and a Moor, who with his Brethren being expell'd their native Country, brought the Egyptian Religion into the Indies, and propagated it there, and this for the following Reasons.[14]

Kaempfer correctly identifies the various statues as representations of the same figure. But he cannot extract consistent information from his informants on either the place or the date of his birth. He thus offers two hypotheses that would hold sway for the next century. We might refer to them as the "two-Buddha theory" and the "African hypothesis." These are often ascribed to Sir William Jones, who presented them to the Royal Asiatic Society in Calcutta in 1786 and 1788. But they were set forth almost a century earlier by Kaempfer, who extended the identification of the various gods all the way to Memphis. He derived the African hypothesis not from texts he read but from things he saw, from statues and what he, and many others, would see as their woolly hair. Although Kaempfer's allusion to dark skin and woolly hair foreshadows the race theory of the nineteenth century, this was not Kaempfer's reference at the end of the seventeenth century. Africa for him meant Egypt, which, as for other scholars of the day, notably the great Jesuit polymath Athanasius Kircher (1602–80), was the source of the pagan religions of Asia. Like Kircher, Kaempfer held that when Cambyses II, son of Cyrus the Great, conquered Egypt (and Memphis) in 525 B.C.E.—the conquest is described by Herodotus—the Egyptian priests who survived escaped to the east, eventually arriving in India, where they introduced their cult of idolatry. This African hypothesis would persist into the nineteenth century; as late as 1810, Edward Moor wrote:

> Some statues of BUDDHA certainly exhibit thick *Ethiopian* lips; but all, with wooly hair: there is something mysterious, and still unexplained, connected with the hair of this, and only of this, *Indian* deity. The fact of so many different tales having been invented to account for his crisped woolly head, is alone sufficient to excite suspicion that there is something to conceal—something to be ashamed of; more exists than meets the eye.[15]

Thus, in 1825, the illustrious French Sinologist Jean Pierre Abel-Rémusat felt it necessary to publish an article entitled "On Some Descriptive Epithets of Buddha Showing That Buddha Did Not Belong to the Negro Race,"[16] where he disputed the hypothesis of Sir William Jones that the Buddha was African. In the first half of the nineteenth century, the country, and even the continent, of the Buddha's origin was a matter of scholarly debate.

Let me inflict one final quotation, a long one I fear, this time from 1844, translated from the French:

It is into the milieu of a society so constituted that was born, in a family of *kṣatriyas*, that of the Śākyas of Kapilavastu, who claimed descent from the ancient solar race of India, a young prince who, renouncing the world at the age of twenty-nine, became a monk under the name of *Śākyamuni* or also *Śramaṇa Gautama*. His doctrine, which according to the sūtras was more moral than metaphysical, at least in its principle, rested on an opinion accepted as a fact and on a hope presented as a certitude. This opinion is that the visible world is in perpetual change; that death succeeds life and life death; that man, like all that surrounds him, revolves in the eternal circle of transmigration; that he successively passes through all forms of life from the most elementary to the most perfect; that the place he occupies on the vast scale of living beings depends on the merit of the actions he performs in this world; and thus the virtuous man must, after this life, be reborn with a divine body, and the guilty with a body of the damned; that the rewards of heaven and the punishments of hell have only a limited duration, like everything in the world; that time exhausts the merit of virtuous actions as it effaces the faults of evil actions; and that the fatal law of change brings the god as well as the damned back to earth, in order to again put both to the test and make them pass through a new series of transformations. The hope that Śākyamuni brought to humanity was the possibility to escape from the law of transmigration, entering what he calls nirvāṇa, that is to say, annihilation. The definitive sign of this annihilation was death; but a precursory sign in this life announced the man predestined for this supreme liberation; it was the possession of an unlimited science, which gave him a clear view of the world, as it is, that is to say, the knowledge of physical and moral laws; and in short, it was the practice of the six transcendent perfections: that of alms-giving, morality, science, energy, patience, and charity. The authority on which the monk of the Śākya race supported his teaching was entirely personal; it was formed of two elements, one real and the other ideal. The first was the consistency and the saintliness of his conduct, of which chastity, patience, and charity formed the principal features. The second was the claim he made to be Buddha, that is to say, enlightened, and as such to possess superhuman science and power. With his power, he performed miracles; with his science, he perceived, in a form clear and complete, the past and the future. Thereby, he could recount everything that each person had done in their previous existences; and so he asserted that an infinite number of beings had long ago attained like him, through the practice of the same virtues, the dignity of Buddha, before entering into complete annihilation. In the end, he presented himself to humanity as its saviour, and he promised them that his death would not annihilate his doctrine; but that this doctrine would endure for a great number of centuries after him, and that when his salutary action ceased, there would come into the world a new Buddha, whom he announced by name and whom, before descending to earth, the legends say, he himself had crowned in heaven, with the title of future Buddha.[17]

Perhaps unusual in its eloquence, this description seems conventional in its content. This is the Buddha that we know. It is important to recall, however, that the Buddha had never previously been described in quite these terms by a European—or by an Asian, for that matter. This is the Buddha of Eugène Burnouf, holder of the chair in Sanskrit at the Collège de France. The passage is drawn from the Ur-text of the academic study of Buddhism, Burnouf's 647-page magnum opus, published in 1844 with the understated title, *Introduction à l'histoire du Buddhisme indien*. Our image of the Buddha, of the simple teacher of morality, seated beneath a tree, derives above all from this book. How Burnouf created this Buddha is a story for another time. We can say in brief that Burnouf could read Sanskrit and that he was a son of the French Enlightenment.

From these desultory quotations, I would hope that the following inferences might be drawn. First, for most of the long history of European contact with what we today call the Buddha image and the person whom this image represents, whom we call the Buddha, this image has been considered an idol, a thing, and those who worship it—whom we call Buddhists—have been considered idolaters, worshippers of things. Second, for most of the long history of European contact with what we today call the Buddha image and the person whom this image represents, Europeans considered the images they encountered in various parts of Asia to depict different gods. That is, they did not conclude that the image of Šakmonia in Mongolia, for example, somehow represented the same god as the image of Godama in Burma. Third, sometime in the late seventeenth century, European missionaries and travelers began to conclude that the many images observed in many nations and the many names recorded in many languages all somehow designated a single figure, though whether he was a figure of myth or history remained undecided. By the beginning of the nineteenth century, his identity was well established, and it was generally accepted that he had been a historical figure, although his origins were debated. The final inference that I hope we might draw from these quotations is that the last quotation, from 1844, is rather different from the rest, both in the detail of its description and in the confidence of its tone. That is, one might conclude that something happened in the first three decades of the nineteenth century that changed everything.

What we have, then, is a familiar, and perhaps fitting, tale. European travelers, first mostly missionaries, merchants, and diplomats, and later colonial officers, encountered Buddhism across Asia. But they could not read Buddhist texts, and hence they harbored many misconceptions about the religion and its founder. Eventually, with the rise of the science of philology and of Oriental scholarship in the nineteenth century, the huge corpus of Buddhist texts began to be read, providing a wealth of new information. The myriad idols coalesced into a single figure, who then became a historical figure, a founder of a religion, and a superstition became a philosophy.

The European travelers of the seventeenth and eighteenth centuries encountered what we today call Buddhism all over Asia, but not in India. The Buddha had lived in northern India in the fifth century B.C.E. Buddhist monks carried texts and images to much of Asia over the next millennium and a half, but by the fourteenth century, and before the arrival of the Portuguese, Buddhism had all but disappeared from India. The reasons for its disappearance were complex (the invasion of northern India by Muslim armies is one of many causes), but its consequences were profound. By the time that European scholars (notably those of the British East India Company) trained in South Asian languages began a sustained study of the culture and history of India, what they would come to call "Buddhism" was an artifact. There were no Buddhists in India, although there were Buddhists almost everywhere else in Asia. Instead, India had monuments (often in ruins), cave temples (overgrown by jungle), and statues (often broken). There were stone inscriptions to be deciphered, and there were Sanskrit manuscripts preserved in Nepal to the north of India and Pali manuscripts in Sri Lanka to the south of India. These were the materials from which European scholars would build their Buddhism.

This Buddhism would be built largely from texts. Because there were no Buddhists living in India during the colonial period, Buddhism, and especially what would come to be called "original Buddhism" or "primitive Buddhism," became the domain of European and later American and then Japanese scholars. They would create a Buddha and a Buddhism that were unknown in Asia and that may never have existed there before the late nineteenth century. Just as there was a quest for the historical Jesus, there was a quest for the historical Buddha, and European Orientalists felt they had found him. This was the human and humane Buddha that Burnouf described in 1844, a Buddha who has remained largely unchanged in the European imagination, or at least the scholarly imagination, since then. This Buddhism then became a model against which the various contemporary Buddhisms of Asia were measured and generally found to be lacking, not only by Europeans but eventually by Buddhist elites in Asia as well.

In closing, we might consider the question of whether something was lost in the march of scholarly progress, whether something disappeared when weathered stone turned to smooth flesh, when the thing turned into an "image." We might consider whether the collapse of many Buddhas into a single archetype effaced a level of detail, of specificity, of locality that is no longer discerned, yet was glimpsed long ago by the eyes of those who could not read, but who could only see.

⚮

A statue of the Buddha, whether in wood or bronze or stone, does not become a Buddha until it has been consecrated. The ceremonies vary across the Buddhist world. In some, the eyes are painted. In others, a blindfold is removed. In Thailand, during the time of Choisy and Kaempfer as well as today, the consecration of a Buddha image is called "opening the eyes of the Buddha." Over the course of the night, monks sit before the statue and recite the events of the Buddha's life to animate his form, like reading a diary to someone emerging from a coma.

Rhetoric of the Heart

Figuring the Body in Devotion to the Sacred Heart of Jesus

David Morgan

Devotion to the Sacred Heart of Jesus originates in its distinctive modern form with the Visitationist nun Margaret-Mary Alacoque (1647–90), whose autobiography and letters document her extraordinary experiences and indefatigable zeal in promoting the object of her life's work, the Heart of Jesus. The history of the devotion since her death presents a varied range of ideas and practices that not only built on her testament but also contested, obscured, and transformed it. This chapter explores the way in which the understanding of the heart has been invested in three different forms of representation—fetish, icon, and symbol—and how these each have been used to craft or a different conception of the body. The body in question is multiform: the body of Jesus, of the saint, of the church, and of the viewer of the image of the Sacred Heart. In every case, the heart is the medium of experience, the chief register of the sacred, one that figures the body of divine presence differently, but without resolving the inherently unstable meaning of the body.

Origins: Sacred Heart as Fetish

From a very early age, according to her autobiography, Margaret-Mary Alacoque experienced a visceral repugnance at sin.[1] Her father died when she was eight years old. The following year she was sent to a convent for education. She remembered herself as a shy, retiring girl there, who for many years struggled with family members, especially with her mother and her brother Chrysostome, who took over as head of the family after her father died, to be allowed to pursue a vocation as a nun.[2] The absent father and oppositional mother became a pattern that structured her relationship to Jesus and the eventual series of mothers superior who were tasked by her extraordinary mortifications and visions for the remainder of her life.

The piety that took shape in Alacoque's experience as a young woman and throughout her years as a religious turned on the twofold nature of Christ as lover and judge, passionate spouse and relentlessly demanding disciplinarian. She longed to be his lover and his slave. Suffering became the medium for satisfying both impulses: crucified and abused to share his suffering, punished and tortured to expiate the offenses made against him—by her own sin and the ingratitude of humanity in general. The visual display of Jesus' suffering served as revelation and medium for drawing near to him. Early on, Jesus would appear to her "under the form of the crucifix or of an Ecce Homo, or as carrying His cross." The imagery filled her with "the ardent desire . . . to suffer" in order that she might render herself "conformable to my suffering Jesus."[3] As much as Jesus demanded her self-mortification and berated her vanity, he also favored her with the assurance that he would deliver her from the travail of her worldly life. As her family arranged to present her with suitors for marriage, the young Alacoque praised Jesus as "the most beautiful, the wealthiest, the most powerful, the most perfect, and the most accomplished amongst all lovers."[4] Wooed by Jesus and horrified by the prospect of being forced to marry another, Alacoque yearned for the religious life and submission to "the Divine Spouse of my soul." Resisting her family's plans, she cultivated an inner life of commitment to Christ, who in time asked her if she would "agree to His taking possession and making Himself Master of my liberty." She "willingly consented" and told her family that "all suitors should be dismissed."[5] Eventually the family relented.

In 1671, she was accepted at the Visitationist house in Paray, where she trained her energies on the bracing relationship she experienced with Christ. "[Jesus] pursued me so closely," she wrote, "that I had no leisure except to think of how I could love Him by crucifying myself."[6] When she received the habit, Jesus revealed that the time of espousal had arrived and he "acquired a new right over me. . . . after the manner of the most passionate of lovers, He would, during that time, allow me to taste all that was sweetest and most delightful in the tokens of His love."[7] Her colleagues and those in charge at the convent were disturbed by the young nun's experiences, excessive zeal, and sometimes bizarre behavior. She was constantly subjected to attempts to induce her to eat and to restrain her from extreme self-discipline. Many, she later reported, came to consider her possessed by the devil.[8] The resistance interposed by authorities at the convent dismayed Alacoque, because she felt it hindered the intimacy and intensity of her relationship with Jesus, whom she consulted. Prudently, he counseled submission to the mother superior.

Yet her compulsion to suffer for and with Jesus was irrepressible. Extreme suffering constituted a kenotic or self-emptying empathy that was the dominant form of Alacoque's intimate connection with Jesus. After professing her vows in 1672, she was favored with the continual presence of her divine lover. The presence "imprinted in me so deep a sense of self-annihilation, that I felt, as it were, sunk and annihilated in the abyss of my nothingness, whence I have not since been able to withdraw myself."[9] This experience led to her first mystical encounter with the Sacred Heart in 1675, which was steeped in the contemplation of the Sacrament of the Altar, abnegation of self, and the erotic pleasure of her paramour:

> One day . . . I was praying before the Blessed Sacrament, when I felt myself wholly penetrated with that Divine Presence, but to such a degree that I lost all thought of myself and of the place where I was, and abandoned myself to this Divine Spirit, yielding up my heart to the power of His love. He made me repose for a long time upon His Sacred Breast, where He disclosed to me the marvels of His love and the inexplicable secrets of His Sacred Heart, which so far He had concealed from me. Then it was that, for the first time, He opened to me His Divine Heart in a manner so real and sensible as to be beyond all doubt.[10]

Jesus told her that his heart was aflame with love for all people, but especially for her, and that he would have this love spread through her to everyone to convey its benefits. "After this He asked me for my heart, which I begged Him to take. He did so and placed it in His own Adorable Heart where He showed it to me as a little atom which was being consumed in this great furnace." Jesus then placed her heart back within her body, leaving a wound in her side, whose pain, he told her, would always remain.

The intermingling of eroticism and pain became most blatant shortly later in a challenging account. Caring for a sick person at the convent who had vomited, Alacoque "was constrained to take it up with my tongue and to swallow it." She wrote that she experienced great "delight" in doing so as an act of conquering herself. But the pleasure was not only hers: "And He, Whose goodness alone had given me the strength to overcome myself, did not fail to manifest to me the pleasure He had taken therein. For the following night, if I mistake not, He kept me for two or three hours with my lips pressed to the Wound of His Sacred Heart,"[11] that is, the wound in the side of his heart, which mirrored the wound in the side of her own body. On another occasion she placed her tongue in some of the discharge of a patient suffering dysentery, then filled her mouth with the fluid.[12]

Alacoque's spirituality was deeply shaped by a long-established adoration of the Host, grounded in the medieval festival of Corpus Christi, which celebrated the holocaust, or sacrificial offering, of Jesus' body and blood in the Eucharist. Alacoque said that it was while stationed before the Blessed Sacrament one day that she felt moved to return her love to Jesus, "rendering Him love for love." It was then that Jesus asked her to set apart the Friday following the period of days dedicated to observing Corpus Christi for "a special Feast to honour My Heart." He asked her to take communion on that day "in order to make amends for the indignities which It [his heart] has received during the time It has been exposed on the altars."[13] Reference to his heart was visualized for Alacoque in the image of a human heart. The Sacred Heart, it would appear, is an iteration of the sacramental host, the body of Christ, contained in the tabernacle and brought out for visual adoration on the altar, where it was placed in a monstrance for display. Alacoque personalized her relation to the host in her visions to such a degree that Jesus himself took the delicate vessel of flesh from the tabernacle of his body and displayed it to her in an act of spiritual intimacy.

Devotion to the heart of Jesus was first visualized in the now-familiar way by Francis de Sales in 1611, the year after he co-founded the Congregation of the Visitation of Holy Mary, or the Order of the Visitation. De Sales wrote co-founder Jeanne de Chantal that God had given him the thought of a blazon or emblem for the order: it would be "a heart pierced by two arrows, enclosed within a crown of thorns . . . surmounted by a cross and engraved with the sacred names of Jesus and Mary."[14] The image that he described conveys the intimacy of Mother and Son in contemporary piety, which was committed to understanding Mary's participation in the Passion of Jesus and assuming the role of co-redemptrice. The harmony of the two also informed the Visitationist ethos and would have greeted Alacoque as she joined the community in Paray-le-Monial. The fervent celebration of the intimate embrace of the hearts of Jesus and Mary was the object of another French figure and older contemporary of Alacoque, Jean Eudes, founder of the Congregation of Jesus and Mary in 1648. "These two hearts," he wrote, "are so intimately joined that the heart of Jesus is the principle of the heart of Mary, just as the creator is the principle of his creature; and as the heart of Mary is the origin of the heart of Jesus, as mother is the origin of the heart of her child."[15] Alacoque first celebrated the devotion to the Sacred Heart in 1685 on the feast of her namesake, St. Margaret, by directing the novices in her house, over whom she had charge, to arrange "a little altar whereon they placed a small ink etching representing the Divine Heart."[16] The image (Figure 1), shows not what Alacoque saw but an ideogram, a diagram of conventionalized portrayals of the heart, a wound caused by the spear of a Roman soldier at the crucifixion to ensure Jesus' death, three nails, droplets of blood and water (which Scripture indicates came from his wounded side), and a cross perched in the aorta, from which arise vaporous flames. Surrounding the heart motif is a crown of thorns intertwined with a crown of *lac d'amours*, or love knots.[17] This highly emblematic image registers the *meaning* of the Sacred Heart through symbolic motifs rather than literally portraying the heart as a human organ, as later depictions would do so carefully.

In accord with the psychodynamics of the oppositional mother, the Marian orientation of the Salesian and Eudist heart piety was subtly displaced in Alacoque's devotion. Mary the mother who shares in the suffering of the son is replaced by Margaret-Mary the daughter-lover-slave-devotee, who joins the Crucified in the painful ardor of the Passion. Jesus sealed their complex, pluriform relationship, addressing her as "My daughter, My spouse, My slave, My victim; a plaything to give pleasure to My Heart," when Alacoque made a will or testament at his direction and sealed the occasion by signing his name with

FIGURE 1 Emblematic image of the Sacred Heart, originally produced in 1685 at
Margaret-Mary Alacoque's direction. Courtesy Peter Nevraument.

a knife on the flesh of her chest.[18] "This divine Heart," she wrote to her Jesuit confessor
late in life, "is the treasury of heaven from which precious gold has already been given us
in many ways to pay off our debt and purchase heaven."[19] In making this claim, however,
she once again affirmed the role that many Marian devotees were enthusiastically ascrib-
ing to Mary, Queen and Treasurer of Heaven.[20]

A psychological interpretation of Alacoque's extreme behavior and visions might suggest that she projected her self-loathing on Christ's intolerance of impurity, making her
self-abuse a form of love for him. His pleasure was her humiliation and his pain was her
pleasure to emulate. Alacoque's self-mortification was considerable. She starved herself
and purged herself after eating; she wrote in her own blood a letter dictated by Jesus, and
on that and another occasion carved the name of the Sacred Heart of Jesus into the bare

flesh of her chest with a penknife.[21] Blood, wounds, pain, vomit, and viscera, most notably the heart, were not simply metaphors in Alacoque's acute spirituality. The heart was more than a figure of love. It was a sublimation of desire expressed in thinly disguised intimacies between the two lovers. Alacoque's *Autobiography* graphically sets out a staunch opposition of self and beloved that was mediated only by suffering. She was adamant: "We can either choose to love God eternally in heaven with the Saints, after having done violence to ourselves, and mortified and crucified ourselves here on earth as they have done; or we can renounce their happiness by granting nature everything it craves. . . . Nature and grace cannot exist together in the same heart. One must always give way to the other."[22] In the zero-sum game of her devotion to Jesus, physical suffering was the medium of satisfying his demand for purity. Penance was measured in pain, which constituted the loss of self. Religious faith was not exhausted by the profession of creeds or the intellectual assent to dogmas or the exercise of volition in the performance of duty. Belief meant the tempestuous cultivation of pathos, an internal, felt-life of experience concentrated on the Sacred Heart. Alacoque repeatedly spoke of it as the place where she went in prayer, where she saw other devotees in worship, and where she entered the presence of the divine. The heart was where her body met his, where he exposed to her his organ of love, and where she joined him by matching her pain to his. Her own body served as the medium for dismantling her self in order to transcend it in the enjoyment of Christ's body.

Alacoque longed for the congress and enjoyed an imagined version of it in the visceral imagery of the heart. But that is not all she wanted. Her religious experience, extreme and extraordinary as it was, remains more than scantily cloaked masochism. It was a persistent quest for spiritual fulfillment in the mystical presence of the deity, a radically embodied spirituality that regarded suffering as the medium of union. Although this is not the ideal or experience pursued by most Catholics, lay or religious, nevertheless, Alacoque was canonized; her autobiography remains in print; and the devotion she founded has flourished around the world. The devout regard this as proof of divine intention. More interesting to the scholar, however, in the success of Alacoque's legacy is what it says about the importance of the body in religion—not just extreme religion, like Alacoque's, but the religion of the laity, popular belief on the scale of millions. The history of the devotion to the Sacred Heart of Jesus offers a rich instance in which to scrutinize the development of belief and practice and the role that images play in marking off discrete moments in the piety's history.

Fetish, Icon, Symbol: An Overview

The piety evolving here begins with Alacoque's erotics of pain, in which she imagines herself to be the spouse, friend, daughter, slave, and lover of Jesus. In this phase, his heart and hers intermingle in a deliberate confusion—his, displayed to her, and hers, passing out of her chest and into his. The heart is a substitute for bisexual organs. In the fervidly envisioned realm of Alacoque's experience, substitution means something akin to an actual switching of one for the other, such that the heart is not a type or symbol or allusion. It is one physical object being used in the stead of another, one that carries a taboo. Though the term is burdened by a problematic history, it would seem that the heart is a *fetish*, if by that we mean a substitute for something that cannot be openly named or embraced.[23] The word *fetish* was first developed to designate the "superstitions" of so-called primitive peoples. A fetish was a charm or amulet, a cult object worshiped for its power to act for good or ill with spiritual force. In latter-day psychoanalytic discourse, the fetish became a substitute object that ascribes to the mother the penis she does not have because she was castrated, the male child fears, by the angry father, who threatens to do the same to the incestuously driven child.[24] Freud used the term because the pathological obsession with the substitute object recalled for him the worshipful attachment to the cult object among "primitives," ensconced in fear and passionate desire. As freighted as the word is, it continues to offer us the ability to signify a fixed concentration of fear and desire whose configuration in an image or object marks a site of enduring power for some devotees. Since I will use the term in a very restrictive sense, and not to generalize the broader devotion to the Sacred Heart, I will risk using it here to designate a particular moment in the devotion's history.

Alacoque's fixation on the heart of Jesus strikes one as fetishistic inasmuch as the heart is a substitute for the passionate connection she longed to enjoy with Jesus as lover. In the frank terms of Freudian theory, the bloody cardiac organ would be the product of the father-lover's violent death—castration, presumably the angry mother's retribution for the father loving the daughter, and for the daughter's desire for the father. But I do not invoke the term *fetish* in order to conduct a Freudian analysis of the Sacred Heart in Alacoque's spirituality. To do so might imply a reduction of religion to illicit or frustrated desire in her case. In the robustly embodied figuration of Alacoque's Baroque spirituality, the heart may take the place of the penis and the vagina (the wound in her body), but it also operates as an embodiment of a relationship that was more than sex, however disturbing or repugnant it was to some contemporaries. The power of the fetish, while not for everyone—indeed, for none but an extreme few—is that it effects a robust and deeply compelling relationship between the lovers by allowing them to engage their passions without limiting their encounter to the strictly genital. The heart marks a visceral connection between Jesus and Alacoque. It is the organ that has passed from the body of one to the other, and therefore operates as a kind of radical empathy, the means of self-evacuation into the other. This empathy is the result of Alacoque's self-loathing: she felt herself out of her own body and into Christ's because she despised herself, denying herself any self-pleasure, any satisfaction in being herself. Suffering assaulted and dismantled the self and projected it beyond itself into identity with Jesus. By ravaging her own body with extreme asceticism, she became the material analogue of Christ's body. The interchange-ability of the heart, or the analogy of her wounded body to Christ's wounded heart, interlocks pleasure and pain in the heart, the meeting point or intercourse of lovers.

As a fetish or substitute, the heart does something that straightforward sexual inti-macy cannot. The fetish plays, scolds, lures, postpones, deflects, intensifies, ritualizes. In short, the fetish takes on a life of its own otherwise denied to the subject. The fetish becomes the thing to which the devotee is devoted. It is the precious gift that the lover leaves behind after their tryst. It is the powerful object whereby the lover is recalled, evoked, summoned, and re-experienced. And for Alacoque, the Sacred Heart was that into which, for which, she welcomed annihilation. It was the bliss of the encounter, both the thing she enjoyed and the token or emblem of what she enjoyed. Using the visual form of an emblem (see Figure 1) allowed her to focus entirely on the object within the allegorical framework of additional devices that added significance to the object without modifying its plain presence.

But the intimacy that the heart meant for her was not what it meant for most other people. During the eighteenth century, the Sacred Heart became a portrait-icon, an image in which the devout saw and were seen by their Savior (see Figure 2). The heart was transposed to a new setting, taking its place within the encompassing and transformative frame of the entire body and person of Jesus. The heart was pictured first in the hand of Jesus and then, in the nineteenth century, affixed to the chest of Jesus, who pulled aside his clothing to reveal a glowing organ (Figure 3), all the while looking steadfastly into the eyes of the beholder. The heart is a material presence, an organ out of place, presented for viewing. But it is not an anatomy lesson that Jesus conducts. His heart is situated within the matrix of his gaze and gesture. In this configuration of showing and gazing, the heart mediates an interactive relation between Jesus and his viewer. This Jesus does not ask devotees to join him by withering away but invites them to recognize a sympa-thetic shepherd, a pastor who seeks them out. Showing the heart qua organ as pulled from its proper place and lodged between Jesus and those looking upon him makes the heart itself part of an iconic gaze. Viewers looked at the heart as Jesus looked at them. The triangulation of heart, Jesus, and viewer made the image of the Sacred Heart more than a sign. It was a revelation, a showing or unveiling that enacted a relational give-and-take. It was not a picture about a theological meaning; it was an *icon* that opened a way to be-holding a vital connection.

In the nineteenth century, the image shifted emphasis from the heart to Jesus the person. Devotees saw the heart not as severed from his body but as hovering mystically on its surface. The difference is noteworthy, because it affected the way the image of Jesus connected with viewers. The move to sympathy as the dominant visual piety of the devo-tion marks the primary framework for the Sacred Heart in the eighteenth and nineteenth centuries. As a more pastoral version of the devotion, sympathy posits an affinity or inclination between Jesus and the soul, but does not aim at canceling their difference in

FIGURE 2   Pompeo Batoni, *The Sacred Heart of Jesus*, 1767,
oil on copper, Il Gesu, Rome.

the destruction of the self. Jesus is shepherd, father, or friend to the soul, not lover. In the visual piety of sympathy, the image of Jesus visualizes the recognition of the soul and Jesus as sympathetic or attuned to one another. The aim is to be recognized and accepted by Jesus, seen by him and drawn close to him. The heart became less organ and more image. It did not become a symbol per se but iconic, the representation that leads to the true heart. In the nineteenth century, the iconography came to picture the heart in the midst of the chest of Jesus, embedded in the person rather than appearing by itself, as it had in the engraving used by Alacoque herself (see Figure 1). The "forgetfulness of self" that Alacoque passionately pursued at Jesus' command ("I was to cling to nothing, to empty and despoil myself of everything, to love nothing but Him, in Him and for the

FIGURE 3   Currier & Ives, *Sacred Heart of Jesus*, hand-painted lithograph,
after 1856. Courtesy Library of Congress.

love of Him, to see in all things naught but Him and the interests of His glory in complete forgetfulness of self"[25]) gradually metamorphosed into a self-effacing modesty palatable to many committed Catholics. Masochistic self-loathing became unassuming meekness, self-humiliation became humility. This was accomplished not by putting new words into Alacoque's mouth but by deftly editing her autobiography. This occurred in 1867, shortly after her beatification, when the Sisters of the Visitation of Paray, the convent in which Alacoque had lived, issued an edition that suppressed certain passages, which were not restored until the sisters issued a new translation in 1924.[26]

As the piety developed during the nineteenth and twentieth centuries, a third moment emerged, which may be called symbolic. This occurred when the icon condensed into a sign, which took place in polemic, in teaching, in commemoration, and in theological discourse. The *symbol* of the heart was used to signify theological meaning. It is an aid to memory, an abstract device, a hieroglyph that stands for an experience as much as for a conviction or a dogma. It is the stuff of catechisms and creeds. The symbol is conducive to education, to teaching children and converts, to the mass circulation that graphic reproduction enables. It corresponds to an explanation that exhausts its meaning. The symbol refers to and endorses dogmas, a corpus of authorized ideas that exerts a powerful structuring effect among large numbers of people, promotes mass movements, and delivers a devotion from one generation to another. During the first half of the twentieth century, devotion to the Sacred Heart came to regard the heart as a symbol of Jesus' compassion, his love for humanity. The heart became a badge or insignia, an increasingly abstract device affixed to the tunic over Christ's chest (Figure 4). Alacoque had overseen the production of small engravings of the heart on paper, which she urged fellow devotees to wear on their clothing, over their heart, as a way of consecrating themselves to the Sacred Heart and promoting the devotion.[27] The nineteenth-century version of the Sacred Heart, which separated the heart from the chest of Jesus as an incandescent device, returned in some sense to this emblematic tradition of a symbolic design. But as a superficial signifier, the image now decorated the body of Jesus rather than symbolizing or disemboweling it. Jesus became transfigured into his own meaning. The sign came to refer to a body of doctrines more than to the body of Jesus.

Avoiding as excessive or even pathological the blood and pain prized by the Baroque versions of the piety, parish priests, religious educators, and catechism teachers used the ubiquitous iconography of the Sacred Heart hanging in classrooms and fellowship halls to teach submission to Christ as Lord and to serve as the emblem of his self-sacrificing love. Many twentieth-century Catholics saw the image as a visual device encoded with meaning that needed to be deciphered. As a symbol, its visceral presence was blunted in order for it to serve as a didactic tool in teaching Catholic doctrine. This also allowed the image to bridge two or three generations of Catholics, especially in America, where the immigrant generation remembered older forms of the devotion, while their children and grandchildren tended to find the penitential practices and Baroque sensibilities repulsive

FIGURE 4   *Sacred Heart of Jesus*, undated lithograph. Collection of the author.

and "Old World." As a way of countering these menacing divisions, the large number of images in circulation, hanging in churches, convents, hospitals, and Catholic homes and schools, were used as teaching devices. In this way, the older piety could be remembered, if dimly, and the imagery could be kept around, even if many educators and priests, especially in the wake of Vatican II, relegated the pictures to back rooms or the edge of consciousness. The use of the image came to turn on memory, especially in rites of commemoration, remembering priests and community figures under the blessing of the Sacred Heart of Jesus.[28]

Debating the Body

Following the great interest that several Jesuit fathers took in the Sacred Heart as confessors of Alacoque and as promoters of the devotion after her death, the Society of Jesus came to make special use of the devotion over the course of the eighteenth century. Jesuits recognized in the Sacred Heart a powerful appeal to a penitential economy that stressed indulgences, the Eucharist, the sacramental life of the Church, and obedience to papal authority over against the movement toward reform undertaken by Protestants, on the one hand, and reformers within the Catholic Church, on the other. The most important example of the latter was the controversy between Jesuits and Jansenists, especially in France, which has been extensively discussed.[29] The debate's relevance for the history of devotion to the Sacred Heart may be summarized here as regards different views on grace, penance, and the material practices of penitence (the works one did to achieve the grace offered by the sacrament of penance). Politically, the controversy dealt with national control of the French Church as a matter of the state versus ultramontane control from Rome. Theologically, the debate centered on the understanding of divine grace. Basing their view of grace on St. Augustine's notion of predestination, Jansenists contended that the saved are elected by God for salvation and that the effect of divine grace upon them is therefore irresistible, in accord with God's sovereignty. All others were rightly damned, irredeemable from their native state of complete corruption. According to Jansenist polemic, Jesuits were latter-day representatives of the Pelagian heresy fought vigorously by Augustine, who opposed his notions of predestination and efficacious grace to the emphasis on the power of human beings to participate in their salvation by virtue of free will, which allowed assent to the gift of divine grace.

The controversy sheds light on the ritual and devotional practices of lived religion and bears directly on differing ideas about the embodied nature of this devotion. Though obviously part of an elaborate theological apparatus, penance was a ritual form of belief that was of ardent practical concern to devout laity as well as to theologians, confessors, religious, clergy, and ecclesiasts. Christianity's core claim was that sin separated humanity from God. Divine grace forgave sin through the sacrifice of Jesus, but the action and application of that grace in daily life was undertaken through penance. It was on this point that Jansenists and Jesuits repeatedly disagreed. According to the latter, God provided sufficient grace for salvation through abundant means for everyone, communicated in the sacraments (one of which was penance). Jesuits urged frequent participation in Holy Communion as a powerful means of receiving forgiveness of sin and bolstering the weak in the struggle for holiness. Jesuits argued against predestination, contending that grace is neither irresistible nor limited to the elect few, but offered to everyone and capable of redeeming all who accepted it. Devotion to the Sacred Heart of Jesus conducted in tandem with frequent Communion was one of the practices encouraged by Jesuits for satisfying the offense of sin. For Jansenists, this made the devotion doubly suspect: it was a way of mechanically usurping divine grace, and it was a devotion endorsed by Jesuits.

One outspoken critic of the devotion and reformer dedicated to Jansenist ideals was Scipio de Ricci, bishop of Prato and Pistoia between 1780 and 1795. In a pastoral letter of 1781, Ricci inaugurated a long campaign for reform, which included a critique of the devotion to the Sacred Heart:

> the object of your adoration and delight is the Holy Sacrament of the Eucharist, where there is not only the Heart of Jesus Christ but the fullness of the Godhead in two natures, hypostatically united and truly present—in the words of St. Augustine, *a symbol of love*, a sacrament of unity . . . what need have you to take on a new devotion to the Sacred Heart of Jesus, without which for all these centuries past the true Faithful attained the highest degree of sanctity?[30]

Ricci repeated a criticism that others had raised, even as early as the 1720s, when the Sacred Congregation of Rites was considering whether or not to support the idea of a universal feast in honor of the Sacred Heart. Archbishop of Ancona Prosper Lambertini was the "promoter of the faith," or official opponent in the case. The postulator of the case was the Jesuit father Joseph-François de Gallifet, who did not hesitate to emphasize the material aspect of the devotion as it was received from Alacoque. Preparing a substantial work to present his case, Gallifet argued that, because the heart is, quoting Thomas Aquinas, "the first source and seat of the natural life" and "the principal organ of the sensible affections," the devotion properly focuses on the heart of Jesus as the material counterpart of his soul.[31] Speaking of the "deified flesh" and "divine body" of Jesus, Gallifet framed the Sacred Heart within the long-established feast of Corpus Christi in order to support his case.[32] Corpus Christi had as its object, he wrote, "the very flesh of Jesus Christ." The Sacred Heart simply focused on the most important aspect of that flesh.[33] Gallifet proposed a syllogism: because the heart is "the noblest part of the body" and "there is nothing in the material creation more excellent than the body of Jesus," then the Sacred Heart merits adoration par excellence.[34]

But both major and minor premises failed to convince Gallifet's opponent. Who could rank Christ's blood, flesh, heart, or wound as greater or lesser in honor? Most were already the object of adoration in feasts and devotions. Moreover, Lambertini feared that establishing yet another official feast in a very crowded liturgical calendar might encourage requests for feasts honoring yet other parts of the Lord's body.[35] The prospect of Christ's body being sundered into smaller and smaller portions, with the almost inevitable scenario of their coming into competition with one another for popular appeal, must have provoked genuine discomfort. As for the heart as the principal seat of the affections, the natural science of the day was calling that into question. Philosophers and physicians over the past century had argued increasingly for the brain as the seat of feelings and the soul, regarding the heart as an organ for pumping blood.[36] Years later, Alphonsus de Ligouri, who authored a *Novena to the Sacred Heart* in 1758, regretted Gallifet's decision to invest the heart in an outmoded science. What Gallifet had thought unassailable, Ligouri wrote, "proved to be, in fact, doubtful. The objection was made, and quite rightly, that it was not at all certain whether all the sentiments of the soul could be said to have their source in the heart and not in the head. . . . Physicians commonly assert nowadays that the heart, to which is attached the arteries and the veins, is the source and principal of the circulation of blood."[37] This very matter, Lambertini had pointed out, was a "philosophical question," that is, one belonging rightly to the domain of natural science. The Church did not want to premise a universal feast on archaic science. In 1727 the Congregation rejected the proposal and upheld its decision two years later when Gallifet solicited a reconsideration.

A third objection emerged early on and was taken up in the subsequent editions of Gallifet's French translation. Early critics worried that devotion to an individual organ of Jesus' body threatened to pull asunder the unique relation of the God-Man by encouraging adoration of a created object that is not identical to Jesus, merely one of his body parts. As Ligouri summarized the argument: "further requests could well be made in the course of time for similar favors in honor of, say, the ribs, the tongue, the eyes, and other members of the human body of Jesus Christ."[38] The result was potentially an idolatrous confusion of a created object with God. Gallifet insisted that "the sacred humanity of Jesus Christ, which is a created object . . . becomes worthy of [adoration] by its union with the divinity."[39] Thus, he reasoned, the two objects of the devotion, "the one sensible and corporeal [the heart of flesh], the other invisible and spiritual [the soul of Jesus]" are united and "honoured with an undivided honour."[40] Gallifet was adamant that the devotion did not rend the heart from the person of Jesus: "The Sacred Heart of Jesus in this devotion must not be considered apart from those things both spiritual and divine with which it is indissolubly connected. We must on the contrary consider it as intimately united to the soul and to the person of our Lord, full of life, of feeling, and of knowledge."[41]

This insistence on the unity of body and person in the Sacred Heart defended a view of the heart as the corporeal touchstone of the spiritual, which lay at the core of a late medieval and Baroque tradition of Catholic mysticism and spirituality that championed a sensuously spiritualized embodiment. Enlisting the testimony of a host of saints, including St. Gertrude, St. Catherine of Siena, St. Theresa of Avila, and St. Philip Neri, Gallifet claimed that "the heart is the place where the Holy Spirit dwells in a sensible manner, and in which Jesus Christ especially makes his presence felt by his spouses. It is there he dwells as *upon his throne* or as in *his garden of delights*."[42] This interior presence of the holy, which emanated into the material universe as by a convection of heat, since the heart was a "furnace" of love, was how Gallifet and many Catholic contemporaries in the early modern world sought to negotiate the sharp difference between the body-soul scheme of Christianity and the increasingly monistic and mechanistic understanding of the human body emerging in eighteenth-century European science. If he endorsed the increasingly outdated view of Aristotle and Galen, glossed in Aquinas, Gallifet was also able to give the materiality of the body considerable due.

Even though he was not prepared to proclaim a feast in honor of the Sacred Heart, Benedict XIII approved the first Roman confraternity in honor of the Sacred Heart in the same year, 1727. Though the devotion continued to lack robust papal support, the faithful were anything but inactive. Between 1733 and 1745 Gallifet published his Latin treatise in expanded editions in French translation. No less important was the steadily growing popular support for the cause. As Gallifet pointed out, in 1726 there were 318 associations dedicated to the Sacred Heart in Europe; by 1745 the number had grown to 702, and the number only continued to expand.[43] Popes after Benedict XIV (1740–1758), who was none other than the former Archbishop Lambertini, were more sympathetic, especially as the monarchies in Spain, Portugal, and France suppressed the Jesuit order and pressured the Vatican to follow suit (which it did in 1773). Support for the Sacred Heart compensated for the bad fortune of the Society of Jesus. By 1765 the Visitationist Order was granted the right to celebrate a feast in the honor of the Sacred Heart. The practice spread, following many requests, until, in 1856, Pius IX granted the petition of the bishops of France to extend the celebration of the Feast of the Sacred Heart to the entire world.

In 1767, registering the mounting enthusiasm for the devotion, Pompeo Batoni was asked to paint a portrait of the Sacred Heart of Jesus for the Jesuit Church of the Gesu in Rome (Figure 2). Jon Seydl has argued persuasively that the image countered criticism about sundering body and Word in the incarnation of the God-Man by showing Christ holding the heart and gazing into the viewer's eyes.[44] Seydl contends that the image presented believers with the importance of affirming the literally corporeal nature of the heart but linked it to the person of Jesus, thereby maintaining the hypostatic union of God and Man in Christ, while refusing the tendency of critics to interpret the heart only as a symbol. Seydl asserts that Batoni's painting shaped the discourse by combining the literal and symbolic aspects of the heart.[45] The idea that the two aspects were not already closely linked would have surprised Gallifet, as we have seen. But he would have welcomed Batoni's picture as an icon of sorts. Indeed, Gallifet could speak of the heart as a kind of icon. He believed that honors paid to the heart did not "terminate precisely and solely in the material heart; they terminate equally and indivisibly in the soul and the person united to this heart."[46] The iconic nature of the heart, however, relied on its material reality. About this, Gallifet left no doubt. He insisted on using the term *metaphor* in the sense of "symbol," an arbitrary signifier: the devotion seized on the heart of Jesus, he said, "in its single and natural sense, and not metaphorically."[47] For Gallifet, the metaphorical domain was meaningful only because it was grounded in the literal. There were long-standing visual consequences to this view. Seydl observes that Batoni's image provided what became the conventional format for portraying the Sacred Heart.[48] This may be due in part to the flexibility of the image: by combining the literal and symbolic, it could service those who preferred literal, symbolic, and iconic interpretations of the Sacred Heart.

The Persistence of Criticism in Nineteenth-Century America

Debate over the meaning of the devotion continued throughout much of the nineteenth century and tended, at least in America, to push public discourse toward the symbolic meaning of the Sacred Heart. In 1874, reviewing a number of recent publications on the devotion, Orestes Brownson, Protestant convert to Catholicism and vociferous polemicist on behalf of his new faith, expressed coolness toward the devotion, repeating (unintentionally) Ricci's criticism by regarding it as a "comparatively new devotion, especially in the form introduced by Margaret Mary [Alacoque], and we are not easily drawn to new devotions."[49] Brownson discounted it as "just now the fashionable devotion," but his coolness toward it had much more to do with the repulsion he felt before its central object. In fact, Brownson returned to Lambertini's criticism of the devotion in the 1720s: "the material heart may be taken as the material seat or organ of the affection; but whether it is so or not is a *philosophical question* which we do not understand the church to have determined in approving the devotion to the Sacred Heart. We have always supposed that in this devotion the Sacred Heart is taken as the material emblem of the affections, the burning love, and infinite tenderness of the God-Man."[50] Brownson objected to the view taken by the Rev. Thomas Preston, whose book *Lectures upon the Devotion to the Sacred Heart of Jesus* was among those Brownson reviewed. "We find Father Preston," he pointed out, "speaking somewhat differently," whereupon he quoted his book: "The *object* of our devotion is the physical, fleshly heart of the Son of God, which beat in his bosom, which was the centre of his vital organism, and through which coursed the most precious blood. When we adore the Sacred Heart of Our Lord, it is no *symbolic* worship; it is a real and true adoration of the actual organ of our Redeemer."[51]

Brownson wondered why the doctrine of the Incarnation required Catholics to worship Jesus' heart qua organ any more than it did his hand or foot. The devotion, he insisted, "requires us to take the heart as standing not precisely for the fleshly organ, but for the affections, the love and will usually regarded as having their bodily seat in the heart." To this he added a personal response that accentuated the shift from fetishized body part to material metaphor: "we confess the picture, the model of which the Blessed Margaret Mary says she was shown by our Lord himself, strikes us not as a heart inflamed with love, but as a wounded and bleeding heart, and which repels rather than attracts us. It does not help our devotion."[52]

Brownson's remarks met with sharp criticism from two readers, both of whom accused him of repeating "Jansenist" errors in criticizing the Sacred Heart. Brownson replied to each, reaffirming that he found the point of the devotion unconvincing and that he "had been repelled by the pictures of the Sacred Heart which we had seen."[53] He also called on the testimony of his spiritual director, "a learned and pious bishop," who told Brownson that "he himself had never been able to look upon those pictures without a shock. The picture always seemed to us the picture of a bleeding, not an inflamed heart, and no picture of mere physical pain, not even the purely physical sufferings of our Lord on the cross, ever deeply moves us."[54] Brownson said he was moved by images of Jesus at agony in the Garden, on the eve before his crucifixion, not because of the physical agony, but rather "by his foresight of how few, comparatively, would profit by his cross and passion, and what numbers . . . would be eternally lost." In other words, Brownson found moving what was not pictured, but only implied, evoked by the suffering in the Garden, but not literally displayed. He corrected his critics by pointing out that he "took not from the Jansenists, but from Benedict XIV," that is, Archbishop Lambertini, who had opposed establishing a feast for the Sacred Heart.[55] He ended his two replies to the letter writers by summarizing his principal point, which goes far toward formulating the symbolic interpretation of the Sacred Heart that emerged strongly in the nineteenth century: "It is only when the heart is taken in union with the living soul which informs it, and transforms it from a mere viscus into a living organ of moral and spiritual affection, that we can see in the devotion any thing to warrant the high eulogiums pronounced on it, or the extraordinary zeal of our friends the Jesuits in spreading it."[56] The heart had to be about more than a body to receive Brownson's veneration.

The transformation that Brownson referred to is precisely the metaphorical or symbolical operation of the image that comes to the fore in the second half of the nineteenth century. Just after mid-century, a related development was unfolding in the iconography of the Sacred Heart, in which we find a striking visual transformation. The timing is significant, since the change took place in the wake of the devotion's formalization and universalization in Pius IX's official elevation of it in 1856. In 1864 Alacoque was declared Blessed by the same Pontiff. The devotion was receiving the highest approbation. But it was also being reshaped to suit the needs of an officially sanctioned popular practice.

Catechisms of the Sacred Heart appearing shortly later reflect and endorse the iconography of the heart emblazoned on the chest of half or full-length portraits of Jesus (Figure 4). In his *Life of Blessed Mary Margaret* (1869), which had been among the books that Brownson reviewed and from which he probably learned about the eighteenth-century official evaluation of the devotion, the Rev. George Tickell observed the now-official pattern of interpretation, the dual aims established in eighteenth-century discourse, as Seydl argued, and reaffirmed in the more popular, often catechetical literature of the nineteenth century: "The spiritual object [of the devotion] is the infinite charity of our Divine Lord; the material or sensible object is His true and real Heart, which is at the same time the symbol of His infinite charity. Both are truly the object of devotion, but the spiritual is the primary object."[57] Figure 4 may reflect this shift in thought. In it the heart rejoins the body of Jesus, but it does so as an emblematic device that lays over the surface of the tunic, subordinate to the body in such a way that the gaze of Jesus remains the primary connection with viewers. In this manner the heart shifts subtly from the focus of the devotion, as in Figures 1 and 2, to become an attribute of Jesus as person.

The heart became a signifier, a symbol, and so began to collect and generate new forms of meaning. If Batoni's picture (Figure 2) had been the dominant model in eighteenth-century Europe, presenting an iconic vision of the heart itself, the nineteenth-century image of the heart flattened the organ against his flesh (Figure 3) and shifted to an effulgent hieroglyph hovering before his tunic (Figure 4), a device that adheres to Jesus as a luminous badge or insignia. The shift was from the heart to what the heart *meant*. The result was a greater emphasis on the person of Jesus, who gestures to the heart. His principal connection to viewers might be said to reside in his gaze. Alacoque referred to the Sacred Heart as "a second Mediator between God and men."[58] But the late-nineteenth-century iconography appears to reintegrate heart and Jesus in a single mediator by reducing the heart to a symbol affixed to the surface of the Savior's body. The force behind this may have been Brownson's modern critical thinking, but it is also likely the application of the piety to the home, where dwelling on the literal organ of flesh would have been unseemly. Beginning in the 1880s, a campaign to "enthrone" the Sacred Heart in Catholic homes probably found a more symbolic image like Figure 4 easier to use than the visceral robustness of Figure 2.[59]

Between Icon and Symbol

Certainly this has been the tendency among many Catholic theologians, liturgists, and clergy in the twentieth century. In his 1899 encyclical, Leo XIII had spoken of the Sacred Heart in iconic terms. He characterized the Sacred Heart as "a symbol and a sensible image of the infinite love of Jesus Christ" and explained the consecration as "nothing else than an offering and a binding of oneself to Jesus Christ, seeing that whatever honor, veneration, and love is given to this divine Heart is really and truly given to Christ Himself."[60] Leo used language traditionally used by proponents of icons to defend their use in the veneration of saints: honor given to the image passes to its prototype in heaven.[61] But if Leo mixed icon and symbol, in the wake of Vatican II Paul VI echoed Leo's characterization of the Sacred Heart as symbol but made no reference to it as icon, calling it "the burning furnace of charity, the symbol and express image of his eternal love."[62] Throughout one encyclical, Paul intermingled reference to Alacoque (who spoke of the Sacred Heart as a furnace) with the Eucharist and the crucifixion, resulting in an affirmation of the devotion that focused attention on the love of Christ communicated to the Church principally in the mass, in effect, the authoritative icon of Christ.

In the twentieth century the papacy repeatedly reflected on how to interpret the devotion, whose popularity only grew. In 1956, Pius XII issued his encyclical "Haurietis Aquas," a substantial theological discussion of the meaning of the Sacred Heart in light of Scripture, Church Fathers, Catholic tradition, and the contemporary world. Pius vigorously defended the devotion, but in doing so set it on a theological foundation that required nothing from the eccentricities of Alacoque. She received honorable mention near the end of the long epistle, but even then only in passing. The real task was to establish the Sacred Heart firmly within the tradition of Catholic teachings about God's love and his action in Jesus Christ. The framework that Pius provided was important because it authorized an official view of the devotion by surrounding it with a rich array of tropes derived from the Bible and from the Church's leading doctors. The result was a decisive shift from the excruciating penance and ascetic self-mortification in Alacoque to a pastoral piety dedicated to the renewal of the Church through a passionate and salutary affirmation of ancient teaching. Pius's method was to unleash a cascade of metaphors, tropes that riffed on love, which showed that the heart was not a new idea but one that "flows from the very foundations of Christian teaching."[63] The heart of Jesus became a master trope, a metaphor of overarching authority, able to gather several tropic regimes under its dominant and unifying register. Pius used the heart to reassert orthodox teaching by fashioning a kind of theological summit at which the heart, symbol of love, meets and embraces other time-honored symbols—most importantly, the Church, the Trinity, and the Cross. Each of these was at one time, during the apostolic period, a contested symbol, debated, even rejected by some. But in time they became more than symbols; they are the bulwark of orthodoxy itself, the pillars of the Church's teaching. By engaging the Sacred Heart with them in a colloquy of symbols, Pius both affirmed the "new" symbol and revivified the old ones.

And yet the newness of the Sacred Heart remained. Repeatedly, Pius had to acknowledge that neither Scripture nor the Fathers referred explicitly to the physical heart of Jesus as the symbol of divine love. Pius was left with the objections raised since the early eighteenth century regarding the physical organ.[64] Yet he insisted that the physical heart of Jesus, "more than all the other members of His body, is the natural sign *and* symbol *of*

His boundless love for the human race.[65] Even this nomenclature was not enough, because he wanted very much to claim that devotion to the Sacred Heart was "in no sense tinged with so-called 'materialism' or tainted with the poison of superstition."[66] The worship of devotees did not culminate in the material organ. Older language used by defenders of the devotion, as we saw, distinguished between the "material" and the "spiritual" object of the worship. But Pius did not avail himself of this terminology. Nor did he rely on the iconic terminology used by Leo XIII, whom he quoted repeatedly. He turned instead to Thomas Aquinas for a comparison to the *Summa*'s very non-Greek justification of venerating images: "Religious worship is not paid to images, considered in themselves, as things; but according as they are representations leading to God Incarnate."[67] This assertion posited a split between matter and spirit that Eastern Orthodoxy was less likely to endorse, since the representation (understood as the image painted on a surface of wood) was itself material, not, as Aquinas seems to think, a cerebral or ideal entity floating somewhere between the material and spiritual realms. The Byzantine defense of icon veneration as justified by the Incarnation itself turned on the materiality of the image. An image, John of Damascus had argued in his classical defense of icons, is not identical to its archetype, "having some *difference.*"[68] Likeness was a ratio of identity and difference. An icon participates in the being of its original by virtue of looking like it. But Pius pushed the image into the spiritual realm rather than understand images as sharing—ontologically, iconically—in what they image. When he spoke of the heart as an "image" of divine love, he switched to the higher heart: "the Heart of the Incarnate Word is . . . the chief sign and symbol of that threefold love with which the divine Redeemer unceasingly loves His eternal Father and all mankind."[69] He stopped short of saying the physical heart could be "the perfect and absolute symbol of His divine love, for no created image is capable of adequately expressing the essence of this love."[70] Without the visual mechanics of the icon to help him explain the relationship between image and referent, Pius was forced into a conceptual scheme that could sound dualistic, which he likely did not intend. Nevertheless, the surfeit of metaphors clustered about the heart and the frequency of "sign," "symbol," and (noniconic) "image" in his encyclical, and the distinctness of physical or material from spiritual in the devotion's meaning, indicate that the Sacred Heart had been officially located in twentieth-century Catholic teaching under the framework of symbol, not iconic portrait, and certainly not fetish.

A return to the mystical and iconic reading of the devotion is found in John Paul II, who endorsed the link between the Sacred Heart and the Eucharist in terms of the adoration of the host associated with Corpus Christi. On the occasion of the centenary of Leo XIII's consecration, John Paul asserted that "the faithful still need to be guided to contemplate adoringly the mystery of Christ, the God-Man, in order to become men and women of interior life, people who feel and live the call to new life, to holiness, to reparation, which is apostolic cooperation in the salvation of the world." He urged Catholics to realize that "contemplation of the Heart of Jesus in the Eucharist will spur the faithful to seek in that Heart the inexhaustible mystery of the priesthood of Christ and of the Church." The battle for the "proper" interpretation of Vatican Council II has not ended, and John Paul framed his view of it within the "Act of Reparation" that resides at the penitential core of the devotion to the Sacred Heart: "Is this not the programme of the Second Vatican Council and of my own Pontificate?" he asked.[71]

The seesaw between tradition and reform in Roman Catholicism persists. Many wish to regard the second half of the twentieth century as having resolved the back and forth in favor of modernity and reform. Yet the resilience of Catholicism consists in its ability to hold opposing elements in tension, to keep in play parts of its tradition that, given free reign, might attempt to eliminate one another, as the long enmity of Jansenism and its opponents suggests. So even as the moderating force of Vatican II and its reform-minded interpreters downplayed the penitential tradition of devotionalism in order to accentuate the common life of the liturgy, popular devotion to Mary, Jesus, and the saints persisted. Though the Sacred Heart does not appear in Mel Gibson's film *The Passion of the Christ* (2004), for example, the surfeit of blood and suffering so graphically portrayed by the film, whose director is notorious for his commitment to traditionalist or preconciliar Catholicism, suggests that the Baroque piety of Alacoque is by no means defunct, but simmering beneath the surface of modernity. The return of the Latin mass, the rise of Marian piety and apparition, and the steady growth of conservative Roman Catholicism around the world indicate that the old penitentialism was not snuffed out by reform, but still pulses within a larger body of faith. As restively as ever, the body's conflicting meanings defy the simplicity of a unitary view.

Idolatry
Nietzsche, Blake, and Poussin

W. J. T. Mitchell

Idolatry and its evil twin, iconoclasm, are much in the news these days. Indeed, it would be no exaggeration to say that the current Holy War on Terror is just the latest engagement in a religious conflict that dates back beyond the Middle Ages and the Christian Crusades in the Middle East, one that centrally concerned itself with the idols worshipped by one's enemies and with the imperative to smash those idols once and for all. While one should be skeptical about reductive ideological scenarios like Samuel Huntington's notorious "clash of civilizations" thesis, it seems undeniable that this thesis has manifested itself in the actual foreign policies of great powers like the United States and its allies, and in the rhetoric of Islamic fundamentalism in its calls to jihad against the West. The fact that an idea is grounded in paranoid fantasy, prejudice, and ignorance has never been a compelling objection to its implementation in practice. The Taliban did not hesitate to carry out the destruction of the harmless Bamiyan Buddhas, and al-Qaeda's attack on the World Trade Center was clearly aimed at an iconic monument that they regarded as a symbol of Western idolatry.[1] The War on Terror, by contrast, first called a "crusade" by the president who declared it, has been explained by some of his minions in the military as a war against the idolatrous religion of Islam.[2] Among the most striking features of the hatred of idols, then, is the fact that it is shared as a fundamental doctrine by all three great "religions of the book," Judaism, Christianity, and Islam, where it is encoded in the second commandment, prohibiting the making of all graven images of any living thing. This commandment launches the age-old *paragone* between words and images, the law of the symbolic and the lawless imaginary that persists in numerous cultural forms to this day.

Among those cultural forms is, of course, art history. Whether regarded as a history of artistic objects or of images, more generally, art

112

history is a field that is centrally concerned with the relation of words and images, and that one might expect to have a powerful account of idols and idolatry. Yet these topics are generally regarded as more properly the business of religion, theology, anthropology, and perhaps philosophy. By the time idols become the subject of art history, they have become art—aestheticized, denatured, deracinated, neutered. Of course, many art historians know this. I could invoke the work of David Freedberg and Hans Belting on the nature of "images before the era of art," and the more specific work by scholars such as Michael Camille (*The Gothic Idol*), Tom Cummins (studies of the Inca idol known as the "Waca"), as well as many others who have attempted to work backward, as it were, from the history of art toward something more comprehensive, something that might perhaps be called an iconology. By *iconology* I mean the study of—among other things—the clash between logos and icon, law and image, which is inscribed at the heart of art history.

We will return to these disciplinary issues presently, in a discussion of Poussin's paintings of two scenes of idolatry and of the ways that art history has danced around the question of word and image in these paintings. As Richard Neer has noted, these discussions have been paradigmatic for the entire discipline, involving its ambivalence about the actual material objects that are so central to it.[3] But before we take up these matters, I want to approach the topic through a fundamental reconsideration of the very concept of idolatry, beginning with the second of the Ten Commandments: "You shall not make for yourself a graven image, or any likeness of anything that is in heaven above, or that is in the earth beneath, or that is in the water under the earth; you shall not bow down to them or serve them; for I the LORD your God am a jealous God, visiting the iniquity of the fathers upon the children to the third and the fourth generation of those who hate Me, but showing steadfast love to the thousandth generation of those who love Me and keep My Commandments" (Exodus 20:4–6).[4] The condemnation of idolatry as the ultimate evil is encoded in this statute with such ferocious militancy that it is fair to say that it is clearly the most important commandment of them all, occupying the central place in defining sins against God, as opposed to sins against other human beings, such as lying, stealing, or adultery. It is difficult to overlook the fact that it supersedes, for instance, the commandment against murder, which, as Walter Benjamin wryly puts it, is merely a "guideline," not an absolute prohibition.[5]

Since idolatry is such a central concept for all the adversaries in the current global conflict, it seems worthwhile to attempt a critical and historical analysis of its main features. What is an idol? What is idolatry? And what underlies the iconoclastic practices that seem invariably to accompany it? The simplest definition of an idol is that it is an image of a god. But that definition leaves open a host of other questions: Is the god represented by the image of a supreme deity who governs the whole world, or a local "genius of the place" or of the tribe or nation? Is the god immanent in the image, its material support? Or is the god merely represented by the image, while the god dwells elsewhere? What is the relation of this god to other gods? Is it tolerant toward other gods, or is it jealous and determined to exterminate its rivals? Above all, what motivates the vehement language of the second commandment? Why is its condemnation so emphatic, its judgments so absolute? Does it not seem that there is some kind of surplus in the very concept of idolatry, a moral panic that seems completely in excess of legitimate concerns about something called "graven images" and their possible abuse? Another way to say this would be to note that *idolatry* is a word that mainly appears in the discourse of iconoclasm, a militant monotheism obsessed with its own claims to universality.

When we move to the moral questions surrounding idolatry, the concept seems to spin completely out of control. Idolatry is associated with everything from adultery to superstition to metaphysical error. It is linked with materialism, hedonism, fornication, black magic and sorcery, demonology, bestiality, fascist führer cults, Roman emperors, and divination. This bewildering array of evils resolves itself ultimately into two basic varieties, which frequently intermix: the first is the condemnation of idolatry as error, as stupidity, as false, deluded belief; the second is the darker judgment that the idolater actually *knows* that the idol is a vain, empty thing, but he continues cynically to exploit it for the purposes of power or pleasure. This is the perverse, sinful crime of idolatry. Thus, there are two kinds of idolaters—fools and knaves—between which obviously there is considerable overlap and cooperation.

Much of the theological discussion of idolatry focuses on fine points of doctrine and subtle distinctions between idolatry as the worship of the wrong god or of the right god in the wrong way.[6] The difference between heretics or apostates within the nonidolatrous community and unbelievers who live outside that community is obviously a critical distinction. But there is a more straightforward approach to the problem of idolatry, what might be called an "operational" or functional point of view. The key, then, is not to focus on what idolaters believe or what iconoclasts believe that they believe, but on what idolaters *do*, and on what is done to them by iconoclasts, who, by definition, must disapprove of the wicked, stupid idolaters. Sometimes the question of belief converges with that of actions and practices: for instance, some iconoclasts believe that, in addition to their wrongheaded beliefs, idolaters commit unspeakable acts such as cannibalism and human sacrifice. This "secondary belief" (i.e., a belief about the beliefs of other people) consequently justifies equally unspeakable acts of violence against the idolaters, which are rationalized as an expression of the just vengeance of the one true god.[7] There is thus a kind of fearful symmetry between the terrible things idolaters are supposed to do and what may be done to them in the name of divine justice.

Another key to thinking pragmatically about idolatry is to ask not just *how* idolaters live (which is presumed to be sinful) but *where* they live. Idolatry is deeply connected to the question of place and landscape, territorial imperatives dictated by local deities who declare that certain tracts of land are not only sacred but uniquely promised to them. Indeed, one could write the history of biblical idolatry and iconoclasm as a collection of territorial war stories—wars fought over places and possession of land. As Moshe Halbertal and Avishai Margalit put it, "The ban on idolatry is an attempt to dictate exclusivity, to map the unique territory of the one God."[8] This becomes clearest when one considers the practical enforcement of the ban on images, which involves destroying the sacred sites of the native inhabitants, "leveling their high places and destroying their graven images and idols."[9] The link between territoriality and idolatry becomes even more explicit when it is invoked as an insuperable objection to any negotiations or treaties. To make a deal with an idolater, especially about land, is to fall into idolatry oneself. The only politics possible between the iconoclast and the idolater is total war.[10]

Idols, then, might be described as condensations of radical evil in images that must be destroyed, along with those who believe in them, by any means necessary. There is no idolatry without an iconoclasm to label it as such, since idolaters almost never call themselves by that name. They may worship Baal or Dagon or Caesar or money, but they do not consider it idolatry to do so; rather, their worship is a normal form of piety within their community. On the side of the iconoclasts, the idolater is generally perceived as beyond redemption. Either the idolater is a traitor to the true God (thus the metaphor of adultery and "whoring after strange gods") or he has been brought up in a false, heathen faith from which he will have to be "liberated"—one way or another.

Iconoclasm, then, betrays a kind of fearful symmetry, mirroring its own stereotype of idolatry in its emphasis on human sacrifice and terrorism, the latter understood as violence against the innocent and the staging of spectacular acts of symbolic violence and cruelty. The iconoclastic stereotype of the idolater, of course, is that he is already sacrificing his children and other innocent victims to his idol. This is a crime so deep that the iconoclast feels compelled to exterminate the idolaters—to kill not just their priests and kings but all their followers and offspring as well.[11] The Amalekites, for instance, are enemies of Israel, so vicious and unredeemable that they must be wiped out. And the emphasis on the cursing of idolaters for numerous generations is, implicitly, a program for genocide. It is not enough to kill the idolater; the children must go as well, either as potential idolaters or as "collateral damage."

All these barbaric practices might be thought of as merely the past of idolatry, relics of ancient, primitive times when magic and superstition reigned. A moment's reflection reveals that this discourse has persisted into the modern era, from Bacon's "four idols" of the marketplace, the theater, the cave, and the tribe, to the evolution of a Marxist critique of ideology and fetishism that builds on the rhetoric of iconoclasm. This latter critique is of course focused on commodity fetishism and what I have elsewhere called the "ideolatry" of market capitalism.[12] One of the strangest features of iconoclasm is its gradual sublimation into more subtle strategies of critique, skepticism, and negative dialectics: Clement Greenberg's kitsch and Adorno's culture industry are producers of idols for the new philistines of mass culture. The endpoint of this process is probably Jean Baudrillard's "evil demon of images," where the Marxian rhetoric rejoins with religion and veers off toward nihilism. But already in his diatribes against the Young Hegelians, Marx made fun of the "critical critics" who free us from images, phantoms, and false ideas.

The greatest break and the most profound critique of idolatry and iconoclasm is Nietzsche's late work *Thus Spake Zarathustra.* Nietzsche turns iconoclasm upside down and against its own roots of authority in the law. The only thing the iconoclastic Zarathustra smashes are the tablets of the law: "Break, break, you lovers of knowledge, the old tablets. . . . Break the old tablets of the never gay," inscribed with prohibitions against sensuous pleasure by the pious killjoys who "slander the world" and tell men "thou must not desire."[13] The only law Nietzsche will tolerate is a positive "thou shalt": he enjoins us "to write anew upon new tablets the word 'noble.'"[14] He criticizes the Manichaean moralism of the priestly lawgivers who divide the world into good and evil:

> O my brothers, who represents the greatest danger for all of man's future? Is it not the good and the just? Inasmuch as they say and feel in their hearts, "We already know what is good and just, and we have it too; woe unto those who still seek here!" And whatever harm the evil may do, the harm done by the good is the most harmful harm . . . the good *must* be Pharisees—they have no choice. The good *must* crucify him who invents his own virtue. . . . The *creator* they hate most: he breaks tablets and old values . . . they crucify him who writes new values on new tablets.[15]

Zarathustra also seems to intuit the connection between the old law of good and evil and the imperative to territorial conquest and "promised lands." He equates the breaking of "the tablets of the good" with the renunciation of "fatherlands," urging his followers to be "seafarers" in search of "man's future . . . our *children's land!*"[16]

So far as I know, Nietzsche never explicitly mentions the second commandment, but it becomes the unspoken center of his great text of 1888, *Twilight of the Idols,* a work that might easily be mistaken for a rather conventional iconoclastic critique. Its promise to "philosophize with a hammer" and its opening "declaration of war" against "not just idols of the age, but eternal idols" may sound like a continuation of the traditional iconoclastic treatment of idolatrous "ideas," like Bacon's critique of "idols of the mind" or the Young Hegelians' war against "phantoms of the brain." But Nietzsche turns the tables on *both* the ancient and modern iconoclasts and the second commandment by renouncing the very idea of image destruction at the outset. The eternal idols are not to be smashed but to be "touched with a hammer as with a tuning fork." They are not to be destroyed but "sounded" with a delicate, precise touch that reveals their hollowness (one recalls the biblical phrase "sounding brass") and perhaps even retunes or plays a tune upon them. Nietzsche's war against the eternal idols is a strangely nonviolent practice, a giddy form of "recreation, a spot of sunshine, a leap sideways into the idleness of the psychologist."[17]

The idolatry-iconoclasm complex has always presented a dilemma for visual artists, who, by professional necessity, seem inevitably to be involved in violating the second commandment. Vasari opens his *Lives of the Artists* with an elaborate set of apologias for the visual arts, noting that God himself is a creator of images, architect of the universe and a sculptor who breathes life into his fabricated creatures. He dismisses the inconvenient case of the Golden Calf and the massacre of "thousands of the false Israelites who had committed this idolatry" by arguing that "the sin consisted in adoring idols and not in making them," a rather stark evasion of the plain language of the second commandment, which says "thou shalt not *make*" any graven images of any thing.[18]

The artist who comes closest to carrying out Nietzsche's inversion and transvaluation of the idolatry-iconoclasm complex is William Blake, who anticipates by almost a century the reversal of values contemplated in *Twilight of the Idols*. Blake famously inverts the moral valences of pious, passive angels and energetic devils in *The Marriage of Heaven and Hell* (1793), and he consistently links the figure of the Old Testament lawgiver with his rationalist Enlightenment offspring in the figure of "Urizen," depicted sometimes as a patriarchal figure dividing and measuring the universe or (in Figure 5) as a reclusive hermit hiding in his cave behind the twin tablets of the law.

Like Nietzsche, however, Blake is not engaged in a simple reversal of a Manichaean opposition of good and evil; he uses a more subtle strategy, rather like Nietzsche's notion of "touching" the idols with a "hammer" or a "tuning fork." Blake's most compelling image of this process is a plate from his illuminated epic poem *Milton* (Figure 6), which shows Los, the artist, as a sculptor engaged in a radically ambiguous act of creation and destruction. We can, on the one hand, read this as an image of Los molding the figure of Jehovah out of the mud on a riverbank, as if we were witnessing Adam creating God out of clay. Or, on the other hand, we can read this as an iconoclastic act, with the artist pulling down the idolatrous statue of the father-god. The image condenses the making and breaking of idols into one perfectly equivocal synthesis of creative activity, a visual counterpart to Nietzsche's acoustical tactic of hammering the idols without breaking them. Blake's portrayal of a musical chorus on the horizon above this scene suggests that he too is "sounding" the idol, not with a tuning fork, but with the bare hands of the sculptor. As a child of the Enlightenment, Blake understood very well that all the idols, totems, and fetishes of premodern, primitive polytheistic societies were the alienated product of human hands and human minds: "The ancient Poets animated all sensible objects with Gods or Geniuses, calling them by the names and adorning them with the properties of woods, rivers, mountains, lakes, cities, and nations, and whatever their enlarg'd and numerous senses could perceive. . . . Till a system was formed, which some took advantage of & enslav'd the vulgar by attempting to realize or abstract the mental deities from their objects; thus began Priesthood."[19]

In the light of this genealogy of religion, which could very well have been written by Giambattista Vico, the development of monotheism is not so much a radical break with

FIGURE 5   Title page, William Blake, *Book of Urizen* (1794).
Lessing J. Rosenwald Collection, Library of Congress, Washington, D.C.

FIGURE 6   William Blake, *Milton* (1804-10), plate 15, Los creating-destroying Jehovah.
Lessing J. Rosenwald Collection, Library of Congress, Washington, D.C.

pagan idolatry as a logical development of its tendency to underwrite the consolidation of political power with absolute religious mandates. It is important to remember that Yahweh begins as a mountain god, probably volcanic, since he is "hidden in clouds" and speaks "in thunder and in fire." The figure of the invisible, transcendent lawgiver, whose most important law is a ban on making images of any kind, is the perfect allegory for an imperial, colonizing project that aims to eradicate all the images, idols, and material markers of the territorial claims of indigenous inhabitants. The fearsome figure of Baal, we should remember, is simply a Semitic version of what the Romans called the *genius loci* or genius of the place—the god of the oasis that indicates the proprietary claims of the nomadic tribe that returns to it every year.[20] Dagon, the god of the Philistines, is characteristically portrayed as an agricultural god, associated with the harvest of grain. The veiling or hiding of the god in a temple or cave is simply the first step toward rendering him (and he is almost always male) metaphysically invisible and unrepresentable. As Edmund Burke noted in his *Enquiry into . . . the Sublime and the Beautiful*: "Despotic governments . . . keep their chief as much as may be from the public eye. The policy has been the same in many cases of religion. Almost all heathen temples were dark. Even in the barbarous temples of the Americans at this day, they keep their idol in a dark part of the hut, which is consecrated to his worship."[21] Kant simply carries Burke's observation to its logical conclusion when he argues that "there is no sublimer passage in the Jewish law than the command, 'Thou shalt not make to thyself any graven image, nor the likeness of anything which is in heaven or in the earth or under the earth.'" For Kant, the secret to the "enthusiasm" of both Judaism and "Mohammedanism" is their "abstraction" and refusal of imagery, together with their claim to absolute moral superiority over heathens and idolaters.[22]

I want to conclude with two scenes of idolatry and iconoclasm by an artist who would seem to be radically antithetical to the antinomian tendencies of Blake and Nietzsche. The work of Nicholas Poussin, as Richard Neer has argued in his work on the painter, is deeply concerned with issues of idolatry and iconoclasm. But the depth of this concern would seem to be expressed, if I follow Neer's argument, by Poussin's determination to remain firmly committed to an orthodox moral condemnation of idolatry in all its forms, at the same time remaining loyal to the most powerful claims of the visual arts as expressed in classical sculpture. One could put this as a paradox: How does a painter endorse iconoclasm and condemn idolatry, at the same time deploying all the graphic visual resources of a thoroughly pagan, idolatrous culture?

Neer takes Poussin's problem not merely as the case of an individual artist but as the central problem of art history as a discipline. As he notes, Poussin scholarship has made him "the most literary of painters," assuming that "to know a picture's literary source is to know the essential thing about it. . . . One gets the impression that he is studied more in the library than the museum."[23] When scholars have broken away from this textually dominated mode of interpretation to identify "visual sources," the usual conclusion is that Poussin's numerous citations of classical imagery are "strictly meaningless." This "bifurcation" of Poussin into the camps of word and image "is in fact exemplary." According to Neer: "It is, in germ, what separates 'the two art histories,' the museum and the academy; the study of Poussin is the grain of sand in which to see a whole disciplinary world."[24] It is as if the *paragone* of word and image that was launched by the second commandment had penetrated into the very heart of the discipline that is supposed to devote itself to the visual arts, confronting it with a version of Poussin's own dilemma: How does one attend to the meaning of an image without reducing it to the mere shadow of a textual source? How does one remain faithful to the claim of the image without becoming an idolater and descending into the abyss of meaninglessness?

Ultimately, I want to propose a third alternative to Neer's division of the resources of art history into the "library" and the "museum." The alternative, unsurprisingly, is the *world*, and the larger sphere of verbal and visual culture within which paintings, like all other works of art, inevitably function, perhaps not merely as what Neer calls "useful evidence in . . . a cultural history" but as *events and interventions* in that history.[25] But this is to get slightly ahead of myself.

Two of Poussin's most famous treatments of the theme of idolatry are *The Adoration of the Golden Calf* (1633–36), now in the National Gallery in London, and *The Plague at Ashdod* (1630–31) now in the Louvre (Figures 7 and 8). Together, the paintings provide a panorama of the fundamental themes of idolatry and iconoclasm. The *Calf* shows the moment of idolatrous ritual and celebration as the Israelites dance around the Calf with the artist, Aaron, gesturing toward it to urge his countrymen (and beholders of the painting) to contemplate his creation. In the darkness of the background on the left, we see Moses descending from Mount Sinai, preparing to smash the stone tablets of the law in fury over the terrible sin of the Israelites. In *Ashdod*, by contrast, we see the terrible punishment for idolatry, as the panicked Philistines realize that they have been stricken by the plague. In the darkness of the left background, we see the fallen idol of Dagon, with its severed head and hands, and behind it the Ark of the Covenant (which the Philistines have seized as a trophy after defeating the Israelites in battle). In the story of the plague (1 Samuel 5:1–7), the Philistines bring the Ark into the Temple of Dagon, where during the night it magically overturns the statue of the Philistine's god and mutilates it.

Neer makes a convincing argument that, from Poussin's point of view and thus from the dominant disciplinary perspective of art history, the principle subject matter of *Ashdod* is not the foreground tableau of the plague but the background vignette of the Ark destroying the idol. The evidence he uses is the contemporary testimony of Joachim Sandrart, as well as Poussin's own title for the painting, *The Miracle of the Ark in the Temple of Dagon*. This argument, depending on verbal evidence, goes directly against what Neer calls the "visual prominence" of the plague narrative, which would seem to undermine his insistence elsewhere in the essay that visual and pictorial elements should be primary.[26]

FIGURE 7　Nicolas Poussin, *The Adoration of the Golden Calf* (1633-36).

But for Neer, Poussin is a painter whose work is governed by signs and citations that point toward an invisible and unrepresentable foundation. Like the motif of the Ark itself, which hides the tablets of the Law, like the hidden God on Mount Sinai, Poussin's painting encrypts a meaning that is evident not to the eye but only to the connoisseur, who is able to reverse the significance of "visual prominence" and see that the primary subject of the painting is "the hiddenness of the divine": "The miracle in the temple is the Second Commandment in action: a battle between statue and sign, ending in the literal destruction of the former," with the plague as merely its outward manifestation.[27] The failure of a beholder to see the plague as a merely secondary consequence or allegorical shadow of the real event in the painting is thus made equivalent to the error of the idolatrous Philistines, who mistake the outward image for the true meaning: "The failure of the literal-minded Philistines to 'read' the plague correctly, to *bien connoistre*, thus amounts to seeing only the Aspect of the plague," rather than the true "Perspective" in which the events and their depiction are to be understood.[28]

Neer shows convincingly that Poussin intended his painting to be an allegorical "machine" that generates a series of "rigidly antithetical" oppositions (which turn out to

FIGURE 8   Nicolas Poussin, *The Plague at Ashdod* (1630-31).

be reversible as well): Ark versus Idol; Imitation versus Copy; Signification over Depiction; Poussin versus the "bestial" Caravaggio. Poussin is doing everything possible to avoid falling into mere copying, mere naturalism or realism. He had an "abhorrence of reproduction, verging on mimetophobia."[29] He must constantly remind us that his scenes are staged and are based in a kind of citational parade of classical figures. The dead mother with her babies starving at her breast is probably a citation of Matthew's Gospel that ironically undercuts the realism of its source in Caravaggio. The hidden truth of the painting, on the other hand, is *literal*; it is a straightforward *istoria*, showing a mutilated idol and an impassive Ark. Like most of Poussin's painting, it is dominated by textualizing practices if not by textual sources, planting subtle clues and citations of previous pictures that will be recognized by the learned viewer. To take the "foreground group" literally, then, not seeing it as a "citational structure" but as "the story it happens to tell," is to miss the point of the painting.[30] This foreground group is "the *allegory of the symbol of the narrative*," a phrasing, as Neer concedes, that is "otiose in a way the picture is not."[31]

I think that Neer has given us the most comprehensive professional reading of this painting we could ask for. As art history, his interpretation is unimpeachable, and as iconology it is incredibly subtle and deft. My trouble begins with his moving of Poussin's theory into the sphere of ethics, where a certain way of reading the painting is reinforced as the morally responsible and even the "pious" way of relating to the picture as a sign or symptom of Poussin's intentions. There is something subtly coercive about this move, and I want to resist it in the name of the painting itself, and perhaps in the name of the "meaninglessness" that scholars like Louis Marin have proposed. In other words, I want to ask *The Plague* (or is it *The Miracle*) of Ashdod what *it* wants from the beholder, rather than what Poussin wants.[32] Since the painting outlives Poussin and participates in what Neer calls a kind of "natural history" (as opposed to its iconological meaning), this means an unleashing of the painting from its own historical "horizon" of possible meanings and allowing it to become anachronistic.

This might be the place to admit that my whole response to this painting is radically anachronistic. I cannot take my eyes off the foreground group. I cannot help sharing in the Philistine gaze that believes this scene is portraying a human reality, an appalling catastrophe that is being reproduced in a kind of stately, static tableau, which is the only thing that makes it bearable to behold. Like William Kentridge's drawings of the atrocities of apartheid, or Art Spiegelman's translation of the Holocaust into an animal fable, Poussin shows us a highly mediated scene of disaster, of a wrathful judgment that is striking down a city and a people in an act of terror that does not discriminate between the guilty and the innocent. The center of this perception is, of course, the most prominent image in the painting, the dead mother with her starving infants at her breast. Neer sees her as a citation to the martyred St. Matthew; I cannot see her without being reminded of a contemporary image that dawned on the world simultaneously with the writing of this text: the image that emerged from Gaza, during the Israeli invasion of January 2009, of "four small children huddling next to their dead mothers, too weak to stand up."[33]

Of course, there is a point of view from which this scene is, like Poussin's, merely an allegory of divine justice in action. The Palestinians, as we have learned recently from a leading Israeli rabbi, are "Amalekites," who deserve the disasters that are being visited on them by an overwhelmingly superior military power that has god on its side.[34] The Hamas movement in Gaza is a terrorist organization that seeks the destruction of Israel. If terrible things like civilian casualties occur, it is the fault of Hamas, which unscrupulously uses civilians as "human shields." (The fact that the fighters of Hamas actually live among and are related by blood and marriage to many of the people of Gaza does not excuse them from the responsibility to stand up and fight courageously in the open, where they can be mowed down by the vastly superior firepower of the Israeli army. Instead, they are understood to be hiding away like cowards in their homes, schools, mosques, government buildings, and community centers, while their women and children are massacred around them.) And if there have been injustices on the Israeli side, they will be "investigated properly, once such a complaint is received formally, within the constraints of current military operations."[35] Justice and the law are being and will be served, if only we have the ability to put this shocking picture in perspective.

Nothing I have said here invalidates Neer's interpretation of Poussin's painting. I think that it probably reflects, for better or for worse, what Poussin thought about his subject, what he thought was expected of him, and what his audience would have understood.[36] My argument is that there is another, contrary perspective on the painting, one in which an "aspect" is not merely an appearance but, as Wittgenstein would have put it, the "dawning" of a new way of thinking about its subject matter and handling. This is the anachronism that disrupts the doctrine or doxa of the painting, calling into question the ethical discipline and piety that it encourages. I would argue further that this sort of anachronistic seeing is inevitable with images, which are open to the world and to history in a way that deconstructs their legibility and certainty. In short, I am on the side of Derrida's abyss and Louis Marin's "meaninglessness" in Neer's argument, not Montaigne's well-grounded faith in the invisible lawgiver. I am also on the side of Foucault's insistence, in his famous reading of *Las meninas*, that we must "pretend not to know" who the figures are in the painting. We must forego the comfort of the "proper name" and the learned citation, and confine ourselves to the "visible fact," described with "a gray, anonymous language" that will help the painting "little by little" to "release its illuminations."[37]

What happens if we follow this procedure with the *Golden Calf*? What would it mean to see this painting through the eyes of Blake and Nietzsche? Does the painting not threaten to be a transvaluation of the idol it is supposed to be condemning? Could Poussin's painting, without his quite knowing it, be *sounding* the idol with a hammer, tuning fork, or (more precisely) a paintbrush? The Calf is gloriously painted and sculpted; it is a wonder, and the festive dance around it is a celebration of pagan pleasure.[38] But up in the dark clouds is the angry patriarch, breaking the tablets of the Law. Nietzsche's pious killjoy and Blake's Nobodaddy converge in Poussin's Moses.

Of course this is all wrong as art history. As iconology or anthropology, however, it may have some traction. Durkheim would have recognized the Calf instantly as a totem animal and would have rejected the category of the idol for the ideological fiction that it is. It is important to note that totemism and fetishism play a distinguished role in disciplines like anthropology and psychoanalysis; idolatry, as a still-potent polemical notion, has rarely been put to technical use by a human science.

So let's consider Poussin's Calf as a totemic image, a figure of the self-conscious projection of a community onto a common symbol (totems were generally plant or animal images). Let's look at it through the eyes of Durkheim, Nietzsche, and Blake, as Poussin's attempt to "sound" the idol with his paintbrush, rather than destroying it. It is important that (in the story) the Israelites have *asked* for this Calf. They have demanded that Aaron, the artist in residence, make an idol "to go before them" as a symbol of their tribal identity. "God is Society" is Durkheim's famous formulation of the concept.[39] One could actually think of this as a kind of democratic emblem, at least partly because it seems to have been a random, chance image, flung out from the fire. As Aaron tells Moses: "I cast the gold into the fire and this Calf came out" (Exodus 32:24).

What if that was Zarathustra up on the mountain, smashing the law and joining in the fun? What if the dark clouds are Blake's Nobodaddy "farting and belching and coughing" in his cave on the mountaintop? Could it be that Poussin was (like Blake's Milton) a true poet-painter, and of the devil's party without knowing it?

"Has this thing appeared again tonight?"

Deus ex Machina and Other Theatrical Interventions of the Supernatural

Freddie Rokem

The *deus ex machina* took the place of metaphysical consolation.
> —Friedrich Nietzsche, *The Birth of Tragedy*

Engel und Puppe: dann ist endlich Schauspiel.

Angel and puppet: a real play finally.
> —Rainer Maria Rilke, *The Duino Elegies*, trans. Stephen Mitchell

The ancient device of the deus ex machina—the appearance of a super-natural being, usually a god, on the stage—rather than gradually disappearing after declarations of the death of God, has shown a surprising persistence on both theatrical stages and movie screens in modern and contemporary fictional stagings. The appearance of supernatural, meta-physical, and transcendental beings and forces is much more common on contemporary stages, as well as in film, than scholars have usually acknowledged.[1] Alluding to the Ur-stage in Western representation, Plato's image of the cave in *The Republic*, Nietzsche announced in *The Gay Science* that "After Buddha was dead, his shadow was still shown for centuries in a cave—a tremendous, gruesome shadow. God is dead; but given the way of men, there may still be caves for thousands of years in which his shadow will be shown.—And we—we still have to vanquish his shadow, too."[2] The modern and contemporary theater has no doubt created many such caves, where we are still struggling with the ghosts of these now no longer existing gods. And in those struggles strange contaminations, partnerships, and utopian hopes can form. The persistence of fictional representations of the supernatural in contemporary performances is remarkable and creates a both uncanny and fruitful discrepancy between these representations and the secular approach with which the theater basically grapples with the world around us, even if its supposed religious/ritual roots are still somehow visible.

My contribution to the investigations of materiality in religion and religious practices will focus on the materialization of the supernatural on the theatrical stage as well as (to some extent) in film, examining the supernatural—"this thing" that, according to Shakespeare's *Hamlet*, is appearing again tonight—in a theatrical context. I am referring to the phenomenon through which the supernatural becomes materialized in an aesthetic medium. I shall return to *Hamlet* in what follows; I will begin by drawing attention to how the arts in general, and theater and performance in particular, have developed a host of possibilities for creating interactions between aesthetic forms of expression and other discursive practices. The discursive interaction I want to explore here is based on an encounter between the "language" of performance, through which a certain dynamics is created in the space we call the stage, on the one hand, and religious discursive practices or belief systems, on the other.[3]

An interesting example of how such an encounter is contextualized through conflicting religious belief systems and how this conflict serves as a source for artistic creativity can be found in the semi-autobiographical film *Fanny and Alexander* (1982), by Swedish director Ingmar Bergman. This film and the many forms of self-reflexive theatrical devices and themes it contains presents a powerful disparity between the ancient cave where the supernatural still holds the characters in its grip and an emergent twentieth-century rational modernity. Some of the most powerful scenes toward the end of this epic film—which unravels the story of the Ekdahl family, who own and run the theater in the small provincial Swedish town of Uppsala during the first decade of the twentieth century—take place in the mysterious cellar in the house of the Jewish pawnbroker Isak Jacobi, after Isak, with the help of magic, has kidnapped and freed the two young protagonists of the film from the sterile home of their stepfather, the bishop, where they have literally been imprisoned.

After the death of their father, who was an actor, Fanny and Alexander had been brought into the household of the bishop by the marriage of their widowed mother, who had to give up her career as an actress in order to join the stern Protestant household of her new husband. Through the juxtaposition between the home of the bishop and the cellar of the Jewish pawnbroker, Bergman presents an almost mythic struggle between a rigorous and sterile form of Protestantism (which for Bergman was epitomized by his own father, a prominent minister in Stockholm) and a world of fantasy, art, and imagination, represented by the secular Jew Isak and his two nephews, Aron and Ismael.[4] *Fanny and Alexander* is a *Bildungsfilm*, showing how the budding artist, Bergman alias Alexander, draws inspiration from a complex fusion of the two opposed worlds of orthodox Christianity and a Judaism associated with other forms of supernatural, spectral, or uncanny being.

Bergman sets up two alternative models of interaction between Christianity and Judaism in his film. Besides the one based on mistrust between the pawnbroker and the bishop, there is also a form of interaction based on mutual respect and even attraction between the representatives of the two religions. It is first presented in the opening scene of the film, where Isak participates in the Christmas celebrations of the Ekdahl family as an intimate friend with romantic ties to the widowed grandmother of both Fanny and Alexander, who, together with her husband, founded the theater. This model of interaction between the two worldviews is the utopian ideal from which, according to Bergman's film, true art will eventually emerge, as opposed to the ascetic denial of life and vitality epitomized by the fanatic bishop whom the children's mother had married after the death of their father. In the cellar of Isak and his nephews, after Fanny and Alexander have been rescued, two worldviews continue to confront one another, mingled with something enigmatic and supernatural and also involving the unexpected intervention of a deus ex machina.

After he has been spirited away from his home with the bishop to refuge in the cellar, Alexander has to get up to go to the toilet in the middle of the night. As he stumbles through the unfamiliar space, he suddenly encounters a huge, speaking doll, which introduces itself as a deus ex machina. The apparition terrifies the young boy, still half-asleep. Aron suddenly appears from behind the doll, however, and calms him by explaining that the doll is merely a human creation, which possesses no real supernatural powers but is merely an instance of human art.

Alexander, both relieved and angry, tries to make light of his former fear. He has already, however, found out that supernatural beings are not just theatrical tricks when he encountered the spirit of his dead father in the corridors of his home. His father, an actor, had died after a heart attack while rehearsing the part of the ghost in *Hamlet*, in rehearsals that Alexander had secretly watched. Thus Alexander is aware of the complexity of the supernatural, situated between dogma and art. Aron, who senses Alexander's dilemma, hovering between skepticism and the acceptance of these theatrical, supernatural phenomena, further complicates the situation by stating that his Uncle Isak claims "that we are surrounded by realities situated one outside each other. And he says that these spheres are full of ghosts, apparitions, dybbuks, souls, demons, angels, and devils."[5] So Alexander is left with the following question: In what sense do we have to take them seriously?

Bergman's film shows how the supernatural intervenes, sometimes quite violently, to create enigmatic disruptions in the immediacy of everyday material reality. Bergman draws attention to the complexity of these phenomena, ambiguously situated between some form of strict religious belief and their appearance as an aesthetic device with a long tradition, beginning in classical Greece. One of the most poignant expressions of this ambiguity takes place after Alexander has learned about the huge deus ex machina doll that Aron has made. This happens when Aron's brother Ismael, who is touched by madness, becomes the supernatural agent for Alexander's revenge on the bishop, his vicious stepfather. Ismael puts his hands on Alexander's forehead, claiming that he will materialize the fantasies and wishes of the young boy. The "result" is a fire in which both the bishop and his retarded sister perish horribly.

Later, at a celebration welcoming two newborn children to which Isak, who has reinforced his friendship to the family by saving them, has been invited as a guest of honor, the supernatural reasserts itself when the ghost of the bishop suddenly appears to haunt Alexander. His apparition is a signal that this budding artist will never completely break free of the cruel Protestantism embodied by his stepfather, the dead bishop, even though he has learned to internalize the playfulness of the pawnbroker (which can also be very dangerous).

Traditionally, the deus ex machina belonged to basic theatrical machinery. It consisted in the sudden and unexpected appearance of a god or a divine figure onstage—usually at the end of the play or performance—in order to unravel and solve the otherwise insoluble predicaments created by human beings. Or, with a more cynical or utilitarian touch, the deus ex machina simply made it possible for the playwright to end the play without having to bother about the details of unraveling the plot through the same human agents who had complicated matters beyond control. Supernatural interventions were quite prominent on Greek and Roman stages, and they continued to be an important theatrical device in the medieval and Baroque theater. From the beginning, however, the device was not universally commended: Aristotle argued that "the unravelling of the plot should arise from the circumstances of the plot itself, and not be brought about *ex machina*."[6] However, as our brief introductory discussion of Bergman's *Fanny and Alexander* has shown, one cannot guarantee that supernatural elements will appear to provide a quick and neat ending. They constitute an integral component of the film's message at the same time as they establish its aesthetic core—and the same can be said of theater as a medium.

During the Middle Ages, Christianity gradually began to leave its marks on theatrical conventions. In the process, the status of supernatural appearances on the stage subtly changed, as new belief systems became integrated into aesthetic form and message. The corporeality of classical gods was simply other as an animal's is other; for an actor to represent a god was a simple instance of the artistic principle of mimesis, which governed all the arts: the actor was making like a god, for the purposes of the audience, closely integrating belief systems with aesthetic form and message, creating challenging encounters between discursive practices. This is a complex development, which I am not examining closely here, whereby the supernatural figures entering the stage had to give credence to the mysteries and miracles on which Christianity was based while enhancing them with an aesthetically appealing form. The "imitation" in mimesis basically meant representation and thus implied a distance from reality, whether as a gradual distantiation from the true forms of reality, as Plato argued, or as an independent aesthetic reality with its own internal laws, a view held by Aristotle. However, the appearance of the divine becomes more flexible in terms of its position in the plot. Now the supernatural could also appear in the beginning of the play, and the notion of metamorphosis and transformation, in particular, the transformation of the body of the actor to a divine fictional character, carrying out a divine mission, such as Mary, Jesus, the Holy Ghost, or even God himself, was developed in a complex dialogue with the notion of transubstantiation.

These issues—and I will present only some very preliminary ideas here—can also be formulated in terms of a related historical dialectics: between the fictional forms of *mimesis* as opposed to the Christian religious notion of *imitatio*. It was through the incarnation of Jesus in the form of a human being, a very special form of divine descent, that the salvation of the individual was made possible. The salvation of each individual was dependent on his ability to create a spiritual relationship of *imitatio* to Christ, a form of spiritual devotion based primarily on acts rather than on faith. Since the historical incarnation of Christ in this world is, at least metaphorically speaking, also a form of deus ex machina, there arose, one could argue, a strong cultural conflict concerning different competing forms of representation. *Imitatio* was perceived as the source of religious elevation and personal salvation through the act of imitating/playing Christ, while *mimesis* was understood as a fundamental aesthetic principle, a more objective and depersonalized mechanism on which playwriting and scenic presentation were based. The distinctions between *imitatio* and *mimesis* are extremely complex and deserve to be discussed and analyzed in much greater detail. But they are clearly connected to the discussion of the deus ex machina, insofar as both *imitatio* and *mimesis* are concerned with different and even competing perceptions and interpretations of how one might theatrically relate to the notion of divine immanence or embodiment.

It is also necessary to make some further distinctions with regard to the positioning of the deus ex machina in the narrative structure itself. Even if the device itself was employed for ending plays, already in classical drama both the Delphic oracle and the riddling Sphinx in the narrative about King Oedipus are, strictly speaking, supernatural beings that have initiated the narrative, even before the plot of Sophocles' play begins. This did not really matter for Aristotle, however, who, with good reason, restricted his discussion of the supernatural to the use of the actual wagons and machineries bringing the gods onstage at the end of a play. The classical gods dwelt in the world, but as part of it. The incarnation of Christ, however, potentially suffused the material world—whether as the body of one man, Jesus, or eventually as all of creation—with a transcendental divine. As a result, supernatural forces transmuted from being a narrative device in which an individual being (a god) would descend to solve a particular, complex problem within forces shaping a material world shared by gods and men to establishing the basic conditions within which the narrative will develop. The Christian narrative of salvation introduced through the birth of Jesus as a divine intervention in the world made a deep impact on early modern and modern drama, including Shakespeare.

The question in the title of my chapter—"Has this thing appeared again tonight?" (*Hamlet* 1.1.21)—poignantly reveals the importance of the supernatural and its aesthetic ramifications, not only in *Hamlet* but in the tradition of Western theater that has emerged from the Shakespearean canon. In the Folio and the First Quarto, this line is ascribed to Marcellus, while in the Second Quarto it is ascribed to Horatio. The question of whether this thing has "appeared again tonight" is posed as these two newcomers arrive on the ramparts to begin their guard duty. They want to know if the ghost of the recently buried king of Denmark has been seen tonight *again*, as it has during previous nights. The appearance of this *thing*, underscoring its material concreteness, activates the play's revenge plot, which ends with the death of all the major characters in the play except Horatio.

It is hard to imagine a contemporary secular spectator refusing to accept the aesthetic convention of the appearance of the ghost in *Hamlet*, even if the notion of ghosts returning from the dead to haunt us is radically opposed to secular belief systems. But I do not think that this bothers us as theatergoers watching this play. *Hamlet* remains a masterpiece because the appearance of this supernatural creature has been integrated within a complex aesthetic framework and because that integration has something to do with the medium of theater itself, at the same time as it raises profound existential issues. The question whether this thing has appeared again tonight echoes the first line of this play— "Who's there?"—as if naively asking what the thing called theater is actually about and what it is we are going to see on the stage. The thing appearing again tonight refers to more than the ghost who has returned from what Hamlet in his "To be or not to be" soliloquy paradoxically terms "The undiscovered country from whose bourn/No traveller returns" (3.1.79–80).[7] How can we be sure that nobody returns from the dead if this thing has appeared again tonight? What and who is it? Or simply, "Who's there?"

The performance itself is also the thing that appears again tonight, and it also possesses powers that can haunt us, though differently from the ghost haunting Hamlet. Actually this thing—the ghost as well as the performance and the combination of both—is materialized every night when *Hamlet* is performed, both on the theatrical stage and in the fictional world of the play, reminding us of the brutal death of the old king at the hand of his own brother and of its tragic consequences. After Hamlet dies, declaring that "the rest is silence" (5.2.337), also meaning that now there will be no more ghosts to haunt us,[8] speaking from the dead, Horatio brings in an additional supernatural dimension:

Now cracks a noble heart. Good night sweet prince,
And flights of angels sing thee to thy death. (5.5.338–39)

It is now the time for angels, not for ghosts. As Fortinbras arrives, Horatio adds that he will take on the task of telling Hamlet's tragic story, telling how "these things came about":

And let me speak to th'yet unknowing world
How these things came about. So shall you hear
Of carnal, bloody, and unnatural acts;
Of accidental judgments, casual slaughters;
Of deaths put on by cunning and forc'd cause;
And, in this upshot, purposes mistook
Fallen on th'inventors' heads. All this can I
Truly deliver. (5.5.358–65)

The ghostly reality Hamlet has experienced will, in Horatio's tale, encompass everything that has happened, while Fortinbras announces that there is no time for lamentation. The new ruler has returned, again, tonight.

It is likely that in Shakespeare's own time there were more people who actually believed in ghosts than there are today. And after the modern declaration of God's death, the deus ex machina took a new turn. It has assumed a career as a powerful metaphor both for an open-ended futurity through which utopian notions are critically reflected and refigured and for ideological, social, and personal conflicts, frequently involving a strong component of violence and cruelty. *Fanny and Alexander* reflects these dimensions of the device. Even where such a utopian fulfillment is radically questioned, the modern and postmodern theater has openly employed many features of the classical deus ex machina device to figure the supernatural on its stages.

Ernst Bloch explored the ways in which the arts can represent a utopian state, a no-place where history can reach its end and fulfillment and where some form of other-worldly, supernatural existence can chronotopically be revealed, in temporal as well as in spatial terms. Jürgen Habermas has emphasized the spatial dimensions of this utopian, open-ended futurity in Bloch's world. His formulations are highly relevant for the modern theater, where the stage can be transformed for a short but powerful fictional moment into a space where the void previously occupied by God is filled by some form of Nietzschean eternal recurrence. According to Habermas, we learn through Bloch that "God is dead, but his locus has survived him. The place into which mankind has imagined God and the gods, after the decay of these hypotheses, remains a hollow space. The measurements in-depth of this vacuum, indeed atheism finally understood, sketch out a blueprint of a future kingdom of freedom."[9]

There are many examples of direct supernatural intervention on modern theatrical stages that confront the vacuous hollow space Habermas diagnosed. I will introduce only two of these here: August Strindberg's *A Dream Play* (1901–6) and An-Ski's *The Dybbuk* (1917). In these examples, just as in those I have already examined, supernatural interventions are closely related to different forms of victimization, serving as a source of violence, aggression, and disruption, but also as a means for trying to confront victimization and violence as they have appeared in history.

The fictional universe of Strindberg's *A Dream Play* is divided between a heavenly sphere and an earthly, everyday world, though the latter is conceived as a world of dreams. In his Preface to the play, Strindberg wrote that he wanted "to imitate the disjointed yet seemingly logical shape of a dream. Everything can happen, everything is possible and probable. Time and place do not exist."[10] In such a world there is obviously room for a transcendental immanence. The play begins with a deus ex machina, the descent of a divine figure, Indra's daughter, from the heavenly spheres against a backdrop of clouds and stars, just as in the Baroque theater. Her aim is to find out whether human suffering is as overpowering and hard to endure as she has heard. Initially hoping to find at least a spark of hope in earthly existence, she soon realizes that the human suffering she encounters and experiences herself is unbearable, and therefore she decides to return to the heavenly spheres from which she came.

In the Prologue to the play, the voice of an invisible Indra warns his daughter:

Thou hast strayed, my child.
Take heed, thou sinkest.
How cam'st thou here? (197)[11]

To which she answers:

Borne on a cloud, I followed the lightning's
blazing trail from the ethereal heights.
But the cloud sank, and still is falling.
Tell me, great father Indra, to what region
am I come? The air's so dense, so hard to breathe. (197)

The descent is slow and painful, and what she sees below is the earth, which, according to Indra, "is the darkest and the heaviest/of all the spheres that swing in space" (197). The descent of the goddess represents the birth of an individual to the pains and sufferings of this world. The deus ex machina thus represents the pangs of birth from the perspective of a newborn baby. But the "birth" of Indra's daughter and her descent into this world in *A Dream Play* are simultaneously equivalent to falling asleep and dreaming, and, according to the Neo-Platonic logic of the play, to the imprisonment of the soul in the material body. However, the curiosity and idealism of Indra's daughter, as well as her desire to change the human condition, transform her into a victim of earthly life, since to wake up from this nightmare means to die. Logically, the play ends with the return of Indra's daughter to the heavenly spheres, a reversed deus ex machina. There had been nothing she could do to relieve the suffering of human beings in this world; the deus ex machina failed to bring about the hoped-for change.

The Dybbuk, written in the wake of the First World War by folklorist and ethnographer Shlomo Rappaport under the pen name An-Ski, takes place in a traditional Jewish religious setting. Originally written in Yiddish, the play received its most important early production in Hebrew, in 1922, by the Habimah Theater, the Jewish theater collective founded in Moscow in 1917 as an integral exponent of the Bolshevik Revolution and the Spring of Nations, on the one hand, and the Zionist revival of Hebrew culture, preparing for the return of the Jews to their ancient "homeland," on the other. During the first years after the 1917 revolution, this combination was actually possible. In the mid 1920s, however, the theater left the Soviet Union, and today it is Israel's national theater. It is quite remarkable that a performance culminating in the exorcism of a "dybbuk," the spirit of a dead person (usually male) that has entered the body of another person (usually female) and speaks through her mouth, was so well received in the early Soviet revolutionary context.

There is an important difference between actual accounts of such exorcisms and An-Ski's play about this custom. According to the sources, the Rabbis usually succeeded in exorcising the unruly spirit that had possessed a young woman, quickly and effectively terminating the period of social and erotic transgression. In An-Ski's play, however, the young woman Leah revolts against traditional social norms. She is penetrated by the dybbuk of Hanan, the man she loves, who had died upon hearing that she had been forced by her father to marry someone with money. Leah more or less consciously chooses to become unified with her dead lover in the next world instead of becoming reintegrated within traditional social norms. Thus *The Dybbuk* fits in well with the zeitgeist of the Bolshevik Revolution, showing how the young couple revolts against traditional bourgeois values. Leah's father forces her to marry for money, despite having earlier made a vow with Hanan's father that the two children should marry when they grew up. The fact that Leah's father has forgotten his vow is the reason for the possession she experiences.

The Dybbuk, bearing the subtitle *Between Two Worlds*, is based on the struggle between earthly and heavenly forces. The Habimah production opened with a mystical chant, accompanied by the music of Yoel Engel, based on Chassidic tunes:

> For what cause, for what cause, does the soul, ho, descend, for
> what cause, for what cause, does the soul descend.
> From the high abode to the deep, ho, abyss, from the high
> abode to the deep abyss.
> Ho-oh, the fall is necessary so that it may rise again.
> Ho-oh, the fall is necessary so that it may rise again.[12]

Hanan's death in front of the synagogue's holy shrine at the end of the first act is the first clearly visible sign of this direct communication between the two worlds. In the second act, as the bridal couple stands under the wedding canopy, which has the bright red color of the revolutionary banner, Hanan's spirit disrupts the wedding ceremony by penetrating the body of Leah as a dybbuk and speaking through her mouth.

Hanan's voice penetrates Leah's body in a gesture that is both erotic and aggressive. He quotes one of the most famous lines from Song of Songs: "Behold, thou art fair, my love" (1:15), his deep male voice emanating from the frail, terrified body of the bride. The intertextual juxtaposition of *The Dybbuk* and Song of Songs is complex, because this biblical dramatic love poem is based on a dialogical strategy whereby the voices of the young woman and her lover are frequently mixed, particularly when she speaks about her love for her lover by quoting him. In An-Ski's original text, the dybbuk speaking through and from Leah's body does not quote from Song of Songs. This interpretation was given by the Habimah production, directed by the renowned director Yevgeny Vachtangov. The words from Song of Songs, coming from Leah but sounding with the deep male voice of Hanan, had an uncanny, disruptive effect. Leah's and Hanan's love for each other is utopian in the sense that it cannot be realized within the confines of existing social structures. They can only be fully united, and not just as an androgyne vocal construct, in the heavenly spheres, the high abode to which the opening lines of the play refer. The kabbalistic oneness of the feminine and the masculine principles realized through the courage of the young couple in their resistance to the old social norms not only corresponded to Bolshevik ideals but also represented the Zionist utopian ideal, in which it is necessary to make *Alijah*—literally, "ascent," referring to Zionist immigration to the Land of Israel (*Ertez Israel*) in order to reach the high abode where a new society in the ancient homeland could be established.

After the Second World War and the Shoah, *The Dybbuk* has continued to have a strong impact, particularly, but not only, in Israel. The Habimah production of the melodramatic story of a young couple who are united in the next world after Leah has become possessed by the spirit of her dead lover was performed more than a thousand times, for more than forty years, up until the mid 1960s. To understand why, it is helpful to recall the original meaning of a dybbuk: the soul of an individual who has not found a final resting place after his death and who therefore in distress tries to enter a living human being. After the Shoah, there were six million potential dybbuks haunting the Jewish people, the state of Israel, as well as all of Europe, and maybe other parts of the world, too—constantly speaking through the survivors.

"I'm not a historian," says Gogo, who, together with Didi in Samuel Beckett's *Waiting for Godot*, is expecting the appearance of some *thing* that we must admit very much resembles a deus ex machina and that, as we all know, does not appear again. But that's exactly Beckett's point: the machinery of the deus ex machina, enabling the appearance of a supernatural being, is finally out of joint. It does not function anymore. Godot will not appear again tonight. And this repeated nonappearance is the core of Beckett's play, reinforcing through its negation the disruptive, uncanny, almost brutal effects of the supernatural in the theater, even when *this thing* does not appear.

Portraits That Matter

King Chulalongkorn Objects and the Sacred World of Thai-ness

Irene Stengs

Researchers such as Birgit Meyer, David Morgan, and Christopher Pinney have argued that sacred portraits belong to a specific category of religious objects.[1] The most important difference between them and other religious images is that they are not just something to be looked at, but possess a gaze of their own. This gives them a particular potency in shaping and sustaining the "given world" of their beholders. Explaining the ontological status of a picture as the concrete, materialized manifestation of an image, W. J. T. Mitchell argues that images are not separately existing immaterial entities like a Platonic Ideal but more like an Aristotelian species, of which a picture is a material specimen.[2] A portrait is thus not a passive reminder of the absent being it depicts; it is, in some way as yet to be determined, an instance of that being, at once material and spiritual, with its own distinct and material history. Mitchell's argument limns a perspective that can allow us to avoid the problematic Platonic and classical Western opposition between material and spiritual worlds, and it sheds light on the surprising ways that in other cultures even the most mundane material objects may exert spiritual power over people.[3] In this chapter, I will explore these insights by examining portraits of the Siamese king Chulalongkorn (Rama V, r. 1868–1910), particularly in light of the deified person he became, as material carriers of a cult that marked the world of the urban Thai middle class in the 1990s.[4]

In the late 1980s, almost eighty years after his death, King Chulalongkorn became the object of a nation-wide personality cult. The development of the cult should be understood against the background of increasing hopes and anxieties about Thailand and Thai identity in a globalizing world. In that respect, the King Chulalongkorn cult can be regarded as one of the many new religious movements that emerged worldwide as a reaction to the booming neo-capitalist 1990s.[5]

To understand why King Chulalongkorn became an object of worship, one must study how he is remembered and how this memory is shaped. On the level of the individual worshipper, the "remembrance of King Chulalongkorn" does not refer to people's personal memories of someone they have known but is "transferred knowledge":[6] although they have never met the king in person, people know who he was, what his achievements and qualities were, and why this makes him a significant figure in their personal, day-to-day lives. A vast corpus of King Chulalongkorn stories circulates through schoolbooks, popular magazines, and radio and television broadcasts. In these stories, several major narratives can be distinguished, each depicting the king in one of his particular capacities. I call these narratives "narrated portraits." The narrated portraits show which aspects of the king's life and personality are so significant for the Thai that the king is generally referred to as the Great Beloved King (*somdet phra piya maharat*, an epithet given him in 1908, on the occasion of the fortieth anniversary of his accession to the throne). As with material portraits, narrated portraits are particular concretizations of an image, textual concretizations, that make the Great Beloved King a part of the world that his worshippers can experience.

The core of what we may call the myth of King Chulalongkorn can be summarized in four narrated portraits. "King Chulalongkorn used to visit the countryside" depicts King Chulalongkorn as a king with such a sincere interest in the needs of his subjects that he traveled the countryside incognito to become involved with them in person.[7] "King Chulalongkorn abolished slavery" tells how the king furthered the well-being of his subjects, ended feudal arbitrariness, and introduced modern individuality. "King Chulalongkorn saved Thailand from becoming a colony" narrates how the king's diplomatic insights and skills maintained the independence of Siam (Thailand) in the era of colonization, the only country in Southeast Asia to manage to do so. The fourth portrait depicts King Chulalongkorn as the kingdom's "Great Modernizer." During the king's reign, a wide variety of typically nineteenth-century modernizations were introduced (railways, electricity, waterworks, and the like), which generally are presented as personal achievements of King Chulalongkorn. Moreover, the king's genius was to be able to select the good that the West had to offer for the benefit of his subjects, while protecting them from the bad.

The worship for King Chulalongkorn takes place in a world saturated with canonical and noncanonical Thai Theravada Buddhist concepts of kingship and the supernatural qualities of Buddhist kings. Buddhist kings are considered to be men with merit and grace, who emanate a benevolent power (*bun barami*) that all the king's subjects throughout his kingdom can experience. Deceased kings continue to protect the kingdom as guardian angels.[8] However, not all Siamese or Thai kings have become the object of a cult. The steep rise of King Chulalongkorn's popularity in the 1990s reflects, rather, the appeal of core elements of his biography in the light of the specific social and economic circumstances of the time.

We may seek to understand the appeal of the Great Beloved King from the narratives, but the vigor of this appeal is immediately apparent from its material manifestation: the omnipresence of King Chulalongkorn portraits. At the time of my research, from 1996 through 1998, the king's portraits were found all over the country, particularly in urban areas. Offices, restaurants, shops, private homes, temples, spirit shrines, railway stations, and other public buildings—there were almost no places without a portrait or statuette of the king. The source of the wide variety of available paintings, photographs, and statues was King Chulalongkorn himself. From the outset of his reign, the king showed a great interest in portraiture and photography, and he had himself depicted using numerous techniques.[9]

The early portraits of King Chulalongkorn and his family were primarily intended to decorate his palaces. Portraits were also sent to European courts as gifts, following a European custom adopted during the Fourth Reign, the reign of King Monkut (Rama IV, r. 1851–68). For the general populace, the abstract image of King Chulalongkorn as "king of Siam" literally got a face in the final decades of the Fifth Reign. On coins and stamps, portraits of the king found their way throughout the kingdom. In addition, these portraits appeared on picture postcards and New Year's greeting cards and were reproduced for widespread distribution, at least in urban and elite environments. There they became objects of worship. In the words of a contemporary observer, Quaritch H. G. Wales:

> One more method of paying homage to deceased kings in Siam remains to be mentioned: the setting of a photograph or lithograph of the particular king on a table, before which are made the usual offering of lighted candles, flowers, and incense. This is now a very popular custom, both in government institutions and private houses, since every Siamese home possesses at least a cheap lithograph and can thus show its loyalty in this easy and practical manner.[10]

As the mass production of portraits began only during the reign of King Chulalongkorn, Wales must be referring to portraits of King Chulalongkorn and his son King Vajiravudh (r. 1910–25), the only deceased kings whose portraits were available. The passage demonstrates that the worshipping of royal portraits—although rather new at the time—predates the development of the King Chulalongkorn cult. At the same time, this passage highlights the power of the alliance between new media, commerce, and religion from the outset. This alliance, therefore, cannot be understood as specific to our time.

The practices for worshipping King Chulalongkorn draw upon popular ideas about the powers of sacred images, a fundamental dimension for understanding the mass production of the king's portrait. Elsewhere I have elaborated on the specific capacities of King Chulalongkorn portraits as, to paraphrase Meyer, objectifications mediating religious experience.[11] Thai people may experience their special relationship with King Chulalongkorn through a portrait of the king—a context-specific encounter with the sublime.[12]

Here I want to highlight the agency of the objects themselves, so as to give insight into how King Chulalongkorn portraits tend to steer their own production, distribution, sustenance, and display. I therefore will take the agency of these objects, their power to affect the world and their significance in the creation of people's life world, as my specific focus.

Moving Objects

King Chulalongkorn portraits have the capacity to transform their environment by radiating their sacredness. The daily practice of the King Chulalongkorn cult consists, therefore, in concrete dealings with things in the world rather than merely spiritual actions. Take the case of Bun, a King Chulalongkorn devotee. His practice demonstrates how his dealings with King Chulalongkorn objects transform his personal world into a sacred space.

Bun is the owner of a well-known flower shop in Chiang Mai, the capital city of Northern Thailand. His small shop—which he runs with his sister—is famous for the quality of its flowers, as well as its flower decorations and garlands. Chiang Mai's elite order their flowers from Bun, particularly on occasions of a formal, "national" character, such as a visit of the queen to Chiang Mai or Chulalongkorn Day.[13] Bun himself is strongly devoted to King Chulalongkorn. This is partly expressed in the eight portraits of the king decorating his shop and its private upper floor. Most of these portraits were presented as gifts to commemorate various occasions, including the opening of the present shop, Bun's birthday, and the New Year. Furthermore, Bun owns a King Chulalongkorn portrait book entitled *Best of the Best: The Great Collection of King Rama V* (*Pramuan Phraboromchai Lakson*).[14]

But Bun's most precious King Chulalongkorn portrait is not on display: it is an original Fifth Reign coin, which he carries always on his body underneath his clothes. An aunt gave him the coin around 1990, in the "knowledge" that he would be the right person to own it. Since then, Bun has taken great efforts to make the coin into a precious medallion (*lokket*).[15] It is encased in elaborately worked gold, and its chain is also made of heavy gold. A small ruby decorates the medallion's top; two rows of small diamonds (brought back from a holiday in Belgium) are inlaid on the left side; and an emerald completes the setting below. The process of embellishing the medallion has been executed bit by bit. Every time Bun has some money or comes across a nice stone, he adds to his design.[16] In its state in 1997, the *lokket* would have cost about a hundred thousand baht. But Bun, of course, has no intention of selling this unique medallion.

Bun owns several other King Chulalongkorn coins and medallions. These objects, however, were newly produced on the occasions of commemorative events or for charities. Occasionally, he buys them from organizations or vendors. In 1996, Bun purchased ten such medallions at prices ranging between one and two thousand baht. Four of the medallions he kept for himself; the other six were gifts. Thus, Bun owns a wide array of

King Chulalongkorn portraits and objects. His desire for portraits, however, never seems to be entirely satisfied. Once he told me that there is one particular King Chulalongkorn portrait he would really like to add to his collection: a good photograph of the equestrian statue. As Bun explained, there is a fundamental difference between the statue and other portraits: the equestrian statue is a portrait of the king as royal Buddha (*phra phuttha chao luang*),[17] whereas the other portraits depict him as royal father (*sadet pho*). The equestrian statue is the "highest" portrait of King Chulalongkorn, because it was erected on the occasion of his fortieth year on the throne; no other king in Thai history had ever ruled so long. This portrait therefore depicts King Chulalongkorn at the peak of his import and power.[18] Apparently, the many widely circulating and easily available photographs of the equestrian statue were not good enough to suit Bun's taste: in his imagination the photograph had to be rare or otherwise impressive.

Bun's story reveals some of the ways in which King Chulalongkorn objects tend to move. First of all, King Chulalongkorn portraits often move as gifts. A portrait is always an apt present for someone who is known to seek special refuge with King Chulalongkorn, and a King Chulalongkorn worshipper presents himself as such to the world by displaying one or more King Chulalongkorn portraits. Consequently, many restaurants, shops, offices, and other semi-public and private spaces are colored by King Chulalongkorn portraits. The body may also serve to show an individual's veneration for the king: although Bun wears his *lokket* under his clothes, most *lokket* owners—women in particular—wear these adornments in plain view, moving with them wherever they go.[19] The *lokkets* are at once material testimonies to their owners' adherence to the king and testimonies to their taste and wealth.[20] The presence of a single portrait may attract many other portraits to arrive around it—on birthdays, shop openings, or other auspicious occasions. Waiting in department stores, religious shops, temple shops, jewelry shops, specialized portrait shops, book stores, and amulet markets, as well as food and household-utensil markets, King Chulalongkorn portraits are for sale in great numbers, with the cheapest items (stickers) costing no more than five baht.[21]

Second, King Chulalongkorn portraits move through door-to-door vending charities and small entrepreneurs. Some of the objects obtained may stay; others may continue their travels as gifts. Sombun, who, together with his wife, runs an architecture and contracting firm in Chiang Mai, obtained his first King Chulalongkorn portrait—a plaster replica of the equestrian statue—from a door-to-door vendor at his office in 1991. Although he said he had not been a King Chulalongkorn worshipper, thinking that King Chulalongkorn "was for the desperate" only, he could not refuse to buy the statuette, "because the vendor was willing to make the price very low." The presence of the statuette changed Sombun's life: he gave the object a respectful place in his office, where he eventually made an altar. Thereupon, their then poorly functioning business improved and began to thrive.

The arrival of the statuette changed Sombun and his wife not only into King Chulalongkorn worshippers but also into disseminators of King Chulalongkorn portraits. In subsequent years, they sent King Chulalongkorn New Year's greeting cards to their friends, relatives, and business acquaintances, sending a different portrait every year. According to Sombun, sending as well as receiving King Chulalongkorn cards is auspicious, which is why it is so important for him to send out these cards.[22]

Third, King Chulalongkorn portraits may seek out their owners themselves. Although Bun's coin was a gift from his aunt, it could not have been given to just anybody: the object was meant to be given to *him*. The same element of destiny is present in Sombun's account of the statuette: why, otherwise, would the vendor have made its price so exceptionally low? A parallel story was shared with me by Nui, a restaurant owner in Chiang Mai, who had been searching for an original King Chulalongkorn coin. He could not afford to buy one, however, as such coins are relatively scarce and therefore expensive. One day an amulet vendor came to his restaurant. The man offered him a one-baht coin for fifteen hundred baht, which was still too expensive for Nui. The vendor rejected Nui's counteroffer of five hundred baht and left the restaurant. Thereupon, Nui turned to King Chulalongkorn for help, at the King Chulalongkorn altar in his restaurant. A fortnight later the vendor returned to sell the coin for a mere five hundred baht. After several years, the vendor returned to ask Nui if he could buy the coin back, offering forty thousand baht, which Nui refused, of course.

Renu's first King Chulalongkorn portrait came to her in the form of a crumpled piece of paper that followed her, steered by the wind, until she could not resist picking it up to see what it was: it turned out to be a portrait of the king, dressed in purple. She ironed the portrait, framed it, and gave it a place in her family's restaurant—and the very next day the king saved her brother from a robber who held him at gunpoint. Her brother saw the king knock the gun out of the robber's hand from the portrait.

The idea of special relationships between specific King Chulalongkorn objects and individual people is widely shared, and it is a recurring theme in people's accounts of experiences with King Chulalongkorn. Importantly, it is the objects that take the initiative in establishing these relationships. As agents, they select their owners (Bun, Sombun), come when they know they are welcome or longed for (Nui), or arrive when help will be needed (Renu), exhibiting social qualities similar to human agents.[23] They assist their owners in constructing their life worlds by providing them with security, economic support, and aesthetic pleasure. In their turn, only through finding their owners can King Chulalongkorn portraits receive the care they "want":[24] an appropriate place, beautification, and reverence. More concretely, King Chulalongkorn portraits, like all sacred objects, "desire" a "high" place, possibly an altar, with incense and candles. In addition, they want pink roses, a glass of brandy, a cigar, apples, young coconut, and traditional Thai sweets, all favorites of the king.[25]

Center of the Cult, Center of the Nation

The equestrian statue in Bangkok is the central portrait in the King Chulalongkorn cult. Since the first King Chulalongkorn Day (October 23, 1912), the statue has been the focus of the celebration that takes place there. Its core is the national wreath-laying ceremony; representatives and employees of national institutions, semi-governmental organizations, the city, the army, scouts, hospitals, schools, banks, and enterprises all present a memorial wreath (*phuangmala*) at the equestrian statue. When presenting their wreath, members of each group kneel down together, bow deeply (*krap*), and salute the king three times (*thawai bangkhom*). Chulalongkorn wreaths are a category of their own, different from both Western memorial wreaths and regular Thai funeral wreaths. Most designs combine a selection of symbols referring to the king and his particularities (royal attributes, symbols of his deeds, roses), with symbols referring to the organization or institution presenting the wreath. The central feature of most wreaths, however, is a portrait of the king. By the end of the ceremony, the equestrian portrait is surrounded by hundreds of King Chulalongkorn portraits, each lavishly embellished with its own specific details. The exhibition reconfirms the general perception that the modern Thai nation-state owes its very

FIGURE 9   Chulalongkorn Day 1996: Schoolchildren kneeling, bowing, and saluting when presenting their school's memorial wreath in honor of King Chulalongkorn at the equestrian statue in Bangkok. Photo by Irene Stengs.

existence to King Chulalongkorn and that, by implication, all the institutions included do as well.

The early 1990s saw a new, unofficial development, however: people began to gather at the statue to approach the king for support in all kinds of personal desires and anxieties. Combining in a single instance both the founding father of the modern Thai secular nation and a meritorious Buddhist king caring for each of his subjects, King Chulalong-korn is a sufficiently ambiguous figure that almost anybody can seek refuge with him. Tuesday evenings became the most significant moments at the statue, as, reputedly, the spirit of the king descends from heaven into the statue on those evenings around 10 P.M. (Tuesdays are auspicious because King Chulalongkorn was born on a Tuesday.) Although any King Chulalongkorn portrait at any time is a divine presence, on Tuesday evenings the equestrian statue *is* the king. The immediate presence of King Chulalongkorn through the equestrian statue both promises the certainty of a caring agency and immediately appeals to ideas and emotions surrounding Thai-ness, of which the king has become the epitome.

The equestrian statue attracts both worshippers and other King Chulalongkorn por-traits. In the late 1990s, when the cult was at its high point, on an average Tuesday evening the statue offered an impressive spectacle. In the candlelit dark, portraits of the king in the thousands gazed back at the onlooker: the part of the square in front of the statue was

FIGURE 10   Chulalongkorn Day 1996: After the wreath-laying ceremony is over, worshippers come forward to present offerings to the king at the equestrian statue in Bangkok. Photo by Irene Stengs.

full of King Chulalongkorn portraits placed on low tables and boxes. They were part of many make-shift altars, surrounded by fruits, sweets, brandy, flowers, incense, and candles. Behind the altars small groups of people were seated on mats—families or groups of friends or colleagues—chanting auspicious formulas (*khatha*), meditating, or chatting. Reputedly, the benevolent power (*bun barami*) radiating from the statue has the capacity to charge everything in its vicinity, people and portraits alike. Yet apparently King Chulalongkorn portraits have a better capacity to store this power.[26] Hence, King Chulalongkorn portraits may be "recharged" regularly at the statue, to continue their positive impact on their owners with renewed force.

As an auspicious object, influencing its entire environment, the equestrian statue has become an important portrait-selling point: in this respect the statue is also a source of auspicious objects. Generally, quite a few pickup trucks are parked next to the statue on Tuesday evenings. Packed with King Chulalongkorn posters, statuettes, and lockets, they serve as moving shops, and many of those portraits find their eventual owners here. Later, depending on their owners' views, they may return to the statue to experience its benevolent power once again.

Thus, the equestrian statue, located in the center of Bangkok, the kingdom's capital city, draws King Chulalongkorn worshippers and portraits into that center, then propels them out again. The statue, therefore, is not just a powerful portrait (a material manifestation) of King Chulalongkorn but also a material center of Thai-ness. Since the idea of Thai-ness virtually coincides with that of the Thai nation, of which the king forms the apex, the statue is thus the material center of the nation. Although the ancient idea that the king is the apex of society has for centuries been a generally shared image, the statue offers for the first time a concrete, approachable picture of that center. Yet it was not planned as the center of the nation, that is, as an objectification of a preexisting idea of such a center.[27] Rather, the situation should be understood from a performative perspective: once the material statue had been created, charged with its new meaning, it made the center come into existence.[28]

From Vision to Portrait

A vital part of my research was to trace the routes of King Chulalongkorn portraits. Where had they come from? How had they ended up in people's houses and shops? In Chiang Mai, many of the King Chulalongkorn portraits in shops appeared to come from a single temple, named Wat Doi Chang.[29] This temple, located at the outskirts of the city, turned out to be a true King Chulalongkorn cult center. A life-size golden King Chulalongkorn statue, housed in a special building, distinguished the temple from other temples; normally, temples do not have King Chulalongkorn statues.[30] The reasons why the statue was created can shed light on the complex interrelationship between the image of the deified

F I G U R E 11   Chulalongkorn Day 1998: The golden statue at Wat Doi Chang, for the occasion decorated with white and red roses, reputedly the king's favorite flower. Photo by Irene Stengs.

king, Thai individuals, and King Chulalongkorn portraits. Here is its story, as told to me by the temple's abbot.

One night in 1992, the abbot had a magnificent vision: King Chulalongkorn, in golden attire, with a golden crown, seated on a golden throne, spoke to him. He told the abbot to create a statue identical to the vision. After the vision, the abbot searched photo books on the life of King Chulalongkorn, to—as he expressed it—"see what I have seen." It turned out to be the king during his "second coronation," as depicted in a specific photograph. In addition to charging the abbot with the erection of the statue, the king had also instructed him to start a relief center and school for orphan boys from hill-tribe villages. The combined project—the intended statue and the orphanage—attracted people to the temple. Yet people also came because it became known that King Chulalongkorn often spoke in person through the abbot. Because Wat Doi Chang was a quiet temple, an increased number of (preferably well-to-do) temple visitors was required to finance the construction of the statue and the orphanage. Within a year, sufficient funds were raised. The statue was made and placed in a temple building (*wihan*) specifically built for the purpose. The abbot insisted that the statue be carved of out of a solid trunk of teak, making it, at that time, unique in all of Thailand.

Importantly, it was the king—not the abbot—who took the initiative in the creation of the statue. This made the initiative a necessity, and auspicious by nature. Second, the king gave detailed visual instructions concerning the eventual appearance of the statue. Hence, like any portrait or photograph created directly after the person portrayed, the statue would truly depict the king and therefore be an "original" portrait, not a mere copy. Third, an existing portrait—the second-coronation photograph; more precisely, a reproduction of that picture—offered material guidance for the making of the statue. Yet again, because not the picture but the vision served as the source of inspiration, the statue is not a copy but an original.

Basically, the account of the creation of the statue is at odds with Western common-sense views. However, for the Thai audience the story follows a familiar idiom (a "recognizable form"),[31] namely, that of a person experiencing the call of a spirit to become its medium and searching for the meaning of an unfamiliar experience or illness.[32] This, however, does not imply that the abbot *is* a spirit medium. In official Buddhism, belief in spirit mediumship is regarded as superstition and hence the rules of the monastic *sangha* (the community of monks and the official Thai religious institution) forbid monks' acting as spirit mediums or practicing other forms of "magic." In addition, an inherent obstacle to a monk's acting as a spirit medium would be that monks vow to wear only robes; an important aspect of Thai spirit-medium possession is changing dress to prepare to receive a spirit. The audiences identify the various possessing spirits that may come by how the medium is dressed during the ceremony. If a medium is not dressed in accordance with the expected attire of a particular spirit, the medium is either not possessed or is possessed by a different spirit. It is in part the same process that makes a monk a monk: a primary

147

differentiating feature between a monk and a layman is the robe. Only in a robe is a man a monk. By implication, a monk can never act as a spirit medium, as that would imply that he literally disrobes.

How, then, are we to understand the relationship between the abbot and the king? Rather than being an instance of spirit mediumship, the link between the two can tell us something about the relationships between persons, images, and portraits, relationships that are fluid and constantly in flux.

A Living Portrait

Jill, a Thai woman living not far from my house, whom I used to visit, asked me one day if I had ever been to Wat Doi Chang. When I answered in the affirmative, she said, "He looks just like him, and like a real womanizer (*chao chu*), too, don't you think?" I had no idea whom she was talking about. "The abbot," said Jill. "The abbot, a womanizer?" Upon seeing my amazement, Jill explained, "Yes, just like King Chulalongkorn. The abbot is exactly the king. And look at his eyes. Womanizers always have those wrinkles around their eyes. He is very attractive."

The next day I went to the temple to see for myself. Did the abbot really look like the king?[33] When I arrived at the temple, the abbot was in the *wihan*, receiving people who had come to consult him and present offerings to the temple. I stayed for almost two hours, continuously observing him, but I was not yet convinced. Then the abbot turned his head to the left, assuming the same pose as the king in a photograph placed behind him. This photograph had been taken during one of the king's visits to Europe. The king, dressed in a Western suit and hat, looks more like an Italian movie star than a Thai king, and certainly nothing in the picture would remind one of a Buddhist abbot. Yet at that moment I saw the resemblance, and I realized that the photograph could not have been placed behind the abbot by coincidence. Whether the abbot was in the *wihan* or in the *sala* (the temple's main building), the photograph was always placed behind him.[34] On another occasion, confirming the abbot's resemblance to the king—and his awareness of the fact—a woman presented him with a small, cross-stitched copy of another portrait, portraying the king's face from the same angle as the Italian portrait. The abbot, with clear appreciation, immediately placed the new portrait next to the other one; it remained there throughout my fieldwork period.

The abbot's physical resemblance to the king helped to circumvent the limitations that being a monk imposes on embodying an entity from the spirit world. The abbot himself, as it were, had become a living portrait of the king—or, in Mitchell's terms, a particular concretization of the image of King Chulalongkorn. However, irrespective of the abbot's particular features, he could not but derive his resemblance from another specific portrait. From this we can conclude that the conflation "king," "abbot," and

FIGURE 12   A "living portrait" of King Chulalongkorn: The abbot of Wat Doi Chang. At right are two portraits of King Chulalongkorn, which highlight their physical resemblance. Photo by Irene Stengs.

"portrait" is unstable and in constant need of reconfirmation by a beholder. The abbot is not always the king's living portrait, and not for everybody. Such conflations therefore are momentary and remain largely implicit.

The Golden Statue, the Abbot, and the King

In this final section, I will compare the roles of the statue and the abbot as movers of people and objects, then return to the issue of the relationship between image and picture, narrowed down to the specific relation between image and portrait.

The temple became a center dedicated to King Chulalongkorn after the king's image found concretization in two extraordinary portraits: the golden statue and the abbot. What, exactly, did that process entail? Without, in Webb Keane's words, exteriorization in a *recognizable form*, the vision would have remained an "idiosyncratic experience" in the abbot's head.[35] The narration of the vision was a first exteriorization: its idiom can be recognized as belonging to the domain of Thai spirit mediumship. The second exteriorization was the vision's materialization in the recognition of the famous coronation picture as the image of the statue-to-be. The constitution of the abbot as a living portrait was the third step in this process, materializing the vision of the king's image in a manner that others could see, hear, and approach.

Does this imply that it would be impossible, finally, to distinguish between the king, the statue, and the abbot? In the *sala*, several portrait compilations visualize the spiritual link between the king, the statue and the abbot—for instance, a portrait of the king at the top, the highest position, with a picture of the (unfinished, not yet gilded) statue in the middle, and lowest—but at the same time most at the fore, and most visible—the abbot. These compositions confirm the conflation. At the same time, however, the different forms in which the image materializes (vision, narrative, statue, face) matter: they have different effects in the world.

The narrative attracted people to the temple and raised donations so that the statue could be realized. Once the statue had been created, it attracted visitors to the temple. It began to take on a life of its own, and new relationships between the statue, devotees, and other King Chulalongkorn portraits started to develop. The statue was worshipped, embellished, and copied,[36] and it attracted many other portraits. Its presence also triggered the carving of other King Chulalongkorn portraits out of wood. These portraits, each carved out of a single block of wood of exceptional size, were commissioned and donated with the specific objective of being placed on a ledge next to the original statue. In consequence, the statute is surrounded by fifteen King Chulalongkorn portraits over one meter tall, which leave no space for the many, many other portraits that have been donated. The abbot complained, one day, that he did not know where to keep all the portraits. The other portraits were initially put on display in the *sala*. The continuous arrival of new portraits eventually led to the construction of a new room, especially designed to store them.

The process of concretizing the statue and its ensuing life made the temple a King Chulalongkorn cult center. The temple, itself a material and visual manifestation of the presence of the image of King Chulalongkorn, allowed the abbot to develop a power of his own, and gradually he performed his spiritual services more and more independently of the golden statue and further away from its immediate vicinity. The portrait compilations mentioned above can also be read as a visualization of this process: King Chulalongkorn's image moves into the background, while the person of the abbot is at the fore as the temple's most prominent attraction, as if having absorbed the king's charisma.

PART III

Sacred Artifacts

Material Mobility Versus Concentric Cosmology in the *Sukkah*

The House of the Wandering Jew or a Ubiquitous Temple?

Galit Hasan-Rokem

In memory of my father
Abraham Hasan

The materiality of things presents us with opportunities to investigate the complex meanings of religious experience in a double perspective, both diachronic and synchronic. Things accumulate traces of lived religious experiences, constituting an alternative and supplementary mode of communicating living experience. The history of religious practice embedded in things is especially important for Jewish culture, since, starting with the Hebrew Bible and elaborated in Rabbinic tradition, Jewish culture embraces a fully embodied and materialized code of religious worship, indeed of sacralized everyday life (in food and bodily purity, laws of agriculture, etc.). Moreover, things bear a special relationship to mobility, as their value, both symbolical and "real," may correlate with their ability to move or to be moved in space.

Concentric Models of Mobility

Yehuda Ha-Levi, a Hebrew poet of eleventh-century Al-Andalus and Castile, coined one of the most striking expressions of the inability, sometimes, of one location to contain the whole meaning of home: "My heart is in the east—/and I am at the edge of the west."[1] The poet's separation of self and heart concretely communicates the feeling of an identity that relates to more than one location at once, a subjective formulation of a consciousness reflecting the mode of existence that we may call diasporic.[2]

Contemporary research has widened the concept of diaspora from its original use in the Greek translation of the Hebrew Bible to refer to the Jews displaced from the Land of Canaan or Israel to include other diasporas, notably the African and the South-Asian.[3] Diasporic consciousness is usually predicated on a clear sense of center and periphery, in which the center is imagined to be the origin of the periphery. In Ha-Levi's line, a polarity emerges between the figurative center of the self, the heart, and the whole body of the self. Contrary to such dichotomous ideas of center and periphery, a model in which center and periphery are correlated in more dynamic and unstable ways can be discerned in many cultural spheres and expressions.

One of the main theoretical inspirations underlying my attempt to introduce a more dynamic view of diasporic phenomena is Michel de Certeau's model for the construction of space in the chapter "Walking in the City" in his classic *The Practice of Everyday Life*.[4] There he suggests that, when a person walks, instead of the walk producing a trajectory in a pregiven framework of space, the spatial framework emerges from the walking itself in an aggregated and cumulative manner. Similarly, diasporic space emerges as an ever-extending universe every time a new location is peopled by individuals or groups derived from an entity experienced as having another location, somehow more original and more central to its identity. In this way, we can begin to conceive the production of a de-centered ontology of exile.[5] A particularly striking formulation for this process has been coined by James Clifford: "In diaspora experience, the co-presence of 'here' and 'there' is articulated with an antiteleological (sometimes messianic) temporality."[6]

In this chapter, I will propose that Jewish culture, as well as the cultural image of Jews conceived by others, has continuously referred to a double diasporic consciousness, in which the dominant narratives propose the concept of a center, while multiple discursive practices, material as well as performative, persistently question and reexamine that notion. Inspired by the trailblazing work of Barbara Kirshenblatt-Gimblett, among others, my focus on material and performative practices seeks to balance the dominant discourse concerning diaspora.[7]

My reflections have grown out of my work on European narrative traditions about the Wandering Jew (see Figure 13). Lutheran attempts to ostracize Jews during the Reformation may have provided some of the impetus for the systematic distribution of the legend about the cobbler who denied Jesus the opportunity to rest against the wall of his house on the way to the crucifixion. Starting with Romanticism and carrying on into modernity, however, the actual effect of these narratives and their accompanying images was to make Jews the epitome of mobility and adaptability, thus of modernity itself.[8] As a figure of thought, the Wandering Jew has thus served to obstruct teleological historiographies, whether apocalyptic or messianic.[9] Consequently, contrary to the socialist plan articulated by Karl Kautsky and reiterated by Ilya Ehrenburg (both themselves of Jewish descent), he was not laid to rest with all other national entities,[10] and, contrary to Zionist

FIGURE 13   Fabian: Ahasver, XI, Zionisten-Kongress, Vienna 1913. Courtesy of the Magnes Collection of Jewish Art and Life, University of California, Berkeley, Acc. no. 80.5.4h.

wishful thinking, articulated too many times to mention, he has not conclusively returned home to stay.

Focusing on the meaning of material things in religion, I want to point to an equally persistent dominant ideological model, one involved less with time than with space. It too is central to the way Western culture has imagined Jews and to how Jews have thought about themselves. This is the model of a cosmic religious center. I hope to demonstrate how certain religious material practices have undermined the dominant idea of a concentric Jewish universe, and therefore the idea of such concentricity in European and Middle Eastern culture in general. Like the Wandering Jew, in its itinerancy the *Sukkah*, the temporary structure built during the fall harvest festival of Sukkoth, calls for perspectives beyond the traditionally historical one, in the deterritorializing spirit of Deleuze and Guattari: "History is always written from the sedentary point of view and in the name of a unitary State apparatus, at least a possible one, even when the topic is nomads. What is lacking is a Nomadology, the opposite of history."[11] In this chapter, I will therefore sacrifice historical linearity and detailed contextualization of specific cases in favor of a problem-centered, "nomadological" discussion of several interlinked religious phenomena. This should, however, not occlude the great complexity inherent in the chronologically and geographically various materials I will be discussing. Obviously, to invoke de Certeau's powerful metaphor, routes other than the one chosen here are possible.

The *Sukkah*—Thing and Practice

One of the material practices that destabilize the clear-cut concentric religious universe of Jewish tradition is the *Sukkah*, the booth associated with the holiday of booths or tabernacles, Sukkoth. The *Sukkah* appears as a particularly complex and varied material sign for similarly complex and varied configurations of mobility. I will suggest analyzing it via a fourfold typology: wandering, nomadism, pilgrimage, and migration. Here, wandering is to be understood as primarily aimless; nomadism as perennial; pilgrimage as temporary and focused on a specific locus; and migration as consisting of complete relocation. In the context of Sukkoth, the model of the centrifugally propelled wanderings of the Jews from one center of national emergence in the land of Israel, more particularly, in Jerusalem, becomes juxtaposed with a nonconcentric model predicated on the kind of cultural adaptation to various locations that, as we will see, characterizes the practices of the *Sukkah*. The material focus of the festival of Sukkoth, the booth itself, has adapted ecotypically to various, sometimes contrasting lifestyles, participating in the shaping of cultural expressions of mobility in Jewish culture and in relation to it.[12]

At a certain date, at the beginning of autumn in the Northern Hemisphere, Jews around the world set out to build temporary constructions designed to remain standing for eight days. The style, size, building materials, and religious practices associated with these constructions vary immensely.[13] One characteristic, however, is a roof made of branches, with or without leaves, or of mats woven of branches (see Figure 14). The interior is often lavishly decorated, expressing the popular crafts and tastes of the place and the period. During seven or eight days, depending on the specific custom adopted,[14] Jews eat and even sleep in the *Sukkah*, in ways that vary individually and locally, and in their degrees of intensity and regularity.[15] Although the construction is taken down after a week, parts of it—such as poles, textiles, and decorations—are often preserved for annual reuse.

Like most Jewish holidays, Sukkoth derives from a Scriptural source, here the third book of Moses, Leviticus 23:39–43. This passage refers to the *Sukkah* only minimally, whereas other references to the festival, such as Exodus 23:16 and 34:22, Numbers 29:12–38, and Deuteronomy 16:13–15, do not mention the booths at all):[16]

> 39 So beginning with the fifteenth day of the seventh month, after you have gathered the crops of the land, celebrate the festival to the Lord for seven days; the first day is a day of rest, and the eighth day also is a day of rest. 40 On the first day you are to take choice fruit from the trees, and palm fronds, leafy branches and poplars, and rejoice before the Lord your God for seven days. 41 Celebrate this as a festival to the Lord for seven days each year. This is to be a lasting ordinance for the generations to come; celebrate it in the seventh month. 42 *Live in booths for seven days: All native-born Israelites are to live in booths* 43 *so your descendants will know that I had the Israelites live in booths when I brought them out of Egypt.* I am the Lord your God. (New International Version, my emphasis)

The seven days of the festival correlate to the seven days of creation in Genesis, thus offering one of the many ritual opportunities for humans to act divine, creating a world and providing a concrete sign of the nexus of linear and cyclical, from an almost divine perspective: the beginning of the major timeline of creation and the eternal return of the annual and the weekly cycles.[17]

Sukkoth is thus a week-long holiday celebrated in the month of Tishrei, nowadays the first month of the Jewish calendar, fifteen days after New Year, Rosh Hashanah. Since the months of the Jewish lunar calendar commence at the new moon, the onset of Sukkoth always occurs on the night of a full moon. In this, it is like a number of other holidays in the cycle of the Jewish year, notably Passover, Pesah, commemorating the Exodus from Egypt. Passover is also a week-long celebration, whose central material expression is unleavened bread, *matsah*. Passover, celebrated in the seventh month of Nisan (the first month of the ancient Hebrew calendar) is the antipodal parallel of Sukkoth, the two holidays being situated exactly half a year apart. The fact that various sources conceptualize both these months as the beginning of the year imparts a certain relativity of time, which dialectically balances—or rather, overturns—the claim that the

FIGURE 14   Sukkot, after Moritz Daniel Oppenheim, c. 1904 (mailed in 1913). Printed by the Sana Gesellschaft, Germany, Cat. No. hof9-0021, The Joseph and Margit Hoffmann Judaica Postcard Collection at the Folklore Research Center of the Mandel Institute of Jewish Studies, the Hebrew University of Jerusalem.

entire calendar is rooted in the seven days of creation. Sukkoth is traditionally celebrated as a harvest festival; as such, it constitutes a triad with Passover and the other harvest festival, Shavuot (Pentecost), or Bikkurim, the feast of the first fruits, celebrated, uncharacteristically, on the fifth day of the ninth month, Sivan.[18] In Ancient Israel, according to the Pentateuchal laws of Moses, these three festivals occasioned the major pilgrimages to the ritual center, the Temple in Jerusalem.[19] Later books of the Hebrew Bible mention their actual celebration: for instance, Passover in Jeremiah and II Chronicles 30:13 and 21, 35:17; Passover and Shavuot in Ezekiel 45:21; Sukkoth in I Kings 8:2, Ezra 3:4, and Nehemiah 8:16–19, as well as in Zechariah 14:16–19; and all three in II Chronicles 8:13. Classical Rabbinical literature, written ca. 250–750 C.E., especially the Mishnah and its companion work the Tosefta, as well as the Talmuds of Palestine and of Babylonia, all devote full tractates to each one of them.[20] The detailed normative ordinances and ethnographic descriptions set forth there include both concrete and imaginative variations and contradictions. They are especially concerned with material details of the *Sukkah* booth itself: its height, the materials that may be used, and the desirable terms of eating and sleeping in it.

Jeffrey Rubenstein's erudite and rich *The History of Sukkot in the Second Temple and Rabbinic Periods* offers a diachronic perspective on the festival by highlighting the dialectics and triple tension built into the *Sukkah*: first, as a memorial site for the desert wanderings of Exodus; second, as a corollary to the Temple worship, emphasizing the concept of an earthly religious center that may denote God's abode with varying degrees of metaphor and symbolism; and third, as a decentered religious practice, stemming from the festival's agricultural genealogy, namely, the ancient booths in the fields that served reapers and pickers.[21] The ancient sources emphasize sacrifices at the Temple as a central aspect of the festival, but this is variously transformed into other aspects of celebration, concretized in the rich and varied material forms of the *Sukkah*.[22] The three aspects in the Sukkah tradition in the Rabbinic era coalesce as a braid of two absences and one strong presence. The two absences are those of the *axis mundi* of the Temple of Jerusalem, including its associations with rain and fertility, and, in the diaspora, the application of the biblical agricultural code, with priestly gifts and so forth. What is massively present, however, is an emphasis on the category of wandering itself, painfully interpreted in the prophetic tradition of the Hebrew Bible and reinforced by Christian theology as exile—and as such a curse and a punishment—however much it is experienced as an exercise in adaptation and sometimes even as a divine mission.[23] The mélange of genealogies produces a combined cultural practice—and an associated material sign—in which the absence of the *axis mundi* is transformed into an alternative cosmology, decentering the earlier concept by enabling the construction of a particular, ad hoc *axis mundi* in each and every Sukkah. Significantly, according to a pervasive tradition, the stars of heaven should be visible as a concrete sign of the axial relationship between heaven and earth.[24]

An Ancient Narrative Dialogue Regarding *Sukkah*

One intriguing instance of *Sukkah* building in Rabbinic literature can be read as an example of "narrative dialogue," a concept that I have proposed for addressing the intercultural contacts and discursive interfaces between Jews and their neighbors, especially in the late Roman and early Byzantine period in the eastern Mediterranean.[25] Here we can watch complex attitudes, both those posing Jerusalem and the Land of Israel as a center and those deconstructing that cosmological centrality, shuttle intertextually between the texts of two religions, Rabbinic Judaism and late ancient Christianity.

The opening paragraph of the third-century Mishnah on the theme of *Sukkah* runs as follows: "A *Sukkah* that is higher than twenty *ama* is invalid [*psula*]. Rabbi Yehuda permits [*makhshir*]."[26] The Mishna then proceeds to set out further rules for the construction, but in the largely contemporary Tosefta this is characteristically—as has been pointed out by Judith Hauptman[27]—followed by a historical narrative in the name of the same Rabbi Yehudah: "'a case [*ma'ase*] regarding the *Sukkah* of Helene that was higher than twenty *ama* and the sages were going in and out there and none of them said anything.' He was told: 'It is because she is a woman and a woman is not required to perform *Sukkah*.' He told them: 'However, she had seven sons who were disciples of the sages and all of them stayed there.'"[28] The Tosefta leaves it at that, whereas the Babylonian and Palestinian Talmud texts elaborating on the earlier text have much more to tell us regarding Helene's *Sukkah*. They also present a variant version concerning who in the family was the real disciple of the sages:

> "A case [*ma'ase*] regarding Queen Helene in Lod, whose *Sukkah* was higher than twenty *ama* and the sages were going in and out there, and none of them said anything to her." He was told: "Is [your] proof from there? She was a woman and a woman is exempt [*ptura*] from performing *Sukkah*." He told them: "However she had seven sons, and moreover: All of her acts were in accord with the opinion of the Sages."[29]

After a short exchange on the ages of the sons, from which it follows that her case is indicative for the consequent deliberations, the discussion continues examining the various views of the earlier sages and the proofs supporting them. For the purpose of the present discussion, we can briefly summarize the Talmudic discussion as dealing with the relations between the height of the Sukkah and its size, as well as the possible internal division of the space into smaller rooms. Throughout the discussion, the Rabbis reveal apparently accepted views about the queen, such as: "All of her acts were in accord with the opinion of the Sages." These include ideas about what befits a queen in general, such as "a queen sits in a *Sukkah* whose walls don't reach the roof for the sake of ventilation," and the rhetorical question "Is it the way of a queen to sit in a small *Sukkah*?" From this it follows that her *Sukkah* must have been big with the necessary implications for Rabbinic ruling. Finally, a moral appreciation of her character is given: "Her sons were sitting in a highly qualified *Sukkah* [*ma'alia*] and she was sitting in a small room [within that same *Sukkah*] owing to her modesty and this is the reason why she was not told anything—i.e. was not corrected by the Rabbis."[30] The emphasis on the relationship with her sons is of particular importance.

The woman who sets in motion the Rabbis' royal imagination is Helene of Adiabene—an ancient kingdom located in what is present Kurdistan or Northern Iraq, also claimed as homeland by the dispersed Assyrians—who converted, together with her sons but without her husband, to Judaism in the first century B.C.E. and visited Jerusalem some ten years after the crucifixion of Jesus of Nazareth.[31] Narrated by Hellenistic Jewish historian Josephus in book 20 of his *Jewish Antiquities*, the conversion story has not been challenged by historians. The Rabbinic accounts are, however, concerned less with the political and religious moves of the royal family than with their piety and especially their devotion to the Temple and to the city of Jerusalem. Josephus, by contrast, emphasizes their financial assistance to the poor citizens of the city and the rebels against Rome.[32] Starting with the early Rabbinic sources, there are numerous accounts of the golden gifts given by Queen Helene, as well as by her sons, especially Monbaz, to the Temple services.[33]

The narrative dialogue performed in the Rabbinic tales about Queen Helene of Adiabene alludes, I would suggest, to another queen with the same name, creating a specific semiotic focus on a continuous and ubiquitous interface and interaction between Jewish and Christian conceptions of diaspora, on the one hand, and sacred space, on the other. Once again legitimacy and being elected share the spotlight, shadowed by their foils, guilt and punishment. This other Helene—or rather, Helena, the mother of Constantine the Great (?273–337 C.E.)—shares a number of characteristics with the Rabbinic Helene, apart from her name (whose possible Greek etymologies include a torch and a basket for fruit): among them a religious conversion, together with her son, that would have major political implications for her son's empire and his political career. In addition, the sons of both queens win great military victories as a consequence of their conversions to a new religion. Both queens also share a predilection for pilgrimage to the Holy Land, especially to Jerusalem, and a practice of making generous gifts to Jerusalem sanctuaries. St. Helena, as she is known in Christian tradition, was instrumental in the Christianization of the Holy Land within the Roman Empire. The conversion of the empire initiated by Constantine and accomplished by his heirs began a new era in Jewish-Christian relations, characterized by a clear hierarchy between the ruling Christian and the ruled Jewish religions, as their institutionalized forms separated further and further, most famously in the Codex of Theodosius (438 C.E.).[34]

It is not easy to claim an unambiguous vector of "influence" between the narrative parallels visible in the tales of the two queens bearing an identical name, although Josephus may be postulated as a source for both. These parallels thus demonstrate the phenomenon of narrative dialogue in its clearest form, since, unlike many other parallels between Rabbinic and Christian traditions, here it is almost certain not only that the Rabbis would have known about the highly public visit of a Roman empress to Palestine but also that the authors of the Christian narratives of Helena Augusta's pilgrimage probably knew about the pilgrimage of Helene, Queen of Adiabene, since Josephus's books were in their libraries.

A particular Jewish-Christian narrative interface is encoded in one of the major versions of the narrative of St. Helena's finding of the True Cross. Some scholars hold that its various narrative formulations elaborate local Jerusalem traditions,[35] in particular, that a Jew living in Jerusalem provided the information that led to her discovery.[36] Jews were guardians of the original revelation, and especially of local knowledge of the Holy Land, which they transmitted on the level of folk wisdom—in fine dialectical contrast to the contemporaneous claims by Christian theologians that Christians were replacing Jews as the "real Israel" (*Verus Israel*).

The later traditions related to the finding of the True Cross—especially the holiday of the Encaenia, instituted to commemorate the dedication of the Church of the Holy Sepulcher on the spot where the cross was found, to serve as a "new Temple"[37]—further support the idea of a narrative dialogue between Christians and Jews. This dialogue was performed in various parallels between the earlier Tannaitic sources and their later Amoraic elaborations concerning Helene of Adiabene's visits in the Holy Land, on the one hand, and the tale of Helena Augusta's trip to Jerusalem, on the other. More importantly for the present discussion, this dialogical cultural creativity—not without polemical undercurrents—further evolved into ritual performance when the Encaenia, which incorporated the commemoration of the finding of the True Cross (*Inventio Crucis*), was instituted.[38] In his *Life of Constantine*, Eusebius describes the initial celebration as occurring on September 13 in the year 335 C.E.. Significantly, according to the extant comparative calendars, in that year the Encaenia corresponded to the eve of Yom Kippur, the Day of Atonement, four days before the eve of Sukkoth, though some scholars believe it may have occurred on Sukkoth itself.[39] Another famous female pilgrim to the city in the late fourth century, Egeria, described the event as consisting of eight days and attracting pilgrims from near and far. She explicitly linked it to a triad with Epiphany and Easter, possibly echoing the three pilgrimages to the Temple in the Jewish calendar.[40]

Narrative dialogue constitutes a complex web of intertextuality, in which it is impossible to define a clear trajectory of influence in any direction. The institutional shaping of the Christian Encaenia consciously acknowledged and capitalized upon the fact that King Solomon dedicated his temple in Jerusalem on the holiday of Sukkoth, celebrated by Jews. It is possible that the universally messianic role of Sukkoth in the book of Zechariah necessitated a Christianized version of Sukkoth, embodied in the Encaenia.[41] Zechariah's prophecy (14:16–19) foretells that "every one that is left of all the nations which came against Jerusalem" will come to the Temple to celebrate Sukkoth, and any who refuse will be punished by withdrawal of rain, the most vital substance in the arid zone of the Holy Land. The prophecy encompasses the double character of Sukkoth: on the one hand, it emphasizes the universal centrality of Jerusalem, while on the other hand, it widens the national framework to a universal one.[42]

A more popular kind of narrative exchange may also have occurred, inspired by local Jewish traditions such as the one hinted at in the narrative of the finding of the True Cross. These traditions may have combined Sukkoth, associated with Solomon's dedication of his Temple (I Kings 8:2; II Chronicles 7:8–10), with the newer festival of dedication, Hanukkah, derived from the historically closer rededication of the Second Temple after its desecration by the Seleucid Antiochus Epiphanes. Already in II Maccabees (1, 9 and 18; 2, 12; 10, 6–8) the two holidays, Sukkoth and Hanukkah, are linked as two festivals of dedication of the same length. This text may have been better known to Christian authors than to Jewish Rabbis at that time, being part of the Greek translation of the Hebrew Bible, the Septuagint, but not part of the Hebrew biblical canon for the Rabbis. For Jews, the recycling of narratives of dedication and rededication may also have suggested the possibility of rebuilding the sanctuary, a possibility raised during the rule of Julian, recorded in ample Christian sources but also in some Rabbinic narratives.[43] Local Jewish traditions may have contributed some elements and articulations to the Christian celebration, then been fed back into the Talmudic tale of Queen Helene's *Sukkah*, imagined high as a palace.

So, what does the *Sukkah* of Queen Helene tell us about religious things in relation to models of mobility? The conversion of the Queen and her sons parallels the collective conversion of the Israelites after the revelation of the Law at Sinai, during the time of their wandering in the desert. In both cases, the burden of the various commandments is accepted; Helene's active support for her sons' circumcision makes this especially emphatic for the royal family of Adiabene.[44] The Temple element is clearly expressed in her and her sons' rich donations of adornment and ritual objects and is manifest in elaborate and imaginative descriptions,[45] possibly echoed by and echoing the growing Byzantine ornamentation of Jerusalem's churches.[46] The competition would have been imaginary, however, since at the time Jews were forbidden to build sanctuaries in Jerusalem. Finally, the decentered element of the *Sukkah* materializes in the Talmudic identification of the *Sukkah*'s place as Lod rather than Jerusalem. Lod was a Rabbinic site west of Jerusalem that flourished long after any conjectural historical date for Helene and served as a meeting place and arena of contestation between Jews and Christians.[47] The decentralized perspective is also evident in the fact that the Rabbinic fantasy of Queen Helene's abode is represented by the ephemeral *Sukkah*, although monumental remains of her actual construction enterprises can be seen in Jerusalem today: namely, the Kings' Tombs, which were built as a gravesite for her and her sons.[48] Finally, and perhaps most importantly, the narrative of Helene and her sons reveals a decentered notion of the emergence of indigenous Jewish diaspora communities, and especially of Jewish sovereignty, outside of Palestine and Jerusalem. At the same time, their pilgrimage and especially their choice to be buried in the city highlights Jerusalem's role as an ideal center. This narrative of the *Sukkah* clearly demonstrates that thinking about Jewish culture through the *Sukkah* leads to a destabilization—one might even say a deconstruction—of the clear-cut concept of the territorial centrality of any one place (in this case, Jerusalem) in the religious universe.

Sukkah as Heterotopia

Anchored in chronologically multidimensional settings, the *Sukkah* is a semiotic bundle of significations of time and space. Borrowing Bakhtin's concept of the chronotope as a recurrent joint encoding of time and space,[49] I would suggest that inhabiting the *Sukkah* involves a continuous chronotopical destabilization of the dichotomy between itinerancy and locality in Jewish culture, and specifically in the lived religious experience of Jews engaging in this practice. Indeed, the complex spatio-temporalities encoded in the *Sukkah* resemble what Michel Foucault has termed a *heterotopia*, a concretely constructed and performed, mirrorlike, inverted reflection of a social situation replete with condensed meanings, here the utopian ideals associated with Jerusalem and the Temple.[50] Thus, for a week every year, this object—this *thing*, in the terminology chosen for the present volume—is constructed, carrying within it the cultural associations of both a utopian religious center in Jerusalem as the goal of pilgrimage and the heterotopian huts of the wanderers in the desert. Some further coordinates in time and space can flesh out in a chronotopical mode what Jews may experience while sitting in the *Sukkah*.

The three Jewish feasts of pilgrimage to Jerusalem are chronotopically connected not only by the practice of pilgrimage itself but also in the way in which they are all associated with the mythical era of the Exodus from bondage in Egypt and the wandering in the desert that ensued.[51] Thus, in narrative terms, the very idea of the religious center to which pilgrimages are directed grows out of the reality of a supposedly toilsome wandering, serving as a grandiose compensation and balancing act and constituting a transformation, indeed a reversal, of it. Passover celebrates the Exodus itself; Shavuot (Pentecost), the revelation of the Laws and the Learning of Moses, the Torah, at Mount Sinai; and Sukkoth, the period of wandering in the desert. Whereas Passover and Shavuot celebrate fixed events in the past, Sukkoth relates to the loosely defined forty years of wandering, especially to the desert environment and specifically to temporary abodes.[52] From early Rabbinic—third-century, Tannaitic—texts on, however, the descent of the divine presence to the Israelites in the form of clouds of glory is correlated with the *Sukkah* huts of the desert wanderers.[53]

These holidays thus introduce into the chronological scheme of the heavenly bodies rooted in the creation of the world, according to which the calendar is supposedly devised, a secondary mythical layer, almost a second creation, in which is formed the identity of the people of Israel as the subject of a particular history. Late ancient Rabbinic literature also reveals the same process of remythicization by consciously conflating the "seven days of creation" with the "ten sayings in which God created the world," paralleling the Ten Commandments given at Mount Sinai.[54] The tabernacles of Sukkoth should not be confused with the Tabernacle, the Ark of the Covenant, which is the major site of worship of Yahweh in the narratives of the desert wanderings: in English, due to the ubiquity of the translation from the Latin Vulgate, the same word is used for both. However, the Sukkoth booths and the desert sanctuary share a confluence of transience and permanence. In the desert, the Ark was an itinerant ritual center, emblematically suggesting the alternative to a reified cultic center, like what Jerusalem was to become, despite the fact that the Ark's teleological trajectory was directed toward its eventual placement in the Temple in Jerusalem, even while it was being carried around in the Sinai desert. Although the festival explicitly commemorates the simple huts of wandering, the pomp and power of the later cultic center of Jerusalem looms in the commandment in Leviticus 23 and certainly in its later ramifications. The splendor of the Temple may, in later Jewish culture, be discerned in the elaborate decorations of the booth, specifically termed *noy sukkah*—the splendor of the *Sukkah*—a special case of *hiddur mitsva*, that is, fulfilling a commandment without sparing expense.

Ethical teachings of Jewish sages in various periods, however, refer to the simplicity and austerity of a desert hut when they suggest that the *Sukkah* may convey a social message: at the period of natural abundance, harvest time, the booths remind one of the meager food of Egypt—however contrary to claims that the Israelites feasted in the flesh-pots of Egypt and dined on miraculously abundant manna and quail sent down from heaven while wandering in the desert.[55] The historical memory should, they have argued, foster empathy with the contemporary poor and encourage almsgiving and social justice, in parallel to the sharing with the poor ordained in the Passover ritual.

The biblical text also suggests (although weakly) an etymology for *Sukkoth* different from the one explicitly mentioned in the commandment. In dialectical opposition to the booths of wandering, the word *Sukkoth* also refers to two place-names. While place-names can intrinsically be held to impart a certain connotation of stability, these particular place-names are both "stations" in the collective wandering: one refers to the first place where the Israelites stopped after having crossed the Red Sea (Numbers 33:5–6); another is a town that refused to provide for Gideon's troops (Judges 8:5), apparently also a site on the route of Jacob's return to Canaan from Mesopotamia, where he erected booths and consequently named the place Sukkoth (Genesis 33:17).[56] Although place-names tend to indicate some kind of stability, the narratives connected to the places called *Sukkoth* refer to passages, border crossings, and impermanence.[57]

Among the triad of pilgrimage festivals, Sukkoth is unlike Passover (for which a particular ritual text, the Haggadah, was composed) and Shavuot (with its marked relationship to the Torah) in having no relationship to a specific text to be performed. Each of these holidays has a tractate in the Mishnah-Tosefta-Talmud libraries, and such tractates exist for most other holidays, as well. Since late antiquity, the liturgical tradition of the synagogue has dedicated various biblical texts from outside the five books of Moses for Sabbaths and holidays. On Passover, the Song of Songs is recited in the synagogue (and, according to some customs, at home too), based mainly on the allegorical interpretation of the Song as a love song between God and Israel, resulting in the "romance" in the desert. On Shavuot, the book of Ruth combines the calendaric etiology of the time of harvest, when the meeting of Ruth and Boaz occurred, with the aspect of conversion common to Ruth and the Israelites at Mount Sinai. Sukkoth, in Ashkenazi tradition, has been allotted Ecclesiastes. The traditional etiology relates the choice to a verse in Ecclesiastes 11:2, "Give portions to seven, yes to eight," supposedly referring to the number of the days of the holiday.[58] Other possible etiologies could include I Kings 8:2, in which Solomon, the legendary author of Ecclesiastes as well as of the Song of Songs and Proverbs, dedicates the Temple he has built in Jerusalem on the holiday of Sukkoth. This tradition, as well as the explicit reference by the first-person narrator of Ecclesiastes to himself as "king of Jerusalem" may subtly evoke the Temple element in the reading of Ecclesiastes in the synagogue on Sukkoth, although the book seems unrelated to any of the themes of the holiday. One may also discern in the text of Ecclesiastes reminders of the futility of building durable structures (2:4), or the futility of durable material belongings in general (2:22; 5:14), or the futility of all of existence (1:1).

A heterotopian perspective enables us to discern and critique the utopian perspective on festivals in general, and pilgrimage festivals such as Sukkoth in particular. On the social level, the utopian ideal of *communitas* has been central in festival and pilgrimage studies, given the inspiration of Victor Turner. But utopia comes accompanied by its discontents, and Sukkoth, like other Jewish festivals—blatantly Purim, but also Passover[59]—has historically also been associated with some forms of violence. One of the earliest accounts of such violence related to Sukkoth is in Josephus's *Jewish Antiquities*, 13.372, which describes the bombarding (usually translated as "pelting") of King Alexander Yannai—pointing out his ritual unsuitability for priestly service—with citrons (*ethrogim*) by the Jews in the Temple. The violence of the people was soon repaid with a royally ordered massacre.[60] Possibly the same event, or a similar one, told in the Tosefta Sukkah,[61] is motivated by a ritual transgression and mentions a Sadducean as the transgressor. The altar was even damaged, putting a temporary halt to the routine of Temple worship until it could temporarily be mended with salt to prevent its exposure as imperfect.[62] A separate study would be needed to address the curious fact that Sukkoth seems not to have attracted the same amount of violence between Jews and Christians as Passover and Purim, although one could imagine that the connection with the Encaenia might have produced a language of symbols for such strife.[63]

Home of the Wandering Jew or Ubiquitous Temple?

Two concepts centrally associated with Jewish culture and history, diaspora and exile, are essential to any consideration of Sukkoth and the construction of the *Sukkah* as a complex sign of stability and instability. From the prophetic books of the Hebrew Bible on, both terms appear often in Hebrew as one—*Galut*—clearly conceptualized as divine punishment. But a close look at the lives of the biblical patriarchs reveals that wandering in and out of the Land—Canaan, Israel, Palestine—was a constant element in their lives. On arrival in Europe, the Jews also told their story as a tale of wandering, as I have shown in earlier work on the legendary figure of the Wandering Jew.[64] Early Christian texts, especially the New Testament, were rooted in the tradition of the prophets and thus perpetuated the idea of Jewish exile as punishment, now motivated by the Jews' refusal to accept the messianic role and the divinity of Jesus Christ. This grew into the doctrine that the punishment of the exiled Jews was a sign witnessing to the truth of the messianic advent of Jesus Christ, linked to the task of the Jews as keepers of Scripture, including the prophecies concerning the revelation of Christ, until the Second Coming. This idea was fortified by the Fathers and the doctors of the Church, especially Augustine, and transmitted in various ways in popular modes of communication and creativity.[65]

However, a prosperous and creative Jewish diaspora existed in the Hellenistic, pre-Christian period in Asia Minor, North Africa, and Babylonia. These Jews did not seem to conceive of their existence as a punishment, and they actually recruited converts, partly constituting the basis for the spread of early Christianity, especially in North Africa. Early Rabbinic literature, by contrast, views *Galut* as a state of political subjugation of the Jews rather than as deportation or displacement from their native land.[66] From the nineteenth century on, Jewish thinkers have also articulated positive approaches to life in exile,[67] however tragically it was cut short by the extermination of the majority of Europe's Jews in the mid-twentieth century, an event that seems clearly to have confirmed the negative view of life in diaspora.

The dynamic, indeed unstable, view of exile in Jewish culture has a bearing on the *Sukkah* in that, paradoxically, the verbal expressions and behavioral and visual symbols connected with it rarely if ever relate it to exile. On the contrary, the unambiguous reference to the mythical wandering in the desert, before settling in Canaan and then the expulsions from it, almost excludes association of the *Sukkah* with exile. Thus, instead of being the imaginary house of the Wandering Jew in the European sense of that image, the *Sukkah* has its roots in the Holy Land. They emerge in the obligatory presence of four other symbolically charged objects at the holiday of Sukkoth: branches of willows, palms, and myrtle, as well as the fragrant citron fruit (*ethrog*), however transposed from the Holy Land to all places. The four symbols function mainly in synagogue worship, but they are also brought into the *Sukkah* and decorate it (see Figure 15). These branches and fruit do

FIGURE 15   *Netilat Lulav* in the synagogue, early twentieth century, P.G.i.F, Germany, Cat. No. hof9-0065, The Joseph and Margit Hoffmann Judaica Postcard Collection at the Folklore Research Center of the Mandel Institute of Jewish Studies, the Hebrew University of Jerusalem.

not usually grow in Europe—the symbolical objects are like the Jews, conceptually if not always realistically from "somewhere else"—and have thus required a lively trade with the Jews of the Holy Land.[68] This reveals that, contrary to the idea that the Roman destruction of Jerusalem, its Temple, and Jewish statehood emptied Palestine of its Jewish inhabitants, actually a period of heightened creativity ensued, producing the lifestyles and foundational texts that have been associated with Judaism ever since, such as the Mishnah, Midrash literature, and the Palestinian Talmud—"Yerushalmi."

The return of Jews to agricultural life in Palestine toward the end of the nineteenth and beginning of the twentieth centuries "revives" the agricultural memory enfolded in the *Sukkah* as a booth used by sedentary peasants. At the same time, the ritual *Sukkah* of the Jews encounters the apparently local tradition of similar structures erected by Palestinian locals, sedentary (*fellahin*) and nomadic (*Bedouin*) alike.[69] But as the *Sukkah* moves back and forth between poles of signification, relocation from inside the home to the temporary structure has itself been interpreted as "going in exile": "so that the symbolical exile . . . expiates sins."[70]

168

As an object that projects a discontinuous and nonteleological model for the conceptualization of sacred space, the *Sukkah* reveals how a concentric model can be destabilized without being completely abandoned. In de Certeau's model for the construction of space,[71] a framework emerges from the walking itself, in an aggregated and cumulative manner, rather than by projecting a trajectory onto a pregiven framework. Similarly, rather than separate *Sukkahs* filling an already-existing picture of the diaspora, the diasporic universe of the religious practices and practitioners of *Sukkah* and Sukkoth emerges with the construction of every new *Sukkah*, as a sign of a decentered ontology of exile. Like de Certeau's urban walker, the diasporic wanderer's prime cognitive tool is memory, linking together space through which he has already walked and places where he has not yet been.

The Sukkoth Thing

Let me return to the material object itself, the *Sukkah*: a construction, a hut, potentially made of various materials, including wooden or metal poles, wooden or textile walls, and, most important, a roof made of freshly cut branches, through which the light of the stars and the moon enters the inner space. The *Sukkah*, as it is most often encountered in contemporary custom, communicates a cosmology or, if you wish, a topography of divine spaces that is semiotically woven into material coordinates: set on the earth, the *Sukkah* incorporates elements of minimally processed natural products (the freshly picked branches); human-made products (such as textiles); artificial products (such as decorations, pictures, and even representations of humans); and, finally, the *axis mundi*, connecting each individual *Sukkah* to the stars, and, both more significant and, for various reasons, more suppressed, to the full moon of the first (seventh) month of the Hebrew calendar Tishrei, considered by some historians of religion to be the embodiment of the Mesopotamian moon goddess Sin, eliminated from the patriarchal religion of Yahweh. A shift in gender can be observed in historical *Sukkah* practices. Rabbinic texts systematically "relieve" or, one may say, exclude women from the *Sukkah*, even though some of the most elaborate late ancient descriptions of *Sukkah* building relate to one constructed for a Hellenistic convert queen, Helene. (See Figure 16 for a representation of this textual norm.) Tension between exclusion and inclusion of women is clearly demonstrated in eighteenth- and nineteenth-century European postcards, which, on the one hand, show the exclusively male practices of the blessings on the four symbols (see Figure 17), and, on the other hand, amply depict mixed company inside the *Sukkah*. In some of these postcards, the matronly wife seated at the table and the young girls playing nearby are accompanied by a younger adult woman, clearly a servant, who brings in food (see Figure 18), or, in a more carnivalesque fashion, stands on the table to hang the decorations (see Figure 19).

FIGURE 16   Taken from Mayer Kirshenblatt and Barbara Kirshenblatt-Gimblett, *They Called Me Mayer July: Painted Memories of a Jewish Childhood in Poland Before the Holocaust* (University of California Press and Judah L. Magnes Museum, 2007); reprinted courtesy of the authors. http://www.maverjuly.com, p. 244.

FIGURE 17   Alphonse-Jacque Lévy, *Sukkot: Netilat Lulav*, 1903(?), ND Phot., France, Cat. No. hof9-0098, The Joseph and Margit Hoffmann Judaica Postcard Collection at the Folklore Research Center of the Mandel Institute of Jewish Studies, the Hebrew University of Jerusalem.

F I G U R E 18   Herman Junker, *Dinner in the Sukkah*, end of the nineteenth century (?), D.G.i.F., Germany, Cat. No. hof9-0062, The Joseph and Margit Hoffmann Judaica Postcard Collection at the Folklore Research Center of the Mandel Institute of Jewish Studies, the Hebrew University of Jerusalem.

FIGURE 19   Herman Junker, *The Decoration of the Sukkah*, end of the nineteenth century (?), D.G.i.F,
Germany, Cat. No. hof9-0061, The Joseph and Margit Hoffmann Judaica Postcard Collection at the Folklore
Research Center of the Mandel Institute of Jewish Studies, the Hebrew University of Jerusalem.

Moving from the material description of the *Sukkah* to its phenomenological attributes, one can observe that it is an ephemeral but perennial construction, constituting a charged nexus of linear time and cyclical time: linear through its historical associations, as well as its brief career as a composite of human-made and natural materials, reminding us of human life's transience; perennial in its cyclical reerection each full moon of the month of Tishrei.[72]

A concrete expression of the transience introduced in material form in the *Sukkah* is the pictorial representations of "guests," known by their Aramaic name *ushpizin*. Traditionally these are seven male figures, each symbolically visiting on one of the days of the Sukkoth holiday. The all-male cast reproduces the male privilege associated with the practices of the *Sukkah*. The dominant grouping consists of Abraham, Isaac, Jacob, Joseph, Moses, Aaron, and David. The tradition is late medieval, and it is first mentioned in the *Zohar*, of thirteenth-century Spanish provenance: "When a person is seated in his *Sukkah*, Abraham and six distinguished visitors partake of his company."[73] The custom of inviting the *ushpizin* into the *Sukkah* became popular in the sixteenth century, in the wake of the kabbalistic revival in Tsfat of the Galilee under the leadership of Rabbi Itzhaq Luria ("Ha-Ari").[74] The historical circumstances of the notion of inviting guests into the *Sukkah* also reinforce the concept of Jews as guests, which has been investigated by Kader Konuk as a cultural memory of their welcome in the Ottoman Empire in the wake of their expulsion from Spain in the late fifteenth century.[75] The nexus of the transient and the eternal reemerges in contemporary contexts in ever-new modes of behavior and expression. Thus commercial genius has constructed what is sold in Israel under the oxymoronic name "eternal *Sukkah*"; elsewhere it can be purchased under the more modest title "*Sukkah* kit." Both monikers unsettle the required temporariness of the object (see Figure 20). In an equal emphasis on stability, in Jerusalem, Orthodox Jews are willing to pay much more for an apartment with a roofless balcony, a "*Sukkah*-balcony," on which a hut can be constructed and from which the stars may be viewed (see Figure 21).

After 1967, in the political context of Jerusalem as an Israeli and Palestinian, Jewish, Christian, and Muslim city ruled by Israeli Jews, *Sukkah* building has taken on a new dynamic. Possibly in reaction to the modest *Sukkah* building practiced before the establishment of the state of Israel, when Jews, especially in the Old City, often had to act as a threatened minority, the mayors of Jerusalem have sometimes exhibited their power by inviting the citizens of the city to a mass *Sukkah* in the courtyard of the Othman building, erroneously named by all the Tower of David (see Figure 22). In this they not only challenged the ethical teachings of austerity associated with the festival since the early texts but also repressed the commandment of the memory of bondage, since for many Jerusalemites, especially Palestinians, the choice of the site was a blatantly oppressive act. The decision of the Mayor Lupulianski to move the site of his *Sukkah* starting in 2006 may have been motivated either by his Orthodox adherence to the exact size of the *Sukkah* or for security reasons. Nevertheless, the positive result, a *Sukkah* of lights at the City Hall

FIGURE 20   An eternal *Sukkah* kit with a leafless roof, Jerusalem 2009,
photograph Gabrielle Berlinger, Indiana University.

square, however temporary, introduced a new level of spiritual symbolism in the public
representation of the festival object (see Figure 23).

The tension between the custom of beautifying the *Sukkah*, the *noy Sukkah*, and the
austere memory of the wandering in the desert may explain some of the peculiarly Jerusalemite customs that have been documented.[76] Specifically Jerusalemite customs of *Sukkah*
are also of interest in examining the tension between the religious center and diasporic
booths. Contemporary interview materials reveal a distinct local self-definition of some
customs: for instance, according to some, a Jerusalem *Sukkah* should be strictly white and
unadorned, and its roof of branches should be naked of leaves, possibly continuing the
centuries-old ascetic practices of local Jewish populations mourning for the lost Temple
and living as a threatened minority. This is especially intriguing in a city whose historical
geography and architecture provide ample material forms for contemplating the religious
yearning for the eternal, as well as endless proof of the inevitable failure of human vanity.
Visible examples are the unspoken competition in the height of church towers, possibly
of competing denominations, in the silhouette of the Old City—or in the limitless wealth
bestowed on the golden cupola of the Haram e-Sharif[77]—and the magnificent and beautiful suspended bridge Gesher ha-Meitarim, by Santiago Calatrava, completed in 2008 and
now the highest structure in the city—all this in a city massively populated by the poor.

FIGURE 21   A *Sukkah* with a leafless roof on a balcony, Jerusalem 2009, photograph Gabrielle Berlinger.

FIGURE 22   Tower of David. From the Jerusalem Municipality Website, 2007.

A much less spiritual idiom is expressed in the ongoing erection of the ugly tool and sign of occupation named the "Separation Fence" or "Security Barrier," which has become a Wall of Separation for the Palestinians, of humans from humans, of family members, of students from their schools and the sick from hospitals, communicating through the ugly concrete of the wall the might of military power, and the nameless fear of terror.[78]

Things direct our attention to the *habitus* of social practices of religion, those locations of religious experience where the topography of divine spaces is transposed into terms of human orientations. The concept of *habitus*, as Pierre Bourdieu has theorized it, can enable us, I hope, to evade the thrust toward purely functionally motivated models of interpretation. The materiality of things offers possibilities and obstacles: such as finitude, wear and tear, the occupation of space, and aesthetic pros and cons. These embody many of the needs that have been identified at the roots of religious phenomena, and above all the yearning for eternity and immortality. On the one hand, the materiality of things creates attachments and dependencies, but on the other hand, it also provides comfort, protection, and intimacy, as well as immediate sensuous pleasure. Unlike most of the artistic and communicative media serving to express religious experience—sounds,

FIGURE 23   *Sukkah* of Light. From the Jerusalem Municipality Website, 2007.

visual effects and objects, verbal texts—things are tangible and operate through our earliest developed, thus sometimes understood as most primordial, sense: touch. To evoke
Bourdieu again: things illuminate the concept of cultural capital in that they often amass
such capital in both symbolic and commercial terms.

I have attempted to show how the religious language and *habitus* associated with the
Sukkah have historically embraced an inner transformation of mobility and stability, inherently connected with the historical self-characterization of Jews, that deconstructs the very
idea of an earthly place as center. The same transformation also accompanies the general
conceptualization of mobility—especially as articulated in the wandering of the Jews and
their exile—as an ambiguous figure of thought encompassing both blessing and curse, both
asset and punishment. Inevitably. some of the paradoxical and troubling concepts that
emerge in the cultural and political context of present claims and practices concerning
Jerusalem as a religious center arose and had to be addressed.[79] In Jewish history and culture,
Jerusalem has been the only canonical religious center. Much has been written about how
nationalism and religion intertwine and complicate each other in the present state of the
world, and the Middle East inhabits a special place in that discourse. The obvious frustration

of those who still harbor a belief in the prevailing of secularization as an offshoot of Enlightenment must have grown immense lately, even in Europe, all the more so in Jerusalem. Given the new facts of the so-called Separation Wall, which created yet another mode of exile for large parts of the Palestinian population, it is hard to concentrate on just one symbol—the *Sukkah*. Still, I have tried to do so without totally losing the connection between a historically evolving religious phenomenon related to exile and wandering and a contemporary situation producing constantly new modes of exile and homelessness. As in the medieval Passover song "Had Gadya," where a fatal chain of actors destroy each other (the cat the lamb, the dog the cat, etc., until one reaches Almighty God) the Israeli settlers of the Gaza strip—and a few from the West Bank—have in the wake of the Israeli "disengagement" in August 2005 become homeless, too. Their situation cannot be compared to the catastrophe experienced by the Palestinian refugees of 1948 or to the plight of those of 1967. But their situation materializes the saying "evil breeds evil."

It is worthwhile to acknowledge the widening usage of the term *diaspora* for multiple cultural and regional contexts, as I did at the outset of this chapter, and to suggest fruitful connections to the study of the Jewish case. The recommendation that we add to the study of "geographical displacement . . . also . . . the possibilities of a transvaluation of *diasporic* sensibility, a metaphorization of deterritorialized critical consciousness in general"[80] is especially useful for studying the transformations of the Jewish perception of diaspora in light of the existence of a Jewish state. To explore what "The diasporic, always in the waiting rooms of the nation-space, . . . preserved at least from the illusion of a fixed identity and a prefabricated cultural role"[81] might mean for studying Israeli Jewish culture at present would be a thought-provoking project. Whereas the end of exile is emphasized in some Jewish prayers and political practices, many others still maintain an awareness of a major Jewish diaspora as a demographical fact, a sensibility, and a dominant cultural *habitus*, a chronotope as well as a heterotopical mirror for utopian dreams and harsh awakenings.

No sign is left of Solomon's palace,[82] not even a pole of his *Sukkah*—if he ever built one. But for some his words are preserved in the books that tradition attributes to him: the erotic Song of Songs written in his youth; the clever Proverbs written in his manhood; and the speculative Ecclesiastes, the fruit of his old age, read in the synagogue at the Sabbath service on the festival of Sukkoth.

It is thus to the relatively comfortable indefiniteness of verbal traditions that I shall return in my pursuit of the meaning of the chronotope of mobility and stability and their relationship to good and evil, but now with a stronger commitment to the messages of *things*. The things of the past are elucidated by verbal information, but they themselves carry complex meanings generated by the human body's movement in its *habitus*, such as the permanent yearning inhabiting transient tabernacles.

The *Tasbirwol* (Prayer Beads) under Attack

How the Common Practice of Counting One's Beads Reveals Its Secrets in the Muslim Community of North Cameroon

José C. M. van Santen

During my many stays in the northern part of Cameroon,[1] I have observed the use of the *tasbirwol*—prayer beads fabricated out of wood, grain, coral, or, recently, plastic—so often, as so integral a part of everyday life in these Islamic communities, that I never gave it a second thought. Only when the call for papers for the yearly NWO conference The Future of the Religious Past tumbled into my mailbox, mentioning that in recent debates in the humanities and social sciences "things" have come to be appreciated as a central dimension of life, one calling for scholarly attention and reflection, did I suddenly realize the importance of these familiar objects. During all my years of research into Islam and Islamic practices, my ethnological questions had been directed toward the spirit, "abstract thoughts," and "thinking," yet the *tasbirwol* was there as a material entrance into a profound spiritual practice. I noticed it but did not see it, and for a long time I was not able to grasp the religious and divine world behind these material objects: it is by meditating with the help of ninety-nine stringed beads corresponding to the ninety-nine beautiful names of Allah that people seek spiritual experience. For Muslims in this region, this world is a material stage in a chain leading to the real "matter": the final judgment, the life hereafter, and reunion with God. To get to this stage, one needs some help, and here the prayer beads come in handy. However, there is more. In this chapter I will explain how, by using this "material entrance," I discovered that Islamic brotherhoods, so much a part of the religious landscape in West Africa, still persist in Cameroon, though they were banned for at least three decades after independence in 1960.

After the recent call for democratization in Egypt, the word for brotherhood, *tarīqa*, has been easily associated with the Islamist transnational movement that was founded in 1928 by an Egyptian schoolteacher, Hassan al Banna, and that, as a political organization, opposes national governments in many Arab states. In West Africa, by contrast, a "brotherhood" connotes the Sufi orders.[2] These have mostly been founded by specific Islamic leaders, cheikhs, as we will discover when we examine the Tijaniyya (Tidja-niyâ) *Sufi* movement.[3] Sufism is considered to be the inner mystical dimension of Islam.[4] In some countries, as in Senegal, where the Mourids may serve as an example,[5] these brotherhoods are neatly organized, having transformed themselves into political forces,[6] and they use modern media to carry out their political aspirations, which need not necessarily aim toward an Islamic state, as we are too eagerly inclined to believe. In other areas this is less the case, but for fear of potential political aspirations, brotherhoods were banned for a time in Cameroon, and they seemed to have vanished from the political landscape.

However, the practice of using prayer beads, which belongs to the mystic forms of Islam, has continued, even among people who are not officially members of a brotherhood and are unaware of the ties of this practice to Sufism. With the recent waves of purification—"fundamentalism," if one likes—the practice of *tashbugo*, counting prayer beads, has come under attack as part of a general assault on mystical Islam, because it is considered to be a relic of an improper Islamic practice.

Mal Baba

Mal Baba, about seventy years of age, is a well-known marabout (religious teacher) in the village of X. Over the decades, he has taught thousands of children how to read and write in Arabic, how to pray, and how to count their beads. Only recently, I found out that since his early youth he had been a member of the Tijaniyya brotherhood. Not even his children (eleven in all, the eldest being over fifty years old) were aware of this fact, although he has never deliberately hidden it from them. When I asked, he said that he never performs the singing of the *dzikr* (the saying of a litany, meditation sessions), "but *tashbugo, tashbugo*, really mattered!" In Fulfulde—the Fulbe language, thus his language as well as the local lingua franca—the word for telling one's beads is *tashbugo*, derived from the Arab word *tashbih*, which means "to praise God" or "to praise God in hymns." His children have all adopted this habit from him, he says, "but getting them to sit down at night in order for me to reveal the secrets of this practice and with it the secrets of religion, life, death, and, most of all, their path to God . . . they never seemed to have the time." Thus, I concluded, Mal Baba influenced his surroundings using Tijaniyya practices without anyone around him being aware of the source of this influence. His story can serve as a point of departure in analyzing the genesis of the prayer-bead spirituality within Islam and the role it plays in everyday religious practice and experience. As we pursue the topic, the amalgam of Islam and political leadership will come to the fore.

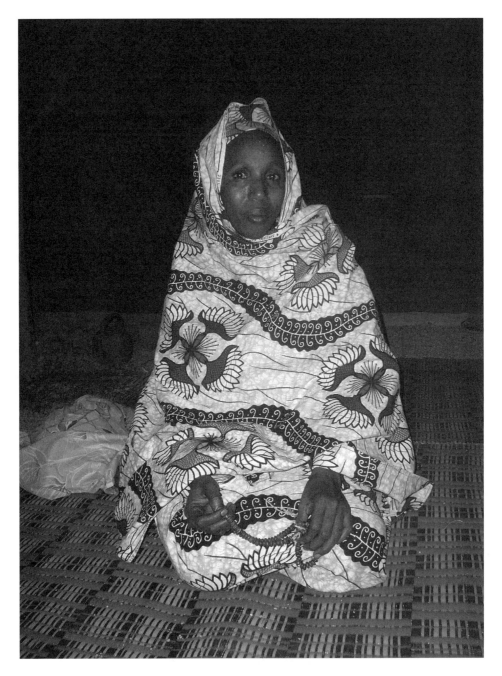

FIGURE 24   Praying woman with beads. After the evening prayers, this woman finishes her day by counting her prayer beads. Photo by José C. M. van Santen, 2008.

FIGURE 25   Mal Baba with his great grandson. Photo by José C. M. van Santen, 2008.

Mal Baba's ethnic background is Fulbe, his clan is Tara.[7] His grandparents came from another region and still "followed their cows,"[8] but his father moved to the village with his family and slaves, first settling on its outskirts, then relocating to its center. His mother comes from a group that still led a nomadic life and went on transhumance at the time she got married (around 1955); she is descended from the clan called Futaare. His father was already a *mallam*, a religious teacher, and he was obliged to learn the Qur'an by heart from a young age, as is the custom in Fulbe society. Had he refused, "he would of course had been beaten." He finished memorizing the Qur'an at the age of thirteen and continued his Qur'anic studies under an *oustas*, a teacher skilled in the Arabic language and Islamic writings, in order to be able to grasp the meaning behind the words of the Holy Book. Eager for more knowledge, he ran away from home at the age of fifteen without telling his parents: "They would have forbidden me to go had I told them beforehand." He walked toward the mountains, passing the town of Mokolo to cross the border into Nigeria, arriving at last in Mobi (a town now in North Nigeria, about a hundred kilometers from his village), because, as he says, "it was commonly understood in our region that 'Islamic knowledge' was to be found in Nigeria."

He stayed there for two years and studied hard. Then his father found out where he was staying and came to fetch him. Mal Baba wanted to return to Nigeria to continue studying, but to keep him in the village, his family gave him a girl "in marriage." As a result, he found that he could no longer leave: that would have meant leaving his wife, and he was all too conscious of the Islamic duty to support one's family, *Debbo bana boggel* (literally, "a wife is like a *boggel*," a rope used to tie calves in the morning so that they do not go out to pasture after their mothers). Thus a wife was supposed to act like a rope to tether him in place. He was eighteen years old when he married; his wife must have been about fourteen, the average age at which a girl got married at that time, although most people did not know their precise age. She soon became pregnant and gave birth. Then his father died. He was nineteen years old, and, being the eldest son, he had to become the head of the household. Quite angry about the way he had been "tied down," he refused to continue studying at all. Instead, he started cultivating the fields of his father. But his wife gave birth again, and again, and when he had about five children, he realized that they needed to be educated. Given that he himself had studied for many years—much more than most religious teachers—he decided to teach his children himself instead of sending them elsewhere, that is, to another *mallam*. Soon other people in the village asked him if their children could join his to be educated, and so began his Qur'anic school, which continues to this day.

His first wife died after having given birth to six children, of whom three died. His second wife has given birth to another eight children. He is very proud of the fact that they are all educated in religious affairs, and that his children by his second wife all have attended secondary school as well. "Knowledge," he proclaims, "is the most important aspect of life, knowledge in all affairs. If you have riches and no knowledge, the money would drain away, wouldn't it? If you have everything in the world but no knowledge, how can you take care of things?" After he decided to teach the children, he himself resumed study of what he calls *taw hid'*, which can be translated as "systematic theology." During his stay in North Nigeria, he had come to know the Tijaniyya and had learned their "way of praying." He remained in contact with other people who followed "the same road," including during the periods when brotherhoods were officially forbidden. The members may come together to pray and *tashbugo*, count their beads. Mal Baba was not the only young person who went in search of knowledge in Nigeria. Many people did so in those days, and they continue to do so.

Mal Baba says that many people no longer use the *tasbirwol* these days. They just say their prayers, finish with *Asala'am Aleikum*, "Peace be with you," and that's that. "It is because," he explains, "there are many roads, because there are so many books available these days, whereas in the past it was difficult to lay your hands on them."

Not only all Mal Baba's children but also the many students who have taken lessons at his Qur'an school have adopted from him the importance attached to the *tasbirwol*. Although Mal Baba has never intentionally hidden his membership in the Tijaniyya brotherhood, none of them know about it, or even that *tashbugo* is a Tijaniyya practice. Indeed, I found out about Mal Baba's Tijaniyya connections from a third person, when an openly Tijaniyya religious leader in the town of Maroua—now that the ban on brotherhoods has been lifted—mentioned that he knew Mal Baba well and that they were on "the same road." Mal Baba is not the only religious teacher to have influenced his surroundings in this way, and the practice of *tashbugo* is a common element of the Muslim community in this part of the world. Now let's turn to the "material thing" and its functions, which are central to this chapter.

Prayer Beads

The prayer beads used in daily Islamic prayers in North Cameroon are a string of ninety-nine shells or beads, with a marker after each thirty-three. By counting them, one performs the act termed *al-tash ih*, that is, repetition of the praises of God. One holds the prayer beads in one's hands and moves the beads along, repeating silently in one's mind the holy phrases. These generally start with saying *subh an Allah*, "God is devoid," or "Glorious is God," thirty-three times.[9] Then one shifts to another phrase, such as *al-hamdu-lill ahi*, "All praise and thanks be to God," saying it thirty-three times, then shifts again to *All ahu-akbar*, "God is great," thirty-three times.[10] Many Muslims do this after ordinary daily prayers. The number ninety-nine is loaded with esoteric significance (its circularity due to its factor of nine) and symbols, and the prayer beads are used to keep a tally of the seemingly endless repetition: it is by meditating with the help of the ninety-nine stringed beads, corresponding to the ninety-nine beautiful names of Allah, that people seek spiritual experience. The threefold division of the beads corresponds to the threefold division of the ninety-nine names, referring to God's power, his wisdom, and his mercy. Bead number one hundred is left out, as it is related to the "Name of the Essential." It is not known to ordinary mortals—only Solomon knew it—and it will be revealed only in Paradise.

The use of prayer beads is said to have arisen in India, whence it was adopted by Christians in the eastern provinces of the Roman Empire. When Islam crossed the borders of Arabia and entered the world of Hellenic-Christian cultures, it may have encountered the use of prayer beads and adopted it in turn. During the Crusades, the beads found their way to the West.[11]

In many Muslim regions, prayer beads are so much a part of everyday life that it is said even the prophet used prayer beads for his daily prayers, although the practice may well have been introduced centuries after the life of Mohammad. Myth has it that after his death one copy of the Qur'an and two sets of prayer beads were found in the prophet's possession. Yet another story says that, when Mohammad saw some women counting their prayers with pebbles, he forbade them to do so, advising them to count the prayers on their fingers. There are also many traditions that recommend counting prayers and praises on one's knuckles (*ya'qidna b'il an amil*), three counts on each finger, and so thirty counts on two full hands, to which one finger is added.[12] For this purpose, a special name was given to each knuckle. Ones and tens are counted on the right hand, hundreds and thousands on the left hand. The prophet would have said:

> Be quiet and pronounce the praises and the mentioning of Allah and of His holiness, and do not forget them, or you will forget mercy. Count them on the knuckles because they are responsible, just as if they really could understand. For the top of your fingers will be witnesses against you on the Day of Judgement.[13]

Some say that the use of prayer beads originated in praying with the help of the knuckles, so the use of beads may also have originally been an Islamic invention.

Praising God is also indicated by the word *subha*, derived from *sabbaha*, "to give praise": that is, to declare God free from every imperfection or impurity or from anything derogatory to his glory. The word was first used for the performance of supererogatory prayer,[14] and then applied to the prayer beads used for this purpose in Sufi circles and, some claim, among the lower classes.[15] Many influential people were opposed to the practice. Abdallah, the son of the Khalif Omar, spoke harshly to one person who had adopted the custom, saying: "Do not do that; it is from the Devil."[16] In the fifteenth century, there was much opposition to it.

Thus religious leaders seem often to have struggled against the use of prayer beads, which was probably first accepted among the lower classes. P. Edgar Schäfer tells us that when the respected ascetic Abu-l-Kasim al Gunejd (297 A.H., 909 C.E.) was seen using a string of beads and criticized for that, he defended himself by saying: "I cannot give up a thing which helps me to approach God." Schäfer therefore concludes that ascetics favored the use of beads. Al Ghazali, the great mystic, propagated meditation on God's character in order to emulate his mercy, compassion, and kindness. It is generally believed that beads are used mostly within Islamic mystical movements. In some Sufi rituals, prayer beads of one thousand beads, called *alf ya*, are used, especially at the funerals of eminent saints. Prayer beads are also used during the *dhikr* and to divine God's will:

> One prays two *rak'as* [a prayer after which one bends and kneels] and reads the verse: "There is no other God etc." Then the beads can be grasped within the palms of both hands, which are then rubbed together; then the *Fatiha* is soberly repeated, after which the user breathes upon the beads in order to put the magic power of the sacred chapter into them. Then he seizes a particular bead and counts toward the "pointer" bead (number one hundred), using the words, God, Mohammad, Abu Jahl. When one terminates with the name of God, it means that the request is favorably received; if it terminates with Abu Jahl it is bad, and if with Mohammad the reply is doubtful.[17]

In many areas within the Islamic world, prayer beads are also used to cure the sick. In that case, the material from which the beads are manufactured is important: the intestinal stones of cattle are supposed to have medical value. Prayer beads are used against the evil eye in India, and in the Maghreb they are supposed to have much holiness or blessed virtue, *baraka*.[18] It is constant prayer that brings *baraka* into the beads. Since their owner has, by much praying, brought *baraka* into them, the beads come to represent his personality. Prayer beads may also be used as an amulet, in which case they have all the virtue, *baraka*, of the names of Allah. Prayer beads' place of origin may convey additional value. Beads from Mecca are most valued by all Muslims, while for members of Sufi brotherhoods, prayer beads from the town containing the shrine of the particular saint who is at the origin of the brotherhood have supplementary significance.[19]

John N. Paden states that: "the core of Islamic mysticism, or Sufism, is a personal relationship with God. An ordinary person is believed to have a third-person relationship with God. An educated person may have a second-person relationship with God, and a trained mystic may have a first-person relationship, 'union,' with God."[20] It requires training to achieve the stage of "union." Having attained a measure of divine grace and having achieved direct communication with Allah is called *wusuli*, "union in God," in the Sufi tradition.[21] Sufi masters have the role of guiding their followers in mysticism and (because the followers still have a third-person relationship with God) of acting as an intercessor between God and the disciples. People in North Cameroon often object to the latter aspect of Sufism, arguing that it leads to an adoration of the "master" rather than of God, whereas adoration of and submission to God is the essence of Islam.[22] The two main brotherhoods in North Nigeria are the Quadiriyya (and related groups such as the Shaziliyya), founded by Abd al-Qadir Jilani of Baghdad, and the Tijaniyya.[23]

Islamization

In the "far north" of Cameroon, Islam has been present since at least the fourteenth century, in a congeries of "empires" that regularly clashed with each other. From 1200 to 1700, the Mandara sultan ruled the region at foot of the Mandara Mountains (with Mora, in the extreme northwest of Cameroon, as his capital); further north, near Lake Chad, the powerful Bornu Empire contributed to the area's wealth. To the west, on the eastern bank of the Logone River, so in present-day Chad, was situated the empire of Barghuirmi.[24]

Islam did not arrive in southern parts of North Cameroon, however, until the early nineteenth century. It was spread by jihads originating in the Sokoto Empire, which had been established in what is now northern Nigeria by Uthman dan Fodio in the eighteenth century. The Islamization[25] of North Cameroon was thus part of a wider process of Islamization in West Africa as a whole.

Uthman dan Fodio (1754–1817) was a Pullo (the singular of Fulbe), and his establishment of the Sokoto Empire in 1809 was part of the eighteenth- and nineteenth-century Islamization of this originally nomadic people, found through West Africa. (The area was, however, also inhabited by the Hausa and people of other groups.) Uthman dan Fodio belonged to the Torodbe, a Fulani warrior class known for its intellectual and religious force and for its many learned scholars. He saw it as his duty to spread Islam by jihad, and he expanded his empire in that way. The specific jihad that Islamized North Cameroon was led by Modibbo Adama, who became the founder of the Adamawa Province of the Sokoto Empire, the central part of present-day Cameroon. All the jihads were carried out by Fulbe leaders, most of whom were trained in Sufism and affiliated to the Quadiriyya brotherhood, as was Uthman dan Fodio, his brother, and his sons.[26] The Fulbe, the ethnic group to which Mal Baba belongs, thus played an essential role in the diffusion of Islam and the teaching of the Arabic script in the region, and many well-known literate "imams" and *oustas* had a Fulbe background.

When the Fulbe invaded the Diamara region, north of the Adamawa Plateau, they subjugated acephalous ethnic groups and entered into power struggles with hierarchically organized populations, some of whom managed successfully to resist their advance.[27] The Sokoto Empire granted the conquerors *tutawal*, the right to install Fulbe chiefs (*laamibe*) in defeated areas after a victory. After the installation of such chiefs, in many affairs of daily life sharia law was applied to all who were living there. Competence in matters concerning the Qur'an was the main qualification for becoming a chief.[28] Evidently an imam had to play a role in these matters, or even to appoint the chief directly. Thus the imam under the first Islamic ruler in Maroua (installed in 1801) had more power than the chief himself.

In 1900 and 1901, German colonizers, who had started arriving in 1868 in the southern parts of Cameroon, marched north and conquered the area. The German colonial system made use of existing political hierarchies to reign over local populations, and the French continued this system when Cameroon was ceded to France after Germany's defeat in the First World War.[29] Only in the 1950s did a religious alternative to Islam in North Cameroon become available, when Christian missionaries settled and started to convert local non-Islamic populations.[30] In earlier periods they had been particularly successful in the south, where today the population is largely Christian. For most people in North Cameroon, political authority throughout the colonial period thus resided in the single person of the chief (or the chief in association with the imam). He exercised all aspects of power: judicial, legislative, executive, administrative, and also religious.

Local rulers were thereby able to hold onto their power for a very long time. After independence, a traditional chief technically became the adjunct of a *maire*, but even today many citizens pay more respect to "local chiefs," who, continuing colonial practice, are still installed and inaugurated by the state, than to administrators of the "modern" political system.

Following the Islamic faith, accepting Islam as a religion, being a Muslim, deepening one's knowledge of the faith, becoming literate by studying the Qur'an, and in former days invading other areas—all have contributed to constructing the identity of the Fulbe. Becoming educated is and was important, which is why Mal Baba, like many other young men, went to Nigeria in search of "Islamic education." Thus Islamic scholarship in the Adamawa subregion is a continuation of the "tradition" founded by the leaders of the nineteenth-century jihads. One of its distinctive characteristics is the use of Fulfulde as the primary medium of religious instruction.[31] Although all Fulbe groups use Islam as an ethnic marker,[32] knowledge of the holy book and the duties, commandments, and prohibitions that come along with Islam differ enormously from group to group, from village to town. Scholars in town even deny that the Fulbe nomads are Islamic at all.

According to Mal Baba, Qur'anic, or elementary, education—which consists of learning the Qur'an by heart—is at the foundation, to be followed by middle-level schooling, for which Mal Baba went to an *oustas*. This is followed by higher education and, at the highest level, *tawhid*, learning systematic theology in order to obtain the status of a *moodibbo* (a scholar of great learning), a process that, according to Mal Baba, never ends; he claims that he is still studying. In Adamawa, acquisition of Islamic learning is itinerant, which means that people go elsewhere to search for knowledge, as did Mal Baba, though at the same time Islamic preachers wander to spread the knowledge they have acquired. The most important activity of mainstream Islamic scholars is the teaching and learning of *fiqh*, basic Islamic theology, jurisprudence, the Arabic language, and poetry.[33] Poetry, *mbooku*, is of great importance in Fulbe society, and it has a written as well as an oral tradition.[34]

Until recently, education meant Qur'anic education, given that "secular" education was associated with the colonial invaders. Refusing secular education is now considered an act of resistance against the colonial government. As a result, non-Islamic ethnic groups had a head start in secular education: they were keen on attending missionary schools and in this way getting rid of their inferior status as "unbelievers" and thus uneducated people.

In North Cameroon, as in many other parts of Africa, the line between indigenous custom and Islam is often ambiguous,[35] although the Fulbe interpretation of Islam has always been regarded as rather orthodox. When colleagues asked whether Tijaniyya brotherhoods were not a part of the Islamic landscape in North Cameroon, I had to admit that I knew little about them, as they did not exist openly; even in the scholarly literature they are seldom mentioned. Of course, I was acquainted with some persons whom I knew to be Tijaniyya, but brotherhoods are less visible in the public sphere there than in other parts of West Africa. Only recently did I find out that the Islamic president Ahidjo, who was in power from independence until 1984, officially forbade brotherhoods. Individuals who I knew favored a brotherhood did not perform activities that differed from those of other people. Perhaps they "counted their beads" a little more often and a little longer than other religious people, but this is difficult to notice if one does not give it any particular attention. Yet I found in researching the topic of this chapter that the use of prayer beads is an important indication of the existence of brotherhoods.

Because the Fulbe had been among the carriers of Islam, in many regions they claim Islam as an "ethnic marker." For a long time, Islamized people of other ethnic backgrounds considered the Fulbe way of life to be tantamount to being a good Muslim. In the plains of North Cameroon and the southern part of the Extreme North province, proselytes claimed Fulbe ethnicity after they converted.[36] In this way the Fulbe, politically dominant but numerically a minority, could increase in number. Fulfulde was not only important in studying religion but also became the lingua franca of North Cameroon.

As a people, however, the Fulbe are far from being homogeneous, either in their lifestyle or in their interpretation of Islam. In North Cameroon I distinguish an elite who ceased being nomadic at an early period and held economic as well as political power. Nomadic Fulbe groups—called M'bororo by other ethnic groups—still wander around with their herds, and there are also poor Fulbe farmers, who settled during the twentieth century yet who are often still semi-nomadic, though their access to pastures is constantly diminishing.[37] Mal Baba is a member of this last group, though he has hardly any cattle left. Agriculture has become his main source of income, and the children from his Qur'an school come in handy in carrying out all sorts of small jobs, like chasing away birds from the dry-season sorghum just before harvest time..

From this overview, we can see that the coming of the Islamic faith to North Cameroon is a good example of how religion and political power go together: Islam came along with political subjugation by Islamic kingdoms that invaded the area and kept control of Islamic teachings. The past, in which the Islamic faith could not be detached from the political situation, is still very much part of the present. Relations between religious and political leaders are still quite close in North Cameroon. This is why politically inspired Sufi brotherhoods, like those that exist in Senegal, are absent from the political scene. Until recently, most chiefs prohibited the brotherhoods, fearing for their own political positions. They thereby followed the politics of the Islamic first president. Since 1984 Cameroon has had a Christian president. Members of the local population discussing these issues—mostly men, though not necessarily propagators of the fundamentalist wave—stress that singing, clapping, and dancing, as members of a brotherhood do in the *dhikr*, is not part of proper Islam. Likewise, Mal Baba, when he admitted he was a Tijaniyya, stated that he did not perform these acts.

Brotherhoods in North Cameroon

Sufi brotherhoods can be autonomous units, like the Qadiriyya, divided into geographically defined areas with an independent leader, the cheikh (*shaykh*). Some of them are more centrally organized orders, like the Tijaniyya, and are consciously missionary in spirit: their followers share a common devotional life. Though the structure of the various orders may vary, the heart of a brotherhood is its cheikh, who is believed to be divinely authorized to teach and guide people in their worldly life and in the hereafter.[38]

Actively searching for brotherhoods, I recently discovered that they now exist more openly than before. A Cameroonian chief named Saidou of town X had been in exile for over ten years (in Nigeria and Central Africa) because he belongs to a brotherhood; now he has been chief of the town for quite a few years and can openly declare his affiliation. As Mal Baba said, "There are many roads these days." Thus, after twenty years, I observed the *dhikr* for the very first time in Maroua in the mosque of a Tijaniyya marabout, who has many disciples and is building a large second mosque next to his house. Many people in the town disparage him for creating such an establishment around himself, saying that "what he is doing is not the real Islam." Yet many people come from as far away as Senegal to visit him, and he teaches his own nearly forty children, as well as many other pupils, "to carry out religion" in the way he believes is best. He discussed with me the existence of brotherhoods in the town of Maroua, and exclaimed when I mentioned Mal Baba's name, "I know him very well, we are on the 'same road'!"

FIGURE 26   *Dhikr* in the mosque of a Tijaniyya marabout. Photo by José C. M. van Santen, 2006.

The Tijaniyya Sufi order was founded in 1782 in Algeria by the Algerian intellectual and mystic Ahmad al-Tijânî (1737–1815). Having seen the prophet Muhammad in a vision in 1782, Ahmad al-Tijânî claimed a rank among saints more or less equal to the rank in prophecy ascribed to Muhammad.[39] In the nineteenth century, the movement made its presence felt across West Africa, from Mauritania to Nigeria, while diminishing in its region of origin, Algeria. It is marked by a long association with the colonial government,[40] an aspect we will not address in this chapter. The direct mystical linkage to the Prophet Muhammad and God through Ahmad al-Tijânî has a deep effect on the social life of those who believe in this linkage and become followers of the Tijaniyya movement.

Other religious leaders within the movement have played important social and political roles, such as cheikh Ibrahim Niass in Senegal, whose movement, called Tijaniyya Ibrahimiyya, had many disciples in North Nigeria, especially in Kano, an important urban center once part of the Sokoto Empire. The movement in Nigeria continued to be of importance after Niass's death in 1975, and its followers remained in contact with the Senegalese base through marriage and informal commercial relations, though this did not lead to a political mobilization, in the way similar movements in Senegal have done.[41]

Kano has been a center of Muslim learning and culture since the fifteenth century, and in the twentieth century it has been a locus of Islamic reform.[42] Though the Fulbe claim to be orthodox, Uthman dan Fodio was trained in Sufism and was affiliated with the Quadiriyya brotherhood, as we have seen.[43] Contact with Tijaniyya in this region dates from the early-nineteenth-century visit of Umar Futi ('Umar al-Futi).[44] This scholar (master) visited Sokoto in 1826 while on a journey to Mecca, and he passed through Bornu and Kano on his return trip in 1837. He married the daughter of Muhammad Bello, son of Uthman dan Fodio. In 1903, on the eve of British occupation (which was violently resisted), many among the ruling religious elite, including the Caliph of Sokoto and the Emir of Kano, opted for a total rejection of European rule. In the period thereafter, religious authorities were tolerated but curtailed.[45] Though the sultan in Sokoto retained spiritual leadership of all Muslims in the region, a partial transfer of power from the aristocracy to a new political class had begun.

After 1954, the Tijaniyya movement took on new life when Emir Abdullahi Bayero, from Kano, renewed his line of authority, *silsila*, from Ibrahim Niass, who had visited Kano in 1937. This set in motion a mass involvement of Kano society, in which the two brotherhoods took the lead in a confrontation with Sokoto religious authority over Islamic hegemony. After that, the Tijaniyya more or less went underground until the death in 1966 of Ahmadu Bello, a *sardauna*, or subchief, of Sokoto who had promoted Islam both as a unifying instrument and as a means of preserving the region's cultural identity. However, his efforts achieved limited results.[46] This may also help explain the movement's invisibility in North Cameroon, as political and religious leaders from both sides of the border regularly meet to discuss their mutual policies in matters concerning the "general well-being of their adherents," which of course include religion.[47]

Islamic Revival Movements in Cameroon

Though Islamic revival movements have always been part of the West African Islamic world[48]—the jihad of Uthman dan Fodio serves as an example—from the 1990s onward Islam in North Cameroon has been receiving new impulses from Islamic "fundamentalist" movements calling for a purification of Islam. This means that many people, women as well as men, demand to be instructed about the "true" path of Islam and that itinerant Islamic "white" preachers travel around, a phenomenon indicated by the Arabic term *daa'wa*.[49] In addition, private Islamic primary and secondary schools have been founded with money from Saudi Arabia, not only in such larger cities as Maroua and Garoua but also in small villages. In 2007, the various regions in the province Extrême Nord counted twenty-eight private Islamic primary schools, seven of which were in the process of being established. There were six secondary schools, with a total number of 1,318 pupils.[50] Officials from the Saudi Arabian and Cameroonian governments preside over the inauguration of secondary schools, alongside many local officials. In 1997, the construction of an Islamic hospital was begun in Maroua; it reached completion in 2007.

FIGURE 27   Islamic secondary school. Photo by José C. M. van Santen, 2005.

Women now cover themselves more, and differently from before; the black *hijab* is for sale in the markets of larger cities and is worn by some. In their homes people listen to cassettes with sermons of various Islamic teachers, and they discuss these teachings. A recent development is searching for Internet sites, but in the north this is still a new phenomenon, due to poor access to the Net.[51]

In general, fundamentalist movements emerge in reaction to an experience of crisis or an external threat. In North Cameroon, the present political hegemony of the Christian South, with its Western-oriented influences, is perceived as such a menace. The Islamic Fulbe were able to hold onto their political hegemony during the reign of an Islamic president. After that, the Christian southerners became more prominent in the public and political arena in the region,[52] and the Islamic community lost its hegemony. Those in favor of a purification of Islam reason that that they are not against development or a move "forward" in history. What they oppose is the fact that, in the present situation, development is oriented to the West. The economic situation has only deteriorated since the 1980s,[53] and—in the eyes of the northern population—this is because Cameroon has

FIGURE 28   New Islamic influences: Videos and cassettes featuring the sermons of various religious leaders and teachers on sale in the Cameroonian capital, Yaoundé. Photo by José C. M. van Santen, 2006.

194

a non-Islamic president, unlike before. They are of the opinion that the present government is ignoring Islamic values and the Islamic lifestyle.[54] Thus they are part of what Louis Brenner calls a "political dynamism," which, though they often claim to be opposed to secularism, contains many secular attributes, among them "rationalization."[55] Sedentary urban Fulbe consider themselves to be more Arab-oriented, using the term *Arab* as something opposed to the West.

This new situation had led, on the one hand, to a more prominent and open presence of brotherhoods—the traditional political leaders have less power. Also, in the Cameroonian capital, Yaounde, the *dhikr* is performed in one of the mosques in the Islamic quarter of town, the Briquetterie. On the other hand, the notion of a purification of Islam has been introduced, with the result that many aspects of Islam in this region are suddenly referred to as "pagan" influences. Thus the director of the Islamic secondary school considers the practice of "counting beads"—though he still performs it himself, as he acknowledges—to be a "pagan" influence. This should have given me second thoughts, but it didn't at the time I spoke to him in November 2006.[56] Only when I reflected on "religious things" as a topic of research did the content of his words fall into place. The same goes for the *doo'wa*, the way, as he explains it, "the old elite finishes prayers." They do so by raising their hands in the air in front of them, palm upward, then rubbing them over their faces and bodies.

Similar observations have been made by Adeline Masquelier in Niger.[57] The yan Izala movement, which is characterized as an anti-Sufi reformist movement, has spread in southern Niger and sparked intense struggles over the meaning of Islam and Islamic identity. It led in 1992 to a violent dispute between *yan* (followers, members of) *Izala*, and *yan Tijaniyya* (members of the Tijaniyya brotherhood) in the main mosque of Dogondoutchi. The incident was followed by further disputes that pitted reformers against traditionalists, contesting the nature of Islamic knowledge and the legitimization of Islamic authority.[58]

The controversy over the use of prayer beads is not something new. In the colonial period, it had to do with the influence of Christian civilization and missions. Thus, in 1912 in an Egyptian magazine titled *El manar*, the editor concluded: "If you mention the names of Allah sufficiently, you need not count them. The counting draws your heart away from the One whom you wish to remember, and you cannot gain your object. It is that kind of *dhikr* of which the poet Muhid bin Arabi says: 'With the remembrance of the names of Allah your sons are multiplied and your spiritual eyes and your heart are blinded.'"[59] Opposition to the use of prayer beads continues, as we can deduce from the words of the director of a private Islamic college in Maroua, who said: "It may help people who can't remember well to count when they pray to God, but it is not an Islamic custom and it is better to count with your hands."

With the new fundamentalist movements and the "Pakistani" preachers,[60] opposition to the practice may grow, as has been the case with the yan Izala movement in Niger and

Nigeria. In particular, the Wahhabi movement (which originated in Arabia in Nedj under Mohammed Abd ul-Wahhab, b. 1691) abominates the use of beads. In Malaysia, too, many Muslims think it remarkable and distracting that Sufi Islam is appreciated in the West, while they themselves consider it to be old-fashioned and conservative. This dissension is expressed in a dispute between followers of Wahhabian Islam and followers of Sufi communities. The Wahhabians complain that the Sufi brotherhoods promulgate un-Islamic practices and that Sufi leaders preach a religion that is antimodern. The followers of the Sufi brotherhoods, for their part, consider the views of the Wahhabians to represent a dangerous trend that preaches intolerance, hatred, and violence.[61]

The common use of the prayer beads in North Cameroon signifies the influence of the Tijaniyya movement. That Mal Baba and the many other people who go to Nigeria in search of knowledge have not openly declared themselves to be part of this Sufi brotherhood is related to its condemnation by the "traditional" political leaders. However, the practices of these people have influenced the majority of the rural and urban populations without people being aware of it. Only when followers of Islamic reform movements condemn this practice does its "mystical" character come to the fore, where it can be remarked by the author, the ignorant anthropologist.

Concluding Remarks: Why Overlook the Obvious?

In this final section I would like to ask why, after having worked for twenty-five years in the region, I had never been aware of the obvious presence of Sufi influence. Of course, I did try to find out, but I was in search of theological discourse, *taw hid*', while all these years there were other indicators—such as, for example, the *tasbirwol*, prayer beads, as a material entrance into a profound spiritual practice. In Sufi practice, as in North Cameroonian society, there is no clear division between the material and the spiritual aspects of religion. As an ethnographer, I was not able to look behind the "matter," although for local Muslims it "mattered" so much. The common use of prayer beads in this part of the world reveals that, although brotherhoods have been openly prohibited in the course of history for political reasons, their influence remains.

During my penultimate research trips (December 2006 to January 2007 and January 2008), I did not even intend to make prayer beads an issue. The observations that I noted down about them were registered unintentionally. Their use and the remarks about it came to mind only when the importance of "religious things" was mentioned. I had been looking for Tijaniyya influence, but I had overlooked the obvious.

As I have explained, the *tasbirwol* is loaded with spiritual importance. It has a profound influence on an individual's divine revelation because it is by using the beads and pronouncing the name of God incessantly that one can reach what the Sufi movements call "union" with God while on this earth. However, the prayer beads are also used for less exalted purposes. One can attach this-worldly material wishes to them. If one has a request to make of God, if there is something one really wants (for a business to succeed, to pass an exam), one can make use of the prayer beads, too. In our case the religious thing, the *tasbirwol*, appears to be key to—indeed *matter* in—the formation of religious subjects in North Cameroon, in their identities and their style of praying.

I am not the only one who has missed the value of these objects. Even in the literature on the Tijaniyya movement I have found no reference to it, though the significance and origin of prayer beads are explained in the literature from around the turn into the twentieth century and in encyclopedias of that period. One may wonder why it was omitted from scientific books thereafter, even though it has never lost its significance in the practices of everyday life. At the time when I was writing this chapter, I once showed prayer beads to two African men, asking: "What do you associate with these?" The Senegalese man immediately said, "Tijaniyya!" The Cameroonian man said, "Evidently, an object to keep your thoughts on the right path." They agreed that it is one's intention while praying or reciting the litany with the help of "counting beads" that is most important. Yet one cannot do without the other: in the literature of the Islamic mystics (and the popular prayer manual called *Ahz ab wa Awr ad, Prayers for Spiritual Practices*),[62] it is revealed that, to approach "union," one should "pray without ceasing." Yet one should not pray in a disorderly manner. One should be in a state of cleanliness, so one should have carried out the ritual washing, but one should also have the intention to carry out the litany. And to maintain order in praying, counting the beads is of great importance.

That prayer beads as an object are mass produced in Asia, brought to Mecca or to the holy towns of the founders of brotherhoods—such as, for the Mourids, Touba in Senegal—and then be bought by pilgrims and handed out as gifts on their return is not an issue. It is the spiritual substance of prayer beads that have sojourned in Mecca, while the recipient of the gift has not yet been in this holy place and perhaps never will have the money to go, that is important. Prayer beads are a spiritual matter in themselves. They derive their importance from their use, and from their association with the litany that leads to union with God.

Contempt for, or even aggression against these objects (as in Niger) is of vital importance for understanding the new fundamentalist movements. The reasoning of the people behind the movements seems to be closer to that of the ethnographer than to that of the people they are trying to re-Islamize—that is, they concentrate too much on "thinking" and "the spirit." But that may be a subjective remark not suitable for a scientist to utter.

Miniatures and Stones in the Spiritual Economy of the Virgin of Urkupiña in Bolivia

Sanne Derks, Willy Jansen, and Catrien Notermans

The ironing board in the corner of Yomar's rented room had been transformed into a personal house altar. Next to a large image of the Virgin of Urkupiña, a miniature suitcase stood open to reveal a tiny university degree, a small identity card, a little plane ticket, and a bundle of fake dollars decorated with a picture of the Virgin. Sticking out of the case were colorful festoons, into which a few stones had been rolled. On the left side of the miniature suitcase, a toy car was displayed, and on the right side, a miniature house. On the other side of the image of Mary stood a vase of flowers. The stones and miniature objects, or *alasitas,* were the material reminders of the requests of Yomar, a twenty-five-year-old medical student in the city of Cochabamba, made during the pilgrimage to the Virgin of Urkupiña at Calvary Hill in Quillacollo, Bolivia.[1] Standing in front of her ironing board, Yomar smiled and explained:

> The stones symbolize health, strength, and work, all necessary to obtain in reality what I bought in *alasita.* Chopping out the stones each year is my promise to the Virgin that I will work hard. In return she blesses my wishes. I would like to have a house with a garden and a jeep to drive to my work in the hospital. But before gaining money, I have to get my degree in medicine. When finished, I need the identity card and the plane ticket to leave for Spain, where I will be able to make even more money. That's why I bought so many dollars.

Alasitas are miniature representations of valuable things like houses, cars, or money. The custom reportedly comes from the Aymaras in La Paz, where in 1781 the first *alasita* market was held in honor of Ekekho, an Andean deity associated with abundance and economic productivity. From there, the custom has slowly been transferred to other religious festivities in the Bolivian highlands, and even to fiestas outside Bolivia, as in Peru.[2] The word *alasita* is not known in present-day Spanish, and its etymological origin may derive from the Aymara word *alathaña*, which means "to buy." *Alasita* would then mean "buy me."[3] Another possibility is that the word derives from the Arabic word *al-asyd*, which means "mediator." The Spanish language uses several originally Arabic words, dating from the Moorish conquest of Spain in the eighth century, and the word *al-asyd* may have spread from there to Bolivia during the colonial era.

This chapter addresses how pilgrims' requests are given material form at this Bolivian Marian shrine by focusing on the *alasitas* bought at the shrine and the stones hammered out of the Lady's mountain as material religious expressions. We will demonstrate that the familiar dichotomy of spiritual versus material does not hold for these religious objects, because pilgrims' material expressions of religion conflate the spiritual and the material.[4] By following the stones and *alasitas*, we will argue, in particular, that they circulate in what we call a "spiritual economy," in which pilgrims trade vows and offerings for Mary's support in order to get what they want.[5] We thus aim to gain insight into objects' roles as symbolic means of exchange and their functioning in the lived religion of the pilgrims.

The Virgin of Urkupiña: Material Prosperity, Stones, and *Alasitas*

The Andean *cosmovisión* is based on harmony and equity in the cosmos, and the Andean people establish reciprocal relations between themselves and the supernatural world to maintain these.[6] The precolonial goddess of fertility, Pachamama or Mother Earth,[7] acts according to this principle of reciprocity, just like other deities in Andean *cosmovisión*. She is, moreover, an independent deity, who does not act on behalf of others. Spanish attempts under colonial rule to convert the *indígenas* to Catholicism by conflating Pachamama and the cult of the Virgin Mary,[8] making use of their similarities as protective and fertile mother figures, have had lasting consequences. They explain why contemporary pilgrims approach Mary with promises and material requests and understand her as having the capacity to intervene in the world of the living independently of God or Jesus: if you treat her well, she will be good to you, if not, you will be punished.[9]

The resemblance between Pachamama and the Virgin Mary explains why pilgrims experience no incongruity in approaching the spiritual world with materialistic requests. Pachamama is a goddess of fertility, and the petitions to Mary are derived from the Andean view of fertility. In the Andean *cosmovisión*, the key value of fertility is experienced as reproduction and prosperity. In a world where money is needed for a fertile life, the initial requests for fertility have expanded into petitions for health and the multiplication of wealth.[10] As materialistic requests are viewed in terms of fertility, for most Bolivians there is no sense of incompatibility in calling upon the supernatural world for upward mobility. This has been demonstrated by Michael Taussig, who explains that, in the Andean interpretation of money, supernatural power should be invoked to obtain the multiplication of money as capital. Religious understandings of the economy prevailed at the beginning of the capitalist era, when Bolivian pilgrims appealed to the supernatural world for money and material goods.[11] With 60 percent of Bolivians living in poverty and 37 percent in extreme poverty,[12] and with the state providing little in the way of social security,[13] this still applies today.

Every Bolivian province has its own patron-Mary with a specific legend, but the Virgin of Urkupiña in the department of Cochabamba is understood to be especially powerful and is famous for her help with economic and material issues. The legend of the Virgin of Urkupiña traces back to the eighteenth century, when, during the Spanish Conquest, the Virgin is said to have appeared to a little Quechua shepherd girl at the outskirts of Cota Hill, near the indigenous market town of Quillacollo, in Cochabamba. There is no exact date of the legend, but its celebration is mentioned in chronicles that date back to 1760.[14] The church of Quillacollo hosts the Virgin's original icon, and the fiesta of the Virgin of Urkupiña is celebrated annually from the 13th to the 16th of August. Until the 1950s, it was celebrated mostly by indigenous Quechua people from the mountain villages around Quillacollo, who saw in Mary an embodiment of Pachamama and came with their music and dances to Quillacollo to venerate their goddess of fertility. After that, Quillacollo's inhabitants, mostly merchants of mixed Spanish descent, became interested in the fiesta and started to organize it, for example, by founding dance fraternities and arranging formal processions.[15] Since the 1970s, the fiesta has begun to attract pilgrims from outside Quillacollo, as well, and it has expanded into a fiesta of national and even international fame.[16]

On the final day of the fiesta, the 16th of August, referred to as "Calvary Day," Calvary Hill, one mile outside Quillacollo, transforms into a veritable ant heap when hundreds of thousands of pilgrims come to Mary to dislodge stones and buy miniatures to seek supernatural blessing for their socioeconomic aspirations. A little chapel, built halfway up the hill, houses a tiny replica of the Virgin. Behind it a path winds further up the hill. At the back of the hill are numerous holes, averaging about ten feet in diameter, where the pilgrims come to hack the stones that symbolize their petitions. The ritual around the stones is found only at this particular pilgrimage site, whereas the miniatures are sold at most Bolivian religious fiestas. Most pilgrims pay their annual visit during Calvary Day, but at least some pilgrims can be found on Calvary Hill every other day of the year. Because of the Andean *cosmovisión*, in which exchanging material things with the supernatural has always played a major role in attempts at improving one's life, pilgrims do not understand their mobilization of the spiritual world for materialistic ends as being at all improper or contradictory.

Religious Objects: Their Meanings and Trajectories

Material things do not have a value in themselves, but derive their meanings from a context of human and religious acts. Although the importance of studying material objects in religion has been emphasized only since the 1990s, in the 1980s there was already a revival of interest in material culture in general.[17] In *The Social Life of Things*, Arjun Appadurai suggested a new approach by proposing that the meanings of objects are inscribed in their uses and trajectories.[18] Igor Kopytoff took this a step further by introducing the notion of a "cultural biography of commodities," that is, by asking questions about things' lives similar to those asked about people's biographies, for example: Where does the thing come from? What has its career been so far, and what do people consider to be an ideal career for such things? How does the thing's use change with its age, and what happens to it when it reaches the end of its usefulness?[19] We will use Kopytoff's notion to understand the relationship between Mary, the pilgrims, and the objects, because it reveals what happens when the things come into contact with Mary and afterward, and what meanings people attribute to the objects and, through them, to Mary. As the stones and *alasitas* derive their meaning from interactions with human persons,[20] following these objects draws us to the "human transactions and calculations that enliven things,"[21] as well as providing insight into the stories, conflicts, and biographies of the pilgrims. While the stones and *alasitas* follow similar and typical trajectories, the personal understandings and interactions of the believers give these objects their singular biographical elements and meanings.

As Jill Dubisch has pointed out, the traveling of religious objects blurs the boundaries of a pilgrimage site, because pilgrims take the sacred home with them.[22] By displaying objects imbued with the sacred on their house altars, they rematerialize the spiritual in another place. In a similar fashion, Colleen McDannell contests the exclusive association of material expressions of religion with the profane and the mundane, pointing out instead that these objects embody the sacred and the spiritual.[23] While the dichotomy of sacred versus profane hence does not hold for these material objects, the fact that it has been overcome does not yet reveal how people experience religion by using them. This study takes previous insights a step further by demonstrating that the Bolivian pilgrims use stones and *alasitas* to combine the supernatural powers of Mary with their own forces in a "spiritual economy" to realize their requests. The miniatures and stones serve as tangible mediators in this spiritual economy and come to symbolize the contract agreed upon with Mary.

At market stalls in front of the pilgrimage place, pilgrims can choose among all sorts of miniature objects and buy items that symbolize their material aspirations. Most pilgrims scrutinize the various objects carefully, as all are convinced that "the Virgin will give exactly what you asked." Little packets of paper money, either in bolivianos (BOB), dollars, or euros, are the best-selling *alasitas*. While bolivianos are used in Bolivia for the daily expenses of food, clothes, and small items, dollars are used for expensive articles, such as cars, houses, televisions, and sometimes rent. Although euros are not used for making real payments, they are also available on the miniature market. Because the euro is strong compared to the dollar and because, as in Yomar's case, it brings about associations with emigration to Europe, piles of miniature European banknotes have become the most-purchased items.[24]

Next to money, miniature credit cards from different companies, certificates for bank accounts, and lottery tickets can be purchased. Flight tickets for various airlines, passports, and identity cards are also frequently sold, expressing desires to emigrate and obtain a better standard of living. In addition, all kinds of cars, motorcycles, and little houses are sold—some of the last plain, others large and palatial. Some have gardens, some even a swimming pool, so everyone can find something that fits his or her personal wishes. Luxury goods, such as microwave ovens, computers, and cell phones, are also for sale in tiny formats. Furthermore, all kinds of certificates and documents can be bought in miniature, such as: birth certificates; health papers; forms needed to open a new business or buy a car, house, shop, or plot of land; university degrees with various specializations, from different Bolivian universities; marriage papers; and even divorce certificates. Precisely because divorce contradicts Catholic ideology, requests for it underscore the wide range of demands that can be given material form in miniature. Virtually everything can be wished for and can connect pilgrims' religion to their everyday lives as lived religion.[25]

Only in recent decades have the miniature objects changed from purely agricultural rural products, such as potatoes and animals, to commercial urban products, such as paper money, cars, and houses, paralleling the transformation from an agricultural to a commercialized society.[26] The trade in *alasitas* has expanded greatly in recent decades, particularly in Cochabamba. According to Bolivian priest Javier Baptista, this is because of its commercial character and the commercial mentality of the *Cochabambinos*.[27] Its fertile climate and central location have made Cochabamba a commercial area, where large markets are held and where most people live from commercial activities.

Nonetheless, one tradition of agricultural *alasitas* is still alive and characteristic of the fiesta of the Virgin of Urkupiña. On the 24th and 25th of August, the main streets of Quillacollo change into a market selling all kinds of real foodstuffs in miniature. Devotees go around the market to buy, for instance, hamburgers, carrots, potatoes, onions, and salt. Miniature domestic articles can also be bought, such as toothpaste, rolls of toilet paper, and corn flakes. With their baskets full, devotees enter the church, where the priest blesses the food in the name of the Virgin. The miniature food is then taken home, cooked, and eaten by all members of the family. The emphasis is on the familiar basket of food, and it is commonly believed that people who join in this tradition will not lack food in the coming year.

A week before, on Calvary Day, however, the stones and nonfood miniature representations are central. With heavy hammers, pilgrims dislodge stones from big rocks on the hill to symbolize their requests to Mary. While many pilgrims refer to the stones as "money" and understand them as a form of wealth, for others they symbolize health or a house. In return for the sacrifice made in extracting the stones, devotees expect the Virgin to help them realize their petitions. Most pilgrims also buy a direct representation of their request in *alasitas*, such as paper money, a house, or health papers, and many explained the relation between *alasitas* and stones in this way: "The stones symbolize the strength and effort I have to make in obtaining what I want." From the energy it costs to dislodge the stones, they can read how much energy it will take to create what they want in daily life. The objects can hence be seen as the currency of the reciprocal relationship. In return for having their wish granted, pilgrims first offer Mary their labor by breaking the rocks with a heavy hammer, with the stones as tangible profit.

The stones are part of the earth, and therefore of Pachamama and the sacred domain, whereas Mary is considered to be the owner of the mine. Because the stones are initially already related to the supernatural world, they are often seen as more powerful than *alasitas*. The miniature objects start their biography in shops and markets, and they do not gain any religious status until they are blessed. From the moment the stones are dislodged and the miniatures bought, they follow the same trajectory and rituals, with blessing acts such as *ch'allas*, prayers, *sahumas*, and sprinkling holy water serving to consecrate the objects and to give them religious meaning.[28] First, a *ch'alla*—a pre-Inca libation offering for blessing and purification—is performed. In it, the rocks and *alasitas* are sprinkled with pure alcohol, wine, and beer, and wrapped with colorful festoons. Usually in the same bag, the miniature objects and stones are taken to the chapel on Calvary Hill that houses the Virgin, where pilgrims pray and burn candles. Next, they often obtain another blessing by asking a *sahumera*—a seller of prayers and blessings—to pray for them. The *sahumera* sings, prays, and calls upon the supernatural power of Mary to bless the pilgrims, while pouring incense on an iron bowl with glowing coals. Afterward, the pilgrims take their objects to the church for yet another blessing, carried out by a priest, who sprinkles the objects with holy water in the name of Urkupiña. During these trajectories, blessings are heaped upon the objects, and with each blessing they become more valuable and spiritually loaded for the believers.

Afterward the objects are taken home. Many pilgrims put the stones and *alasitas* in the same place they keep their money—in a drawer, for example. Others display them on their house altars or put them close to a statue or picture of the Virgin, as Yomar did.

Some pilgrims display flowers and burn candles on their altars throughout the year. When a year has passed, the pilgrims return the stones and miniature objects to Calvary Hill, where they once again perform blessings in the form of *sahumas* and *ch'allas* and then destroy their dollars, cars, houses, and papers, and leave their stones behind. By destroying the miniatures and getting rid of the stones, the devotees show that the lifetime of their symbolic requests has terminated. Even pilgrims who do not return their miniatures and stones told me that the objects lose their religious status after a year.

The religious life of the objects is hence limited. They are included in the spiritual economy established with the Virgin for one year only. After that, a new cycle begins, with new offerings and new requests. On the same day that last year's miniatures lose their religious status and are destroyed by the pilgrims, the ties with Mary are reestablished through a new pilgrimage, new offerings, and new requests made for the coming year. The trajectory of *alasitas* and stones demonstrates that all sorts of material things can be incorporated in the spiritual economy: they need only to be bought, offered, blessed, displayed, and prayed over.

Escarlent's Pilgrimage to Calvary Hill

The biographies of things do not, however, consist only of a trajectory. They also include the human interactions that give them their spiritual significance. In addition to the general trajectory of the objects, the personal perspectives of pilgrims add meaning to every single object. The personal interpretations give a thing its biographical data.

Escarlent is a twenty-five-year-old woman from a middle-class family from Cochabamba. Every year since she was very young, she has gone to Calvary Hill to perform her rituals. She explains that the pilgrimage is both a social and a religious ritual:

> I have grown up with Urkupiña. When my grandmother was alive, every year she invited all her children with their families to go together on pilgrimage. The Day of Calvary was one of the happy occasions when the whole family was together. I also liked the fiesta, but more because that day my mother gave me her old *alasitas* of the previous year, so I got presents to play with. I still like to go. Over the years my faith in the Virgin has increased, and this special day gives me the opportunity to reflect on my life, on what is missing, on what I want to change, and to find new directions.

Escarlent still makes the pilgrimage, together with her mother's family, and they turn it into an annual, entertaining day trip. In 2007, Sanne Derks joined them on their pilgrimage.

At the entrance to Calvary Hill, Escarlent bought a little bar, a packet of dollars, and a university degree from two different stands. She explained: "This year I want to open a bar. This tiny one has beer on every table, it has a huge fridge, and they have a food menu. That's exactly what I would like to see in my real bar! I will change it, and also the name. Now it is called San Lorenzo." While scratching off the *n* of *San*, she continued: "I will call it Sas, as my friends used to call me Saskaya. Therefore I need a lot of money, so I bought these dollars. The university title degree is not to graduate, as I have at least two years to go. For me it symbolizes that I will enroll for next year and study."

After lunch at the picnic space on Calvary Hill, the group went up the road to the hill behind the chapel to hack out new stones and return the old ones. Everyone had to dislodge her own stones. Escarlent's mother, who went first, had some trouble chopping off parts of the rock. She laughed about it and joked, "I don't need that much, I'm not too ambitious." For her, extracting only tiny fragments of the stones meant she would have only a bit of "money and luck" in the coming year. Escarlent, by contrast, smashed down powerfully on the same rock, and with her first blow she dislodged a big piece. She smiled proudly and said with relief: "Yes! That is exactly what I need! Now I know I can stop being so stressed, everything will turn out all right!" She continued until she had collected so many stones that her big bag was half full.

When all had "worked in the mine," as they call the dislodging of stones from the holes, all started making *ch'allas* to their stones.[29] Escarlent rolled her stones up in colorful festoons, sprinkled confetti on top of them, dribbled pure alcohol on them, and lit some firecrackers. According to Escarlent: "The bangs will call Mary's attention to my wishes. The festoons and confetti show that it is a fiesta, and the alcohol is to please Mary." After making her own blessing, she went to the bags of her family and sprinkled beer over them while saying prayers. While Escarlent was performing her *ch'alla*, a piece of stone from another mine fell into her lap. She smiled and joked, "Look, the money is just falling from the sky," and she put the little stone in her bag. One of her uncles called a *sahumera* to perform a blessing on their stones and miniatures. Escarlent said, "I usually do not do a *sahuma*, as I do not trust other hands with my wishes."

The old stones had not yet been returned to the Virgin. They moved to a place away from the mine, and all the bags with old stones were emptied out on the same heap. The big stones were pulled out, and together the family started building a little house with a fence around it. "It is our own custom. Every year we construct a house together, just for fun." When the house was finished, another *ch'alla* was performed. Afterward everybody turned to go down the hill. Derks walked with Escarlent a little behind the rest, chatting. When they finally arrived at the picnic spot, the group was not yet there. "Ay," Escarlent said, "I forgot to take my stones and *alasitas* to the Virgin. Well, I am not going back. I will let them be blessed next week in the fiesta of *alasitas* in church."

A few days later the miniature food market took place in Quillacollo, and together with her mother Escarlent collected the necessary miniature foods. Escarlent explained, "We have thrown away the old, rotten, and discolored packages from our *alasitas* provision cupboard, and we made a list of all the things that are missing." At a stand of plastic and paper packages, they bought about thirty items, such as toothpaste, washing powder, cornflakes, canned tomatoes, and oil. While shopping for real miniature potatoes, meat, and groceries, Escarlent discovered a stand with miniature alcoholic beverages. Unhesitatingly, she bought two little bottles for the bar. After the purchase of little loaves and sugar, they entered the church. Both Escarlent and her mother had also brought their stones and *alasitas*. They put all their things on the ground, lit candles, and prayed to the image of the Virgin. After a few minutes, they asked the sacristan to bless their objects. Escarlent wanted to be sure that all objects would be blessed, so she clutched all her items in her arms, the dollars and university papers in her left hand, the bag of stones around her wrist, the bar tucked under her arm, and the bag of packages in her other hand. Her mother had put her car and dollars on top of the vegetables in the basket of foods. After the blessing, they sat at a table at the miniature eatery stand, where a miniature meal was shared. Escarlent explains:

> There are always days that you cannot eat at home and you have to eat in the streets. Therefore we have this meal, so we will always be able to find food easily on these days. We will eat the vegetables, meat, and bread we bought during this week. We do not make a special meal with it, but just use the ingredients when we cook. The other things are just symbolic, we do not eat them. But really, it works. One year we did not join this tradition, and the whole year we had problems. We forgot to buy sugar, for example, or when we wanted to buy bread, there was no bread left, things like that. Always something was lacking. But now, with the blessing of Urkupiña, we can be sure that everything will turn out fine.

In her house the *alasitas* are placed in different spots. One shelf of the provision cupboard was dedicated to all the *alasitas* from the food market in Quillacollo. The miniature bar was put on her desk in her bedroom. She had drawn a new name and signboard, and also changed the menu. Her bag of stones, together with the university title and dollars, was put in the living room, under a little table that served as a house altar. Under a picture of the Virgin, her bag was placed next to those of her brother and mother. Escarlent explained, "So Mary can watch over our wishes."

Class and Materialistic Aspirations

The pilgrims who come to the fiesta to dislodge stones and buy *alasitas* are a heterogeneous group, from all socioeconomic and ethnic backgrounds. As M. L. Lagos points out, pilgrims "learn to ask for gifts they may reasonably expect to receive."[30] Rich pilgrims ask for luxury articles, such as cars, big houses, and swimming pools—objects they would be in a position to buy anyway before going to the fiesta. Poor pilgrims ask for basic things, according to their needs. Presidential candidates ask to become president, for example; students ask for higher grades; shopkeepers, for improved trade; young couples, for babies, a house, or land; and petty traders for *pan del dia*—daily bread. The pilgrims adjust their petitions according to the possibilities afforded by their circumstances, and in this way everybody can receive something from the Virgin. For years, for example, Escarlent had dreamed of opening a bar in the city. During that time, she had saved some investment capital, and she was already looking for a place. She bought a bar in miniature to ask Mary for her blessing on her new project. Sometimes pilgrims buy *alasitas* of many more things than they actually expect to receive. Of the many miniatures Yomar bought, only a few will become reality, but by buying so many miniatures, she can give direction to her life. Yomar also explained that it was the fourth time she asked for a car: "Sometimes the Virgin does not make it possible the first time you ask for it, but she wants you to put more effort in it."

While poor pilgrims are aware that others ask for impressive luxury goods, they tend to accept these differences. A poor petty trader explained this attitude: "Some pilgrims are too ambitious and ask too much. They ask for more than they need. However, if you have more, your life is also more complicated, as you cannot be satisfied anymore. You always want to have more. This can be dangerous, because the Virgin will know when your requests are not sincere anymore." By contrast, the rich justify their requests in terms of the faith they have in the Virgin and the hard work they have put in to reach their material goals. The rich also have more money to invest in rituals, in the miniature objects, *sahumas*, and *ch'allas*. For them, making bigger offerings justifies their larger requests. Escarlent's miniature bar, for example, cost 30 BOB, around a day's salary for people from the lower class. She also bought a bundle of 50,000 dollars for 5 BOB; poorer pilgrims can buy 10,000 dollars for 1 BOB. They offer less and hence receive less. The *alasitas* also promote a sense of well-being, because by buying 10,000 dollars in miniature for one boliviano, poor people can feel rich for one day in the year. This way they are able to give expression to their desires and aspirations to have access to large amounts of money.

It is hard to draw a line between material necessities and merely materialistic desires. In general, lower-class pilgrims tend to take the rituals more seriously. For them there is more at stake, and they hope to obtain what they need so desperately in their daily lives. Pilgrims from the higher class are more likely to parody the rituals when performing them; they joke about it, but just in case, they perform all the necessary steps in the right order to make sure they are able to receive what they want. Escarlent's mother joked when she did not manage to dislodge big pieces from the rocks, for example, but she still followed the entire trajectory with her objects. This also demonstrates that those who already have most of the things they need confirm their relationship with Mary in order to maintain the status quo or to improve their fortunate situation.

The church takes an ambivalent attitude toward the materialistic requests of pilgrims. On the one hand, every year during the fiesta of Urkupiña, an article appears in the newspaper that calls upon devotees to "leave behind their materialistic interests" and preaches about "spiritual values" of love, respect, and harmony. In a similar fashion, not all priests agree with the ritual of dislodging stones. One of the priests in charge in 2005 denied the existence of such a ritual completely. Another priest who worked in the parish in 2007 spoke of "pagan rituals that have to stop":

> These rituals will stop in a few years, as we have already started to build a large basilica at the top of Calvary Hill. We have already closed more than half of the mines by putting sand in them. We want to change the sanctuary into an absolutely spiritual one, like Lourdes in France or Guadalupe in Mexico. When the basilica is there, there will be no mines left, and the pilgrims will stop dislodging stones. They will only come with spiritual intentions.

On the other hand, most priests do not have a problem with blessing the objects. One priest explained: "What can I do? If I make these people feel better by blessing their items, why not?" Another priest explained: "Well, they make materialistic requests, but all people come together with their families to buy the paper money and other *alasitas*. The practice of *alasitas* contributes to the unity of the family, and therefore it is no problem at all." The practice is thus variously condemned or condoned by representatives of the Church, and varying social positions influence the meanings given to these religious artifacts and the practices that surround them. While for some the meanings are related to survival, for others they represent general feelings of security, or a mere joke or toy.

Collaborative Mary

The tangible miniature objects and stones make the requests more vivid and solid, and their materiality makes them appealing. As we have seen in the case of Escarlent, all members of the family make their personal requests, hack out their own stones, buy their own *alasitas*, and even personalize them, as Escarlent did by changing the bar's name and menu. The personal relationship with the objects symbolizes the intense, unique, and personal relationship between Mary and the pilgrims. The case also shows how the trajectory of the stones and *alasitas* turns into a personal biography, as every person decides what steps to take and in which order. Escarlent and her family extracted new stones before returning the old ones, for example. Escarlent did not find it necessary to perform a *sahumera* or return for a blessing, but her relatives did. Still, Escarlent prays, burns candles, makes numerous *ch'allas*, and takes her objects to be blessed by the priest. Despite numerous variations, a dominant line can be discerned in investing objects with religious meaning.

In fact, faith is invested in the objects. But what role do the objects play in the relationship between pilgrims and Mary? What are pilgrims' perceptions of the objects? All pilgrims who bought the *alasitas* explained, "You have to have faith, otherwise it will not work." Just buying the miniature objects is not enough; you have to believe in the possibilities and pray. Escarlent's aunt explained: "Miracles won't fall from the sky. But because we cannot make it in daily life, we look for other possibilities. Religion is one of them. It is the only hope we have!" She continued: "The people have to make the effort. If one wants to buy a house, for example, one can buy it as a miniature, but one also has to search and earn money to buy land and a house oneself. It is the Virgin who makes the person continue his search." This is in line with what Karen McCarthy Brown has written about voodoo religion. The spirits function as a catalyst in confronting problems yourself and making your own goals clear in your mind.[31] As Escarlent explained: "The university degree, for example, symbolizes my wish to enroll at university. Together with the effort of dislodging stones, it functions to encourage me to study. Of course, if I do not study, I will not pass. But I don't want to disappoint the *Virgencita*. When I asked her help in front of her image, I also promised her that I would do my utmost in studying."

Interestingly, pilgrims use the objects to remind them of their own goals. By displaying them on the house altar and renewing them after a year, they are again and again confronting their ideals and aspirations, and the need to work toward fulfilling them. After a year they are able to evaluate their projects and, if necessary, adjust their aims. With Mary as witness, pilgrims feel empowered to work toward their goals. The pilgrims do not attribute success to Mary's powers alone. All emphasized that they themselves have to make an effort. In the reciprocal relationship with Mary, the pilgrims have to promise something in return for her help. As Escarlent said: "It is not an unconditional gift of the Virgin. No, I promise her to study, to work, to make money and search for a bar." Evidently, pilgrims expect the Virgin to work with them in the realization of their requests. Before Mary, the pilgrims create a spiritual economy in which they promise her, and themselves, to continue their steps in striving for upward mobility.

If their requests are not realized after a year, the relationship with Mary is not affected. The pilgrims always blame themselves for failure. They say they did not have enough faith in Mary or explain their disappointment by the way they performed their rituals. Sometimes pilgrims make the same requests for many years. If they have invested enough, they are able to receive from Mary.

The objects function as reminders, both for the pilgrims and for Mary. A pilgrim's account illustrates this: "In our house we have a little shelf with a painting of Mary. I put the miniature house in front of her, so she won't forget about us. She will see the house and that will remind her to help us. At the same time, we see the little house. It reminds us what we are working for." This way, the objects are not only used as a tangible reminder to Mary but also function as reminders for the pilgrims to keep their goals in mind. Both Mary's effort and that of the pilgrims are necessary to convert the miniatures into what they represent. Thus the pilgrims take a collaborative approach in their relationship with Mary.[32] They do not take a "deferring approach," in which the outcome of their request is passively handed over to Mary's judgment, but they expect Mary to shape the circumstances for them to realize their goals. The pilgrims take the steps necessary to finish a study, buy a car, or construct a house, and the Virgin intervenes by creating the conditions necessary to achieve the particular goal. Pilgrims do not change the structures of inequality that underlie their petitions, but in the sacralization of things, they can find a stimulus for their own actions, creativity, and inventiveness to change what is in their power.

Mary makes it easier for pilgrims to accomplish what they want. When Escarlent was able to dislodge a big part of the rock in a single stroke, she felt reassured that in real life it would likewise be easy to obtain what she wanted. Pilgrims' belief in Mary's help offers them trust, patience, and confidence in their actions. It gives them faith in the feasibility of their projects. By making Mary part of their struggles, pilgrims actively try to change their situations. By engaging in a public act of extracting stones and offering miniatures, they experience a sense of control: they are no longer the victims of circumstances, but their narrators.[33] Furthermore, the objects ensure that the relationship with Mary is not limited to a few moments at the pilgrimage shrine but continues at home. The objects function as a vehicle of empowerment in a spiritual exchange economy between the pilgrims and Mary.

Conclusions

In this chapter, we have looked at the materialization of pilgrims' requests in stones and *alasitas* at the pilgrimage site to the Virgin of Urkupiña in Quillacollo and tried to give insight into what these objects reveal about the relationship between pilgrims and Mary. We have employed Kopytoff's notion of the biography of things to do so, as the trajectory of the objects, together with human interactions with them, construct meaning in the objects and thus can reveal much about pilgrims' relations with Mary. The biographies of objects show that the Bolivian pilgrims construct a spiritual economy in which they appeal to the spiritual world to improve their chances of upward mobility. In doing so, they collaborate with Mary. Stones and *alasitas* embody not merely a simple wish for divine intervention in one's economic distress but a complete intertwining of the religious, social, and economic domains, whose joint forces allow the pilgrims to cope with the difficulties of life and motivate them to work toward solving them.

For most of the pilgrims, there is no contradiction in approaching Mary for materialistic improvement. Due to the conflation of the Andean goddess of fertility Pachamama with the Virgin Mary during the colonial era, the material domain is conflated with the spiritual domain as well. The pilgrims' investments in objects and offerings are exchanged for Mary's intervention in bringing about the conditions necessary to accomplish their goals. The objects function as the currency of these transactions, but, like modern currency, their real value lies in the faith placed in them.

A spiritual economy is established in which pilgrims negotiate with Mary for intervention in their daily lives. All pilgrims emphasized that they themselves had to make an effort to realize their requests. They work together with Mary in a collaborative relationship, in which she has the power to shape possibilities and empower the pilgrims to continue their own steps toward the fulfillment of their economic aspirations. This study thus demonstrates religion's empowering role: by making Mary part of their problems, the pilgrims become active agents in changing their class position within the boundaries of their personal possibilities. The stones and *alasitas* operate as reminders of this relationship. During the pilgrimage, personal meanings are attributed to the objects, and the objects' biographies show how they are tangible mediators between Mary and the pilgrims. Back home, the objects are displayed on home altars, where they serve as reminders both for Mary to help the pilgrims and for themselves to remember what goals they had in mind. The use of miniatures and stones offers pilgrims trust and confidence in the feasibility of their projects, and in them they find spiritual encouragement to take the steps necessary to realize their economic aspirations.

At the same time, however, this chapter shows that pilgrims ask for things they can reasonably expect, and, when they cannot turn their requests into reality in the coming year, they do not lose trust in Mary but rather readjust their goals and wishes. To a certain extent, they have to accept their own economic limits in the relationship with Mary. Poor people cannot ask Mary for villas, nor do they have the assets to find, buy, or build a villa. They are encouraged to accept their own poor economic situation and the differences between theirs and that of others. Their negotiating power in improving their individual class position is hence not really sufficient to bring about changes in structural inequalities. This means that empowerment and disempowerment go hand in hand. Pilgrims motivate and activate themselves with the *alasitas* and stones, but at the same time they keep realistic considerations in mind when confronted with inequalities, and they accept their economic circumstances. While the rich justify their privileged class positions by the hard work they have done to achieve their goals, the poor accept economic inequality and try to keep their heads above water by making tiny offerings to Mary in the hope that she will reciprocate.

PART IV

Bodily Fluids

Fluid Matters

Gendering Holy Blood and Holy Milk

Willy Jansen and Grietje Dresen

Bodily substances figure prominently in Christian and Islamic beliefs and practices. At the intersection of the physical or material and the symbolic, they provide an interesting starting point for a discussion of the material dimension of religion.[1] In this chapter, the bodily fluids blood and milk will be singled out for closer scrutiny. Christians see in the blood of Jesus Christ a source of redemption. He is seen as having sacrificed his blood for the salvation of humankind, and American fundamentalist Baptists, for example, narrate their conversion in terms of being "washed in the blood of Christ."[2] Catholic believers symbolically drink the blood of Christ during mass; venerate relics of the Precious Blood in places like Saintes, Bruges, Mantua, or Boxmeer; organize themselves in devotional societies such as the Missionaries of the Precious Blood, and celebrate commemorative feasts of the Precious Blood on the first Sunday of July.[3] The sacrifice of blood for atonement, for forgiveness for one's sins and reconciliation with God, is an equally important symbolic complex in Islam. By following the Qur'anic example of Ibrahim, who showed his surrender to God by his willingness to offer his son but was allowed by God instead to make a "noble sacrifice,"[4] Muslims ritually slaughter an animal during the Feast of Immolation so that the blood can run free in an offering to God. Shi'ite Muslims participating in the Ashura ritual in Iran, Iraq, Lebanon, and other countries scourge their backs in submission to God until they bleed, while others touch this sacrificial blood and smear it on themselves or their infants in order to partake in its blessing.[5]

Whereas the religious connotations of blood abound, at first sight those of mother's milk seem less plentiful. In Christianity, holy milk is especially associated with the Virgin Mary nursing her child. The image of Maria Lactans, probably modeled after the goddess Isis suckling the infant Horus and showing parallels with other lactating goddesses, such as Yashodă and Hariti, was popular in early Christianity and in the late Middle Ages, as can be seen in several beautiful artworks in which Mary feeds her child or shares her milk with saints. As in the case of the Precious Blood, relics of Holy Milk have attracted pilgrims and been venerated at many sites, including Bethlehem, Walsingham, Chartres, Laon, Genoa, Rome, Venice, Padua, Avignon, Aix-en-Provence, Toulon, Paris, and Naples.[6] In Islam, animal milk is considered a gift from God. Officially, Islam has no female deities whose holy milk is especially blessed, yet in everyday lived religion, Mary is considered a prominent feminine model, leading Muslim and Christian women to engage in similar devotional practices.[7] Suckling is discussed extensively in religious sources, as we will show below. This raises the question of how and why bodily fluids of blood and milk figure so prominently in Christianity and Islam. Why do bodily fluids matter in religion? What makes them susceptible to religious meaning?

The important role of the material body and bodily fluids in religious thought, and the mutual impact and, at times, conflation of substance and symbol deserve attention in our efforts to understand the materiality of religion. Bodily metaphors in religion provide models for, as well as models of, experience.[8] Bryan Turner has noted that "we use the body as a convenient way for talking or thinking about the moral and political problems of society. Our sense of good and evil has also drawn heavily on bodily metaphors."[9] Strangely, in his article Turner disregards Mary Douglas, who sees the body as a natural symbol for the social order.[10] It is also interesting to examine possible parallels between the discussion of bodily substances in kinship studies and their symbolic use in religion. Before elaborating on the substantive discourse on blood and milk in Catholicism and Islam, we will review these theories to explore how they can help us understand why bodily fluids matter, and what makes them useful concepts to think with in religion.

Human bodies are usually male or female, and bodily metaphors build structures of masculinity and femininity upon the body. Whereas blood seems gender neutral, milk is feminine. Bodily metaphors can function as gender scripts that express as well as prescribe people's experience and behavior as gendered beings.[11] So, how do specific metaphors of blood and milk and their uses in religion construct men and women as religious beings? We will argue that the religious meanings given to these substances contribute to constructing men and women as different and hierarchically placed religious and social subjects. On a more material level, these fluids operate to limit women's religious space in comparison with that of men. An analysis of holy texts and visual arts in Christianity and Islam that refer to bodily fluids, as well as actual religious beliefs and practices, as observed in Europe by Grietje Dresen and in Algeria and Jordan by Willy Jansen, can offer insight into the system of meanings embodied in these symbols and their implicit gender messages.

The Substance of Religion

In her study of kinship, Janet Carsten has shown that anthropologists have regarded substance in different ways.[12] The concept can denote a separate thing (such as the blood of a woman), a vital part or essence of that thing (as when the woman points at her daughter and says, "That's my blood"), or the fluid of which her body is composed (as when she uses the same expression to discuss the medical aspects of this matter). This interest in substance evolved from anthropological research into the cultural perceptions of the properties of blood, milk, saliva, and sexual fluids, in an effort to determine how their mutability and transformative potential contributes to constructing kinship.[13] By the transmission of bodily substances—semen during intercourse and conception, blood and milk during a child's growth—both a new child and its kinship relations are created. In the process, one substance is transformed into another, as the mother's milk that feeds the baby is transformed into its blood and bones. Gendered substances—semen, milk—thus are changed into gender-neutral substances, and vice versa. David Schneider, perhaps the first anthropologist to use substance as an analytical term, points out that family members are related by the fact that "they share in some degree the stuff of a particular heredity. Each has a portion of the natural, genetic substance."[14] He distinguishes this "natural substance" from "blood," which he terms a "symbolic substance." In Schneider's eyes, it is important to differentiate between the symbol and what is allegedly symbolized. Carsten criticizes him for maintaining this dichotomy too strictly. These insights from kinship studies are relevant to a discussion of the role of substances in religious studies because they point to lines of thought that can help us understand why and how substances matter. First, we can say that substances matter in creating relatedness, and second, we can affirm that any analytical distinction between the symbolic and the material should take into account their conflation in actuality.

In religion, too, relatedness is created by the transmission of substances. By sharing ritual food during the Feast of Immolation, Muslims connect with each other and with Allah. Catholics eat bread and drink wine in the sacrament of the Eucharist, during which, according to the Catholic doctrine of "the mystery of transubstantiation" and the "real presence of Christ," these foods are transformed into Christ's body and blood. The worshippers who consume these substances believe that they ingest the Word incarnate and obey the scriptural injunction to "bear God in your body" (1 Cor. 6:20). In this ritual, we see the transformation from material to symbolic substance and vice versa, and with the movement of the substance between the priest and the believers, a relation is established between Christ and humans, who now share in his holiness and embody his sacrifice. By sharing the same religiously imbued material substance, religious kinship and community are created. The fluid matters now really matter, not merely as a symbolic act of transmission but as an embodiment of the spiritual. This ritual transmission and transformation of substance fortifies the individual believer bodily, creates spiritual bonds of relatedness between believers and the supernatural and a sense of community among them, and materializes the spiritual connection, thus conflating the symbolic and the material.

"Matter out of place" That Really Matters

Certain bodily substances are central in the ideological order of relatedness, but the dominant substance may change over time and place. In perceptions of kinship, blood is still a dominant concept for expressing relatedness, but recently it is coming to be replaced by the notion of genes. In both Catholicism and Islam, a strong blood discourse still exists, but a discourse of milk has decreased in importance, as we will see. Among bodily substances, fluids especially seem to matter. In particular, all substances related to sexuality— such as semen, vaginal secretions, (menstrual) blood, or human milk—are prone to playing a metaphorical role. In order to understand why and how human "wetware" provides such apt and readily available material for making moral judgments, expressing and imposing social hierarchies, and expressing religious values, we need to look more closely at Mary Douglas's theory of "matter out of place."[15]

Douglas points to the important symbolic function of bodily substances that are no longer contained within the body. She terms them "matter out of place" because they are physically outside the body and argues that they serve a crucial role by functioning as metaphors for things that are outside the social order. In many cultures, matter out of place is ambiguous and taboo; it can lead to ritual impurity and danger but also to its opposite. She puzzles over the fact that abject substances like pus or blood outside the body are sometimes seen not as defilement, as an impurity opposite to holiness, but as part of holiness: for instance, one of the markers of St. Catherine's holiness is that she deliberately drank a bowl of pus to punish herself for the revulsion she felt at the wounds she was tending. Bodily matter out of place can thus be seen as sacred or polluting, pure or impure, powerful or dangerous.[16] Its classification is not fixed and may change with how fluids have left the body, or whose body they come from. Given the potency of bodily fluids in evoking a sense of ambiguity and taboo, it is interesting to see what effect they can have on gender.

Holy Blood, Polluting Blood

Blood is frequently used as a metaphor in social life. Close ties and similar identities (or the lack thereof) may be expressed as: "She is of my blood"; "They have blue blood"; or "This is a bloodless relation." In different areas or religions it can have different meanings.

Whereas in Western Europe the heart is seen as the center of life in the body and the seat of feelings, elsewhere this role can be played by the liver or the intestines. Instead of speaking of a "bleeding" or "broken heart," an Arab might say that his liver hurts, and in the biblical book of Jeremiah the intestines are allotted this function, much to the bewilderment of exegetes and translators. Blood symbols therefore gain meaning only in specific cultural or religious contexts. This fluidity, however, should not blind us to structural similarities.

Douglas states: "The metaphors of the physical body and of the new undertaking relate to the perfection and completeness of the individual and his work. . . . Holiness requires that individuals shall conform to the class to which they belong. And holiness requires that different classes of things shall not be confused."[17] Although blood may indicate the essence of life, identity, and belonging, blood that has left the body confuses categories, and thus the social and religious order. Yet such disorder, which disturbs pattern, also provides the material of pattern. It "has potentiality. It symbolizes both danger and power. Ritual recognizes the potency of disorder."[18] Blood that has crossed the boundaries of the body fills us with ambivalent emotions. It reeks of danger, affecting the sensorium in ways that surpass the merely rational. Some people faint when they smell or see blood; others feel disgusted or shocked. After an accident, spilled blood is washed away quickly. Yet blood is simultaneously and typically seen as very powerful. Exchanged, it creates blood relations or blood brotherhood. It is used in magic spells and sacrifices.

Douglas presents a number of recurrent ways in which humans deal with such matter out of place.[19] A first way to assuage the unease and disturbance caused by lost blood in society, and to control the anomaly, is to ignore it or remove it from sight. Good girls do not show that they are menstruating; media advertisements for hygienic products use blue rather than red ink to show their absorption power; and politicians speak of precision bombing or collateral damage rather than the spilling of human blood. During wars, whether the media can show blood is a hotly contested issue: both parties try to control the showing of blood because it can have important political effects, both for the struggle and for its legitimation.

A second way to control the anomaly of blood is to sequester its danger and potential power through ritual. The anomalous substance that creates impurity must be cleansed through a ritual of purification. The impurity caused by all bodily excretions—not only the blood of menstruation, childbirth, disease, or violence, but also semen, vaginal fluids, urine, excretions, vomit, and pus—must be washed away and then ritually cleansed. Through this ritual, the anomalous impurity strengthens and affirms what is pure. In Islam, blood is a pollutant that has to be cleansed away before religious acts. All mosques have fountains for minor ablutions and showers for a major purification. Moreover, blood is a forbidden food.[20] In Judaism impure persons cleanse themselves through the *mikvah*, the ritual bath, and in Catholicism the holy-water fonts near the entrance of churches, although nowadays often standing dry, are reminders of this cleansing ritual.

Douglas also suggests a third reaction to deal with anomalies that disturb the social order: to reclassify the abnormality and bring it into a higher order, that of the divine. This occurs in Christianity when the blood shed by Christ is reclassified as Precious Blood, a sacred substance and the source of redemption. In the writings of the Apostles, it is regarded as synonymous with Jesus' Passion and Death.[21] In contrast to the blood removed from sight, this blood is shed publicly, like the blood spilled in honor killings and ritual beheadings.

These examples show that the structural aspect of blood is not that it can be holy or polluting but that it is a fluid that matters because it is out of the normal order, and as such imbued with religious power. Just like fluid matters themselves, the symbolic significance with which it is invested is not immutable and permanent. When we look at blood, how can its symbolic meaning fluctuate with gender?

Gendering Blood in Christianity

On the one hand, in many ways women and men have similar bodies, and blood seems to be a gender-neutral fluid. On the other hand, men and women are not the same in the ways they lose blood and in the ways meanings are attributed to this blood. For women, bleeding indicates the rhythm and phases of their fertile life. The menarche (first bleeding) signals the onset of the reproductive phase and menopause (last bleeding) indicates the end of it. Blood can stand for life power and reproductive health. Blood out of place, however, could indicate the loss of this life power—lack of conception, miscarriage, infertility, abortion. Female bodies suffer more frequently than male bodies from uncontrollable blood loss, because women menstruate and give birth, resulting not only in blood loss during labor but also in lochia until forty days after delivery. Moreover, their social role as carers means that they handle blood in daily life more often than men. They attend more regularly to the wounds of their children and partners, or do so more often professionally as nurses. They clean up the fluid matter left by family members, the sick, and the wounded. Women's ability to give birth, but also the monthly "curse" and their caring activities, are part of a culturally prescribed femininity that defines them as "Woman."

Women's bleeding and women's handling of blood seems to have influenced women's space in Catholicism in a number of ways. At present, women and women's blood are not defined as impure by the Catholic Church, but certain religious texts, rituals, and arguments still remind us of such a connotation. The Scriptures mention women's impurity due to menstruation and childbirth. Leviticus 12:1–5 states:

Yahweh said to Moses: Tell the Israelites: If a woman conceives and bears a male child, she shall be ceremonially unclean seven days; as at the time of her menstruation, she shall be unclean. On the eighth day, the flesh of his foreskin shall be circumcised. Her time of blood purification shall be thirty-three days; she shall not touch any holy thing, or come into the sanctuary, until the days of her purification are completed. If she bears a female child, she shall be unclean two weeks, as in her menstruation; her time of blood purification shall be sixty-six days. When the days of her purification are completed, whether for a son or for a daughter, she shall bring to the priest at the entrance of the tent of meeting a lamb in its first year for a burnt offering, and a pigeon or a turtledove for a sin offering. He shall offer it before the Lord, and make atonement on her behalf; then she shall be clean from her flow of blood.

According to this part of the Old Testament, a woman's birthing and loss of blood during and after giving birth defiled her and excluded her from sacred spaces, rites, and functions until a male priest made an offering on her behalf. They constituted a gender-based pollution that needed purification. Moreover, not only her own sex but also that of her children was involved. The defilement was twice as long when the child was a girl. Leviticus specifically informs Judaic law and, to a much lesser extent, Catholic doctrine. Officially these rules do not apply to Catholic women. Nevertheless, such texts are present in the Old Testament, which people may have in their houses and read. Moreover, it seems to have informed the ritual of churching, although the Catholic Church does not explicitly refer to Leviticus in this context.

Until the 1960s, it was common among Dutch Catholics for a woman to undergo the ritual of churching (*Benedictio mulieris post partum*) about a month to forty days after giving birth.[22] Only she and the priest participated, on a normal weekday, in this non-obligatory, simple, and scarcely noticed ritual. Women commonly understood it to be necessary before they could enter the church and, especially, partake of communion again. This meant that mothers were not present at the baptism of their babies, as this needed to be done as soon as possible after birth to save the soul for heaven in case the infant died. In the churching ritual, the woman knelt with a burning candle outside the door of the church until the priest came to bless her with holy water. He read Psalm 23, let her touch the end of his stole, and led her into the church, guiding her to the altar while saying: "Enter into the temple of God, and adore the Son of the Blessed Virgin Mary, who gave you fruitfulness of offspring." Normally the new mother would offer her burning candle and/or some flowers to Mary and make a donation to the church. At the conclusion, she would be sprinkled with holy water again and blessed.

Since Pope Paul V (1605–21), the churching ritual has been presented simply as an act of thanksgiving.[23] Before that, the clergy plainly considered it a purification rite, as historical sources show. Paula Rieder, for example, describes how in 1270 Bishop Nicholas Gennent of Angers sought to control the churching ritual in order to avoid mothers of illegitimate children also purifying themselves in this way.[24] Despite the Church's repeated insistence that it is no longer a purification ritual but a rite of joy and thanksgiving to God for the birth of a child, many of the women who underwent churching nevertheless considered it to be a rite of transition and purification.[25] They were given the impression that this ritual was needed for them to be reintegrated into the religious community and to be considered worthy of participating in the Eucharist again. Some women found it humiliating, because they had to wait outside at the door of the church—in our own mothers' case, the side door—because they were not allowed to enter the church before the priest permitted them to. Dutch Catholic women increasingly started objecting to this rite. Why, they asked, did they need to be reintegrated into the church in this humiliating way after having given birth? Since the 1960s, this ritual has disappeared in the Netherlands, and the baptism of new-born babies has been delayed so that mothers can participate in the ritual and their motherhood be blessed.[26]

The early Christian and medieval idea that a woman becomes impure because of the blood she loses during and after childbirth recalls Judaic law. Mary, being a Jewish woman, followed this law and was ritually purified before she entered the Temple forty days after the birth of Jesus, when she presented her son to Simeon. The churching ritual imitates this event, which is commemorated on Candlemas (February 2). According to later Catholic doctrine, as in the dogma of Mary's Immaculate Conception, Mary as mother of God was born without original sin and therefore not subject to the pains of childbirth and other physical inconveniences of ordinary women, and thus never impure. The issue of whether Mary menstruated led to heated debates in the Middle Ages, because some assumed that she needed to have menstruated in order to be able to produce milk to feed her child.[27] According to the dogma of Perpetual Virginity (affirmed at the Lateran Council of 649), her hymen remained intact during both conception and birth. That she nevertheless followed the purifying rite was explained and valued as a sign of obedience to the priestly laws. This explanation was convenient when the Catholic Church wanted to uphold Mary's example to women.

A more fundamental impact of women's bleeding on women's place in Catholicism lies in reference to their bodies as an argument for why they cannot become priests, bishops, or popes. The fact that a woman's body—in particular, her menstruating and birthing body—does not resemble that of Christ disqualifies her for the priesthood. In Catholic doctrine, women are not allowed to perform the sacrament of consecration because they do not resemble Jesus, as males do. They have a different body, a body that may pollute the holy altar when they menstruate. In Douglas's terms, this would confuse categories and mix the holy with the impure.

Men's dealings with blood are quite different from women's. Men bleed more often on the battlefield or spill blood as soldier, terrorist, executioner, or as the groom who deflowers his bride. The authority to kill, butcher, or deflower is what in many cultures defines men as "Man"; militarism and sexual prowess are recurrent aspects of hegemonic masculinities. Women can also be killers, soldiers, or terrorists. Their share in such things is even on the increase, but they are still a minority there. Displaying male blood, provided it is in the proper context, such as heroes who have sacrificed their lives for their nation or martyrs who have died for their faith, has historically been seen as more appropriate than displaying female blood. Such blood becomes a sign of men's uncommon sacrifice or holiness. In this line of thought, all the blood seen in depictions of the suffering Christ as he is tortured and crucified accrues to his holiness. At times, reclassification strategy conflicts with the removal strategy that is intent on moving all spilled blood out of sight, leading to heated discussions—for instance, on the violence and blood shown in the movie *The Passion of the Christ*, by Mel Gibson.

It is through consuming holy male blood that salvation can be reached. It is the male fluid that matters most. The bleeding heart of Christ is sometimes accompanied by the bleeding heart of Mary, but it is Christ's blood that is consumed, not Mary's. Thus blood also matters in defining gender, because male blood is valued more highly than female blood, making the first more often holy and precious, and the latter more often abject. This expresses an unequal gender valuation. Moreover, it helps to exclude women from the priesthood.

Gendering Blood in Islam

In Islam, the limitation of women's religious practice due to their impurity caused by blood is much more explicit. Pollution is a part of everyday life; the normal functioning of the body brings impurity upon it. The Qur'an admonishes believers to wash themselves before praying when they are polluted (S. 4:43 and 5:6). The main verse on pollution does not specify the blood of menstruation or childbirth:

> Believers, do not approach your prayers when you are drunk, but wait till you can grasp the meaning of your words; nor when you are polluted—unless you are traveling the road—until you have washed yourselves. If you are ill and cannot wash yourselves; or, if you have relieved yourselves or had intercourse with women while traveling and can find no water, take some clean sand and rub your faces and your hands with it. Gracious is God and forgiving.

Although the verse addresses male believers, it is not gender specific. Pollution is a fact of life for both sexes, and both need to purify themselves. Only pure believers can pray or fast, touch the Qur'an, enter the mosque, or go on pilgrimage to holy places. A minor ablution will purify the uncleanliness incurred by contact with unclean substances such as: pus; alcohol; solid, liquid, or gaseous emissions from the body; the hands of non-Muslims; or forbidden foods. A major ablution is needed after sexual intercourse, menstruation, childbirth, or death.

During research in Algeria in the 1980s, Willy Jansen found that Muslim women closely associated ritual ablution and sexuality, in particular, having had sex or preparing for sexual intercourse. The word for washing had the double meaning of having sex.

Women who allowed outsiders to see their wet hair or who went too frequently to the bathhouse were talked about as being very sexually active. One woman said she preferred to get up in the middle of the night to wash herself after intercourse, in order not to expose her nightly activity. Another woman reported that it was very improper for a young wife to let her father-in-law see her carrying washing water in the morning, as he was supposed to remain oblivious of the possibility that she had had sex with his son. Washing was also a euphemism for menstruation. A woman who said that it had been seven weeks since she washed meant that she did the ritual purification after her last menstruation seven weeks ago, and thus let it be known that she was probably pregnant. Women had to purify themselves more frequently than men both because they menstruated, gave birth, or had polluting caring roles and because they had less control over intercourse. Although men also became impure by intercourse, women saw their lack of control over sexuality as a lack of control over being religious. As one woman exclaimed: "A woman is like a sink. Her husband dumps everything in her and she has to wash and wash. A woman keeps washing. When I was young I had to sleep every night with my husband and went every two or three days to the bathhouse. I had to because I prayed."[28] Women's reproductive bodies and roles meant more impurity for them, and as a result more restrictions on their religious activity. Praying, fasting, or making a pilgrimage are not valid acts when performed in an impure state. During the month of Ramadan, many women lost a few days because they were menstruating. They had to make up for this later, when it was much more difficult, because they had to do it alone. Given the difficulties of remaining pure as a young wife and mother, many Algerian women in their child-bearing years temporarily gave up praying five times a day, although they practiced fasting, because they found it too inconvenient to continually be cleansing themselves. It was mostly postmenopausal women who could fully commit themselves to religion.[29] Due to the purity rules, women had more days with no access to or protection from the supernatural than men, and as such were de facto lesser as religious persons. Moreover, this more frequent impurity of women led in practice to a common perception of women as impure beings.

Male blood, although in principle similarly polluting, has been invested with other meanings. Martyrs for the faith, mostly male, are not considered to have become polluted by their death, as other people are, but go straight to heaven. The blood drawn by male Shi'ite participants in the passion play in Karbala on the 10th of Muharram, commemorating the death of Ali's son al-Husain, is considered sacrificial blood. It is invested with powerful meanings, and some onlookers take some of this blood to bless their children. In a similar vein, followers collect the blood that flows from the bodies of flagellating Sufis in Morocco to gain protection from the evil eye,[30] and only males are allowed to slaughter a sacrificial animal—preferably a ram, free from any physical defects, whose blood must flow unhindered. According to Anton Blok, the ram is the meritorious animal for sacrifice. It is known for its "virility, sacrality, beauty, strength, and fierceness," and it is closely identified with human males, especially male heroes. He found evidence for the ritual prominence of rams and their close identification with male leaders and heroes in art, myths, legends, and narratives. According to Genesis (22:9–13), Abraham sacrificed a ram caught in a thicket by its horns instead of his son Isaac, a substitution that is commemorated every year by millions of Muslims in the slaughter of sheep during the Feast of Immolation. In Blok's words: "no other animal came so close to epitomizing the character of what was considered the ideal and quintessential male leader."[31]

The greater value placed upon the male sacrifice and the male sacrificer serves as a model for gender differences, but it works only on a symbolic level, not a material one. Paradoxically, the ram's virility—only one male is required to cover roughly fifty ewes—makes male sheep also the relatively dispensable sex. Not many rams are needed for the reproduction of a flock of sheep, and so they can readily be used up as objects of consumption and ritual. In many other sectors of animal husbandry, such as chickens, pigs, or cattle, males also face an early death: but then the scarcity of male animals can help to boost their ritual value again. This paradox is rarely discussed in analyses of such systems of classification. It shows that ritual value need not necessarily be correlated with material value and actual substance.

Milk

In the history of Christianity, milk had life-giving meanings similar to those of blood. The promised land is described as the land of milk and honey in the Old Testament (Exodus 3:7–8). Human milk was physical and spiritual nourishment for God and ordinary mortals. In the New Testament, milk stands for the beginnings of belief in the word of God (1 Cor. 3:1–2). In Islam, the fast during Ramadan is broken with milk and dates, and in the Qur'an milk is considered a prized food: "In cattle too you have a worthy lesson. We give you to drink of that which is in their bellies, between the bowels and the blood-streams: pure milk, pleasant for those who drink it."[32] In paradise, believers are promised that they will find "rivers of milk for ever fresh."[33] As a bodily fluid, milk seems to be feminine par excellence. The high value attributed to milk in both religions leads to the expectation that it could counterbalance the gender imbalance created by blood.

Holy Milk in Christianity

In early Christianity and the Middle Ages, Mary's milk functioned as a key icon of relatedness—between Mary and her child, between Mary and God the Father, and between God, Mary, and devotees. The oldest representations are found in Byzantine and Coptic icons of the Galaktotrophusa (Mother of God as Milk Giver). In a Florentine painting of ca. 1402, now in the Cloisters in New York, Mary's milk is presented as on a par with Jesus' blood. In this painting we see a kneeling Jesus, who shows his wounds to God above; opposite him kneels Mary, of a similar size, who shows her right breast to God and simultaneously points her right hand toward the sinners kneeling at their feet to ask mercy for them. Their holy fluids form the connection between the believers and their Lord. That the milk has a very strong appeal can be read in the inscription: "Dearest son, because of the milk I gave you, have mercy on them."[34] In his *Confessions,* Augustine compares mother's milk with heavenly consolation, and elsewhere he cannot decide whether to receive nourishment from the wound in Christ's side or from Mary's breast. Here he too puts holy blood and holy milk on the same level.[35] In the writings of theologians such as Clement of Alexandria, Anselm, and Bernard of Clairvaux, God's breasts are conflated with Mary's breasts. In Ode 19 of the Odes of Solomon, an early Christian collection, the masculine and feminine aspects of the Holy Trinity transform into each other. The milk of salvation, which imparts life, proceeds from the Father, but the womb of the Virgin received it, and she underwent conception and gave birth.[36] In the words of Margaret Miles: "In communities under siege from plague, wars and malnutrition, the Virgin's breast was a symbol of God's loving provision of life, the nourishment and care that sustain life, and the salvation that promises eternal life."[37]

In pictorial art, this symbol of God's loving provision of life was long present in the representation of Mary's breast—a male provision embodied in a female fluid. Mary's bare breast while suckling her child can be admired in such paintings as: Ambrogio Lorenzetti, *Madonna of the Milk* (fourteenth century); Filippino Lipi, *The Virgin and Child* (ca. 1457); Jacopo Tintoretto, *Nursing Madonna* (sixteenth century); Jean Fouquet, *Madonna Surrounded by Seraphs and Cherubs* on the Melun Diptych (ca. 1450); Hans Memling, *Tondo with Nursing Madonna* (1485–90); Pieter Coecke van Aelst, *Holy Family* (ca. 1525); Joos van Cleve, *The Holy Family* (ca. 1512–13); Peter Paul Rubens, *The Madonna with the Periwinkle* (sixteenth century); and Rembrandt van Rijn, *The Holy Family in the Carpenter's Shop* (ca. 1634). The lactating Mary is also represented in statues, such as the *Lady of the Cloister* in the cathedral of Tarragona and the *Virgin of the Port* in Plasencia, Spain, and in frescoes by unknown artists in fourteenth- and fifteenth-century churches such as St. Proculus in Naturns or the Basilica of San Zeno in Verona.

Some early images seem either to lack craftsmanship or to express a certain discomfort with showing a lactating mother. Mary's body is rigid and straight. Her breasts seem dislocated, either placed near her shoulder (Memling, van Aelst) or too far apart (Fouquet). They are partly covered by her hand or by an oversized baby Jesus, are blackened, as if their skin differed from the rest of her body (the statue in Tarragona), or are privatized by the protective presence of Joseph. Fouquet's painting has been discredited by the rumor that the nursing woman it depicts is actually Agnès Sorel, the mistress of Charles VII, who so bewitched his treasurer, Étienne Chevalier, that he commissioned the painting.[38] Yet the very sight of a lactating Mary is powerful, as it is reminiscent of people's earliest experiences and so connects with the intimate life of common believers, drawing parallels between everyday and supernatural relatedness, between physical and spiritual relatedness.

Depictions of a lactating Mary become even more powerful when she does not reserve her milk for Christ but shares it with special devotees. In the painting *Madonna of Grace* (ca. 1508), by Filotesi dell'Amatrice, Mary squeezes her bountiful milk out of both breasts in a half circle of rays into the mouths of the souls in purgatory. Such representations of Mary were quite common in the fifteenth and sixteenth centuries in Italy.[39] Miracles are attributed to Mary's milk. She is reputed to have spilled some milk while nursing Jesus in a cave in Bethlehem on their flight to Egypt, and this miraculously turned the black cave walls white. From the twelfth century on, lactating women visited this Milk Grotto, as they believed that eating some of the white powder from the walls would increase their supply of milk.[40] In the English fourteenth-century *Queen Mary Psalter*, one illustration shows "How a monk with an ulcerated mouth was laid out as dead, and how the Virgin healed him with milk from her breast."[41]

Mother Mary's breast and milk were also central in the Dominican cult of the Virgin's milk. Mary was believed to have shared this milk of paradise with such saints as the Blessed Paula of Florence (who received it in a vision in 1368) and St. Bernard of Clairveaux (1090–1153), in what is called the Lactatio of St. Bernard. In some early depictions of his adoration of Mary as intercessor to the Savior, the passing on of the faith is given visual form by a Holy Mother who spouts milk from her breast into St. Bernard's mouth or onto his head.[42] In other depictions, he merely watches devoutly while she nurses her baby.

Unlike blood, milk has lost much of its meaning in Christianity. Mary's bare breasts and her milk have undergone a process of resignification, followed by erasure from religious art. In the late fifteenth century, techniques of graphic representation improved, and Mary's breasts were depicted more and more realistically. They took on the softness and roundedness of real breasts and came to evoke feelings of domestic intimacy. Moreover, female breasts gained other meanings in artworks of that time: they signified penitence, served as erotic assets, or became objects of study. Reacting to this development, the Catholic Church banned the nudity of sacred figures in art at the Council of Trent in 1593.[43] Not only naked breasts but also physically well-endowed and motherly feminine forms receded into the background in religious art, to be replaced by an elfin, childlike Virgin. Images of the frail and ephemeral Virgin of Lourdes or Fatima are now the most popular, and reproductions of such images can be found in many churches and homes. In the late twentieth century, women's visits to the Milk Grotto in Bethlehem also declined sharply, and knowledge of the shrine is dying out. According to Susan Starr Sered, most Christians in the area now "have either never heard of it or claim that it is a place visited only by superstitious women."[44] Believers have distanced themselves from the bodily materiality of Mary, and her feminine forms are more and more disguised.[45]

Today, the lactating Mary appears only in provocative and, in the eyes of believers, blasphemous art, such as the photograph *Untitled #223*, by Cindy Sherman, in which a plastic breast is offered to a baby; a series of icons by the Dutch artist Myrna Rasker, in which Mary suckles a green, monstrous animal; or in the elephant-dung-covered black breasts of *The Holy Virgin Mary* (1996), by the British-Nigerian artist Chris Ofili. Cardinal O'Connor called this painting "an attack on religion," and the Catholic mayor of New York, Rudy Giuliani, found this work so offensive and disgusting that he threatened to stop the subsidy of 7.2 million dollars to the Brooklyn Museum if they dared to display it in their exhibition *Sensations* in 2000.[46]

Religious as well as nonreligious art depicting the nursing Mary, as well as the reactions to it, demonstrate two of the ways of dealing with matter out of place explained above: reclassifying it as holy, or labeling it as degrading and removing it from sight. In the late Middle Ages, milk was represented as the nourishment of God and a sacred substance. It stood on a par with blood and could even be conflated with it, as when Christ was described as a nursing mother by mystics such as Catherine of Siena and Juliana of Norwich.[47] Yet when women's breasts came to be associated too closely with sexuality, prostitution, and nakedness, Mary's milk lost its former power and was largely obliterated from religious discourse. At the same time, the presentation of the Holy Blood in crucifixion scenes became increasingly strong and violent. Rather than analyze this straightforwardly as a unilinear marginalization of the feminine, however, we should take a more complex view. Carolyn Walker Bynum, for instance, has shown that these changes varied considerably across regions and that at times gender differentiation was far from clear.[48] Gail Paterson Corrington warns that the models provided by bodily metaphors should not be assumed to be the "true" representation of "the way things are." For instance, motherly metaphors might serve as models for how women ought to be, rather than being based on women's experiences and being representations of them, or they might symbolize something other than what we expect. In her alternative, critical-feminist interpretation, pre-Christian metaphors derived from childbirth and nursing, once applied to female deities, were "appropriated for application to male models as descriptive of modes of communicating divine wisdom and protection."[49] In her view, the metaphor of nursing described the saving activities of the male savior-deity, not those of Mary, as Mary is not the savior. This gender reversal, however, is an uncomfortable metaphor, and thus does not dominate early Christian art. Moreover, she argues, "the motif of the lactating mother was eschewed in Mary's case because she is a model for "overcoming" the material by the spiritual, the female by the male."[50] In other words, in early Christianity, first, the symbol of women's milk, indicating women's divine power, was appropriated and resignified to indicate the milk of salvation emanating from the divine father and later the divine child, as male deities were substituted for female deities, and second, the substance of women's milk lost its role as religious signifier.

The Milk of Relatedness in Islam

Islamic doctrine has never given any place to female deities or holy figures with blessed milk. Yet the Qur'an, even more often than the Bible, heralds Mary as a worthy example for women. This respect for Mary has occasionally led to devotional practices among Muslim women similar to those among Christians, including ones connected with Mary's milk.[51] In western Turkey, Muslim women are known to visit a Milk Grotto to partake in the healing powers of the fluid seeping through the stones.[52] And the Milk Grotto in Bethlehem is also visited by Muslim women.[53]

In Islam the religious investment in mother's milk has taken a different turn, however. The symbolic role of human milk has gained special meaning because of Qur'anic verse 4:23. This verse specifies the marriage partners that are forbidden, and these include a foster mother and foster siblings. Glosses on this verse say that women who suckle children who are not born to them establish kinship relations with these children. Through the milk it ingests, a child who has been suckled takes in the essence of its nurse and her family, thus becoming related to them. A woman's milk, transmitted to a child, transforms their relation into a kinship relation, one with religious approval. Children will always recognize and respect their foster mother and her family, and the tie between them is so strong that it is considered incest for them to intermarry.[54]

Islamic jurisprudence raised the question of who owns human milk and established a claim that a husband owns his spouse's milk. In everyday life, women managed to gain some control over their milk, and they used it subversively to include outsiders in their kinship network or exclude others as marriage partners for their children. With the arrival of bottled milk, the need for fostering was reduced, as was the ability of women to create relatedness through their milk.

Conclusion

Analysis of the religious meanings given to blood and milk in holy texts and religious practices in Christianity and Islam shows that these bodily fluids matter in creating cogent links between people and their religion. In them, a conflation of material and spiritual substance embodies and anchors religion. This is not necessarily a direct and clear connection with only one interpretation, but rather an ambiguous, complex, and fluid process. In the symbolic universe of Christianity and Islam, conflicting and at times opposing connotations are given to blood and milk. Blood can refer to holiness, purification, and salvation, life-giving qualities. But it can also take on the opposite connotations, being regarded as a destructive, polluting substance. Milk can represent God's love, divine intimacy, or motherly protection, on the one hand, and nakedness, blasphemy, or offensive sexuality, on the other. Meanings given to matter are fluid and subject to change.

In the process of the transmission and transformation of bodily liquids, people are constructed not only as believers but also as men and women. The gendering of blood and milk functions to represent, on a symbolic level, the social hierarchy between men and women. According to Douglas, ideas and rituals about purity and impurity caused by bodily fluids work on both expressive and instrumental levels. On the first level they "are used as analogies for expressing a general view of the social order," and on the second level "we find people trying to influence one another's behaviour."[55] The different evaluation given to male and female blood thus expresses and constructs the hierarchical social order between the sexes.

Some scholars who have discussed the pollution caused by female blood have warned against automatically reading into it gender inequality and the submission of women. Elizabeth Faithorn suggests that substances are polluting, not the people who secrete them. Male substances, such as semen, can be as polluting as female substances, such as menstrual blood.[56] We have seen above that this also is true for the substances considered polluting in Islam. Thomas Buckley and Alma Gottlieb warn that the focus on the polluting and disempowering aspects of menstruation has prevented us from seeing that in some contexts it can have the opposite meaning and effect—that of celebrating and effectuating women's power.[57] We agree with these authors that masculine pollutants should not be neglected and that women should be seen not only as victims in the cultural constructions of purity and taboo but as active agents participating in creating these cultural constructs and thereby gaining empowerment. Women's active role in Marian pilgrimage, for example, expresses a preference for the female mediator over the male God, and attributing alternative meanings to Mary, in line not with doctrine but with women's own aims and empowerment, indicates a clear religious agency and interpretative power.[58]

Gendering is neither automatic nor static, but fluid and dependent on context. Yet despite the fact that it is substances, not people, that are considered taboo and despite women's own interpretations of blood and milk as life-giving and indicative of their reproductive role in society, we should not ignore the underlying tendency to devalue female blood and laud male blood, as well as the effects this has on women as believers. The gender connotations encased in the religious meanings given to blood and milk do express different power positions in society and religion. Indeed, both textual data and believers' experiences show that impurity through the fluids related to sexuality, excretion, illness, and death is not gender neutral, because women, due to menstruation, childbirth, submission to their husbands in sexual matters, and caring tasks have far less control over their impurity and are far more frequently impure. As a result, not just their fluids but women themselves are at times considered impure beings and as such considered religiously less worthy.

In speaking of gender, Douglas prefers to remain on the symbolic level, as can be seen when she discusses the dangers attributed to sexual fluids: "I suggest that many ideas about sexual dangers are better interpreted as symbols of the relation between parts of society, as mirroring designs of hierarchy or symmetry which apply in the larger social system."[59] By contrast, we have argued that the idiom of blood and milk also functions on the material level, influencing people's behavior and actual access to religious practice and ritual. Because of their blood, women cannot perform the sacrament of transubstantiation in the Catholic Mass or the sacrificial killing of sheep at Islamic feasts. It significantly limits women's space to practice their religion or become religious leaders, compared to that of men. Thus cultural constructs have consequences in the material world.

The relation between the diminished religious power of feminine fluids and changing power relations between the genders is less clear. The dominance of male blood over female blood and female milk is certainly an expression of gender and gender inequality, but in two ways it is a contested dominance. First, secularization has significantly decreased the impact of such religious symbols and beliefs on actual gender relations. Second, our research has shown that many of those Catholics who still believe—in particular, women—prefer the alternative religious practice of Marian pilgrimage over going to church and obeying religious authorities.[60] In doing so, they empower and resignify Mary and endow her with other and more powerful feminine qualities than the Church has done. In other pilgrimages, we found women who no longer reinterpreted Mary to regain respect for their body and bodily fluids, such as the Swedish middle-aged women who discovered themselves as big, strong, and happy on the way to Santiago, or the Spanish and American women who deposited their menstrual blood on the altar in the cave of Mary Magdalene in France as a way to connect with mother earth and the forces of life.[61]

"When you see blood, it brings truth"

Ritual and Resistance in a Time of War

Elizabeth A. Castelli

In the opening years of the twenty-first century, we find ourselves in a reenchanted world, a world distinctively different from the one foretold just a few decades ago by social scientists who were convinced that religion was a withering vestige of an bygone era and sensibility, on its way to cultural extinction. We could have a long and energetic debate about why and how these social scientists got it wrong. But whether religion was really ever on its last legs, or merely escaped notice, or was overshadowed by other global forces during the last half of the last century, most would now agree that religion is back—with a vengeance. We tend to notice religion's resurgence on the global stage as it has come to be interwoven with militant nationalist politics, whether the Hindutva movement in India, Islamist movements throughout the Middle East and elsewhere, or Christian dominionism in the United States. Less visible at the moment are the ways in which religion comes to be mobilized in opposition to nationalism, militarism, and state violence, and it is this less visible form of religious activism that I am interested in exploring here.

I will focus on a group of pacifist Catholic activists who drew upon their theological and sacramental traditions in an attempt to render the effects of war making and violence visible and to challenge the logical underpinnings of state violence. They did so through an act of political provocation that focused on the most intimate material element of war: human blood. Although the *materiality* of the blood was not in itself of primary concern to the activists, its status as a substance—whether a religious and symbolic substance or an illicit and infectious one—came to play a central role in the subsequent federal trial of the four defendants, all members of the Catholic Worker movement, in a federal court two and a half years after the action itself. Here we will seek to understand the work that blood performs in this religiously inflected act of political protest and to set that performance in a broader historical and interpretive frame.

The opening scene is an Army-Marine Recruiting Center in the Cayuga Mall in the village of Lansing in upstate New York, in the days just before the U.S. attack on Iraq in March 2003. The main players in the drama are four members of the Catholic Worker Movement (Peter De Mott, Clare Grady, Daniel Burns, and Teresa Grady) and a Sergeant in the U.S. Army named Rachon Montgomery, who worked as an army recruiter. The Army-Marine Recruiting Center in the Cayuga Mall had been the setting for numerous antiwar demonstrations and actions in the months leading up to the Iraq war, including a die-in on December 21, 2002, a vigil on Good Friday 2003, and an action on St. Patrick's Day 2003, which became the focus of a federal indictment and prosecution.

On March 17, 2003, just days before the U.S. invasion of Iraq, Peter De Mott, Clare Grady, Daniel Burns, and Teresa Grady entered the recruiting center and poured small amounts of their own blood in protest of the impending invasion. They read this short statement, which opens with a quotation from St. Patrick:

"Killing cannot be with Christ."

"Our apologies, dear friends, for the fracture of good order." As our nation prepares to escalate a war on the people of Iraq by sending hundreds of thousands of US soldiers to invade, we pour our blood on the walls of this military recruiting center. We mark this recruiting office with our own blood to remind ourselves and others of the cost in human life of our government's war making. Killing is wrong. Preparations for killing are wrong. The work done by the Pentagon with the connivance of this military recruiting station ends with the shedding of blood, and God tells us to turn away from it. Blood is the symbol of life. All life is holy. All people are created in the image and likeness of God. All people are family and everyone is loved by God. Dr. Martin Luther King reminds us that "we are called to speak for the weak, the voiceless, for the victims of our nation, for those it calls enemy, for no document from human hands can make these humans any less our brothers [and sisters]."

We come here today with pictures of Iraqi people—mothers, children, those who have been the victims of US bombardment and sanctions for the last twelve years. We come here with love in our hearts for the young US service people, also victims of war making.

We find hope in these dark times when sisters and brothers around the world resist the spirit of hatred and violence, lift up prayers for peace—together with works of peace.[1]

After reading this statement, the protestors then knelt down and prayed. Soon afterward, they were arrested by Tompkins County sheriffs and charged with trespass and destruction of property. They were subsequently tried in a county court, where a hung jury resulted in no conviction.[2]

Scene two is a federal courtroom in Binghamton, New York, September 2005. After the local court's nonconviction of the St. Patrick's Four, as De Mott, Burns, and the Grady sisters came to be known, the U.S. Justice Department stepped in and charged the four with trespass, destruction of property, aiding and abetting, and conspiracy to impede a federal officer in the discharge of his official duties. The last was a federal felony charge, one carrying the threat of a multiyear prison sentence.

How scene one (the St. Patrick's Day action) came to be recalled and interpreted in scene two (a federal courtroom two and a half years later) is at the heart of the drama.

The basic facts of the matter were not in dispute in the federal trial of the Catholic Workers in September 2005. The defendants in the trial consistently admitted their involvement in the action, but they argued that their actions were lawful under—indeed, required by—the U.S. Constitution and international law, since their actions were aimed at interrupting illegal activity on the part of their government.[3] Invoking the example of Nazi Germany and the moral failures of that country's complacent and complicit citizenry in the1930s and 1940s, the St. Patrick's Four argued that their action was not only legally defensible but legally required. Moreover, they all identified their religious convictions and communal religious experiences as the moral grounds for their action. As Catholic Workers, the four were committed to nonviolence, antimilitarism, and pacifism. Clare Grady described the contours of the Catholic Worker commitment in her opening statement: "In the Catholic Worker tradition, we seek to practice the works of mercy and turn away from the works of war. Works of mercy are to feed the hungry, give drink to the thirsty, clothe the naked, visit the imprisoned, care for the sick, and bury the dead. And the works of war destroy crops and land, seize food supplies, destroy homes, scatter families, contaminate water, imprison dissenters, inflict wounds, burn and kill the living and terrorize all."[4]

By situating their actions within the tradition of the Catholic Worker, these activists aligned themselves with a movement founded in New York City in the 1930s by Dorothy Day and Peter Maurin at the height of the Great Depression.[5] The movement is rooted equally in a religious insistence upon the dignity of each individual person and a political critique of all economic and social relations that undermine individual human dignity. Religious commitment and political critique then come together in action in the world: the "works of mercy" of which Clare Grady spoke in her opening statement and nonviolent acts of resistance. Indeed, nonviolence is the hallmark of the Catholic Worker ethos. From the 1930s onward, Dorothy Day insisted upon a complete rejection of all forms of violence and promoted the view that radical social change can be brought about by individuals who undertake a daily practice of radical nonviolence, consisting of traditional Christian spiritual practices (e.g., praying and fasting), traditional forms of political protest forms (e.g., picketing), and complete noncooperation with evil. The Catholic Worker movement initially attracted a considerable following in the 1930s, with its penny-a-copy newspaper called *The Catholic Worker* (in conscious imitation of *The Daily Worker*), but it experienced a significant drop in adherents during the Second World War, when its radical pacifism remained unwavering even in the face of the rise of fascism. Indeed, Dorothy Day's commitment to nonviolence was absolute, and it overrode all other considerations. Insofar as nonviolence was, for Day, the bearing required of Christians, her concern was, as Anne Klejment puts it, "moral purity, not victory."[6] By the 1960s, the movement regained a place of influence in the antiwar movement, advocating a wide range of nonviolent actions to protest the U.S. war in Vietnam, including refusal to participate in the system of military conscription or to pay taxes related to military spending, as well as the destruction of draft cards.[7] Men who were closely affiliated with the Catholic Worker were among the first to destroy their draft cards; David Miller, a member of the Catholic Worker, was the first to be sentenced to prison for damaging a draft card.[8] As the history of the Catholic Worker unfolded in relation to the antiwar movement, however, significant fissures emerged between the Catholic Worker, on the one hand, and, on the other, what became known as the "ultraresistance," a movement that was more willing to embrace some forms of property damage and yet still lay claim to the mantle of nonviolence. In the early twenty-first century, after the death of Dorothy Day and the dispersal of authority to individual Catholic Worker communities, the question of the character of nonviolence came to be answered locally.

Catholic Workers call upon the sacramental and liturgical elements of their tradition far more than upon the Bible, though they make general references to sacred texts, especially the stories of Jesus in the gospels, and they certainly ground their identity and practice in an ethic derived from the Sermon on the Mount (e.g., "blessed are the peacemakers"). But the Catholic Worker is not a biblicist movement, and although scripture plays a critical role in its liturgical and contemplative life, the actors in this story are far less likely than, say, Protestant evangelical activists to turn to the Bible for prooftexts. Interestingly, however, they were at one point, at least, misapprehended and derisively dismissed as Bible readers. Tompkins County Deputy Sheriff Jeffrey Baker was questioned about the two men—Peter De Mott and Daniel Burns—whom he encountered in the lobby of the recruiting station:

Q: And what were these individuals doing when you observed them?

A: They were either sitting or kneeling on the floor reading some type of propaganda.

Q: What do you mean by that?

A: Scriptures or I don't know.[9]

Rooted in the Catholic pacifist tradition, the St. Patrick's Four drew upon the concept of the mystical body of Christ and the traditional sacramental theology of Catholicism to articulate the rationale for their action. These theological notions emphasize the interconnectedness of the human and the divine in the mystical body, the sacrificial efficacy of symbolic reenactments of the spilling of blood through the sacrament of the Eucharist, and the centrality of an imitation of Christ's suffering in the everyday lives of Catholic Workers—a suffering for others. In a sense, these activists place themselves symbolically in a genealogy of Christian martyrdom. Just so, a Catholic Worker who was in the audience in Grinnell, Iowa, when I spoke about this case in November 2006 offered his own testimony concerning an occasion in which he and others had used their own blood in a similar action. As he explained it, their purpose in pouring their own blood was to demonstrate their difference from those whose action they protested: as he put it, "we wanted to show that we were willing to spill our own blood but not the blood of others." This claim echoes that of longtime Catholic Worker activist Tom Cornell, who, writing in 1968 about a shift in tactics in the nonviolent antiwar movement, argued, "Even a nonviolent revolution, or rather, especially a nonviolent revolution will demand blood, our blood, not theirs, and that's the difference."[10] This symbolic expression, by which blood stands simultaneously for self-sacrifice and the refusal to shed the blood of others, is also frequently repeated by members of the antinuclear Plowshares movement. As Greg Boertje-Obed, a Plowshares activist and ex–army officer, put it in an October 2000 interview with sociologist Sharon Nepstad, "When we pour blood, we are saying that we are giving our lives and we will not shed anyone's blood."[11]

While situating themselves within the framework of Catholic liturgical and sacramental thought, the St. Patrick's Four also see themselves in the lineage of other American activists for radical social change: direct-action abolitionist Harriet Tubman, civil rights workers Martin Luther King, Jr., and Rosa Parks, advocates for women's suffrage such as Susan B. Anthony, and social critics like Henry David Thoreau.[12] In their defense, they sought to bring into view the extended networks of affect and solidarity in which their lives are embedded—their natal families, their families formed through marriage (indeed, they all emphasized their experiences as parents as formative of their pacifism), their Catholic Worker communities, and their sense of connection to and solidarity with the victims of U.S. military action around the world. One or more had spent time in Central America in the 1980s; in Vieques, Puerto Rico in 2000; and in Iraq after the Gulf War.

The action of the St. Patrick's Four can be plotted on a historical trajectory that runs from the antiwar movement during the Vietnam era, with its spectacles of resistance (such as the burning of draft records with homemade napalm by activist Catholic priests Philip and Daniel Berrigan and seven others at Catonsville, Maryland, in May 1968[13]) through the antinuclear activism of the Plowshares movement, which in the 1980s began performing gestures that were simultaneously literal and symbolic, seeking to enact the biblical prophecy "hammer swords into plowshares" by applying their own homely hammers strategically to B-52 bombers and nuclear-weapon-bearing submarines and often pouring blood onto the instruments of war.[14] The first use of blood in such protests took place in what has come to be called the Baltimore Customs House Action on October 27, 1967, when four men entered the government building and poured blood on the draft files for 1-A (ready for service) conscriptees. The idea of spilling blood in a symbolic gesture of protest emerged in a meeting between members of the Baltimore Peace Mission, led by Philip Berrigan, and a lawyer named Philip Hirschkop. According to the biographers of the Berrigan brothers, Hirschkop had suggested the use of blood as an alternative to more radical ideas for the destruction of property at the draft-record site. Initially, Philip Berrigan rejected the idea as "the tepid proposal of 'just another bourgeois lawyer,'" but in discussion with fellow activist David Eberhardt, who saw "pouring blood in a draft office . . . as a prophetic stroke worthy of Amos and Hosea," Berrigan not only was persuaded but began to elaborate a consciously theological interpretation of the act: "The blood could be seen as a surrogate for the blood of Christ, he envisioned, and its pouring could be interpreted as a symbolic act of Christian purification—a kind of echo of the sacrifice of the Mass."[15] The statement of purpose distributed to reporters at a nearby rectory can be seen as a model for the statement of the St. Patrick's Four thirty-five years later, beginning with a characterization of the act of voluntary blood spilling: "*We shed our blood willingly and gratefully in what we hope is a sacrificial and constructive act. We pour it upon these files to illustrate that with them and with these offices begins the pitiful waste of American and Vietnamese blood 10,000 miles away. That bloodshedding is never rational, seldom voluntary—in a word—non-constructive. It does not protect life.*"[16]

The actions of the St. Patrick's Four, then, can be plotted genealogically back to these earlier antiwar actions and read as a reenactment of them in a new political context. And yet the theological, liturgical, and historical framework of the St. Patrick's Four, not surprisingly, came into serious and ongoing conflict with the rules of evidence and the constraints inherent in the judicial process that was their federal trial. Like their predecessors who saw the courtroom as itself a space for activism,[17] the St. Patrick's Four sought repeatedly to enter into evidence their lifetimes of learning and lived experience—from the politics and activism of their parents during the Cold War and the Vietnam War to their own experiences in Nicaragua and El Salvador in the 1980s, at actions staged at the School of the Americas at Fort Benning, Georgia, and more recently in Iraq in the wake of the Gulf War. Peter De Mott, a veteran of both the Marines and the Army (and also a participant in Plowshares actions in the 1980s[18]), spoke of his growing recognition of his own complicity in the conduct of that war, for which, he said, "The realization that I share in the guilt for the slaughter of innocents . . . causes me to feel remorse and sadness and experience the pangs of a grief-stricken conscience."[19] The court repeatedly instructed the defendants that they had a right to say what they "believed" or "felt" about the impending war in Iraq—that is, that they believed or felt the war to be illegal—but they were barred from introducing evidence that would establish the factual bases of these beliefs and feelings. The court did, however, also allow the defendants considerable latitude to enter into testimony their own personal narratives, despite expressing exasperation at times at the level of detail the defendants offered up in evidence.

While the defendants struggled to put their actions in the broadest possible pacifist context, the prosecution worked equally hard to reframe the actions of the Catholic Workers as extremist violence and even, implicitly, terrorism. What follows is an analysis of the terms of the debate within the trial, focusing in particular on the contestation over the status of the activists' blood, with a brief reflection on the broader implications of this particular example for thinking about embodied religion in public zones.

The evidence I draw upon is the transcript of the federal trial of the St. Patrick's Four. The document runs to almost nine hundred pages, recording verbatim a five-day trial. The transcript is a wonderful document, for it preserves verbal tics, moments of frustrated inarticulateness on the part of some of the participants, occasional flashes of eloquence and humor, glimpses of ordinary humanness displayed even between adversaries, and struggles over the terrain of justice and making bodies count.

The actions of the St. Patrick's Four and their allies on December 21, 2002, on Good Friday 2003, and on March 17, 2003, made strategic use of individual bodies in order to try to make visible what business as usual in a militarized society seeks to obscure. The action on December 21, for example, was a die-in at the recruiting center, during which individuals lay down on the floor and thereby placed their bodies both physically and symbolically in the way. Placing their bodies in the way, performing death, enacting and thereby experiencing an uncanny stilling in the midst of the "just doing my job" recruiting activities of the station, the Catholic Workers sought to dramatize and make visible the materiality of death. But in the testimony one also encounters the ordinariness of bodies, their limitations, their capacity to tire and to require various forms of relief. Thus, as Danny Burns testifies about the action on December 21, he observes:

> There was a march at the mall across the street which was organized very quickly using E-mail. . . . Parked at YMCA across the street wearing black with signs pinned to our shirt saying No War to Iraq. No War to Iraq. Another—other signs asking the government not to go to war. And we marched in the mall, which is very similar to Oakdale Mall. I think it's owned by the same company, actually. And we just walked around like, you know, if we walked around the mall in single file like, you know, see folks getting exercise at the malls going on. That's what we did. And we shopped and I did my Christmas shopping after, you know, while I was there, and we spent a little money, but at the same time we showed in the spirit of Christmas that, you

know, shopping isn't the only thing. That we have to stop and think about what—what our government is doing and ask them not to do it. Peaceful ways. . . . We walked into the recruiting center and we lied [*sic*] down. I got as comfortable as I could because I didn't know how long I was going to be there, and some people did take down posters and put up some of the posters we had that were brought, that we used in the march across the street. And we read Martin—Dr. Martin Luther King's Christmas sermon, which calls for Americans to speak out against war, especially during the Christmas season. And I didn't expect to be arrested. I thought they would leave us there for a couple hours and then eventually we'd all have to go to the bathroom, we would leave.[20]

Burns's description of this action juxtaposes and analogizes one kind of bodily performance with another—walking in the mall to protest, walking in the mall to exercise, walking in the mall to shop. He also focuses in his description of the die-in on the profound ordinariness of bodies—their need for comfort and relief. Anyone with experience in civil disobedience will recognize this kind of focus on the bodily details: at the same time as one prepares to carry a message, to bear witness, to perform an act of noncooperation or resistance, one is also thinking "What kind of clothes and shoes should I wear? What should I carry in my pockets? What if I have to go to the bathroom?"

But if Burns's description emphasizes the ordinariness of bodies and ties the actions of daily life to the action of protest in a more or less seamless and routine fashion, the action of March 17 was of a different order altogether because of the provocative introduction of a particular bodily element into the action: blood.

Blood is central to the events of March 17, 2003. For the defendants, blood is a rich and evocative symbol that draws upon Catholic theology and liturgy. It is also a sacramental element. As we have already seen, its use in this context has numerous historical precursors in the antiwar actions of Catholic activists, going back to what became the "ultraresistance" during the Vietnam era and the antinuclear actions of the Plowshares. The action on March 17 was a demonstration against the impending war, but it was also a carefully orchestrated sacramental performance—the pouring out of blood recalling ancient practices of sacrifice and the Christian Eucharist, the prayers spoken after the pouring of blood onto the walls, the doors, the flag. The defendants speak repeatedly about the sacrificial, sacramental character of the blood and by doing so evoke the atoning and purifying qualities attributed to sacrificial blood in their tradition.

If the blood generates such sacrificial, purifying associations for the defendants, it does quite the opposite for the other side. The prosecutor, Miroslav Lovric, and the prosecution witnesses focused relentlessly on the fact that the blood was out of place—as if they had collectively been longtime disciples of anthropologist Mary Douglas and her classic slogan for explaining purity systems, "Dirt is matter out of place." The blood was also, in the prosecution's account, itself a weapon—thrown, splattered, spattered, dumped. (These are the verbs the prosecutor used repeatedly to describe how the blood was handled by the St. Patrick's Four.) Blood was, for the prosecution, one of the elements of the crime, a potent weapon in the destruction of government property, a nefarious tool used to impede and intimidate the recruiting officers in the execution of their duties. In making his case, the prosecutor swelled the quantity of blood, speaking in his opening statements of "bottles of blood," conjuring up mental images of brimming sanguinary containers, setting off an intuitive purity alarm: human blood doesn't belong in bottles, except in the antiseptic setting of a lab or a hospital. What was it doing here? Later, the prosecutor repeatedly called the blood a "biohazard" and emphasized the recruiting officer's anxiety that he might have been infected by exposure to this purportedly impure substance. Eventually, we learn from the testimony of one defendant after another that the blood had been carried to the site in small jars, that we are talking about sixteen ounces of blood altogether—two cups, one pint—not super-sized soda bottles or gallon jugs, images the prosecutor conjured up by using the term *bottles* and the verbs *throw*, *splatter*, and *dump* to describe the dispersal of the blood in the recruiting center.

From the prosecution's point of view, the very presence of the blood in this space constitutes a provocation; an act of force, intimidation, and threat (to use the language of the indictment); a source of injury and anarchic disruption; a biohazard. (The use of the term *biohazard* was, I believe, an effort to create an imaginative link between this action and terrorism, but more on that in a moment.)

During the prosecution's case, Sergeant Rachon Montgomery, the recruiting officer at the center that day, emphasized the upsetting character of his own encounter with the Catholic Workers' blood. Pointing to a picture, he said:

> That is the red substance, blood, that was splashed on the windows. The blood that was on the door, as I was locking the door, some actually did get on me when I was locking the door.[21]
>
> Basically, I locked the door, took the key with me. You know, I had a conversation, if I'm not mistaken, with Mr. De Mott based on, you know, what is the point, what are you doing? And he said, you know, basically they were there for whatever their reasons were. Mr. Burns continued to splash whatever blood he had left. Then the two of them on that paper basically began to read prayers and poems and different things like that and at that point, I kind of realized I had blood on my hands. I went in the office so I was kind of, you know, getting upset . . .
>
> Q: What were you upset about?
>
> A: Well, I was upset that, you know, I had blood put on my hand, you know. I don't know what type of diseases or anything so I was pretty upset about that. I was also upset they were actually there, you know, as we are trying to do our normal, you

know, normal duties. Nobody comes to work to go through, you know, this type of event. So it kind—it was upsetting to have to go through that when I'm just there to do my job.[22]

When Rachon Montgomery says, "I kind of realized I had blood on my hands"—not as an epiphany or a shift in consciousness but rather as a literal statement of fact and fear— one sees the action of the St. Patrick's Four distilled down to its essence, and on one reading, the failure of the action to achieve its intended goals. While Montgomery is clearly and sincerely shaken by the materiality and the proximity of the blood, he shields himself from it with expressions of anxiety about potential infection, desire for restored normalcy, a sense of duty interrupted. The hoped-for pricking of conscience has not occurred; indeed, in reporting his conversation with Peter De Mott, in which he asked him why the four were doing what they were doing, Montgomery can only narrate that "basically they were there for whatever their reasons were."

And yet, on another reading, this moment in the trial transcript signals the success of the action *as a ritual*, if a deferred success. That is, insofar as the action of the St. Patrick's Four was a ritual, it shows itself here actually to have performed the work of ritual: the actions of the St. Patrick's Four, like any good ritual, provoked an utterance ("I had blood on my hands"), whether or not its speaker believes or comprehends the deeper significance of the utterance. But, of course, the register of ritual is only one register in this drama: there is also the judicial register, by which the state sought to reframe the ritual act in felonious terms.

Indeed, probably the most pressing prosecutorial goal was to prove the existence of a felony conspiracy involving the blood. Here, the mechanics of the transfer of the blood from the bodies of the Catholic Workers into the jars that they carried to the recruiting center became a critical element in the case. How had the blood flowed from their bodies into the jars? Who drew the blood? Where was the blood drawn?[23] The prosecutor, who alleged on behalf of the government—the people of the United States—a criminal conspiracy, wanted details: places and names. The prosecutor and Danny Burns had an exchange about the matter during Burns's cross-examination, an exchange that has the makings and markings of a vaudeville act. The prosecutor has been trying unsuccessfully to elicit the address of the place where Burns's blood was drawn, and he gives it another try:

Q: And where was it again this blood was drawn?

A: In Ithaca, New York.

Q: I'm asking for a specific location.

. . .

241

A: From my arm. Right here (indicating).

Q: Okay. I was looking for the other location.

A: From my heart.

Q: Mr. Burns, you know what I'm asking. I want to know where you were when the blood was drawn. Whose house was it?

A: I know the house. I know whose house it was. I know their names. I know that the Attorney General of the United States is named Alberto Gonzales. I know that when he—before he was your boss—

MR. LOVRIC: Judge, I object.

A:—he signed a memo declaring the Nuremberg Principles moot and therefore—

THE COURT: Mr. Burns, please stop talking.

A: I don't trust to give you those names, sir.

THE COURT: You refuse to tell him the names?

THE WITNESS: I refuse to tell the government of the United States, this government, not the next one.[24]

So, while the prosecution seeks to prove a conspiracy and to treat the blood as in essence an illegal substance, Burns resists the efforts to compel him to implicate others. For his refusal, he is held in contempt of court and fined for that as part of his sentence at the end of the trial. And while the prosecutor repeatedly seeks to characterize the blood as a weapon, for the defendants, the blood remains a powerful and irreducible symbol. As they testified repeatedly during the trial, blood communicates in graphic and immediate terms. The goal of the March 17 action was to make the blood of war visible. As Peter De Mott testified: "I thought that the blood would serve as a very visual and graphic reminder of what happens in war. The loss of life that would occur. . . . A graphic reminder of the destruction and suffering and horror of war. . . . I used the blood to convey that message. And to remind others . . . and myself that life is precious. Life is sacred. Life is holy."[25] Later, he would testify: "I could see [the slaughter of innocents] that was coming if this war were to start so I used that blood to say no"; "The plan was, as I've said already, to bring the blood to the recruiting station, to pour it there and to use it as a marker, as a reminder, as an impassioned plea to turn away from the war before it would begin and not only to ourselves and to the recruiters, to recruits, but also to people around the world."[26]

Daniel Burns described his actions on that day, pouring his own blood in an effort to make present a studied absence, to give voice to the silence about blood in the materials about enlistment that were available in the recruiting center:

> I poured blood carefully. I didn't throw it or splash it; exaggerations. And it dropped down. And then I saw the flag; I poured it on the flag. And then I went over to the literature and I poured it on the literature and I poured it on cutouts I saw in the corner. And then I went to the front window and I poured blood on a sign that said $50,000 for college, $10,000 bonus sign on. And then I wondered why we just can't give them money for college and we have to risk them, our precious soldiers, precious children, why do we have to send them to war to give them college education? In that room, in all that literature, there's not one mention of blood. There's not one mention of shedding blood.[27]

Later, Burns situated his use of blood and its symbolism within a Catholic liturgical context. Blood's immediacy, Burns argued, makes it an especially effective mode of communication: "Well, I'm Catholic and it's part of our ceremony, the blood of Christ. Blood tells the truth very quickly. It tells the truth about war, and we were about to invade another country, and symbolically the use of blood in my religion, and it gets through all—it gets right to the heart. You know, when you see blood, it brings truth, and I want to bring truth about the war, and again, in that recruiting center there's no mention of blood."[28]

When the Catholic Workers poured their blood on the U.S. flag, the purity anxieties of the prosecutor and the prosecution witnesses became enflamed by the resulting stain. "Defacing and damaging the very symbols of peace and independence of our country was reprehensible," the prosecutor intoned during his summation.[29] As for the main prosecution witness, Sergeant Montgomery, the act of pouring blood on the flag and the "Army of One" banner that also hung in the recruiting center was especially egregious and upsetting to him. During her defense testimony, meanwhile, Clare Grady offered a counter-reading of the bloodied flag. As she put it, "On March 17, I poured my blood in this peaceful, nonviolent, symbolic action, to call attention to the supreme crime being committed in my name. . . . And that blood was already on the flag. We just made it visible. And I am so sad for all the blood that has been spilled in our name."[30] Later on in her testimony, she elaborated, focusing in particular on the sacrality accorded to the flag by many and her desire not to damage the sacred symbols revered by others: "I value life more than pieces of cloth. I also never wanted to disrespect someone's very sacred object . . . there is blood on that flag, and pouring it as we did was not the part that disrespected the flag. It's when we bloody that flag with criminal acts that shed the blood of the innocent, that's when you disrespect the flag."[31]

Meanwhile, under redirect questioning, Daniel Burns carried the argument a step further, making an almost magical claim about the blood poured out at the recruiting center.

Q [BY DE MOTT]: Do you believe you damaged property?

A: No, I don't believe I damaged property. I believe that—I believe that I didn't bring the blood to the recruiting center. I didn't put it there. I just made it so you can see it.[32]

The prosecutor sought throughout the trial to reframe the symbolic pouring of blood as a violent, even terrorist act. In his narration, the blood constitutes a biohazard, and its pouring out dangerously threatens the U.S. military in its pursuit of its goals, goals that he believes should always be preeminent. (As he put it in his summation, "The men and women in our armed military forces who fight to preserve those laws and the liberties that those laws guarantee to each of us must always prevail."[33]) As the prosecutor frames the action in his closing argument, military order, the recruiter's work ethic, and honor and purity are all disrupted by the pouring of blood:

I'm going to mention something and I only mention it because of the act. Think about what they did when they poured blood in that recruiting center. Rachon Montgomery I think said it best. You don't expect something like that when you come to work. Now Rachon Montgomery is doing his job. He's doing his duty. He's performing what all of us expect him when he enlists in the US Army and he is doing his duty for all of us. And then these people come in and pour blood and expose him to a biohazard. He goes to the doctor to get himself tested because now he's worried about contracting a disease because of these people. He inhales that stuff as it's in the office and being cleaned. That is absolutely disgraceful. Absolutely disgraceful.[34]

The prosecutor returns to characterize the defendants' action as violence and as a profound threat to the health of the recruiting officer when he summarizes the crime: "They threw a biohazard substance in Rachon Montgomery's space."[35]

The language of biohazard is, I venture, just one of several attempts by the prosecutor to gesture towards terrorism—without, mind you, ever using the word—in his framing of his case against the defendants. Indeed, throughout the trial and especially in his summation, the prosecutor sought to place De Mott, Burns, and the Gradys in a quite different political historical lineage from the one they claim for themselves: the defendants, according to the prosecutor, are not heirs to the legacies of Martin Luther King and other "patriots" (as he calls them) but are instead like the Ku Klux Klan, the bombers of abortion clinics, and the Aryan Nation—all of whom use murderous violence and terror against African Americans, abortion providers, and Jews in the service of their convictions. The prosecutor's rhetoric reaches a particular crescendo in his rebuttal closing argument:

> I submit to you, it will be a sad day in our history when somebody says to people like these defendants, it's okay to do this. . . . I submit to you it will be what I said before. It's anarchy. It's chaos. It's lawlessness. . . . People blow up abortion clinics in this country because of their view. Is that okay? Is it okay to burn—blow up an abortion clinic because you believe personally that doctors are committing murders in there? Is that okay? No, it's not. It's against the law. You're entitled to your view. You're entitled to your opinion. You're entitled to your driven thoughts on this topic of abortion but you can't blow up, burn down abortion clinics. Are you entitled, like a lot of extremist groups—Aryan Nation, they go around killing Jews. They blow things up. They demolish things. Timothy McVeigh. I'm not comparing anybody in here with Timothy McVeigh. I want to be clear about that.[36]

But then, disavowal notwithstanding, the prosecutor proceeds to argue that the defense's logic calls Timothy McVeigh to mind. "I'm sure Timothy McVeigh right now in hell thinks that he was right. That doesn't make it lawful."[37]

This argument rather remarkably remaps the conceptual and moral world to render the world's most powerful military the hapless victim of threatening, anarchic, violent extremists. And lest one misapprehend, the prosecutor has already laid out the relevant alliances and affiliations in the opening of his summation, where he addresses the jury in these words: "You, the jurors, in my view are serving a democratic, Constitutional process that is probably only superseded or more—the only other process that I can think of that's more important is if you serve in the armed forces. If you put your life on the line for this country and for our values."[38] And so, by this argument, the jury and the military are poised on one side of the equation, protecting the nation and "our values" against those on the other side: biohazard-splattering anarchists whose violence puts them in league (or at least on a par) with white supremacists, anti-Semites, and domestic terrorists.

The St. Patrick's Four were convicted of three of the four counts against them, but were found not guilty of the felony conspiracy charge. All four were sentenced in late January 2006 and served prison terms in federal penitentiaries. Daniel Burns received two six-month sentences to be served concurrently; Peter De Mott received four months in a federal penitentiary and four months of community confinement (a form of house arrest). Both Burns and De Mott were incarcerated in the Metropolitan Detention Center in

Brooklyn. Clare Grady received a six-month sentence, which she served in a federal detention center in Philadelphia. Teresa Grady served her four-month sentence in the Federal
Correctional Institution in Danbury, Connecticut. All four returned home.[39]

It is difficult to draw definitive conclusions about the meanings of this action by the St.
Patrick's Four and its judicial aftermath. According to certain measures, the action was a
failure: the recruiting efforts of Rachon Montgomery and his colleagues continue, unim-
peded by the actions of De Mott, Burns, and the Grady sisters; Montgomery's own sense
of obligation to do his job appears unshaken. On the other hand, the jury's refusal to
convict the four on the most serious charge—the felony conspiracy to impede through
force, intimidation, threat, or injury an officer of the United States in the discharge of his
official duties—suggests that the prosecution was unpersuasive in its efforts to criminalize
conversation and affiliation amongst these activists.

It also should be noted that the practice of using blood as a symbol in religiously
inflected political protest has never been uncategorically embraced, whether by Catholics
of less radical political persuasions or by activists who share the radical political vision
but question the efficacy of blood to communicate.[40] Interesting gender differences also
emerge in responses to these radical tactics; it is clear that some women, at least, were
often more suspicious of them, as Dorothy Day herself most certainly was.[41] As far back
as the antiwar actions of the Vietnam era, activists like the Berrigan brothers and other
members of the Catholic ultraresistance often found themselves on the defensive for their
political provocations. Philip Berrigan's well-known "Letter from a Baltimore Jail," a clear
evocation of Martin Luther King, Jr.'s "Letter from a Birmingham Jail," expresses anger
at the critique that came in the wake of the Baltimore Customs House action and the
Catonsville action:

> Some of you have been sorely perplexed with me; some of you have been angry,
> others despairing. One parishioner writes of quarreling with people who thought me
> mad. After all, isn't it impudent and sick for a grown man (and a priest) to sloth
> blood . . . on draft files; to terrorize harmless secretaries doing their job; to act without
> ecclesiastical permission and to disgrace the collar and its sublime office? . . . You had
> trouble with blood as a symbol—uncivilized, messy, bizarre. . . . You had trouble
> with destruction of property, with civil disobedience, with priests getting involved,
> and getting involved this much. Let's face it: perhaps half of you had trouble with us
> acting at all."[42]

Even Dorothy Day, the founder of the Catholic Worker movement, felt considerable
ambivalence about actions involving the spilling of blood and did not herself participate
in antiwar actions that involved the destruction of property. Her commitment to nonviolence was absolute, and this commitment extended, it seems, to objects as well as human

beings. She also harbored the anxiety that the destruction of property could lead to "the real thing." Yet, she also offered public support to the Catonsville Nine after their arrest and observed to one interviewer in 1971, about activist Catholics who were engaging in such actions: "Those priests and sisters! I admire their courage and dedication but not their arrogance."[43]

Finally, it is worth observing that the use of blood in such religio-political performances is not only a deeply Catholic tactic but appears to been a singularly American one. In comparing the American and European antinuclear Plowshares movements, sociologist Sharon Nepstad highlights the general rejection by European activists of the use of blood in their actions. As she documents the explanations offered for this difference, one encounters a distancing from Catholicism and even from religiosity altogether, as well as the worried sentiment that blood is, in fact, contaminating and unclean. "From the beginning, we never used blood," one Swedish activist tells Nepstad. "Blood does not have the same kind of meaning to Protestants as it does in the Catholic tradition. . . . People wouldn't really understand it here." Another Swedish activist cited by Nepstad observes: "It is difficult to say how people understand the symbols in an action. However, I think blood can actually be dangerous from a contamination point of view, and it gives also associations to religious fanaticism which creates an unnecessary polarization to the opponent."[44] Meanwhile, a Dutch activist whom Nepstad interviewed observes: "I'd like to [spill blood] but I've never been in a group with people who would agree. They say it's a very Catholic thing and Europe is very secular. People wouldn't understand that symbolism. . . . Europeans just associate it with something very unsanitary."[45]

Postscript

In the fall of 2005, at a lecture at the Center for Religion and Media at New York University, the art critic and activist Gregg Bordowitz began by saying that he had decided to take every occasion for speaking publicly as an occasion to speak about the war in Iraq. His statement was a kind of scholarly provocation, and it has operated as a kind of inspiration for this project.

But this work was also inspired as a kind of counterpoint to work in which I have also been engaged in the last few years, an exploration of another group of American Christian activists, the "persecuted church" movement.[46] Within this movement, American Christians—like the St. Patrick's Four—call upon the image of the body of Christ and articulate a theology of the imitation of Christ. But unlike the Catholic Workers, the persecuted church movement places itself in a martyrological lineage that ironically links Christian identity with the project of the American state. In its more extreme expressions, the movement specifically aligns Christianity and advocacy for "the persecuted church" with the international war on terror, as the cover of a 2006 publication from the organization, named the Voice of the Martyrs (whose tagline reads "serving the persecuted church since 1967"), demonstrates. In the background of its collage image, Osama bin Laden raises his hand in exhortation to gun-toting Muslim boys (recognized by the semiotics of their headgear and the tanks they stand near). In the foreground, two young boys with Western-style haircuts and clothing examine a Bible picture book, which they have apparently received from the Voice of the Martyrs. In the lower left-hand corner appear the words: "The Gospel—Winning the War on Terror." This framing of a choice—between a bin Laden–inspired army of jihadi children or an army of Bible-wielding Christian children—is addressed specifically to American evangelical and fundamentalist Christians and drafts them as symbolic foot soldiers into the war on terror. So conscripted, Christians must remain ever vigilant, contributing to the offensive in the war on terror abroad but also on the defensive in the so-called war on Christians at home. Since this movement sees Christians under siege everywhere, it is no surprise to hear a repeated call for the rearmament of Christians, readying themselves for battle against their perceived enemies.

But working on the two things simultaneously, I cannot help but reflect more and more on the routinization of militarism in U.S. culture as a whole. Even with the promise of the withdrawal of American troops from Iraq by 2010, the U.S. economy continues to be held hostage to the war project, while domestic politics and foreign policy in the first eight years of the twenty-first century were foundationally organized around imperial war logics and the space for dissent has narrowed dangerously, justified by the fact that "we are at war." But language itself becomes militarized, as even the language of "the culture wars" suggests. Our thinking and creative energies, too, get pulled into the circuit of the war logic—even as we try to turn these efforts toward its critique and its subversion.

My own small effort to get out from under this dominating regime is to try not to let it all have the last word. And so I wish to close with a story that picks up on many of the themes that emerge from my account of the St. Patrick's Four—the costs of acting against violence and standing instead in solidarity with its victims, the creative and resourceful adaptation of traditional Catholic liturgy to render violence visible and remembered, and, importantly, the mobilization of the material in the enactment of a religious-inflected politics.

In the spring of 2006, I was in the company of a certain Sister Mary Reilly, a member of the order of the Religious Sisters of Mercy in Rhode Island, a woman well into her senior years. Now retired, at the time she was the executive director of a nondenominational middle school for girls from low-income families in Providence called Sophia Academy, a school she created from nothing after she had officially gone into retirement for the first time some years before. I met Sister Mary at a lunch where she was receiving an award entitled "Leadership for Change through Education." In my conversation with Mary Reilly, I mentioned that I had, many years ago, worked with a member of her community, Peggy Langhammer, who had been the executive director of the Rape Crisis

Center in Providence at the same time that I was the director of the coalition of shelters for battered women in the state. My own position was, ironically enough, underwritten by a grant from Catholic Church. In one of those holy zones of weirdness, as religionist and lawyer Kathleen Skerrett calls them, the Catholic Church was paying me to coordinate the efforts of groups one of whose main goals was to help women leave their husbands.

When I mentioned Peggy Langhammer to Sister Mary, she responded with a clear Irish lilt in her voice, "Oh, Peg's a great friend of mine." In our conversation, I recalled an incident that occurred while Peggy and I were working together: a rape case had gone to trial, and in the course of the trial, the notes taken by a counselor at the rape crisis center in her work with the victim had been subpoenaed by the defense. The center refused to turn over the notes, and in consequence Peggy Langhammer, Religious Sister of Mercy, was found in contempt of court and sent to jail at the Adult Correctional Institute in Cranston, Rhode Island. (A side note to this story: Peggy had, prior to her work at the Rape Crisis Center, been the women's chaplain at the prison, so her incarceration—with many of the women whom she had served as chaplain—was a rather different experience from what the judge had probably intended.) As I recounted this story to Mary, she too recalled it, and she said, "And do you know where those notes were hidden?" "No," I replied. "In my kitchen cupboard!" she announced, with an unmistakable note of pride. "Before, that is, they went into the fireplace." She then confided that, after burning the notes, she had collected up the ashes and kept them. As she explained it to me, to this day she uses these ashes in her own private anointing ceremony on Ash Wednesday, tracing a cross of ashes on her own forehead. How better to commemorate the opening of Lent, the season of the Passion in the Catholic liturgical calendar, she asked, than to use in a homemade ritual—a women's ritual, she specified—the ashes produced out of the story of this one woman's suffering?

We live in a time and place dominated by the logic of violence, the logic of the body count, as the statistical overwrites and overwhelms substance, sentience, and sentiment. The spectacular action of the St. Patrick's Four, pouring their own blood in order to render the bloodiness of war visible; the private ritual act of Sister Mary Reilly, turning words into ash and then wearing them, an open secret, on her forehead—both of these particularizing acts draw upon rich liturgical traditions, reinscribe them in an idiom crafted for their own particular political moment, and mobilize materiality in moments of religious and political signification. Both operate in counterpoint to the deadening bureaucratic operations of the body count. Both issue a challenge to imagination and to allegiance. What difference, indeed, would it make to decide—as a matter of ethics and economics, politics and sociality—to make bodies count and, in consequence, to refuse to live in and by the logics of violence? What truth becomes visible when you see blood?

A Pentecostal Passion Paradigm

The Invisible Framing of Gibson's Christ in a Dutch Pentecostal Church

Miranda Klaver

> It has the power to draw you in and have you experience something on an
> emotional level that you may not be able to logically explain. However, it
> will leave you with a set of images or an experience or feeling that may
> make you to look further. That's all, the film is just a jumping-off point.
>
> —Mel Gibson

Pentecostalism is often described as a religion of the ecstatic, of experience and bodily manifestations in opposition to images or icons. Its
emphasis on direct communication with God seems to privilege the
inspired Word and the Spirit over mediation through visual symbols
or material objects. Members of the Dutch Pentecostal church where I
conducted my research from September 2006 to June 2007, for example,
claim to have unmediated access to God. However, at the outset of my
fieldwork I was struck by the central place of the communion ritual in
the life of believers. Shortly thereafter, the church sponsored a series of
sermons, together with a seven-step program conducted in small
groups, that centered on the Passion story of Christ, with particular
emphasis on the seven times that Jesus bled. During this period of
intense fieldwork, the image of the blood-covered face of Christ from
the movie *The Passion of the Christ* came repeatedly to my mind.
Clearly, for me the Pentecostal narratives and practices I observed were
evoking material religious forms—here images from a movie and the
viscerally empathetic bodily sensations I had felt while viewing it. How
was I to relate the Pentecostal emphasis on immediacy of experience to
the ways believers talked about the blood of Christ as a substance and
the role of the communion ritual as a religious practice? And how was
I to understand the role of Gibson's movie in the practices I was studying? Were the same images evoked for the believers as for me?

These questions brought me face to face with the material aspect of religion—in this case, with that of Pentecostalism, despite its iconoclastic Protestant tradition.[1] In this chapter, I will examine how the substance of the blood of Jesus operates as a material dimension in Pentecostalism, despite believers' claims to unmediated access to God, and how they use their experience of Gibson's film to enhance their understanding of that substance. Using the concept of semiotic ideology, I will address the interplay of meaning attribution, social interaction, and sensory modalities in believers' experience of the transcendental. I will start with a brief sketch of Pentecostal spirituality, followed by a theoretical discussion of material religion. I will then look at the concern with the Passion in the Dutch Pentecostal church and examine the responses of believers, especially women, to the Passion narrative. This case study will enable us to see material aspects of religion as an important extra-linguistic realm that is nonetheless an intrinsic part of signifying processes.

Pentecostal Spirituality

Accounts of transformational encounters with God are to be found at the heart of Pentecostal religiosity.[2] For many Pentecostals, the life of faith is initiated by conversion as the essential spiritual experience. The individual is brought into a relationship with God through the Holy Spirit and by acceptance of Jesus as Lord and Savior of one's life. But the experiential aspect of faith is not limited to the "crisis experience" of conversion: continuing spiritual encounters of varying intensity with the Holy Spirit and its manifestations mark the lives of Pentecostal believers. They see themselves as reenacting first-century Christianity, awaiting supernatural signs and miracles like those recorded in the New Testament.[3] This expectation that God will intervene in the mundane world of the believer generates a dynamic interplay of anticipation and experience as a way of reinforcing spirituality.

However, while Pentecostal spirituality can be characterized as a spirituality of encounter or an interventionist piety,[4] among themselves Pentecostals are divided over the issue of religious experiences and their precise significance, as well as the range of experiences that are allowable and to be recognized as authentic expressions of biblical faith.[5] Despite the attempts of Pentecostals to use the schema of the early Church recorded in the New Testament, the varieties of Pentecostal expression indicate the impossibility of an unmediated access to the past through biblical texts. Since claims of direct access to God through the Spirit minimize the role of Christian tradition and place the individual at the forefront, differences among Pentecostals often emerge over time, as some individuals stress some topics at the expense of others within the broad range of the Pentecostal movement. This is visible, for example, in the shifts that have taken place in the charismatic movement since the 1980s in the United States. Heightened attention to deliverance through exorcism and the gifts of the Spirit as taught by the Pentecostal innovator John Wimber moderated the emphasis on baptism with the Holy Spirit and the conversion experience.[6]

The Dutch Pentecostal church accentuates the call to conversion and infilling or baptism by the Holy Spirit as distinct religious experiences that initiate one into the Pentecostal faith. We encounter a third phase in the Pentecostal faith, however, in repeated practices of deliverance, expressed as "setting the captives free." The dominant discourse used in sermons, songs, and meetings builds an identity for the Pentecostal believer via notions of freedom from "the bondage of the past" through attempts to lead a perfect life, rather than in terms of being saved. Interestingly, the theme of "deliverance" is strongly connected to an emphasis on the power of the blood of Jesus. Images of the Passion story—interestingly informed by Gibson's movie—substantialize the blood of Christ and anchor it in the material world. Before exploring specific links between Gibson's movie and Pentecostal practice, however, let us take a look at some theoretical questions about the relationship between religion and material forms and expressions.

The Material Dimension of Religion: Semiotic Ideology

In the contemporary study of religion, we can observe a shift from symbolic approaches to an emphasis on processes of mediation. Among other things, this draws attention to the concrete, material dimension of religion.[7] From different angles, questions regarding the relationship between spiritual and material aspects of religion are being addressed, concentrating on the dynamic role materiality plays in the formation of religious subjects and communities. While "material religion" has become a new catchword, the concept recalls old discussions concerning how to overcome the dichotomies between subject and object, mind and body, or actor and structure.

Webb Keane suggests rethinking or breaking down the distinction between object and subject by emphasizing the objectlike qualities of humans and the ways in which objects seem to contain some of the attributes that define human agency: "The subject is not simply constructed through its opposition to and encompassment of the object; rather it is amplified by merging with the object."[8] Therefore, in the case of charismatic/Pentecostal Christianity, it is important to look beyond the characterization of Pentecostalism as an experiential mode of religion. Simon Coleman, in his study of the Ulf Eckman's Faith Church in Sweden, illustrates how the text-based charismatic prosperity discourse is clothed with material features that constitute a particular form of literacy. He argues that evangelical practices encourage externalizing aspects of the self in linguistic and material forms.[9] When believers describe the process of reading the Bible as a form of ingestion akin to eating, the Bible as the Word of God is invested with physical qualities. One can get filled with the Word or hunger after the Word, and in this way the text comes to be embodied in a person, who becomes the walking, talking representation of its power. At the same time, in Pentecostal discourse and language, disembodied concepts such as faith, trust, and surrender are often combined with sensory metaphors, which can be seen as the critical meeting ground between textuality and embodiment.[10] When religious language is framed in such a way that words become materialized in the self and in the environment, practices involving words and things are captured in what Keane calls a semiotic ideology. Borrowing from linguistic ideology, he suggests using the term *semiotic ideology* to avoid the problematic distinction between what counts as language and what does not—after all, not only this distinction but also what counts as categories of words and things are not given but culturally constructed: "Like language ideology, then, semiotic ideology is a reflection upon, and an attempt to organize, people's experiences of the materiality of semiotic form. Not only language, but also music, visual imagery, food, architecture and gesture and anything else that enters the actual semiotic practice function within perceptible experience by virtue of its material properties."[11]

From this broad, dynamic concept, Keane argues that material things not only express past acts, intentions, and interpretations but also invite unexpected responses by their opacity and ineffability. This sparks a dynamic interplay between ideal and material domains, which inform, interact, and influence each other but at the same time reveal the ways people are connected to the world around them. In studying the Dutch Pentecostal church, Keane's concept of semiotic ideology can be a source of inspiration in addressing the material aspects of an experience-based form of religion.

A Church in Transition: The Book, the Movie, and the Blood

In 2007, Dutch Pentecostal churches celebrated their centennial. However, the church where I conducted my research belongs to a more recent phenomenon of independent Pentecostal churches, loosely connected in transnational networks. The church was founded in the early 1980s, the result of a schism in a Dutch Reformed Church. It clearly distinguishes itself from "old Pentecostalism," understood as "traditional" denominational Pentecostal churches, such as the Dutch Assemblies of God. In the mid-nineties, this church introduced the Toronto Blessing, which turned into a dividing line within the Dutch Pentecostal movement.[12] For some time, the Sunday night revival meetings were a great national attraction for believers, though they incited controversy among Pentecostal leaders because of the unusual behavior that occurred and manifestations like "holy laughter" and "animal noises." After "Toronto," the church received visiting prophets and apostles loosely connected or aligned with the New Apostolic Reformation movement, but when it introduced the fivefold ministry, church leadership ran into trouble.[13] Three years earlier, a pastor from a Pentecostal church in the region had been asked for help. He became the interim pastor of the church, while continuing to pastor his own church. He introduced a rigorous cell church model and envisioned merging the two churches into one megachurch in the near future. Both plans, however, turned out to be a fiasco.[14] At the beginning of my fieldwork, the interim pastor resigned for health reasons, and the youth pastor, Hans, who was both young and successful, was asked to be the new pastor of the church. After the interim pastor's attempts to develop "renewal" and "revival," as in the days of the Toronto Blessing, the church had fallen into crisis. Pastor Hans assumed his leadership role by attempting to reestablish belief in the church. He introduced a new book, entitled *The Miracle of the Cross*, written by a successful emerging Dutch Pentecostal pastor and national conference speaker, Wilkin van der Kamp.[15] From Christmas until Easter, Pastor Hans preached seven times on *The Miracle of the Cross*, following the chapters of the book. He used most of the book's content in his sermons, and the author of the book was invited to preach one Sunday morning during that period.

The book is constructed around seven moments in the Passion story when Jesus bled and the seven miracles stemming from that. The author stresses the importance of what really happened to Christ by compiling the four gospels into one Passion story. In each chapter, the physical suffering of Christ is described in great detail and connected to one of the miraculous meanings of the cross. The cross-centered devotion invites the believer to meditate on each wound on the body of Christ.

Jesus bled seven times:	*Miracle of:*
Sweat like blood in the garden	Forgiveness of all sin
Maltreatment by high priest	Redemption of feelings of guilt
Maltreatment during interrogation	Cleansing of consciousness
Flagellation	Healing
Crown of thorns	Liberation from the curse
Nailing of feet	Atonement
Spear in the side	Regeneration[16]

At first, I assumed that, in the emphasis on the blood and suffering of Christ, a Catholic practice was being introduced into a Pentecostal context. Following the Passion story greatly resembles the Catholic ritual of the Stations of the Cross. But when I read the book (before the sermons started), the picture of Gibson's Christ came to my mind straightaway, even though I had not even seen the movie myself. The few times I had seen its trailer during commercial breaks on TV were sufficient to imprint this image in my mind.

The subtitle of the book, "The Last Eighteen Hours Before Jesus Died," made me wonder about Gibson's influence on the Pentecostal author, since Gibson claims to give an accurate account of the last twelve hours of the life of Christ. What I assumed to be a reinvention of a Catholic tradition was thus probably influenced more by Gibson's movie

The Passion of the Christ, which had been a great success among evangelicals and Pentecostals in both the United States and the Netherlands, since it articulates theological themes that are important to them. However, van der Kamp does not mention Gibson's movie in his book, and in an interview he stressed the supernatural revelation and inspiration he had received while writing. The fact that his book was published a year after the release of Gibson's movie was directed from above and without his doing, he assured me.[17]

However, when the author preached in the Pentecostal church on one of the seven miracles, he made a strong connection between his book and the movie: the sermon started with two anecdotes regarding the film *The Passion*. In the first story, the preacher emphasized the importance of the authenticity of the movie: "It is not about the goriness, but about what really happened." In the second anecdote, the supernatural power of the movie was stressed. Van der Kamp told the story of a woman who had been deeply involved in the occult; when she watched the movie, "God broke through the walls of her heart." After she read his book, she understood why she needed such a violent movie.

Through these anecdotes, van der Kamp suggested that the movie does more than inspire reflection. When the authenticity of the movie is emphasized, the historical and biblical accuracy is implied without questioning the central emphasis on physical suffering. This is typical of Passion literature throughout history,[18] since in it details of torture are elaborated far beyond the descriptions in the gospels.

Gibson's reconstruction of the four gospel narratives into one Passion account accords well with Pentecostal hermeneutical practices in dealing with biblical texts.[19] Moreover, according to the preacher, the movie mediates the sacred and serves as an instrument for bringing the sacred into the ordinary, everyday life of people, with dramatic consequences. Just like the movie, the book *The Miracle of the Cross* promises to change one's life: it offers a road to freedom by means of the seven miracles of the cross. At this point boundaries become fuzzy: the boundaries assumed to exist between film reality and ordinary reality, between scripted, filmed interpretation and historical accuracy, between popular culture and religious expression, between the material world and the believing subject.

The strong parallel between Gibson's movie and the book, surrounded by an aura of authenticity, amplified the impact of the book in the church. One could not read the book or listen to the sermon without thinking about the blood-covered face of Christ as portrayed in the movie. "This is what our faith is really about," was often said. Like the movie, the book focuses on the physical suffering of Christ, forging a strong relationship between violence and atonement: the greater the suffering, the more powerful the redemption. However, the emphasis on violence and suffering has consequences for the understanding of redemption: redemption is not only primarily located in the death of Christ, but extended or even shifted to the magnitude of His suffering, concentrated on and even materialized in the blood of Christ, which atones for the sin of man. Supported by the imagery of Gibson's movie, the book provokes—by focusing on seven moments of Christ's bleeding—the powerful and compelling symbol of blood sacrifice, which adds greatly to the sense that one's own sins are responsible for the suffering and crucifixion of Christ. While Gibson's movie offers viewers a "way of seeing" that engages their bodies, the book not only adds a "way of knowing" but also reinforces a "way of feeling," which evokes emotional responses of compassion and guilt. In terms of Keane's concept of semiotic ideology, a shift in doctrine, by emphasizing the sacrificial aspect of Christ's death, opens up Pentecostal practices to a reinterpretation of the conversion experience, to new religious experiences and to a rearticulation of notions like the power of the blood.

Apart from the sermons, an outline of the *Miracle* book, published in a booklet called *Seven Steps on the Road to Freedom*,[20] was discussed in approximately twenty small groups in the church. Indeed, all church members were encouraged to buy it. The questions at the end of each chapter in the booklet contributed to group discussion and self-reflection. A written prayer at the end of each chapter was sometimes used as a common prayer, but in general one was encouraged to use it at home. I attended two small groups: a women's group, which included a few new believers; and a mixed group, with core members of the church. In both groups, themes connected to the suffering, wounds, and blood of Jesus were discussed biweekly and related to personal beliefs and daily life. But it was in the women's group that the book was embraced and applied most intensively.[21] The meaning of Jesus' blood was addressed explicitly in conversation and expressed in practices within the women's group. Unlike most small groups in the church, the women's group celebrated communion each time they met.

A Pentecostal Women's Group

The small women's group met every other week at lunchtime at one of the women's homes. They had lunch together, read and discussed the Bible, took communion together, and closed with a time of prayer for each other's needs. During lunch, everyone was encouraged to express and share personal concerns. Struggles with relatives, children, husbands, and parents were, next to health and illness, the topics most frequently addressed among the women. The communion ritual was a set custom at the meetings. It was important in the spiritual life of the women, not only in the group but also in the private sphere at home.

Before I joined the group, the women had read a book by a Mexican charismatic prophetess called Ana Mendez,[22] who had visited the church the year before. Her book, *Eat My Flesh, Drink My Blood*,[23] had convinced them of the importance of the communion ritual, and as a group they had decided to take communion every time they came together. Mary, raised in an Assemblies of God church, told the group about her communion practices at home. Being a divorced mother of three teenage sons, she struggled with raising her boys. But through Mendez, she started taking communion with her sons at home. Since that time, she testified to the group, her situation had changed remarkably. Her boys were easier to handle, and she derived strength from the bread and wine. "There is so much power in the blood of Jesus," she often said to the group. Other women in the group were also familiar with communion practices in the private sphere. Laura, the group leader, encouraged the women to take communion during their quiet time,[24] particularly when they face difficult situations. "It is to nurture the soul," she emphasized, "and it gives you spiritual strength." She recalled several situations in her life when she took bread and wine "just to be with Jesus" and stressed the intimacy of having a meal together with Jesus. It is through the power of the blood of Jesus that her life is being restored, strengthened, and even healed.

The women's understanding of the communion ritual, with its emphasis on the power of the blood of Jesus, led them to give *The Miracle of the Cross* a warm reception. The women could easily relate to its concentration on the blood and suffering of Christ and apply the seven miracles to their own life situations. For every meeting, Laura asked one of the women to summarize a chapter of the book and share some personal thoughts and reflections about its content. Several times women in charge referred to Gibson's movie. When Jenny was leading the meeting, she encouraged the women to watch it again and stressed how film makes you aware of the intense suffering of Christ and how the book and the film were all about the same things.

In their discussions, the struggle with the past was a recurrent theme, particularly a tension between what was promised through conversion and the reality of everyday life. The overall message of the book is that it is God's purpose for his children to be "free from bondage" and "the past." At the same time, the author emphasizes the causal relationship between the providence of the cross and the responsibility of believers to experience God's blessings. Through the different chapters and by means of a checklist, the women of the group were encouraged to face their past, their childhood, family relationships, their character, and their physical condition in order to trace possible causes for not experiencing full freedom and blessings from God. During the meetings, some of the seven miracles turned out to be more relevant than others in the lives of the women. Three stood out: the miracle of forgiveness of sins, the liberation from the curse, and the miracle of healing.

Above all, the book stresses the power of the blood for the forgiveness of the believer's sins, the primary meaning of conversion. While this was understood as liberation from the past, it was not without conditions: the book emphasizes that the Bible teaches that God cannot forgive those who do not forgive others. This aroused a lot of emotion and led to much discussion in the group, since it called up painful past experiences, traumas, and memories. While the divine power of the blood was presented as a power available for redemption, believers were made responsible for not having applied this power in their lives. Failure to forgive, according to the book, gives the devil legal grounds for afflicting a believer.[25] Believers were urged to reconcile themselves with the past by confronting it, but past experiences became problematic again precisely through this attempt. Although forgiveness was understood to be an act of the will, several women were not sure whether they had really forgiven those who had caused them so much pain in the past.

The second "miracle" that attracted a lot of attention among the women was liberation from the curse through the blood of Jesus. The notion of the curse is often addressed in the church: in sermons, prayers, and conversations among believers. The meaning of the curse, however, varies from a strong connection with the power of words—like the influence of parents' negative judgments on children—to the concept of generational curses. In the struggle to overcome such problems as bad habits and addictions, the power of evil is often located in a believer's former generations, who have somehow been allied with evil or dark forces. Laura, the group leader, told the group that her family had been afflicted by a power of poverty for several generations. After conversion, she found out that one of her forefathers had been a dowser. By making a surrogate confession of guilt for him, she had broken the curse over her life: there was no longer any legal ground for its power. Invoking Exodus 20:5 and 34:7, she explained that it is a spiritual law that the sins of the forefathers afflict future generations up to the tenth generation. By the act of undoing the curse in the spiritual world, the believer cuts off his or her family and blood ties to gain spiritual freedom from bondage. The blood of Jesus plays a significant role in the prayer for breaking the power of the curse. Phrases such as "we plead on the blood of Jesus" and "cover us with your blood" as means of protection against evil, treat the blood of Jesus as a force and a power, appropriated by the believer as a spiritual attribute or object. While this practice promises a break with the past, paradoxically, it keeps the past continuously present as a source of causal explanations for all kinds of affliction—past, present, or future.

As a source of protection against evil, in terms of breaking the curse, the book also understands the blood of Christ in relationship to the realm of the occult, which ranges from Harry Potter to engagement in divination practices. It is also connected to certain objects. Saskia, a new convert in her early fifties who was caught up in a conflict at home over her daughter's Buddha statue, was advised by the group to "bring the Buddha under the blood of Jesus." When she spoke these words, the negative power of the Buddha would be neutralized and would not affect her. Another woman confirmed this practice by citing the example of her son's Satanic Bible.[26] She clearly did not want it in her house, but she could only "bring it under the blood of Jesus." This was done by an act of proclamation, since it was believed that the act of speaking the name of Jesus and pleading on His blood would drive demons away.

Besides forgiveness and liberation, the blood of Jesus, understood as life giving and a source of healing, was the third miracle emphasized among the women. The scriptural passages "By His wounds we are healed" (Isaiah 53:5) and "For the life of a creature is in the blood and I have given it to you to make atonement for yourselves on the altar; it is the blood that makes atonement for one's life" (Leviticus 17:11) form the foundation for a conviction that in the severe physical suffering of Christ those who believe have available a source of healing for all diseases.

Here the tension between promise and reality was most visible. Joan, suffering from chronic illness and unable to work, struggled with the fact that her healing failed to occur. She often asked for prayer at the end of the Sunday services, and she really believed God could heal her. Eventually, she attended a healing service in another church with a Pentecostal preacher known for his healing ministry. Nothing miraculous happened to her that night, but she told the women that God had spoken to her and told her that her healing had begun. At the next meeting, she admitted that she still suffered from a lot of pain but would nevertheless hold onto what God had promised her. When she started to doubt, she said, she rebuked the devil and held onto the power of the blood of Jesus and the promises of God. The issue of forgiveness was intertwined with her story because she had been abused as a child. Several times she mentioned that she had forgiven her abuser, but she also displayed her doubts because healing had failed to come.

During the small group meetings, the Pentecostal women discussed several themes and doctrines implicit in the general discourse of the church. In the book these beliefs are integrated and explicated in relation to the physical suffering and the blood of Christ. At the same time, believers were encouraged to examine their lives within the context of the event of the crucifixion. Especially in the communion ritual, believers appropriate the power of the blood when the wine they drink is invested with the material qualities of Christ, to be incorporated into their own bodies. This ritual practice is complemented by the material reproduction of static "text" in living, sacralized words as believers call upon the blood of Jesus. In this context, one can see how the strongly affective movie images of Gibson's interpretation of the Passion story subtly pervade practices and verbal expressions of belief. Emphasis on the physical suffering of Christ as concentrated in His wounds provokes the women to focus their attention on the material properties of the blood of Christ.

Passion Paradigm as Semiotic Ideology?

We have encountered various different media and material forms in this Dutch Pentecostal church: the imagery of Gibson's movie; a book directing a particular, Pentecostal interpretation of the Passion story by evoking these images; and the objectified power of the blood of Jesus. Gibson's claims about the film's historical accuracy,[27] together with the film's hyperrealism, strongly resonate with Pentecostal forms of biblical literalism. Therefore, it is no coincidence that Pentecostal believers understand Gibson's movie as authentic and real. Here, emphasis on the "real"—as historical account as well as true meaning—limits or even denies a metaphorical interpretation of the Passion narrative.[28] Focusing on language, one can argue that the characteristic prevalence of metonymy within Pentecostal religiosity[29]—the world is experienced as full of signs referring to God—encourages a tendency toward objectification. We can see this, for instance, in the Pentecostal understanding of evil spirits as actual spiritual beings. But Pentecostals' metonymic understanding of the biblical blood of Jesus appeals to more encompassing forms of sense making beyond the assumption that language literally refers to God and the world. An emphasis on language, indeed, enables us to understand the affective power of Gibson's imagery, concentrated in the extraordinary physical suffering of Christ, as the change from a metaphoric to a metonymic interpretation of the blood. However, it is important to see how this difference in the understanding and interpretation of language collapses two domains of reality into one—and that is only one part of the story. Keane's concept of semiotic ideology offers a comprehensive way of analyzing the interrelatedness of the domains of practice, doctrine, and material forms present within a religious context. When we take into account the connections between words and things, and relate the meaning of signs to their materiality, we can observe how signs intensify and alter categories of material and immaterial reality. When we extend this to a materiality beyond words, we open up a dynamic field of interpretation of the material relations of signs.

Charles Sanders Peirce's distinction of a trichonomy of sign relations—*icon*, *index*, and *symbol*—can be helpful here.[30] Whereas Peirce understands indexicality as a form of naturalness and deeply felt fitness in the relationship to the sign, and hence as close to metonymy,[31] iconic features of signs have the potential to disclose complex constellations of meaning. I would argue that Gibson's *The Passion* functions here as a religious icon, thus acting as more than a mere representation of the biblical narrative: it is invested with spiritual power and with supernatural qualities. Indeed, as an icon, the movie opens a gateway for entering the Pentecostal world of the miraculous and the supernatural. The Passion paradigm laid out in the book offers a framework for a Pentecostal understanding of the world and a powerful narrative emplacement for reflection on one's life. The particular way the author of the book stresses the "real" meaning of the event of the crucifixion displays the paradox of Pentecostal biblical literalism:[32] although biblical texts are valued for their literal meaning, they are also in need of the sort of extensive exegesis performed in the book, including such techniques as written prayers. Indeed, Pentecostal forms of literalism manifest a dynamic interplay of literal and experiential understandings of the text, in which illumination by the Spirit contributes to enlarging a text's meanings.

We can see from this that religious ideas and texts are indisputably subject to forms of embodiment and material expression beyond the scope of language. While the Passion movie upholds the metaphoric characteristics of language, as religious icon it offers lay spectators an opportunity to practice a way of seeing that engages their bodies. It thus operates as a powerful agent of visual piety, influencing the way people encounter devotional objects.[33] The familiarity of the movie's narrative serves to structure Pentacostal believers' corporeal and emotional identification. At the same time, the portrayal of the extreme physical suffering of Christ, made visually potent in His blood-covered body, offers an intensification of the ordinary experience of suffering, potentially pushing the believer toward a limit experience,[34] a sense of being overwhelmed by wonder and awe. The movie as technological medium enhances this corporeal, visceral power as it represents the mediation performed by Gibson's Christ.

In a less evocative way, the author of the book *The Miracle of the Cross* uses the Passion narrative as a starting point, then intensifies the storyline by cumulatively repeating the seven times Jesus bled. What started out with biblical texts is being amplified by tapping into the imaginary of Gibson's movie. The effect of this cumulative intensification of signs and mobilization of deeply embodied sensations via the phenomenological aspects of the movie as medium contributes to a sense of religious awe and affectivity concentrated in the blood of Jesus. The blood no longer holds its metonymic quality as linguistic formation but is transformed into matter. This is what the book displays: within a Pentecostal discourse, the central concept of atonement is surrounded and embodied by the strong affective notion of the blood. Moreover, believers understand the blood not only in an immaterial, spiritual, or divine way but also as a substance, crucial for redemption and as payment for the sins of the world. The blood conveys objective power, bringing about protection, healing, and forgiveness of sin and breaking evil bondage from the past. In this sense, the objectification of the power of the blood can be seen as the opposite of the objectification of evil spirits, namely, as the power to counter evil.

Pentecostal groups promote emotion and feeling as a means of approaching the divine, appealing to the senses, activating sensuous forms of knowing, and giving the body the central role as a primary mediator of religious experience. Multisensory religious experiences create affective bonds, enabling Pentecostal believers to speak of and experience the power of the blood in a concrete and material religious form. The appropriation of this power is centered in believers' bodily experiences and is twofold, relating to both their outer and their inner worlds. It is in the act of speaking, through proclamation, that the power of the blood is externalized in the world. The power of words in the spiritual world is an important instrument in the battle against evil and a source of protection against evil. At the same time, the power of the blood is internalized by the act of eating in the communion ritual, which is understood as taking in spiritual food. Such food nurtures and strengthens the soul, but also cleanses and heals both the soul and the body. Since access to the communion ritual is not constrained by clerical control and individual use of the ritual is encouraged, these practices are an important source of personal empowerment. In the practices of Pentecostal women, the blood of Jesus operates both as a powerful force they use to change themselves and as a power to gain some sense of control over issues in their lives where they feel powerless or afflicted.

In the tensions believers encounter after conversion in dealing with their past—whether family ties, relationships, or the confrontation with their own sinfulness—the concept of the power of the blood of Christ turns out to be a source of potential renewal and power and thus mediates in a rather paradoxical way.[35] On the one hand, the believer is addressed as a responsible person, who can choose to make the right decision, decide to forgive others, and exercise self-control through the power of the Holy Spirit. On the other hand, the believer is approached as vulnerable and gullible, constantly under attack by the forces of evil and in need of protection in the battle with them. The power of the blood mediates the tension between these positions and restores the believer from vulnerability to strength. This is enacted in the communion practice, which enables the believer, in times of failure and affliction, to reenact the conversion experience by applying the blood of Jesus as a source of cleansing, healing, and protection. Communion is therefore a means to regain strength and power.

During the time when the Pentecostal Passion discourse was being introduced and discussed in the church, an emphasis on the power of the blood of Christ was not connected to the Pentecostal understanding of the Holy Spirit. In the lived theology of believers, however, the power of the blood and the power of the Spirit were employed side by side. Keane states that the idea of a semiotic ideology should not be taken to imply totalization: different semiotic ideologies can be in play in a religious group at the same time. An emphasis on the power of the blood of Christ can therefore be interpreted as an alternative semiotic ideology in times of restoration and the routinization of charisma at the level of the local church as a whole. This particular church is known for its past successes. It has recovered from several crises, and it is haunted by a number of prophesies promising that it will become a center of the Holy Spirit's power for the entire nation and beyond. Thus a return to roots, with a particular emphasis on the blood of Christ, can be understood as a kind of "cleansing ritual for the whole church," or a reconversion ritual for sanctification, inviting God to pour out His Spirit so that the predicted revival will come.

In the emphasis on the power of the blood as a material force, the boundaries between the material and the immaterial are redefined and reconstructed according to situation and context. Keane's argument that words and things are mutually constitutive and that the significance of signs cannot be divorced from their material qualities is highly relevant here. However, although Keane includes visual imagery in his concept of semiotic ideology, he tends to neglect other sensuous experiences. I am convinced that the picture will not be complete without attention to the other aesthetic and sensuous dimensions at work in the formation of religious bodies within a religious group.[36] As Tanya Luhrmann points out: "the experiential dimension of religion rests upon the way people learn to use cognitive concepts to interpret their minds and bodies, and the practices people learn which change bodily experiences in relation to these concepts, to make those concepts real."[37] In a Pentecostal context, through social interaction people learn to develop a new orientation to the body and new forms of knowing, thus opening up the body as a vent for fears and desires, both to the sacred world and also the outer world. This opening of the body makes it possible to transgress the boundaries between the immaterial and the material. It creates the conditions for experiencing the merging of object and subject as a permeation of the sacred into the world, including the lives and bodies of believers.

Conclusion

We have seen that Pentecostalism as an experiential mode of religiosity does not exclude material representations. Within the boundaries of a Dutch Pentecostal church, we have encountered expressions of materialization framed within a particular Pentecostal ideology and discourse. These are, not by accident, found in the power of the blood. The scope for such material expression is limited within Pentecostal discourse by a fierce resistance to church tradition and ritual and by an emphasis on unmediated access to God. However, Pentecostal believers adopt Gibson's representation of the Passion story as being genuine and authentic.

The particular understanding of the blood of Jesus as an embodied, directly experienced, and unlimited source of material power that is personally available to believers enables a believer to mediate between the ideal sanctified life of a convert and the reality of everyday life, including her own past. This also applies to the church as a whole. The corporate engagement of believers in the Passion story as a living reality serves as a collective cleansing ritual aimed at regaining the fire of the Holy Spirit.

This clearly reflects an important characteristic of Pentecostal spirituality: one cannot experience the world in a metonymic way, as full of signs indicating the presence and intervention of God in everyday life, without negotiating the material contingency of signs. Multisensory processes of signification induce a reconstruction of the Pentecostal body beyond its physical boundaries. Particular Pentecostal forms of embodiment are intertwined with distinct material forms, which bind people's sensory and sensuous bodies together through an engagement with the sacred and the world, including the material world. While Keane's concept of semiotic ideology is very useful in understanding the dynamics of signs and their material qualities, bridging between material aspects of religion and its other discursive domains, the sensuous character of signs and their effect on forms of knowing and embodiment needs to be addressed as well.

Afterword

After writing this chapter, I asked Pastor Hans to read my text and give me his comments. "This is what I do not want to happen," he told me. He could imagine that people could understand the blood of Christ to be a powerful substance, but he was troubled by the fact that believers might attribute "magic" power to the blood of Jesus as a substance in words and actions. Perhaps material things are subject to forces not only beyond the control of believers but also beyond the control of pastors.[38] Or even of researchers.

PART V

Public Space

The Structural Transformation of the Coffeehouse

Religion, Language, and the Public Sphere in the Modernizing Muslim World

Michiel Leezenberg

In recent years, the myth that only the Western world has effectively and successfully modernized has been reproduced in the oft-heard claim that the Islamic world has not experienced the (or an) Enlightenment. Although this myth has been challenged both by area specialists and by the emerging world-history paradigm in historiography, these insights have yet to reach philosophical debates. Thus, even an eminent philosopher like Jürgen Habermas argues in his recent writings on post-secular society that the Islamic world remains trapped in a premodern, religion-based constellation and has not become truly modern and secularized, let alone entered a post-secular phase of the kind he sees emerging in Western Europe.[1]

As an empirical historical claim, this is so seriously flawed that one may well ask how far its falsity affects Habermas's conceptual and normative argument more generally. I will do so only indirectly, however—by sketching an alternative to Habermas's famous account of the rise of a modern public sphere.[2] My central historical claim will be that the Islamic world has witnessed processes of Enlightenment, modernization, or secularization that were not merely derived from European influence but driven by an internal dynamic; moreover, this dynamic was not driven primarily by the state. More concretely, I will argue that something much like a secular public sphere for literary and political discussion emerged in early modern Ottoman coffeehouses. Among historians and area specialists, this may be relatively uncontroversial knowledge; but these insights have yet to make it to philosophical discussion. My central conceptual and normative concern is to uncover the deep secularist and Eurocentric assumptions in the work of liberal thinkers like Habermas. For liberally inclined philosophers, the secular character of critique, philosophical reason, and public debate may be a necessary if not self-evident requirement, but on closer inspection, and seen in a broader perspective, the secular character of philosophical critique turns out to be a matter more of historical contingency than of conceptual or normative necessity.

In anthropology, this contingency has influentially been explored in Talal Asad's genealogies of religion, secularism, and the concept of the secular.[3] Asad, however, still appears to see an asymmetry between Western and non-Western histories: "the history of Western thought . . . can be (and is) written on its own, but not so the history of Arab thought."[4] I have no intention of contesting the enormous—and often destructive—societal and political importance of Western colonial and imperial domination, but the asymmetry between the Western and the non-Western world is all too often taken as a conceptual given, and thus risks unwittingly reproducing the very Eurocentrism it sets out to criticize. As such, it may be said to form part of what Bruno Latour calls the "modern constitution,"[5] by which was effected not only a new conceptual separation or, as Latour calls it, "purification," consisting of the three axes of modernity—nature, society, and discourse, religion being strangely absent among them. In addition, and simultaneously, the modern constitution involves a separation or "Big Ditch" between the modern and the traditional, and between Western and non-Western societies or cultures: the latter are then represented as not yet modern and as a fit object for anthropological research.[6]

Below, I will tackle this alleged asymmetry from the intersection of linguistics, anthropology, philosophy, and religious studies. Thus, I will argue that European modernity has at least in part been constituted by a non-Western phenomenon or institution, namely, the coffeehouse. The fact that something like an Ottoman public sphere emerged prior to any substantial European influence, let alone hegemony, provides a strong argument against the assumption of asymmetry and against the still-widespread assumption that "modernization" crucially if not exclusively involved the importation of European conceptions and practices. Crucially, however, the Ottoman public sphere was not as strongly anticlerical as the European ones. Moreover, language played a rather more—or more visibly—central role in the Ottoman case than in the European experience. Thus, the character and role of the Ottoman coffeehouses have nontrivial implications for the normative notion of the public sphere as theorized most famously by Jürgen Habermas. My question here is not how much early modern Ottoman realities embody a public sphere in Habermas's sense, but rather how much this philosophical conception is itself up for reconsideration in the light of non-Western experience. Similarly, the Ottoman coffeehouse experience problematizes some of the main tenets of Talal Asad's genealogical critique of liberal and secularist assumptions. It will also emerge that the abstract discussion of a disembodied public sphere cannot stand entirely apart from the materiality of lived and experienced public space.

Tea or Coffee? The Emergence of the Public Sphere in Europe

Michel Foucault once remarked that analytic philosophy involved "the analysis of discursive strategies followed over a cup of tea in an Oxford salon"; these strategic games, he continues, are not without interest, but have a very limited empirical range.[7] Foucault's bon mot is undoubtedly an oversimplification, but it points to the possibly premature universalization by analytical philosophers of some historically and culturally very particular linguistic practices. Thus, among twentieth-century Western philosophers with a background in the analytical tradition, the notion of rational and cooperative communication, which is dominated by the force of arguments rather than the social power of speakers, has come to figure as a timeless and universal normative ideal. Probably the most influential statements of such views are H. P. Grice's theory of conversational implicature and Jürgen Habermas's theory of communicative action.[8] Despite their differences, both authors pursue an—ultimately Kantian—project of uncovering the universal features of communication as a particular form of rational action. Yet it appears that these allegedly universal principles of rational communication have clearly traceable historical roots. It may be worthwhile to trace these roots in order to uncover some deep ethnocentric, language-ideological, and secularist assumptions in these allegedly universal theories of communicative action.

Polite speech emerged in England during the seventeenth and eighteenth centuries, where periodicals such as *The Spectator* and *The Guardian* propagated a reform of good manners, especially as an alternative to the often less than polite—not to say violent—religious disputes of the seventeenth century. The prime locus for this new form of polite conversation was the coffeehouse, which emerged in the seventeenth century and was to become the main location where one could exchange information about economic and political developments.[9] The new sociability of the coffeehouse also brought along new civilizational and conversational ideals, when authors not belonging to the nobility attempted to banish the specter of the fierce and often bloody religious discord that had characterized seventeenth-century England. In the nineteenth century, however, the London coffeehouses gradually disappeared as a major institution of the new public sphere. According to some historians, this decline is due in part to the rise of tea as a beverage, it being cheaper and easier to prepare at home than coffee.[10] The rise of teatime, with its concomitant polite conversation, nowadays seen as a prototypically if not quintessentially British phenomenon, thus coincides with the decline of the classical public sphere and the growth of a new bourgeois British domestic or private sphere. Undoubtedly, the bourgeoisie's gradual withdrawal into the privacy of domestic life has rather more complex causes, but it is tempting to visualize it as accompanying a shift in tastes from coffee toward a preference for tea. With some oversimplification, then, one might say that coffeehouse talk embodies or exemplifies the new public sphere in the eighteenth century, and teatime conversation characterizes the nineteenth-century bourgeois private sphere. More generally, polite conversation may be seen as a way of domesticating, avoiding, or exorcising social conflict. In the seventeenth-century British experience, this conflict was of a specifically religious character: one key ingredient of civil talk was the avoidance of contentious religious topics of conversation, which could lead to verbal animosity and even to physical violence.[11]

In many respects, the German and French experiences of this period were rather different from the British, but they appear to share its anticlerical or even antireligious character. Thus, one can see the coffeehouse as an embodiment or emblem of a secularized public sphere, which in the English case banished potentially dangerous religious disputes in favor of rational philosophical argument, or in the French and German cases employed the notion of reason as a means of countering clerical authority. This particular historical experience also appears to inform Kant's 1784 essay "What is Enlightenment?" a text that crucially shaped Habermas's 1962 study; in it, Kant argues that Enlightenment requires, first and foremost, the freedom to make "public use of reason."[12] Three features of this view of reason and its public use stand out, and all are to some extent reproduced by Habermas. First, Kant's position is explicitly anticlerical, aiming at restricting the social power of the church; at the same time, and equally explicitly, Kant abstains from claiming the right to criticize publicly absolutist but enlightened worldly rulers—witness his praise of Frederick II of Prussia as an enlightened ruler who can say, "Argue as much as you like and about whatever you like, but obey!"[13]

Second, what Kant calls the "public use of reason" involves a highly idiosyncratic notion of the public. For Kant, reason is used privately when employed in one's status as a civil employee of state, church, or school during working hours; thus, soldiers, religious officials, and school teachers should as such not question or criticize but merely obey the orders of their employers.[14] One is allowed, Kant continues, to doubt or criticize such doctrines only when making public use of one's reason, that is, as a man of learning, in one's free time, and to an audience of educated persons (*Gelehrten*). The elitist character of Kant's conception has been pointed out before: thus, the notion of a public of *Gelehrten* presumes literacy if not higher education, and indeed contains a hidden gender dimension. Kant holds it to be rather unlikely, if not undesirable, that women can or should enlighten themselves by the public use of reason.

Third, and perhaps most importantly, Kant is blind to language. Nowhere in his short essay on Enlightenment or in his far lengthier *Critiques* does Kant treat language as a philosophically complex or politically relevant question. This silence on questions of language (or what Jürgen Villers calls Kant's "speechlessness") has been seen as typical of Enlightenment universalism and contrasted with a Romantic emphasis on locality, particularity, tradition, and national language; in fact, however, the Enlightenment witnessed intense speculation on questions concerning both the origin of language and its relation to national character.[15] Thus, to mention but one example, both Kant's great source of inspiration Rousseau and his pupil and later rival Johann Gottfried Herder wrote in great detail about the origin of language in relation to the origin of society; the doctrines of both authors were in part shaped by Condillac, whose influential writings in turn build on Locke's *An Essay Concerning Human Understanding*. It is downright astonishing to see that this entire tradition is completely ignored by Kant; after all, what he calls the public use of *reason* is more adequately characterized as a highly regimented way of using *language* in public.

Kant's speechlessness is reproduced, surprisingly perhaps, by the latter-day Kantian Habermas. Historically Habermas traces the emergence of the public sphere to the rise of coffeehouses and salons in the seventeenth and eighteenth centuries, but philosophically he clearly grounds it in Kant's notion of the "public use of reason." Likewise, his more general concept of communicative action as guided by an ideal speech situation free of power relations and violence, and subject to no force or coercion other than that of rational argument and consensus-oriented discussion, is obviously inspired by the historical experience of the eighteenth-century public sphere as embodied in coffeehouses and salons, and by Kant's philosophical writings.[16]

Both Habermas's historical analysis of the emergence of the public sphere and his philosophical accounts of the public sphere and communicative action, however, reproduce some of the problematic features of Kant's Enlightenment essay.[17] At first sight, Habermas's self-proclaimed linguistic and pragmatic turn to an essentially Kantian program seems to reflect an attempt to incorporate language as a factor; yet on closer inspection Habermas turns out to pay insufficient attention to the constitutive qualities of language. Although he discusses this constitutive character generically in the Heideggerian terms of the "world-disclosing" capacities of language, Habermas wholly ignores the effect of the choice and use of particular languages. Thus, he fails to address or even to raise the question of which language should be used in public debate, apparently presuming a monolingual environment in which an official and standardized language is simply given. This is, of course, a serious oversimplification, which does not hold unproblematically even for eighteenth-century London, Paris, or Berlin, let alone a multilingual metropolis such as Istanbul. In Berlin, for example, French was the preferred language of learning and debate for much of the eighteenth century. Thus, the Prussian ruler Frederick the Great wrote most of his books and letters in French rather than German, and the Prussian Academy of Science in Berlin initially conducted its sessions in French.

The central point I would like to raise here is that the distinction between public and private space is not only conceptualized *in* language but in part constituted *by* language. It is tempting to take this claim as implying that language is something like a transcendental condition of possibility for public reason, but crucially, language itself is not a given, either. Rather, it is itself conceptualized, reconceptualized, and contested in and through human practices; an especially important role in these reconceptualizations and contestations is played by so-called linguistic ideologies or, as Webb Keane more generally calls them, semiotic ideologies. These are popular doctrines or folk theories of what words are and do, which appear to help in shaping both linguistic practice and language structure.[18] Thus, the argument presented here should not be mistaken for a Kantian or structuralist thesis that reason or thought is constituted by linguistic structures; rather, it redirects attention to embodied linguistic practices in concrete and material spaces.

The Oriental Roots of the Western Public Sphere

Before discussing the constitutive role of language and linguistic ideologies, however, I would like to raise another point. Habermas and others see the secular and liberal public sphere, as it emerged in Western and Central European coffeehouses, as typical of, if not unique to, Western modernity; both coffee and the institution of the coffeehouse, however, are non-Western imports, originating in the early modern Ottoman empire. Significantly, one of the first London coffeehouses was owned by the merchant Daniel Edwards, a long-time resident of Smyrna, and run by his servant Pasqua Rosee, a Smyrna-born Greek; another was, equally significantly, called The Turk's Head.[19] That is, both the beverage of coffee and the institution or space of the coffeehouse have their origins in the Islamic world. This makes it worthwhile to ask, first, whether the vicissitudes of the coffeehouse in the Ottoman empire have shaped the Western notion of the public sphere rather more extensively than Habermas allows and, second, whether Habermas's notion is conceptually and normatively adequate to deal with the experience of the non-Western world. Thus, the non-Western background of an allegedly uniquely European innovation implies more general questions concerning modernity at large. Below it will appear, most importantly, that in the Ottoman coffeehouses language plays a rather more prominent role than in the European experience as construed by Habermas and that a number of secularist assumptions that appear relatively unproblematic in eighteenth-century Europe appear not to hold in the Ottoman empire.

Coffee had been consumed from the Middle Ages on, but in the mid-sixteenth century the coffeehouse emerged as a particular public space that was distinct from both the domestic sphere and other public spaces such as the mosque and the bath house (*hammam*).[20] Relatively many coffeehouses were run by (former) Janissaries, who by the late eighteenth century had lost their privileged position as part of the military elite (*askeri*). There had been some early attempts by religious scholars, notably a fatwa by the empire's highest religious authority, Sheykhülislam Ebu's-Su'ûd, to declare the consumption of coffee forbidden by religious law, but these were largely ineffective (and, in fact, were challenged even on religious grounds[21]). In seventeenth- and eighteenth-century writings, it appears that it was increasingly the coffeehouses, rather than the use of coffee, that were being perceived as a threat to the social order; this threat concerned not only (sexual) morality but also, and especially, the "subversive political talk" (*devlet sohbeti*) one could encounter there.[22] Thus, in 1633 Sultan Murat IV ordered all coffeehouses in Istanbul to be closed. But this, too, proved to be a temporary and largely ineffective measure. Murat was quite right, however, to fear the coffeehouses as hotbeds of sedition; in 1730 a rebellion started in a coffeehouse and actually headed by a coffeehouse owner, Patrona Halil, forced Sultan Ahmed III to abdicate. The Ottoman rulers saw a clear link between the coffeehouses, the Janissaries, and social unrest: according to the local historian Mehmed Dânish Bey, when they crushed the Janissaries in 1826, they also demolished more than ten thousand coffeehouses in Istanbul alone.[23] Until the very end of the Ottoman empire and even beyond, however, traditional coffeehouses continued to exist and attract their clientele.

Now, which novel linguistic practices appear in the Ottoman coffeehouses? First, and perhaps most importantly, various different languages were spoken in them. Thus, the famous Çardak coffeehouse in Istanbul is reported to have been frequented by visitors of various ethnic, linguistic, and religious backgrounds. On various occasions, spies' reports note that conversations eavesdropped upon and reported elsewhere have been translated from local languages such as Arabic, Persian, and Greek, as well as foreign languages such as Russian, French, or English.[24] Cengiz Kirli argues that this interaction between different ethnic and religious groups in the coffeehouses belies the once-widespread view that social life in the Ottoman empire (and in Muslim societies more generally) was largely divided along confessional lines. Instead, he argues, urban contacts were in part shaped by regional networks rather than ethnic, religious, or national identities.[25]

Second, and undoubtedly most importantly from the perspective of the state authorities, there was gossip about court affairs, or *devlet sohbeti*, already mentioned above. Government bureaucrats and aspiring officials in search of a job would meet in coffeehouses, where they could exchange the latest news and court gossip. Third, there were more literary practices, such as reciting poetry and/or singing songs and performing puppet plays (most famously, the occasionally rather obscene shadow plays of Karagöz, in which stock characters represented government officials and the different ethnic groups in the empire). From the 1860s on, a more strictly literary coffeehouse, the so-called *kiraathane* ("reading room"), where one could read the newspaper at ease, emerged as a alternative to the *mahalle kahvehanesi*, or neighborhood coffeehouse. This does not mean, however, that literary activities, such as singing or reciting poetry, had been absent from the traditional coffeehouses. Rather, it involved a stricter regimentation of earlier literary practices, such as those of, in particular, the Karagöz plays, which at times had been obscene enough to scandalize European visitors.[26]

Ottoman coffeehouses were characterized not only by a vernacularization of linguistic practice, in which new varieties and registers of language came to be used for literary, educational, and scholarly purposes, but also by novel ideologies of simplification, which decreed that literary and other texts had to be understandable for a wider audience. Serif Mardin has argued that the eighteenth-century expansion of the Ottoman bureaucracy necessitated the admission of less thoroughly educated officials, and hence the simplification of the language of official documents.[27] This simplification of language, however, did not occur in state circles only; the coffeehouses, too, saw the appearance of new forms of public recital of literary texts, which increasingly anticipated that their audience would not be highly educated. Somewhat later, in the early nineteenth century, the first printed newspapers appeared; in the coffeehouses, these would often be read aloud for those who could not read. Hence, and contra Benedict Anderson,[28] one might argue that the rise of secular nationalisms is not triggered simply by the mere presence of a particular technology, such as printing, but is shaped in and by particular practices that make use of those technologies. It was not just new practices of language that appeared, but also new ideologies: the new public use of language also brought along new demands for the simplification of language, with an eye to an audience that was fluent in different languages but not necessarily schooled in the languages of religious learning and high literature—in fact, an audience that was largely not even literate. Thus, new registers of literary Turkish gained ground, ones that did away with the flowery borrowings from Arabic or Persian that had characterized the classical language of Ottoman bureaucracy and elite poetry. Likewise, new forms of publicly used Modern Greek emerged that were closer to the spoken language than to the koine Greek taught in the religious schools. The practice and ideology of simpler registers of language, intended to be more easily accessible to the population at large rather than the jealously guarded privilege of a small elite, do not yet amount to the later Romantic-nationalist glorification of the language of the common people as the purest expression of the national soul or later attempts to purify national languages from allegedly alien borrowings. But they did pave the way.

Ottoman Coffeehouses: Secular Public Sphere or Heterotopia?

Coffeehouse culture cannot simply be called a form of civil society. In a very real sense, the eighteenth-century Ottoman empire knew no such thing as a generic Ottoman "society"; likewise, something like an Ottoman state, as distinct from the personality of the ruler, was very much in the process of being institutionalized during this period. Thus, the subject population was not seen or governed as a whole but divided along religious lines separating Muslims from protected non-Muslims (*dhimmis*). Perhaps more importantly, it was divided into a class of soldiers (*askeri*), as opposed to the "flock" (*re'aya*) of the civilian population, and into an educated elite (*khâssa*) and an illiterate mass (*'âmma*). Needless to say, these distinctions did not coincide; thus, in the eighteenth century the Greek-speaking Christians governing the Danube provinces were *askeri* ruling over a partly Muslim *re'aya*. More directly relevant to our discussion, since many coffeehouse keepers came from the ranks of the Janissaries, in theory they belonged to the *askeri*, though they were generally considered part of the illiterate masses.

Ottoman coffeehouses cannot unproblematically be seen as public spaces, either. It is tempting to oppose the coffeehouse as a typically male public space to the harem as typically female and private, but that would be a serious error. Not only did women often participate in coffeehouse activities, these activities also included practices that amounted to an extension of the domestic or private sphere and forms of communication (such as, most prominently, gossip) that tended to be associated with women; on the other hand, as Leslie Peirce has argued, inside the sultan's harem women often wielded real power that was effective in the "public" world of Ottoman high politics. This insight has led Alan Mikhail to argue that the Ottoman coffeehouse does not qualify as a public sphere in the Habermasian sense and that the very distinction between public and private is untenable in the Ottoman case: at different times, the coffeehouse served purposes of business or entertainment, of domestic affairs or matters of government.[29] The same holds, of course, for European coffeehouses and salons. Mikhail appears to miss Habermas's point that the public sphere is primarily a normative notion concerning legitimate discussion of matters political and only secondarily a descriptive historical category. Thus, my point here, *pace* Mikhail, is, first, that something novel and much like the European public sphere did indeed emerge in the eighteenth- and nineteenth-century Ottoman coffeehouses and, second, that its particularities force us to revise the Habermasian concept of the public sphere itself. With its rigid conceptual dichotomies, it may be less than useful even in abstract and analytic, let alone normative terms: thus, Mikhail has argued that, in a number of respects, the Ottoman coffeehouse might more fruitfully be seen as what Foucault has called a "heterotopia,"[30] that is, a real or enacted utopia or counter-site, in which other sites (such as, most relevantly, mosques, churches, or palaces) are simultaneously represented, contested, and inverted.

A heterotopia, according to Foucault, is simultaneously real and mythic or illusory. It offers an escape from, or contestation of, state power. As such, it has nontrivial normative implications, but it is less centrally based on a normative idea of the "public use of reason" or rational debate than is Habermas's notion of the public sphere. Now, some of the more distinctive features of the Ottoman coffeehouses emerge clearly when we consider them as heterotopias rather than asking whether or not they fit Habermas's normative and ethnocentric criteria of the public sphere: as we will see below, they were marked less by "rational debate" than by other linguistic practices that might be characterized as "secular" or anticlerical. Already by their very physical location, however, they could be seen, and were in fact seen, as a challenge to religious authority: significantly, a good many coffeehouses appeared near, or even adjacent to, mosques. Religious scholars and historians of the time were quick to notice that they involved a new kind of sociability, which formed a secular rival to the mosque as a public space.[31] Thus, the Ottoman historian Ibrahim Peçevi, writing around 1635, describes how, since their introduction in Constantinople, coffeehouses had attracted customers from the higher as well as the lower classes and how they had come to be seen as serious rivals to the local mosques:

These shops became meeting-places of a circle of pleasure-seekers and idlers, and also of some wits from among the men of letters and literati. . . . Some read books and fine writings, some were busy with backgammon and chess, and some brought new poems and talked of high literature. . . . It became so famous that, besides the holders of high offices, even great men could not refrain from coming there. The imams and muezzins and pious hypocrites said: "People have become addicts of the coffeehouse; nobody comes to the mosques!" The ulema said: "It is a house of evil deeds; it is better to go to the wine-tavern than there." The preachers in particular made great efforts to forbid it. . . . After this time, it became so prevalent that the ban was abandoned. . . . Among the ulema, the sheikhs, the viziers, and the great, there was nobody left who did not drink it.[32]

Peçevi and others appear quite aware that the increasing popularity of such secular spaces or heterotopias undermines religion, not only by drawing people away from the mosques but also by bringing the literate ulema and others together with the commoners. One of the central tenets of the premodern and early modern Islamic world was the strict separation between illiterate mass (*'âmma*) and literate or learned elite (*khâssa*). The masses were generally thought of as unfit for religious learning; thus, to mention but one example, Ibn Rushd (Averroes), in his famous fatwa on the legitimacy of philosophy, *Fasl al-maqâl* (*The Decisive Treatise*), expressly forbids the study of philosophy for the masses:

In general, everything in [revealed texts] which admits of allegorical interpretation can only be understood by demonstration [i.e., philosophical reasoning]. The duty of the elite here is to apply such interpretation; while the duty of the masses is to take them in their apparent meaning in both respects, i.e. in concept and judgment, since their natural capacity does not allow more than that. . . . The masses, who are incapable of more than rhetorical arguments, have the duty of taking these texts in their apparent meaning, and they are not permitted to know such interpretations at all.[33]

Ibn Rushd's views bear some resemblance to Kant's idea of the "public use of reason," which, as noted above, likewise restricts critique and the discussion of philosophy to a literate audience of *Gelehrten*.

Now, crucial to the emergence of the Ottoman coffeehouses and of a local public sphere is the increasing visibility and participation of illiterate or uneducated commoners in political and other discussions. Paired with this shift is a gradual change in meaning of the conceptual pair *'âmma-khâssa* from "mass-elite" to "public-private" in the modern, liberal sense. Although this change is not complete until the twentieth century, it already appears in the mid-nineteenth-century neologism *efkâr-i umumiyya* for "public opinion," in which the adjective *umumi* is based on the same verbal root as *'âmma*.[34]

The Ottoman coffeehouses involved not only increased contacts between mass and elite but also new public talk of matters of government. This becomes quite clear from a work of advice (*nasîhat*) written by Koca Sekbanbasi for the Ottoman sultan and signifi-cantly entitled *Hulâsat ül-Kelâm fi redd-ül avâm* ("Summary of the Discourse in Refuta-tion of the Commoners"), which alludes to the coffeehouse as a place where commoners (*awâm*) publicly talk about matters of government. Although he does not mention them by name, Sekbanbasi suggests that the Janissaries are commoners (*avâm*) rather than members of the literate elite (*khâssa*) and hence have no right to speak about matters of government in public. His comments are worth quoting in detail: "For some time past, a rabble composed of the dregs of the populace, setting themselves up for judges of the times, and assembling in the coffee-houses, barbers' shops, and taverns, have, in vain speeches, unbecoming their station, indulged themselves in the liberty of abusing and calumniating the Sublime Government."[35]

Clearly, Sekbanbasi sees public opinion as by definition illegitimate. He has no doubts, either, as to how Sulayman the Magnificent, the often-idealized ruler of the Otto-man empire's golden age, would have dealt with it: he would have ordered the tongues of those who spoke of politics, and the ears of those who listened, to be cut off and nailed on one of the city's gates for public display. His reasons for rejecting public opinion are what we would nowadays call religious: he argues that those commoners who criticize and vilify the Ottoman authorities are unwittingly themselves the true cause of the "cor-ruption of the world" (*fesâd-i âlem*): they are outwardly Muslims but "ignorant of the religious purities."[36] Thus, Sekbanbasi virtually identifies religion (*dîn*) with obedience to the ruler. At the same time, however, he appears to reflect the broader trend toward an expanding public, explicitly indicating that he writes in a simple and more broadly acces-sible language: "a correct statement of some events which ought to be made public, . . . we have undertaken to write it in a style which is simple, and easy to be understood."[37]

In other words, despite his resistance to the practice of public discussion of matters political, Sekbanbasi clearly shares the new ideology that public language should be more easily accessible and understandable to commoners. It was not until later that the Otto-man authorities started viewing public opinion (*efkâr-i umumiyya*) as a source of policy making rather than a cause for repression or punishment. Thus, Kirli notes that by the mid-nineteenth century the sultan sent spies to the coffeehouses not with the intention of punishing those speaking about matters political, as Sekbanbasi had recommended, but to sound out popular support for impending policy decisions; increasingly, such poli-cies were actually based on public opinion, albeit not through any formal process of consultation.[38]

Coffeehouse Culture: Between Western Hegemony and State Policies

Whether conceived of in Kantian and Habermasian terms as a public sphere or in a more Foucauldian vein as a heterotopia, the Ottoman coffeehouses provided a secular counterpart to the religious spaces of the mosques and the dervish lodges. The historical background from which they emerged, however, was quite different from that of contemporary Western and Central Europe. Hence, it should cause no surprise that the practices one encounters are different from the those seen in Europe. Obviously, one should not ask how far they live up to Habermas's notions of public reasoning and public critique but rather study them as locally developing practices.[39] Insofar as the Western European public sphere was in fact shaped and legitimated by an idea of the public use of reason and by norms of rational, polite discussion, as Habermas holds, this reflects the very particular historical constellations of early modern Europe, which should not tacitly be transformed into normative ideals without further ado. Unlike seventeenth-century England, the early modern Ottoman empire was not marked by pervasive religious conflicts that threatened to escalate into an all-out civil war, and unlike eighteenth-century Prussia, it was not marked by a struggle between an absolutist ruler and a socially powerful—and largely autonomous—clergy.

Thus, it was rather less anticlerical or antireligious than its European counterpart; moreover, public debate did not so much involve subjecting religion, or religious authority, to a secular rational critique but rather focused on ridicule, satire, and gossip, as becomes clear, in particular, from the Karagöz plays. This does not reflect the lack of critical reflection often alleged to be inherent in Islamic culture, however: witness the long-standing tradition of *munâzarât*, or public theological debates, which is attested in locations as far apart in space and time as early 'Abbâsid Baghdad and Emperor Akbar's India and which at times involved more radical critiques of prophethood and revealed religion than was possible in Europe until early modern times. One question to be explored on another occasion is how far and in what respects Ottoman coffeehouse culture, with its new and expanding public, actually differed from these premodern debates.[40]

One question left implicit by Habermas is how far the rise of a secular public sphere affected the sphere of religion; here, I would like to phrase this question in terms of how the novel linguistic practices and ideologies encountered in the Ottoman coffeehouses affected the category of religion itself, most importantly, through the gradual change in meaning of the *'âmma-khâssa* opposition. The new public spaces undermined or transformed the traditional religious opposition between mass and elite, and they paved the way for the new conceptions and practices of mass mobilization and a sovereign people that would characterize the late nineteenth and early twentieth centuries. Kirli argues that the emergence of public opinion led to the redefinition of public space as political, a change that he sees as more important than the formal introduction of citizenship rights by the Ottoman authorities in the late nineteenth century.[41] By extension, one might also argue that the emergence of a domain of literary practice and criticism, and of political commentary and gossip, implies the formation of a public sphere as a primarily secular arena. Religion was not seen as part of this newly emerging public sphere. Indeed, religion did not really enter this public sphere until much later, at least as a political ideology: a good case can be made that this process did not really materialize until well into the twentieth century.[42]

Thus, the emergence of something like a public sphere in Ottoman coffeehouses provides counterevidence to the claims, first, that modernity is an exclusively or even primarily Western phenomenon and, second, that in the Islamic world this process of modernization was shaped by the state rather than by society. The first point should be clear by now: both coffee as an article of consumption and the culture of the coffeehouse came to Europe from the Muslim Middle East, rather than vice versa. The second point concerns the claim, made by Talal Asad and some of his followers, about the character of legal and religious modernization in the Islamic world as imposed from above by states under Western hegemony or, as Asad puts it: "The translation of modern Western categories into the administrative and legal discourses of the non-Western world is a familiar story. It was through such discursive powers that people undergoing modernization were compelled to abandon old practices and turn to new ones."[43] Further, he argues that the constitution of the modern state required the "forcible redefinition of religion as belief" and of religious belief as not only a personal or private matter but also as primarily symbolic and irrational in nature.[44] In a later essay, he traces the redefinition of the category of religion (*dîn*) in the modern Islamic world to nineteenth-century changes in state power;[45] what Sami Zubaida has called the "etatization of the law," that is, the fact that the Ottoman state tried to make juridical practice more uniform and more directly under its control, is part of this broader process. Asad seems, however, to overemphasize the duration, uniformity, and pervasiveness of both the alleged Western hegemony and the state's role in these processes of modernization. Here, I would like to argue that the category of religion was not only redefined by the state but also affected by processes in society, or perhaps more precisely, by the very emergence of something like a civil society or public sphere. If this analysis holds, the Ottoman experience suggests that new secular spaces and a reconceptualization of religion may also have come about in relative autonomy from, or even in spite of, any state interference.

Thus, a new sense of public space and of distinct public uses of language, such as emerged prototypically in the Ottoman coffeehouses, was also instrumental in reconceptualizing the societal place and role of religion. Crucial to this process were changing ideologies of language, that is, folk-theoretical beliefs about what language is and how it functions and should function, in the world. Linguistic or more generally semiotic ideologies have in recent years become a major object of study in anthropological linguistics; they may also help us to refocus on the materiality of both language and religion. A focus on such ideologies should also caution us against structuralist (and more generally post-Enlightenment) construals of both language and religion as abstract, disembodied, and conceptually autonomous spheres of experience. The historical development of the Ottoman coffeehouse suggests that neither the religious nor the secular should be treated as a given.

Similar points about the historically contingent and variable character of such abstractions as *nature* and *society* have been raised by Bruno Latour, as noted above, but his discussion in *We Have Never Been Modern* does not make clear how religion fits in with what Latour calls the "modern constitution" articulated along the three axes of nature, society, and discourse.[46] If the religious and the secular are indeed interrelated entities mutually implied in defining and redefining each other, then the emergence of a new secular space like that of the coffeehouse will inevitably be accompanied by a redefinition of the religious. I would claim that linguistic ideologies and practices played a crucial role in the redefinition of the spheres of both the religious and the secular in the modernizing Ottoman empire.

My claims go beyond the increasingly widespread line of critique, pursued by Wendy Brown and Saba Mahmood, for example, that tends to dismiss secularism as an instrument of empire (or, more correctly, imperialism): the suggestion implicit in such criticism, that secularism is a purely Western invention, unwittingly reproduces the very ethnocentrism it sets out to criticize and ignores or downplays the early modern societal dynamisms in the non-Western world.[47] My point here, however, concerns the more general question of the rise of nation states out of the early modern Ottoman empire, which was in theory and practice more multilingual and multireligious than the Habsburg empire and Tsarist Russia. The early phases of this process lie in the eighteenth century and set off a concomitant reconceptualization of language, religion, and, indeed, the public.

Conclusion

The early Ottoman public sphere poses important conceptual and normative questions both for liberal conceptions of the modern secular public sphere and for genealogical critiques of secularism; moreover, the materiality of both the coffeehouse as a public space and of the embodied use of language encountered there calls for more systematic attention. I have argued that Ottoman coffeehouse culture crucially involved new public uses of language. These uses are mostly literary and otherwise "nonfunctional." Especially in the early stages, they are scarcely if at all conditioned by what Benedict Anderson calls "print capitalism," but they are partly constitutive of the public sphere and germane to later forms of cultural and political nationalism, even if they do not inherently lead to them. The Ottoman coffeehouses may also be called a secular public sphere insofar as they formed a public space that acted as an alternative or rival to religious spaces such as mosques and churches; more fruitfully, however, they may be described as a secular heterotopia, where both worldly and religious authority could become the object of gossip, literary representation, or lampoon-style mockery.

If this is so, the onset of this transformative process antedates by almost a century the "politicization of religion" that Kemal Karpat describes as occurring primarily during the Hamidian era and may be less the result of Western conceptual hegemony than Asad believes. My argument complements studies such as Richard Bauman and Charles L. Briggs's *Voices of Modernity: Language Ideologies and the Politics of Inequality* and Tomoko Masuzawa's *The Invention of World Religions: Or, How European Universalism Was Preserved in the Language of Pluralism* in that it explores more systematically changing forms of local agency, specifically, forms of agency that are autonomous—or at least distinct— from the developing state.[48]

Two features of the Ottoman public sphere stand out. First, it is more visibly multilingual than the public spheres emerging almost simultaneously in Paris, London, and Berlin. This suggests that, more generally and more systematically than Habermas would allow, public languages are actually *constitutive of* public spheres. Second, the Ottoman public sphere is less clearly secularist or anticlerical than its European counterpart. One reason for this may have been the fact that the Ottoman empire had a more clearly articulated, and more enduringly institutionalized, multilingual and multireligious character than, say, early modern France or England: the Ottoman religious hierarchy, with its supreme leader, or *sheykhülislam*, at its apex, was subordinate to the sultan and was generally seen as part of the state apparatus rather than as an independent societal power.

Both these features emerge more clearly when studied with an eye to the materiality of linguistic practices and ideologies. The new public use of both official and vernacular languages, paired with the ideology that such language should also be understandable for commoners (*awâm*)—indeed, the very fact of commoners speaking up in public at all, especially on matters of government—all had a direct bearing on the rearticulation of the religious as opposed to the secular and of religious authorities and elites.

The new public usages of languages or linguistic registers that had hitherto been considered unworthy by learning and literature, and the new ideologies that public language should be more widely understandable, also made possible some of the later developments. The public use of languages in coffeehouses paved the way for their later use by the state in education and mass communication, and the ideology that language should be understandable by the common people anticipates, but does not yet embody, both the practice of national languages and the Romantic-nationalist notion of the pure and uncontaminated language of the people as embodying the national soul or spirit. Such Romantic usages and ideologies did not gain currency, in the Ottoman empire as in Europe, until the latter part of the nineteenth century; thus they fall outside the scope of the present paper. What all this does make clear, however, is that secular nationalism in the Islamic world has roots that lie too far back in the past to be explained entirely as resulting from European influence and that it does not appear to have been imposed from above by the state.

The Affective Power of the Face Veil
Between Disgust and Fascination

Annelies Moors

In December 2005, the Netherlands became the first country where a parliamentary majority voted in favor of a ban on face veiling in all public space. Although for legal reasons this general ban was not implemented, in the years to follow partial, functional bans on face coverings were put into effect.[1] Elsewhere, too, bans on the face veil are debated and sometimes implemented. The face veil certainly is a thing that disturbs.

Dutch debates about face veiling are far removed from the Habermasian ideal-typical formation of public opinion through the rational exchange of points of view. Rather, feelings of discomfort, disgust, fear, and resentment among the majority public have come to be considered grounds for legal intervention, with debates increasingly characterized by the use of a strongly affective language. Such an affective turn in public debate fits well with the broader process of the culturalization of citizenship, with citizenship being defined not only in terms of legal rights and duties but also as requiring evidence of the acceptance of Dutch values.[2]

Simultaneously, theory in the social sciences and the humanities has witnessed a renewed interest in feelings, emotions, and affect. This concern extends even to law. Martha Nussbaum has criticized the commonsense notion "that the law is based on reason and not passion."[3] Taking issue with the idea that all emotions are irrational, she argues that it would be difficult to conceive of a system of law that "did not include a substantive normative role for certain sorts of emotions, and for norms of reasonableness in emotion."[4] More generally, critical thinkers such as William Connolly and Wendy Brown have emphasized that, by presenting itself as separate from and even the opposite of passion and emotion, rationality has concealed how emotions affect and are intertwined with reason.[5]

Apart from Nussbaum's strongly cognitive theory of emotion, others have turned to the notion of affect to refer to the nondiscursive sensations and intensities that objects generate.[6] They are critical of post-structuralist theories of subjectivity, which they consider to be too concerned with language and discourse. Rather than focusing on cognition and signification (with its dichotomies of subject and object), they turn to corporeal experience and recognize the affective power of things and the need to examine how people experience this affective power.

At first sight, such a turn to the affect of things seems particularly fortuitous for the case of face veiling, as the face veil has certainly engendered strong feelings and sparked public displays of emotion. However, I will argue that a paradigmatic shift from cognition and discourse to affect and experience does not work very well when we attempt to understand the affect face veiling produces. It is true that a focus on the affective power of things is certainly helpful in analyzing the work face veiling does. However, discourse, subjectivity, and signification do matter. As Yael Navaro-Yashin has argued, neither things nor people "are affective on their own or in their own right, but both produce and transmit affect relationally."[7] Understanding the affective power of things, especially items of dress, whose effect is closely tied to the idea that they are to be worn, also requires understanding how subjects constitute themselves and are constituted through their dealings with these things.[8]

In investigating how both people and things, subjects and objects, work as circuits for, produce and are produced by, affect, I will ask how a rather insignificant piece of cloth becomes such a tremendously powerful, affective object once people use it to cover (part of) the face in public. In order to better understand what is at stake, I will present three perspectives from which to discuss this vexed issue. The first, "naming/framing" centers on how things are qualified and contested through language, with the various parties concerned holding strong and divergent points of view. The particular term used to label the piece of cloth covering part of the face has a strong effect on its affective power. In other words, language matters. I will then turn to how the face veil is experienced. Not only in public debate but also in everyday life the face veil is evaluated very differently by the women who wear it (and those supportive of this practice) and the majority public. Although those who wear face veils consider them both morally desirable and aesthetically pleasing, the majority public is affected in a very different way. To the latter, the sight of someone wearing a face veil has a thoroughly disturbing effect, often phrased in terms of discomfort, dislike, or even disgust. In conclusion, I will focus on how face veils have become a source of fascination and a visual icon par excellence through the work they also do in framing the eyes and drawing attention to the body. Yet neither disgust nor fascination is simply experiential: both are part of cultural histories of contestation, which acquire a particular saliency at moments when citizenship is culturalized.

Naming as Framing: Language Matters

The face veil is an utterly insignificant thing, consisting of one or more pieces of cloth. It may be simply a long, rectangular piece of material, which turns into a face veil only when it is wrapped around the face in particular ways. It may also be a small piece of cloth with straps or snaps attached to the back that make it easy to put on quickly, so as to cover the lower part of the face, and to take it off. Some face veils consist of two or three layers of cloth with a slit for the eyes, the semi-transparent top layer attached in such a way that it can either show or cover the eyes. The material itself comes in a variety of thicknesses and may be opulent or partially transparent. Depending upon the nature of the cloth and its texture, whether it be thin cotton or various kinds of synthetics, it has a particular feel. Face veils also come in different lengths, from those that just cover the face and the neck to ones that are much longer. Whereas they are often a single color—usually black—white, pastels or darker, subdued colors, occasionally with designs or decorations, are also used. Some models are part of a larger garment covering the head and body and have mesh in front of the eyes. In Muslim-majority countries, various terms are used to describe these items of dress.[9]

In the Dutch context, labeling these items "face veils" turns out to be far from neutral. This becomes evident when one traces shifts in the terms used, from the moment when the face veil emerged as a major topic of public concern. This happened in December 2002, when three sixteen- and seventeen-year-old Dutch-Moroccan students who had come to school wearing face veils were refused entry to the school grounds. Two of them subsequently raised a complaint with the Equal Treatment Commission (CGB), claiming that they had been discriminated against on the grounds of religion.[10] The school, however, argued that this was not so, as its ruling prohibited the wearing of *any type of face covering*. In its verdict, the Equal Treatment Commission supported the school's line of argumentation. Both the ruling against wearing face coverings at school and the decision of the Equal Treatment Commission to uphold it gained wide public support, including among Muslim organizations.

Why did the school use *face coverings* in its ruling rather than *face veils*? The school used this neutral term, which can also refer to masks, visors, and so on, in order to counter the accusation of direct discrimination on the grounds of religion. This is important, because there is no legal justification for direct discrimination. It is true that a ruling against face coverings may still be considered *indirect* discrimination, as it disproportionately affects those who adhere to a particular religion. This was indeed the point of view held by the CGB. However, indirect discrimination is allowed if an "objective justification" makes such a ruling necessary. The school's arguments that wearing face coverings impedes communication central to the education process, hinders identification and hence poses a security risk, and strongly diminishes the girls' chances for internships and future employment were accepted as objective justifications. Not surprisingly, then, in following years the term *face coverings* (in Dutch *gelaatsbedekkende kleding* or GBK) has become the term used in official documents and among civil servants, with all parties concerned well aware of the fact that the real target is Islamic face veils.

When newspapers started to report on this case, many terms were used to describe the piece of cloth with which the young women covered (part of) their faces. These terms included *gezichtssluier* ("face veil"), *chador*, *niqab*, and *burqa*, in various spellings. "Face veil" refers to a piece of cloth that covers (part of) the face. *Niqab* is the term the women themselves used for the particular style of face veils they were wearing; it is also the term widely used for such face coverings in the Arab world. It is true that in some parts of the Arab world the term *burqu* is also used for face veils, but the women concerned never used this term, as in the Netherlands (and elsewhere in the West) it is conflated with the term *burqa*, which refers to the all-covering, light-colored Afghan garment that is pulled over the head and has mesh in front of the eyes.[11] Whereas the term *burqa* is used for such a garment in Pakistan and Northern India, in Afghanistan itself the term *chadari* is far more common. This may in fact have been the reason why some journalists at first used the term *chador*. In the Dutch context, however, that is again rather confusing, as the term *chador* is commonly used to refer to the all-enveloping cloak women wear in Iran, which typically does *not* cover the face.

If at first journalists used these terms interchangeably, within a few years this had changed. Whereas in 2003 the term *niqab* was used far more often than *burqa* to refer to the style of face veils worn, by 2006 the variety of terms had narrowed down to one preferred term, the *burqa*, which by then was used far more often than *niqab*. In part this happened because a central player in the debates about face veiling, Geert Wilders, has consistently employed the term *burqa* in public debate. In 2005, he proposed a resolution explicitly asking for a prohibition on publicly wearing the *burqa*, not face coverings in general.

The widespread use of the term *burqa* in public debate is remarkable. First, most face-veiling women in the Netherlands cover the forehead and the lower part of the face with a thin piece of cloth, often leaving the eyes visible. This is far more like Middle Eastern and North African styles of face veiling than the Afghan-style *burqa*. Second, the use of the term *burqa* is not a matter of ignorance. Newspaper editors are well aware of the differences between the *burqa* and the *niqab*. Nearly every time face veiling is discussed, either an article is published that explains the names used for different styles of covering or a letter to the editor points to the fact that women in the Netherlands do not wear a *burqa*, but a *niqab*. The stylebook published by the editor-in-chief of *De Volkskrant* also explains that the *burqa* is an Afghan garment, which is hardly ever worn in the Netherlands. It criticizes the intermingled use of the terms *burqa* and *niqab*, and explains that the former has a slit that leaves the eyes visible, adding that it is the *niqab* that is actually worn in the Netherlands.[12] Nonetheless, *Volkskrant* journalists too mainly employ the term *burqa* for face veiling.[13]

The use of the term *burqa* for face veils in the Netherlands is not innocent. When the first face-veiling case emerged in 2003, the term *burqa* was already known to the public. Newspaper articles from 2001 and 2002 commonly used the term *burqa* in articles about the Taliban regime in Afghanistan, which had come to be defined as the most repressive regime for women ever, with the *burqa* as visual proof.[14] Not only would the media, in subsequent years, reiterate this link of face veiling to the Taliban and women's gender oppression, but in parliamentary debates the term *burqa*, with all its associations, worked in a similar way. This was, for instance, evident in the course of a 2008 parliamentary consultation on face coverings, when not only the representative of Geert Wilders's Party for Freedom but also the representative of the right-wing Liberal Party repeatedly used the specter of Afghanistan and the Taliban regime to argue for a general ban on the *burqa* as "this is not something that we should want in the Netherlands."

In other words, language does matter. Qualifying things through words may have a societal effect, and the *burqa* is a particularly strong case. Naming a piece of cloth or an item of dress a *burqa* when this has already come to stand for the oppressive gender regime of the Taliban conjures up a world in itself. Things do not simply produce affects or function as nodes in circuits in which affect circulates: the affect things evoke may also be grounded in discourse, in the language through which these things are qualified or framed. This certainly has been the case with the face veil turned *burqa*. The point is not that an incorrect term is used but rather that it is an overdetermined term that evokes Muslim women's gender subjugation.

Experiencing the Power of Face Veils

Face veiling does not have affective force only through the terms used to refer to this practice. A major way in which face veils evoke particular feelings and engage in the production and circulation of affect is through corporeal experience, which includes both the tactile and the visual. The act of wearing a face veil affects both those who are themselves involved in the practice (or want to do so) and the majority society in very different ways.

Wearing a Face Veil: What Does It Do?

What do face veils do to or for those who wear them? Face veils, worn on the body, belong to a particular category of artifacts, that is, items of dress. To a woman wearing it, a face veil is not only a matter of how she looks, but also of how a face veil feels and acts upon her body. Although practicality is only one argument in discussions of choice of dress, it is an issue to which face-veiling women regularly refer. One dimension of practicality pertains to the legal field, and to public space. In the Netherlands, some institutions—such as some universities, schools, and banks—do not allow people with face coverings to enter their premises. A practical compromise solution for face-veiling women is then to wear a style of face veiling that allows them easily to cover and uncover the lower part of their faces. More important, however, to the women concerned is the "feel" of face veils, which brings in tactility. When selecting a face veil, women not only check whether "the look" fits with their intentions but also whether the texture of the material is such that they can breathe easily, that their skin does not become irritated, and that they are able to move around with relative ease. Only then is face veiling a practice that can be sustained over a long period of time.

Women who wear face veils express strongly positive feelings about face veiling. For them, to do so is first and foremost to engage in a highly desirable religious practice. As they told me in the course of our conversations, they consider wearing a face veil to be an act of worship and a means of expressing their love for God. "It is a way to get closer to God, it is a way to experience again the intense feeling of being in love with Islam." As most women consider wearing a face veil an act that is recommended rather than obligatory, this means that they are doing "something extra." Engaging in such a moral act, they feel strongly and positively affected, which they experience and express in a variety of ways. Some turn to a spiritual language, saying they experience a sense of "floating through the air," or refer to "experiencing a feeling of inner peace." Others point to how wearing a face veil makes them feel good: "I felt really, wow, this is it. I felt strong." Such statements may also refer to having been able to overcome many obstacles to dressing in this way. In contrast to the majority public's view that these women are forced to wear a face veil by their kin or husbands, many face-veiling women emphasize that they have to face considerable resistance from their families and from society at large.

There are also other ways in which face veiling affects them. As in Saba Mahmood's analysis of the effects of veiling on Egyptian women in the piety movement, face veiling not only produces certain feelings but also has an effect on women's behavior.[15] As the women with whom I talked pointed out, "You are not only more at peace with yourself, more quiet, but you also act that way." After all, "if you wear a *niqab* you should not hang around and talk loudly, that does not go together with wearing a face veil, even if there are some sisters who do so." To the women concerned, wearing a face veil is evidently a self-disciplinary practice. Still, it is not simply a corporeal practice that affects one's inner state of being. They simultaneously emphasize that, in order for face veiling to have such an effect, it is crucially important that one wears a face veil with a pure intention: "Everything you do needs to be based on a pure intention; that means that you do it only for Allah and not, for instance, because of social pressure or because it is a trend." In other words, only when one has developed the required mind-set does face veiling have the desired effect. Moreover, such an inner state of being can be the effect of both affective experience and cognitive reasoning. Some women started to cover and wear the face veil because of an intensely felt need to do so, "that is why it is called belief, not knowledge." Only later would they study the correct forms of wearing *hijab*. For others, through gaining Islamic knowledge they came to understand that they needed to change their styles of dress: "It starts in the heart, but now I realize that if it is in your heart, it will also become present in your appearance."

Given that face veiling is considered a highly appreciated moral act, it is no surprise that these women enjoy the presence of others wearing face veils and the accompanying forms of strictly covering dress. They not only express their pleasure in sharing the same moral universe but also highlight the beauty of such styles of dress: "I find it fascinating, totally covered, it looks so complete; I find that very very beautiful." They appreciate the simplicity of Islamic dress: everything is in one or at most two colors. They love the flow of the long, loose garments, sometimes pointing out that they had already been impressed by such styles of dress even before they became committed Muslims. In other words, they engage in a sartorial aesthetics that, by striking contrast to many Western styles of women's dress, refuses overt public display of their bodies. They experience this style as manifesting a pure and mysterious form of beauty, one that demands spiritual growth and self-discipline. Such a style of appearing in public is very different from a contemporary secular morality that considers the visibility of women's sexualized bodies to be a measure of their freedom and gender equality.[16]

The Sight of a Face Veil: The Discomfort of the Majority Public

Whereas women wearing face veils consider this practice to be both religiously recommended and aesthetically beautiful, the majority public holds a diametrically opposite view: they evaluate face veiling very negatively, both in moral and in aesthetic terms. Such a strongly negative affective register can be seen not only in letters to the editor, responses on populist websites, or statements by ordinary people, but also in parliamentary debate and in public statements made by politicians and others in positions of authority. Moreover, not only those who would like to ban face veils from all public space but also those who are very critical of such a general ban feel the need to state publicly their lack of appreciation for this sartorial practice and to express strong feelings of discomfort and anxiety. The chair of an expert committee, for instance, who had strongly criticized attempts to ban the face veil, was quoted in a major daily as stating "I find a face veil a terrible sight."[17] Job Cohen, then mayor of the city of Amsterdam, who was well known for his nuanced stance on public Islam and who also strongly opposed a general ban, stated publicly: "Personally I find it horrible to see a woman in a *burqa*."[18] While he was the Dutch prime minister, Jan-Peter Balkenende felt the need to express his personal feelings, saying: "Once I saw a woman wearing a *burqa*, and I did not like that."[19] To the majority public, face veils are evidently an offensive sight.

Although legislators do not explicitly refer to disgust, subjective feelings of unsafety and a sense of discomfort have been presented as grounds for making laws against face veiling. Such a line of argumentation became particularly popular once it had become clear that face veils could not be prohibited on the ground of their being an objective threat to security, given that the authorities concerned—such as public transportation and border control—publicly denied the existence of such a threat. A strong example of how such subjective feelings entered the realm of parliamentary deliberation is the Cabinet letter sent to parliament on February 8, 2008, that argued for specific, functional bans on face veiling rather than for a general ban.[20] Explaining its arguments for such functional bans, the Cabinet highlighted the importance of open communication for the interaction between people in society, starting with the general observation: "The mutual acceptance of difference and commonality emerges when people are able to get to know and relate to each other without hindrance. Wearing face coverings strongly impedes such open communication." Turning from face coverings in general to Islamic face veils, the Cabinet then analyzed the problems the latter cause in society. They "evidently hinder open communication, . . . are considered oppressive to women, and, to many, are a symbol of a fundamentalist Islam that does not suit Dutch society." Recognizing that this style of dress evokes in many "a feeling of anxiety and unsafety," the Cabinet explained that it "considers open communication between citizens, participation, and equal chances for men and women essential values of Dutch society and our democratic rule of law." It saw itself as responsible "for guaranteeing such open communication where that is essential for the development and functioning of the democratic rule of law." In short, the Cabinet considered "wearing such clothing undesirable and intends to actively oppose it wherever necessary."

The idea that face veiling is an obstacle to open communication and related to such undesirable phenomena as women's subjugation and Islamic fundamentalism is widespread. For many, the moral rejection of face veiling is based on the assumption that face veiling is a strong sign, instrument, or symbol of women's gender oppression, a notion already evoked by the use of the term *burqa*. When, in response to the Cabinet's 2008 plans for partial functional bans, Wilders proposed a draft bill that would instate a general prohibition, it was grounded in such assumptions. Moreover, many who would reject a general ban still supported an analysis that linked face veiling with women's oppression. Not only in parliament but also in popular culture this has become a common trope. In a best-selling booklet of cartoons by Peter de Wit, called *Burka Babes* and featuring as central characters two women in black outfits and face veils, women's gender oppression, as well as a link with radical Islam, are common themes.[21] One cartoon, for example, features two face-veiled women talking to each other in the pouring rain. One asks, "Looking forward to spring?" The other answers, "Not sure. I'll have to ask my husband."[22] A second example depicts two face-veiled women addressing a third one, who is carrying explosives—a rocket launcher and a machine gun. They say, "O I get it, the boys go all fundamentalist and you're left to do the donkey work."[23] If face veils are perceived as a strong sign of women's oppression, then it is not surprising that people experience a sense of discomfort or even disgust and anger when confronted with someone wearing a face veil.

The strongly affective language used in public debate and the use of feelings of dislike and discomfort to ground lawmaking make this a strong instance of the performativity of discourse.[24] Expressing feelings of dislike and even disgust about face veiling structures the perception of face veils and contributes to the production of such feelings. In the words of Sara Ahmed: "It is not making something out of nothing. But to say something is disgusting is still to make something; it generates a set of effects, which then adheres as a disgusting object."[25] This is obviously what has happened with respect to face veiling. Whereas it is true that face veiling in itself may evoke a feeling of discomfort, the discourse linking women's oppression and radical Islam, as well as expressions of disgust by those in positions of authority, have certainly contributed to and helped normalize this.[26]

Labeling face veiling as disgusting has a strong societal effect. Talking about disgusting things is always already social, as it is necessarily shared with others, "whose shared witnessing of the disgusting thing is required for the affect to have an effect," as Ahmed writes.[27] Labeling something as disgusting "generates more than simply a subject and an object; it also generates a community of those who are bound together through the shared condemnation of a disgusting object or event."[28] Nussbaum is also highly critical of the use of disgust—which she considers an irrational emotion—as a basis in lawmaking. Highlighting that those who defend the appeal to disgust in making laws have all been communitarians, she argues: "What their thought shares is the idea that society ought to have at its core a homogeneous group of people whose ways of living, of having sex, of looking and being, are defined as 'normal.' People who deviate from that norm may then be stigmatized and penalized by law, even if their conduct causes no harm."[29]

This is very much what happened in the case of face veiling in the Netherlands. The assumption that we need to see each others' facial features for open communication to occur does not recognize that the display of emotions may conceal as well as reveal. That face veiling touches upon something else became clear during discussions with university teachers who had among their students two girls wearing face veils.[30] In general conversations about face veiling, they would indeed raise the problem of communication, but when they discussed their personal experiences, such practical problems either did not occur or turned out to be only a minor issue. What mattered most to those objecting to face veiling was, as they phrased it, the girls' refusal "to accept our values," the fact that they did not want "to make an effort to integrate in society" and that they "purposely and provocatively set themselves apart." In other words, it is the refusal to accept mainstream Dutch values that matters.

This brings up the issue of how certain effects are linked or adhere to specific categories of people. Why does face veiling evoke women's gender oppression, a major ground for considering it a disgusting act? I would argue that it is not so much the act in itself but rather the fact that Muslim women engage in this practice that almost automatically turns it into a sign of women's oppression. In other words, it is the category of women involved that makes the link between covering part of the face and women's gender oppression self-evident, despite the fact that they themselves consider it above all a religious practice in which they have chosen to engage. To a liberal secular public, engaging publicly in religious practices in itself already stands in a tense relation to the notion of the free, autonomous subject. This is all the more so in the case of Islamic practices such as face veiling, shaped by a long colonial history that has naturalized the notion of Muslim women as the victims of their own men or culture.[31]

Whereas disgust is above all about taste, smell, and touch, in the case of face veiling it works through the visual. As William Miller has argued, the visual can "horrify in its own right independently of suggestions from other senses."[32] It functions as a means of social control, confirming others as belonging to a lower status. At the same time, however, the fact that Muslim women cover their faces in public clashes with the long-standing convention that those in power may choose to remain invisible, while subaltern populations are turned into objects of scrutiny. The moral condemnation of the act of face veiling, engaged in by Muslim women, who are already defined as the victims of gender oppression, stands in a tense relation to their defiantly visible presence in the public space. Appearing in public wearing a face veil works as a corporeal challenge to Dutch normativities of gender and sociality, and hence evokes feelings not only of discomfort but also of resentment and anger. This is the more so at a moment when the shift toward the culturalization of citizenship increasingly puts pressure on Muslims to accept and incorporate Dutch cultural values.

The Face Veil as a Source of Fascination

In the course of the first decade of the twenty-first century, the term *burqa* has become firmly inserted into the Dutch vocabulary. It has become the preferred term for referring to the face veil among the majority public, and it is also increasingly used metaphorically as a means of attracting public attention. It has become a popular term in titles of largely unrelated theater plays, performances, films, books (such as Ebru Umar's *Burka en Blahniks*), and television programs (*Bimbo's en Boerka's*), as well as in wordplay and jokes. Although some of these—like the cartoons mentioned earlier—amplify the discourse of dislike and disgust, it may also be argued that the routinization of the term *burqa* has to some extent emptied it of meaning.

Next to the verbal *burqa*, there is also another *burqa* present in public space: the ubiquitous visual imagery of face-veiling women, as on posters and book covers. In a few cases, such imagery actually depicts a woman wearing an Afghan-style *burqa*. A strong example is, for instance, the poster a Dutch university produced to announce a public lecture by Dr. Asma Barlas about Islamic feminism: it foregrounds a picture of a woman wearing an Afghan *burqa* and carrying a small child.[33]

Most of this visual imagery, however, depicts women wearing a *niqab*-style face veil that leaves the eyes visible. These face-veil images are in some cases used to convey a message that is intended to be related to the practice of face veiling: for instance, an image of two women, presented as jigsaw puzzle pieces, one with a face veil, the other with piercings, is part of a government job-advertisement campaign to present the diverse issues (puzzles) civil servants deal with in their work. Another poster, produced by a development NGO, employs a picture of a face-veiled woman in a campaign to defend the rights of lesbians. These two images are obviously linked to public debate, but in ambivalent ways. Whereas the "puzzle poster" was explicitly intended to refer to issues with which civil servants must deal, many viewers interpreted it quite differently, analyzing it as conveying the message that everyone is welcome to work as a civil servant.[34] In the case of the NGO poster, the use of an image of a face-veiled woman, even if the setting was South Asia, should be seen within a context in which the acceptance of homosexuality has become a litmus test for Muslims to prove their integration into Dutch society.

However, just as with the verbal use of the term, there are also many instances where such visual imagery is simply used to catch public attention. A university website employs a stylized image of a face-veiled woman as its frame; a poster for a film screening about migrant women and sports uses the image of face veiling (although none of the women concerned wears a face veil), and a veiled face was also used to draw attention to a thematically unrelated university lecture series on Asia. What is most striking is how, in all these cases, face veils frame and highlight beautiful, or beautifully made-up, eyes.[35] Such attractive, mysterious, partially covered faces are also prominently present on the covers of popular books that focus, often in stereotypical ways, on women's oppression in the Muslim world.[36] These face veils are highly ambiguous, because they are simultaneously employed to emphasize women's oppression visually and to attract public attention. William Miller has argued that, even as the disgusting repels, "it rarely does so without also capturing our attention. It imposes itself upon us. We find it hard not to sneak a second look."[37] But these images of face-veiling women work in a different way. They do not make one at first recoil and pull away, rather, they intend, through their aesthetic appeal, to catch the eye and become a source of fascination. They are fascinating visuals.

Whereas in public debate the face veil is associated with Muslim women's gender oppression, such visual imagery evokes attractive and seductive Oriental women. The movie *Submission*, produced by Ayaan Hirsi Ali and the late Theo van Gogh and shown on television in 2004, brings these two discourses together: gender subordination is central in the text, while the visual imagery draws attention not only to beautiful eyes but also to a highly sensual female body.[38] The textual narrative of the movie is straightforward. Four women recount how they have been victimized through forced marriage, rape by a family member, the punishment of whipping for a sexual relation outside of marriage, and domestic violence. References are provided to Qur'anic verses, and the message is hard to miss: Muslim lives are determined by Islam, and violence against Muslim women is causally linked to the Qur'an. To bring this message home, the visual imagery shows Qur'anic verses and traces of whippings on the skin of the women's bodies, underneath transparent gowns.

Yet the visual imagery does more than show these traces of violence. Whereas their bodies are exposed, the faces of these women are covered, except for their beautiful eyes. Such a simultaneous covering and uncovering of the female body through the use of semi-transparent forms of dress or veiling has long been a trope of Orientalist painting, as well as of popular visual imagery, such as colonial postcards.[39] In *Submission*, the fact that the women's faces are partially covered draws attention not only to their eyes but also to their bodies. While the verbal narrative highlights Muslim women's suffering, the visual imagery does not picture downtrodden women, but rather seductive, eroticized, and exotic bodies.

The bringing together of face veiling, nudity, and sexuality is most explicit in the field of humor. In the *Burka Babes* booklet, references to sexuality are one of the most common themes, including sexy underwear and visible breasts and buttocks. One cartoon, for instance, depicts one of the face-veiled characters saying to the other: "You should wear a thong under that burka. You've got a visible panty line."[40] Another has one of the characters wearing a tiny bikini on top of her all-covering outfit, explaining: "It's a burkini."[41] This kind of imagery—linking face veiling with sexuality—goes against the grain of what face-veiling women aim to achieve, namely, the ability to enter public space without having imposed upon them an imperative to sexual display.

There are, however, also alternative ways of picturing face veils. In his analysis of nondocumentary *burqa* pictures on the Internet, Pekka Rantanen has argued that, whereas documentary *burqa* pictures are rather uniform representations, nondocumentary *burqa* pictures are "in many ways ambivalent representations," which may encourage the public "to think reflectively and turn one's attention to the very legitimacy of stereotypical representation."[42] Some of de Wit's cartoons may individually function as such, especially the ones playing with the fashion concept—for instance, the cartoon on the cover of the book, where two veiled characters exclaim "Snob!" at the sight of a third one wearing an all-covering Burberry-print *burqa*. A stronger example is how artist and fashion designer Aziz Bekkaoui has used the *burqa* in his visual art. In his exhibit *Times Burka Square*, he employed glossy billboards with elegant, playful women modeling black face veils and long gowns in combination with slight adaptations of famous advertising slogans, such as "Because I'm more than worth it," a play on L'Oréal's original slogan "Because I'm worth it," in order to normalize the presence of the *burqa*. Other examples are "Let's make things beautiful" (adapted from "Let's make things better"—Philips), "I'm just loving it" (referring to "I'm loving it"—McDonalds), and "Just do it right" (playing on "Just do it"—Nike). Whereas these images also present attractive bodies, they do so by creatively playing with the fashion-advertising genre.[43]

In other words, the face veil as a source of fascination can do different kinds of work. The term is often used simply to attract public attention without any particular relation to content. Visual imagery of face veils framing beautiful eyes may work in a similar way. Both women wearing face veils and religious scholars are well aware of this. They cannot help feeling uncomfortable, however, when face veils are combined with revealing styles of dress or, as in cartoons, with explicit references to nudity and sexuality, which mock what many face-veiling women aim to achieve: that, again, is the ability to be present in public without being put sexually on display.

Conclusion

Face veils evoke strong affective sensations. They certainly disturb, but they do not disturb everyone. The women who wear face veils or would like to do so stand in a profoundly different relation to face veils from the majority public. For the former, covering one's face in public is a morally recommended religious practice, wearing a face veil affects their behavior in a positive sense, and they experience face veils as aesthetically beautiful. The majority public, by contrast, experience face veils as producing discomfort, disgust, fear, anger, and resentment. Such feelings do not just occur naturally. Part of the story is that politicians actively engage in producing such feelings among their constituencies through the use of affective language. In producing feelings of disgust vis-à-vis an exceedingly small group of people, they simultaneously produce a strong sense of bonding among the majority public. In other words, affect works to produce both the objects of this discourse and the subjects themselves.

But this still begs the question of why face veils work *so well* as things that disturb. I would argue that they do so because they are inseparable from Muslim women as objects of a deeply ingrained and sedimented Orientalist discourse that a priori defines such women as victims of their own culture. This also explains why the term *burqa* has, after taking a detour through the Taliban regime in Afghanistan, become so quickly the preferred term for face veils in the Netherlands. Such forms of signification turn face veiling—a specific sartorial practice—into something that is experienced as morally reprehensible.

Face veils do not disturb simply because the majority public considers them to be a sign of or mechanism for Muslim women's oppression. It is the dissonance between framing face-veiling women as victims and the perception of their public presence as challenging Dutch sociabilities that evokes resentment. Such disturbing effects are also due to the particular historical moment. Starting in the 1990s, there has been a growing unease with the presence of Islam and Muslim migrants in the Netherlands.[44] Following the Rushdie affair and the fall of the Berlin Wall, Islam became newly targeted as the enemy, and people who were formerly defined in terms of ethnicity now came to be labeled Muslims. The ensuing decade witnessed a double move toward the culturalization of citizenship—demanding some measure of cultural assimilation—and the explicit call among policy makers for a stronger national identity. Under such conditions, defining face veiling in public debate as simultaneously a sign of gender oppression and an active refusal to integrate in Dutch society produces a profound sense of discomfort and resentment.

To complicate matters further, whereas in public debate face veiling is morally condemned and aesthetically devalued, in the world of the visual imaginary face veils work in more diverse ways. It is true that some of these images only amplify feelings of fear and discomfort or mock face-veiling women.[45] However, face veils also fascinate, drawing attention to the eyes as well as the body. In doing so, they evoke a different strand of Orientalism, that is, the trope of the seductive Oriental or Muslim woman, highly popular in the nineteenth century as a counterpoint to the ideal of the chaste and virtuous Victorian woman. Yet whereas in those days such a seductive presence was accompanied by moral condemnation, in contemporary Western societies the visible presence of women's sexuality is celebrated. To understand how face veils disturb requires, then, not only the recognition of agentic power among those who are supposedly ruled by and victims of their culture and religion but also the acknowledgment that affect is inscribed both discursively and nondiscursively in the "rational" field of the political in societies that define themselves as liberal and secular.

"There is a spirit in that image"

Mass-Produced Jesus Pictures and Protestant-Pentecostal Animation in Ghana

Birgit Meyer

In southern Ghana, where I have been conducting research on the genesis of popular Christianity for almost twenty years, Christian imagery is everywhere. The Ghanaian state readopted a democratic constitution in 1992, and this was followed by a liberalization and commercialization of the mass media, which in turn facilitated the spread of Pentecostalism in the public sphere.[1] Within this process, Christian pictures have become ubiquitous. Pentecostal-charismatic churches assert their public presence and power via television, radio, posters, and stickers, and there has also emerged a new public culture rife with Christian imagery. This visual and aural expansion of Christianity and its particular aesthetic severely challenges what is being called African Traditional Religion and clashes with initiatives developed by the state and intellectuals to secure a national heritage.

The spread of Christian imagery via mass media testifies to a remarkable alignment of religion and technologies of mass reproduction. However, it would be mistaken to understand this alignment in terms of a loss of substance, as if in "the information age" religion is bound to erode.[2] On the contrary, the successful public presence of religion today depends on the ability of its proponents to locate it in the marketplace of culture and to embrace audiovisual mass media so as to assert their public presence.[3] Placed within a thriving mass-mediated environment, mass-produced pictures are an intriguing case in point. These pictures, far from featuring as mere depictions bereft of an aura and looked at with a distant, objectifying gaze (as an admittedly too simple understanding of Benjamin might suggest[4]), can be unsettling presences that bring their beholders under their spell. This pertains not only to pictures of evil, which may easily slip into evil pictures and render present the dangerous forces they depict, but also to pictures of

Jesus. Although Jesus pictures have an overwhelming presence in public and private spaces as posters, stickers, paintings, and calendars, many staunch Pentecostals criticize such pictures as illicit representations that may be hijacked by Satan and lead people astray.

At first glance, the dismissal of Jesus pictures as potentially satanic seems to run counter to the dualism of God and the Devil, which is at the base of Pentecostals' attitude toward the world and which features supremely in their urge to make Christian imagery materialize in the public sphere. But the iconoclastic attitude toward these mass-produced pictures is part of a broader Pentecostal crusade in southern Ghana against a particular kind of material culture associated with shrines and artifacts of local religious traditions, as well as with items such as tourist masks and other things associated with Ghanaian cultural heritage. To "take Jesus Christ as your personal savior" is the central tenet of Pentecostal conviction and is thought to be a viable mode of protecting oneself against evil spirits. Born-again believers hail Jesus, yet they tend to consider pictures of him dangerous, because such pictures have a remarkable potential to become demonic presences. This is not simply a matter of a pictorial representation becoming the actual presence of what is depicted (the logic of the icon, as it were); rather, it is a radical reversal through which what looks like Jesus becomes the Devil. Not all Pentecostals endorse this view, and some say Jesus pictures are signs of the victorious outreach of Christianity. But the suggestion of a possible slippage epitomizes a deep ambivalence people have regarding the spread and power of pictures. Pictures serve to index Pentecostal presence in the public sphere, but they may nonetheless appear excessive and uncontrollable, as unleashing the very forces against which Pentecostals are fighting their "spiritual war." How to make sense of this slippage is the central concern of this chapter.

This focus requires attention to three related issues. One concerns what I will call "the materiality of pictures." Inspired by recent debates in the fields of visual and material culture, in my first section I argue that pictures should not be understood simply as depictions subject to the beholders' gaze, but instead should be taken seriously as things that may evade human control. Here I do not simply reverse received ontological claims about the superiority and control of subjects over objects and beholders over pictures. Rather, I stress the importance of scrutinizing how pictures are embedded in particular social practices of acting and looking. Only in this way can we fully grasp the role and place of religious pictures as they evolved as Africans encountered Protestant Christianity.

Second, I will explore, in historical perspective, how Protestant conceptions of and attitudes toward things and pictures were conveyed to the Ewe in what is today southeastern Ghana. I will show that, despite the aggressive attitude regarding religious things (including pictures) and their dismissal as "fetishes" and "idols" in the nineteenth-century encounter between missionaries and local populations, these things were not entirely stripped of their power. I examine clashes between missionary Protestantism and local attitudes about the place and role of things in religion and conclude with a brief sketch of the views of religious things held by historical mission churches, African Independent Churches, and Pentecostal-charismatic churches, respectively, highlighting similarities to and differences from indigenous attitudes and perspectives.

Third, I will scrutinize contemporary Pentecostalism to address attitudes toward and debates about mass-produced Jesus pictures and explore the tensions on which Pentecostal audiovisual strategies thrive in Ghana's contemporary media-saturated environment. This is my main focus—the complicated relation between Protestant, and especially Pentecostal Christianity and African indigenous religious traditions.[5] While the former polemically charged the latter with idolatry and Devil worship, their relation is best understood not as an opposition but as an unavoidable and, as it were, symbiotic entanglement. This means that the epistemic nature of pictures is unstable, hence the potential of Jesus pictures featuring as signs, or indices, of Christian outreach to slip into icons that render present not the depiction itself but a dark force hiding behind it. Understanding this potential for slippage is key to understanding how Christian imagery is situated in Ghana's current public sphere.

My main overall concern is to sketch the pivotal, albeit paradoxical role of Protestant Christianity in what W. J. T. Mitchell calls the "visual construction of the social field,"[6] in which pictures may become powerful things. I will show that current Pentecostal anxieties regarding Jesus pictures as potentially demonic are rooted in longstanding, inherently paradoxical views of religious things that impinge on the new public sphere that emerged in Ghana after the turn to democratization. While this study spotlights one location, comparing different attitudes to religious things in the spectrum of Christianity and African indigenous religious traditions in historical perspective, it is inspired by and speaks to broader debates about the reconfiguration of religions in the face of new media and technologies of mass reproduction and circulation.[7] I seek not only to shed light on religious audiovisual culture in Ghana, but also to contribute to developing a better conceptual framework for exploring comparatively the intersection of outreaching religions, including Pentecostalism, and the new technologies that allow for the circulation of religious pictures. Grasping this intersection is a *conditio sine qua non* for understanding the spell of pictures in our time.

Beyond the Gaze: Pictures as Animated Things

The potential of a slippage of pictures of Jesus into demonic presences resonates with recent suggestions made by scholars in the emergent field of visual and material culture that pictures need to be understood not simply as depictions but also as "things" that may impress themselves on their beholders, instilling sensations ranging from blissful amazement to sheer anxiety. Anthropologists have long been interested in alternative conceptions of the relation between people and things, including pictures.[8] Outside of

298

anthropology, as well, scholars are increasingly questioning the adequacy of the modern object-subject distinction and are developing alternative understandings of "what things do."[9] In order to account for the power and agency of objects, Bill Brown has suggested that we imagine things "as what is excessive in objects, as what exceeds their mere materialization as objects in their mere utilization as objects—their force as a sensuous presence, the magic by which objects become values, fetishes, idols, and totems."[10] This is a stimulating suggestion, certainly as it invokes the notion of the fetish that has long been employed to proclaim a distance between Western and non-Western people. If "To be sensuous is to suffer, in the sense of being acted upon" (as Patricia Spyer paraphrases Marx and Pietz[11]), then acknowledging the "sensuous presence" of things challenges modern models of agency that regard the relation between persons and the world in terms of subjects wielding power over objects and beholders fixing pictures via the gaze.

Anthropological work in the wake of Marcel Mauss highlights the conceptual grounding of the relation between persons and things in historically and culturally specific settings.[12] From this perspective, what we need is not simply one more adequate ontology (premised, for instance, on a view of things as excessive, as suggested by Brown). Rather, we require detailed insights into the different modes through which relations between people and things are shaped and transmitted in particular settings.[13] At the same time, the awareness of alternative ontologies that demand our thorough ethnographic attention (as suggested by many anthropologists) should not blind us to the fact that contestations over the nature of human-artifact relations have been central to Western colonial expansion. Therefore, it is important to acknowledge that Western models of these relations— though problematic conceptually—are not merely misguided fictions bereft of any reality. They have been called upon time and again to mark the difference between "modern" and "primitive" people. As part and parcel of missionary Protestantism, for instance, ideas about proper and improper relations between "things" and "persons," and the proper designation of agency and control, traveled all over the world and were grafted onto settings in which such relations had hitherto been thought about and organized in quite different ways. While Westerners (or at least modern Protestants) were held to be able to maintain the boundary that separates subjects from objects, "primitive" people were charged with confusing it, thus submitting themselves to a "fetish."[14]

Tomoko Masuzawa has pointed out that the very idea of the "fetish" (i.e., mistaking a "mere" object for an animated being) presupposes an opposition of spirit and matter, and of subject and object, which the "fetish" scandalously blurs yet also sustains.[15] The blurring and by the same token reinstatement of this opposition, Masuzawa suggests, is at the heart of modernity's "troubles with materiality," according to which matter was understood as dead, inanimate, and disenchanted, while people increasingly were coming under the spell of commodities in the rising capitalist economy. This is the limbo in which the notion of the "fetish," born in the encounter between Africans and Westerners, is situated.[16] Attempts to wield power over things by a process of "purification"—which

posits a strict distinction between subjects and objects and denies agency to the latter[17]—
are as central to the project of modernity (and were, for that matter, to nineteenth-century
Protestant missions) as are the notions of "fetish" and "idol" that indicate objects' illicit
yet persuasive and partly inescapable animation. The very designation of an object as a
"fetish" implies a call for unmasking this mystification, while acknowledging the mysterious power of things to put persons under their spell.

Therefore, Brown's assertion that things, due to an excessive potential that resists full
objectification, may appear as "fetishes, idols and totems,"[18] can only be a starting point
for a serious inquiry into the power and agency of things.[19] We need to pay attention to
both indigenous conceptualizations of the nature of things *and* to the impact on these
conceptualizations of modern Western views of subject-object relations. In many cases,
such as the one I focus on here, these include Protestant views.

Pictures are particular kinds of things, situated in specific visual (and sometimes
audiovisual) regimes that stipulate the nature and status of pictures and organize practices
of looking.[20] Acknowledging the materiality of pictures calls forth a critique not only of
modern models of agency but also of models of the gaze as the prime relation between
beholders and pictures. According to modernist ocularcentric ideologies, vision, in the
sense of a distant and distancing gaze, achieved the status of the master sense through
which beholders wield control over yet also experience an unrecoverable separation from
the world.[21] Recent work in the fields of visual culture, cinema studies, and the anthropology of media has moved beyond taking modern ocularcentrism at face value. Merging the
hitherto separate fields of visual and material culture and adopting a sensory approach
has allowed us to recognize the materiality of pictures[22]—their capacity to engage the
senses and touch the beholder.

While we must take into account differences between material pictorial forms such
as icons and statues, painted stills, photographs, or mass-produced pictures, it is important to realize that understanding these forms as material—as things—blurs radical distinctions between such forms and questions their categorization into different spheres
and distinct modes of analysis, such as material culture, art, visual culture, and so on.
Approaching these different forms as "pictures," I follow Mitchell's understanding of
pictures as material concretizations of images. While images are more abstract—"what
can be lifted off the picture"—"the picture is the image plus the support; it is the appearance of the immaterial image in a material medium."[23] Adopting this approach allows us
to transcend misleading oppositions such as spiritual and material, and situates our
inquiries right at the heart of the confluence of the study of visual and material culture.
A key concern of this chapter is to show that attitudes developed toward "fetishes" (and
"idols"—in the setting I studied, both terms were used interchangeably) extend into
attitudes toward mass-produced pictures and even film. The point is to investigate how
these different material forms assume a sensuous presence for their beholders via specific

ideological—in our case religious—regimes that organize the ways in which people engage pictures with their senses.[24]

Several authors have called attention to a broad range of visual engagements that far exceed the gaze that dominates ocularcentric models.[25] Approaches that appreciate the multi-sensory impact of pictures in constituting a sense of being in the world are particularly relevant for religious pictures and attitudes toward pictures from a religious perspective. In my understanding, pictures do not have an intrinsic power but appear as powerful in the context of specific social settings that mobilize particular conceptions of the nature of pictures and things. In other words, people are taught to approach, value, treat, and look at pictures in specific ways, and this ensues in a process of animation through which pictures may (or may not) become agents who impress themselves on their beholders.[26]

Religions, I propose, authorize particular traditions of looking, upon which the sensorial engagement between people and pictures is grounded, and through which pictures may assume a particular sensuous presence (or be deliberately denied one) and mediate what remains invisible to the eye.[27] In this way, spirits and the spiritual are made to materialize in a picture and thus become approachable. Being authorized as leading to a realm beyond, even a mass-produced picture is considered to be more than itself, since it points to something transcendental. Different conceptions of human-things relations and the nature of religious pictures offer entry points for comparison, but they also open up a minefield of contestations over and paradoxes of pictures that arise in the interface between different religious traditions, such as missionary Protestantism, local African religions, and Pentecostalism.

Jesus pictures in a Protestant-Pentecostal setting, such as that in Ghana, are a particularly interesting research focus because, while they express a search for the presence and power of God via pictures of Jesus, they are also, paradoxically, haunted by the fear that the Devil may hijack them, even when they are intended to draw people closer to God.

Paradoxes: Protestantism and Things in Ghana

Much has been written about Protestantism's iconoclastic attitude regarding pictures of God. As Max Weber pointed out,[28] this attitude instigated a new disenchantment with religious objects and has been vital for the genesis of modernity. Protestant attitudes concerning religious objects and pictures were and are far more diverse than common stereotypes suggest,[29] but it is nonetheless true that Protestant critiques of religious pictures as inappropriate representations of divinity have tended to be mobilized in clashes with other, more "thing friendly" religions such as Catholicism and indigenous religious traditions. All around the globe, nineteenth-century Protestant mission societies fiercely attacked "heathen" religion for its obsession with "fetishes" and "idols" and its deplorable materiality. In settings such as contemporary Ghana, this attitude is kept alive by churches and movements in the Pentecostal-charismatic spectrum. This generates constant debates about the alleged danger enshrined in all kinds of objects associated with older indigenous religion, drums and masks made for tourists, and, most pointedly, Jesus pictures.

Protestantism is one of the settings in which attitudes about things and pictures—including those pertaining to religious beliefs and practices that are to be "left behind"—are generated and endorsed. Generating and endorsing such attitudes is grounded in a particular "semiotic ideology," that is, the way in which distinctions between words, things, persons, and spirits are sorted out and their relations organized materially.[30] In his insightful examination of the encounters between Dutch Protestant missionaries and their Sumbanese converts in Indonesia, Webb Keane has shown how Protestantism's semiotic ideology is constantly thwarted and in need of reaffirmation. Dismissing Sumbanese, who assigned agency to things, as "fetishistic" was not sufficient to maintain the stable distinction between subjects and objects that the missionaries had in mind. Instead, Keane's study of the encounter lays bare the ultimate impossibility of such categorical distinctions and of the overall project of modern purification of which they are part. While Keane pays much attention to language, his notion of a semiotic ideology that stipulates proper relations between people, spirits, words, and things is also useful for examining mass-produced pictures of Jesus in Ghana and the attitudes toward and practices surrounding such pictures there. The point I wish to make in this section is that these attitudes and practices are grounded in early contacts between Protestant missionaries and local people. A brief glance at their encounter reveals interesting differences as well as—on a more hidden level—similarities between their respective semiotic ideologies.

Despite some regional differences, Protestant missionary activities among the Ewe, Ga, Krobo, and Asante in the mid-nineteenth and early twentieth centuries have much in common. This is partly due to the central role of the Basler Mission, which collaborated with the Norddeutsche Missiongesellschaft (NMG) in spreading Pietism on the Gold Coast. Both mission societies, whose missionaries were all trained in the same mission school at Basel, adopted a similar strategy in that they sought to translate the Bible into the respective mother tongues and took a harsh stance against local gods and spirits. This stance can best be summarized as "diabolization," a process by which these entities were declared to be demonic, but retained all the more as truly existing powers from which pious Christians were to dissociate themselves.[31] Of particular interest here are missionary attitudes concerning religious things, which were despised as "fetishes" or "idols" that would surely bind people to Satan. In the diabolizing assault on local Ewe, Ga, Krobo, and Asante religious traditions, the organizing theme appears to have been missionaries' crusade against the religious things associated with the "heathens." In the historical material I know best, concerning the activities of the NMG among the Ewe, local people and Christians often clashed over "fetishes" and "idols."

Before turning to missionary ideas about such things, it is important to note that Ewe ideas about them were not grounded in a "fetishistic" attitude but rather in an alternative ontology that emphasized that invisible forces and spirits became tangible via things in which they dwell.[32] The eminent missionary ethnographer Jacob Spieth,[33] who offered the first substantial description of Ewe religion, introduced *trɔwo* as spirits that are invisible but nonetheless have hands and feet and can hear and see; they inhabit the sky but also have abodes on earth "that are prepared for them with human hands. These [abodes], however, are just signs that have the purpose of reminding human beings of the *trɔ*. When the priest calls the *trɔ*, the latter comes down to the earth, so as to listen to the matters of the human beings and to convey their voice to God. It is only through their mediation that God listens to the voice of the human beings, and he receives the sacrificial gifts from human beings through their hands."[34]

Of special importance here is the role of human beings in creating particular abodes to host, and even fix, a spirit for some time on earth.[35] Spieth's rendition of spirits as mediators between human beings and God is also fascinating. It is difficult to assess how important the notion of the distant High God was in the Ewe cosmology or whether its importance was exaggerated by Western Protestant missionaries, who introduced an alternative, Christian way to reach God without relying on spirits that would need to have abodes and be worshipped, and without employing sacrifice. What is clear is the specific entanglement of spirit and matter in Ewe religious practice.

In her study of the Ewe Gorovodu cult, Judy Rosenthal explains that West African concepts of power imply "forces and domains that are invented by humans as surely as humans are shaped by them," and thus "people are conscious of the fact that they have a hand in the creation of divinities and the sacred."[36] This Ewe understanding is quite removed from Western conceptions of spirit and matter, and God and humans, which stress the distinctiveness of these two dimensions. It is not a matter of *mistaking* a thing for a spirit, as the term *fetish* implies, but rather of recognizing the material dimension and human intervention as necessary for the articulation of spirits and invisible powers on earth.

Missionary attitudes concerning religious things—that is, objects, substances, pictures, and natural sites considered to be dwelling places of spirits or spiritual powers by the local people—were complex. I want to distinguish three. First, missionaries engaged in what I will call *the disenchantment of natural substances*. In building new mission sites, for example, the missionaries over and over again came across restrictions on the use of certain materials and access to natural resources.[37] On the whole, the missionaries espoused a disenchanting attitude toward natural substances, which often met with serious protest from local people, who viewed this as desecration or even pollution.[38] Similarly, the missionaries preached against obeying certain taboos, for instance, interdictions against fetching water from the river on certain days, using modern containers, or allowing menstruating women to touch the water. On the whole, the missionaries sought to introduce a utilitarian attitude regarding matter, which, to invoke Brown again, would reduce things to mere objects with a certain use and purpose. While this implied a critique of local cosmology, with its sacred sites and taboos, it is important to realize that ultimately the missionaries regarded their own work on nature—the cultivation of the bush, the construction of Christian villages, in short, the transformation of wilderness into civilization—as a religious activity that would reveal the presence and power of the Christian God.

Second, the missionaries were *iconoclastic*. This attitude pertained to things the Ewe considered sacred that could not be reduced to a utilitarian purpose because they had no use value that could be recaptured by stripping them of their spiritual dimension. Certain things, such as the objects stored in the interior of shrines, dwelling places of spirits, amulets, powerful costumes, and other magical devices (*dzo*) that would protect or do harm simply stood in the way of the proper worship of God as envisioned by the missionaries. The Protestant critiques of Catholicism and "heathendom" correspond in interesting ways that culminate in the rejection of the use of things to access the divine. The mission records register numerous acts of violence vis-à-vis shrines and objects used in worshipping gods. If they agreed to convert, local priests were asked to burn their shrines and all their paraphernalia.[39] This yielded spectacular performances that not only asserted the superiority of Protestant Christianity (as a religion that could do without "idols") but, by the same token, confirmed the very power of these objects, which could not simply be abandoned or forgotten.[40] Similarly, the missionaries encouraged public acts of disposing of one's personal magical items (*dzo*).[41] In short, and reminiscent of Latour's analysis of the Protestant "iconoclash,"[42] missionaries' often-violent attitudes against religious things kept alive and even emphasized the power of things.

Third, along with these downright assaults, which ultimately affirmed the power of what had been destroyed (and thus fit perfectly with the logic of diabolization), the missionaries also engaged in unmasking the supposed power of fetishes and their priests. Stories abound about brave evangelists who dared to challenge obnoxious priests and exposed them as mere liars and fakes, unworthy of the awe and appreciation bestowed on them. They charged them with employing fraudulent devices—special effects, as it were—that produced sounds and visions alluding to the spiritual realm. But then Satan himself, in whose league these priests and their spirits were held to stand, was regarded as the master of deception. In this way, "fetishes" and their priests were not simply waiting to be unmasked as unreal or "fake" but above all were condemned as dangerous and wrong. In preaching the Gospel, the missionaries shifted easily between a view of "fetishes" and "idols" as "false" in the sense of fake or unreal and "false" in the sense of "wrong" and hence real, yet devoted to satanic powers. Thus even projects of *unmasking* would not necessarily reduce an excessive thing loaded with power to a mere object. On the contrary, the act of unmasking was part of a dialectic of revelation and concealment that in the end did not introduce a prosaic attitude towards religious things as mere human-made objects.[43] Indeed, in an indirect manner the missionaries charged objects and matter with precisely the excessive potential that, according to Brown, distinguishes objects from things and makes the latter assume a sensuous presence.

If in their approach to nature and natural substances the missionaries sought to reveal God's presence in the world, in their attacks on "fetishes" they ultimately found Satan's power at work. In both cases—the disenchanting (though on a higher level resacralizing) attitude toward nature and the unmasking of "fetishes"—we encounter an underlying attitude that acknowledges the presence of God, or the Devil, in and through things. The missionaries' semiotic ideology, not unlike that of Dutch Protestant missionaries among the Sumbanese analyzed by Keane, thrived on contradictions: on the one hand, they propagated a prosaic perspective on things, as objects to be controlled and utilized by humans, while on the other, they regarded the world, and hence the relation between people and things, as subject to an invisible spiritual force: God or the Devil is at work through matter. This understanding was not so far removed from that of the Ewe view that matter and spirits were fully entangled.

Despite missionaries' fierce stance against "idol" worship, things played an important role in their practice. Within the mission churches a Protestant material culture emerged that placed great emphasis on Christian modes of dress and architecture, which became outward signs of Christian identity.[44] Certain artifacts, such as the Bible, storybooks, and pious Jesus pictures, played a central role in Christian worship, but these remained *unacknowledged* in their materiality. In addition, many converts sought to invent more practical acts than prayer alone to contact God and make him affect people's lives and well-being. These ran counter to missionary Protestantism's dominant semiotic ideology, which dismissed the value of things in the worship of God, but which ultimately was not realized in practice. Any contact with invisible spiritual forces, including the Christian God, was predicated upon practices of mediation through which it became possible to address, touch, or otherwise sense these forces in the first place. African converts, who had been socialized in alternative, indigenous semiotic ideologies, which acknowledge the importance of material mediations in contacts with spirits, realized this more clearly than did the missionaries. Nevertheless, the missionaries claimed a strict distinction between immaterial Protestantism and the fetishistic materiality of indigenous cults, which was the foundation of Protestantism's alleged superiority.

Especially in times of crisis, however, converts felt the urge to "slide back" into "heathen" repertoires that would offer more tangible remedies in the battle against sickness and insecurity.[45] Within the confines of this article, I cannot present a history of the development of Protestant Christianity in relation to the question of materiality. Still, I would like to propose that the numerous conflicts between missionary Christianity and the African Independent Churches—or "spiritual churches," as they are also called in Ghana—that occurred as part and parcel of processes of Africanization and "enculturation" can at least in part be attributed to tensions surrounding the valuation of things and concrete ritual action.[46] Unlike Protestant mission churches, such as the Evangelical Presbyterian Church, the "spiritual churches" that emerged in the 1930s and spread after independence in the late 1950s were characterized by the use of elaborate paraphernalia, including white crosses in the bush, white gowns, incense, and florida water, and by their more ritualistic religious practices. Objects and substances were employed to invoke the power of God to effect healing and protection. These churches redeployed the missionary semiotic ideology in such a way that they could be Christian and yet allow the use of effective material things. Otherwise, they believed, it would be impossible for them to counter "traditional religion," which was framed, still in line with missionary preaching, as the realm of Satan.[47]

To make a long story short, the Pentecostal-charismatic churches that became phenomenally popular in Ghana during the 1980s and gained a strong presence in the aftermath of democratization in the early 1990s initially distanced themselves from both missionary Christianity, with its strong reliance on the Bible and reading at the expense of the power of the Holy Spirit, and from "spiritual churches," with their emphasis on objects, through which they were said to indulge in "idol worship." The Pentecostal-charismatic churches' self-presentation as anti-idolatrous even instigated a number of "spiritual churches" to do away with the use of religious objects in worship and to refashion themselves as Pentecostal.[48] What moved to the fore was an emphasis on the human body as a harbinger of the power of God; the Holy Spirit would work through the touch of the hand.

It seems that Pentecostals are now reconsidering this rejection of the use of religious objects. Some of the more recently founded charismatic churches are moving away from a sole reliance on the embodied power of the Holy Spirit. During my last visit to Ghana in January 2008, I noticed a subtle shift toward the use of, for instance, Italian olive oil, which is prayed over and used to anoint born-again believers.[49] When I asked Pentecostal pastors and believers about this, they told me, much to my surprise, that things such as olive oil, holy water, and even black stones were "symbols" that can convey and transport the power of God. While such "symbols" were effective and good, they said one had to stay away from the "worship of idols," as practiced in "traditional religion," "spiritual churches," and Catholicism. This fundamental distinction between "symbols" and "idols" highlights a Pentecostal semiotic ideology that appears to struggle against, yet also accommodates, certain material forms and espouses significant similarities with "spiritual churches," "traditional religion," and, to some extent, even Catholicism.[50] I will now turn to examine this semiotic ideology in order to elucidate the potential for slippage enshrined in mass-produced Jesus pictures.

Pictures of Jesus

Notwithstanding the Second Commandment, popular Protestantism has produced an audiovisual material culture of its own, in which mass-produced pictures of Jesus abound.

While these pictures are only rarely displayed in churches, they feature in prayer books and Protestant homes, and they sustain a popular Protestant aesthetic in which pictures play a central role in generating what David Morgan calls "visual piety."[51] This is a distinct Protestant didactics of looking, through which representations of Jesus are addressed in a specific manner. On the basis of rich historical and ethnographic material, Morgan has argued that, in American popular Protestantism, pictures of Jesus are personal sites of veneration. Correcting stereotypical views of Protestantism as radically iconoclastic, Morgan asserts that we need to pay attention to the specific ways through which Jesus pictures are legitimized as suitable for inducing sensations of a divine encounter. The point, then, is not the presence of pictures per se but rather the value attributed to them and their modes of use. Particularly interesting for my purposes is his argument that pictures of Jesus are not viewed as divine objects of worship, as "idols," but rather are approached as pictures that allow access to Him by inducing contemplation and generating "visual piety." Jesus pictures, in short, are part and parcel of a popular Protestant aesthetic with its own "sensational forms," which makes it possible to experience the divine by way of a picture.[52]

Note that the role of vision in the context of this popular Protestant aesthetic poses a challenge to facile associations of modern mass-produced visual culture with the eye and with a particular kind of distant, objectifying gaze. Morgan's notion of looking as a particular kind of religious practice, which needs to be learned and which involves both disciplining and extending the sense of vision, resolutely moves us beyond preconceived ideas about the role of vision in modern mass-mediated culture.[53] Many of the pictures Morgan discusses—for example Warner Sallman's famous *Head of Christ*[54]—can also be found in Ghana, where they are traded via Christian bookshops and roadside poster stalls. But we also find there Jesus images from the Catholic traditions, such as the Sacred Heart of Jesus, especially on calendar posters, paintings, cars, canoes, and even clocks (see Figures 29 and 30).[55]

In these popular, mass-produced materials, I have never come across any picture of a black Jesus, but only endless repetitions of the usual appearance of Jesus as a man with long, usually blond hair and white skin.[56] I am wary, however, of reducing this to a racial inferiority complex fed by Christianity. We need to be aware that Jesus may well be framed by analogy to the figure of the white traveling spirit, which owes its power to its foreign, distant place of origin. (Dente, Tigare, and many other "white" spirits were considered powerful because they came from neighboring peoples.) White is also a color associated with peace and coolness. The color white thus sets Jesus apart, suggesting an analogy with "white" spirits and an extraordinary power.[57] My point here is not to dismiss issues of race but to suggest that historically there has been a convergence of "white" spirits and "white" as a dominant racial category and that depictions of Jesus as "white" cannot be reduced to either discourse.

FIGURE 29   Jesus Posters, Accra, 2008. Photo by Birgit Meyer.

How are these well-known and popular pictures of Jesus used, and looked at in the Ghanaian setting? Quite in line with Morgan's analysis of the United States, in Ghana too pictures of Jesus adorn people's halls or bedrooms, often as calendar posters. I found such pictures in both Catholic and Protestant households. As a friend told me, "Having pictures of Jesus in your room is a way to show one's Christianity." Although I did not conduct detailed research on how people converted these pictures from mass-produced commodities into personal items, in casual conversation I found that, certainly in the Catholic homes, pictures of Jesus were sites of personal worship, a place to pray. Many Protestants, too, have these pictures, which indicates that they are less iconophobic than a strict Protestant stance might lead us to expect. I also found that a Protestant background would not lead people to choose a more Protestant image, such as those derived from Sallman; they might well buy calendar posters with a Sacred Heart of Jesus, which was taken up by the Jesuits and spread as part of popular Catholicism.[58] Furthermore, some of my Pentecostally inclined acquaintances had Jesus pictures, though they stressed that these were not "idols to be worshipped" but "symbols." Taking a Jesus picture to be a "symbol" implied that one would not pray to it but use it as a reminder for oneself to

FIGURE 30   Jesus painting on a canoe, Winneba, 2009. Photo by Birgit Meyer.

do good. One friend, an electrician attending a Pentecostal church, told me he had a Jesus calendar in his bedroom, and explained to me, "One may have something bad in mind, but seeing the picture reminds one that this is no good."

I was told that people pray in front of Jesus pictures, but I have never seen this, since it takes place in the seclusion and intimacy of the bedroom. That is why, in order to provide a glimpse of this practice, I will invoke a scene from a "Ghanaian film,"[59] in which a person prays in front of a Jesus picture. It corresponds well with what I have heard people say about these pictures. While films can, of course, not be taken as immediate mirror images of popular religious practice—they dramatize, condense, and offer a specific perspective—I do not think they should be regarded as inferior to so-called first-hand information generated by participant observation and interviews. As I have argued elsewhere,[60] many of these locally produced movies convey a Christian and often a Pentecostal perspective. While these movies, in visualizing a Christian perspective on indigenous cults, "misrepresent" such religions in the eyes of their practitioners, they remain interestingly close to Christianity in that they not only mirror but also instigate religious practice.

For instance, in *Women in Love* (1996),[61] there is a scene in which a desperate woman called Sabina awakes from a terrifying dream announcing an upcoming disaster. She immediately turns to the picture of Jesus above her bed and prays. In her prayer, she surrenders herself to Jesus as her savior, and implores him to protect her against evil.[62] The director renders the picture of Jesus transcendental by the camera angle and accompanying music. He thereby attributes to it the power of revelation in a dream, recalling the practices of visual piety outlined by Morgan. The picture of Jesus is not venerated per se, as if it were an "idol," nor is it presented as a mere representation separated from what it depicts. Jesus' image instills feelings of awe precisely because Jesus is understood to be uncontainable by the frame, without which the image could not be and which it nonetheless exceeds, and to have the power to interfere in the believing person's everyday life. Sabina is shown to be overwhelmed by this spiritual experience, and the camera sets out to invoke the experience for the spectators too, actualizing their memory of having been involved in such practices. Since films do not offer individual artistic representations but are deeply entangled with everyday experiences in that they mirror as well as instigate them, this scene can be regarded as representing a common practice, albeit one that here is framed and dramatized, and it shows the efficacy of praying in front of the picture of Jesus.

Centered in the popular imagination, this dramatization reveals how Jesus pictures can induce spiritual experience. When I talked to people—both ordinary born again believers and some Pentecostal pastors—about the use of Jesus pictures to direct one's prayers, they continually stressed that such pictures "are just symbols, the only thing is *not* to worship them." This insistence, of course, indicates the perceived need to indulge in a typically Protestant anti-idolatric discourse, according to which traditional religion thrives on worshipping man-made things while Protestant Christianity leaves this behind by moving from "idol" to "symbol." The point is to pray not *to*, but *in front of* a picture. When one distinguishes between these types of signs, the same object—a Jesus picture—is assigned a very different value and meaning, which imply a different set of attitudes and practices. This exemplifies how the meanings of religious things can be construed in different ways and backed by different semiotic ideologies. At the same time, the somewhat diffuse category of the "symbol"—referring to an object that does not itself have power but reminds the spectator to do good and that expresses a person's Christian identity to visitors—seems prone to mutate into an "idol." Why otherwise would the discourse of anti-idolatry be mobilized so strongly to stress the distinct character of the "symbol"?

Indeed, the portrayal of Jesus pictures as "symbolic" is heavily contested in less compromising Pentecostal circles.[63] In a conversation with a bookseller in the bookshop of the Action Faith Chapel in Accra, for instance, I was given to understand that charismatic Pentecostals do not appreciate Jesus pictures at all, because people may "easily start worshipping them." In addition, he said, "We do not even know how Jesus looked, since in those days there were no cameras to take his picture," so "why make a point of inventing how he looked?" Moreover, he explained, evil spirits might hijack the picture, and in this way it may be taken over by a demonic presence and become dangerous. I encountered this stance many times, even in people whom I interviewed because they sold things such as clocks adorned with Jesus pictures. It was repeatedly stressed that these depictions were not true to Jesus' real appearance and, in addition, that they might lead people astray. The point was to not make pictures of Jesus but instead accept him as one's personal savior, to pray to him without material mediation, and to call on his name in times of need.

I present these less compromising perspectives that reject even the view that Jesus pictures are "symbols" because I want to underscore that there are different positions with regard to such pictures. Over time, and probably pressed by particular anxieties, the same person may adopt a less compromising stance. The point is that different positions are available, highlighting the problematic values of pictures as either indices of divine presence or instances of idolatry.

The problems that may result from engaging a Jesus picture are made clear in the movie *The Beast Within* (1993).[64] A set of scenes portrays a desperate Christian house-wife praying in front of, or perhaps even to, a picture of Jesus in her living room, unaware that a *juju* (an object embodying magical power) is hidden behind it. This *juju* is the real power in the house. In the end, only a *juju*-man from the village is able to control this power; the prayers to Jesus do not help solve the problem and possibly even increase it by rendering the *juju* behind the picture more powerful. In the film's climax, the *juju*-man, dressed in traditional style, insists that the picture of Jesus must be taken down. While the woman stands in front of the picture, screaming "Don't touch my Jesus with your demonic hands," her husband pushes her aside and lifts the picture. A small object is revealed, evoking a cry from another person in the room: "Jesus Christ!" (See Figure 31.)

As I have explained elsewhere, this movie, though well made, was not very successful because of these very scenes.[65] The young Pentecostals with whom I watched the movie (in 1996) did not at all like the suggestion that prayer to Jesus could be less effective than the actions of a local priest. This clearly went against the common idea, endorsed by many movies, that Christianity was far more powerful than local religious traditions, which were dismissed as diabolic. Interestingly, this criticism still maintains the Jesus picture as a suitable point of veneration—a site of visual piety. The struggle in the film is seen as one between Christianity and "traditional religion," here represented by two material forms, a picture and a *juju*, in which the former is supposed to be superior.

While the film fails to assert this superiority—hence the criticisms—it does reproduce the familiar understanding that "traditional religion" is not as visible as Christianity but thrives in its shadows. In this sense, Christianity and African indigenous religious tradi-tions do not simply exist separate from and next to each other but are connected in a

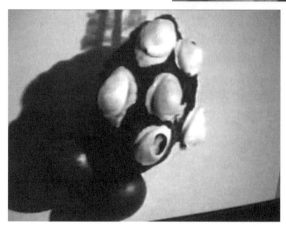

FIGURE 31a–c   Stills from *The Beast Within*.

more complex manner. Nothing could express this better than the location of the *juju* hidden behind Jesus' picture, which for it is a perfect concealment. The power of traditional spirits thus operates *from behind* and *through* a Christian picture.

This harmonizes with the missionary attitudes regarding religious things that I outlined earlier. As I explained, missionaries introduced a particular semiotic ideology, which asserted God could not be made present through religious things (though he might reveal himself through matter in the world), but they also stressed that things can embody or even become what they represent, especially in the case of indigenous religious objects. This underpins a complex perspective, according to which indigenous religious things appear to be vested with power, and raises questions about how Christian power becomes manifest, given that things are not the appropriate place to host the power of God. The fear of powerful things, hidden in private space and affecting unsuspecting people, runs like a red thread through popular Christianity in Ghana. Christians, it seems, never feel completely and safely beyond the unsettling spiritual power of indigenous religious things, which are even more potent when secreted from view. Therefore they have to be unmasked. Far more than mainstream Protestantism, Pentecostal-charismatic churches linked up with these fears, and by affirming the fears they confirmed the existence of the powers that raised them.

The reason why pictures of Jesus are considered problematic in Pentecostal circles became clear to me through a conversation I had with an actress named Roberta on the set of the movie *Turning Point*, in October 2002.[66] Roberta belonged to the Winner's Church, a popular Pentecostal-charismatic church that originated in Nigeria, and she told me that, upon the advice of her born-again sister, she had gotten rid of the Jesus picture in her room. Her sister had told her: "There is a spirit in that image, not the spirit of God, but a devilish thing. The problem is that the spirits can look at you through images and masks, and the like. They use the eyes." When I did not get the point, she immediately brought a photograph and, pointing to the eyes, said: "Wherever you are in the room, the image will look at you, so you are seen." This blurring of the distinction between a picture subject to a person's gaze and the picture looking back is attributed to the power of the Devil, who, it is believed, can appropriate even the eyes of Jesus in a picture so as to observe and confuse a Christian. This is why it is dangerous to have religious pictures—especially those depicting beings that might look back—in one's house, even, or even especially, ones depicting Jesus.[67]

Roberta initially put a Jesus picture in her room not as decoration but as a focal point in her practice of visual piety, much as Sabina looked at her picture of Jesus to direct her prayer. However, having been warned by her sister that the spirit of the Devil might occupy such a picture, she began to sense the presence of an uncanny force operating from behind Jesus' dear and familiar face, and even appropriating the picture's eyes. After removing the picture, she felt relieved. Her narrative reminded me of the accounts of Christian converts, past and present, who felt a pressing need to get rid of certain powerful

313

objects, even though they no longer believed in them or had any intention of employing them as a focus of veneration. The striking difference, however, is that in Roberta's case it was the familiar and supposedly protective picture of Jesus that had become uncanny and dangerous, because of its possible occupation by a demonic spirit. Whether the picture of Jesus is approached as a center of veneration or feared as a hideout for Satan, it is not simply an object of the beholder's gaze; when one looks at the object, it becomes a spiritual presence that comes to the beholder as a sensation that disrupts the hierarchical relation between beholder and the object of her gaze. In both cases, we encounter instances of what Laura Marks has called "haptic visuality," a sense of being touched by looking at a picture.[68]

Marks differentiates modes of looking in the context of "optic" and "haptic" visuality. In optic visuality, one perceives a distant object by gazing at it. This engenders a modern mode of knowledge production, geared toward symbolic representation that is able to maintain a stable distinction between the viewing subject and the object looked upon. Haptic visuality, by contrast, entails a sense of being gripped by a picture. This yields an affective, visceral, and emotional experience that is instigated by looking yet encompasses the body as a whole and confounds the beholder/picture or people/thing distinction that I examined earlier in this paper.[69] Within the semiotic ideology we are analyzing here, looking at Jesus is construed as a haptic sensation, through which the beholder expects to feel the ungraspable presence of God, yet fears that the unsettling presence of Satan may take His place.

This resembles modes of looking at statues and figures in indigenous religions. In her analysis of *bocio* figures among the Ewe and the neighboring Fon, Susan Preston Blier explains that they are intended "to address the full range of human senses—visual, acoustic, olfactory, tactile, and gustatory."[70] Viewers are positioned in such a way that they feel addressed "at the rawest sensorial level." Thus these figures "comprise an art whose full aesthetic can be understood not only by seeing, but also by tasting, and if one recalls their original offertory dedication, hearing and smelling."[71] It is an aesthetic that binds beholders by inducing strong feelings of admiration or fear in the process of looking. Despite the fact that Jesus is presented as counter to the Devil, Jesus pictures are found to operate in a way similar to these figures in that both possess a strong affective potential to bring people under their spell through a dense synaesthetic experience. In other words, the African figures seem to underlie—and even reinforce—the fear of the pictures of Jesus.[72] This reveals a process of assimilation in which the difference between the production and provenance of indigenous sacred and mass-produced objects is transcended. Even though former objects of worship are made and animated by humans, while mass-produced pictures of Jesus have been printed by machines and are available as commodities, the anxiety about the latter depends on a similar process of animation, which should caution us against attributing too much power to technologies of mass production as such to change people's views. In the present case, mass-produced pictures are framed by and regarded from a Protestant-Pentecostal aesthetic.

In the context of this religious aesthetic, the experience of the haptic is heightened by sustained reflections on why the picture that looks like Jesus yet truly embodies Satan is looking back.[73] I was often told that *both* God and Satan observed human beings with cameras that could look into people's deepest and darkest secrets and that would produce films of people's lives. As Roberta put it: "The Devil and his demons are very smart. They have pictures of all of us and see us, because they still have the power they had as angels. And they can see. They will always try to get those who are born again and not too strong; they work on them, not on nominal Christians [i.e., people who are held not to have made a personal choice for God—"born into," rather than "born again"], because they belong to them already."

Because, like God, Satan has the power to see everything, believers are asked to create zones of seclusion. One way to hide from his gaze is by refusing to look into the eyes of an "idol" that is mistaken for a "symbol" of Jesus. Despite such measures, however, Satan is a master of deception, as his parasitical appropriation of Jesus pictures perfectly shows. For this reason, pictures are deceitful: "never trust appearances!" By contrast, being observed by God is regarded as desirable, since he keeps an eye on his followers and protects them in times of need (though he is also witness to their going astray and may punish them in turn).

According to this understanding, the relationship between beholders of pictures and those present in or behind them reverses the direction of the gaze central to optic visuality. While the beholders feel that they are touched by the picture through all their senses (or, in the case of the Devil, fear that they may be), both God and Satan are supposed to look at human beings in order to observe and control them. In a sense, whereas in the popular Protestant-Pentecostal semiotic ideology people partake in a kind of haptic visuality that leaves them little control over a clear object of vision that can be seen and surveyed, the same people are objects of the optic visuality of God and Satan. Human beings appear as moving images that are subject to the gaze of a spiritual power. This capacity of religious pictures to look, rather than being merely objects of the gaze, is visualized in an evocative manner in popular posters that have long been used for advertising Ghanaian and Nigerian movies (see Figure 28). Two streams come from the pictures' eyes, targeting innocent onlookers. Like movies, the posters claim to make visible such acts of looking, which otherwise remain invisible to the naked eye. That lines similar to the streams emanating from the eyes are also used in posters to depict the power emanating from the hands of people or spiritual beings (see Figure 29) underscores the notion that haptic visuality is a matter of touch.

Interestingly then, by contrast to Morgan's analysis, in which Jesus pictures function in the context of certain religiously authorized practices of looking, the Pentecostal suspicion vis-à-vis pictures suggests an understanding of pictures as potentially prone to "going wild." Pictures, in this view, cannot be fully contained and easily act out their excessive potential.[74] This, again, leads us to missionary Protestantism's paradoxical attitude toward pictures, according to which they may easily slip from being mere depictions or symbols of divinity into idolatrous materializations of satanic power. The excessive potential attributed to Jesus pictures refers back to the simultaneous rejection and encapsulation of local religious traditions as the powerful realm of Satan.

The frequent reference made to God and the Devil as observing people via film technologies raises questions about the role of film in the contemporary Pentecostal semiotic ideology. Pentecostals' resistance to or at least questioning of the appearance of still religious pictures is grounded in a strong emphasis on looking practices, and the relation between picture and beholders brought about by these practices. From this perspective, the medium of film is embedded in Pentecostal views of vision as a religious practice. The capacity to look into a realm that is invisible to ordinary sight is likened to the medium of film, while by the same token film is regarded as a medium of revelation. Hence film is invoked as a trope for describing how God and the Devil look at people, meticulously recording their secret actions. At the same time, as I have explained in detail elsewhere,[75] films are presented, and often looked upon, as laying bare what happens in the realm of the invisible. Audiovisual technology thus acts to support religious revelation: special effects both indicate and transcend the distinction between the visible and invisible. In many films, the camera offers spectators the perspective of the omniscient eye of God.

Thus, while Jesus pictures are felt to be potentially dangerous, film is appreciated as a suitable mediation device because it offers a vision. Unlike mass-produced pictures of Jesus, films are understood not as prone to becoming idols but rather as visionary devices that offer insights and perspectives unattainable—and thus all the more desirable—in everyday life.[76] By contrast to single pictures of Jesus, which capture and fix the eye, thereby potentially subverting the power relation between viewer and picture, Christian-style films claim to offer above all a superior perspective, a revealing view. Framed as divine revelations that unmask and by the same token affirm the machinations of the Devil, this kind of movie claims to offer the possibility of *experiencing divine vision in action*. These movies thus are grounded in and invoke religious acts of looking that are embedded in a popular Protestant-Pentecostal aesthetics out of which they arise and which they affirm, and which encapsulates and at the same time challenges traditional ideas about religious things.

Conclusion

In examining the important role of Protestant-Pentecostal Christianity in generating the host of still and moving mass-produced pictures that populate Ghana's public sphere, I have taken as my point of departure the social embeddedness of the relations between

FIGURE 32 Video poster 1 (collection of Many Elsas).

people and things, and between beholders and pictures. I have explored how this is framed and transmitted in the sphere of religion. In Bill Brown's analysis, the excessive dimension of things is proper to his understanding of them, and thus in a sense is natural to them. I have shown, however, that religions play a central role in creating the very possibility of excess by enveloping people and things, beholders and pictures, in a structure of mutual animation.

317

FIGURE 33   Video poster 2 (collection of Many Elsas).

Focusing on differences and similarities (though the latter may initially be hard to see) between the semiotic ideologies of missionary Protestantism, traditional religion, and contemporary Pentecostal-charismatic churches, I have explored the remarkable slippage through which pictures of Jesus may cease to be "symbols" that index Christian presence and identity, and become instead dangerous "idols" through which beholders are subject to the gaze—and thus the power—of the Devil. In the case of missionary Protestantism and later Pentecostalism, this slippage generated a complex situation, in which the potential excess of pictures thrived on the simultaneous valuation of local spirits as false in the sense of both fake and wrong. This entails an entanglement of Christianity and indigenous traditions, in which the latter hide and flourish behind the former, while the former stresses its superiority. The opposition between them, which is rigorously maintained in dominant discourse, is constantly thwarted, as is perfectly highlighted by the fear that pictures of Jesus—who is hailed as the central warrior against and ultimate defeater of Satan—may be occupied by the Devil himself.

Approaching pictures as things and analyzing them as embedded in religious semiotic ideologies clarifies our understanding of the relationship between religion and media technologies. Instead of viewing the adoption of new media technologies into religious practice in terms of a loss of substance—as if mass reproducibility could, in itself, collide with religious concerns—I call for detailed analyses of how still and moving pictures are framed religiously. While print allows for an endless recycling and spread of Jesus pictures from the repertoire of popular Christianity, for many people these pictures still serve as sites of prayer and contemplation, as ethical reminders, or as expressions of a Christian identity. Whereas they seem unbothered by the Second Commandment, they insist that Jesus pictures should by no means serve as "idols." This points to an oppositional structure, in which a thing that is coded as a "symbol" is on the side of Christianity, whereas the "idol" belongs to the realm of "paganism" and even the "powers of darkness." In the strict antipicture stance held by some staunch Pentecostals, Jesus pictures do not feature as "symbols" but as "idols," which are dangerous by definition. That these "idols" have eyes to fix innocent beholders and envelop them in a haptic, visceral gaze emphasizes the need to analyze pictures as things. At the same time, the emphasis on looking and being looked upon also indicates the importance of religiously induced modalities of vision. These modalities are not only ascribed to Jesus pictures but are also invoked in relation to Christian-oriented movies. These also operate within a logic of unmasking and revelation that is reminiscent of the missionary attitudes regarding local religious traditions.

These findings speak to broader questions about Protestantism and materiality. The point is not only that religious things and pictures are despised as illicit forms of "idol worship," and yet have attributed to them—and hence are loaded with—a mysterious power that may run wild and act upon people. The more important point is that the idea of an immaterial religion is a fiction; even a semiotic ideology that denounces religious things and pictures cannot do without material forms. In this respect, local ideas about the interdependence of spirits and matter highlight the need to transcend the misleading contrast between matter and spirit that has informed missionary Protestant semiotic ideologies that spread around the world in the course of missionization and engendered highly problematic conceptions of local religious traditions as "fetishistic" and "material." Certainly, at a time when religions embrace modern media technologies and religious pictures have become a bone of contention in struggles to define blasphemy,[77] we need to re-materialize our understandings of both religion and media.

The FedEx Saints

Patrons of Mobility and Speed in a Neoliberal City

Maria José A. de Abreu

In this chapter, I will assess the role and place of modern religious iconography in a time of electronic media by examining the complex interactions between Catholic Charismatics in Brazil and the sacred images they employ. I will pay particular attention to the perceived temporality of the media in which these images are presented—whether they appear as sculpted and "still," or as fleeting and in motion. Sacred images are problematic for Charismatics because of their emphasis on the gifts of the spirit, also known as charismata. By definition, they thus value the body of the believer more highly than iconographic representations as a site of religious power. Nowadays, however, religious images have been reconceptualized as they are transferred to the electronic mass media, with their connotations of contemporaneity and speed. These two aspects—emphasis on the spirit and the use of new technological media—both enhance and respond to an ongoing demand for mobility in the thriving socioeconomic urban sphere of São Paulo. The importance of *pneuma*, the Greek term for breath, air, or spirit, within the Catholic Charismatic Renewal (CCR), on the one hand, and its increasing mediatization through electronic technologies, on the other, not only run parallel to but build upon each other's materialities. We will see how the motion of the spirit—understood as a sort of fluidity—comes to be apprehended through electronic media, such as radio, television, DVD, and Internet, all of which have been employed by the CCR since at least the mid-eighties.

Relying a great deal on Pentecostal elements and practices, the Catholic Charismatic movement arrived in the State of São Paolo, Brazil, in the late sixties. Pentecostalism emphasizes the transformative powers of the Holy Spirit when embodied through the charismata. While the pneumatic dimension of the Movement has been present from the outset, only when Charismatics began to employ electronic media in the eighties and nineties did *pneuma* receive a prominent place in the organization of the relations between religion, technology, the body, and space. In assessing the role traditional iconography has played for the CCR in an age of electronic media, I will first describe and analyze the place of the "charismatic" body, that is, a body that has been infused with the graces of the Holy Spirit, in the overall image economy of the Movement. In sum, my essay aims to assess ideas about images and to examine the extent to which electronic imagery helps to sustain, question, or weaken a principle of liveliness, upholding an injunction against freeze-frames and static images.

Electronic media have altered the ways in which Catholic Charismatics access both the materiality of the icon and the significations that undergird it. Electronic imagery is in motion—images appear and disappear, come and go—and this introduces a new life and dynamism that problematizes the stasis governing conventional ideas about traditional religious imagery. That is to say, the slippage of images on the TV screen—the fact that they are made up of thousands of discrete shots that move by so quickly the eye sees them as more or less continuous—disintegrates the sense of completion we get when looking at a sculpted image. Technically speaking, however, the sense of liveliness and animation in the TV image is possible only because of the disruptions and tracking through which electronic images come to pass. In electronic (as in cinematic) movement, interruption is presence insofar as the only way for the image to come together is by structuring the forces of arrest and fragmentation (e.g., editing out, framing, cutting, etc.) that constitute it. In other words, the liveliness of the electronic image is, paradoxically, predicated on a sort of serialized iconoclasm—a continuous, sequential breaking up—that undergirds it.

The media presentations of Pentecostals have yet to acknowledge the specific materialities and movement associated with electronic imagery, particularly in light of the dialectic between destruction and construction in the very creation and perception of such imagery. One can see this in a televised episode that took place during the series of provocations between Protestants and Catholics known in the mid-nineties as Brazil's Holy War. The pastor of an evangelical church, the worldwide Universal Church of the Kingdom of God, kicked a statue of Our Lady of Aparecida, Brazil's patron saint, in front of the cameras of one of Brazil's main TV channels, claiming to demonstrate thereby the powerlessness of the statue, on the grounds that it could not move, whereas he, a living body, could.[1] He did not seem to realize that, for the viewers, he and the statue were both images mediated through the TV cameras. What seemed to matter to him was that he could direct his body to move, could feel that he was alive (and kicking)—in emblematic redundancy to the "live" structure of the broadcasted event, yet oblivious to the fact that his impact on the viewers was that of yet another televised image (an image in passing, indeed) not so very unlike the statue that he kicked. What was at issue was not only a battle between competing denominations, as many tended to read it, but also a debate about the materiality of images in an age of mass electronic media and about how motion is apprehended in the modern city. This perception is conditioned not just by contemporary media technology but also by the state's warnings about and attempts to combat economic stagnation.

Many Catholic Charismatics own traditional religious statuettes, busts, and sculptures. They display these in their private homes, during public celebrations, or within media settings such as recording studios. As I have explained elsewhere, the aspiration to be a "Charismatic," that is, to embody charismata through baptism in the Holy Spirit, has been a major source of contention with the local Church establishment with regard to perceptions of sanctity and traditional forms of representing saints.[2] By claiming that the body, and not static images, is the site of sacred power, the CCR movement has incited controversy with both the Brazilian Church hierarchy and popular Catholicism. Born-again Catholic Charismatics face the predicament of needing to dispense with graven images without jeopardizing their identity as Catholics. They have been called by their Pentecostal progenitors to reformulate the traditional status of the image as a site of mediation—to replace it with a direct and unmediated experience of the divine—and yet, they must do so in terms that will not betray their Catholicism. Indeed, many of the newly baptized who previously have owned and venerated religious objects are uncomfortable with the call to rid themselves of images as testimony to their new condition as inspirited and born anew. They may have been baptized in the Holy Spirit, but they are still Catholics.

Admittedly, I have never come across any born-again Catholic Charismatic who has purposely destroyed a religious object because of the commandment not to venerate graven images. More interesting, however, is how the very conceptualization of iconography and the relation to religious images is changing under the influence of electronic images—not just on a semiotic level, but on a material one, as well. Starting in the nineties, the growing popularity of the so-called expeditionary saints, such as St. Expeditus, St. Judas Tadeu, or St. Edwiges, attests to how saints and their images are becoming increasingly imbued with "electronic presence," not only among Catholic Charismatics but also among the larger urban population of São Paulo. This is not to say that traditional iconography is being swept away by the force of electronic regimes. On the contrary, electronic images are nuancing and enlivening the features of traditional imagery. In other words, the ambiguities generated at the core of the electronic image—expressed in the possibility of being an image and an animated body, freeze-frame and motion at once—has helped to make more explicit a tension between presence and absence *that sculpted images already had*. Recognizing the indeterminate nature of the image, which electronic mediation enhances, performs, and materializes, may increase our sensitivity to the originary breach that always afflicts not only identity but also the images we seek to keep sacrosanct—just as Catholic Charismatics have had to come to terms with their ambiguous identity as both Catholic and Pentecostal, maintaining a respect for religious objects while venerating more highly the inner experience of the spirit. There is, perhaps, no better icon to convey this complex field of forces and changes in iconography than the hugely popular St. Expeditus, "the saint for the urgent causes," also known as the FedEx saint.

A Requiem for St. Expeditus

On April 12, 2001, I paid a visit to Dona Claudia Moriz Xavier. She had invited me for lunch at her posh residence in the Jardins neighborhood of São Paulo. Even though we were approaching the dead of Brazilian winter, the air was hot and humid. I could not wait for the moment I could refresh my parched throat with some fresh water or lemonade. Dona Moriz opened the gate, while taking off her apron. As though reading my thoughts, she welcomed me with some freshly prepared *suco de laranja*, an orangeade, which she served in a fine glass. The temperature in the patio was tempered by a roof of aging grape leaves. So attentive was I to refreshing my throat that I did not notice a huge and grisly pit bull moving swiftly in my direction. Seeing the approaching animal, I flinched and choked. The nearly empty glass slipped from my hands and fell to the tiled floor, shattering into a myriad tiny shards. Slipping after it, my left foot smashed into a little statuette tucked into a niche in the wall by the main entrance. After some minutes of apologizing to and fro—Dona Moriz for the unleashed dog (which keeps robbers at bay), me for all the damage—we finally moved inside, as if in search of a new start. And, although I had come to visit Dona Moriz to talk about her experiences as an active member in one of the *groups de oração* ("prayer groups") within São Paulo city, St. Expeditus, whose image I had just inadvertently kicked, became the main theme of our conversation. (See Figure 34.)

I feared that the accident with the image upon my arrival would constitute a bad omen for a Catholic Charismatic. Aware that Charismatics filter events through the motto that "nothing is coincidence, everything is providence," thus reading signs into everything, I was wary of her "discernment" (which is how Charismatics speak). To my relief, however, Dona Moriz treated the incident rather like those sayings that evoke good luck by naming disaster, such as "Break a leg!" As Dona Moriz confirmed, St. Expeditus is one of the most popular saints within contemporary urban São Paulo. The saint's popularity grows despite—or perhaps because—of his undefined status within the Roman Catholic Church. As my hostess explained, the Church does not know what to do about him. On the one hand, the story of St. Expeditus is widely questioned, including whether he really existed. On the other, precisely this indefinition surrounding the saint, in addition to all the stories built around him, has endowed him with aura and helped spread his cult throughout southern Europe, in New Orleans, and in Latin America.

FIGURE 34   St. Expeditus.

Legend has it that St. Expeditus was a Roman centurion in Armenia who became a Christian, a fact that led to his being beheaded during the Diocletian Persecution of 303. The image of the saint depicts a young soldier holding a cross (in the past, it used to be a clock) with the inscription *hodie* (the Latin word for "today") in his left hand. On the ground lies a dying crow, trodden under the soldier's right foot. A bandarole with the word *cras* ("tomorrow") emerges from the crow's mouth. For this reason, many consider St. Expeditus to be the saint opposed to pro*cras*tination or, alternatively, the saint for urgent causes—in short, the saint who responds *expeditiously* to petitions. Many conflicting narratives about the origin and spread of the saint's popularity exist, working both to discredit and to publicize him. The funniest of all tells how, in the year 1781, a package was sent to a community of nuns containing the body of a saint that had been buried in the Denfert-Rochereau catacombs of Paris. The story goes that the nuns identified the corpse as that of St. Expeditus after seeing the word *expedite* on the package, to ensure a quick delivery of the bodily remains.

The uncertainty about the saint's actual existence, his nonrecognition by the Church, and the anecdotal repertoires he has inspired have by no means shattered his credibility. On the contrary, they have contributed to his popularity across a wide spectrum of religions, where he is best known as "the saint against procrastination," "the speedy centurion," or "the FedEx saint." Merchants, sailors, shopkeepers, dealers, examinees, and schoolboys have long adopted St. Expeditus as their special protector. More recently, he has been designated the "unofficial" patron saint of Internet nerds and computer hackers—as well as anyone who needs a "soft" or "hard" solution to a problem. There are readymade litanies and prayers to the saint. Here is a typical one:

> Saint Expeditus,
> Noble Roman youth, martyr,
> You who quickly bring things to pass,
> You who never delay,
> I come to you in need—
> (State your petition)
> Do this for me, Saint Expeditus,
> And when it is accomplished,
> I will as rapidly reply, for my part,
> With an offering to you.
> (State your vow or promise)
> Be quick, Saint Expeditus!
> Grant my wish before your candle burns out,
> And I will magnify your name.
> Amen.

Such a prayer should be followed by a small ritual, usually performed around a few objects, including the saint's statue or holy card, a St. Expeditus holy candle, flowers, and sometimes pound cake. The unofficial nature of the saint makes room for iconoclastic vengeance when deliveries happen slowly or, indeed, not at all. The saint can receive a kick, as though to coerce him to act speedily, while reminding him that he has a reputation to keep up. Curiously, instead of being chucked, the broken pieces of the saint's statues are often placed within roadside altars, shrines built beside the road whose origins go back to colonial days. Once in these rustic altars, the fragments of saints' images again attain a new status vis-à-vis the devotee.[3] Specifically, the shrines and the images placed therein—not all of which are broken—reinforce Catholic laypeople's aspiration to have unsupervised access to the saints, especially when it comes to judging their efficacy in delivering on their reputation by intervening in human affairs. In other words, roadside altars are alternative spaces to display (broken) images that, on the one hand, acknowledge the alternative nature of the saint and, on the other, submit him to the power of laypeople to expose his debris. This practice of humiliating the saints—which, as Aron Gurevich and others have described, goes back to the Middle Ages—has the paradoxical effect of contributing to the saint's popularity for, as Gurevich suggests, humiliation is intrinsic to a saint's capacity for humility.[4] A saint worthy of the name is always already a disfigurement of himself.

Whether coincidence or providence, my kicking the statue of St. Expeditus did not set things off on the wrong foot, as it were. To the contrary, it awakened me to an unanticipated existing parallel between broken statuettes and the ongoing conceptualizations of the image among Catholic Charismatics. Admittedly, it taught me less about the difficulties of being a dog when thirsty strangers happen by.

The Body/Image Predicament

Arriving from the United States into the State of São Paulo in 1969, the Catholic Charismatic Renewal, then known as the Catholic Pentecostal Movement, announced itself as the expression of a second Pentecost designed to recreate that original descent of the Holy Spirit on a global scale. In the pursuit of that ambition, it teaches that all individuals should become receptive to the experience of baptism in the Holy Spirit, which comes down upon the individual or community of individuals in the form of graces or gifts of the Spirit. The gamut of the charismata of the Holy Spirit is described in Mark 16:17–18 and the First Letter to Corinthians. Charismata can be divided into those of the word (the ability to prophesy and to speak in tongues), those of action (performing miracles and charity) and those of cognition (the gift of knowledge, discernment). Catholic Charismatics usually refer to the teachings in St. Paul's epistles, where he states that, though everyone can be endowed with charismata, these nonetheless follow a hierarchy in importance: charity being the highest, with glossolalia, or speaking in tongues, the lowest. Charismatic graces are understood to be faculties that are in principle accessible to all who allow themselves to be guided by the Holy Spirit. They are both personal and contextual: they are manifested in particular situations and for particular purposes, and some people might be predisposed to embody and manifest some charismata rather than others.[5] By embodying and practicing the gifts of the Spirit, Charismatics claim that a more direct and personal relation with the divine is not only possible but desirable.

In its emphasis on embodied charisma, the CCR challenges some of the principles of mediation established by institutional Catholicism in late-nineteenth-century reforms designed to consolidate the Church's control over the sacraments and the cults of saints and their images. These reforms aimed to extend the power of the Church (and of the State) to areas that had been evolving largely outside the purview of ecclesiastic power. For four long centuries of colonial rule, most communities had lived outside the direct control of the Church. *Muito padre, pouca reza* ("Much priest, little prayer") was a widespread saying among laymen. The priest would visit certain villages once a year, when he would cobble together a hodgepodge of sacramental ceremonies for the locals—baptisms, marriages, and funerals—all administered within the scope of two or three days. In the absence of the priest, during most of the year communities organized their religious lives around the supernatural gifts ascribed to, and owned by, particular individuals, who cured or prophesied.

Standing above these gifted individuals in assisting local people were only the saints. And the power of the imagination to represent them in the form of sculpted images compensated for their absent bodies. The proliferation of images fulfilled both religious and decorative functions in private households, chapels, or public shrines. In the context of colonial authority, where priests avoided most rural areas, workers expected landowners and servants expected their masters to build chapels and to pay tribute to a saint by constructing a shrine or altar for the workers, mostly slaves, and residents of the *fazenda*, coffee plantations created in the nineteenth century. In this climate of relatively unsupervised Catholicism, many iconoclastic episodes took place, with violence inflicted on saints and their images not only by Catholic devotees but also by those who saw in this practice of positive iconoclasm an opportunity to renounce Christianity—paradoxically, through methods that were themselves Catholic.[6] Avenging oneself on a saint worked to restore one's sense of empowerment when a petition was not answered in time or not at all, yet the disfigurement of the image, both verbal and physical, helped to enhance the saint's prestige in local hagiographies.

This practice of tacitly giving laymen socially accepted authority over matters of sanctity and agency would vastly change in the latter half of the nineteenth century. At that time, Roman Catholicism advanced into the countryside and put into operation a modern reform. The protagonists of this reform were, by and large, European-ordained and trained priests—German, Italian, and Polish. Most notable was the Order of the Redemptorists, who moved to Brazil in an attempt to recover, control, and take command of the power that, they claimed, was flowing about haphazardly in the rural areas.

Among the most prominent consequences of this new European reform was the elimination of many saints from local pantheons all around Brazil. Reformers advanced the argument that those saints, although venerated, were pagan and profane, as were their cults, to which the Roman Catholic Church had not given official recognition. This is how the term *popular Catholicism* came into being as a modern category. As the anthropologist Pedro Oliveira explains, it came into existence as a hegemonic strategy of the Church, created in order to distinguish it from "official Catholicism."[7]

It is this aspect of nonofficial sanctity and nonsacramental intervention that the Charismatic movement is now recovering, while articulating its own specificities vis-à-vis both popular Catholicism and the Church establishment. Thus if, on the one hand, the CCR takes up features that are identifiably premodern—for example, its strong lay matrix, cult of sanctity, and belief in miracles—on the other, it expands on modern reformist ideals. Like the latter, Charismatics endorse the Augustinian principle of *imitatio dei*, the aspiration to divine qualities to which all humans should be entitled.[8] They do so, however, through the mediation of the Holy Spirit, which blows where it will, and not through the Church's sacramental mediation. Especially in the movement's early stages, Charismatics contended that the canonization of saints is an obstacle to the *imitatio dei* ideal insofar as it undermines the democratic potential inherent in such a notion. As historian Kenneth Woodworth explains, the decision-making process in the canonization of saints is a highly bureaucratic and controversial mechanism, which at once promotes and limits the scope of *imitatio dei*.[9]

Charismatics in their turn relate to charisma as a substance through which divinity can be cultivated. While striving to intensify this dimension of *imitatio dei*, they also create new limits, borders, and judgments concerning what defines the condition of being well cultivated in sanctity. Thus, while in its early years the CCR was still striving to be accepted by the local Catholic establishment, spiritual presence could be detected in charismatic exteriorizations like "irreverence" or "intrepidness," whereas once the movement grew in popularity and acceptance within the Catholic ranks—and as Brazil moved into an increasing neoliberal sphere—those qualities give away to "flexibility," "pliability," and "fluidity." From a force opposed to the system, *pneuma*, the substance of the Holy Spirit, transmuted into an energizing resource for a society in which mobility, malleability, and speed had become paramount. In a changing cosmopolitan environment, procrastination becomes the sin one must avoid.

Against Procrastination

Popular saints like St. Expeditus thus exist in the tradition of an unofficial class of saints created apart from the institutional aegis of sanctity, yet they function in a particularly modern way. The cult of St. Expeditus became especially visible starting in the mid-nineties, especially in São Paulo. Wherever one turns in the city, one sees the image of the saint, as if he were stalking you: a statue, a poster, a banner bearing the words *Agradeço a St. Expedito pela graça alcançada* ("I thank St. Expeditus for grace attained"). There are small, improvised altars and even a small chapel honoring and publicizing the saint. The shrines and the hundreds of banners, which often hang from an electricity pole or a tree—or sometimes from a bridge or tunnel—are made and displayed by urban laypeople as a form of gratitude. They are, moreover, a form of publicity that has become integrated into the economy of exchange between saint and devotee. Another common form of payment to the saint is to put an ad in the newspaper acknowledging the miracle. Others do so even before they attain grace, for it is believed that to invest in the saint's publicity encourages him to come through. These practices have stimulated an industry in holy cards, known in Brazil as *santinhos*—8-cm-x-10-cm colorful printed images of the saint. A man in the southern region of São Paulo has set up a printing business as both a petition and promise to St. Expeditus. Nowadays, St. Expeditus's *santinhos* are found scattered in cafés, butcher shops, restaurants, hairdressing salons, and boutiques, or are simply distributed on the street. They are printed on such objects as bumper stickers, calendars of all sizes, key chains, car statuettes, empty candle holders, mugs, wallets, T-shirts, soaps, oils, and incense. They can function as a bookmark, a decoration for pen and paper, or a computer screen saver. The postmen love him.

Adopted by thousands of Paulistanos, the frenetic speed of the saint in his travels awakens particular sympathy among Catholic Charismatics. Although they are predisposed to relinquish the use of graven images, St. Expeditus has successfully entered their horizon of piety. As Dona Moriz observed, "Images ought to condense meaning rather than condense sacredness." The vitality, youthfulness, and, above all, expediency of St. Expeditus have relieved him of the conventional gravitas associated with saints. His ubiquity and timeliness excel in their capacity to transcend place and, paradoxically, time. The fact that he embodies qualities to which many Brazilians aspire—or at least are expected to aspire—in their professional and personal lives redeems him from the pedestal of sanctity while inspiring ordinary mortals to transcend their daily gravities. St. Expeditus is a saint or messenger who moves in the midst of urban Paulistanos, bringing and taking news, slipping in under the most unexpected circumstances, embodying the minimal space between promise and deliverance.

The fact that St. Expeditus has never been officially recognized by the Catholic Church, that he is interdicted from integration into the pantheons of sanctity or having his statue displayed in churches, only contributes to his popularity among both Charismatic and non-Charismatic Catholics. The saint's indeterminate position has led to his adoption as a kind of "anti-icon" icon. He even has his unofficial feast day, on April 19, and, in some parts of São Paulo (e.g., as it happens, around the Church of Tiradentes), all over Brazil, and in other parts of the world, a novena is performed to the saint just before that date. St. Expeditus's unofficial status explains why not only Catholics but also individuals of other creeds, including evangelicals, *umbandistas* (that is, practitioners of the Umbanda Afro-Brazilian religion), and even confessed atheists, can relate to the saint. While he is remembered as a Christian martyr, he is equally associated with African and Afro-Caribbean spiritual entities—tricksters and messengers such as Legba Barros, Samedi, or Bonsu.

While many Catholic Charismatics are wary of or defensive about owning images, many carry with them in their wallets a holy card of St. Expeditus. Sculpted images of him are also unproblematically present in the domestic sphere of Catholic Charismatics. As Dona Moriz explained, "St. Expeditus is not contained in the statue. Before you finish saying his name, he is already somewhere else!" The integrity of the image, she suggests, "is false," because St. Expeditus is never arriving but always and already departing. As she suggests, no matter how long one looks at the image, one's look is always located in passing, in the verb tense *having looked*. The image unpresents itself, as it were. The image is *there* only in order to stress its capacity for being *not there*—but in passing, like a visitation. And yet, despite this constitutive internal negation, a whole array of new materials and techniques are employed in producing the image of the saint. These vary from the heavier, solemn, artisanal authenticity of a statuette to the lighter, thinner body of a printed image. The use of printed reproductions of the saint is at once practical and performative:[10] practical because they are easy to carry; performative because they express how the saint's lightness and expeditiousness become incorporated into their very form. Parallel to the printed format, St. Expeditus has entered the digital universe through the phenomenon of cyber-altars and website petitions.[11] From statuettes to wax, from the press to the world of electronic and digitalized images, St. Expeditus's popularity has spread like that of no other contemporary urban saint. There is no technological evolution; no one technique eliminates another. Rather, as electronic figurations come to dominate the arena, they inflect the meanings associated with sculpted images, so that they come to share the spatiotemporal qualities attributed first to print and then to electronic images. Conversely, one becomes ever more aware of the still or frozen image within moving images. As a result, clay, plastic, print, and digital media all coexist nowadays as possible inscriptions, borrowing from each other's materialities and semiotic potentials. It is as though the variety of materialities involved in making images itself performs the malleability of the saint. Or, to put it differently, it seems as if images are becoming increasingly aware of their own lives and regimes.

In the early stages of the movement, many Catholic Charismatics kept their statues in the closet, feeling that they impeded rather than expressed sanctity, but in the nineties those statues gradually came into the open. The popularity of St. Expeditus has, in the meantime, mobilized the Catholic Church to promote other competing but official expeditionary saints into the local hit parade of sanctity. Examples of this are St. Judas Tadeu, the saint for "impossible causes," or St. Hedwig of Andechs, known in Brazil as St. Edwiges, who is the "saint for the beholden." Like St. Expeditus, they are invoked to provide immediate solutions for urgent missives, but unlike him they remain under the aegis of institutional control.

The tendency toward speedy saints reflects and helps organize the busy lifestyle and fast-going rhythms experienced by urban Brazilians. In the last three decades, São Paulo has evolved into one of the major world's economic hubs, becoming a cosmopolitan, high-tech metropolis. The city vibrantly welcomes icons that challenge their own iconicity, icons that, in their passing, are at once an image and its impossibility, iconic and aniconic. Largely made up of a burgeoning middle-class population, São Paulo city responds to the incentives posed by the government of Lula da Silva to embrace mobility and speed, not quite in the military sense, as Paul Virilio describes in his book *Speed and Politics*, discussing the aftermath of the events of 1789, but in terms of the contraction of time and space through global technologies; roads and even aerial avenues for private jets and helicopters; the expansion of the market; an acceleration in lifestyles; more intense competition for jobs; social mobility; the development of media channels; and, last but not least, sports. With its massive size and high population density, São Paulo demands mobility and agility, not only in the circulation of information, goods, and people but in the traffic between this and other worlds. "Never put off until tomorrow what you can do today" runs the old proverb, and that applies to people as much as to saints.

The upper-middle-class origins of the CCR place it on a cusp where the demands for mobility are particularly pressing: the university, the stock market, the media. The skill (or charisma) of an enhanced, embodied elasticity and ability to adjust to new and unpredictable situations has inspired a whole range of viscous practical metaphors, with enough ambivalence to lubricate the various domains of the social and the religious. The association of the Holy Spirit with breath is often translated into a fluid discharge. Thus baptism in the Spirit, the supernatural moment when a person is endowed with the gamut of spiritual charismas, is also described in terms of "unction," and a person whose giftedness is particularly recognizable by others in the community is referred as "the anointed," turning to metaphor the literal oil of biblical times. Having sprung from the need for an expression of Catholicism unfettered by the Church hierarchy and the modern state, Catholic Pentecostalism has chosen a more bodily conception of sanctity, one in which the qualities of resolution and resilience were first valued as signs of inspirited anointment, to be replaced by motility and malleability. In the process—as is frequently the case within Catholicism—the movement has started to reincorporate older features, if also submitting them to new transformations.

This is how, parallel to the viscous nature of the Spirit among Catholic Charismatics, starting in the nineties there has appeared a new St. Expeditus Oil—a product inventoried in the array of products offered by Red Fast Luck Oil. The oil can be used in lighting small lanterns at home, at work, or on public altars. Others place a few drops of St.

Expeditus oil in the tanks of their automobiles, for both protection and speed, (or protection in speed) within the chaotic traffic of São Paulo; in the keyholes of their domiciles, to ward off robbers; and in their places of work. Last but not least is the popularity of a whole range of commodified cosmetic products, advertised under such alluring labels as "Botânica Saint Expedito Oils," all of which respond to an increasing demand for wholesome, fast solutions in the spiritual, bodily, and practical dimensions of everyday life.[12]

For all the popularity and fame of St. Expeditus, he cannot outshine the young, athletic, and media-savvy Padre Marcelo Rossi, a Catholic Charismatic priest. Nowhere are elasticity, cosmetics, and ethics as powerfully conjoined as in his hugely popular religious celebrations called "the aerobics of Jesus." A former bodybuilder and apprentice in a beauty parlor, Padre Marcelo became a priest in 1994 in a small parish in the southeastern region of São Paulo. Throughout the years, he has become a living icon of fluidity, a lifter of all sorts of social, physical, and psychological gravities. People keep coming back to him, either via the media or by visiting his mega-sanctuary: a gym like structure with a fifteen-meter altar, from which he coaches thousands. On Sundays, his "aerobics of Jesus" are transmitted live on TV to the whole nation.[13]

What makes Padre Marcelo so famous are the ways in which he has managed to synthesize in his persona a number of issues that have been at work as points of contention between various Catholic groups, between them and other Christian Pentecostal denominations,[14] and between Christians and other religious and nonreligious groups— above all, the media. It is as if the suppleness he praises and organizes in the context of his aerobics also endows him with the pliability necessary to stretch, morph, and slide through and into other repertoires, while maintaining, justifying, and, indeed, quite successfully harmonizing these through a dynamic and resilient Christianized logic of *pneuma*. Padre Marcelo's emphasis on breath and rhythm—patented in all sorts of musical compositions, techniques of prayer, and Orthodox-based meditations he has himself configured and disseminates through the media and religious shows—underscores the idea of "urgency" that a saint like St. Expeditus so popularly articulates. Inasmuch as his aerobics help to situate the body in the "here and now," Padre Marcelo is not only attaining the desirable (mediated) immediacy claimed by Catholic Charismatics in the context of contemporary Catholicism but also picking up on premodern ideals of unmediated (i.e., nonsacramental) religion that had become subsumed under the category of the popular. Above all, he does so through the breath's inalienable association with movement and liveliness. Indeed, it is at this conceptual juncture—namely, that of mediated immediacy, movement and liveliness—that the dialogue between sculpted images, broken images, and the disruptive rhythms of electronic media, as well as between different factions in Catholicism, becomes productive in the larger conceptualization of the religious image in an age of mass media.

Images in Passing: Conclusion

Given what we have seen so far, how can we reassess the question of religious images, including the classic iconoclasm debates, within contemporary Brazil as a whole? What might my fortuitous kick to the statue of St. Expeditus—and the reflections that followed—tell us about the ways in which electronic media are changing our perceptions not only of the image and the body but also of sanctity? Broken into fragments, the statue of St. Expeditus vividly opens to view the motion of the icon and, in that, unexpected parallels to the living qualities of televised imagery. Samuel Weber speaks of mediatized images as "coming to pass."[15] His ideas about television as a medium can help us to grasp the relation between integrity and separation, between being there and not being there (already and only in passing) within the context of electronic media. He writes: "the space defined by the television set is already fractured by the undecidability of that which appears on the screen. Is it taking place here, or there, or anywhere? The development of video, and above all, of the digitalization of images, renders the question even less susceptible of an unequivocal answer."[16]

What television renders as fractured—and what video and digital media intensify—is no less present in the vast pantheon of sculpted images that lurk and prowl in almost every corner in Brazilian private and public spaces. The ubiquitous presence of images—sometimes tucked away in the most unexpected places—and the plasticity that undergirds their simultaneous proliferation and trivialization, their hubris and humiliation, creation and destruction, parallels and enhances the equally fracturing nature of the television medium. This explains why anthropologist Rafael Sánchez, in his study on the serialization of images and the televised media in the context of the María Lionza possession cult in Venezuela, can state: "No wonder that earlier I was able to describe the splitting effects of possession in the María Lionza cult with quotes from Samuel Weber, without saying that they referred to television and not to spirit possession."[17] As Sanchez argues, the tantalizing proliferation of statues and figures around the saint is analogous to the flickering process, effect, or event of "channel-surfing." That, in turn, is a part of, as much as a reaction to, the equally fleeting quality of time and space within urban areas like Caracas and São Paulo, one that demands from its urban dwellers and passersby—and the saints that they beseech—an aerobiclike flexibility in delivering solutions and answers within what Sanchez designates "spaces of alteration":

> Within such a space of alteration, subjects are not just passively jolted or split by displacement, mobility, and their manifold violences. They also become suckers for speed, addicted, so to speak, to shock and displacement as means of enjoying and reinventing themselves in circumstances where the vagaries of the job market, the indeterminancies of space, the telegraphics of power, and the media all intimate that if you stay put or stay the same, you might as well give up.[18]

Along similar lines, Bruno Latour and Peter Weibel, in the catalogue to the exhibition *Iconoclash: Beyond the Image Wars in Science, Religion, and the Arts*, consider the disjointed, fractured, and cascading nature of televised images in order to question whether in fact sculpted images have not always been internally fractured, thus making any act of iconoclasm redundant. The ambivalence of the icon stems from the fact that images are never adequate to themselves. And so, just as electronic images owe their motion to the operations of arresting, cutting, and sampling, so the stillness of sculpted images may result from the impasse, hesitation, if not paradox involved in what we take to be presence. In that sense, perhaps, a small degree of procrastination or deferral within the image itself is always unavoidable.

PART VI

Digital Technologies

Enchantment, Inc.

Online Gaming Between Spiritual Experience and Commodity Fetishism

Stef Aupers

> A world awaits. . . . Descend into the World of Warcraft and join thousands of mighty heroes in an online world of myth, magic and limitless adventure. . . . An infinity of experiences await. So what are you waiting for?
> —From the cover of World of Warcraft (Blizzard Entertainment, 2005)

In the field of new media entertainment, the computer gaming industry is booming. In the United States alone, $9.4 billion was spent on games in 2003 (topping Hollywood's movie industry by $1 billion), while 60 percent of all Americans (about 145 million people) play console and computer games on a regular basis.[1] Among the fastest growing genres are "Massively Multiplayer Online Role Playing Games" (MMORPGs). What distinguishes this new generation of online games from "console games" is that they are shared (the game worlds are "inhabited" by millions of players at the same time), that they are persistent (the three-dimensional environment is online twenty-four hours a day and continues to exist even when players are not interacting with it), and that they generate a unique culture, social structure, economy, and ecology, which changes over time. As such, they are generally described as "virtual worlds" or "synthetic worlds."[2] And most importantly for our topic here, they are defined by their otherworldliness. Johan Huizinga famously argued that play in general invokes a "magic circle" that stands in opposition to the "ordinary world": "Into an imperfect world and into the confusion of life it brings a temporary, a limited perfection."[3] MMORPGs or virtual worlds are "magical worlds" in the most literal sense. More than 95 percent of them are based on the fantasy genre:[4] virtual worlds display Tolkienesque environments brimming with mythical creatures, mysterious forces, and magical opportunities.

Players, who play on average more than twenty-three hours a week in the game,[5] are totally immersed in a magical or otherworldly environment.

From a classical social-scientific perspective, these "otherworldly" worlds can nonetheless never belong to the realm of religion or spirituality. In a "disenchanted world" reigned over by science and technology, Max Weber famously argued, "there are no incalculable forces . . . one can, in principle, master all things by calculation."[6] More specifically, the argument goes that magic and enchantment have literally been banished to the world of fiction—the realm of poetry, literature, television, and, more recently, computer games. Fiction, Coleridge argued famously in *Biographia Literaria* (1817), encourages a "willing suspension of disbelief" and induces "moments of poetic faith," but it can never seduce its secular readers to believe in the supernatural events described in the text. This "willing suspension of disbelief" is a typical product of the modern Enlightenment and can be understood as an attempt to defend and legitimate supernatural discourse in literature in a secular or "disenchanted" age. It "enables us to engage with a more richly imaginative world than the one in which we live under rational truth,"[7] but it leaves the strict modern divide between reality and fantasy, fact and fiction, intact.

From this perspective, the current popularity of *Lord of the Rings*, *Harry Potter*, *Charmed*, *Buffy the Vampire Slayer*, or games like World of Warcraft may demonstrate that lost magical worldviews are appealing to a large audience. At the same time, however, it confirms rather than contradicts Max Weber's classical thesis. After all, while reading, watching, or consuming fantasy, the audience is expected to uphold the modern, secular divide between the real and the simulated, fact and fantasy. As Simon During argues: "once the difference between fiction and non-fiction is grasped, and a particular text is deemed to be fiction, then it is impossible simply to believe in the reality of fictional events, whether they are supernatural or not."[8] A disenchanted world, then, is completely based on the dichotomy of (religious) "belief" versus (secular) "disbelief," with the latter understood as temporarily suspendable in engagements with fiction. Against this background, I will discuss an undertheorized epistemological shift in the religious climate from (religious) belief to (spiritual) experience that both motivates an unexpected reenchantment and opens the door to a spiritual engagement with a commercialized form of fiction that goes beyond the "willing suspension of disbelief." I will use the newest genre of online computer games, MMORPGs, as an empirical case study.

Reenchantment: From Religious Belief to Spiritual Experience

Max Weber's thesis of the disenchantment of the world holds that the Western Judeo-Christian tradition, and in a later phase the scientific worldview, erodes belief in metaphysical worlds, spirits, and magical means of controlling such mysterious entities: "it means that there are no mysterious incalculable forces that come into play."[9] Before examining the question of whether this thesis is applicable to the contemporary Western world, one may wonder whether it holds true for Weber's own time.

Max Weber and the New Age

The beginning of the twentieth century is often described as a period brimming with alternative, non-Christian forms of religiosity—a period when "countless small religions" flowered.[10] Especially widespread were esoterical doctrines and currents like the new theosophy of Helena Petrowna Blavatsky (who founded the Theosophical Society in 1875), the anthroposophy of Rudolf Steiner, spiritism, and pantheistic perspectives on nature derived from Romanticism. Many of Weber's contemporaries, including intellectuals, artists, philosophers and psychologists, were engaged in and freely experimented with these alternative forms and varieties of religion. Max Weber definitely knew about these initiatives of reenchantment. In 1914, for instance, he visited Ascona, a small village in the Alps where contemporaries experimented with spirituality and free sexuality. In "Science as a Vocation," he noted that "many old gods ascend from their graves" and pointed out, more specifically, that the "idols whose cult today occupies a broad place on all street corners and in all periodicals" are "personality and personal experience."[11] This interest in new, post-Christian "lived religion" was especially prominent among youngsters in his time: "They crave not only religious experience but experience as such."[12]

Although Weber emphasized that this phenomenon of reenchantment was a "crowd phenomenon," he never systematically elaborated upon this trend in his academic work—let alone problematized his own assumption of the disenchantment of the world. The main reason for this blind spot in his work seems to be his moral position. Weber theorized that a "disenchanted world" meant essentially a world without meaningful illusions, since science can describe the world objectively as it "is" but can say nothing about its inherent meaning (if there is such a thing). Weber argued that people should "heroically" face this meaningless "disenchanted world," without taking refuge in "surrogate" experiential religions: "The ubiquitous chase for 'experience' stems from . . . weakness: for it is this weakness not to be able to countenance the stern seriousness of our fateful times."[13] And more bluntly: "this is plain humbug or self-deception," and one should "bear the fate of the times like a man."[14]

His moral position vis-à-vis the trends of reenchantment in his time, as explicitly expressed in "Science as a Vocation," seems to inform a blind spot in his academic work. By condemning the widespread interest in esotericism and spiritual experience, he seemed to fall into the trap of mixing up moral values and science, "ought" and "is," in his work—two domains, he advocated repeatedly, that should be clearly separated, since morality clouds objective science and science can never objectively legitimate a chosen moral stance in the public debate. Dutch historian Patrick Dassen goes so far as to argue that his diagnosis of a disenchanted world was to a large degree intended as a provocation to those who sought refuge in new utopias and religions.[15] Whether this is the case or not, the dialectic of "disenchantment" and "reenchantment," source of the "ghosts" that perpetually "haunted modernity,"[16] has not been systematically discussed in his work.[17]

Yet the interest in esoterical currents and "lived experience" Weber observed was not just a temporary outburst or a fin-de-siècle phenomenon. Since the beginning of the last century, it has remained a stable feature of modern life, and it has—especially since the counterculture of the 1960s and 1970s—only increased in popularity and significance. The protest of the counterculture, mainly represented by young, white, middle-class people, was aimed both at the Christian tradition and at the "technocratic" and "dehumanizing" machineries of modernity,[18] which were understood as reducing people to "one-dimensional" men and women.[19] Informed by this antimodern stance, countercultural gurus like Ken Kesey and Timothy Leary advised their fellow hippies to "drop out" and experiment with cocktails of LSD, spirituality, and esoteric wisdom, while "beat poets" such as Jack Kerouac and Allen Ginsberg mixed esoterical and oriental religious worldviews. Alan Watts, in turn, introduced Buddhism to a larger audience.[20] Looking at this development in retrospect, the spiritual wing of the counterculture made way for a broad "cultic milieu"[21]—a milieu that, despite its heterogeneity, has become "conscious of itself as constituting a more or less unified movement" since the 1980s.[22]

This movement is generally referred to as the New Age movement. It has grown rapidly in the past decades: while secularization, referring to the decline in church membership and the belief in a Christian God, has steadily advanced, New Age spiritualities have blossomed in northwestern Europe and especially in the countries where traditional values have eroded most: France, Great Britain, Sweden, and the Netherlands.[23] Such spiritualities are not exclusively privatized manifestations of religiosity, as is generally assumed, since they increasingly seem to find their way into the public realm and into the heart of modern institutions.[24] In this respect, Steven Sutcliffe and Marion Bowman argue that "contrary to predictions that New Age would go mainstream, now it's as if the mainstream is going New Age."[25] Indeed, New Age spirituality features prominently in the media nowadays—in bestsellers like *The Celestine Prophecy* or *The Da Vinci Code* and television shows like *Char*, *Medium*, or the *X-Files*—and has found its way into modern business organizations, where managers are encouraged to participate in spiritual courses to increase both well-being and profits.[26] And last but not least, the countercultural promises of New Age spirituality are, paradoxically, incorporated by and institutionalized in mainstream marketing, branding and advertisement.[27] Concluding with David Lyon that "the late twentieth century witnessed a widespread reenchantment, in ways that might well have surprised Weber"[28] hence seems like an understatement: New Age spirituality has become an intrinsic part of Western culture.

New Age: The Epistemology of Experience

> Only personal experience . . . can provide immediate and uncontaminated
> access to truth.
>
> —Christopher Partridge, *The Re-Enchantment of the West*

What, then, is New Age, and how exactly does it constitute a "reenchantment of the world?" In most of the social-scientific literature, the term *New Age* is used to refer to an apparently incoherent collection of spiritual ideas and practices. Most participants in the spiritual milieu, it is generally argued, draw upon multiple traditions, styles, and ideas simultaneously, combining them into idiosyncratic packages. New Age is thus referred to as "do-it-yourself-religion," "pick-and-mix religion," "religious consumption à la carte," or a "spiritual supermarket."[29] In their book *Beyond New Age: Exploring Alternative Spirituality*, Sutcliffe and Bowman even go so far as to argue that "New Age turns out to be merely a particular code word in a larger field of modern religious experimentation."[30]

These accounts of the New Age are certainly not wrong: participants in the spiritual milieu are inclined to "bricolage"—the construction of strictly personal packages of meaning, based on individual tastes and preferences.[31] Underneath this diversity, however, one can find commonly held assumptions that have all too often been neglected. Interestingly enough, these main features of the New Age coincide to a very large extent with those witnessed by Weber in his time. Above all, New Age is a secularized manifestation of the esoteric tradition that has existed as an undercurrent in Western culture at least since the Renaissance.[32] Moreover, like German young people at the beginning of the twentieth century, contemporary New Agers worship mainly the idols of "personality" and "personal experience," manifest in a "sacralization of the self."[33] This widely shared doctrine not only provides a substantial explanation for the bewildering diversity of the spiritual milieu but also contradicts the alleged "individualism" of New Agers, since basically *all* New Agers understand themselves collectively as essentially "authentic" and "divine" beings.[34] "We are all gods!" one of my New Age respondents once typically stated. And indeed, following Paul Heelas: "The great refrain, running throughout the New Age, is that we malfunction because we have been indoctrinated . . . by mainstream society and culture."[35] Mainstream society is thus conceived of as an alienating force, which estranges one from one's "authentic," "natural," "real" or "higher" self—from who one "really" or "at deepest" is:

> Perfection can be found only by moving beyond the socialized self—widely known as the "ego" but also as the "lower self," "intellect" or the "mind"—thereby encountering a new realm of being. It is what we are *by nature*. Indeed, the most pervasive and significant aspect of the *lingua franca* of the New Age is that the person is, in essence, spiritual. To experience the "Self" itself is to experience . . . "inner spirituality." . . . The inner realm, and the inner realm alone, is held to serve as the source of

authentic vitality, creativity, love, tranquility, wisdom, power, authority and all those other qualities which are held to comprise the perfect life.[36]

This, then, is the main tenet of New Age spirituality: the assumption that in the deepest layers of the self the "divine spark"—to borrow a term from ancient Gnosticism—is still smoldering, waiting to be stirred up and to succeed the socialized self. As such, New Age by and large coincides with the "cult of personality" that Weber witnessed in his age. Following Emile Durkheim, it can also be portrayed as a "religion of which man is, at the same time, both believer and God."[37]

Although a *collective belief* in a sacred self thus, paradoxically, constitutes the core doctrine of the New Age from an etic perspective, this picture becomes problematic from the emic point of view because, epistemologically speaking, New Agers eschew belief. Instead, they consider the self the locus of *experience* and argue that no truth, beauty, or reality exists independently of the self and that reality in all its forms can only be experienced. And vice versa: everything that is known through "unmediated" experience cannot be false or falsified. Informed by an esoteric critique of Western culture, then, New Agers radically problematize every belief in an external truth—indifferent to whether this truth is formulated in a scientific or a Christian religious milieu. Based on an analysis of the "narratives of experience" in the esoteric tradition and New Age, Olav Hammer notes, in *Claiming Knowledge: Epistemologies from Theosophy to the New Age*: "There is no real need to believe in any particular doctrines, nor is one obliged to trust in their antiquity or their scientific basis. The ultimate litmus test is whether you can experience their veracity for yourself."[38]

As such, post-Christian spirituality entails an epistemological third way of "gnosis," rejecting both religious faith and scientific reason as vehicles of truth. Rather, it is held that one should be faithful to one's "inner voice" and trust one's "intuition":

> According to [gnosis] truth can only be found by personal, inner revelation, insight or "enlightenment." Truth can only be personally experienced: in contrast with the knowledge of *reason* or *faith*, it is in principle not generally accessible. This "inner knowing" cannot be transmitted by discursive language (this would reduce it to rational knowledge). Nor can it be the subject of *faith* . . . because there is in the last resort no other authority than personal, inner experience.[39]

Gnosis, Wouter Hanegraaff states, retreats from the notion that such a thing as a truth independent of the individual exists, because "truth" can only be experienced subjectively. In various New Age courses, personal truth is even displaced by *experience for the sake of experience*. In a case study on reincarnation therapy, for instance, I found that "past-life experiences" were surrounded by radical suspicion and skepticism by both the providers of these therapies and their clients.[40] The Atma Institute (a spiritual New Age center specializing in reincarnation therapy) typically argued in their mission statement: "With reincarnation therapy it is not important whether the experiences of a client are based on the truth." In a similar vein, one client stated: "I can not say that I really believe [in reincarnation]. It feels like a subjective reality that works for me." These examples demonstrate that experience is considered meaningful in and of itself—it exceeds the importance of objective truth or even personal truth. This variety of New Age spirituality coincides with Zygmunt Bauman's work on the postmodern (pseudo) religious quest for "this-worldly ecstasy," "peak experiences," and the "flow of sensations": "Each new sensation must be 'greater,' more overpowering and exciting than the one before, with the vertigo of 'total,' peak experience looming always on the horizon."[41]

Belief in magic, spiritual entities, and a metaphysical world may have eroded, as Weber noted, but the undertheorized epistemological shift from religious belief to spiritual experience has outlasted his theory. In addition to critiques of theories of secularization that point out that there remains a "believing without belonging,"[42] I propose that *experiencing without believing* may provide yet another fruitful avenue for empirical research. This proposition is formulated from an "emic" perspective, of course, since from a more detached "etic" perspective, "authentic" spiritual experiences are not possible without preceding New Age beliefs and cognitions.[43]

Paradoxically, this primacy of spiritual experience in contemporary society can be explained by the "disenchantment" thesis of Weber. As noted, disenchantment is accompanied by problems of meaning, since "objective" meaning can no longer be grounded in metaphysical and religious realms. Sciences like astronomy, biology, physics, or chemistry may describe the world as it is, but they can (and should) not teach anything about the meaning of the world. In a totally "disenchanted world," Weber argues, "the world's processes simply are . . . and happen but no longer signify anything."[44] A radicalization of this assumption can be detected among postmodernists like Jean-Francois Lyotard, Fredric Jameson, and Jean Baudrillard. The abandonment of universal truth and the destruction of interpretation, they argue, lead us to an emphasis on "surface" and "desert-like and indifferent forms" without any inherent meaning.[45] It is exactly this "disenchanted" worldview that provides a fertile ground for New Age. As the example of reincarnation therapy demonstrates, New Agers are skeptical about believing in every external truth—whether metaphysical or empirical. They therefore seek "depth" within the self and are immersed in personal experience. The "disenchantment of the world," then, goes hand in hand with a reenchantment through spiritual experience.

The Spiritual Experience Economy

The epistemological shift from belief to experience has important ontological implications, since it defies the clear-cut modern distinctions between fantasy and reality, fact and fiction, on which a "disenchanted world" is based. Moreover, it breaks with the "willing suspension of disbelief" proposed by Coleridge in 1817 to defend supernatural literature in a secular age, since experience can not be "suspended" or "falsified." As Annette Markham observes: "When experiences are experienced, they cannot be 'not real.' In a broader sense, terms such as *real*, *hyperreal*, *not real*, or *virtual* are no longer valid or meaningful as definitions of our experiences because our experiences are not easily separated in these binary oppositions."[46]

Starting from this theoretical assumption, I will demonstrate on an empirical level that this epistemological stance opens the door to a spiritual experience of fiction—a development that brings the countercultural New Age movement to the heart of modern capitalism.

The Market in Spiritual Fiction

Although New Age gained momentum in the counterculture of the 1960s and 1970s, its tension with mainstream culture and their mutual demonization has diminished since the 1980s, when New Age gradually came to adapt to the market. During this period, it changed from an alternative "cult movement" into a commercial "client and audience cult."[47] Rodney Stark and William Bainbridge write about "audience cults": "Most who take part in audience cults do so entirely through the mass media: books, magazines, newspapers, television . . . and the like."[48] And indeed, New Age bestsellers like *The Aquarian Conspiracy* (1980), *The Dancing Wu-Li Masters* (1979), *You Can Heal Your Life* (1984), and, most notably, James Redfield's *The Celestine Prophecy* (1993), as well as magazines like *Body Mind Spirit*, *Kindred Spirit*, and *Insight Network* popularized New Age spirituality. In addition, television shows like *Char*, *Medium*, and the talk show of Oprah Winfrey (who blends New Age with a Christian message that claims "God wants you to be yourself"[49]) have propelled this mainstreaming of the New Age and as a result contributed to the loss of its countercultural potential.

Spiritual experiences, whether sought by Heelas's "full-time New Agers," "part-time New Agers," or Bauman's "sensation seekers,"[50] are, in short, mediated by the market and instigated by books, magazines and television shows. The supply on the spiritual market ranges from genres making factual claims about a "spiritual" truth to full-fledged fiction without a clear referent, with the two genres often converging or even being conflated. Dan Brown's bestseller *The Da Vinci Code* stands out as a good example. It has been described as an "esoterical novel" or "fact-fiction novel," since it consciously blends historical facts, esoteric claims, and fiction. For New Agers, there is no need to disentangle fact from fiction, since literally everything, including fiction, can be considered "real if it feels real." This typically relativistic stance, which I have elsewhere described as "ontological pragmatism,"[51] is motivated by the primacy of experience. In particular, the long-standing genres of "fantasy fiction" and "science fiction" have become a locus of spiritual experience. These and many other manifestations of popular fiction, Adam Possamai and Christopher Partridge argue convincingly,[52] may be increasingly understood as religious texts, containing sacred narratives that provide spiritual inspiration and invoke spiritual experiences.

Science fiction is widely read in the spiritual milieu and has fueled the imagination of many New Agers, especially (neo)pagans.[53] The Church of All Worlds, a California community of pagans established in 1967, is even completely based on Robert Heinlein's *Stranger in a Strange Land*, and its members greet each other with the catchwords "Thou Art God." Like several other pagan groups, they consider science fiction to be "the new mythology of our age," and one participant declared she was "seized with an ecstatic sense of recognition" while reading Heinlein's novel.[54] A more famous example is, of course, Scientology, which was founded by science fiction writer Ron Hubbart. Like New Age, Scientology promises salvation through unmediated experience, self-actualization, and personal growth, although these "authentic" experiences are in fact mediated by Hubbart's worldview, which is, in turn, based on his own science fiction novels. More recently, the Raelian cult (made famous by the media because it announced it had created the first cloned human baby) has been involved in constructing cosmologies based on Ufology, digital technology, science fiction, and New Age. Rael's message reads: "Now it's time to stop believing and begin to understand . . ."

While these examples illustrate the trend toward a spiritual experience of (science) fiction, they may be considered somewhat exotic and deviant. A similar development, however, can be detected in the cultic milieu and in fan cultures clustering around main-stream Hollywood blockbusters and series like *Star Trek*, *Star Wars*, and *The Matrix*.[55] *Star Trek*, for instance, attracts a fandom that hovers "between cult and culture,"[56] while its hardcore fans, "the Trekkies," are "textual poachers" who try to unravel the mysteries of these series.[57] George Lucas, the director of *Star Wars*, explicitly based the movies on Jungian archetypes and the perennial myth of "the hero's journey" derived from the work of Joseph Campbell.[58] In addition, he fueled its cosmology with a New Agey holistic worldview ("the Force"), thereby causing an unforeseen cult of the Jedis or "Jediism."[59]

While the line between science fiction and fantasy fiction is hard to draw—as *Star Wars* demonstrates—"fantasy" has been at the heart of the spiritual imagination from Theosophy to the New Age. An early mystery novelist like Rosicrucian Edward Bulwer Lytton, whose narratives were filled with sorcery and magic from Egypt and India, inspired Madame Blavatsky's invention of the Theosophical Masters.[60] Since the 1960s, New Agers and pagans have been fueled by fantasy fiction, ranging from the work of J. R. R. Tolkien to movies like *Charmed* or supernatural "pulp horror" like *Buffy the Vampire Slayer*: "Witchcraft, or Wicca, is the fastest growing 'religion' in the USA today. It is estimated that around a million and a half teenage Americans, often as young as thirteen, are practicing Wiccans. Television programs such as *Sabrina the Teenage Witch* and films like *The Craft* have sparked continent-wide interest in witchcraft and awarded the official Hollywood stamp of 'cool.' "[61] The most important influence in the field is, of course, the work of Tolkien. *The Lord of the Rings* is based on multiple sources, including Anglo-Saxon legend, art, and literature and Norse mythology, and its world, Middle Earth—inhabited by hobbits, elves, and wizards—was immediately embraced by the spiritual counterculture when it was published as a paperback in 1965. It was, as Warren Hinckle states, "absolutely the favorite book of every hippie,"[62] since he would feel "immediately familiar, upon first reading, with an apparently imaginary place and/or time."[63] This identification with Middle Earth may partly be explained by its enchanting content, which nonetheless approaches the "consistency of reality" through the technical skills of the writer. *Lord of the Rings* contains, more than any other work of fantasy, incredibly detailed and precise descriptions of the historical background, language, and customs of the different races inhabiting Middle Earth.[64] Tellingly, Tolkien himself explicitly refuted the assumption that his work is fiction that motivates a temporary escape in an "unreal" world. A good author of fantasy, he wrote in his essay "On Fairy Stories," is the "subcreator" of "a secondary world that your mind can enter. Inside it, what he relates to is true: it accords with the laws of that world."[65]

This understanding of worlds of fiction as "true," I hope to have demonstrated, stems to a large extent from the primacy of experience, which defies the divide between reality and fantasy, fact and fiction, on which a disenchanted world is based. Religious beliefs, motivated, legitimated, and guarded by the Christian church, cannot easily transgress such boundaries, because they are always restricted by boundaries between what is sacred and what is profane, what is holy and what is not. Once experience reigns, however, the "real" becomes simply "what feels real"[66]—a situation in which even fiction can obtain spiritual significance.

Online Games: Spirituality Enters the Experience Economy

Joseph Pine and James Gilmore claim that we are living nowadays in an "experience economy."[67] Our economy has shifted from providing goods and services on the basis of use value to the provision of compelling experiences. Today's market, then, is based on the same epistemological premises as New Age. After all, in the contemporary "experience economy," Pine and Gillmore argue: "There is no such thing as an artificial experience. Every experience created within the individual is real, whether the stimuli be natural or simulated."[68] "Cyberspace," they add, "is a great place for such experiences."[69]

The computer-gaming industry exemplifies this "elective affinity" between the epistemological premises of New Age and today's experience economy. In general, *experience* and *immersion* are among the main catchwords in the industry: "complete immersion in the gaming experience has become the Holy Grail among video game designers."[70] More than that: the new generation of online games that has been available on the Internet since the end of the 1990s has totally blown apart the distinctions between disenchantment and reenchantment. Ultima Online, the first such game, issued in 1997, advertised: "If you've ever felt like you wanted to step out of yourself, your life, into one that was full of fantasy and adventure—virtual worlds offer you this opportunity. . . . You choose your own virtual life and immerse yourself into the mystical, medieval world of Britannia. . . . Ultima Online is the place where you can be whatever you want to be." When one looks at the history and genealogy of online role-playing games, it is not surprising that today's virtual worlds promise "enchantment" and a paradoxical salvation from modern life.[71] There is much evidence that many of today's major game designers were part of the spiritual counterculture of the 1960s and 1970s and were, in particular, strongly influenced by the work of Tolkien.[72] Sherry Turkle argues: "The personal computer movement of the 1970s and early 1980s was deeply immersed in Tolkien and translated his fantasy worlds into hugely popular (and enduring) role-playing games."[73] Richard Bartle confirms: "The single most important influence on virtual worlds from fiction is J. J. R. Tolkien's *The Lord of the Rings* trilogy."[74]

Indeed, by the time Tolkien died in 1973, his enchanting world had been reproduced in cyberspace. In 1976, Stanford hacker Donald Woods and programmer Will Crowther developed Adventure, the first text-based fantasy role-playing game. An essential contribution was made during the 1980s by Roy Trubshaw and Richard Bartle, who developed the Multi-User-Dungeon, a textual environment that could be played by several players at the same time on the Arpanet. After Ultima Online, designed by Richard Garriot to be the first full-fledged virtual world, was launched on the Internet in 1997, its popularity triggered other designers and companies to create online worlds: most notably, Everquest, in 1999 (a game produced by Sony and, at the time of writing, still "inhabited" by about five million players); Dark Age of Camelot (two million players); and, more recently, World of Warcraft (no fewer than fourteen million players in 2011).

From the birth of online worlds in the alternative counterculture up to their major role in the contemporary experience economy, online role-playing games have been depicted as "otherworldly" and spiritual.[75] These speculations were instigated both by New Agers—such as LSD guru Timothy Leary, who converted from "psychedelia" to "cyberdelia" in the 1980s[76]—and game designers. Especially in the 1990s, virtual worlds were depicted as environments for "spiritual growth," a "home of the mind," a "metaphysical space," or a realm above and beyond "the problems of a troubled material world."[77] Game designer Brian Mortiarty claimed at a conference in 1996: "Spiritual experiences are, in fact, our business. . . . If we could design reality for our minds, what powers would we grant ourselves? . . . Why should we settle for avatars when we can become angels?" Moreover, virtual worlds were sometimes understood as countering the "disenchantment of the world." As one designer argued in an online discussion of "magic" in virtual worlds: "Magic is . . . a very compelling way to view the world and can provide more meaning and agency than a viewpoint that is strictly materialist. In a nutshell, we want the magic that was stripped by rational materialism to return back into our lives. Immersive 3D worlds provide a nice playground to this end."[78]

These quotes from game designers demonstrate, in short, that virtual worlds of fiction are constructed as spaces for magical and enchanting experiences. When one looks more substantially at online worlds like World of Warcraft, Dark Age of Camelot, and Everquest, this does not seem far-fetched. They are infused with the religions, legends, myths, sagas, and "ultimate and . . . sublime values" that, Weber argued, have retreated from modern life.[79] Dark Age of Camelot, for instance, claims to be informed by "King Arthur legends," "Viking mythology," and "Celtic lore." Recent expansions have added new environments, such as the "superior civilization of Atlantis" and others where one can encounter the ancient Greek Minotaur and "creatures from Egyptian mythology." The worlds display polytheistic and animistic religions, in particular. In World of Warcraft, for instance, players are encouraged to search for "spiritual objects," "totems," or weapons imbued with "mana." Unencumbered by historical accuracy, then, game designers cut, paste, and sample various "premodern" religions, popular legends, and myths and combine them into new, idiosyncratic worlds. As such, these designers are very much like New Age teachers on today's spiritual market, who rely on a bricolage of multiple traditions to produce spiritual experiences for their clients.[80]

The question remains whether and how players identify with these spiritual worlds and start to experience them as "real." Do they indeed experience them as truly enchanting? In line with the Weberian "disenchantment thesis," it is important to note that the majority of the players of World of Warcraft I interviewed see themselves as incapable of believing in "supernatural" or "transcendent" realms. They see themselves as "too sober" (in Dutch, *nuchter*) to believe, and they often claim that scientific knowledge essentially can solve and demystify all mysteries. But there's another side to their story. Like FBI agent Fox Mulder in the *X-Files*, gamers generally see themselves as victims of their rationality: they cannot believe but actually "want to believe." One gamer typically argued: "I would really like it if there was more than we can see in life: telepathic connections between people, or special superpowers that people are born with—forces that would be prominent in everyday life." "Magic," "telepathic connections," and "superpowers"—such mysterious elements may be scarce goods in the real modern world, but they are virtually omnipresent in World of Warcraft's fantasy online worlds of Azeroth. Quotes such as these demonstrate that online games provide the opportunity to experience meaningful enchantment without believing. After all, the primacy of experience turns the enchanting world into a real environment. In the words of one of my respondents: "You know that it is a world of make-believe—that it is just not real, but it feels like very real to me."

Playing the Spiritual Self?

How is this ontological turn from fiction to reality invoked in the concrete process of playing? First, it is instigated by role playing. By choosing a role before the game starts—a

"character" or "avatar," such as a "sorcerer," "warlock," "wizard," "enchanter," "illu-
sionist," "coercer," "summoner," "necromancer," "conjurer," "druid," "warden,"
"fury," "shaman," "defiler," or "mystic"—players become active subjects in the online
world. This is very much built into the design of these online games: players can make
seemingly endless choices about the gender, race, class, work, and physical appearance of
their characters. Thus everyone can in theory be a truly "authentic" individual in the
game world. As the game Asheron's Call comments on its website: "Enter the vast and
magical world of Dereth, where a new and heroic identity awaits you! . . . After selecting
your attire and facial features from millions of possible combinations, customize your
skill set to make your character truly unique." In the game, individual players are linked
to and embedded in the broader narrative of the game world—its imagined history, tales
about violent wars between good and evil alliances, and so on. Moreover, they become
part of clans, tribes, or guilds with other players—groups that constitute the social structure of the world. This construction of both "agency" and "structure" is a defining characteristic for real *and* virtual worlds and contributes to the experience of the latter as
real.[81]

Second, role playing has in itself often been described as causing vivid experiences
that mark a transformation from "play" to "serious play,"[82] or as invoking an ontological
transformation from "playing" to "being." As Huizinga notes in *Homo Ludens*: "The
disguised or masked individual 'plays' another part, another being. He is another being."[83]
In the context of online gaming, Bartle refers to this as the "role-playing paradox":

> You're not role-playing as a being, you *are* that being; you're not assuming an iden-
> tity, you are that identity; you're not projecting a self, you are that self. If you're
> killed in a fight, you don't feel that your character has died, you feel that you have
> died. There's no level of indirection, no filtering, no question: you are there. . . .
> When player and character merge to become a persona, that's immersion; that's what
> people get from virtual worlds that they can't get from anywhere else; that's when
> they stop playing the world and start living it.[84]

My own research validates this point to a large extent. Players of World of Warcraft
emphasized that they increasingly identified with their avatars. "A hero that follows his
own path and does his own thing—that's the way I have designed him. And I like playing
with the idea that I am him. He is a part of me, something that I would like to be," one
player contends. "You can be someone else. I think it is a beautiful world full of fantasy—a world that you encounter only in books. Unlike in real life, you can become a
real hero," says another. A third respondent states, "It says something about your dreams:
you play the person that you cannot be in real life but would like to be."

The experience of the enchanting world as real is thus mediated by role playing. More
substantially, the study of online gaming reveals an elective affinity between New Age

experiences and gaming experiences. Like "soft" New Age techniques, such as rebirthing, aura reading, visualizations, or neo-hypnotherapy, the activity of role playing on the screen provides an opportunity to experience and access the "higher," "deeper," or "spiritual" Self. In New Age activities and gaming alike, people willingly incarnate a second identity that is imagined to be "higher" than the self experienced in everyday life. From an etic perspective, however, this "second self" may be equally perceived as an other—an internalized heroic identity derived from popular culture, literature, or media. To take the example of reincarnation therapy again: could it be that the alleged "authentic" experience of being a knight in a former life, a princess in medieval times, or a witch burned at the stake is actually informed by popular novels and historical images in the media?[85] Titus Rivas, for example, convincingly demonstrates that the Hollywood blockbuster *Titanic*, directed by James Cameron (1997), motivated many people to believe that they had actually died on the Titanic in a former life—a claim that was dubbed "The Titanic Complex." The first symptom: while watching the movie, they experienced the "physical sensation" that they had actually been there.[86] In a similar vein, Tanya Luhrmann has argued that neo-pagans explicitly adopt role models from fiction in their magic: "Magic involves and encourages the imaginative identification in which the practitioner 'plays at' being a ritual magician or a witch. . . . Here the role models are taken from fiction: the magician fantasizes about being Gandalf, not about being his coven's high priest."[87]

These cases may be theoretically instructive, since they demonstrate the intimate connection between New Age experiences and media experiences. This raises the question: Could the locus of "authenticity" in the spiritual milieu—the alleged "unmediated" higher self—actually be a Self mediated by popular culture? Questions such as these are complex to answer, since, as Birgit Meyer rightly notes, "it is neither enough to deconstruct and dismiss these experiences as 'made up' and 'faked' nor to take their authenticity at face value."[88] In online computer games, however, this mediation of experience is obvious and seemingly uncontested: the played characters, or "avatars," that generate genuine feelings of "authenticity" and even give rise to a magical "omnipotence of thought" in the Freudian sense are, in the end, mass-produced by game designers, companies like Sony, Microsoft, Blizzard Entertainment, and other representatives of the contemporary experience economy.

Commodity Fetishism New Style?

The case of online gaming demonstrates that the experience economy hovers between meaningful or even spiritual experiences, on the one hand, and commodity fetishism as theorized by Marx, on the other. As Stephen Klein et al. state: "There is a slippery slope from conceptions of a digitally empowered player to a doctrine that blindly accepts whatever the market dispenses as right and good."[89] Marx argued that *every* commodity sold on the market is *in itself* a fetish, because people *by definition* forget about the circumstances under which it was manufactured, produced, and sold. Don Slater notes: "the true source of their value—human labour—is not visible," and people therefore perceive them as "forces beyond human making."[90] Hence the mystification. The case of online games demonstrates, however, that designers *explicitly and purposely* imbue their products with mysterious, enchanting qualities, thereby multiplying their fetish character—a sort of *commodity fetishism new style.*

From this perspective, it is fascinating that game designers state that immersion in games through identification with avatars helps people to become more like "who they really are."[91] Despite this much-emphasized personalization, avatars nonetheless remain artificial constructs engineered by designers, so that even players' "authentic" experiences, feelings, and emotions are to a large extent subjected to and disciplined by technical regimes. David Freeman has dubbed this "Emotioneering," which relies on "the vast body of techniques . . . that can create, for a player or participant, breadth and depth of emotions in a game or other interactive experience, or that can immerse a player in a world or a role. . . . The goal of Emotioneering is to move the player through an interlocking sequence of emotional experiences."[92] So what happens when people fully identify with their in-game characters? It seems just as logical to reverse the reasoning set out by many of the designers: these commodities do not necessarily bring personal "authenticity" but rather transform the person himself or herself into a full-fledged commodity. This is, on an empirical level, confirmed by Robert Marks, who argues: "But who owns a player's creation inside a game? When a player spends months on end creating the perfect Everquest character, does the character belong to Sony or to the player? The short answer is, it belongs to Sony."[93]

Spiritual experiences and enchantment are to a large degree mediated, incorporated, and produced, as the case of online gaming demonstrates. In addition, since the 1970s and 1980s the marketing strategies, advertisements, and methods of branding in today's experience economy have been explicitly influenced by and infused with countercultural values. Aware that many people nowadays are disenchanted with modernity and that "the rejection of limitless consumption becomes as central to the modern social imaginary as consumption itself,"[94] many companies have, paradoxically, incorporated this antimodern stance. These companies thus aim to "out-counterculture one another" and turn "all the complaints about conformity, oppression, bureaucracy, meaninglessness, and the disappearance of individualism that became virtually a national obsession during the 1950s into rationales for consuming."[95] The marketing and branding of online gaming provides an excellent example of this. Advertisements of these mass products paradoxically promise their consumers an enchanting world of spiritual freedom beyond alienating modern society: "limitless possibilities with only your imagination to bridle them" (Ultima Online), a "personal saga" (Asheron's Call), or an "infinity of experiences" (World of Warcraft). These experiences are no longer the result of long-term ascetic training, rituals, or spiritual exercises; spiritual salvation, game producers promise, is just a few dollars and a mouse-click away.[96]

How, then, can this development be understood? It would, I think, be a mistake to fall back on the simple neo-Marxist reflex of understanding this development in online gaming as the latest trick of the "culture industry" to colonize and commodify the hearts and minds of the individual, an attempt to immerse them in the market's "spectacle," or a simulated and hallucinating "hyperreality."[97] The problem with these theories is that they can, by their very nature, never be falsified, because in a commodified context even the most meaningful spiritual experience is understood as the ultimate proof of alienation on a priori grounds. These theories are, as such, strongly informed by the modern moral and nostalgic assumption that "real" enchantment and the economy are, just like "true" spirituality and commodities, *by definition* mutually exclusive categories. Since meaningful experiences can in fact be experienced in a totally commodified context, as I hope my empirical exploration of online games has demonstrated, I propose to go beyond this "modern divide."[98] If as social scientists we take the accounts of our respondents seriously (and as a sociologist of culture I propose that we do), we may obtain more insight into how the production and consumption of spiritual experiences interact than if we simply condemn spiritual experiences that depend upon commodities as deeply alienating in advance.

Conclusion

Weber's theory of the "disenchantment of the world," I conclude, has become problematic in two ways. First, the epistemology of belief—which is what the theory addresses—has become increasingly obsolete due to its supersession by the epistemological premise of spiritual experience that is at the heart of the growing New Age movement. Second, this epistemological turn has important ontological implications, since it defies the boundaries between fact and fiction, spirituality and commodities, and, ultimately, the sacred and the profane, on which the modern disenchanted world is supposedly based. The institutionalization of New Age assumptions in today's experience economy has, in particular, blurred distinctions between the sacred and the profane. Online computer games, such as World of Warcraft, have been used as a case study: although they are commodified environments on the Internet, they do provide truly enchanting experiences that cannot easily be distinguished from the experiences produced and consumed in today's spiritual New Age milieu. As Danielle Egan and Stephen D. Papson state about religion in general: "Religion and its discursive structures have moved into the marketplace and are being subjected to and reinscribed within its logic."[99]

This relocation of the sacred to the market in general and to the world of commodified fiction in particular makes the relevance of this chapter quite clear, I hope. While

Marx's work on commodity fetishism already indicates that "spirit" and "matter" are not mutually exclusive categories,[100] I hope to have demonstrated that today spiritualization and commodification reinforce one another. Until now, discussion in the social sciences has focused mainly on the commercialization of spirituality—a development discussed over and over again since Thomas Luckmann first wrote about an emerging "market of ultimate significance," in which the New Age movement plays such an important role.[101] In this discussion, there is disagreement less about *whether* New Age is commercialized— most authors agree that it is—than about whether or not this degrades spirituality to triviality, insignificance, or even an irrelevant consumer item. The main question in this debate, then, is: Does the commercialization of New Age indicate a process of secularization, or does it not?[102]

In this chapter, I have gone beyond this seemingly endless debate and moved in another relevant direction: the spiritualization of commodities, a development that remains by and large unnoticed in today's academic world. The case of online computer gaming seems just one empirical example among many. Commodities have been suffused with countercultural values and ideas about the liberation of human potential ever since these ideas were developed in the 1970s and popularized in the 1980s.[103] The most obvious examples are, of course, Apple's computers ("Think Different") and Nokia's mobile phones ("Connecting People"), but even ordinary beauty products like shampoos, body lotions, and perfumes promise nowadays to "heal" consumers' personal lives, thanks to their basic ingredients, which supposedly stem from ancient, long-forgotten, and above all "authentic" civilizations and cultures of the East.[104] Values associated with the modern Enlightenment, such as progress, efficiency, and functionality, are, of course, also still salient,[105] but they are increasingly complemented by these romantic and spiritual values. The commodities of "New Age capitalism," Kimberly Lau has argued, "circle back to an imagined past existing prior to industrialization, a past epitomized by references to more integrated relationships and the interconnectedness of all living things." By incorporating these values and perspectives, she adds, companies "exploit . . . anxieties about risk society and the diseases of modernity."[106] Now that mass-produced commodities increasingly promise consumers authentic experiences and spiritual liberation from the modern disenchanted world, academic attention should turn to this spiritualization of commodities rather than endlessly debating the commodification of spirituality as evidence for secularization.

Fulfilling the Sacred Potential of Technology

New Edge Technophilia, Consumerism, and Spirituality in Silicon Valley

Dorien Zandbergen

The New Age movement was one of the outcomes of the process of religious redefinition initiated by "countercultural" spiritual seekers in the 1960s and 1970s in northern Europe, Australia, and North America.[1] The manifestations of New Age differ somewhat between regions,[2] yet, as Wouter Hanegraaff shows: "what connected adherents of the New Age is the sharing of several worldviews and techniques all aimed to realize the 'New Age,' or a New World whether through an apocalypse, or in the here and now."[3] As such, the New Age is a culture-critical spiritual movement that ultimately seeks the overthrow of the cultural system of the mainstream. Two prime ways in which this culture criticism manifests itself are in the rejection of consumerist values and in an emphasis on the use of "natural means" for realizing the New Age.[4]

When we focus on this culture criticism, the New Age movement in Northern California presents us with a puzzling situation: it is characterized by discourses of "naturalness" and anticonsumerism, but it was decisively shaped in intimate relationship with the computer industries of "Silicon Valley"—the Santa Clara Valley, on the San Francisco Peninsula. One indication of the entwinement of New Age with the high tech industries of this area is the fact that in the late 1980s cultural actors in this area launched the term *New Edge* to refer to their brand of New Age spirituality. This term expresses the belief that the New Age will be realized through the "cutting edge" technologies and sciences pioneered in Silicon Valley.[5] In this chapter, I will ask how Northern Californian New Edgers reconcile their embrace of naturalness and their anticonsumerist ideals with their enthusiasm for the products pioneered by the technology industries of Silicon Valley.

The New Edge spiritual embrace of computer science and technology implies defining the nature of the sacred and the nature of computer technology in relation to one another. This means, in the first place, that these technologies are constituted as natural and as giving sacred perception. Second, it involves a reflexive stance that imagines the sacredness of computer technology in terms of its "potential": this makes it possible to critique the corporate system in which computer technologies are created while holding onto the ideal that these technologies are in and of themselves capable of transcending the cultural system of the mainstream. As such, the New Edge is engaged in a struggle over the definition of the nature of the "things" that are produced by the Silicon Valley industries: while defining computer technologies as sacred technologies, the New Edge is at times opposed to the conventional treatment by corporate industries of computer technologies as consumer products. At other times, however, the New Edge imagines the sacred potential of computer technologies in surprising harmony with the consumerist ethos of the Silicon Valley industries. The aim of this chapter is to gain insight into the circumstances in which New Edgers forge relationships between the sacred and the corporate, the materialistic and the spiritual.

In the following account of the entwinement between New Edge and the Silicon Valley computer industries, I support the insight produced by a wide variety of scholars in the past few decades that—contrary to the way in which processes of secularization have conventionally been understood and described—neither religion and technology nor religion and technological consumerism intrinsically exclude one another.[6] A study of the New Edge shows how technologies of mediation are presupposed in experiences of the sacred and how certain forms of spirituality can be at home in consumerist and technological environments. An ethnographic study of New Edge is, furthermore, a study of how a religious imaginary and practices are implied in the creation and use of certain artifacts and of how the choice of particular technical artifacts in turn shapes a religious imaginary and practices. The following account of the New Edge, in other words, discusses religion as part of a *technological system*, defined by the anthropologist Marcel Mauss as a "total social phenomenon that marries the material, the social and the symbolic in a complex web of associations."[7] This definition of a technological system a priori acknowledges that the sacred, the material, and the social continuously shape each other. It defies any deterministic conceptualization of either "technology" or "religion" as phenomena with fixed properties.

In this sense, the following discussion of the New Edge breaks with earlier academic reflections on the religious correlates of digital technology. In the early 1990s, various scholars theorized the Internet as a technology with intrinsic religious characteristics. Examples can be found in Michael Benedikt's collection *Cyberspace First Steps*, in which he describes cyberspace as the latest stage in an evolutionary movement from matter to spirit, with "the ballast of materiality cast away—cast away . . . perhaps finally."[8] Such characterizations are quite close to New Age conceptualizations of the Internet: in 1994, the former Harvard psychologist, "psychedelic explorer," and New Ager Timothy Leary argued that the "electronic-digital" domain of the Internet is inherently spiritual because of its "mythic, magical, ethereal, incorporeal, intangible, nonmaterial, disembodied, ideal, platonic" attributes.[9] Such understandings are technologically deterministic in the sense that they treat the Internet as a technology with intrinsic characteristics that have an impact on social and cultural life in a definite way.[10] As such, these understandings disguise the way in which technological artifacts such as the Internet are socially and culturally constructed as spiritual. They also conceal the way in which the religious experiences generated by the "immaterial realm" of the digital are still dependent on the specific materiality of digital technologies, as shaped in a specific historical context. In more recent years, some of the "first-generation" scholars of "cyber-religion" have exchanged their religious depictions of the Internet for more dystopian and secular versions.[11] Yet ethnographic accounts of high-tech spirituality that bring spiritual interpretations of digital technology into perspective as being constituted within a historically, socially and culturally contingent network of people, institutions, discourses, and practices are still relatively scarce. In this chapter, then, I will discuss the New Edge as a historically emergent, locally produced set of discourses and practices by identifiable networks of people, institutions, and events in the San Francisco Bay Area.

In his book on the New Age published in 1996, Hanegraaff dubs the New Edge, in a footnote, a "recent development."[12] Yet, as I will show, historical and ethnographic research suggests that the origins of this development can be traced back to at least the late 1960s. Since this period, spiritual seekers in Northern California who adhere to New Age doctrines and epistemologies have sought to create sacred spaces and moments of divine awareness by embracing technologies pioneered and mass-marketed by research centers and corporations in this area. In this chapter, I use the term *New Edge* to refer to this long-term relationship between New Age spirituality and "high tech." I base this account of the New Edge on a nine-month period of fieldwork conducted in 2005 and 2006 in the San Francisco Bay Area, on archival research, on network analysis, on a close analysis of "New Edge texts," and on other histories of the relationship between Silicon Valley and the "counterculture" in general.[13]

New Edge and New Age

In the San Francisco Bay Area, New Edge discourses and practices can be found within several overlapping networks of people and institutions.[14] Stretching across at least three generations, these networks trace their roots back to the California countercultural movements of the 1960s and 1970s and still consider themselves decidedly countercultural. One of these networks comprises San Francisco's contemporary self-described "psychedelic community." Members of this community prefer to refer to psychedelic drugs as "entheogens"—a term that expresses the notion that psychedelic drugs "bring out the divine within."[15] For this reason, the community also refers to itself as the "entheogenic community." The entheogenic community has clear genealogical lines with what was referred to as San Francisco's "rave movement" in the 1990s, consisting of various "tribes" or "rave collectives" that organized all-night parties during which electronic music, "mind-altering" drugs such as XTC, and computer animations served to create all-immersive environments. Whereas not all of these "tribes" characterized themselves as "religious" or "spiritual," a few of them explicitly profiled their rave activities in such terms and have continued to do so.[16]

Overlapping with the entheogenic community and the rave movement is the "cyberpunk movement," which took shape in the Bay Area in the mid-1980s. Cyberpunk is a genre of science fiction that emerged in response to the rise of global computer information networks and was pioneered by the writers William Gibson, Rudy Rucker, Vernor Vinge, John Shirley, and Robert Anton Wilson. In contrast to older forms of science fiction and various contemporary genres, cyberpunk stories are situated in the near rather than a distant future. Furthermore, whereas older forms of science fiction center on large spaceships and robots, cyberpunk focuses on networked or small-scale and prosthetic information technologies.[17] A theme that typically characterizes cyberpunk fiction is the way that information technologies—whether injected in the body or when immersing bodies as information networks—"enhance" humans in ways that transform them into a new kind of species. When we trace even further back the networks in which New Edge discourse has emerged, we come across various cultural "movements" that explored psychedelics, alternative kinds of spirituality, and politics in the 1960s and 1970s.

Starting in the 1960s, artists, journalists, computer engineers, computer scientists, and scholars affiliated with these overlapping countercultural movements have prefigured the contemporary New Edge. Through magazines, manifestos, novels, websites, mailing lists, conferences, and events, they have expressed their understanding of the potential of information technology. In it, we can recognize the basic composites of New Age thought. As I will show, this understanding imbues information technologies with the capacity to connect people to a sacred reality that is otherwise deeply hidden inside the self and in the wider universe. In "reconnecting" people with this sacred reality, information technologies are seen as capable of realizing "natural" and "authentic" ways of being.[18] This understanding of information technology resonates with two basic premises of New Age: gnosticism and holism.

Gnostic epistemology, as various scholars have pointed out, presupposes the idea that true reality—the sacred order of the universe—can only be known through experience. For New Agers, Hanegraaff emphasizes:

truth can only be found by personal, inner revelation, insight or "enlightenment." Truth can only be personally experienced: in contrast with the knowledge of *reason* or *faith*, it is in principle not generally accessible. This "inner knowing" cannot be transmitted by discursive language (this would reduce it to rational knowledge). Nor can it be the subject of *faith* because there is in the last resort no other authority than personal, inner experience.[19]

Second, in the treatment of technologies as gnostic, we can discern the New Age holistic worldview, which is rooted in a rejection of the "dogmatic rationality and dualism" of Western culture. According to the New Age worldview, this dogmatic dualism—apparent in the Christian separation of man and nature, mind and body, spirit and matter—"brainwashes" and indoctrinates people into seeing reality in restrictive ways.[20] The central aim of New Agers is, therefore, to restore an authentic awareness of the holistic nature of reality by making people aware of the interconnection between their own selves and other people, nature, and God.[21] The holistic idea that the self and God are intrinsically connected exhibits, furthermore, the New Age worldview in which the self is considered divine. As Paul Heelas phrases this New Age idea of "self-spirituality": "to experience the 'Self' itself is to experience 'God.'"[22]

New Agers world-wide enact and affirm the gnostic, holistic, and self-spiritual worldview of New Age through practices such as meditation, yoga, or dance. In addition, particularly in Northern California, New Age beliefs have been enacted through engagement with information technology. A New Age worldview has thereby been modified into a New Edge worldview, as some self-consciously refer to it. In what follows, I will present a brief chronology of the way in which certain technologies have been constituted as "gnostic" by Northern Californian New Edgers. I start with the New Edge embrace of electric technologies by the "Merry Pranksters" in the 1960s. Then I move to the New Edge use of electric and digital biofeedback technologies by countercultural computer advocates in the early to mid-1970s. Finally I discuss the New Edge embrace of Virtual Reality and Virtual Worlds technologies in the 1980s and 1990s.

Bypassing the Reducing Valve: The Technological Way to Gnosis in the 1960s

During my research in Silicon Valley in 2005, I regularly met with Bruce Damer, someone whose worldview I came to characterize as New Edge. Damer is an engineer at NASA and speaks regularly at conferences organized by the entheogenic community of Northern California. During these conferences, as well as in interviews with me, Damer is continuously developing a vision of a future empowered by science and technology in which the universe will achieve a higher level of consciousness.

Damer is quite reflective about his own position in a historical line of other high-tech spiritual pioneers, particularly the "Merry Pranksters." In *The Electric Kool-Aid Acid Test*, American novelist and journalist Tom Wolfe documented the activities of the Pranksters.[23] Wolfe based his novel largely on writings, film footage, and audio tapes produced by the Pranksters themselves. One important story line in this documentation is a cross-country bus ride from San Francisco to New York undertaken by the Pranksters in 1964, in their bus called "Furthur." Damer, in possession of the Pranksters' videotapes of this bus ride, is also the proud owner of a replica of their bus, which sits in the garden of his farm and which he has—referring to its mechanical defects—named "No Furthur." This identification of a contemporary New Edger with the Merry Pranksters induced me to explore the Pranksters' approach to technology.

As Wolfe documents, the Pranksters had gathered around the novelist Ken Kesey. In the late 1950s, when LSD had not yet been criminalized, Kesey had volunteered for LSD experiments conducted by a mental health clinic in Menlo Park. His acid trips, in combination with his work as a night watchman at the Menlo Park clinic, inspired him to write *One Flew Over the Cuckoo's Nest* (1962). The book was so successful that in 1962, after Kesey and others were evicted from where they had been living, on Perry Lane in Palo Alto, he could afford to buy a cottage in the town of La Honda, in the Santa Cruz Mountains to the west of Palo Alto. A group of around twenty other "acid-heads" came to live with him there. Together, they formed the Merry Pranksters.

At La Honda, the Pranksters continued what they referred to as their LSD "experiments" or "acid tests." One of the things they "tested" was their view of reality. Through the use of psychedelic drugs, the Pranksters discovered what was to become one of the key ideas of the New Age: "with these drugs your perception is altered enough that you find yourself looking out of completely strange eyeholes. All of us have a great deal of our minds locked shut. We're shut off from our own world. And these drugs seem to be the key to open these locked doors."[24]

The Pranksters framed this insight in terms laid out by the novelist Aldous Huxley in *The Doors of Perception* (1954), in which Huxley writes about his experiences with the drug mescaline. Huxley writes: "The function of the brain and nervous system and sense organs is in the main *eliminative* and not productive. Each person is at each moment capable of remembering all that has ever happened to him and of perceiving everything that is happening everywhere in the universe. . . . According to such a theory, each one of us is potentially Mind at Large."[25] Huxley defines the human brain and nervous system as a "reducing valve," which allows only a "measly trickle" of consciousness. This "reduced awareness" is taken by most people to be the one and only reality, because humans have invented elaborate "symbol-systems and implicit philosophies, which we call languages" to "formulate and express the contents of this reduced awareness." This language "tricks" and "bedevils" people into believing that "reduced awareness is the only awareness" and that words are "actual things."[26] For Huxley, self-transcending experiences such as mescaline-induced ones make people conscious of the "totality of reality . . . of the Mind at Large." For him, this awareness is clearly religious in nature, because what it reveals is "the glory, the infinite value and meaningfulness of naked existence, of the given, unconceptualized event. In the final stage of ego-lessness there is an 'obscure knowledge' that All is in all—that All is actually each."²⁷ This experience, for Huxley, entails true salvation, since it delivers one from "the world of selves, of time, of moral judgments and utilitarian considerations, . . . of self-assertion, of cocksureness, of over-valued words, and idolatrously worshipped notions."²⁸ Instead, an "inner world [that is] self-evidently infinite and holy" can be discovered.²⁹

As Wolfe reports, the Pranksters took such spiritual cosmologies to heart. During their LSD trips, they reported a "bottled-up God inside . . . that is whole, all-feeling, complete and out front."³⁰ They also experienced that they were one with a supreme, awe-inspiring divine reality that governs all and that, they imagined, formed the essence of all world religions: "Gradually the Prankster attitude began to involve the main things religious mystics have always felt, things common to Hindus, Buddhists, Christians, and for that matter Theosophists and even flying-saucer cultists. Namely, the experience of an Other World, a higher level of reality. And a perception of the cosmic unity of this higher level."³¹

A Cybernetic Ecology

Electric technologies played a major role in Prankster practices aimed at restoring connection with the divine and experiencing "cosmic unity." They used electric technologies to overcome the "faulty body interface." One of the Prankster dreams was, for example, to build a high-tech geodesic dome:

> A geodesic dome on top of a cylindrical shaft. It would look like a great mushroom. Many levels. People would climb a stairway up to the cylinder . . . and the dome would have a great foam rubber floor they could lie down on. Sunk down in the foam rubber, below floor level, would be movie projectors, video-tape projectors, light projectors. All over the place, up in the dome, everywhere, would be speakers, microphones, tape machines, live, replay, variable lag. People could take LSD or speed or smoke grass and lie back and experience what they would, enclosed and submerged in a planet of lights and sounds such as the universe never knew. [It would be] a fourth dimension.³²

The dome was realized at the "acid tests." By immersing themselves in interactive environments with cameras, sound recorders, and stroboscopes, the Pranksters sought to create direct feedback loops between inner signals and outer ones, in complete synchronization, thus bypassing the impulses of the physical body and creating a full experience of "a higher level of reality . . . in the supreme now . . . of cosmic unity."³³

According to Wolfe, the Pranksters modeled their imagination of technological salvation on Arthur C. Clarke's science fiction novel *Childhood's End* (1953). In this book,

Clarke describes the "Breakthrough Generation" of "the Children of the Earth [who] ultimately rise from their bodies, and set out for the stars." The children of the Breakthrough Generation are born on Earth, but already as infants show "powers of mind far beyond their parents."[34] While still living on Earth, the children form their own colony, from which they eventually "return" to the stars to become part of the Overmind. The Pranksters identified with this Breakthrough Generation, in part because Clarke's story resonated with their own sense of being at the leading edge of a "mind-powered," spiritual evolution. Yet another reason for their identification resides in the fact that the story of the Breakthrough Generation was framed as a science fiction story, rife with extremely fast and powerful machines (spaceships), capable of breaking through time into the future. This framing seamlessly fitted the Pranksters' postwar generation—in particular, its enthusiastic embrace of the fast, powerful technologies that contributed to the wealth of postwar America and that provided a way of "breaking free" from the older generation. As Wolfe writes:

> It was very Heaven to be the first wave of the most extraordinary kids in the history of the world—only 15, 16, 17 years old, dressed in the haut couture of pink Oxford shirts, sharp pants, snaky half-inch belts, fast shoes—with all this Straight-6 and V-8 power underneath and all this neon glamour overhead, which somehow tied in with the technological superheroics of the jet, TV, atomic subs, ultrasonic–Postwar American suburbs–glorious world! One's parents remembered the sloughing common order, War & Depression—but Superkids knew only the emotional surge of the great payoff, when nothing was common any longer—The Life! A glorious place, a glorious age, I tell you! A very Neon Renaissance.[35]

Various historians of the counterculture have pointed out that such technological optimism and utopian expectations of postscarcity and material abundance are major features of the "first phase of the counterculture," lasting from 1964 until 1968.[36] Two stanzas of a poem by the Californian poet Richard Brautigan from 1967 capture this optimistic imagination of a future harmonious relationship between human beings and technology:

> I like to think
> (right now, please!)
> of a cybernetic forest
> filled with pines and electronics
> where deer stroll peacefully
> past computers
> as if they were flowers
> with spinning blossoms.

I like to think
(it has to be!)
of a cybernetic ecology
where we are free of our labors
and joined back to nature,
returned to our mammal
brothers and sisters,
and all watched over
by machines of loving grace.[37]

Brautigan's poem communicates a romantic futurism that would continue to characterize New Edge in the following decades: it posits a state of natural and authentic being from which man has fallen and to which he can hope to return through technology.

While the use of technology in spiritual celebration should not necessarily surprise us, a more puzzling element of New Edge is the way its countercultural embrace of technology also implies an embrace of consumerism and hence of the logic of mainstream society. To be sure, the Pranksters were motivated by a desire to break free from mainstream norms and "roles," and from mainstream ways of relating to production and consumption. Yet this did not imply a rejection of consumer items as such. Rather, it entailed a call for *active*, "Do It Yourself," or "participatory" consumerism. It implied a kind of consumerism that "liberated" commodities from imposed conventions about their use. By disconnecting technologies from their mainstream context and by appropriating them in different, creative ways, the Pranksters made them, as they put it, "part of their own fantasy."

One of the Prankster "fantasies" was to use technology to return to authentic ways of being. Paradoxically, this depiction depended on the explicit acknowledgement that people live in an artificial world of fantasy *already*. Wolfe described this awareness, conveyed to him by Kesey, as follows:

The incredible postwar American electropastel surge into the suburbs!—it was sweeping the Valley, with superhighways, dreamboat cars, shopping centers, soaring thirty-foot Federal Sign & Signal Company electric supersculptures—Eight New Plexiglas Display Features!—a surge of freedom and mobility, of cars and the money to pay for them and the time to enjoy them and a home where you can laze in a rich pool of pale wall-to-wall or roar through the technological wonderworld in motor launches and, in the case of men like his [Ken Kesey's] father, private planes . . . you're *already* there, in Fantasyland.[38]

The Pranksters combined this hyperbolic celebration of high-tech consumer goods with the notion that genuine experiences of the sacred can be produced by "pushing this high-tech world to its limits." As described by Wolfe, the Pranksters sought to "juice up the world," to transform it into "what it's already aching to be."[39] The New Age rhetoric of "becoming your true self" rings through this Prankster narrative of "transforming things into what they are already aching to be." The Pranksters felt that, much like people, technologies can be "brainwashed" into being things that have more limited capacities than they inherently possess. This is because mainstream corporations design technologies in such ways as to fulfill only one specific purpose, in carefully prescribed ways. By removing the brakes from the bus, by using microphones and cassette tapes to "wire up" the woods around La Honda, or by cutting up the American flag into costumes, for example, the Pranksters broke things free from their single-purpose applications and made them "part of their own fantasy." They thus hoped to overcome alienation from society, a common theme of the 1960s and 1970s counterculture, not by rejecting technology and consumption but by personalizing technology and actively engaging in the process of consumption—by pushing both technology and the human mind "to their limits." In the process, the Pranksters transformed symbols of mainstream power (the American flag or cars and television sets as symbols of postwar affluence) into symbols of their own individual and spiritual power.

The Prankster approach to technology is thus characterized by two sets of paradoxes. The first consists of the fact that, on the one hand, technology is treated as an extension of the human senses and as part of the sacred order of the universe. As such, technology transcends its artificial status. On the other hand, their embrace of fast technologies as a way of "breaking through" social conditioning is rooted in the notion that such breaking through cannot be established by "natural" means. The second paradox consists of the Pranksters' celebration of mainstream American consumerism, on the one hand, while operating in an environment that opposes mainstream America, on the other.

These two paradoxes are shaped as part of a countercultural imaginary that resists both the mainstream enslavement of commercial and technological forces and the "naïve" rejection of consumption and technology that the Pranksters encountered in their own countercultural milieu. Wolfe describes one encounter between the Pranksters and followers of psychedelic guru Timothy Leary on the East Coast. As the Pranksters came to think of the "Learyites": "they have turned back into that old ancient New York intellectual thing, ducked back into the romantic past, copped out of the American trip [looking for] another country . . . where it is all better and more philosophic and purer, gadget-free." The Learyites use "no tapes, video tapes, TV, movies, Hagstrom electric basses, variable lags, American flags, no neon, Buick Electras, mad moonstone-faced Servicecenters, and no manic buses."[40] In self-conscious contrast to Leary's followers, the Pranksters turned technologies into fetishes of the sacred. By breaking them apart from mainstream conventions of use and production, they made them and themselves part of a cosmic, science-fiction story of salvation.

As historians of the counterculture point out, the optimistic spirit that supported the unabashed celebration of consumption, abundance, and technical progress during the "first phase" of the counterculture was tempered during its second phase. This phase began in the late 1960s and was characterized by the criminalization of LSD, the declaration of the "Death of the Hippie" by the so-called Yippies,[41] economic recession, the election of Republican President Richard Nixon, and the exodus of the "hippies" from the cities into newly formed communes.[42] Yet the paradoxical embrace of technology by the Pranksters continued to characterize the countercultural approach to technical artifacts in the following decades.

In the following discussion of the ways in which technological gnosticism continued in the 1970s and 1980s, I will introduce one more characteristic of New Edge discourse concerning technology, namely, its "hopping" from one "cutting-edge" technology to another. I will argue that this "hopping" sheds light on how New Edge negotiates its relationship with mainstream Silicon Valley.

The Portola Institute

In 1968, along with other Merry Pranksters, biology student and journalist Stewart Brand organized one of the biggest "acid tests" ever. Today, now that he has founded the Global Business Network and organizes lectures about the future of technology and business at the Long Now Foundation, he takes some distance from his "wild hippie years." When Brand speaks about his involvement with the counterculture, it is in a critical tone.[43] Yet this tone already characterized his countercultural activities in the 1960s. Because, according to Brand, the "back to the land communes" had "no knowledge and understanding of technology,"[44] he set himself the task of making the counterculture more technology minded and science savvy. One of the ways in which he did so was by joining the Portola Institute, founded in Menlo Park in 1966 by engineer Bob Albrecht.

The Portola Institute supported all kinds of educational organizations and publications dedicated to "appropriating" "cutting-edge" technologies for political and spiritual purposes. Albrecht himself was particularly interested in "bringing computers to the people," and this interest remained the main focus of the institute in the decades to come. At the time, the popular imagery of computers was rather negative: countercultural youth targeted computer centers as part of their antiwar protests, motivated by the fact that most, if not all, computer research was funded by the Pentagon. For the public at large, computers represented the rise of bureaucracy and the loss of individual control. As journalist Steven Levy put it: "Every time an inaccurate bill arrived at a home, and the recipient's attempts to set it right wound up in a frustrating round of calls usually leading to an explanation that 'the computer did it,' and only herculean human effort could erase the digital blot, the popular contempt toward computers grew."[45]

This popular contempt formed the starting point for the alternative approach that volunteers for Portola sought to take to computing. In an article in a magazine called

People's Computers, one engineer, for example, laments the tendency of engineers to want to adapt people's behavior to computer systems. Instead, he argues, people should shape computer systems in ways that serve their human needs.[46] Members of the Portola Institute proposed to reorganize the social setting in which technology is developed as a way of making computers more "humane." As engineer Andrew Clement wrote in *People's Computer* in 1977: "The social and organizational settings in which micro-computer technology is developed and used will define precedents of some lasting effect. If the work is done in an environment of relaxed and open exchange of information by people in small local groups that are in close communication with each other, then the results are likely to be more humane than if it is done in a competitive and secretive atmosphere."[47]

A similar call for the humanization of computer technology was made by Theodore Nelson, a regular vistor at Portola. As Nelson wrote in his manifesto *ComputerLib*: "Computers can be many different things and what they are depends on those who design them. Roughly they are designed by two kinds of people: people who dream ('lunatics, idealists and dreamers') or 'profit-hungry companies and unimaginative clods.'"[48] Computer idealists such as Clement and Nelson envisioned a future in which people without technical training would not have to depend on engineers for their access to computers. As Nelson urged these people: "You can and Must understand computers NOW." The Portola Institute facilitated this vision by supporting computer centers and hobby clubs that offered people "hands-on," "Do It Yourself" engagement with computer technology. The slogan that announced the arrival of the *People's Computer* magazine captured the spirit of Portola well (Figure 35):

> Computers are mostly
> used against people instead of for people
> used to control people instead of to *free* them
> time to change all that—
> we need a . . .
> PEOPLE'S COMPUTER COMPANY

While volunteers at Portola showed awareness that the meaning of computer technology depends on the social context in which it is developed, they were informed by a rather contradictory understanding of computer technology. They also considered computer technology to have intrinsic spiritual potential. As communicated within the Portola network in a variety of ways, the idea was upheld that, if created in the right setting by the right people, the computer will "offer us the first real chance to let the human mind grow to its full potential." The ultimate purpose of computer technology was to guarantee the "Wholiness of the human mind."[49] Portola volunteers thus harbored the paradoxical understanding that computers, on the one hand, acquire meaning in specific social contexts of production and use, while, on the other hand, computer technology is considered to have the teleologically defined goal of attaining New Age salvation.

FIGURE 35   Front cover, *People's Computer Company*, Issue 1, October 1972.

A periodical that treated technology in a similar paradoxical fashion was the *Whole Earth Catalog*, produced by Stewart Brand on behalf of the Portola Institute starting in 1968.[50] The subtitle of the *Whole Earth Catalog*, *Access to Tools*, reflected its main purpose: to present knowledge, tools, and technologies that would support a self-reliant and spiritual life-style. Addresses of tool distributors were listed alongside practical advice on how to use the tools. In his statement of purpose, published on the first page of the *Catalog*, Brand wrote: "We are as gods and might as well get good at it. . . . a realm of intimate, personal power is developing—power of the individual to conduct his own education, find his own inspiration, shape his own environment, and share his adventure with whoever is interested. Tools that aid this process are sought and promoted by the WHOLE EARTH CATALOG."

Among the tools and technologies for self-reliant living discussed in the *Catalog* were rustic artifacts such as spades, tents, and wooden stoves, but also high-tech products such as radios, calculators, and computers. This characteristic combination of romanticism and futurism is particularly present in the opening pages of its issues, invariably dedicated to the ideas and inventions of Buckminster Fuller. Fuller was an engineer who was embraced as a visionary by countercultural youth in the 1960s and 1970s . In his writings, many of which were reprinted in the *Catalog*, Fuller expressed an understanding that was typical of the gnostic counterculture overall: he felt that humans are born with perfect perceptive capacities, yet brainwashing by mainstream culture and society invariably hampers these capacities. Or, as he put it in his own intricate language: "We could, of course, hypothesize that all babies are born geniuses and get swiftly de-geniused. Unfavorable circumstances, shortsightedness, frayed nervous systems, and ignorantly articulated love and fear of elders tend to shut off many of the child's brain capability valves."[51] Fuller argued that thus far humanity had managed to live without scientific and technological "compensation" for its shortcomings. As he wrote in his *Operating Manual for Spaceship Earth* (1969), nature had been sufficient "to allow us to carry on despite our ignorance." However, "just as a bird inside of the egg is provided with liquid nutriment to develop it to a certain point," now our "nutriment is exhausted." According to Fuller, we need to "locomote on [our] own legs" and we must act like a bird who must "step forth from its initial sanctuary and forage on its own legs and wings to discover the next phase of its regenerative sustenance."[52] For Fuller, this next phase was only conceivable by means of science and engineering. Fuller considered himself a person who had been "lucky enough to avoid too many disconnects during his upbringing," and he had set himself the task of leading the scientific and technological way. By equating human technical inventions and physical innovations with the development of wings and legs by birds, Fuller indicated that he understood technology to be part of a natural and spiritual evolutionary development: "I see God in the instruments and the mechanisms that work reliably, more reliably than the limited sensory departments of the human mechanism."[53]These words underscore what most Portola volunteers imagined as the true potential of the various high technologies that fascinated them: their capacity for "healing" human awareness of the sacred and for moving humanity onto the spiritual ladder of evolution.

Biofeedback

Biofeedback was one of the technological concepts to imagine a restoration of human awareness that was discussed in the *Catalog*.[54] In a biofeedback setting, various kinds of technical artifacts can be used to "sense" signals from the human "autonomous system." Outputs of these measurements are registered on paper; through sound or light devices—or (as described in Portola's magazine *People's Computer*) as images on a computer screen. In this way, people could become aware of various types of physical activity, such as heart rate, blood pressure, and brain waves.[55] In the early to mid-1970s, biofeedback was a burgeoning practice in psychology and medicine, and it became constitutive of New Edge.[56] (See Figure 36.)

Whereas some biofeedback manuals at the time seemed to struggle with the terminology to describe the process being measured ("consciousness," "awareness," "intent," or "will"), other manuals did not hesitate to present biofeedback, in characteristic New Age terminology, as a technique for obtaining a "real knowledge of the self"—a knowledge that "has been lost by humanity over centuries by civilization."[57] In the latter type of manuals, biofeedback is presented as a modern and scientific way of regaining awareness of who we truly are and as a solution to alienation from the body.

One manual describes, for instance, how a stressful society that emphasizes only rational thought has induced "us" to lose "touch with our bodies."[58] Biofeedback, then, is imagined as a modern technology for returning to authentic ways of being in a manner that is congruent with the demands of a fast-paced society. It is a technique, one manual writes, that "many claim to be capable of producing the same effect as meditation but at a considerably accelerated pace."[59] We can read in another manual:

> It is . . . considered by some people to be a means of reaching, in a matter of hours, that state of inner awareness and peace, spiritual and mental, which the practitioners of yoga, Zen and other forms of meditation reach only after many disciplined years. . . . Perhaps this is one very positive contribution that biofeedback can make. For to get in touch with the inner workings of one's psyche requires far more time and discipline than many Americans are able to put in after an exhausting day. For many the process of meditation is incomprehensible and, for many others, the nearest they can come to satori is a few minutes spent on yoga exercises every week or so.[60]

Biofeedback is, furthermore, imagined to be congruent with a consumption-oriented society: "the gadgetry involved in biofeedback makes it highly sympathetic to the American character. Rather paradoxically, that gadgetry may be one product of the very technology that has made our lives so complex, which will lead us to a reconsideration of the

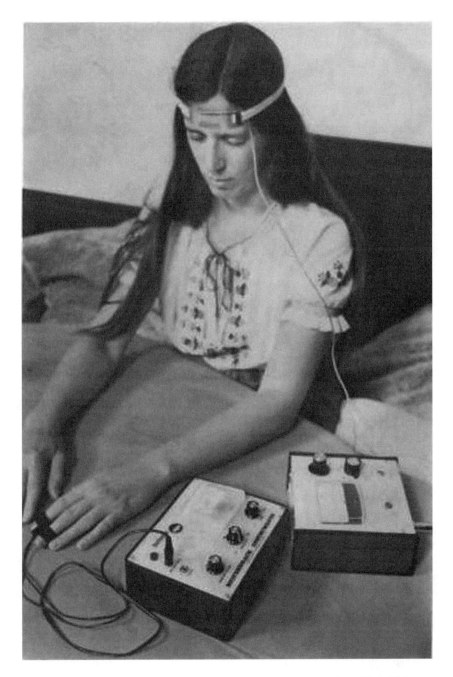

FIGURE 36   Biofeedback practitioner. From D. B. Payne and C. T. Reitano, *BioMeditation: The Scientific Way to Use the Energy of the Mind* (Brookline, Mass.: BFI, Inc., 1977), ii.

quality of life."[61] In a language reminiscent of Arthur C. Clarke's description of the "breakthrough generation," this manual predicts that the "powers of mind," freed through biofeedback, will lead humanity in an accelerated pace towards a new level of evolution.

Yet another manual expresses the same idea as follows: "Biofeedback is a new tool in developing the energies of the mind, body, and emotions. These energies, once brought under control and integrated with the wisdom of our higher minds or Spiritual selves may help bring mankind into a new level of evolution. It's an exciting world!"[62] Many of the periodicals produced by Portola emphasized that biofeedback could be used as a "Do It Yourself" technology—as something that could be individually created and controlled. One Portola volunteer told me how she had used toothpaste and salt "to attach the electrodes to our heads; it took weeks to get it out of our hair."[63]

These portrayals of biofeedback once again feature the paradoxical countercultural treatment of technologies. While they are treated as "Do-It-Yourself tools" that need to be controlled by people, they are simultaneously imagined as transcending the artificial world and transporting people into an ultimate spiritual reality. Furthermore, biofeedback was recognized as merely a mainstream gadget, on the one hand, yet on the other it was imagined as a tool for transcending American brainwashing. Indeed, the concept of "feedback" as a way of imagining human-technology relationships as inherently openended developed into an important imaginary, by means of which New Edge distinguishes itself from mainstream understandings of the human-technology relationship. Through this open-endedness, I will argue in the next section, New Edge authenticates certain technologies as sacred. Because of this, it opposes processes of commoditization that fix technologies in their "thingness." We can observe this in New Edge's reactions to the commercialization of Virtual Reality (VR).

Virtual Reality

Starting in the late 1960s, the notion of feedback became an important mechanism in countercultural celebrations of various kinds of high tech. In the 1960s, the Pranksters used feedback technologies such as stroboscopes and cameras as a way of breaking through social conditioning, and in the early to mid 1970s, biofeedback technologies served a similar purpose. Since the mid 1970s, personal computers have increasingly been explored as spiritual feedback systems, and in the mid 1980s various artists started experimenting with immersive feedback environments. Like earlier biofeedback technologies, these environments were imagined as spaces in which older forms of being and knowing could be restored.

While biofeedback has remained a New Edge theme, the technical artifacts used to celebrate and exemplify the ideal spiritual relationship between humans and technologies have changed across time. Looking at the recent history of New Edge, we may conclude that gnostic celebrations of specific technologies often ended when these technologies became commercialized. When personal computers became commercial products in the early 1980s, many of the volunteers at the Portola Institute became disillusioned and lost belief in their transformational quality.[64] Throughout my research, I also encountered expressions of New Edge disillusionment when VR (also referred to as "Artificial Reality" or "Virtual Worlds") turned into a commercial hype in the early 1990s, to be followed by the Internet "dotcom boom" soon thereafter. Though this disillusionment is due to a complex of economic, psychological, and social factors, I will discuss only its relationship to spiritual expectations about artifacts.

One of the first artists to create immersive environments for New Edge purposes was Myron Krueger. In the 1970s, Krueger explored the concept of Artificial Reality environments—or, as he also labeled them, "responsive environments." In these environments, he explained in his book *Artificial Reality* (1983), "human behavior is perceived by a computer, which interprets what it observes and responds through intelligent visual and auditory displays."[65] Krueger imagined these environments as capable of restoring older states of being: "Artificial reality reintegrates the mind and the body, which have been estranged since the printing press created the sensory-deprivation, black-and-white world of the intellect, and offers a knowledge environment in which the mind, the body, and the full sensorium are employed."[66] Artificial Reality, according to Krueger, extends human sensorial capacities considerably: "We are no longer creatures of five senses. Technology has given us hundreds. We can sense the universe throughout the electromagnetic spectrum. We can hear vibrations, from the infrasound of the seismologist to the ultrasonics used in destructive testing. We can see molecular and cosmological structures. We can sniff the stars through spectral analysis. We can feel the age of ancient objects."[67]

One of the dancers who performed in Krueger's artificial-reality environments—Galen Brandt, partner of the engineer Bruce Damer—experienced Krueger's immersive environments as restoring a deep memory of her true self, about which she had forgotten:

> When I was moving . . . I became the me that I had known myself to be . . . I never felt so alive as when I was doing that, ever. . . . I lost my recent memory of my body's limitations, and refound my deeper memory of its limitless beauty and power. My body became a true "body of knowledge" which knew itself as spirit, reborn, embodied and moving.[68]

Another VR performer who spoke of virtual worlds in this way was Verona, who had studied anthropology in the 1980s and specialized in "art, ritual and dance in the Megalithic culture of South-East Asia."[69] She studied this out of a sense of "nostalgia"—a search for "a deeper way of being human, that you just couldn't find in this culture." She added, "now I really think we can find it in technology." In the early 1990s, Verona became involved in the creation of virtual worlds for the University of California, Santa Cruz. She explained her experiences with virtual worlds as creating a "visceral type of experience" that helped her to "get out of linearity" and "experience something larger than yourself of a spiritual nature." Arguing that virtual worlds "take us to the next dimension" and help us "get used to a part of reality that we just don't get yet," Verona compared the experiences people can have in VR to the change of perspective when artists and scientists moved from two to three dimensions during the Renaissance.

Most such narratives emphasize that human beings are physically transformed by their interactions with these sensorial technologies. Galen Brandt, for example, used the terms *rebiologization* and *recorporealization* to refer to her experience in virtual worlds. As she told me: "the collaboration with machines reconstituted me . . . so that I had become the me that I had known myself to be."[70] In a discussion of the impact of graphic technologies, graphics researcher Thomas West understands their effect on the human species to be neurological: "The more our technologies change (and also change us), the more we can see that the newest computer data visualization technologies draw on some of our oldest neurological resources—more like those of the hunter-gatherers than those of the scribes, schoolmen, and scholars of more recent times."[71]

In these ways, spiritual seekers in Silicon Valley who imagine a return to authentic ways of being through technology often evoke the ideal of human-computer symbiosis as a form in which this can be realized in the future. Myron Krueger depicted his artificial reality environments in these terms, for instance, with "man and machine . . . joined to form a single functioning unit, a symbiotic entity in which both perform the task suited to their abilities."[72]

"We weren't done yet"

Artists and performers such as Myron Krueger, Galen Brandt, and Verona worked with VR before it became a hype in the early 1990s, with an explosive growth in the number of VR corporations and the establishment of VR theme parks. Whereas Galen Brandt earlier had experienced the VR world as a true community ("We had all seen exactly the same thing; it was like we all had the same hallucination, and we all knew where we fit"), she recalled that the group of artists and computer scientists she had been cooperating with had to sign nondisclosure agreements "when the money came in":

> everybody stopped talking. And you would go to parties and everybody would say the same thing, cheap-shit horrible stuff, like, "Well, I am working on something but if I told you I'd have to kill you." And everybody talked about their IPO's. . . . it is true, it was like the dark ages. A lot of people went underground and a lot of people got very nervous, and a lot of people made a ton of money, it was a very dark time.[73]

Another early VR developer and New Edger, Brenda Laurel, was not fond of this period either. Like various other early VR pioneers, she remembers being taken by surprise when the hype washed over Silicon Valley:

> As the VR meme started to flame out in northern California in 1992, many of us involved began scrambling to change our shingles from virtual reality to something roughly synonymous, but less tainted—telepresence, augmented reality, immersion technology. Anything to get some distance from the all-too-vivid spectacle of the hype-fueled, VR road-and-media show that rocketed VR pundits to the pinnacle of pop culture and then sent us burning back into the atmosphere, noticing too late that we were in the decaying orbit of a fad. "Hey guys," little voices shout from the capsule as it begins to glow, "We weren't done yet . . . we were just beginning . . ."[74]

The New Edge withdrawal from VR when it became commercialized and popularized is only one example of a general trajectory. At first sight, this New Edge reaction appears to affirm the classical binary oppositions of spirituality and materiality and idealism and materialism. Yet the fact that New Edge has historically developed as a form of spirituality that has in itself never rejected commercialism and materialism suggests that this might not be the prime reason for the New Edge withdrawal. Reflections on commercialization by New Edgers themselves indicate, rather, that their real problem was the way in which nondisclosure agreements, copyright licenses, and material restrictions (programmed or engineered in hardware) socially, materially, and religiously "close off" technological development. Things constituted through New Edge discourse and practices as "open-ended" became "fixed" in their thingness when they were sold as consumer products. We can thus see that the ideology of "open-endedness" is central to the way in which New Edge constitutes technical things as sacred.

As I have already suggested in my narration of the Prankster involvement with technology, according to New Edge ideology, technology can fulfill its highest purpose only by being open-ended, by inviting active engagement and unlimited registers of use. As such, technology is understood as containing promises of constant surprise and the transformation of social, material, and sacred reality—an open-endedness that precludes the idea of technology as "passive" entertainment.

In VR developer Brenda Laurel's words: "Virtual Reality may be many things. It may become a tool, a game machine, or just a mutant form of TV. But for virtual reality to fulfill its highest potential, we must reinvent the sacred spaces where we collaborate with reality in order to transform it and ourselves."[75] According to Laurel, whereas TV invites consumption, real VR invites playlike interaction with technology:

> it may be that the nature of VR makes it inappropriate to think of it as an entertainment medium at all. Entertainment—at least mass entertainment—implies the consumption of some performance by a large audience. Roughly speaking, the size of the

audience is inversely proportional to the degree of influence over the course of events that can be afforded any one person. . . . If, on the other hand, what you want is to create a technologically mediated environment where people can play—as opposed to being entertained—then VR is the best game in town.[76]

Laurel's understanding of human interaction with artifacts as "play" resembles the Pranksters' conceptualization of their interactions with technologies as "experimental" and Galen Brandt's notions of VR as "transformational": they all refer to the ideal of technologies as being open-ended.

New Edgers often emphasize the fact that their technologies are—and all technologies ought to be—open-ended. In his manifesto *ComputerLib*, Theodore Nelson, for example, celebrates computers as the first tool to "let the human mind grow to its full potential" and relates this to the fact that the computer is an "All-Purpose machine"—a machine that has every potential meaning and significance, depending on the way in which it is produced and used.[77] Artificial reality developer Myron Krueger equally emphasized that his immersive environments did not have just one single purpose. He defined artificial reality as a "generalized concept that separates technology from any single application, enabling us to examine its broad implications." For him, artificial reality is a "medium of experience," "an incarnation of the imagination," and "a paradigm for our future interaction with machines." As he also puts it: "It is a laboratory for philosophy where we can ask basic questions such as, 'What is reality?,' 'What is perception?,' 'Who am I?,' in fundamentally new ways."[78] Such New Edge foregrounding of "open-endedness" also implies the idea that technologies lead humanity into an as yet unknown future of spiritual salvation: an infinite amount of experience and knowledge can be channeled when humans and technologies are interconnected in open-feedback loops. Hence, New Edgers feared that the VR hype would turn a technology with gnostic potential into an entertainment medium for passive consumption and entertainment, with copyright restrictions and clearly prescribed purposes, thus robbing VR of its promise of spiritual transformation.

New Edge Fetishism

The New Edge forms an intrinsic part of the technological system of Silicon Valley, and I have encountered the examples used in this chapter in contexts as diverse as academic research institutes, nonprofit institutes, cyberpunk literature, and cyberculture magazines. They have been expressed by artists, teachers, computer engineers, scientists, journalists, and entrepreneurs alike, most of whom operate in the everyday corporate and academic environments of Silicon Valley. Moreover, the self-conscious spiritual discourses of New

Edge are often indistinguishable from the discourses and practices that guide technological development in Silicon Valley at large. New Edge understanding of certain technologies as extending people's sensory devices—as helping people to "see more," "become aware," and "bring out one's true self"—is part and parcel of a marketing rhetoric that promises that technology will "bring out the artist within." The New Edge exists in a continuum with wider Silicon Valley society, then, with people, concepts, technologies, and tropes continuously "traveling" from a space set apart as sacred to spaces not imagined as such. I was intrigued during my fieldwork, for example, by the way Moore's Law, coined by Intel-founder Gordon Moore in 1965 and predicting accelerated growth of computer power in the next few decades, was translated across these various domains and cultural spheres. Moore's Law turned out to be enthusiastically embraced at both "purely technical" conferences about technological change and "spiritual or psychedelic" ones, where it is used to legitimate claims of accelerated spiritual evolution.

Such examples, of course, pose the problem of drawing boundaries around New Edge and of clearly marking off "spiritual" uses of technology from "merely technological," "corporate," or "purely scientific" ones. It is thus difficult if not impossible to delineate a bounded social space in which New Edge lives, which implies that its discourse is only recognizable as "sacred" by the fact that some people at some moments define it as such and oppose it to its secular rendition. As I have attempted to show, this is not done by rejecting things for their commercial or materialistic qualities but through a much more subtle process, in which a distinction is made between technologies that fulfill their "true potential" by being transformational and technologies that have lost their "true power" by being "brainwashed" through copyright restrictions and single-purpose definitions of use. Seen in this way, it becomes understandable why it is that New Edge has attached itself to certain technologies at moments when these technologies were not yet popularized as consumer products. New Edge technologies are either used in explicitly experimental settings (such as biofeedback in the 1970s) or are just beginning to be discovered by the larger public (as in the embrace of personal computing in the late 1970s, VR in the late 1980s, and the World Wide Web in the early 1990s).

In their many reflections on technology, New Edgers are conscious of the fact that "technology can be many things," as Nelson said about computers in the 1970s. The New Edge expresses a conscious desire to control the creation of technology socially and to make, as the Pranksters put it, technology "part of their own fantasy." This recognition that the world is artificial and socially constructed makes the New Edge ultimately at home in the materialistic environment of Silicon Valley and at ease with media technologies that blur the distinction between reality and fantasy. New Edge ideology is based on the sense that "we live in a fantasy world already," as the Pranksters put it in the 1960s, or, as Myron Krueger wrote in the 1990s:

> The promise of artificial realities is not to reproduce conventional reality or to act in the real world. It is precisely the opportunity to create synthetic realities, for which

there are no real antecedents. . . . To an overwhelming degree, our daily experiences take place in a reality of our own construction. We live our lives in the automobile, the home, the office, and the shopping mall. Through the spoken word, the written word, and the television broadcast, we experience a conceptual world that is every bit as real to us as the physical world. As the rate of technological change accelerates, it becomes increasingly difficult to understand the changing culture that technology defines. This ignorance makes us uneasy. However, it is as foolhardy to yearn for a benign Nature, which never existed, as it is not to accept technological developments that make us anxious.[79]

Yet New Edge's awareness of the constructed nature of things—and, by implication, its critique of technological determinism—doesn't make it any less deterministic. Although New Edgers consider everything to be socially constructed, they still operate with the understanding that technology has a "true" and "essential" property. This essential property is imagined in terms of the sacred, a characterization that makes technologies transcend their artificial, constructed nature. As such, the New Edge grants the presence of spiritual forces in an artificial and ultimately constructed world.

In Their Own Image?

Catholic, Protestant, and Holistic Spiritual Appropriations of the Internet

Ineke Noomen, Stef Aupers, and Dick Houtman

The notion that modern technology and religion are incompatible because—in sociologist of religion Bryan Wilson's words—"technology is itself the encapsulation of human rationality" and because "the instrumentalism of rational thinking is powerfully embodied in machines" has long been a social-scientific mainstay.[1] The implication of this notion that religion will inevitably suffer from encounters with technology has, however, been challenged by historical studies demonstrating that the two have in fact often developed in tandem and that their potential for peaceful coexistence has become even more evident since the emergence and widespread religious use of the Internet starting in the 1990s.[2] Well-established religious traditions such as Roman Catholicism, Protestantism, Buddhism, Hinduism, and Islam are now communicating their messages online, just like neo-pagans, witches, and others who identify with the field of holistic spirituality. Going online is, however, by no means automatic for religious groups, and it is unlikely that the Internet means the same to all of them, irrespective of their historical particularities, national backgrounds, and other offline features. In this chapter, we will study how the Internet is dealt with in Dutch Catholic, Protestant, and holistic spiritual milieus and, more specifically, what dilemmas and struggles each of these encounters in appropriating it.[3]

After setting out the relevance of our study and describing the context of the Dutch religious and media landscape, we will study in empirical detail how web designers in these three religious fields understand the Internet and what problems and dilemmas they encounter in appropriating it.

Religion Online and Offline

From Technological Determinism to Cultured Technology

Since the 1990s, the relation between religion and the Internet has been hotly debated. The earliest studies were still enraptured with utopian views of cyberspace, imputing to it all kinds of spiritual and liberating qualities.[4] It was often portrayed as an other-worldly realm in and of itself—as a "paradise," a "new Jerusalem," "metaphysical," or a "technological substitute for the Christian space of heaven."[5] Other scholars have conducted empirical and descriptive case studies of online religions, in particular, exotic breeds that they assumed would become substitutes for traditional, offline types of religion.[6]

These early studies emphasizing the transformative powers of the Internet or even considering cyberspace a spiritual place in and of itself generally were technologically deterministic in flavor. Even where offline religious traditions were considered, it was postulated that "the question is not whether but how and when religious traditions and religious organizations will change and be changed by involvement in the online world."[7] More recent studies on religion and the Internet typically break with such technologically deterministic assumptions in two different ways. First, they are less focused on the question of how new cyber-religions "naturally" or "inevitably" emerge online, concentrating more often on how established religions cope with and appropriate the Internet.[8] Second, following computer-mediated communication (CMC) studies and science and technology studies (STS), they have emphasized the importance of offline contexts for understanding how religion manifests itself online. It is argued that the roots in the offline world of long-standing religious traditions like Christianity, Buddhism, Hinduism, and Islam cause them to differ markedly in their understandings and appropriations of online environments. Karine Barzilai-Nahon and Gad Barzilai use the idea of "cultured technology" to communicate this insight that "cultures modify technologies and endow them with a communal context,"[9] whereas Heidi Campbell has developed the notion of "spiritualizing the Internet" to emphasize that different religious traditions speak, think and act fundamentally differently on the Internet.[10]

Comparing Religious Traditions Online

Empirical studies aimed at comparing whether and how different religious traditions appropriate the Internet in different ways are still remarkably rare and tend to remain theoretically underdeveloped. Two shortcomings are particularly important.

First, many of the otherwise relevant studies focus on single cases. There have been studies of Islam and the Internet, online Christian communities, and modern pagans on the Internet[11]—all of which raise important theoretical issues about the prominent role of religious authority, identity, and community online for the particular religious move-ment they address.[12] Yet, because these are studies of single cases, their findings cannot reveal whether and how the types of appropriations of the Internet that they have found are typical for the religious tradition at hand or apply more generally.

Second, there are studies that do compare different strains of religion on the Internet, but these have often focused on describing similarities rather than explaining differences. Randolph Kluver and Pauline Hope Cheong, for example, have studied the understand-ings and uses of the Internet by six different religious traditions in Singapore (i.e., Islam, Protestantism, Catholicism, Taoism, Buddhism, and Hinduism) to find out "how differ-ent religious communities appropriate technology differently."[13] In the end, however, they draw conclusions about the general compatibility of religion and the Internet, thus disregarding—as they generously admit themselves[14]—the question they initially set out to answer: namely, whether different religious dispositions yield different outcomes online, and how. Likewise, Cheong and Jessie Poon compare Christian and Buddhist organizations on the Internet and draw general conclusions about the relation between religious social capital and technology, but do not achieve their initial ambition of fleshing out the differences between the two.[15]

These studies focus on similarities rather than differences, leaving unanswered the question of how different religious traditions may appropriate the Internet differently. In this chapter, we will follow the lead of the few comparative studies that do focus on these differences in a systematic way.[16] We will compare the two dominant strains of Christian-ity in the Netherlands, Catholicism and Protestantism, with the field of holistic spiritual-ity. We will do so because the latter differs in striking ways from the former two in terms of its understandings of religious community, religious authority, and religious texts.[17] To enable a meaningful interpretation of our interview data, we start with a description of the context of the Dutch religious and media landscapes and how these have historically come into being.

Religion and Media in the Netherlands

In the past half-century, processes of secularization and the commercialization of the broadcasting media have—even apart from the emergence of the Internet—caused major changes in the religious and media landscapes in the Netherlands. Due to secularization, Catholics and Protestants have lost much of their former television airtime and easy access to newspaper audiences, and this period has also witnessed a major increase in the num-ber of nonreligious persons, alongside the rise and spread of holistic spirituality as a new religious competitor to the Christian churches.

The Dutch Religious and Media Landscape

Until well into the 1960s, the system of "pillarization" (in Dutch, *verzuiling*), a type of societal organization peculiar to the Netherlands, was still firmly in place. It consisted of a handful of vertically arranged religious and political segments, or "pillars" (in Dutch, *zuilen*), which existed side by side, with people identifying with only one of them throughout most of their lives. The system of pillarization has deeply affected the religious, political, and media landscapes of Dutch society. Catholics and Protestants had their own newspapers and broadcasting organizations, which catered to their own people and depended on the size of their constituencies for airtime and financial resources. When processes of secularization sparked a process of "de-pillarization" (in Dutch, *ontzuiling*) in the 1960s, new religious and nonreligious competitors gained ground, which has made it more difficult for the Christian churches to cater to the religious needs of their crumbling constituencies.[18] Since the 1980s, moreover, the increased importance of ratings and the introduction of commercial television in 1989 have led to an even further decline in airtime for Catholic and Protestant broadcasting organizations.

The consequences of the process of de-pillarization are basically twofold. On the one hand, the Christian churches now need to compete with new secular ideologies and with newly emergent and less institutionalized holistic spirituality. Yet loss of their guaranteed mass media access has ironically strengthened the felt need of Catholics and Protestants to make themselves heard among the resulting cacophony of secular and religious voices. Even though holistic spirituality has in the past never had the luxury of having its "own" national newspaper or broadcasting organization, those in the holistic milieu also experience this urge, as we shall see. The emergence of the Internet in the 1990s has filled a significant media gap for all three of these religious groups.

Catholicism, Protestantism, and Holistic Spirituality in the Netherlands

Dutch Catholicism, Protestantism, and holistic spirituality have all developed in a unique fashion, which reflects Dutch culture and history. The Dutch Catholic province, particularly in comparison to its southern and central European counterparts, is renowned for its critical stance toward Roman hierarchy, orthodoxy, and authority. Many Dutch Catholics welcomed the Second Vatican Council in the 1960s, which marked the onset of an age of *aggiornamento* that promised to modernize traditional Catholic teachings and placed an emphasis on openness and dialogue. Many Dutch Catholics and non-Catholics alike deplored the waning of this progressive pontifical policy, and their discontent reached a climax during the visit of Pope John Paul II to the Netherlands in 1985. Yet there have, of course, always been more orthodox Catholics in the Netherlands, too, who are quite critical of the calls for openness and dialogue by their progressive counterparts. Despite the Catholic Church's theologically informed aim of uniting the global community of

Catholic believers, then, polarization between a more progressive and a more orthodox wing has always existed in Dutch Catholicism.

The history of Dutch Protestantism is characterized by innumerable conflicts and schisms motivated by theological disputes, because Protestantism, unlike Catholicism, emphasizes believers' individual relationships with God. In the Netherlands, this has sparked a proliferation of competing theological interpretations and the fragmentation of Dutch Protestantism into numerous congregations and churches. The largest branch of Dutch Protestantism is the PKN (Protestant Church in the Netherlands), which is a coalition of Reformed (in Dutch, *Hervormd*), Dutch Reformed (in Dutch, *Gereformeerd*) and Lutheran (in Dutch, *Luthers*) churches, comprising about eighteen hundred congregations with liberal, mainline, and conservative outlooks. After decades of exploratory and nonobligatory alliances, this coalition was finally settled in 2004, leaving ample room for difference and religious diversity. It is still rejected, however, by many (particularly more orthodox) Protestant churches, which have refused to join. The Protestant Church in the Netherlands characterizes itself as a church "in unity and variety" and a "community centered on the Word."[19] Although declining church attendance and church membership are a major concern for the Protestant churches, they nonetheless appear to feel less challenged by contemporary religious and ideological pluralism than the Catholic Church does, because historically they have always found themselves in such a situation. Religious pluralism is a natural condition for Dutch Protestants.

Finally, in the 1960s holistic spirituality emerged as a new competitor on the Dutch religious scene when the first New Age centers were established in Amsterdam.[20] Instead of shared loyalty to a particular religious body of thought, this type of spirituality is based on the notion that all religious traditions are man-made constructions that at bottom refer to the same underlying spiritual core. This notion of "perennialism" implies receptivity to a broad range of spiritual and religious traditions, with individuals seen as free to choose their own spiritual paths.[21] This explains why New Age and holistic spirituality have been characterized as a "cultic milieu"[22]—a loose network that comprises all kinds of small organizations and single-person businesses providing spiritual workshops, courses, therapies, books, and art. In the last decades of the previous century, this cultic milieu expanded tremendously in the Netherlands, transforming the field of holistic spirituality into a sizable component of the Dutch religious landscape.

Research Design and Data Collection

In this chapter, we analyze in-depth qualitative interviews with twenty-one web designers who—either professionally or on a voluntary basis—work in the Dutch Catholic, Protestant, or spiritual milieus. Since we aim to unravel how the Internet is received and dealt with in these milieus, we have chosen to focus our study on religious web designers, because they work at the junctions of these religious milieus and the Internet. They are, as it were, mediators, who typically work in organizational contexts in which they find themselves faced with competing ideas, demands, and conflicts regarding the purposes, contents, functionalities, and visual outlooks of the websites they are working on. They provide us with an excellent source of data for our study of religious appropriations of the Internet at the point where these processes most decisively take place: in the minds and hands of the people who build the religious websites that confront Internet users.

Nine of our interviewees are engaged in the Catholic field. Three of these are directly professionally affiliated with the Catholic Church in the Netherlands (Hendrikjan, Jeroen, and Sanne), and two are priests involved with Internet projects (Martijn and Stephan). Two others work for the broadcasting organization that hosts the Dutch Catholic Church's official website, KRO/RKK (Alex and Bas). Richard was formerly involved with KRO/RKK as well, but he is now preoccupied with an ecumenical web project of Catholic and Protestant churches. This leaves one web designer who is professionally unaffiliated with the Church yet hosts one of the largest and most successful Dutch websites on Catholicism (Jan).

Because the Protestant milieu is more fragmented, with multiple religious organizations and media companies, the six web designers in this field are less easy to pin down. Connie works for the PKN; Klaas is involved in a Protestant website initiated by a cluster of Protestant organizations; Emma is professionally affiliated with the liberal Protestant broadcasting organization IKON; and Mark is involved with a foundation that closely relates to the Liberal Protestants in the Netherlands. Two interviewees in this field do not work for Protestant organizations: one used to host the website of a large Protestant church in Utrecht (Henry), and another works for a small-scale media company that builds websites for nonprofit religious, cultural, and ideological organizations (Dirk). The last has worked with organizations from different religious currents but is now involved with a large Protestant web project for PKN.

Finally, our six interviewees in the field of holistic spirituality (Annemarie, Caroline, Daan, Erwin, Patrick, and Ronald) are part of small-scale cooperative networks. Most of them own their own businesses in spirituality. Because of this, they tend to host more than one website for the different projects they are involved in.

The interviews had an open character and addressed general ideas about the meaning of the Internet for the future of religion or spirituality, the aims and aspirations that made the various religious groups decide to go online, the main objectives and target groups of the websites, and considerations about functional and visual design. In addition, respondents' websites were thoroughly explored before the interview, to enable detailed questions about them. All interviews (except one, which took place by telephone) were conducted face-to-face in the period between September 2008 and April 2009 by Ineke Noomen. On average, interviews lasted about an hour and a half. All interviews were recorded and transcribed verbatim, and all quotations used in this paper have been translated from Dutch by Noomen. Respondents have been given fictitious names so as to safeguard their privacy.

Religious Dilemmas in Appropriating the Internet

Because going online is by no means a "natural" thing to do, we first discuss how the pluralized Dutch religious and media landscapes have led various religious and spiritual groups to embrace the Internet. We then explore the problems and dilemmas web designers confront and how these stem from typical offline features and conflicts characteristic of the respective religious fields.

The Web as a Last Media Resort

All religious groups we have studied face the difficulty of insufficient television airtime and access to newspaper audiences. Richard, who works in the Catholic confines, explains that "previously we of course had Catholic newspapers and the like . . ., but, well, these are practically all gone." He infers that "right now the Internet is the only channel left through which the church can directly address an audience." In a similar vein, holistic web designer Patrick had been striving for a program on national television, which proved, however, very difficult to achieve. For him as well, the web has become an attractive alternative for sharing his ideas, since "through the Internet I could still reach my audience." In this way, the Internet virtually serves as a "last resort" for all religious groups under study—as the only viable option left to them if they want to make themselves heard.

In contrast to the traditional mass media, moreover, the Internet is quite hospitable to small groups addressing niche audiences. Broadcasts for highly specific audiences can no longer be afforded in national programming, but they can easily be offered online. Hendrikjan explains how Church topics "that bite the dust again and again" in national programming can easily be "transmitted through the Internet and watched very well." Bas, who works at the Internet department of the Dutch Catholic channel, gives the example of their bimonthly online broadcasts of the Pope's Wednesday general audiences and his Angelus prayers on Sundays: "we would say that it is not expedient to broadcast it on television. But there is an audience for this, and that's why we offer it through the Internet," Bas explains, concluding that this "certainly caters to a need." Similarly, a recent Dutch newspaper article reports a boom of orthodox Protestant radio stations on the Internet, serving groups that "are lacking their own news, opinion and music at the national channels."[23] It concludes that the web enables programmers to "make their own choices" regarding the Christian music, church news, psalms, and organ concerts they want to broadcast, "without interference of a public net manager" or non-Christian music or advertising "being imposed" upon them.[24]

The experienced lack of viable media alternatives stems from a strong motivation to make oneself heard in the cacophony of secular and religious voices that already exists online. This is because respondents from all three fields, even though they expressed it somewhat differently, conceive of the Internet as a stage where sometimes highly idiosyncratic or over-simplified thoughts, opinions, and dissatisfactions are disseminated. Emma, for example, speaks of "very scary weblogs, indeed about people who tell you with red-hot flames when the end of the world is near," and Hendrikjan notices "people who, well, do really weird things" online and "all kinds of evil sites." Like these two respondents, who work in the Protestant and Catholic domains, respectively, Erwin, who works in the field of holistic spirituality, speaks of "that negativity on the Internet . . . all kinds of excesses which are there," available "through a single click of the mouse." Considerations such as these do not cause religious groups to avoid the web but actually give them reason to counterbalance these voices in the Internet "jungle" (Bas) by providing reliable information or statements of a more positive kind. Emma argues that the Church should realize that it "needs to put a balanced answer up against this, on a site that looks professional, of which people will think 'Oh, this has authority.'" Martijn reasons that the Catholic Church should "put [its] own stall" in this "large market, where there are all kinds of stalls," because otherwise "everyone can be found out there, except for the Church." In a similar fashion, Erwin explains that he has made a number of websites only to "show positive messages and beautiful things: nice pictures, nice texts," "purely to just put positive things on the Internet." Unlike Emma and Martijn, he is part of the spiritual milieu and as such not constrained by any organizational authority structure, yet he understands it as his personal responsibility to counterbalance content that contradicts his personal values and ideals.

In sum, people from distinct religious fields experience a need to provide web users with "reliable" religious or spiritual content, because they are well aware of the everyday significance of the Internet as a source of information, communication, and entertainment. As we shall see, however, this consensus about the importance of the Internet does not mean that its religious appropriation is an easy process. Quite the contrary: each tradition faces its own typical dilemmas and struggles in appropriating and culturalizing the Internet through web design.

Catholic Struggles with Authority

The pluralism of the Dutch religious landscape poses more of a challenge to Catholics than to either Protestants or those who identify with the spiritual milieu. This is because Catholicism is historically and theologically a monopolistic creed, whose aim has always been to unite a global community of believers representing God's Kingdom on earth, which now finds itself in decline and facing an increase in pluralism—in the Netherlands even more so than elsewhere. Referring to this situation, priest and web maker Martijn therefore claims that "the church as an institution that provides meaning" is only "one party in a competitive market," a view that is shared by independent Catholic web designer Jan, who conceives of Catholicism as "one of the parties on the reli-market."

The notion that Catholic community and identity are under threat is omnipresent in Dutch Catholicism, and the Internet is understood as a means to counter this problem.[25] Jeroen, initiator of a Catholic news site, wants to "show what [is] going on in the Church," intending to "stimulate the self-awareness of Catholics." Likewise, Alex aims to "make people more conscious of our values" and to demonstrate that Catholicism concerns "a tradition that isn't frozen, but one that still lives on and constantly gets reinterpreted." Such a rejuvenation of Catholic identity, moreover, is experienced as a necessary basis for more encompassing missionary goals put forward in Pontifical documents that designate modern media like the Internet as "'gifts of God,' which, in accordance with His providential design, unite men in brotherhood and so help them to cooperate with his plan for their salvation."[26] Our respondents express a similar emphasis on the need for a shared Catholic identity. Stephan argues that "if you want to survive as a church, then you need that clear identity again," and Sanne explains that the Catholic youth forum she is involved with aims to "make [youngsters] surer of themselves," so that "we'll get a larger group of Catholics who know how to stand their ground, and then you have people to go and face the world."

Reaching out to a mixed audience of adherents and potential believers through the Internet, however, also demands reflection on and redefinition of "who we are," "what we believe in," and "what we stand for." Questions such as these invoke contrasting ideas about what exactly constitutes—or rather: *should* constitute—Catholic identity nowadays and how it should be articulated on the web. On the one hand, there are quite orthodox voices that try to transpose Church authority, tradition, and hierarchy onto the Internet by way of regulation and control of online information, whereas on the other hand, there are more progressive pleas for openness and dialogue.

One way to accomplish control over online information is to use a strict linking policy. The Vatican website, which lacks any web links to external websites, is a paramount example of this. Hendrikjan, an official in the Dutch Catholic Church, recounts how this issue caused "quite some discussion" when the official website of the Catholic Church in the Netherlands was launched. To avoid bringing in "organizations that you're rather not be associated with," they decided "after long talks" to link only to websites "for which we can take responsibility ourselves." Martijn gives another example when he tells about his participation in an ecumenical Catholic-Protestant foundation that had been registering Dutch religious domain names in the early stages of the Internet. Its aim was to prevent these domain names from falling into the hands of so-called "domain grabbers" and to assure that these web domains would lead only to "what we judge is good information," which, however, caused disputes with Christian organizations that wanted to use these domain names.

Contrary to these initiatives, Richard, who is also active in Dutch Catholicism, feels that people should be allowed "to exercise their personal responsibility," because it "would really not be a good thing" if the Church were in a position to control the information supply. Jan recounts how contrasting ideas about how to handle online information have hindered online cooperation between Dutch Catholic organizations: "the main current was conservative" and proposed to work out "a traffic-light system to indicate the reliability of Catholic information," whereas he himself "really was not into that." Hence this consortium fell apart "because there were too many different opinions on how one should manage this on the Internet." Jan personally holds the view that the Internet "really works democratizing" and firmly believes that "that's the way it works: if I don't find it here, I might find it there, or elsewhere, or hold my own opinion about it."

To sum up, the traditional dilemma of Dutch Catholicism—of either "conservatively" holding on to Church authority or "progressively" providing opportunities for dialogue, diversity, and openness—is revived in the dilemmas faced by web designers, who need to make decisions about the functionalities, web links, and contents of Catholic websites.

Communicating a Fragmented Protestant Belief

The fragmented nature of the Dutch Protestant landscape seems at first sight to fit the Internet quite well, because it provides each of its often small congregations with a means to communicate its own message to its adherents as well as to a broader audience of potential believers. Next to Evangelical Protestant groups that are quite successful in communicating their beliefs to new audiences in religiously pluralistic contexts,[27] there are Liberal Protestants without any missionary goals who use the web primarily as an "important informational site for materials, a range of ideas, texts, etcetera" that "provides people within a tenth of a second with information about something they want to know" (Mark), thus using it as a tool to find and exchange information of all sorts.[28] Even orthodox Calvinist congregations that condemn media like television for their opportunities for entertainment and their role in distracting believers from more important things have quite easily found their way online. Through their own websites, these orthodox Protestant groups serve their adherents with highly specific media menus, adapted to their moral standards and interests.

The Internet thus provides Protestant organizations of quite different sorts with a convenient platform to serve their specific audiences. The presence of the web also challenges Protestant groups to present themselves in a unified manner to a lay audience that is typically ignorant of this internal diversity. Several of our respondents are responsible for representing the Protestant Church in the Netherlands (PKN), or mainline Protestantism generally, online, and they unanimously characterize this as a difficult task because of the differences between various Protestant churches.

Dirk, who designs websites for various religious groups and ideological organizations and is currently involved with an all-embracing PKN Protestant web project, admits that "it wasn't as easy as one would think to choose the words . . . to indeed create a sort of collective appearance," characterizing it as "a very, very vulnerable balance that one needs to find." Connie, an employee at PKN, also underscores the difficulties that stem from conflicting religious interests and identities. When talking about a collective representation of the Protestant church online, she states: "that's what *we* would like, but the congregations, they couldn't care less. They have their own particular character." Klaas, moreover, hosting a general informational website about Dutch Protestantism and aiming to represent "the breadth of Protestantism," has experienced similar difficulties with Protestantism's fragmented nature: "It's not my point to represent 'the churches.' Because if the website was meant to represent *the* Protestant church, then I could forget it! Then there would be quite many pulling out immediately, saying: but I won't be a party to that!" This eventually gave rise to a strictly informational website, without any religious or missionary aspirations, that explains the different standpoints and views within Dutch Protestantism. It apparently proves much easier in the broader Protestant field to offer "clean" information or technological and organizational facilities online than to present substantial religious content, because the latter is almost inevitably contested and bound up with religious conflicts and theological disputes.

A struggle of a different kind concerns the strongly visual character of Internet culture. Having a mainly text-based creed, non-Evangelical Protestant groups appear less conscious of their visual presentations than their Catholic and holistic spiritual counterparts, which creates difficulties for web designers in this field. Mark claims that for him it was a "conscious choice" to "immediately confront people with content" on the homepage, and in like manner Conny confines her visual design to a "nice picture" to go with the text, but "nothing more." Yet others feel that their websites need to be visually attractive to reach a public not as yet involved. Emma and Dirk, both professional web designers who have also worked in other religious fields, stress the importance of a visually attractive website in the online market and explain how difficult this actually is in a strongly text-based religious tradition like Protestantism.

Emma, who has previously worked for a Catholic organization, explains that it is very difficult to "visualize" Protestantism, because it "lacks any rituals and images, no pictures of Mary, no saints and the like." She advocates "visually modern" religious websites ("So, not like, 'well, OK, we put an image of our church building on it, and that's it'") and Dirk holds the same view, criticizing Protestant websites that portray "pale clergymen" or "the interior of a church holding just four people." Like Emma, he thinks the Protestant church should create a more "modern" and "contemporary" look for itself, a process in which, according to him, it has so far taken only the first few small steps. Protestantism's internal fragmentation and its uneasiness about and lack of familiarity with the predominantly visual culture of the Internet create, in short, problems and dilemmas for Protestant attempts to appropriate the Internet.

Holistic Spirituality: Sharing and Connecting through the Web

Apart from hesitations relating to people's distraction from their offline everyday lives or the distortion of fields of spiritual energy by computer radiation (both echoes of holistic spirituality's fears of alienation by modern technology), there are few contestations about the use of Internet in the field of holistic spirituality, particularly in comparison with the Catholic and Protestant milieus. The dominant view in the field of holistic spirituality is that the Internet gives groups and individuals room to voice their criticisms of modern society and its dominant culture and provides them with a platform to connect, share their ideas, and reach out to others.

The web designers in this field view the Internet as an environment for disseminating spiritual ideas and selling their products and services. Most of them run their own spiritual businesses and consequently do not have to communicate ideas on behalf of larger organizations or religious traditions, as web designers in the Catholic and Protestant fields must do.

Annemarie, who hosts several websites on spiritual matters and sells her spiritual books through them, explains how much she enjoys how through these websites she can "live my passion" and "just disseminate the things I want to share." Similarly, Caroline uses her website as an outlet for her spiritual artwork, for providing information about related joint projects, and for her work as a therapist. She understands her website as representing her personal spiritual identity ("at once you're showing: 'this is me!'"), and she realizes that "this is what I stand for; this is what I have on offer." Rather than expressing a shared religious identity, those involved use the web to channel their personal views and practices, while intending to inspire their online visitors and stimulate them in their personal development. Caroline, for instance, explains that on her website she puts forward that "it is possible to communicate with elemental beings" and "that the world consists of energy" in order to "wake people up" and "give them that nourishment." Consistent with this, various neo-pagan authors have celebrated the web as "an incredible resource," "a beautiful chaos . . . where anyone can share anything," and "an endless source of sustenance."[29]

Using the web as a platform for sharing and connecting, then, feels almost like a natural thing to do for them, and it does not cause the types of struggles and dilemmas faced by Catholic and Protestant web designers. Holistic spiritual web designers often design their online spaces in such a way as to help others to share their ideas and experiences, and to sell their products and services, too. Daan claims that "everything is aimed at this exchange . . . and the website is of course ideal for that, right?" Ronald likewise has created "a platform where people can respond to each other's statements," explaining that "in this way discussions and networks will arise and things will get connected" and adding that "that actually is what the Internet very much is intended for at the moment."

Ronald has designed what he calls a "spiritual marketplace" on one of his websites, where spiritual providers are invited to advertise their products and services. Unlike the Catholics, who try to control online information, Ronald does not want "to make any judgments about soundness" concerning all the healers, mediums, therapists, and coaches who make use of his service. He does not want to "deliver any warranty of quality," either, because "it's not up to us to give a value judgment." Annemarie, who is involved in an online spiritual radio station with an online forum for its listeners, explains that "we want to offer a platform, and that doesn't have to mean that we agree with it. Because exactly spirituality is just something so individual."

All in all, the Internet is appreciated in holistic spiritual circles as a platform for sharing spiritual wisdom and connecting to others to enrich people's spiritual lives. What is more, the web's visual culture is in striking accordance with holistic spirituality's marked focus on intuitive knowing and spiritual experience. Ronald, for example, stresses the importance of the "look and feel" of his websites, and Patrick claims that "images provide a much nicer way . . . to take in information." As such, and in striking contrast to typical Protestant understandings, spiritual messages need, not to be understood, but rather to be experienced.

Conclusion

Now that the Internet has come to pervade the lives of almost all people in the West, and now that its use increasingly appears practical and profane rather than liberating or otherworldly, the focus in Internet studies has shifted to understanding online practices as embedded in offline routines and values. Offline-based aspirations, it is held, need to be taken into account in order to understand online participation in virtual communities.[30] In the study of religion and the Internet, these pleas have resulted in notions of "cultured technology" and the "spiritualizing of technology."[31] Scholars stress, not that online religion is determined and shaped by technology, as earlier studies in the 1990s suggested, but rather that digital technologies are culturally and religiously appropriated.

Guided by this perspective, we have studied religious appropriations of the Internet in Dutch Catholicism, Protestantism, and the holistic milieu. We find remarkably similar reasons for going online in the first place: it is universally felt that this is by now the only remaining viable way to reach out and make oneself heard in the radically pluralist cacophony of voices that has resulted from processes of secularization and religious change.

Consistent with theories about "cultured technology" and the "spiritualizing of technology," we have found that the offline religious heritage matters a lot when religions seek to culturalize, spiritualize, and appropriate the Internet through web design. We have also seen, however, that coherent offline traditions do not smoothly translate into a new online context. Rather than shaping virtual environments "in their own image," contestations about what this "own image" actually is pose major difficulties to Catholic and Protestant web designers. Conflicts among Dutch Catholics about the desirability of whether to follow Roman orthodoxy or create room for dialogue and diversity pose dilemmas to web designers, who need to decide about the functionalities, web links, and contents of the Catholic websites on which they are working. Catholic websites are thus not simply the result of a smooth transposition of a neat, coherent, and uncontested religious tradition, but rather the outcome of religious conflict, power, and contestation.

Protestant web designers face their own dilemmas. Because of Dutch Protestantism's history of fragmentation and theological dispute and disagreement, it is difficult to build websites that transcend the particular religious identities of specific Protestant congregations. Designing websites that are acceptable to all, or even a majority, of Protestant congregations demands so great a sacrifice of content that the resulting websites become disappointingly empty, flat, and neutral. In appropriating the Internet, Protestants are hence spared the conflicts found in Catholicism only to the extent that they are prepared either to let a thousand flowers bloom or to surrender to a watered-down Protestantism. The decentralized, network structure of the milieu of holistic spirituality, finally, makes the Internet an almost natural habitat for connecting and sharing spiritual wisdom. None of the problems faced by Catholics and Protestants are experienced here, which means that holistic spiritual appropriations of the Internet are less conflict-ridden and smoother than those of their Catholic and Protestant counterparts.

Consistent with theories of "cultured technology" and the "spiritualizing of technology," in short, it is quite clear that offline context does matter for how the Internet is appropriated. It is, however, equally clear that the religious culturalization of the web is typically a conflict-ridden process in which power and contestation play decisive roles.

Notes

Introduction: Material Religion—How Things Matter, by Birgit Meyer and Dick Houtman

NOTE: We would like to thank Petra Gehring, Galit Hasan-Rokem, Niklaus Largier, David Morgan, Mattijs van de Port, Irene Stengs, Terje Stordalen, and Jojada Verrips for helpful suggestions and encouragement in writing this Introduction. Birgit Meyer wishes to acknowledge that she worked on this text during her affiliation as a fellow of the Institute for Advanced Studies, Berlin (2010–11).

1. See: Dick Houtman and Stef Aupers, eds., *Religions of Modernity: Relocating the Sacred to the Self and the Digital* (Leiden: Brill, 2010); Peter van der Veer, "Spirit," *Material Religion* 7, no. 1 (2011): 124–31; Peter van der Veer, "Spirituality in Modern Society," in *Religion: Beyond a Concept*, ed. Hent de Vries (New York: Fordham University Press, 2008), 789–98; Peter van der Veer, "Spirituality: East and West," *Eranos Yearbook* 69 (2010): 45–61; Paul Heelas, *The New Age Movement: The Celebration of the Self and the Sacralisation of Modernity* (Oxford: Blackwell, 1996); Paul Heelas, Linda Woodhead, et al., *The Spiritual Revolution: Why Religion Is Giving Way to Spirituality* (Oxford: Blackwell, 2005); Stef Aupers and Dick Houtman, "Beyond the Spiritual Supermarket: The Social and Public Significance of New Age Spirituality," *Journal of Contemporary Religion* 21, no. 2 (2006): 201–22.

2. Such debates echo what has become known as the *Materialismusstreit* in nineteenth-century Germany. The polemical debate between zoologist Carl Vogt, who defended a materialist worldview that strictly relied on the natural sciences, and physiologist Rudolf Wagner, who insisted that the natural sciences had nothing to say about the existence of God, shaped public discussions about the consequences of increased scientific knowledge starting in the 1840s. The rather simplistic opposition between matter and ideas was transcended by dialectical materialism. Nonetheless, this opposition has continued to shape public opinion up to our time, as, for instance, the antireligious polemics of Richard Dawkins and pro-atheist campaigns show. Recent research on the brain, e.g., the question of a "religion gene," is also often mobilized in this framework.

3. Edward B. Tylor, *Primitive Culture*, 2nd ed., 2 vols. (1873; New York: Brentano's, 1924). See also Talal Asad's famous critique of Geertz's definition of religion in terms of "belief": Clifford Geertz, "Religion as a Cultural System," in *The Interpretation of Cultures: Selected Essays* (New York: Basic Books, 1973), 87–125; Talal Asad, *Genealogies of Religion: Discipline and Power in Christianity and Islam* (Baltimore: Johns Hopkins University Press, 1993), 27–54. See also Rodney Needham, *Belief, Language, and Experience* (Chicago: University of Chicago Press, 1972).

4. Although within Christian discourse the terms *belief* and *faith* are used interchangeably, *faith* is more intimately and exclusively connected to Protestant religiosity than *belief*, which is also used in a general sense, as a host of definitions of religion show, from Tylor to Clifford Geertz. On the distinction between faith and belief, see W. C. Smith, *Faith and Belief* (Princeton, N.J.: Princeton University Press, 1979). See also David Morgan, "Introduction: The Matter of Belief," in *Religion and Material Culture: The Matter of Belief*, ed. David Morgan (New York: Routledge, 2010), 2–3.

5. See Tomoko Masuzawa, *The Invention of World Religions; or, How European Universalism Was Preserved in the Language of Pluralism* (Chicago: University of Chicago Press, 2005), and Donald S. Lopez, Jr., "Belief," in *Critical Terms for Religious Studies*, ed. Mark C. Taylor (Chicago: University of Chicago Press, 1998), 21–35.

6. Lopez, "Belief," 33.

7. See, e.g. José Casanova, *Public Religions in the Modern World* (Chicago: University of Chicago Press, 1994); José Casanova, "Religion, European Secular Identities, and European Integration," www.eurozine.com, 29-7-2004; and José Casanova, "Public Religions Revisited," in *Religion*, ed. de Vries, 101–19. On modern religion as essentially privatized religion, see esp. Thomas Luckmann, *The Invisible Religion: The Problem of Religion in Modern Society* (New York: Macmillan, 1967).

8. See: Hent de Vries and Lawrence Sullivan, eds., *Political Theologies: Public Religions in a Post-Secular World* (New York: Fordham, 2007), esp. Jürgen Habermas, "On the Relation Between the Secular Liberal State and Religion," 251–60 (also in *The Frankfurt School on Religion: Key Writings by the Major Thinkers*, ed. Eduardo Mendieta [New York: Routledge, 2005], 327–38); Charles Taylor, *A Secular Age* (Cambridge: Harvard University Press, 2007); Peter Achterberg, Dick Houtman, et al., "A Christian Cancellation of the Secularist Truce? Waning Christian Religiosity and Waxing Religious Deprivatization in the West," *Journal for the Scientific Study of Religion* 48, no. 4 (2009): 687–701.

9. Morgan, "Introduction," 6. See also Robert A. Orsi, "Belief," *Material Religion* 7 (2011): 10–17.

10. See: Jonathan Z. Smith, "Religion, Religions, Religious," in *Critical Terms for Religious Studies*, 269–84; Jonathan Z. Smith, *Imagining Religion: From Babylon to Jamestown* (Chicago: University of Chicago Press, 1982); Talal Asad, *Formations of the Secular: Christianity, Islam, Modernity* (Stanford, Calif.: Stanford University Press, 2003); Oscar Salemink, "Framing Religion: The Human Rights Encounter and the Transformation of Religion in Vietnam," inaugural lecture, University of Copenhagen, June 17, 2011.

11. Hent de Vries, "Introduction: Why Still 'Religion'?" in *Religion*, ed. de Vries, 1–98.

12. Ibid., 5; our emphasis. Therefore, de Vries argues: "only by being willing to move beyond the concept as we (think we) know it can we open ourselves up to a phenomenon or set(s) of phenomena whose simultaneous density ('thickness') and elusiveness ('thinness') belong to the 'heart' of its 'matter' and constitute its references in their very 'essence,' that is to say, their logic and grammar" (ibid.).

13. Ibid., 6.

14. Ibid., 66.

15. In his recent inaugural lecture, Mattijs van de Port introduced the notion of "the rest of what is" to indicate the shortcomings of language and other symbolic registers for capturing religious experience. "The rest of what is" is beyond signification yet present in a negative, indirect manner. See Mattijs van de Port, "Dat wat rest: Over sacralizering en de ongerijmdheden van het bestaan," inaugural lecture, VU University, March 26, 2010; see also Mattijs van de Port, *Ecstatic Encounters: Bahian Candomblé and the Quest for the Really Real* (Amsterdam: Amsterdam University Press, 2011). This perspective resonates with Meyer's approach to religion as entailing authorized "sensational forms" that induce a sense of a limit from which experiences of the sublime arise. See her "Religious Sensations: Why Media, Aesthetics, and Power Matter in the Study of Contemporary Religion," in *Religion*, ed. de Vries, 704–23. Like de Vries and van de Port, Meyer takes "religion" as one of the sites that open up toward a "beyond" that is registered as indeterminable. Resisting

full—exhaustive—signification, a sense of this "beyond" is generated through shared, repetitive forms.

16. See, e.g., the recent critical comments by Charles Hirschkind, "Media, Mediation, Religion," and the response by Matthew Engelke, *Social Anthropology* 19, no. 1 (2011): 90–102.

17. The series includes: de Vries, ed., *Religion*; Meerten B. ter Borg and Jan Willem van Henten, eds., *Powers: Religion as a Social and Spiritual Force* (New York: Fordham University Press, 2010); and forthcoming volumes entitled *Words*, ed. Ernst van den Hemel, Asja Sjafraniec, and Jan Bremmer, and *Gestures*, ed. Anne-Marie Korte and Martin van Bruinessen.

18. Cf. Morgan, "Introduction: The Matter of Belief."

19. A genealogy of scholarly engagement with materiality and materialist approaches and the quite different dualisms entailed by them—materialist vs. idealist, material vs. spiritual, object vs. subject, matter vs. spirit, nature vs. culture, concrete vs. abstract—still needs to be written.

20. See: Daniel Miller, *Material Culture and Mass Consumption* (Oxford: Blackwell, 1987); and Daniel Miller, ed., *Materiality* (Durham, N.C.: Duke University Press, 2005). See also Fred Myers, ed., *The Empire of Things: Regimes of Value and Material Culture* (Santa Fe: School of American Research Press, 2005).

21. Judith Butler, *Bodies That Matter: On the Discursive Limits of "Sex"* (New York: Routledge, 1993).

22. See: Hans Belting, *An Anthropology of Images: Picture, Medium, Body* (Princeton, N.J.: Princeton University Press, 2011); David Freedberg, *The Power of Images: Studies in the History and Theory of Response* (Chicago: University of Chicago Press, 1989); Alfred Gell, *Art and Agency: An Anthropological Theory* (Oxford: Oxford University Press, 1998); W. J. T. Mitchell, *Picture Theory* (Chicago: University of Chicago Press, 1994); W. J. T. Mitchell, *What Do Pictures Want? The Lives and Loves of Images* (Chicago: University of Chicago Press, 2005).

23. Bruno Latour, *Reassembling the Social: An Introduction to Actor-Network-Theory* (Oxford: Oxford University Press, 2005).

24. See: Daniel C. Dennett, *Consciousness Explained* (Boston: Little, Brown, 1991); Douglas R. Hofstadter and Daniel C. Dennett, *The Mind's I: Fantasies and Reflections on Self and Soul* (New York: Basic Books, 1981).

25. See Bo Dahlbom, ed., *Dennett and His Critics: Demystifying Mind* (Oxford: Blackwell, 1993).

26. See also Birgit Meyer, "Introduction: From Imagined Communities to Aesthetic Formations: Religious Mediations, Sensational Forms and Styles of Binding," in *Aesthetic Formations: Media, Religion and the Senses in the Making of Communities*, ed. Birgit Meyer (London: Palgrave Macmillan, 2009), 5–11.

27. The tangibility of construction is depicted vividly in the cover image of a building site on Latour's book *Reassembling The Social*.

28. Butler recurs here to the classical Greek conception of *hyle* ("wood"; *Bodies That Matter*, 31–32). For Aristotle, matter is a potential that is to be shaped by form. Form organizes matter in a particular way. This is a very fruitful starting point for thinking about the nexus of matter and the social.

29. The term *Materialismus* was used as an insult, to refer to a misguided stance based on a problematic mistake. Only in the course of the *Materialismusstreit* (see n. 2, above) was materialism invoked as a positive self-description. The problem with current mobilizations of the materialist stance is that they rely on an outdated view of matter. See Mario Bunge, *Matter and Mind: A Philosophical Inquiry* (Dordrecht: Springer, 2010).

30. David Chidester, "Material Terms for the Study of Religion," *Journal of the American Academy of Religion* 68, no. 2 (2000): 374.

31. Tellingly, the issue of materiality was not marked in the introduction to Taylor's volume.

32. Note that scholars tend to use terms such as *materiality* or *material culture*, rather than *materialism*. Might this be an echo of the eighteenth- and nineteenth-century use of *materialism* as an insult? Does it signal some distance from Marxian dialectical or historical materialism?

33. See, e.g.: Caroline Walker Bynum, *Christian Materiality: An Essay on Religion in Late Medieval Europe* (New York: Zone Books, 2011); Matthew Engelke, "Material Religion," in *The Cambridge Companion to Religious Studies*, ed. Robert A. Orsi (Cambridge: Cambridge University Press, 2012); Webb Keane, *Christian Moderns: Freedom and Fetish in the Mission Encounter* (Berkeley: University of California Press, 2007); E. Frances King, *Material Religion and Popular Culture* (New York: Routledge, 2010); Karl-Heinz Kohl, *Die Macht der Dinge: Geschichte und Theorie sakraler Objekte* (Munich: Beck, 2003); Colleen McDannell, *Material Christianity: Religion and Popular Culture in America* (New Haven, Conn.: Yale University Press, 1995); David Morgan, *The Sacred Gaze: Religious Visual Culture in Theory and Practice* (Berkeley: University of California Press, 2005); David Morgan, ed., *Key Words in Religion, Media, and Culture* (New York: Routledge, 2008); Morgan, *Matter of Belief*; Robert A. Orsi, *Between Heaven and Earth: The Religious Worlds People Make and the Scholars Who Study Them* (Princeton, N.J.: Princeton University Press, 2006); Jeremy Stolow, *Orthodox by Design: Judaism, Print Politics, and the Artscroll Revolution* (Berkeley: University of California Press, 2010); Elizabeth Williamson, *The Materiality of Religion in Early Modern English Drama* (Farnham: Ashgate, 2011). See also: Richard M. Carp, "Teaching Religion and Material Culture," *Teaching Theology and Religion* 10, no. 1: 2–12; Arie Molendijk, ed., *Materiel Christendom: Religie en materiële cultur in West-Europa* (Hilversum: Verloren, 2003).

34. Birgit Meyer, David Morgan, Crispin Paine, and S. Brent Plate, "The Origin and Mission of *Material Religion*," *Religion* 40 (2010): 209.

35. Elisabeth Arweck and William Keenan, "Introduction: Material Varieties of Religious Expression," in *Materializing Religion: Expression, Performance and Ritual*, ed. Elisabeth Arweck and William Keenan (Aldershot: Ashgate, 2006), 2–3.

36. Webb Keane, "On the Materiality of Religion," *Material Religion* 4, no. 2 (2008): 230.

37. Bruno Latour, "What Is Iconoclash? Or, Is There a World Beyond the Image Wars?" in *Iconoclash: Beyond the Image Wars in Science, Religion, and Art*, ed. Bruno Latour and Peter Weibel (Cambridge: MIT Press. 2002), 14–18.

38. De Vries, "Introduction," 11.

39. Max Weber, *The Protestant Ethic and the Spirit of Capitalism* (1904–5; London: Allen & Unwin, 1978). In the German original, Weber uses *Glaube*, echoing Luther's *sola fide*.

40. In *The Romantic Ethic and the Spirit of Modern Consumerism* (Oxford: Blackwell, 1987), Colin Campbell argues that Weber overlooked the importance of consumption for the rise of capitalism. Launching the notion of the "romantic ethic," Campbell seeks to complement Weber's undue emphasis on ascesis at the expense of consumption.

41. Max Weber, *Economy and Society*, 2 vols. (1921; Berkeley: University of California Press, 1978), 506.

42. The following discussion of Weber relies on a section in Birgit Meyer, "Aesthetics of Persuasion: Global Christianity and Pentecostalism's Sensational Forms," *Global Christianity, Global Critique*, special issue, *South Atlantic Quarterly* 9 (2010): 744–50. For a similar analysis of Weber's view of religion and art, see Ernst Müller, *Ästhetische Religiosität und Kunstreligion in den Philosophien von der Aufklärung bis zum Ausgang des deutschen Idealismus* (Berlin: Akademie, 2004), xxi–xxiv.

43. Max Weber, "Religious Rejections of the World and Their Directions," in *From Max Weber: Essays in Sociology*, ed. and introd. H. H. Gerth and C. Wright Mills (1948; London: Routledge & Kegan Paul, 1970), 341.

44. Ibid. Bernice Martin, in "The Aesthetics of Latin American Pentecostalism: The Sociology of Religion and the Problem of Taste" (in *Materializing Religion*, ed. Arweck and Keenan, 141) points out that that Pentecostalism "embodies multiple paradoxes" and does not fit neatly into Weber's model. Obviously, this challenges the model itself.

45. Max Weber, *Economy and Society*, ed. Guenther Roth and Claus Wittich (1968; Berkeley: University of California Press, 1978), 399–634.

46. Ibid, 608–9.

47. Weber submitted that, in practice, the relation between art and religion can be restored. The renewed synthesis comes about when religions aspire to spread out: "the more they wished to be universalist mass religions and were thus directed to emotional propaganda and mass appeals, the more systematic were their alliances with art" (Weber, "Religious Rejections," 343). See Meyer, "Aesthetics of Persuasion," 745.

48. Here lies another difference between Tylor and Weber. Whereas the former, as Peter Pels argues, prefigures semiotic approaches to the social, the latter, as Stef Aupers argues, prefigures postmodern thinkers like Jean-François Lyotard, Fredric Jameson, and Jean Baudrillard. This is why Weber's work has remained so stimulating. See: Nicholas Gane, *Max Weber and Postmodern Theory: Rationalisation Versus Re-Enchantment* (London: Palgrave, 2002); Dick Houtman, *Op jacht naar de echte werkelijkheid: Dromen over authenticiteit in een wereld zonder fundamenten* (Amsterdam: Pallas Publications, 2008).

49. Webb Keane, "Sincerity, 'Modernity' and the Protestants," *Cultural Anthropology* 17, no. 1 (2002): 71.

50. For a critique of this stance, see Matthew Engelke and Matt Tomlinson, eds., *The Limits of Meaning: Case Studies in the Anthropology of Christianity* (Oxford: Berghahn, 2006).

51. An inspiring starting point could be the work of Niklaus Largier on medieval mysticism, with its emphasis on the materiality of experience and sensation in spiritual practice. See esp. Niklaus Largier, "Mysticisms, Modernity, and the Invention of Aesthetic Experience," *Representations* 105 (2009): 37–60. In this article, Largier addresses the profound transformation of medieval mystical practices after the sixteenth century, in the aftermath of Luther's distinction between the secular and the spiritual realm, taking mysticism and spirituality out of the realm of ordinary practice. See also Niklaus Largier, "A 'Sense of Possibility': Robert Musil, Meister Eckart, and the 'Culture of Film,'" in *Religion*, ed de Vries, 739–49, and M. B. Pranger, "Religious Indifference: On the Nature of Medieval Christianity," in ibid., 513–23.

52. See, e.g.: Keane, *Christian Moderns*; Matthew Engelke, *A Problem of Presence: Beyond Scripture in an African Church* (Berkeley: University of California Press, 2007); Birgit Meyer, *Translating the Devil: Religion and Modernity among the Ewe in Ghana* (Edinburgh: Edinburgh University Press, 1999); Joel Robbins, *Becoming Sinners: Christianity and Moral Torment in a Papua New Guinea Society* (Berkeley: University of California Press, 2004).

53. Keane, *Christian Moderns*, 16. See also Meyer's essay in this volume.

54. Meyer, *Translating the Devil*, esp. 83–111, 213–16.

55. Engelke, *Problem of Presence*; see also his essay in this volume.

56. See also Miranda Klaver, "This Is My Desire: A Semiotic Perspective on Conversion in an Evangelical Seeker Church and a Pentecostal Church in the Netherlands," Ph.D. thesis, VU University, Amsterdam, 2011.

57. This is the key concern of the emergent "anthropology of Christianity," which largely focuses on Protestantism and Pentecostalism. See, e.g.: Fenella Cannell, *The Anthropology of Christianity* (Durham, N.C.: Duke University Press, 2006); Joel Robbins, ed., *The Anthropology of Christianity*, special issue, *Religion* 33, no. 3 (2003); Jon Bialecki, Naomi Haynes, and Joel Robbins, "The Anthropology of Christianity," *Religion Compass* 2, no. 6 (2008): 1139–58.

58. David Morgan, "Imaging Protestant Piety: The Icons of Warner Sallman," *Religion and American Culture: A Journal of Interpretation* 3, no. 1 (Winter 1993): 29–47; David Morgan, *Visual Piety: A History and Theory of Popular Religious Images* (Berkeley: University of California Press, 1998); David Morgan and Sally M. Promey, eds., *The Visual Culture of American Religions* (Berkeley: University of California Press, 2001).

59. Mitchell, *What Do Pictures Want?* 188.

60. For Christian painters, the issue was how to frame the act of painting in such a manner that it would not contradict the Second Commandment. See Christiane Kruse's excellent investigation of how the origins of art are featured in paintings and in discourses about art in the period between 1100 and 1650 (*Wozu Menschen malen: Historische Begründungen eines Bildmediums* [Munich: Wilhelm Fink, 2003]).

61. William Pietz, "The Problem of the Fetish," pt. 1, *Res* 9 (1985): 5–17; pt. 2, *Res* 13 (1987): 23–45; pt. 3, *Res* 16 (1988): 105–23. See also: Patricia Spyer, ed., *Border Fetishisms: Material Objects in Unstable Spaces* (New York: Routledge, 1998); Tomoko Masuzawa, "Troubles with Materiality: The Ghost of Fetishism in the Nineteenth Century," in *Religion*, ed. de Vries, 647–67.

62. Böhme links *fetish* etymologically to *factitious* (Latin), "what is made," by contrast to *terrigemus*, "what grows naturally" (Hartmut Böhme, *Fetischismus und Kultur: Eine andere Theorie der Moderne* [Reinbek: Rowohlt, 2006], 179). See also Kohl, *Die Macht der Dinge*, 69–118; Christine Weder, *Erschriebene Dinge: Fetisch, Amulett, Talisman um 1800* (Freiburg: Rombach, 2007).

63. Bruno Latour, "Fetish-factish," *Material Religion* 7, no. 1 (2011): 44.

64. Böhme agrees with Pietz's view that the notion of "fetish" emerged in a context of cross-cultural encounters but is critical of Pietz's reading of the "fetish" as posing a challenge to European rationalism. Instead, Böhme shows that the notion of the "fetish" and charges of "fetishism" were initially mobilized in a religious framework of "superstition." Also, Protestants adopted the notion of the fetish to critique what they regarded as Catholic idol worship. In this sense, the theological discourse on idolatry contributed to the notion of the fetish. According to Böhme, only in the eighteenth century did an understanding of the fetish as challenging a rational outlook that insists on things as inanimate emerge (Böhme, *Fetischismus und Kultur*, 182–85).

65. Karl Marx, "The Fetishism of Commodities and the Secret Thereof," *Capital*, vol. 1, section 4 (http://www.marxists.org/archive/marx/works/1867-c1/ch01.htm#S3a4). The German original puts this even more evocatively: "voller metaphysischer Spitzfindigkeiten und *theologischer Mucken*" (*Karl Marx*, Das Kapital: Kritik der politischen Ökonomie [1885; http://www.mlwerke.de/me/me23/me23_049.htm#Kap_1_4; checked on 11 August 2011; an on-line version of Karl Marx and Friedrich Engels, *Werke*, vol. 23, *Das Kapital* (Berlin, 1968)], 1:85). *See also Kohl*, Macht der Dinge, 92–98.

66. Don Slater, *Consumer Culture and Modernity* (1997; Cambridge: Polity Press, 2008), 111–12 (quoted in Aupers's essay).

67. Benjamin writes: "One can behold in capitalism a religion, that is to say, capitalism essentially serves to satisfy the same worries, anguish and disquiet formerly answered by so-called religion. The proof of capitalism's religious structure—as not only a religiously conditioned construction, as Weber thought, but as an essentially religious phenomenon—still today misleads one to a boundless, universal polemic" (Walter Benjamin, "Capitalism as Religion," in *The Frankfurt School on Religion*, ed. Mendieta, 259).

68. Böhme argues that placing the fetish at the center of modernity necessitates an alternative theory of modernity: "Modernity means that self-enchantment and enlightenment belong together, like fetishization and the critique of fetishization" (Böhme, *Fetischismus und Kultur*, 75; our translation). See also Jane Bennett, "Commodity Fetishism and Commodity Enchantment," in *The Enchantment of Modern Life: Attachments, Crossings, and Ethics* (Princeton, N.J.: Princeton University Press, 2001), 111–30.

69. See: Campbell, *Romantic Ethic*; Miller, *Material Culture and Mass Consumption*.

70. See Jean-Luc Nancy, "A Deconstruction of Monotheism," trans. Gabriel Malenfant, in *Religion*, ed. de Vries, 380–91, and in Jean-Luc Nancy, *Dis-Enclosure: The Deconstruction of Christianity*, trans. Bettina Bergo, Gabriel Malenfant, and Michael Smith (New York: Fordham University Press, 2008), 29–41. See also Alena Alexandrova, Ignaas Devisch, Laurens ten Kate, and Aukje van Rooden, eds., *Re-treating Religion: Deconstructing Christianity with Jean-Luc Nancy* (New York: Fordham University Press, 2011).

71. See Marcel Mauss's essay on the gift, in which he explains the logic of gift exchange without having recourse to distinctions between religious and socioeconomic spheres (*The Gift: Forms and Functions of Exchange in Archaic Societies* [1954; London: Routledge, 1970]). Famously, he shows that valued articles (*taonga*) in Maori gift exchange are identified with the "spirit of the gift"(*hau*), making a strict distinction between gift, giver, and receiver impossible. Placed beyond a religious framework of "bad objecthood," the notion of the gift is a fruitful starting point for an alternative approach to "things" in the study of religion. See also the essay by Derks, Jansen, and Notermans in this volume.

72. Bill Brown, "Thing Theory," *Critical Inquiry* 28, no. 1 (2001): 1–22. See also David Morgan, "Thing," *Material Religion* 7, no.1 (2011): 140–47, and the essay by Meyer in this volume.

The Modern Fear of Matter: Reflections on the Protestantism of Victorian Science, by Peter Pels

NOTE: This essay was previously published as Peter Pels, "The Modern Fear of Matter: Reflections on the Protestantism of Victorian Science," in *Material Religion* 4, no. 3 (2008): 264–83. © 2008 Berg Publishers, an imprint of Bloomsbury Publishing.

1. I use "Occidental" whenever I want to refer to the "imaginary figure" that Dipesh Chakrabarty, in *Provincializing Europe: Postcolonial Thought and Historical Difference* (Princeton, N.J.: Princeton University Press, 2000), 4, refers to as "Europe"—a virtual reality that one cannot afford *not* to think with when analyzing the constitution of modernity (see also Bruno Latour, *We Have Never Been Modern*, trans. Catherine Porter [Cambridge: Harvard University Press, 1993]).

2. Mary Poovey, *A History of the Modern Fact: Problems of Knowledge in the Sciences of Wealth and Society* (Chicago: University of Chicago Press, 1998).

3. Peter Pels, "The Spirit of Matter: On Fetish, Rarity, Fact and Fancy," in *Border Fetishisms: Material Objects in Unstable Spaces*, ed. Patricia Spyer (New York : Routledge, 1998), 91–121; William Pietz, "The Problem of the Fetish, I," *Res* 9 (1985): 5–17; William Pietz, "The Problem of the Fetish, II: The Origin of the Fetish," *Res* 13 (1987): 23–45; William Pietz, "The Problem of the Fetish, IIIa: Bosman's Guinea and the Enlightenment Theory of Fetishism," *Res* 16 (1988): 105–23; William Pietz, "The Fetish of Civilization: Sacrificial Blood and Monetary Debt," in *Colonial Subjects: Essays in the Practical History of Anthropology*, ed. Peter Pels and Oscar Salemink (Ann Arbor: University of Michigan Press, 1999), 53–81.

4. Pels, "The Spirit of Matter," 94.

5. See George W. Stocking, "Philanthropoids and Vanishing Cultures: Rockefeller Funding and the End of the Museum Era in Anglo-American Anthropology," in *Objects and Others: Essays on Museums and Material Culture*, ed. G. W. Stocking, Jr. (Madison: University of Wisconsin Press, 1985), 114.

6. Pels, "The Spirit of Matter."

7. Webb Keane, "Sincerity, 'Modernity' and the Protestants," *Cultural Anthropology* 17, no. 1 (2002): 71.

8. Poovey, *A History of the Modern Fact.*

9. Webb Keane, "Materialism, Missionaries and Modern Subjects in Colonial Indonesia," in *Conversion to Modernities: The Globalization of Christianity*, ed. Peter van der Veer (New York: Routledge, 1996), 137–70; Bruno Latour, "What Is Iconoclash? Or, Is There a World Beyond the Image Wars?" in *Iconoclash*, ed. B. Latour and P. Weibel (Cambridge: MIT Press, 2002); Margaret J. Wiener, "Hidden Forces: Colonialism and the Politics of Magic in the Netherlands Indies," in *Magic and Modernity: Interfaces of Revelation and Concealment*, ed. Birgit Meyer and Peter Pels (Stanford, Calif.: Stanford University Press, 2003), 129–58.

10. Latour, "What Is Iconoclash?"

11. Pels, "The Spirit of Matter."

12. Daniel Miller, *Material Culture and Mass Consumption* (Oxford: Blackwell, 1987), 107–8.

13. Pierre Bourdieu, *Outline of a Theory of Practice*, trans. Richard Nice (Cambridge: Cambridge University Press, 1977).

14. Alfred Gell, *Art and Agency: An Anthropological Theory* (Oxford: Oxford University Press, 1998).

15. Pels, "The Spirit of Matter."

16. Quoted in William Pietz, "Fetishism and Materialism: The Limits of Theory in Marx," in *Fetishism as Cultural Discourse*, ed. E. Apter and W. Pietz (Ithaca, N.Y.: Cornell University Press, 1993), 144.

17. In recent work on material culture, some stress discourses of the object's or "fetish's" agency (Gell, *Art and Agency*; Pels, "The Spirit of Matter"; Pietz, "The Problem of the Fetish, I; II; IIIa"; Pietz, "The Fetish of Civilization"), whereas others (Arjun Appadurai, "Introduction: Commodities and the Politics of Value," in *The Social Life of Things*, ed. A. Appadurai [Cambridge: Cambridge University Press, 1986], 3–63; Fred. R. Myers, "Introduction: The Empire of Things," in *The Empire of Things: Regimes of Value and Material Culture*, ed. F. R. Myers [Santa Fe: School of American Research Press, 2001], 3–61, and, to a lesser extent, Webb Keane, *Signs of Recognition: Powers and Hazards of Representation in an Indonesian Society* [Berkeley: University of California Press, 1997]) stress the human regimes of value to which objects are subordinated. The remarkable thing about this literature, however, is a recent convergence of human and objective agency and intention (see esp. Gell, *Art and Agency*; Miller, *Material Culture*; Keane, "Materialism"; Webb Keane, "Money Is No Object: Materiality, Desire and Modernity in an Indonesian Society," in *The Empire of Things*, ed. Myers, 65–90; Spyer, ed., *Border Fetishisms*).

18. Pels, "The Spirit of Matter."

19. Ibid.

20. Peter Pels and Oscar Salemink, "Introduction: Locating the Colonial Subjects of Anthropology" in *Colonial Subjects*, ed. Pels and Salemink, 1–52.

21. Keane, "Materialism"; Webb Keane, "Calvin in the Tropics: Objects and Subjects at the Religious Frontier," in *Border Fetishisms*, ed. Spyer, 13–34.

22. As Emile Durkheim (*The Elementary Forms of the Religious Life*, trans. Joseph Ward Swain [French pub. 1912; New York: Free Press, 1965], 144–45), and, commenting on Durkheim's work, Michael Taussig ("Maleficium: State Fetishism," in *Fetishism as Cultural Discourse*, ed. Apter and Pietz, 217–47) bring out, the relationship is much more complex, especially when one considers its historical layering (see, e.g., Fred R. Myers, "The Wizards of Oz: Nation, State, and the Production of Aboriginal Fine Art," in *The Empire of Things*, ed. Myers, 165–204; Patrick Wolfe, *Settler Colonialism and the Transformation of Anthropology: The Politics and Poetics of an Ethnographic Event* [London: Cassell, 1999]).

23. Keane, "Money," 70.

24. See Gell, *Art and Agency.*

25. See Carlo Ginzburg, "Clues: Freud, Morelli, Sherlock Holmes," in *The Sign of Three*, ed. U. Eco and T. Sebeok (Bloomington: Indiana University Press, 1983).

26. Peter Pels, "Spirits of Modernity: Alfred Wallace, Edward Tylor, and the Visual Politics of Fact," in *Magic and Modernity*, ed. Meyer and Pels, 241–71.

27. Keane, "Materialism," 139.

28. See the discussions of virtuality and "virtualism" in James G. Carrier, "Introduction," in *Virtualism: A New Political Economy*, ed. J. G. Carrier and D. Miller (Oxford: Berg, 1998), 1–25; and Daniel Miller, "Conclusion: A Theory of Virtualism," in the same book, 187–215. I have neglected to discuss these notions, as well a number of other relevant concepts (such as "idealism," "metaphysics," or "theory" versus "empiry"). I readily admit, however, that such different vectors of contest may generate important modifications of my present argument.

29. See Pietz, "Fetishism and Materialism," 144–50.

30. For details, see Pels, "The Spirit of Matter"; Pietz, "The Problem of the Fetish, I; II; IIIa"; Poovey, *A History of the Modern Fact.*

31. Cf. Mary Poovey, *Making a Social Body: British Cultural Formation, 1830–1864* (Chicago: University of Chicago Press, 1995).

32. Such conjecture is, among other things, the standard operation in medical diagnosis—when based, that is, on finding out what ails living organisms (see Ginzburg, "Clues"). One can find its equivalent in social science in the conjecture of evolutionist schemata, cultural patterns, or functional relationships on the basis of their perceived effects (as in Wallace and Tylor: see Pels, "Spirits of Modernity"). See the remarks, below, on Durkheim's "hyperspiritual" *conscience collective* and Tylor's notion of "culture."

33. For nineteenth-century occultists and Indian nationalists, see: Partha Chatterjee, *Nationalist Thought and the Colonial World: A Derivative Discourse* (London: Zed Books, 1986); Peter van der Veer, "The Spirits of the Age: Spiritualism and Political Radicalism," in his *Imperial Encounters: Religion and Modernity in India and Britain* (Princeton, N.J.: Princeton University Press, 2001). For twentieth-century nationalism and "New Age religion," see: Wouter Hanegraaff, *New Age Religion and Western Culture: Esotericism in the Mirror of Secular Thought* (Leiden: Brill, 1996); Paul Heelas, *The New Age Movement: The Celebration of the Self and the Sacralization of Modernity* (Oxford: Blackwell, 1996); Joel Kahn, "Anthropology's Malaysian Interlocutors: Toward a Cosmopolitan Ethics of Anthropological Practice," in *Embedding Ethics: Anthropological Moralities at the Boundary of the Public and the Professional*, ed. L. Meskell and P. Pels (New York: Berg, 2004).

34. Miller, *Material Culture.*

35. Pels, "The Spirit of Matter."

36. Poovey, *A History of the Modern Fact*, 9.

37. See Charles Taylor, *Sources of the Self* (Cambridge: Cambridge University Press, 1989), for an analysis of the emergence of the interior, autonomous self in Western philosophy.

38. This is, of course, ideology: as I have argued in juxtaposing Alfred Wallace's spiritualism and Edward Tylor's taxonomic schemes, all determinations of the material or the factual involve moral and political decisions (Pels, "Spirits of Modernity").

39. Latour, "What Is Iconoclash?" 18. I use the gender of the "man-made" intentionally, as "male" mechanical manufacture and "female" natural procreation have long been opposed in the hegemonic discourses that I target. By contrast, see Donna Haraway's exploration of the liberating possibilities of the person that is both "made" and "grown"—the cyborg (Donna Haraway, *Simians, Cyborgs, and Women: The Reinvention of Nature* (New York: Routledge, 1991).

40. Keane, "Materialism," 139.

41. Keane, "Money," 86.

42. John Stuart Mill, *Utilitarianism*, ed. and introd. R. Crisp (1863; Oxford: Oxford University Press, 1998), 55.

43. Hermann Braun, "Materialismus—Idealismus," in *Geschichtliche Grundbegriffe: Historisches Lexikon zur politisch-sozialen Sprache in Deutschland*, ed. O. Brunner, W. Conze, and R. Koselleck (Stuttgart: Klett-Cotta, 1982), 977–1019.

44. I use "Science"and "Scientific" with a capital *S* when referring to the ideology of science current in the Victorian era, to distinguish it from more general scientific practice (which has, to me, no definable unity).

45. Quoted in Adrian Desmond, *Huxley: From Devil's Discipline to Evolution's High Priest* (Reading, Mass.: Addison-Wesley, 1994), 319.

46. Thomas Henry Huxley, "Agnosticism," in his *Essays upon Some Controverted Questions* (London: Macmillan & Co, 1892), 362.

47. Huxley, "Agnosticism."

48. Desmond, *Huxley*, 625.

49. See Noel Annan, "The Intellectual Aristocracy," in *Studies in Social History*, ed. J. H. Plumb (London, 1955), 243–87.

50. Alfred Russel Wallace, *Miracles and Modern Spiritualism*, 3rd rev. ed. (1874; London: George Redway,1896), vi–vii.

51. Pels, "Spirits of Modernity"; see Poovey, *A History of the Modern Fact*.

52. See Peter Pels, "Occult Truths: Race, Conjecture, and Theosophy in Victorian Anthropology," in *Excluded Ancestors, Inventible Traditions: Essays Toward a More Inclusive History of Anthropology*, ed. R. Handler (Madison: University of Wisconsin Press, 2000), 11–41; Pels, "Spirits of Modernity"; Steven Shapin and Arnold Thackray, "Prosopography as a Research Tool in History of Science: The British Scientific Community, 1700–1900," *History of Science* 12 (1974): 6, 11.

53. Helena Petrovna Blavatsky, *The Key to Theosophy* (1889; Ayar, Madras: Theosophical Publishing House, 1987), 87; my emphasis.

54. Wallace, *Miracles*, 211.

55. Edward B. Tylor, "Ethnology and Spiritualism," *Nature* 5 (1872): 343; Edward B. Tylor, *Primitive Culture*, 2nd ed., 2 vols. (1873: New York: Brentano's, 1924); see also George W. Stocking, "Animism in Theory and Practice: E. B. Tylor's Unpublished 'Notes on Spiritualism,'" *Man*, n.s. 6 (1971): 88–104.

56. I borrow these terms from Johannes Fabian's analysis of anthropological rhetoric in *Time and the Other: How Anthropology Makes Its Object* (New York: Columbia University Press, 1983).

57. But see Pels, "Spirits of Modernity," and Stocking, "Animism."

58. Quoted in Pietz, "Fetishism and Materialism," 131.

59. See: Pietz, "Fetishism and Materialism," 142; Pietz, *The Fetish of Civilization*, 59–60.

60. As far as I can tell, Tylor used "Materialism" only once in *Primitive Culture*, as a way to define "the deepest of all religious schisms, that which divides Animism from Materialism" (Tylor, *Primitive Culture*, 1:502). One wonders whether this—obviously radical—pronouncement, placed at the end of vol. 1, was too controversial to be repeated (especially for someone who could still be banned from an academic position by the Oxbridge religious establishment because of his Dissenting background).

61. Desmond, *Huxley*, 427, 464.

62. See Pietz, "Fetishism and Materialism," 132.

63. See: Lorraine Daston, "Marvelous Facts and Miraculous Evidence in Early Modern Europe," in *Questions of Evidence: Proof, Practice, and Persuasion Across the Disciplines*, ed. J. Chandler, A. I.

Davidson, and H. Harootunian (Chicago: University of Chicago Press, 1994), 243–74; Lynne Williamson, "Ethnological Specimens in the Pitt Rivers Museum attributed to the Tradescant Collection," in *Tradescant's Rarities: Essays on the Foundation of the Ashmolean Museum*, ed. A. MacGregor (Oxford: Oxford University Press, 1983), 338–45.

64. Tony Bennett, "The Exhibitionary Complex," in *Culture/Power/History*, ed. N. Dirks, G. Eley, and S. Ortner (Princeton, N.J.: Princeton University Press, 1994), 124–54; see also William Ryan Chapman, "Arranging Ethnology: A.H.L.F. Pitt-Rivers and the Typological Tradition," in *Objects and Others*, ed. Stocking, 15–48.

65. Pels, "Spirits of Modernity."

66. Tylor, *Primitive Culture*, 1:1.

67. Ibid., 1:12.

68. Poovey, *A History of the Modern Fact*, 3; see, for his love of statistics, Edward B. Tylor, "On a Method of Investigating the Development of Institutions, Applied to Laws of Marriage and Descent," *Journal of the Anthropological Institute* 18 (1888): 245–72.

69. Talal Asad, "Ethnographic Representation, Statistics, and Modern Power," *Social Research* 61 (1994): 55–88.

70. See Carrier, "Introduction."

71. Marginalized, that is, from mainstream Science. Despite the overwhelming philosophical literature on hermeneutics, phenomenology, and like approaches, the social history of the survival of the more phenomenological and democratic attitudes toward research in scientific disciplines vis-á-vis the "hard sciences," in the humanities, in the field of anthropological method (see Asad, "Ethnographic Representation"), and in popular science, including occultism (see: Pels, "Occult Truths"; Pels, "Spirits of Modernity"), is still in its infancy.

72. See: Emile Durkheim, *Professional Ethics and Civic Morals*, ed. and introd. Bryan S. Turner (London: Routledge, 1992); Poovey, *Making a Social Body*; Taussig, "Maleficium."

73. Emile Durkheim, "Individual and Collective Representations," in his *Sociology and Philosophy*, ed. D. Pocock and J. G. Peristiany (1898; New York: Free Press, 1974), 34, emphasis in original; see also Dick Pels, "Het project als object: Durkheims kennispolitiek in relativistisch perspectief," *Amsterdams Sociologisch Tijdschrift* 10, no. 1 (1983): 51–91.

74. Timothy Mitchell, "Society, Economy, and the State Effect," in *State/Culture: State-Formation after the Cultural Turn*, ed. G. Steinmetz (Ithaca, N.Y.: Cornell University Press, 1999), 76–97; Timothy Mitchell, *Rule of Experts: Egypt, Techno-Politics, Modernity* (Berkeley: University of California Press, 2002).

75. Max Weber, "Die Wirtschaftethik der Weltreligionen," in *Gesammelte Aufsätze zur Religionssoziologie* (Tübingen: J. C. Mohr, 1947), 1:245–46.

76. Max Weber, "Die protestantische Ethik und der Geist des Kapitalismus," in *Gesammelte Aufsätze zur Religionssoziologie*, 1:203.

77. See Pietz, "Fetishism and Materialism," 122, 129.

78. Tylor, *Primitive Culture*, 2:576.

79. Ibid.

Dangerous Things: One African Genealogy, by Matthew Engelke

NOTE: The main body of this chapter is a revised and edited version of Matthew Engelke, "Sticky Subjects, Sticky Objects: The Substance of African Christian Healing," in *Materiality*, ed. Daniel

Miller (Durham, N.C.: Duke University Press, 2005), 118–39. Copyright © 2005 Duke University Press. It was reprinted, in edited form, in Matthew Engelke, *A Problem of Presence: Beyond Scripture in an African Church* (Berkeley: University of California Press, 2007), 224–43. The final two sections are taken from Engelke, *A Problem of Presence*, 20–27. I would like to thank Duke University Press and the University of California Press, respectively, for permission to reprint the material here.

1. Edwards, quoted in Margaret Aston, *England's Iconoclasts: Laws Against Images* (Oxford: Oxford University Press, 1998), 1:13.

2. See Daniel Miller, "Materiality: An Introduction," in *Materiality*, ed. Daniel Miller (Durham, N.C.: Duke University Press, 2005), 7.

3. See: Webb Keane, "Calvin in the Tropics: Objects and Subjects at the Religious Frontier," in *Border Fetishisms: Material Objects in Unstable Spaces*, ed. Patricia Spyer (New York: Routledge, 1998), 13–34; Colleen McDannell, *Material Christianity: Religion and Popular Culture in America* (New Haven, Conn.: Yale University Press, 1995); S. J. Tambiah, *The Buddhist Saints of the Forest and the Cult of Amulets* (Cambridge: Cambridge University Press, 1984).

4. See Keane, "Calvin in the Tropics," 29.

5. Miller, "Materiality," 41.

6. For "relative" materialities, see Michael Rowlands, "A Materialist Approach to Materiality," in *Materiality*, ed. Miller, 72–87. For "plural" materialities, see Fred Myers, "Some Properties of Art and Culture: Ontologies of the Image and Economies of Exchange," in *Materiality*, ed. Miller, 88–117.

7. Matthew Engelke, *A Problem of Presence: Beyond Scripture in an African Church* (Berkeley: University of California Press, 2007).

8. Miller, "Materiality," 16; Rowlands, "A Materialist Approach," 80–84.

9. For the *benge*, see E. E. Evans-Pritchard, *Witchcraft, Oracles, and Magic among the Azande*, abridged ed. (Oxford: Oxford University Press, 1976), 122–48. For Buddhist amulets, see Tambiah, *The Buddhist Saints*, 243–57.

10. Evans-Pritchard, *Witchcraft*.

11. See Engelke, *A Problem of Presence*, 79–108.

12. McDannell, *Material Christianity*, 8.

13. Ibid., 15.

14. Engelke, *A Problem of Presence*, 46–78.

15. Jean Comaroff, "Healing and the Cultural Order: The Case of the Barolong boo Ratshidi," *American Ethnologist* 7, no. 4 (1980): 639. See also: John Janzen, *The Quest for Therapy in Lower Zaire* (Berkeley: University of California Press, 1978); John Janzen and Steven Feierman, eds., *The Social Basis of Health and Healing in Africa* (Berkeley: University of California Press, 1992); Victor Turner, "The Waters of Life: Some Reflections on Zionist Water Symbolism," in *Religions in Antiquity: Essays in Memory of Erwin Ramsdell Goodenough*, ed. Jacob Neusner (Leiden: Brill, 1968); Tracy Luedke and Harry West, eds., *Borders and Healers: Brokering Therapeutic Resources in Southeast Africa* (Bloomington: Indiana University Press, 2005).

16. Matthew Schoffeleers, "Ritual Healing and Political Acquiescence: The Case of the Zionist Churches in South Africa," *Africa* 60, no. 1 (1991): 4.

17. File S138/22 in the National Archives of Zimbabwe, Harare (hereafter NAZ).

18. Blair Rutherford, "To Find an African Witch: Anthropology, Modernity, and Witch-Finding in Northwest Zimbabwe," *Critique of Anthropology* 19, no. 1 (1999): 98.

19. Munjeri's interviews with Gombera were conducted on February 8 and May 3, 1979. The quotes in this paragraph are taken for the corresponding NAZ file, AOH/49.

20. See: Harri Englund, "Witchcraft, Modernity and the Person: The Morality of Accumulation in Central Malawi," *Critique of Anthropology* 16, no. 2 (1996): 257–79; Peter Geschiere, *The Modernity of Witchcraft: Politics and the Occult in Postcolonial Africa* (Charlottesville: University Press of Virginia, 1997); Harry West, "Sorcery of Construction and Socialist Modernization: Ways of Understanding Power in Postcolonial Mozambique," *American Ethnologist* 28, no. 1 (2001): 119–50. See also Henrietta Moore and Todd Sanders, "Magical Interpretations and Material Realities: An Introduction," in *Magical Interpretations, Material Realities: Modernity, Witchcraft, and the Occult in Postcolonial Africa*, ed. Henrietta Moore and Todd Sanders (New York: Routledge, 2001), 14–18.

21. Isabel Mukonyora, "The Dramatization of Life and Death by Johane Masowe," *Zambezia* 25, no. 2 (1998): 191–207; Isabel Mukonyora, "Marginality and Protest in the Wilderness: The Role of Women in Shaping Masowe Thought Pattern," *Southern African Feminist Review* 4, no. 2 (2000): 1–22; Richard Werbner, "The Argument of Images: Zion to the Wilderness," in *Theoretical Explorations in African Religion*, ed. Wim van Binsbergen and Matthew Schoffeleers (London: Kegan Paul International, 1985), 253–86.

22. Werbner, "The Argument of Images," 251.

23. Johanna Drucker, *The Visible Word: Experimental Typography and Modern Art, 1909–1923* (Chicago: University of Chicago Press, 1994), 14.

24. Although it was never explicitly mentioned, some prophets may forbid the men to carry staffs because spirit mediums use them, too.

25. The fact that bamboo grows near rivers and streams is important to note. As I discuss in more detail later in this chapter, water is an important kind of *muteuro*, and things that are associated with water are often invested with a spiritual significance.

26. McDannell, *Material Christianity*, 8.

27. Keane, "Calvin in the Tropics," 28.

28. I am using the word *pebble* here because this is how the apostolics referred to them. Technically, however, not all the "pebbles" they used were in fact pebbles (rounded stones shaped by flowing water); some were chips of rock, some were little crystalline bits. However, I could not discern a pattern to their use that reflected a conscious differentiation of material properties at this level of specificity.

29. This would not be the case in West Africa, where stones do, in fact, play an important role in religious therapeutics. See Michael Jackson, *Paths Toward a Clearing: Radical Empiricism and Ethnographic Inquiry* (Bloomington: Indiana University Press, 1989). See also Keane, "Calvin in the Tropics," on the ritual use of stones in Sumba, and Richard Parmentier, *The Sacred Remains: Myth, History, and Polity in Belau* (Chicago: University of Chicago Press, 1987), on their use in Belau. As Terence Ranger, in *Voices from the Rocks: Nature, Culture, and History in the Matopos Hills of Zimbabwe* (Bloomington: Indiana University Press, 1999), has shown, rocks are integral to the southern African religious imagination, but more in terms of what they tell us about space and place than in their materiality per se. Bengt Sundkler, *Zulu Zion and Some Swazi Zionists* (London: Oxford University Press, 1976), as well, has written of the Zionist prophet John Mtanti, who, in the mid-1920s, found holy stones in a river with which to build "the new Jerusalem": "They looked like ordinary stones to ordinary people, but Mtanti discovered a message in them, or rather *on* them" (135). The message was a linguistic one; each stone was marked by a letter of the Roman alphabet, to be deciphered as a source of biblical revelation. This case is again different from that of the apostolics. For Mtanti, only particular stones were of interest, and only because they charted a predetermined "supernatural drama" (ibid.), which he was, in effect, reading like the New Testament.

30. In Drucker, *The Visible Word*, 34. The literary critic John Frow uses the example of the pebble to make a similar point about its objective insignificance. He cites a poem by Zbigniew Herbert

that describes the pebble as "filled exactly / with a pebbly meaning" (John Frow, "A Pebble, a Camera, a Man Who Turns into a Telegraph Pole," *Critical Inquiry* 28, no. 1 [2001]: 271) to highlight the more general problem of representing "things" in literature. "This is the paradox of the key fascination with the thingness of things: that things posited in themselves, in their distinctness from intention, representation, figuration, or relation, are thereby filled with an imputed interiority and, in their very lack of meaning, with a 'pebbly meaning' which is at once full and inaccessible" (ibid., 272).

31. Webb Keane, "Money Is No Object: Materiality, Desire, and Modernity in an Indonesian Society," in *The Empire of Things: Regimes of Value and Material Culture*, ed. Fred Myers (Oxford: James Currey, 2001), 87.

32. Gordon Chavanduka, *Traditional Medicine in Zimbabwe* (Harare: University of Zimbabwe Press, 1994), 46.

33. Pamela Reynolds, *Traditional Healers and Childhood in Zimbabwe* (Athens: Ohio University Press, 1996).

34. Joost Fontein, *"Traditional Connoisseurs" of the Past: The Ambiguity of Spirit Mediums and the Performance of the Past in Southern Zimbabwe* (Working Paper of the Centre of African Studies, University of Edinburgh, 2004); Marja Spierenburg, *Strangers, Spirits, and Land Reforms: Conflicts about Land in Dande, Northern Zimbabwe* (Leiden: Brill, 2004).

35. David Lan, *Guns and Rain: Guerrillas and Spirit Mediums in Zimbabwe* (Berkeley: University of California Press, 1985), 55.

36. See Ranger, *Voices from the Rocks*.

37. Michael Gelfand et al., *The Traditional Medical Practitioner in Zimbabwe: His Principles of Practice and Pharmacopoeia* (Gweru: Mambo Press, 1985); Reynolds, *Traditional Healers*.

38. Reynolds, *Traditional Healers*, 158–60.

39. For mediums, see Lan, *Guns and Rain*. For the Mwari cults, see: Ranger, *Voices from the Rocks*; Richard Werbner, "Tswapong Wisdom Divination: Making the Hidden Seen," in his *Ritual Passage, Sacred Journey: The Process and Organization of Religious Movement* (Washington: Smithsonian Institution Press, 1989).

40. Christopher Taylor, *Milk, Honey, and Money: Changing Concepts in Rwandan Healing* (Washington: Smithsonian Institution Press, 1992), 36.

41. Another kind of *muteuro*, which is closely associated with water and which reinforces Judeo-Christian imagery, is reeds. At Juranifiri Santa, the elders tended a patch of water reeds, which were used in healing services for the protection of children. The reeds were not given to the children, but they were asked to pass through the reed patch at certain times of the year, usually before school exams. This was said to "hide" the children from witches and vengeful spirits that might be looking to disrupt their academic progress. In explaining the importance of this *muteuro*, several apostolics drew attention to the story of Moses being hidden from Pharaoh in the bulrushes as a baby in Exodus 3. This was never explicitly remarked upon in the course of the ritual "hidings," but it serves as an example of how biblical knowledge was incorporated into church life (see Engelke, *A Problem of Presence*, 185–99).

42. See NAZ S138/22.

43. Hans Belting, *Likeness and Presence: A History of the Image Before the Era of Art* (Chicago: University of Chicago Press, 1994), 465.

44. Ibid., 465.

45. Aston, *England's Iconoclasts*; Belting, *Likeness and Presence*, 458–90; Joseph Koerner, "The Icon as Iconoclash," in *Iconoclash: Beyond the Image Wars in Science, Religion, and Art*, ed. Bruno Latour and Peter Weibel (Cambridge: MIT Press, 2002), 164–213; John Phillips, *The Reformation of Images: Destruction of Art in England, 1535–1660* (Berkeley: University of California Press, 1973).

46. John Milbank, *The Word Made Strange: Theology, Language, Culture* (Oxford: Blackwell, 1997), 95.

47. Phillips, *The Reformation of Images*, 202. See also Aston, *England's Iconoclasts*, 234–44. It should not be forgotten that Henry VIII's and Edward VI's iconoclasm also benefited the royal treasury: precious metals in the religious art and objects destroyed were melted down and recast, and bishops' lands were confiscated by the crown. (See Phillips, *The Reformation of Images*, 97–100.)

48. Koerner, "The Icon as Iconoclash," 178.

49. Ibid., 179.

50. Hans-Georg Gadamer, *Truth and Method*, 2nd ed., rev. trans. Joel Weinsheimer and Donald Marshall (1960; New York: Continuum, 1989), 165.

51. Ibid., 187.

52. Vincent Crapanzano, *Serving the Word: Literalism in America from the Pulpit to the Bench* (New York: The New Press, 2000), 10.

53. Simon Coleman, "When Silence Isn't Golden: Charismatic Speech and the Limits of Literalism," in *The Limits of Meaning: Case Studies in the Anthropology of Christianity*, ed. Matthew Engelke and Matt Tomlinson (New York: Berghahn, 2006); Susan Harding, *The Book of Jerry Falwell: Fundamentalist Language and Politics* (Princeton, N.J.: Princeton University Press, 2000), 61–82.

54. Crapanzano, *Serving the Word*, 34.

55. Ibid., 59.

56. Ibid., 54.

57. Ibid., 56.

58. Friedrich Schleiermacher, *On Religion: Speeches to Its Cultured Despisers*, trans. J. Oman (1799; New York: Harper & Row, 1958), 91.

59. Ernst Troeltsch, *The Christian Faith*, trans. Garrett E. Paul (1925; Minneapolis: Fortress Press, 1991), 14.

60. Gadamer, *Truth and Method*, 191.

61. Troeltsch, *The Christian Faith*, 15.

62. Ibid., 18.

63. Ibid., 15.

64. Ibid., 30.

65. Ibid., 30–31.

66. Miller, "Materiality," 28.

67. Webb Keane, *Christian Moderns: Freedom and Fetish in the Mission Encounter* (Berkeley: University of California Press, 2007), 10.

68. Daniel Miller, *Material Culture and Mass Consumption* (Oxford: Blackwell, 1987); Miller, "Materiality"; Keane, *Christian Moderns*.

69. Miller, "Materiality," 81.

70. Bill Brown, "Thing Theory," *Critical Inquiry* 28, no. 1 (2001): 5.

71. Ibid., 4.

72. Rowlands, "A Materialist Approach," 80; see also Miller, "Materiality," 16.

Things That Matter: The *Extra Calvinisticum*, the Eucharist, and John Calvin's Unstable Materiality, by Ernst van den Hemel

1. Brian Cummings, *The Literary Culture of the Reformation* (Oxford: Oxford University Press, 2002), 45. In this excellent study, Cummings emphasizes that the Reformation, with its claim to

return to Scripture. was as much about literary truth as about literal truth. The struggle to return to Scripture opened up questions of interpretation that are of great importance to the study of literature. Cummings discusses at length how the sixteenth-century crisis of meaning is connected to the act of writing (and thinking about) literature. See esp. the second part of the prologue ("Words and Things: Montaigne on Language") for an interesting discussion of the tension between language and expression.

2. See Max Weber's famous *The Protestant Ethic and the Spirit of Capitalism.*

3. See Charles Taylor, *Sources of the Self* (Cambridge: Cambridge University Press, 1992), esp. pt. 3, "The Affirmation of Ordinary Life," 211–305.

4. See Louis Dupré, *Passage to Modernity* (Yale: Yale University Press, 1995), 209.

5. For the charge of combining philosophy and theology, see David Andersen, "A Critique of John Calvin's Philosophical Axiom *finitum non capax infiniti," Global Journal of Classical Theology* 3, no. 2 (2002): http://www.trinitysem.edu/journal/andersenv3n2.htm. For these writings as a threat to Calvin's theological system, see E. David Willis's monograph on Calvin's writings on the Eucharist, *Calvin's Catholic Christology* (Leiden: Brill, 1966): "In approaching the so-called extra Calvinisticum one is faced with what is admittedly a potential weakness in Calvin's thought. . . . The so-called extra Calvinisticum . . . has not been sufficiently scrutinized to see if it can indeed bear the weight imposed upon it by the rest of his system" (6).

6. The Marburg Colloquy, cited in Alister McGrath, *Reformation Thought* (Oxford: Blackwell, 1993), 181.

7. One of the clearest formulations of this part of Luther's theology is found in Luther's polemical piece *Das diese Wort Christi "Das ist mein Leib" noch fest stehen, wider die Schwärmgeister,"* in *Martin Luthers Werke: Kritische Gesamtausgabe* (Weimar: Böhlau, 1901), 23:38–320. See also Oswald Bayer, "Luther as an Interpreter of Holy Scripture," in *The Cambridge Companion to Martin Luther,* ed. Donald McKim (Cambridge: Cambridge University Press, 2003), 73–85. For a more general discussion, see Lee Palmer Wendel, *The Eucharist in the Reformation* (Cambridge: Cambridge University Press, 2006).

8. See McGrath, *Reformation Thought,* 180.

9. Cummings, *The Literary Culture of the Reformation,* 24, 25.

10. Ibid.

11. Thomas More, "Responsio ad Lutherum," in *The Complete Works of Saint Thomas More,* vol. 5, ed. John Headley (New Haven, Conn.: Yale University Press, 1969), 240–41. Quoted in Cummings, *The Literary Culture of the Reformation,* 44.

12. Cummings, *The Literary Culture of the Reformation,* 29.

13. Michel de Montaigne, *The Complete Essays* (London: Penguin Books, 1993), 1213.

14. See McGrath, *Reformation Thought,* 181.

15. John Calvin, *Institutes of the Christian Religion,* trans. Henry Beveridge (Grand Rapids, Mich.: William B. Eerdmans Publishing Company, 1989), 4.14.1–2 (p. 492).

16. Ibid.

17. Ibid.; my emphasis.

18. Ibid., 2.6.1 (p. 293); my emphasis. For an excellent and detailed discussion of Calvin's cosmology as the theater of divine glory, see Susan E. Schreiner, *The Theater of His Glory: Nature and the Natural Order in the Thought of John Calvin* (1991; rpt. Grand Rapids, Mich.: Baker Academic, 1995).

19. Calvin, *Institutes of the Christian Religion,* 2.13.4 (p. 414).

20. E. David Willis traces the muddy heritage of the term *extra calvinisticum* back to the debate between the theologians of Giessen and Tübingen. For a history of its use and for the Lutheran background of the resistance against it, see Willis, *Calvin's Catholic Christology,* 11–13.

21. Andersen, "A Critique of John Calvin's Philosophical Axiom *finitum non capax infiniti.*"

22. Ibid.

23. Calvin, *Institutes of the Christian Religion*, 4.17.5 (p. 532).

24. Ibid., 33 (p. 590).

25. Wendel, *The Eucharist in the Reformation*, 163.

26. Calvin, *Institutes of the Christian Religion*, 2.16.2 (p. 435).

27. Paul Helm, *Calvin's Ideas* (Oxford: Oxford University Press, 2004).

28. David C. Steinmetz, "Calvin as an Interpreter of the Bible," in *Calvin and the Bible*, ed. Donald McKim (Cambridge: Cambridge University Press, 2006), 290.

29. Calvin, *Institutes of the Christian Religion*, 4.14.2 (p. 492).

30. Heiko Oberman, *The Dawn of the Reformation* (Grand Rapids, Mich.: William B. Eerdmans Publishing Company, 1991), 255. Oberman devotes pt. 10 of this book to the *extra calvinisticum.* He divides it into four sections: "Etiam extra Ecclesiam," "Etiam extra Coenam," "Etiam extra Carnem," and "Etiam extra Legem." Due to a lack of space, I do not have the time to devote more attention to these sections, although they merit closer scrutiny.

31. Calvin, *Institutes of the Christian Religion*, 1.4.11 (p. 59).

32. John Calvin, *Commentary on Genesis* (Grand Rapids, Mich.: Christian Classics Ethereal Library, 1999), 38; my emphasis.

33. Calvin, *Institutes of the Christian Religion*, 4.17.32 (p. 587).

34. Dupré, *Passage to Modernity*, 209.

From Stone to Flesh: The Case of the Buddha, by Donald S. Lopez, Jr.

1. Clement of Alexandria, *Stromata*, bk. 1, chap. 15.

2. St. John Damascene, *Barlaam and Ioasaph*, trans. G. R. Woodward and H. Mattingly (Cambridge, Harvard University Press, 1983).

3. See John Andrew Boyle, "The Journey of Het'um I, King of Little Armenia to the Great Khan Möngke," *Central Asiatic Journal* 9 (1964): 188–89.

4. *The Book of Ser Marco Polo the Venetian Concerning the Kingdoms and Marvels of the East*, 2 vols., trans. and ed. Sir Henry Yule, 3rd ed., rev. Henri Cordier (1926; New York: AMS, 1986), 2:316–17. See also the extensive notes of Yule and Cordier, 320–30.

5. Francis Xavier, *The Letters and Instructions of Francis Xavier*, trans. and introd. M. Joseph Costelloe, S.J. (St. Louis: The Institute of Jesuit Sources, 1992), 336–37.

6. Robert Knox, *An Historical Relation of Ceylon* (Glasgow: James MacLehose and Sons, 1911), 116.

7. Daniel Defoe, "Confucius," in his *Dictionarium Sacrum Seu Religiosum: A Dictionary of All Religions, Ancient and Modern, Whether Jewish, Pagan, Christian, or Mahometan*, expanded ed. (1704; London: James Knapton, 1723).

8. See Tomoko Masuzawa, *The Invention of World Religions: Or, How European Universalism Was Preserved in the Language of Pluralism* (Chicago: University of Chicago Press, 2005).

9. Abbé de Choisy, *Journal of a Voyage to Siam, 1685–1686*, trans. and introd. Michael Smithies (Kuala Lumpur: Oxford University Press, 1993), 175–76.

10. Alvara Semedo, *The history of that great and renowned monarchy of China wherein all the particular provinces are accurately described, as also the dispositions, manners, learning, lawes, militia, government, and religion of the people: together with the traffick and commodities of that countrey* (London: Printed by E. Tyler for Iohn Crook, 1655), 89.

11. Nicolas Gervaise, *The Natural and Political History of the Kingdom of Siam* [1688], trans. Herbert Stanley O'Neill (Bangkok, 1928), 74–77.

12. Father Fernaõ de Queyroz, *The Temporal and Spiritual Conquest of Ceylon,* trans. Father S. G. Perera (Colombo, 1930), 141.

13. On this notion of "demonic plagiarism," see Donald S. Lopez, Jr., *Prisoners of Shangri-La: Tibetan Buddhism and the West* (Chicago: University of Chicago Press, 1998), 27–28.

14. Engelbert Kaempfer, THE HISTORY OF JAPAN, *Giving an Account of the Ancient and Present* STATE *and* GOVERNMENT *of that* EMPIRE; *Of Its Temples, Palaces, Castles and other Buildings; Of Its Metals, Minerals, Trees, Plants, Animals, Birds and Fishes; Of the Chronology and Succession of the* EMPERORS. *Ecclesiastical and Secular; Of the Original Descent, Religions, Customs, and Manufactures of the natives, and of their Trade and Commerce with the Dutch and the Chinese. Together with a Description of the Kingdom of Siam,* trans. J. G. Scheuchzer (London: 1727), 1:35–37.

15. Edward Moor (1771–1848), *The Hindu Pantheon* (1810; New York: Garland Publishing, 1984), 231–32.

16. Jean Pierre Abel-Rémusat, "Sur quelques épithètes descriptives de Bouddha qui font voir que Bouddha n'appartenait pas a la race nègre," in his *Mélanges Asiatiques* (Paris: Librarie Orientale de Dondey-Dupré Père et Fils, 1825), 100–28.

17. Eugène Burnouf, *Introduction à l'histoire du Buddhisme indien* (Paris: Imprimerie Royale, 1844), 152–53. Translation by Katia Buffetrille and Donald Lopez. For a translation of the full text, see Eugène Burnouf, *Introduction to the History of Indian Buddhism,* trans. Katia Buffetrille and Donald S. Lopez, Jr. (Chicago: University of Chicago Press, 2009).

Rhetoric of the Heart: Figuring the Body in Devotion to the Sacred Heart of Jesus, by David Morgan

1. *The Autobiography of St. Margaret Mary Alacoque,* trans. The Sisters of the Visitation (Rockford, Ill.: TAN Books and Publishers, 1986). The French original, *Vie de Sainte Marguerite-Marie écrite par elle-même,* appears in Sainte Marguerite-Marie, *Oeuvres choisies* (Paray-Le-Monial: Monastère de la Visitation Sainte-Marie, 1962), 1–119.

2. On the family's opposition, see A. Hamon, *Histoire de la dévotion au Sacré Coeur,* 5 vols. (Paris: Gabriel Beauchesne, 1923), 1:49–53.

3. Alacoque, *Autobiography,* 25.

4. Ibid., 40.

5. Ibid., 41.

6. Ibid., 52.

7. Ibid., 53.

8. Ibid., 89–90.

9. Ibid., 59.

10. Ibid., 67.

11. Ibid., 82.

12. The passage is expunged from the English translation, *Autobiography,* 83–84. The original French can be found in *Vie,* 73.

13. Alacoque, *Autobiography,* 106.

14. Letter of Francis de Sales to Jeanne de Chantal, June 10, 1611, quoted at La Dévotion au Sacré-Coeur, www.spiritualite-chretienne.com/s_coeur/chrono_d1.html.

15. Jean Eudes, "Le divin Coeur de Jésus," in *Oeuvres choisies de Saint Jean Eudes* (Paris: P. Lethielleux, 1937), 9–10.

16. Alacoque, *Autobiography*, 108.

17. For a description of one of the earliest images of the heart emblem, which clearly informed the version reproduced here in Figure 1, see *The Letters of St. Margaret Mary Alacoque* (Rockford, Ill.: TAN Books and Publishers, Inc., 1997), 72–73 and 275n.26.

18. *The Letters of St. Margaret Mary Alacoque* (Rockford, Ill.: TAN Books and Publishers, Inc., 1997), 231.

19. Ibid., 221.

20. See, e.g., St. Louis Marie Grignon de Montfort, "True Devotion to the Blessed Virgin," in *God Alone: The Collected Writings of St. Louis Marie de Montfort* (Bay Shore, N.Y.: Montfort Publications, 1988), 296: "God the Son imparted to his mother all that he gained by his life and death, namely, his infinite merits and his eminent virtues. He made her the treasurer of all his Father had given him as heritage." The book was written sometime between 1710 and 1715.

21. For her account of refusing to eat and vomiting after meals, see Alacoque, *Autobiography*, 89; on self-mutilations, see 97, 115.

22. Alacoque, *Letters*, 103.

23. For a discussion of the term's lineage in anthropology and the study of religion, see Tomoko Masuzawa, "Troubles with Materiality: The Ghost of Fetishism in the Nineteenth Century," in *Religion: Beyond a Concept*, ed. Hent de Vries (New York: Fordham University Press, 2008), 647–67.

24. See William Pietz, "Fetish," in *Critical Terms for Art History*, ed. Robert S. Nelson and Richard Shiff (Chicago: University of Chicago Press, 1996), 197–207.

25. Alacoque, *Autobiography*, 105.

26. Ibid., 15.

27. See Alacoque, *Letters*, 67, 70–71, 193, 230.

28. I have considered the commemorative aspects of the imagery in David Morgan, "The Sacred Heart of Jesus: The Visual Evolution of a Devotion," *Meertens Ethnology* 6 (Amsterdam: Meertens Institute and Amsterdam University Press, 2007).

29. Important studies of Jansenism include: Dale K. Van Kley, *The Jansenists and the Expulsion of the Jesuits from France, 1757–1765* (New Haven, Conn.: Yale University Press, 1975); Henry Phillips, *Church and Culture in Seventeenth-Century France* (Cambridge: Cambridge University Press, 1997); Dale K. Van Kley, *The Religious Origins of the French Revolution: From Calvin to the Civil Constitution, 1560–1791* (New Haven, Conn.: Yale University Press, 1996); and John McManners, *Church and Society in Eighteenth-Century France*, 2 vols. (Oxford: Oxford University Press, 1998), esp. 2:345–69.

30. Quoted in Charles A. Bolton, *Church Reform in Eighteenth-Century Italy (The Synod of Pistoia, 1786)* (The Hague: Martinus Nijhoff, 1969), 10–11; my emphasis.

31. Father Joseph de Gallifet, *The Adorable Heart of Jesus* (Philadelphia: Messenger of the Sacred Heart, 1890), 50–51. This is an English translation of the third French edition (Nancy, 1745) of the original Latin work: Joseph de Gallifet, *De cultu Sacrosancti Cordis Dei ac Domini nostri Jesus Christi* (Rome: Joannem Mariam Salviorii, 1726). The first French edition was *L'excellence de la devotion au Coeur adorable de Jésus-Christ* (Nancy: Veuve Baltasard, 1733).

32. Gallifet, *The Adorable Heart of Jesus*, 65–67.

33. Ibid., 66.

34. Ibid., 68.

35. "The Devotion to the Sacred Heart: Historical Sketch," *The Messenger of The Sacred Heart of Jesus* 5, no. 2 (February 1870): 67–79; referred to hereafter as *Messenger*. This article drew from the

work of an English Jesuit, the Rev. George Tickell, *The Life of Blessed Margaret Mary, with Some Account of the Devotion to the Sacred Heart* (London: Burns, Oates, 1869).

36. Hamon, *Histoire*, 4:44; Jon L. Seydl, "Contesting the Sacred Heart of Jesus in Late Eighteenth-Century Rome," in *Roman Bodies: Antiquity to the Eighteenth Century*, ed. Andrew Hopkins and Maria Wyke (London: The British School in Rome, 2005), 218.

37. Alphonsus de Ligouri, "Novena to the Sacred Heart," in *Selected Writings*, ed. Frederick M. Jones (New York: Paulist Press, 1999), 223.

38. Ibid.

39. Hamon, *Histoire*, 4:40.

40. Ibid., 45.

41. Ibid., 48.

42. Ibid., 74; for his discussion of saints on the heart of Jesus, see 114–60.

43. Gallifet, *The Adorable Heart of Jesus*, 22; Hamon, *Histoire*, 4:59.

44. Seydl, "Contesting the Sacred Heart of Jesus," 215–27.

45. Ibid., 221.

46. Gallifet, *The Adorable Heart of Jesus*, 48.

47. Ibid., 44.

48. Seydl, "Contesting the Sacred Heart of Jesus," 224.

49. *Brownson's Quarterly Review* 23 (July 1874): 421–24. His notice of books on the devotion was reprinted in *The Works of Orestes A. Brownson*, ed. Henry F. Brownson, 20 vols. (Detroit: H. F. Brownson, 1887), 20:418–20.

50. Brownson, *Works*, 20:419; my emphasis.

51. Ibid.; Rev. Thomas S. Preston, *Lectures upon the Devotion to the Most Sacred Heart of Jesus Christ* (no publisher, 1874).

52. Brownson, *Works*, 20:420.

53. Ibid., 415.

54. Ibid.

55. Ibid., 417.

56. Ibid., 434.

57. *Messenger* 5, no. 2 (February 1870): 76.

58. Alacoque, *Letters*, 65.

59. For a discussion of the campaign, which continued into the twentieth century in Europe and America, see J. V. Bainvel, *Devotion to the Sacred Heart of Jesus: The Doctrine and Its History*, trans. E. Leahy, ed. Rev. George O'Neill (New York: Benziger Brothers, [1924]), 328–33.

60. Leo XIII, "Annum sacrum," May 25, 1899.

61. The classic discussion is John of Damascus, *Three Treatises on the Divine Images*, trans. Andrew Louth (Crestwood, N.Y.: St. Vladimir's Seminary Press, 2003), who quotes Basil the Great: "For the honor given to the image passes to the archetype" (35).

62. Pope Paul VI, "Investigabiles divitias Christi," February 6, 1965: "In the first place we desire that the Sacred Heart of Jesus, whose greatest gift is the Eucharist, receive stronger devotion through participation in the august sacrament. . . . May it be valued by everyone and approved the true form of piety, which in our time, especially as set down by the Second Vatican Council, must be rendered to Christ Jesus, the king and center of all hearts, who is the head of the body, the Church, the beginning, the first born from the dead, that in everything he might be first (Colossians 1:18)."

63. Pius XII, "Haurietis aquas," May 15, 1956, para. 98.

64. Ibid., para. 23 and 52.

65. Ibid., para. 22; my emphasis.

66. Ibid., para. 101.

67. Ibid., para. 103.

68. John of Damascus, *Three Treatises*, 25; my emphasis.

69. Pius XII, "Haurietis aquas," para. 54.

70. Ibid., para. 104. Two thick volumes of theological reflection on the Sacred Heart and Pius XII's encyclical appeared shortly after the letter's publication: *Cor Jesu Commentationes Litteras Encyclicas PII PP. XII "Haurietis Aquas,"* 2 vols., ed. Augustinus Bea, Hugo Rahner, Henri Rondet, and Friedrich Schwendimann (Rome: Herder, 1959).

71. Pope John Paul II, "His Heart Is the Heart of the Church," June 11, 1999.

Idolatry: Nietzsche, Blake, and Poussin, by W. J. T. Mitchell

NOTE: This chapter first appeared as "Idolatry: Nietzsche, Blake, and Poussin," by W. J. T. Mitchell, in *Idol Anxiety*, ed. Josh Ellenbogen and Aaron Tugendhaft (Stanford, Calif.: Stanford University Press, 2011), 56–73. Copyright © by the Board of Trustees of the Leland Stanford Jr. University.

1. Denounced, of course, as idols by the Taliban. It is important to note, however, that a Taliban spokesman who toured the United States prior to the destruction of the Buddhas claimed that the statues would be destroyed, not because there was any danger of their being used as religious idols, but (on the contrary) because they had become secular idols for the West, which was expressing interest in pouring millions of dollars into Afghanistan for their preservation. The Taliban blew up the "idols," in other words, precisely because the West cared so much about them.

2. See the remarks by General William Boykin, undersecretary of defense during Donald Rumsfeld's tenure as secretary of defense. For a discussion of the response to Bush's declaration of a "crusade" of "good against evil," see (among numerous commentaries) Peter Ford's piece in the *Christian Science Monitor*, September 19, 2001: "Europe Cringes at Bush 'Crusade' Against Terrorists."

3. Richard Neer, "Poussin and the Ethics of Imitation," in *Memoirs of the American Academy in Rome*, ed. Vernon Hyde Minor, vols. 51–52 (2006–7): 297–344.

4. Revised Standard Version.

5. Walter Benjamin, "Critique of Violence," in *Reflections*, ed. Peter Demetz, trans. Edmund Jephcott (New York, 1978), 298.

6. The best study of this sort is Avishai Margalit and Moshe Halbertal, *Idolatry*, trans. N. Goldblum (Cambridge: Harvard University Press, 1992), which surveys the major themes of idolatry and iconoclasm from the rabbinical commentators through the history of Western philosophy.

7. For a fuller discussion of the concept of "secondary belief," see "The Surplus Value of Images," chap. 4 of my *What Do Pictures Want? The Lives and Loves of Images* (Chicago: University of Chicago Press, 2005).

8. Margalit and Halbertal, *Idolatry*, 5.

9. See my "Holy Landscape: Israel, Palestine, and the American Wilderness," in my *Landscape and Power*, 2nd ed. (Chicago: University of Chicago Press, 2002), 261–90.

10. As Halbertal and Margalit note, "the prophets speak of protective treaties with Egypt and Assyria as the worship of other gods" (*Idolatry*, 5).

11. The second commandment makes explicit the mandate of collective punishment: "You shall not bow down to them or serve them; for I The Lord your God am a jealous God, visiting the

iniquity of the fathers upon the children to the third and the fourth generation" (Revised Standard Version).

12. See my "The Rhetoric of Iconoclasm: Marxism, Ideology, and Fetishism," chap. 6 of my *Iconology: Image, Text, Ideology* (Chicago: University of Chicago Press, 1986). For a survey of the sublimated, immaterialist concepts of idolatry, see Margalit and Halbertal, *Idolatry.*

13. Friedrich Nietzsche, *Thus Spake Zarathustra*, in *The Portable Nietzsche*, ed. Walter Kaufmann (New York, 1954), 317.

14. Ibid., 315.

15. Ibid., 324–25.

16. Ibid., 325.

17. *Twilight of the Idols*, in *Portable Nietzsche*, 466.

18. Giorgio Vasari, *The Lives of the Artists* (New York, 1991), preface.

19. *The Marriage of Heaven and Hell*, pl. 11, in *The Poetry and Prose of William Blake*, ed. David V. Erdman (Garden City, N.Y.: Doubleday, 1970), 37.

20. See W Robertson Smith, *The Religion of the Semites: The Fundamental Institutions* (1889; rpt. New York: Schocken, 1972), 93: "In semitic religion the relation of the gods to particular places . . . is usually expressed by the title Baal."

21. Burke is, of course, speaking here of the idols of *Native* Americans in this passage. Edmund Burke, *A Philosophical Enquiry into the Origin of Our Ideas of the Sublime and Beautiful* (1757), ed. James T. Boulton (South Bend, Ind.: University of Notre Dame Press, 1968), 59. See my discussion in "Eye and Ear: Edmund Burke and the Politics of Sensibility," in *Iconology*, chap. 5, 130.

22. Immanuel Kant, *Critique of Judgment*, trans. J. H. Bernard (New York, 1951), 115.

23. Neer, "Poussin and the Ethics of Imitation," 297.

24. Ibid., 298.

25. Ibid., 299.

26. Ibid., 312.

27. Ibid.

28. Ibid.

29. Ibid., 309.

30. Ibid., 313.

31. Ibid., 318.

32. This shift of the question from the meaning of the painting to "what it wants" is, of course, the procedure I have advocated in *What Do Pictures Want?*

33. It is hard to ignore the fact that Ashdod is located in the short space of land (about twenty miles) between Tel Aviv and Gaza. During the invasion of Gaza in January 2009, it suffered rocket attacks from the Palestinians in Gaza.

34. See Nadav Shragal, "An Amalek in Our Times?" *Haaretz*, January 21, 2009.

35. Alan Cowell, "Gaza Children Found with Mothers' Corpses," *New York Times*, January 8, 2009.

36. In a fuller exposition, I would explore the relation between the dogmatic historicism of art history, its assumption of a proper "horizon of meaning," and the closely related problems of anachronism and intentionalism. Richard Wollheim is among the most prominent supporters of a strict historical psychologizing of pictorial meaning, which in his view "always rests upon a state of mind of the artist, and the way this leads him to work, and the experience that the product of this work brings about in the mind of a suitably informed and sensitive spectator," *Painting as an Art* (Princeton, N.J.: Princeton University Press, 1987), 188. See my forthcoming essay, "The Future of the Image," for a discussion of the inevitability of anachronism and unintentional meaning in

pictures; see also Georges Didi-Huberman, "The History of Art Within the Limits of Its Simple Practice," in *Confronting Images: Questioning the Limits of a Certain History of Art*, trans. John Goodman (University Park: Pennsylvania State University Press, 2005), 12–52: "Anachronism is not, in history, something that must be absolutely banished—in the end, this is no more than a fantasy or an ideal of equivalence—but rather something that must be negotiated, debated, and perhaps even turned to advantage" (41). We should note as well that, when Wollheim asks himself, "Where have I seen this face before?" in Poussin's *Rinaldo and Armida*, his answer is—of all things—Courbet! See *Painting as an Art*, 195.

37. See Michel Foucault, *The Order of Things* (New York, 1994), 10, and my discussion in *Picture Theory: Essays on Verbal and Visual Representation* (Chicago: University of Chicago Press, 1994).

38. The Israelites dancing around the Golden Calf, like the Palestinians in terror at the plague, are both depicted as classical figures—as Greeks, in other words. As it happens, contemporary archeological research suggests that the Philistines were, in fact, Myceneans who migrated from Greece down to Palestine. This fact gives the historical dimension of Poussin's painting an uncanny accuracy in relation to modern historical knowledge that he could not have known. Thanks to Richard Neer for this factoid.

39. Émile Durkheim, *The Elementary Forms of Religious Life*, trans. Karen Fields (New York, 1995). The totem "expresses and symbolizes two different kinds of things. From one point of view, it is the outward and visible form of what I have called the totemic principle or god; and from another, it is also the symbol of a particular society that is called the clan. . . . God and society are one and the same" (208).

"Has this thing appeared again tonight?": Deus ex Machina and Other Theatrical Interventions of the Supernatural, by Freddie Rokem

1. The handbook by Karl Beckson and Artur Ganz, written a few years after Beckett published *Waiting for Godot*, sweepingly brushes aside the deus ex machina as a more or less nonexistent phenomenon in the modern theater, claiming that "Serious modern writers avoid the *deus ex machina*, though it has sometimes been used in comedy" (Karl Beckson and Artur Ganz, *A Reader's Guide to Literary Terms* [London: Thames and Hudson, 1961], 48).

2. Friedrich Nietzsche, *The Gay Science*, trans. Walter Kaufmann (New York: Random House, 1974), 108, 167.

3. In my books *Performing History: Theatrical Representations of the Past in Contemporary Theatre* (Iowa City: University of Iowa Press, 2000) and *Philosophers and Thespians: Thinking Performance* (Stanford, Calif.: Stanford University Press, 2010), I analyze the relations between theater/performance and the discursive practices of history and philosophy, respectively.

4. Isak was played by one of Bergman's oldest friends, the Jewish actor Erland Josephson, who created much of the Isak character himself.

5. Ingmar Bergman, *Fanny och Alexander* (Stockholm: Månpocket, 1984), 201; my translation.

6. Aristotle, "On the Art of Poetry," in *Classical Literary Criticism*, trans. and introd. T. S. Dorssch (Harmondsworth: Penguin Books, 1965), chap. 15, 52.

7. All citations from Shakespeare are from *Hamlet, Prince of Denmark*, The New Cambridge Shakespeare (Cambridge Cambridge University Press 1989); line numbers appear in the text.

8. For additional interpretations and contextualizations of Hamlet's last words, see chap. 2 of my *Philosophers and Thespians*.

9. Jürgen Habermas, "Ernst Bloch—A Marxist Romantic," *Salmagundi* 10–11 (Fall 1969–Winter 1970): 313.

10. August Strindberg, Preface to *A Dream Play*, in *Six Plays of Strindberg*, trans. Elizabeth Sprigge (New York: Doubleday, 1955), 193.

11. Translations of *A Dream* Play are taken from ibid. Page references are given in the text.

12. This translation is based on the Hebrew text used by the Habimah Theater, which is a transcription of a phonographic recording of their 1922 production (CBS Records, 1952). It differs at several points from the recently published Hebrew version, *Ha-Dybbuk: Bein Shnei Olamot*, trans. Chaim Nachman Bialik (Tel Aviv: Or-Am, 1983), as well as from the English translation of this passage in *The Dybbuk*, published in *The Great Jewish Plays*, trans. Joseph C. Landis (New York: Avon Books, 1966).

Portraits That Matter: King Chulalongkorn Objects and the Sacred World of Thai-ness, by Irene Stengs

1. Birgit Meyer, "'There is a spirit in that image': Mass-Produced Jesus Pictures and Protestant-Pentecostal Animation in Ghana," in this volume; David Morgan, *The Sacred Gaze: Religious Visual Culture in Theory and Practice* (Berkeley: University of California Press, 2005); Christopher Pinney, "Piercing the Skin of the Idol," in *Beyond Aesthetics: Art and the Technologies of Enchantment*, ed. Christopher Pinney and Nicolas Thomas (Oxford: Berg, 2001), 157–80.

2. W. J. T. Mitchell, *What Do Pictures Want? The Lives and Loves of Images* (Chicago: University of Chicago Press, 2005), 85–86.

3. See also Meyer, "'There is a spirit in that image.'"

4. The material for this chapter was collected in Thailand between September 1996 and December 1997, and in October and November 1998. That research was funded by the Program on Globalisation and the Construction of Communal Identities, of the Netherlands Foundation for the Advancement of Tropical Research (WOTRO). I have summarized the ethnographic material from my earlier publications, especially Irene Stengs, "Modern Thai Encounters with the Sublime: The Powerful Presence of a Great King of Siam Through His Portraits," *Material Religion* 4, no. 2 (2008): 160–71, and Irene Stengs, *Worshipping the Great Modernizer: King Chulalongkorn, Patron Saint of the Thai Middle Class* (Singapore: NUS Press, 2009). The interpretation developed here has been expanded and adapted for the purpose of the present publication.

5. See Richard H. Roberts, "Introduction: Religion and Capitalism—A New Convergence?" in *Religion and the Transformations of Capitalism*, ed. Richard H. Roberts (London: Routledge, 1995), 1–18; Jean Comaroff and John. L. Comaroff, "Millennial Capitalism: First Thoughts on a Second Coming," in *Millennial Capitalism and the Culture of Neoliberalism*, ed. Jean Comaroff and John L. Comaroff (Durham, N.C.: Duke University Press, 2001), 1–56.

6. See Paul Connerton, *How Societies Remember* (Cambridge: Cambridge University Press, 1989), 36–40.

7. See Prince Damrong Ratchanuphap, *Sadet praphat ton, phra niphon somdet krom phraya damrong ratchanuphap* [Touring the Countryside, Writings of Prince Damrong] (1912; Bangkok: Sinlapabannakan, 1976).

8. Michael Aung-Thwin, *Pagan: The Origins of Modern Burma* (Honolulu: University of Hawai'i Press, 1985); Prince Dhani, "The Old Siamese Conception of the Monarchy," *Journal of the Siam Society* 36, no. 2 (1946): 91–106; Charles F. Keyes, "Millennialism, Theravada Buddhism and Thai

Society," *Journal of Asian Studies* 36, no. 2 (1977): 283–302; Stanley J. Tambiah, *World Conqueror and World Renouncer: A Study of Buddhism and Polity in Thailand Against a Historical Background* (Cambridge: Cambridge University Press, 1977); Stanley J. Tambiah, *Culture, Thought, and Social Action: An Anthropological Perspective* (Cambridge: Harvard University Press, 1985).

9. See Maurizio Peleggi, *Lords of Things: The Fashioning of the Siamese Monarchy's Modern Image* (Honolulu: University of Hawai'i Press, 2002), for a detailed study and interpretation of the conscious use of modern Western practices, techniques, and objects by the Siamese monarchy (in particular during the reign of King Chulalongkorn) in shaping and refashioning the royal elite's image and identity.

10. Quaritch H. G. Wales, *Siamese State Ceremonies: Their History and Function (with Supplementary Notes)* (1931; Richmond, Surrey: Curzon Press, 1992), 173.

11. See Birgit Meyer, "Religious Sensations: Why Media, Aesthetics, and Power Matter in the Study of Contemporary Religion," in *Religion: Beyond a Concept*, ed. Hent de Vries (New York: Fordham University Press, 2008), 708.

12. See Stengs, "Modern Thai Encounters with the Sublime."

13. Upon her arrival, the queen receives a garland (*phuangmalai*) from those awaiting her. King Chulalongkorn is commemorated on October 23 (Chulalongkorn Day), the day the king died. The most important commemorative ritual is the presentation of wreaths (*phuangmala*) at the equestrian statue in the early morning. For more elaborate descriptions and interpretations of Chulalongkorn Day celebrations, see Stengs, *Worshipping*, 127–75.

14. Apart from the title, the book contains no further English text. I interpret the regular appearance of English words on King Chulalongkorn objects as reflecting the king's association with modernity.

15. From the English "locket." Like any Thai noun, *lokket* denotes both the singular and the plural.

16. Bun beautified the *lokket* in a way strongly reminiscent of how he beautifies himself. When I became acquainted with him, he had just had his third facial plastic surgery (costing fifty thousand baht). As with the coin, a little beautification is added now and again, but the project as a whole is never complete.

17. *Phra phuttha chao luang* is another title used to address King Chulalongkorn or to speak about him. This title, which literally means "Royal Buddha," reflects the idea that a Buddhist King is a future Buddha. Although every Thai or Siamese king is a *phra phuttha chao luang*, at present the title specifically refers to King Chulalongkorn. See Walter Skrobanek, *Buddhistische Politik in Thailand (mit besonderer Berücksichtigung des heterodoxen Messianismus)* (Wiesbaden: Franz Steiner, 1976), 23.

18. Having ascended the throne in June 1988, King Bhumibol Adulyadej has now been the longest-ruling monarch in Thai history. He is presently also the world's longest-ruling living monarch.

19. Whereas wearing powerful amulets and collecting them are typical male interests (see Stanley J. Tambiah, *The Buddhist Saints of the Forest and the Cult of Amulets: A Study in Charisma, Hagiography, Sectarianism and Millennial Buddhism* (1984; Cambridge: Cambridge University Press, 1988), the wearing and beautifying of King Chulalongkorn *lokket* have become particularly popular pursuits among middle-class women. The *lokket* is an opportunity to wear a jewel and an amulet at the same time. For a more elaborate analysis of the gender dimensions of the King Chulalongkorn cult, see Stengs, *Worshipping*, 172–75.

20. Ibid.

21. Many temples have a modest "temple shop," which is often run by lay people actively involved with the temple. Such shops sell statuettes, holy water, candles, incense, and amulets. I use

"religious shops" to refer to independent shops run by lay owners in town. These shops sell a large variety of religious or temple necessities, such as statues, temple decorations, monks' robes, and Buddhist flags, as well as ordinary household utensils needed by the temple and the monks. The customers, usually lay people, buy the articles as offerings to the temples.

22. Nonetheless, Sombun sent me a quite common New Year's greeting card in Western design in 1998. He had already warned me in advance that, due to the economic crisis, they could not afford to send the more expensive King Chulalongkorn cards.

23. See Alfred Gell, *Art and Agency: An Anthropological Theory* (Oxford: Oxford University Press, 1998), 18–22.

24. Cf. Mitchell, *What Do Pictures Want?*

25. Pink is the color related to Tuesday, the king's day of birth, rather than a historically confirmed favorite of his. The Western attributes relate to the king's modernity.

26. This transfer of the king's charismatic power into the objects at the square can be compared with the sacralization of objects (*pluk sek*) in consecration ceremonies (*phithi pluk sek, phutthaphisek*) at temples. See Nithi Aeusrivongse, "Lathi phithi sadet pho ro ha," [The Cult of King Rama the Fifth], *Sinlapa Watthanatham chabap phiset* [special edition of Art and Culture Magazine], Matichon, August 1993, 27. In such ceremonies, people also bring their images (whether Buddhist amulets, statuettes of monks, or portraits of Thai kings) to be sacralized and charged with beneficial power. The fundamental difference, though, is that in the King Chulalongkorn cult people do not depend on expert intermediaries, such as monks (ibid.).

27. See Daniel Miller, *Material Culture and Mass Consumption* (Oxford: Blackwell, 1987).

28. I owe the inspiration for this line of thought to Maartje Hoogstcyns, *Artefact Mens: Een interdisciplinair onderzoek naar het debat over materialiteit binnen de material culture studies* (Alphen aan de Maas: Uitgeverij, 2008).

29. For reasons of privacy, the name of the temple is fictitious.

30. The exception is when such statues have been commissioned by the king himself, as, for instance. the King Chulalongkorn statue in the Marble Temple (Wat Benchamabophit) in Bangkok.

31. Webb Keane, "On the Materiality of Religion," *Material Religion* 4, no. 2 (2008): 230–31.

32. See Walter Irvine, "Decline of Village Spirit Cults and Growth of Urban Spirit Mediumship: The Persistence of Spirit Beliefs, the Position of Women and Modernization," *Mankind* 14, no. 4 (1984): 315–24; Rosalind C. Morris, *In the Place of Origins: Modernity and Its Mediums in Northern Thailand* (Durham, N.C.: Duke University Press, 2000); Gehan Wijeyewardene, *Place and Emotion in Northern Thai Ritual Behaviour* (Bangkok: Pandora, 1986).

33. I interpret Jill's depiction of the abbot as a womanizer as referring only to his looks, particularly the wrinkles he shares with the king.

34. To put this in the proper context, the temple owns an enormous number of King Chulalongkorn portraits.

35. Keane, "On the Materiality of Religion," 230.

36. In addition to miniature plaster copies of the statue produced and sold by the temple, and in contradiction to the abbot's original intention to create only a single, unique statue, two exact copies were made. This shows how everything having power exerts a pressure to be copied.

Material Mobility Versus Concentric Cosmology in the *Sukkah*: The House of the Wandering Jew or a Ubiquitous Temple? by Galit Hasan-Rokem

NOTE: This chapter was initially written for presentation at the conference Religion and Things, organized by Birgit Meyer and Dick Houtman at University of Amsterdam in June 2007. I thank the organizers for the invitation and the NWO and the programme committee of The Future of the Religious Past for wonderful cooperation, especially Hent de Vries and Jan Willem van Henten. Since then I have had the opportunity to share it with colleagues and wider audiences at the Department of Classical, Near Eastern, and Religious Studies at the University of British Columbia (thanks to Professor Robert Daum), as the Max and Gianna Glassman Israel Exchange Scholar at the University of Toronto in November 2007 (thanks to Professors Derek Penslar and Hindy Najman), and last and not least as Diller Family Professor at the Folklore Program of the Department of Anthropology (thanks to Professor Charles L. Briggs) and the Center of Middle East Studies (thanks to Professors Nezar Elsayyad and Emily Gottreich) at the University of California, Berkeley, my longtime academic haven in the United States, where I have benefited from the wisdom and generosity of too many to mention. I thank especially those friends, colleagues, and relatives who read versions of the chapter and contributed substantially from their knowledge and wisdom, my dear *ushpizin* in the *Sukkah* (alphabetically): Daniel Boyarin, Ron Hendel, Dale Loepp, Na'ama Rokem, Ariel Rokem, Ishay Rosen-Zvi, Hagar Salamon, Dani Schrire, Sasha Senderovich, Avigdor Shinan, Dina Stein, Haim Weiss, Israel J. Yuval. Moran Banit, Miki Joelson, and Yaniv Messinger are thanked for research assistance. All errors and folly remain mine.

1. Peter Cole, ed. and trans., *The Dream of the Poem: Hebrew Poetry from Muslim and Christian Spain 950–1492* (Princeton, N.J.: Princeton University Press 2007), 164.

2. The names *Al-Andalus* and *Castile* encode to this day a historical memory as well as a poetic fantasy of a fruitful, although at times in reality uneasy, cultural coexistence of Muslims, Jews, and Christians. A pertinent question one might put to that historical past—though it lies beyond the scope of this chapter—could be: Which of the three major groups there was in exile, and which not?

3. For the Jewish diaspora, see Menahem Stern, "The Jewish Diaspora," in *The Jewish People in the First Century*, ed. Shmuel Safrai and Menahem Stern (Assen: Van Gorcum, 1974), 1:117–83. See also: Isaiah M. Gafni, "Punishment, Blessing or Mission—Jewish Dispersion in the Second Temple and Talmudic Period" (Hebrew), in *The Jews in the Hellenistic-Roman World: Studies in Memory of Menahem Stern*, ed. Isaiah M. Gafni, Aharon Oppenheimer, Daniel R. Scwhartz (Jerusalem: The Zalman Shazar Center for Jewish History, 1996), 229–50; another version, titled "Jewish Dispersion in the Second Temple and Talmudic Periods: Punishment, Blessing or Universal Mission?" has appeared in Isaiah M. Gafni, *Land, Center and Diaspora: Jewish Constructs in Late Antiquity* (Sheffield: Sheffield Academic Press, 1997), 19–40. Gafni's tripartite classification tacitly exposes the lack of correlation between dispersion and suffering, since, as he mentions on p. 33, it is the Jews in Palestine who suffer the most, i.e., under the Trajanic and Hadrianic persecutions.

For other diasporas, see Paul Gilroy, *The Black Atlantic: Modernity and Double Consciousness* (Cambridge: Harvard University Press, 1993); Ronald Segal, *The Black Diaspora: Five Centuries of the Black Experience Outside Africa* (New York: Farrar, Straus and Giroux, 1995); Dominic Thomas, *Black France: Colonialism, Immigration, and Transnationalism* (Bloomington: Indiana University Press, 2006); Rajagopalan Radhakhrishnan, *Diasporic Mediations: Between Home and Location* (Minneapolis: University of Minnesota Press, 1996). Kevin Kenny observes, in "Diaspora and Comparison: The Global Irish as a Case Study," *Journal of American History* 90, no. 1 (2003): 141: "If the semantic span of diaspora in its classical sense was arguably too narrow, it has in recent years become remarkably broad."

4. Michel de Certeau, *The Practice of Everyday Life*, trans. Steven Randall (Berkeley: University of California Press, 1984), 91–110.

5. Among the studies that have inspired my work, some of which will be quoted later in this chapter, I wish at this point to acknowledge the earlier achievements and thoughts of scholars and

beloved friends, Barbara Kirshenblatt-Gimblett, "Spaces of Dispersal," *Cultural Anthropology* 9, no. 3 (1994): 339–44, and Daniel Boyarin and Jonathan Boyarin, *Powers of Diaspora: Two Essays on the Relevance of Jewish Culture* (Minneapolis: University of Minnesota Press, 2002), without, however, fully accepting their programmatic visions.

6. James Clifford, *Routes: Travel and Translation in the Late Twentieth Century* (Cambridge: Harvard University Press, 1997), 264. I am aware of the distinctions that could be made between exile and diaspora but choose not to delve into them here. Clifford is right about the relatively less central status of the legend of the Wandering Jew in the non-Christian world, although he does not acknowledge the Christian source of the legend (ibid., 274).

7. Barbara Kirshenblatt-Gimblett, *Destination Culture: Tourism, Museums, and Heritage* (Berkeley: University of California Press, 1998).

8. Galit Hasan-Rokem, "Ex oriente fluxus: The Wandering Jew—Oriental Crossings of the Paths of Europe," in *L'orient dans l'histoire religieuse de l'Europe*, ed. Mohammad Ali Amir-Moezzi and John Scheid (Turnhout, Belgium: Brepols, 2000), 153–64; Galit Hasan-Rokem, "L'image du Juif errant et la construction de l'identité européenne," in *Le Juif errant—un témoin du temps*, ed. Laurence Sigal-Klagsblad and Richard I. Cohen (Paris: Musée d'art et d'histoire du Judaïsme & Adam Biro, 2001), 45–53; Galit Hasan-Rokem, "Contemporary Perspectives on Tradition: Moving On with the Wandering Jew," *Konstellationen: über Geschichte, Erfahrung und Erkenntnis*, ed. N. Berg, O. Kamil, and M. Kirchhoff (Göttingen: Vandenhoeck & Ruprecht 2011), 309–31.

9. George K. Anderson, *The Legend of the Wandering Jew* (Providence: Brown University Press, 1965); Galit Hasan-Rokem and Alan Dundes, eds., *The Wandering Jew—Essays in the Interpretation of a Christian Legend* (Bloomington: Indiana University Press, 1986).

10. Karl Kautsky, "Are the Jews a Race?" originally published in German in 1914, English translation: http://www.marxists.org/archive/kautsky/1914/jewsrace/index.htm. See the reference to Kautsky's use of the metaphor of the dying Ahasver in Paul Mendes-Flohr, "The Throes of Assimilation: Self-Hatred and the Jewish Revolutionary," *European Judaism* 12 (1978): 38. The Soviet Jewish writer Ilya Ehrnburg denied being a Wandering Jew, as he had been called by the editor of the French newspaper *Liberation*. Ehrenburg admitted that he was a traveler, but he also said that he possessed "a country, a garden, roses." The columnist of the Israeli daily *Davar*, who reported Ehrenburg's views. commented that "many Jewish writers in exile had thought this," but that "it seemed strange that anybody in the second half of the twentieth century should still think so." The newspaper clip (in the column "Be-shulei Dvarim" ["In the Margins"], in *Davar*, May 19, 1963) is part of the vast material in Yom Tov Lewinsky's archives of the Wandering Jew, donated by his family to the Folklore Research Center at the Mandel Institute for Jewish Studies of the Hebrew University of Jerusalem. See Galit Hasan-Rokem, "The Wandering Jew—A Jewish Perspective," in *Proceedings of the Ninth World Congress of Jewish Studies*, Division D (Jerusalem, 1986), 2:190.

11. Gilles Deleuze and Félix Guattari, *A Thousand Plateaus: Capitalism and Schizophrenia*, trans. Brian Massumi (Minneapolis: University of Minnesota Press, 1987), 23. The analytical procedure of this article may thus sacrifice historical linearity and concentration in specific cases in favor of a problem-centered discussion of religious phenomenology.

12. Regarding "ecotype," see: Carl Wilhelm von Sydow, "Geography and Folk-Tale Oicotypes," in *Selected Papers on Folklore* (Copenhagen: Rosenkilde and Bagger, 1948), 346–55 (originally published in *Bealoideas* 7 [1932]; rpt. New York: Arno Press, 1977); Lauri Honko, "Four Forms of Adaptation of Tradition," *Studia Fennica* 26 (1981): 18–33; Galit Hasan-Rokem, "Ökotyp," in *Encyclopädie des Märchens* (Berlin: Walter de Gruyter, 2000); and Galit Hasan-Rokem, "Aurora Borealis: Trans-formations of Classical Nordic Folklore Theories," in *Norden og Europa: Fagtradisjoner i nordisk etnologi og folkloristikk*, ed. B. Rogan and B. G. Alver (Novus, Oslo, 2000), 269–85.

13. See, e.g., Haym Soloveitchik's review of a book on Jewish customs, *Olam ke-Minhago Noheg*, by Yizhaq (Eric) Zimmer, in *A[ssociation for]J[ewish] S[tudies] Review* 23, no. 2 (1998): 228–29.

14. The number of days varies in different sources and customs. One of the differentiations marking Jerusalem and the Land of Israel is that some holidays are shorter by a day than in other places. This underlines the particularity of these spaces in Jewish cosmology, possibly also concentrically.

15. Daniel Sperber, *Jewish Customs* (Hebrew) (Jerusalem: Mossad Harav Kook, 1994), 75–77.

16. Mark S. Smith, *The Pilgrimage Pattern in Exodus, with Contributions by Elizabeth M. Bloch-Smith*, ed. David J. A. Clines and Philip Davies, supplement, *Journal for the Study of the Old Testament* series 239 (Sheffield: Sheffield Academic Press, Ltd, 1997), 65–73, reviews the material on Sukkoth in the Hebrew Bible.

17. Incidentally, some late ancient Rabbis debate whether the world was created in the month of Tishrei, when Sukkoth occurs, or in the month of Nisan, when Passover occurs, both week-long holidays. Both these months served as the first month of the Hebrew calendar: Nisan in biblical times, Tishrei from rabbinical times onward. See: Palestinian Talmud tractate yRosh Hashana 1, 5 (f. 56b); yAvodah Zarah 1, 2 (f. 39c); Babylonian Talmud tractate bRosh Hashana f. 8a; f. 10b; bAvodah Zarah f. 8a; and the midrashic compilation on Genesis Bereshit (Genesis) Rabbah 22, 3, Theodor and Albeck's critical edition, 207. On the importance of the number seven as rooted in the number of the days of Creation, see, e.g., the elaborate calculations mentioned in Rachel Elior, *The Three Temples: On the Emergence of Jewish Mysticism*, trans. D. Louvish (Oxford: Littman Library of Jewish Civilization, 2004), esp. chap. 1, though it contains few references to Sukkoth.

18. However, in the Dead Sea sectarian literature (e.g., the Book of Jubilees) on the fifteenth of the third month (i.e., Sivan, since Nisan is the first), Shavuot was celebrated as the major annual festival. See Elior, *The Three Temples*, esp. chap. 6. The calendaric disagreement, particularly concerning the festival connected to the revelation on Sinai, is a major issue that cannot be discussed here. The Book of Jubilees also contains pre-Mosaic genealogies of the festivals: Shavuot since the time of Noah (*The Old Testament Pseudepigrapha*, ed. James H. Charlesworth [New York: Doubleday, 1985], 67–68); Sukkoth celebrated by Abraham (ibid., 89). Abraham's Sukkoth observance consists mainly of sacrifices (like the pentateuchal version in Numbers 29) and other offerings.

19. For the multiple meanings of the Temple in Jerusalem, and temples in general, see, e.g., Raphael Patai, *Man and Temple* (1947; New York: Nelson, 1967).

20. Unlike the specificity of the tractates Sukkah and Pesahim, the tractate Bikkurim, discussing the offering of first fruits at the Temple of Jerusalem, is not exclusively devoted to the festival of Shavuot.

21. Jeffrey L. Rubinstein, *The History of Sukkot in the Second Temple and Rabbinic Periods* (Atlanta: Scholars Press, 1995). See also: Håkan Ulfgard, *The Story of Sukkot: The Setting, Shaping and Sequal of the Biblical Feast of the Tabernacles* (Tübingen: Mohr Siebeck, 1998). Ulfgard discerns three different historical contexts for the holidays: in the Hebrew Bible, the Exodus from Egypt and the Temple of Jerusalem, and in later apocryphal texts, the age of Noah and the patriarchs. The Alexandrian Philo viewed Sukkoth, as well as other festivals, with a double emphasis on universal and national values. Steven Weitzman writes, in "From Feasts into Mourning: The Violence of Early Jewish Festivals," *The Journal of Religion* 79, no. 4 (1999): 561: "whereas Josephus stressed the role of the festivals as unifying Jews, and whereas the author of Jubilees saw in the festivals evidence of intracommunal divisions, Philo seized on the festivals as a way to connect Jews and non-Jews." The emphasis on the booths as a particular custom of the "returnees from Babylonia" in the Nehemiahan account (Ulfgard, *The Story of Sukkot*, 87) further underlines the link between booths and mobility.

22. David Henshke, *Festival Joy in Tannaitic Discourse* (Hebrew) (Jerusalem: The Hebrew University Magnes Press, 2007), 85–159. Henshke's work demonstrates not only the enormous changes that the regulations regarding this festival (and festivals in general) underwent historically but also the rich synchronous variation in any given period.

23. See, however, Tim Whitmarsh's illuminating discussion of exile as a topos in his *Greek Literature and the Roman Empire: The Politics of Imitation* (Oxford: Oxford University Press), esp. 134–78. I thank Tali Artman for this reference and her wisdom. See also Nancy Sultan, *Exile and the Poetics of Loss in Greek Tradition* (Lanham, Md.: Rowman & Littlefield, 1999).

24. Albeit seemingly a minority view in Rabbinic literature, this tradition is documented in both Talmuds, supported by later authorities, reported in medieval sources, and, above all, persistent in custom to this day.

25. Galit Hasan-Rokem, "Narratives in Dialogue: a Folk Literary Perspective on Inter-Religious Contacts in the Holy Land in Rabbinic Literature of Late Antiquity," in *Sharing the Sacred: Religious Contacts and Conflicts in the Holy Land*, ed. A. Kofsky and G. Stroumsa (Jerusalem: Ben-Zvi Institute, 1998), 109–30. The concept of narrative dialogue suggests less dichotomous modes of interaction, more closely connected with everyday life, than those suggested by some other close colleagues, although we share a similar basic approach to cultural interaction between Jews and Christians. In choosing my concept, I seek to view the interaction less as polemics (in Israel Yuval's formulation) or as theological concatenations (in Daniel Boyarin's version) and more as shared cultural baggage being constant transformed and adapted, including in polemical interactions. For their views, see Israel Jacob Yuval, *Two Nations in Your Womb: Perceptions of Jews and Christians in Late Antiquity and the Middle Ages* (Berkeley: University of California Press, 2006), and Daniel Boyarin, *Border Lines: The Partition of Judaeo-Christianity* (Philadelphia: University of Pennsylvania Press, 2006). See also Israel Jacob Yuval, "The Other in Us: Liturgica, Poetica, Polemica," in *Heresy and Identity in Late Antiquity*, ed. Eduard Iricinschi and Holger M. Zellentin (Tübingen: Mohr Siebeck, 2008), 364–85. I have earlier pointed out the special value of narratives in investigating the less confrontational modes of cultural interaction, as well as the apparently high frequency of narratives about women, without, however, claiming that this implies totally irenic attitudes: Galit Hasan-Rokem, *Tales of the Neighborhood: Jewish Narrative Dialogues in Late Antiquity* (Berkeley: University of California Press, 2003).

26. Mishna Sukkah 1, 1.

27. Judith Hauptman, *Rereading the Mishnah: A New Approach to Ancient Jewish Texts* (Tübingen: Mohr Siebeck, 2005), 21. Hauptman considers the Tosefta older than the Mishnah in its present formation.

28. Tosefta, S. Lieberman's edition, 1, 1. Cynthia M. Baker insightfully correlates this text with two other texts on women in the same tractate in her "The Queen, the Apostate, and the Women Between: (Dis)Placement of Women in Tosefta *Sukkah*," in *A Feminist Commentary on the Babylonian Talmud: Introduction and Studies*, ed. Tal Ilan et al. (Tübingen: Mohr Siebeck, 2007), 169–81. See also Shulamit Valler, "Women and Dwelling in the *Sukkah* in the *Bavli*," in ibid., 151–67.

29. BT Sukkah 2b.

30. Ibid. 3a.

31. Josephus, *Jewish Antiquities*, with an English translation by Louis H. Feldman (Cambridge: Harvard University Press, 1960), chap. 20, 17–96, pp. 399–440; Jacob Neusner, "The Conversion of Adiabene to Judaism: A New Perspective," *Journal of Biblical Literature* 83, no. 1 (1964): 60–66. See also: David A. Barish, "Adiabene: Royal Converts to Judaism in the First Century c.e.—A Study of the Sources," Ph.D. dissertation, Hebrew Union College—Jewish Institute of Religion (Cincinnati Ohio, 1983); Lawrence H. Schiffman, "The Conversion of the Royal House of Adiabene in

Rabbinic Sources," in *Josephus, Judaism, and Christianity*, ed. Louis H. Feldman and Gohei Hata (Detroit: Wayne State University Press, 1987), 293–312, referring amply to earlier historiography; Martin Goodman, *Mission and Conversion: Proselytizing in the Religious History of the Roman Empire* (Oxford: Oxford University Press, 1994), 47, 62–65, 84, 136. Tal Ilan, *Integrating Women into Second Temple History* (Peabody, Mass.: Hendrickson, 2001), 25–26, integrates Queen Helene into her feminist revision of the Second Temple period's history as an unusual case highlighted by the Rabbis. It is not necessary to assume (as Ilan does) that Helene adhered to Pharisaic Judaism, as being the only possible motivation for including her in Rabbinic literature—although her indication does not indicate that she did not, either. Unlike Ilan's claim, Izates is mentioned once, however, in a strange disguise in the report of the circumcision of Monbaz and Zwytws (the vocalization is indecisive; Schiffman glosses "Zoitos", the sons of King Ptolemaios (sic) in Bereshit (Genesis) Rabbah 46, 11, p. 467 in Theodor and Albeck's critical edition, including a detailed entry in the notes.

32. Josephus, *Jewish Wars*, bk. 5.

33. See, e.g., Mishnah, mYoma 3, 10 and versions: Tosefta, tYoma (Kippurim), Lieberman's edition 2, 3; Babylonian Talmud bYoma f. 37a-b; Palestinian Talmud yYoma 3, 8 (f. 40b; 41a). The contemporary municipal toponymy of Jerusalem has grouped *Helene* and *Monbaz* as street names around the Russian Compound, curiously correlating them with an Eastern Church. I am not aware of a street honoring the memory of victorious Izates.

34. See D. Boyarin, *Border Lines*, 214–220, esp. the references to Amnon Linder's work on p. 217.

35. Primarily in the writings of Gelasius, Ambrose, Eusebius, Rufinus, Theodoret, Sozomen, and Paulinus. See: Jan Willem Drijvers, *Helena Augusta: The Mother of Constantine the Great and the Legend of Her Finding of the True Cross* (Leiden: Brill, 1992; Dutch original 1987); Stephan Borgehammer, *How the Holy Cross Was Found: From Event to Medieval Legend* (Stockholm: Almqvist & Wiksell, 1991). See also Joan E. Taylor's illuminating review article of both books in *Bulletin of the Anglo-Israel Archaeological Society* 12 (1992–93): 52–60. E. D. Hunt, *Holy Land Pilgrimage in the Later Roman Empire AD 312–460* (Oxford: Oxford University Press, 1982), 36–49, elaborates the local Jerusalemite elements of the legend. Another "narrative dialogue" pertaining to the royal family of Adiabene is detected in Daniel R. Schwartz, "God, Gentiles, and Jewish Law: On Acts 15 and Josephus' Adiabene Narrative," in *Geschichte—Tradition—Reflexion: Festschrift für Martin Hengel zum 70. Geburtstag*, ed. Peter Schäfer (Tübingen: Mohr Siebeck, 1996), 263–82. Another intercultural connection exists between Helena Augusta and the Georgian Saint Nino: see *The Wellspring of Georgian Historiography: The Early Medieval Historical Chronicle "The Conversion of K'art'li" and "The Life of St. Nino,"* trans. Constantine B. Lerner (London: Bennett & Bloom, 2004), 37, 55–65, 161; see also 233. For an extensive discussion of the imbrications of the traditions of the two queens in a particular instance of Jewish-Christian inter- and intra-textuality, see Galit Hasan-Rokem, "Polymorphic Helena—Toledot Yeshu as a Palimpsest of Religious Narratives and Identities," in *Toledot Yeshu ("The Life Story of Jesus") Revisited: A Princeton Conference*, ed. Peter Schäfer, Michael Meerson, and Yaacov Deutsch (Tübingen: Mohr Siebeck, 2011), 247–82.

36. Sozomen's active rejection of this element is telling (Drijvers, *Helena Augusta*, 105).

37. Robert Wilken, *The Land Called Holy: Palestine in Christian History and Thought* (New Haven, Conn.: Yale University Press, 1992), 93ff.

38. Hunt, *Holy Land Pilgrimage*, 39.

39. Charles W. F. Smith, "No Time for Figs," *Journal of Biblical Literature* 79, no. 4 (1960): 325, claims that the first Encaenia was celebrated on Sukkoth. Daniel Stökl Ben Ezra, *The Impact of Yom Kippur on Early Christianity* (Tübingen: Mohr Siebeck, 2003), points out a number of textual and

ritual convergences of Sukkoth and Yom Kippur, e.g., 39n132, 41, 68. Stökl Ben Ezra pays special attention to the connection of the Encaenia (and from the sixth century onward the Exaltation of the Cross, which branches out of the Encaenia but is less relevant to our discussion) to Yom Kippur (ibid., 290).

40. See: *Egeria's Travels to the Holy Land*, trans. John Wilkinson (Jerusalem: Ariel Publishing House, 1981), 71, 79, 146 (as a generic term), 167; *Egeria: Diary of a Pilgrimage*, trans. George E. Gingrass (New York: The Newman Press, 1970), chaps. 48–49, pp. 126–27; Joshua Schwartz, "The *Encaenia* of the Church of the Holy Sepulchre, The Temple of Solomon and the Jews," *Theologische Zeitschrift* 43 (1987): 265–81. Schwartz, however, mentions that September 13 was also the *dies natalis* of Capitoline Jupiter (ibid., 270); cf. *Egeria's Travels*, trans. Wilkinson, 60n1. In the annotated Hebrew translation, Ora Limor, *Holy Land Travels: Christian Pilgrims in Late Antiquity* (Jerusalem: Yad Izhak Ben-Zvi Press, 1998), 113–14, the translation for the Encaenia is "Hanukkah," since the Latin name for Hanukkah was *dies encenarium*. See also: Ben Ezra, *The Impact of Yom Kippur*, 294, 294n12, 295; *Étherie, journal de voyage*, trans. Hélène Pétré (Paris: Cerf), 264–65n1: "The word *enkainia* designates in the Greek of the Septuagint and the New Testament (John 10:22) the Jewish festival of the dedication of the Temple. It was conserved in the language of Christians and applied for the dedication of churches." Another famous Christian woman pilgrim, Paula, also noticed Helene's tomb, cf. Jerome's letter 108, quoted in Limor, *Holy Land Travels*, 142.

41. Smith, "No Time for Figs," 315–27, discusses the use of Zechariah's prophecy by the evangelists and the centrality of Sukkoth for the presentation of Jesus' attitude to the Temple.

42. In John, Jesus metaphorically transforms his own body into the Temple, or rather, into the gift of waters ensured by the Temple worship during Sukkoth. Among the many studies of this text are: Joel Marcus, "Rivers of Living Water from Jesus' Belly (John 7:38)," *Journal of Biblical Literature* 117, no. 2 (1998): 328–30; Michael A. Daise, "'If Anyone Thirsts, Let That One Come to Me and Drink': The Literary Texture of John 7:37b–38a," *Journal of Biblical Literature* 122, no. 4. (2003): 687–99. Dale Loepp has suggested, in a private communication: "in many ways, biblical Israelite religion was one of radical 'centering.' Israel's God, at least in the Biblical text, comes to dwell in the Temple of Jerusalem. That God lives in a house is not unusual in Ancient Near Eastern culture, but that he lives in only ONE exclusively particular house would have been a claim that many would have (and certainly did) resist.—Qumran community, Samaritans, etc. The subsequent destruction and total appropriation of this radical center (by Romans and later Christians) leads to what I would see as this equally radical de-centering expressed in the Sukkah." The parallel existence of "decentering" tendencies is indeed visible in some Jewish communities, such as the dwellers of Qumran and the Samaritans (who, however, suggest an alternative center . . .). This is too wide a theme to investigate here. See also: Ulfgard, *The Story of Sukkot*.

43. For Julian, see Ammianus Marcellinus, *History* 23.1.2–3, quoted in A. D. Lee, *Pagans and Christians in Late Antiquity* (London: Routledge, 2000), 155–56. See also D. Levenson, "Julian's Attempt to Rebuild the Temple: An Inventory of Ancient and Medieval Sources," in *Of Scribes and Scrolls*, ed. H. Attridge et al. (Lanham, Md.: University Press of America, 1990), 261–79. For the Christian sources, see Robert L. Wilken, "The Jews and Christian Apologetics after Theodosius I Cunctos Populos," *The Harvard Theological Review* 73, no. 3–4 (1980): 451–71. For the Rabbinic narratives, see, e.g., Genesis Rabbah 64, 29, in Theodor and Albeck's critical edition, 710–12.

44. Genesis Rabbah 44, 11, in Theodor and Albeck's critical edition, 467–68. Note Egeria's mention of the emphasis on newly converted Christians during the Encaenia; see Schwartz, "The *Encaenia*," 268.

45. See, e.g., Mishnah Yoma 3, 10; Tosefta Yoma (Kippurim), Lieberman's critical edition, 2, 3; Palestinian Talmud Yoma 3, 8 (f. 41a); Babylonian Talmud Yoma 38, 2.

46. Some of the descriptions in Egeria's account of the liturgical year in Jerusalem correlate with the golden treasures of Helena of Adiabene's gifts to the Temple in early Rabbinic sources (*Éthérie, journal de voyage*, 20), http://users.ox.ac.uk/~mikef/durham/egetra.html (viewed July 11, 2008). See esp. Vespers; Egeria's *Description of the Liturgical Year in Jerusalem* §4 and §7; Epiphany §8 and §9. Emperor Justinian's building projects, 530 c.e., are reported in Procopius of Caesarea, *De Aedificiis* (558 c.e.); http://homepages.luc.edu/~avande1/jerusalem/sources/procopius.htm (viewed July 11, 2008). For the richness of Empress Helena's adornment of Jerusalem's churches, see Eusebius, *Life of Constantine*, trans. Averil Cameron and Stuart G. Hall (Oxford: Oxford University Press, 1999), 135–36, 138.

47. Joshua J. Schwartz, *Lod (Lydda), Israel: From Its Origins Through the Byzantine Period, 5600 B.C.E.—640 C.E.* (Oxford: Tempus Reparatum, 1991); Ben-Zion Rosenfeld, *Lod and Its Sages in the Days of the Mishnah and the Talmud* (in Hebrew) (Jerusalem: Yad Izhak Ben-Zvi, 1997). However, in the commentary to his edition of the Tosefta, Lieberman argues that the word *Lod* is an addition.

48. Maximilian Kon, *The Tombs of the Kings*, introd. E. L. Sukenik (in Hebrew) (Tel-Aviv: Dvir, 1947). Kon gives a detailed account of the ancient sources mentioning the tombs as an introduction to his archaeological study of the compound (1–10). He notes the scarcity of sources from the end of the fifth century c.e. until the sixteenth century. However, the earliest medieval tradition identifying them as the tombs of the kings of Judea is by a Jewish writer in the fourteenth century (11); it was later transmitted by Jews and Christians alike. It is not completely clear from Kon's exposition when the tombs were again attributed to the royal house of Adiabene, since his account focuses on the material condition of the structure. See also Ruth Jacoby, "The Decoration and Plan of Queen Helena's Tomb in Jerusalem," *The Real and Ideal Jerusalem in Jewish, Christian and Islamic Art*, ed. Bianca Kühnel, special issue, *Jewish Art* 23/24 (1998): 460–62. Today access to the tombs is physically possible but "diplomatically" sometimes complex. The Jewish family that owned the site in the nineteenth century bestowed it in 1886 on the government of France, and the key is now held by the man living closest to the tombs, who has to be contacted by telephone prior to any visit.

49. Mikhail M. Bakhtin, *The Dialogic Imagination: Four Essays*, trans. Caryl Emerson and Michael Holquist (Austin: University of Texas Press, 1981). The chronotope provides a particularly powerful tool for clarifying "the articulation of different temporalities," in Michael Lambek's astute formulation (Michael Lambek, "The Sakalava Poiesis of History: Realizing the Past Through Spirit Possession in Madagascar," *American Ethnologist* 25, no. 2 [1998]: 106).

50. For heterotopia, see Michel Foucault, "Of Other Spaces (1967), Heterotopias," http://www.foucault.info/documents/heteroTopia/foucault.heteroTopia.en.html (last viewed July 12, 2008). The notion of a heterotopian practice of a utopian idea seems to characterize the festival of Sukkoth, which Henshke, in *Festival Joy* (130–32), refers to as a commandment addressing "All native-born Israelites," thus one to be fulfilled by the community as an entity rather than by each and every individual. He refers especially to the work of historian Shmuel Safrai. Whereas the heterotopian status of the Sinai desert in extra-pentateuchal biblical texts (e.g., Isaiah 40:3 and Jeremiah 2:2) has been extensively treated and discussed, though not necessarily with reference to this theoretical framework, the postbiblical occurrences have been largely neglected. The Talmudic tall-tale narrator Raba Bar Bar Hana, for instance, is led by an Arab (*taya*) to a site where he can view Mount Sinai and the dead generation of the desert-wandering giant Israelites (bBava Bathra 73b–74a). There the heterotopian aspect is emphasized by the introduction to "our" mythological sources by an "other." See my discussion of this topic in Galit Hasan-Rokem, "*Homo viator et narrans*—Medieval Jewish Voices in the European Narrative of the Wandering Jew," *Europäische Ethnologie und Folklore im*

internationalen Kontext, ed. Ingo Schneider (Frankfurt am Main: Peter Lang, 1999), 93–102, esp. the reference to Dina Stein's substantial Hebrew article on the Talmudic Raba Bar Bar Hana texts, "Believing Is Seeing: A Reading of Baba Batra 73a–75b," *Jerusalem Studies in Hebrew Literature* 17 (1999): 9–32.

51. See Ronald Hendel, "The Exodus in Biblical Memory," *Journal of Biblical Literature* 120, no. 2 (2001): 601–22. See esp. his reference to Fernand Braudel's "tripartite rhythm of historical time . . . event, conjuncture and *longue durée*," which emphasizes an ethnographic perspective on the study of culture like the one I take here.

52. Some philological studies, however, have attempted to identify this place with the first rest after the crossing of the Red Sea, e.g., David Elgavish, "Sukkot—a Placename or a Term for Temporary Structures?" (in Hebrew) *Beyt Miqra* 39 (1996): 367–76. These suggestions have no base in the tradition or historical memory.

53. Jeffrey L. Rubinstein, *The History of Sukkot in the Second Temple and Rabbinic Periods* (Atlanta: Scholars Press, 1995), 17, 324. Regarding the association of the desert with divine revelation in the Hebrew Bible and Second Temple Judaism, see (the scholarly polemical framework notwithstanding) Daniel R. Schwartz, "Whence the Voice? A Response to Bruce Longenecker," *Journal for the Study of Judaism in the Persian, Hellenistic and Roman Period* 31 (2000), 42–46.

54. Genesis Rabbah, 17, 1; in the critical edition of Theodor and Albeck, 151. Genesis Rabbah is generally dated to the fifth century C.E. in the Galilee. For remythicization, see Galit Hasan-Rokem, "Myth," *Contemporary Jewish Religious Thought*, ed. Arthur A. Cohen and Paul Mendes-Flohr (New York: Charles Scribner's Sons, 1987), 660.

55. Note that at the other end of the calendrical pole, on Passover, we find "the bread of affliction."

56. See Elgavish, "Sukkot—a Placename."

57. As Dani Schrire reminds me, naming places also very strongly indicates the constructedness and temporariness of human geography. See Amer Dahamshy, "Name for a Place: The Names of Arab Settlements in the Galilee and the Names of Natural Features in the Folk Narrative," Ph.D. dissertation, Hebrew University of Jerusalem, 2009.

58. On the complex negotiations of the number of the days of Sukkoth, whether seven or eight, in early sources, see Henshke, *Festival Joy*, 160–231.

59. David Nirenberg, *Communities of Violence: Persecution of Minorities in the Middle Ages* (Princeton, N.J.: Princeton University Press, 1996), and Elliott Horowitz, *Reckless Rites: Purim and the Legacy of Jewish Violence* (Princeton, N.J.: Princeton University Press, 2006), each exquisitely demonstrate two different perspectives on festival violence with regard to Jews: Nirenberg stresses the intergroup, interactive perspective; Horowitz focuses on Jewish subjectivity and moral responsibility.

60. Josephus, *Jewish Antiquities*, 13.373.

61. Tosefta Sukkah, Lieberman edition, 3, 16.

62. The incident is repeated in Babylonian Talmud tractate Sukkah f. 48b; a less detailed account can be found in the Mishnah tractate of Sukkah 4, 9. Steven Weitzman, "From Feasts into Mourning," mentions (547) another violent incident related to Sukkoth from Tosefta Sukkah 3:1, as the Boethusian priests prevented the people from erecting one of the symbols of the festival, the *lulav* palm branches, around the altar. See also Weitzman's reference to the utopian function of festivals, and Sukkoth in particular, in creating an image of the ideal society, and to violence as representing an alternative vision of the same (ibid., 562–65), associated with the messianic tones echoed in the political events of the period, especially the Bar-Kokhva uprising.

63. However, see Ben Ezra, *The Impact of Yom Kippur*, 295, referring to John Chrysostom's polemics against the Jews with reference to Sukkoth (*Against the Jews* 7:1, *Patrologia Graeca* 48:915). I am tempted to refer here to the universal prophecy of Zechariah, but this question needs further consideration.

64. See Hasan-Rokem, "*Homo viator et narrans*" and "*Ex Oriente Fluxus.*"

65. "But it was not enough that he should say, 'Slay them not, lest they should at last forget Thy law,' unless he had also added, 'Disperse them'; because if they had only been in their own land with that testimony of the Scriptures, and not every where, certainly the Church which is every-where could not have had them as witnesses among all nations to the prophecies which were sent before concerning Christ" (Augustine, *City of God*, 18.46, taken from Nicene and Post-Nicene Fathers, first series, ed. Philip Schaff [Peabody Mass.: Hendrickson, 1994], 2:389). See the classic work on this: Bernhard Blumenkranz, *Die Judenpredigt Augustins, ein Beitrag zur Geschichte der jüdisch-christliche Beziehungen in den ersten Jahrhunderten* (Basel: Helbing & Lichtenhahn, 1946; rpt. with a preface by Marcel Simon, Paris: Études Augustiniennes, 1973); Bernhard Blumenkranz, "Augustin et le Juifs: Augustin et le judaisme," *Extrait de Recherches augustiniennes*, supplement, *Revue des études augustiniennes*, vol. 1 (Paris, 1958); Jeremy Cohen, *Living Letters of the Law: Ideas of the Jew in Medieval Christianity* (Berkeley: University of California Press, 1999); and, by contrast, Franklin T. Harkins, "Nuancing Augustine's Hermeneutical Jew: Allegory and Actual Jews in the Bishop's Sermons," *Journal for the Study of Judaism* 36, no. 1 (2005): 41–64, esp. his discussion of Sermon 4 (50–53), using Jacob and Esau as an example of how the older will serve the younger, like the Jews will serve the Church, Jacob being a prefiguration for Christ. See also Paula Fredriksen, *Augustine and the Jews: A Christian Defense of Jews and Judaism* (New York: Random House, 2008). However, Michael Frassetto, in his "Doctrine of Witness and Attitudes Toward the Jews in the Eleventh Century," *Church History and Religious Culture* 87, no. 3 (2007): 287–304, states that, although throughout the Middle Ages Augustine of Hippo's doctrine of witness shaped theological attitudes toward the Jews and moderated Christian behavior toward them, Christian authors some-times turned away from the doctrine to create a new theological image of the Jew that justified contemporary violence against Jews, discussing especially the impact of the writings of Ademar of Chabannes (989–1034), during a time of heightened apocalypticism and attacks on Jews.

66. Chaim Milikowsky, "Notions of Exile, Subjugation and Return in Rabbinic Literature," in *Exile: Old Testament, Jewish and Christian Conceptions*, ed. James M. Scatt (Leiden: Brill, 1997), 265–96. See Gafni, *Land, Center and Diaspora*, 19–40. As mentioned above, Gafni's tripartite classi-fication tacitly exposes the lack of correlation between dispersion and suffering, since, as he men-tions (33), it is the Jews in Palestine who suffer the most, i.e., under the Trajanic and Hadrianic persecutions. See also Daniel R. Schwartz, "From Punishment to Program, from Program to Pun-ishment: Josephus and the Rabbis on Exile," in *For Uriel: Studies in the History of Israel in Antiquity Presented to Professor Uriel Rappaport*, ed. Menahem Mor et al. (Jerusalem: The Shazar Center for Jewish History, 2005), 205–26 (however, I think that scholarship in general disagrees with Schwartz's claim [221] that the priesthood practically lost its status after the fall of the Temple).

67. See, e.g.: Simon Dubnow, "The Affirmation of the Diaspora" (a reply to Ahad Ha-Am's "Negation of the Diaspora"), in *Nationalism and History: Essays on Old and New Judaism*, ed. and introd. Koppel S. Pinson (Philadelphia: Jewish Publication Society of America, 1958), 182–91; Simon Dubnow, "Autonomism," in *The Jew in The Modern World: A Documentary History*, ed. Paul R. Mendes-Flohr and Jehuda Reinharz (New York: Oxford University Press, 1980), 337–39.

68. Alfred C. Andrews, "Acclimatization of Citrus Fruits in the Mediterranean Region," *Agricul-tural History* 35, no. 1 (1961): 35–46; Erich Isaac, "Influence of Religion on the Spread of Citrus," *Science*, n.s. 129/3343 (1959): 179–86. Incidentally, nowadays (especially in *shmita* years, when there

are serious limitations on agriculture in Israel) *lulavim* are imported to Israel from Egypt: http://www.moag.gov.il/NR/rdonlyres/925D9A93-8F99-43A1-A0FA-D68DE 2F27D2D/1352/ BulletinSeptember2007.pdf. In the late summer of 2011, as a result of tension on the Egyptian-Israeli border, the Egyptian export was halted and Israeli growers had to make extra efforts to satisfy the need for millions of *lulavim*.

69. The topic opens up the entire question of how the early Jewish colonizers/pioneers assumed local dress and lifestyles, sometimes posing in Arab attire. The *kufyeh* headgear was a mark of identity for members of Jewish socialist youth movements until the late sixties and was apparently wiped out by the encounter with the "'67 Palestinians" after the Six-Day War. On the *kufyeh* (spelled *kafiya*), see Yael Zerubavel, "Memory, the Rebirth of the Native, and the 'Hebrew Bedouin Identity,'" *Social Research* 75 (2008): 315–52, 337–39. See also a very different perspective on that conflation in Zeev Meshel, "Wilderness Wanderings: Ethnographic Lessons from Modern Bedouin," *Biblical Archaeology Review* (July/August 2008), which explores ethnographic parallels between the Bedouin and ancient Israelites. I thank Ronald Hendel for this reference.

70. Sperber, *Jewish Customs*, 116, quotes the sixteenth-century Kabbalist from Tsfat in the Galilee, Rabbi Itzhaq Luria ("Ha-Ari"), as well as his own father.

71. De Certeau, *The Practice of Everyday Life*, 91–110.

72. Israel J. Yuval has wisely suggested that the language of the religious practice of Sukkoth as formulated in early Rabbinic texts and their later interpreters would be a rich mine for the analysis of elements of temporariness. This task lies ahead.

73. *Zohar*, Emor, 5:103b.

74. Israel J. Yuval urged me to go further in investigating the *ushpizin and* also alerted me to the fact that their emergence in the practices of Sukkoth belongs to the same historical era in early European modernity when the Wandering Jew becomes a central figure in popular discourse. I have, in parallel, investigated the contemporaneous appearance of the Dybbuk phenomenon in written Jewish sources as a possible cultural negotiation with the Wandering Jew: Galit Hasan-Rokem, "Dybbuk and Wandering Jew: No Rest Either in Life or Death," paper delivered at the Scholion Conference Between Heaven and Earth, Jerusalem, June 2008, forthcoming in a volume edited by Yoram Bilu.

75. Kader Konuk, "Eternal Guests, Mimics, and Dönme: The Place of German and Turkish Jews in Modern Turkey," *New Perspectives on Turkey* 37 (2007): 5–30.

76. The contemporary information is based on ethnographic fieldwork initiated and sponsored by the Smithsonian Institute in Washington, D.C., in the context of an aborted project to represent Jerusalem at the American Folklife Festival in the summer of 1993 as a joint American, Israeli, and Palestinian enterprise. For a detailed analysis of the complex interactions during the research, as well as a focused analysis of the material on Sukkoth, see Galit Hasan-Rokem, "Dialogue as Ethical Conduct: The Folk Festival That Was Not," in *Research Ethics in Studies of Culture and Social Life*, ed. Bente G. Alver, Tove I. Fjell, and Ørjar Øyen (Helsinki: Academia Scientiarum Fennica, 2007), 149–61. I am deeply grateful to my friends and colleagues Dr. Suad Amiry, Dr. Amy Horowitz, and especially Dr. Hagar Salamon, who coordinated the fieldwork of the Israeli partners.

77. See Tim Jon Semmerling, *Israeli and Palestinian Postcards: Presentations of National Self* (Austin: University of Texas Press, 2004), 141–42.

78. http://www.ir-amim.org.il/Eng/?CategoryID = 173; http://www.stopthewall.org/downloads/pdf/book/jerusalemandbethlehem.pdf.

79. For a disinterested exposition—if such is possible—of the history of Jerusalem in correlation to all groups imperial, national, and religious that now have or have had interests in Jerusalem, see Karen Armstrong, *Jerusalem—One City, Three Faiths* (New York: Ballantine Books, 2005).

80. Samir Dayal, "Diaspora and Double Consciousness," *The Journal of the Midwest Modern Language Association* 29 (1996): 46–62. The undefined caveat about mixing "real" diaspora with a "particular danger . . . of facile and rootless cosmopolitanism masquerading as transvalued diaspora" seems, however, to reveal a partisanship that echoes too many unpleasant past voices.

81. Ibid., 51. Serious attempts have been initiated in Hebrew by Amnon Raz-Krakotzkin, in his "Exile Within Sovereignty: Toward a Critique of the 'Negation of Exile' in Israeli Culture," *Theory and Criticism—An Israeli Forum* 4 (1993): 23–55, and by Israel J. Yuval in his "The Myth of Exile—Jewish Time and Christian Time," *Alpayim* 29 (2005): 9–25. See Daniel Boyarin and Jonathan Boyarin, *Powers of Diaspora*.

82. Although some archaeologists still ardently search for it.

The *Tasbirwol* (Prayer Beads) under Attack: How the Common Practice of Counting One's Beads Reveals Its Secrets in the Muslim Community of North Cameroon, by José C. M. van Santen

1. I started my fieldwork in North Cameroon in 1986; in the years following 2006 it was carried out as part of the NWO Program Islam in Africa, Moving Frontiers, part of the overall program The Future of the Religious Past.

2. Sufism is a movement of organized brotherhoods, who are grouped around a spiritual leader, or *sheik*. Sufis organize themselves into "orders" or groups, called *tariqas*. These groups are headed by a leader, called a *shaykh*, who is considered the most spiritual man, with the most *taqwa*, among them. See http://www.globalsecurity.org/military/intro/islam-sufi.htm, accessed October 7, 2011.

3. Ali Salih Karrar, *The Sufi Brotherhoods in the Sudan* (London: C. Hurst and Co, 1992).

4. Alan Godlas, *Sufism's Many Paths* (Athens: University of Georgia Press, 2000).

5. Cheikh Gueye, *Touba, la capital des Mourides* (Paris: Karthala, 2002).

6. See Cheikh Gueye and Olivia Gervasoni, "The Mourid Brotherhood at the Center of Senegalese Political Life: A Dialectic of State and Religious Power," in *Powers: Religion as a Social and Spiritual Force*, ed. Meerten B. ter Borg and Jan Willem van Henten (New York: Fordham University Press, 2010), 134–48.

7. Clan descent is a way to determine the origins of certain populations in this part of the world. The Tara clan came from the northern regions of Nigeria and from Niger (*Atlas de la Province Extrême-Nord Cameroun*, Paris: IRD, 2005).

8. Mal Baba means that they went on "transhumance," that is, migrated during certain seasons in search of fodder for their cattle.

9. Although this phrase can be translated "Glorious is God," its root is *sabh*, "voidness," or *tasbeeh*, "making something void." Thus the literal meaning of the phrase is "God is devoid." It also implies what is expanded in *al-hamdu-lill ahi* (literally "void of all evil," but translatable as "All praise and thanks be to God"). *Al-hamdu lillahi rabbil 'alamin* is the first Ayah of the first Surah of the Qur'an.

10. Clifford Geertz, *The Religion of Java* (Chicago: University of Chicago Press, 1976), 183.

11. C. H. Becker, "Islam und Christentum," *Der Islam*, January 1913; Samuel M. Zwemer, "The Rosary in Islam," in *Studies in Popular Islam: Collection of Papers Dealing with the Superstitions and Beliefs of the Common People* (Northumberland: Sheldon Press 1939).

12. Geertz, *The Religion of Java*, 183.

13. P. Edgar Schäfer, "The Rosary in Islam," *The Muslim World* 3, no. 3 (1913): 246–49.

14. Edward William Lane (1863), *Lane's Arabic Lexicon*: http://books.google.nl/books?id = 3R7g 2U0l9-8C&pg = PA202&dq = Lane%E2%80%99s + Arabic + Lexicon# *PPA198,M1.*

15. Ignác Yitzhaq Yehuda Goldziher, *Vorlesungen über den Islam* (1910), ed. Frantz Babinger, vol. 1 of Religionswissenschaftliche Bibliothek (Heidelberg: Carl Winter, 1925). Ignác Yitzhaq Yehuda Goldziher (June 22, 1850–November 1921) was a Hungarian orientalist who is widely considered to be among the founders of modern Islamic studies in Europe. Some regard him as the most important Jewish interpreter of Islam (see Maxime Rodinson, "Western Views of the Muslim World," in *Europe and the Mystique of Islam*, ed. Roger Veinus [Seattle: University of Washington Press, 1987], 3–82). Martin Kramer ("Introduction," in *The Jewish Discovery of Islam: Studies in Honor of Bernard Lewis*, ed. Martin Kramer [Tel Aviv: The Moshe Dayan Center for Middle Eastern and African Studies, 1999], 1–48) claims that Goldziher regarded Judaism and Islam as kindred faiths. During his stay in Damascus, Goldziher's assimilation of the two faiths reached a point where "I became inwardly convinced that I myself was a Muslim." In Cairo he even prayed as a Muslim: "In the midst of the thousands of the pious, I rubbed my forehead against the floor of the mosque. Never in my life was I more devout, more truly devout, than on that exalted Friday."

16. Schäfer, "The Rosary in Islam," 248.

17. http://answering-islam.org/Books/Zwemer/Studies/chap1.htm.

18. E. Westermarck, *Ritual and Belief in Morocco*, vol. 1 (London: Macmillan and Co, 1926).

19. The Mourids in Senegal, for example, always use prayer beads, and in the streets of Touba, the town of Hamadou Bamba, the founder of this brotherhood, one can buy prayer beads every few yards near the main mosque. But there are differences here: Mourid prayer beads have sixty-six beads, while those used by the Tijaniyya have ninety-nine. Great masters may use strings with a thousand beads (999 "plus the not counted top-one," as the Tijaniyya leader in Maroua explained to me in an interview (November 2007). See also the film *Knowledge That Came from Nigeria: Islam, Brotherhoods, and Moving Frontiers in Cameroon* (José C. M. van Santen, 2007)

20. John N. Paden, *Religion and Political Culture in Kano* (Berkeley: University of California Press, 1973), 65.

21. Roy Dilley, *Islamic and Caste Knowledge Practices among Haalpulaar'en in Senegal* (Edinburgh: Edinburgh University Press, 2004), 148.

22. See also Heinz Kimmerle, "Einflüsse des Islam und afrikanische Weisheitslehre: afrikanische Moslems, Marabuts, Weisheitslehrer," *Zeitschrift für Afrikastudien* 15/16 (1992): 63–72.

23. John N. Paden, *Religion and Political Culture in Kano* (Berkeley: University of California Press, 1973), 64–82.

24. A. Lebeuf, "L'origine et la constitution des principaux kotoko (Cameroun septentrional)," in *Contributions de la recherche ethnologique à l'histoire des civilisations du Cameroun* (Paris: CNRS, 1980), 1:209–18; Vivan Paques, *Le Roi Pecheur et le Roi Chasseur* (Strasbourg: Travaux de l'Institut de l'Anthropologie de Strasbourg, 1977).

25. I use the concept "Islamization" and the verb *Islamize* to indicate that the transition from one religion (the so-called "traditional" religion) to another, the world religion Islam, has the character of a process. The verb *Islamize* is, moreover, a direct translation of the Fulfulde word *silmugo*. A further discussion of this point can be found in José C. M. van Santen, *They Leave Their Jars Behind: The Conversion of Mafa Women to Islam (North Cameroon)* (Leiden: Vena Publications, 1993), and José C. M. van Santen, "Islamization in North Cameroon: Political Processes and Individual Choices," *Anthropos* 7 (2002): 67–97.

26. H. R. Palmer, "An Early Fulani Conception of Islam," *Journal of the African Society* 13 (1913–14); Paden, *Religion and Political Culture*, 410.

27. The Guiziga were one such acephalous ethnic group; see Eldridge Mohammadou, *Les royaumes Foulbe du Plateau de l'Adamaoua au XIX siècle* (Tokyo: ILCAA, 1978); *Le Royaume du Wandala ou Mandara au XIXe siècle* (Tokyo: ILCAA, 1982); *Les Lamidats du Diamare et du Mayo Louti au XIXe siècle* (Tokyo: ILCAA, 1988). The Mundang, by contrast, had a hierarchical organization; see van Santen, *They Leave Their Jars Behind*; Kees Schilder, *Quest for Self-Esteem: State Islam and Mundang Ethnicity in Northern Cameroon* (London: Avebury, 1994). The Fulbe of Diamaré and Kalfou did not succeed in penetrating the regions adjacent to the Logone River, where the Massa and Toupouri lived.

28. For a thorough description, see Olivier Iyébi-Mandjek and Henry Tourneux, *L'école dans une petite ville africaine Maroua, Cameroun* (Paris: Karthala, 1994).

29. See Philip Burnham, *The Politics of Cultural Difference in Northern Cameroon* (Edinburgh: Edinburgh University Press, 1996), and van Santen, *They Leave Their Jars Behind*. During the colonial period, acephalous ethnic groups were at first ruled by Islamic chiefs of the hierarchically organized Fulbe people. In due course—and here the mountain population of the Mafa may serve as an example—they no longer accepted rule by the Fulbe chiefs, whereupon they got their own, though also Islamized, chief (van Santen, "Islamization").

30. Van Santen, *They Leave Their Jars Behind*, 28.

31. Hamman Tukur Saad and Isa Alkali Abba, "Islamic Scholarship across the Nigeria-Cameroon Border: The Case of the Old Adamawa Emirate," *Frankfurter Afrikanistische Blätter* 6 (1994): 23–52.

32. Kees Schilder and José C. M. van Santen, "Etniciteit en Gender: Een verkenning in de Afrikanistiek," *Tijdschrift voor Vrouwenstudies* 19 (1994): 123–38.

33. Saad and Alkali, in "Islamic Scholarship across the Nigeria-Cameroon Border," remark that Islamic scholars are also involved in the *tariqah* (brotherhood), or Sufi orders, and in *dibbu* (the use of supernatural agencies to control the natural environment). The Islamiyya system of education developed in the 1950s and 1960s. In this system, secular education and Islamic education are integrated, as they are in the new private Islamic school system mentioned in this chapter.

34. As J. Boyd and A. Shagari, "The Fulani Women Poets," in *Pastoralists of the West African Savannah*, ed. Mahdi Adamu and A. H. M. Kirk-Greene (Manchester: Manchester University Press, 1986) state, "in the Fodio family the intellectualism of five generations of women can be traced" (127). One of Uthman dan Fodio's daughters, Nana Asmaou, studied poetry.

35. E. E. Rosander and D. Westerlund, *African Islam and Islam in Africa, Encounter Between Sufis and Islamists* (London: Hurst & Company, 1997), 6.

36. E. Schultz, "From Pagan to Pullo: Ethnic Identity Change in Northern Cameroon," *Africa* 54, no. 1 (1984): 46–64.

37. See: José C. M. Van Santen, "Garder du bétail, c'est aussi du travail: Des relations entre pasteurs foulbé et agriculteurs du Centre du Bénin et du Nord-Cameroun," in *L'ethnicité peule dans des contextes nouveaux*, ed. G. Schlee and Y. Diallo (Paris: Karthala, 2000), 129–60; Jan Willem Molenaar and José C. M. van Santen, "'Maami Wata's kingdom underneath the water': Perceptions of Water in a Hydrological and Ecological Changing Context; The Case of the Logone Floodplains in Cameroon," *Geographical Journal* 127, no. 4 (2006): 331–47; Paden, *Religion and Political Culture*, 32.

38. Salih Karrar, *Sufi Brotherhoods*, 125.

39. Patrick J. Ryan, "La Tijâniyya: Une confrérie musulmane à la conquête de l'Afrique," *Journal of Religion in Africa* 30, no. 2 (2000): 208–24.

40. David Robinson and Jean-Louis Triaud, eds., *Le temps des marabouts: Itinéraires et stratégies islamiques en Afrique occidentale (v. 1880–1960)* (Paris: Karthala, 1997).

41. Ousmane Kane, "La confrérie 'Tijaniyya Ibrahimiyya' de Kano et ses liens avec la zawiya mère de Kaolack," *Islam et sociétés au Sud du Sahara* 3 (1989): 27–40.

42. Paden, *Religion and Political Culture.*

43. Ibid.; Palmer, "An Early Fulani Conception of Islam."

44. Paden, *Religion and Political Culture*, 74; John Ralph Willis, *In the Path of Allah: The Passion of al-Hajj 'Umar: An Essay into the Nature of Charisma in Islam* (London: Frank Cass and Co. Ltd, 1989). The political and religious direction of the 'Umarian Jama'a was dominated by the Torodbe clerisy (Uthman dan Fodio came from this group), whose acceptance of the Tijaniyya litany bestowed upon it its peculiar character. The persona and charisma of al-Hajj 'Umar, the mystic shaykh, provided the binding element (Willis, *In the Path of Allah*).

45. Bawuro M. Barkindo, "Growing Islamism in Kano City since 1970: Causes, Form and Implications," in *Muslim Identity and Social Change in Sub-Saharan Africa*, ed. Louis Brenner (Bloomington: Indiana University Press, 1993): 98.

46. Because this chapter deals with the *tasbirwol*, I will not pay attention to the difference made in the scholarly literature between traditional Tijaniyya and reformed Tijaniyya. The latter emerges in the Salgawa movement, initiated by Muhammed Salga (d. 1938), whose son Abdullahi submitted to Ibrahim Niass in 1937 and whose brother became the leader of Tijaniyya youth activities (Paden, *Religion and Political Culture*, 90).

47. Personal communication from local *laamibe*, chiefs (Mokolo, Pette, Mindif, Mafa Kilda).

48. Youssef M. Choueiri, *Islamic Fundamentalism* (London: Pinter Publishers, 1990), 20–21; van Santen, *They Leave Their Jars Behind*, 69–101; Roman Loimeier, *Islamic Reform and Political Change in Northern Nigeria* (Evanston, Ill.: Northwestern University Press, 1997).

49. They are called "white people," *nasaara*, by the local population. Paradoxically, the term *nasaara* has been derived from the town of Nazareth—the hometown of Jesus. It means "those who follow him from Nazareth"—thus, Christians. These preachers, however, come to preach Islam. Another local term for them is "Pakistani," or "Wahhabi," regardless of the fact that they in fact come from Pakistan.

50. In all the provinces of Cameroon, there are sixteen private Islamic secondary schools. A report containing these numbers was given to me by the Secretary of Islamic Education for the Province Extrême Nord. Despite their private founding, the schools are now coordinated by the Ministry of Education.

51. Cheikh Gueye and José C. M. van Santen, "Internet or the Mirror on the World: How Youth in Senegal and Cameroon Reshape Their Muslim Identity," paper for the conference Youth, Dakar, October 2006.

52. In the colonial period, tribal courts were installed for the non-Muslim ethnic groups.

53. Mentan Tatah states: "40% of the rural people and 15% of those in 'urban' areas live below the poverty line. . . . Though the number of unemployed is growing by leaps and bounds, 'capital flight' is above 150 milliards FCFA per annum, which accounts for about one quarter of the national annual budget. . . . It is thus understandable why Cameroon's Gross Domestic Investment would be 1989 (16.5% of GDP), 1990 (14.6%), 1991 (12.6%), 1992 (11.1%), 1993 (10.8%) as it deteriorates with the years" ("The Political Economy of Regional Imbalances and National Integration in Cameroon," in *Regional Balance and National Integration in Cameroon: Lessons Learned and the Uncertain Future*, ed. Paul Nkwi, Paul Nchoji, and Francis B. Nyamnjoh [Yaoundé: ICASSRT Monograph 1, 1997], 17–29).

54. These remarks were made long before the unhappy events of September 11, 2001, and such reactions come from different sides. The Gulf crisis may have had some effect, though in all these years—I have regularly lived in and visited North Cameroon since 1986—it has hardly been discussed.

55. Louis Brenner, ed., *Muslim Identity and Social Change in Sub-Saharan Africa* (Bloomington: Indiana University Press, 1993).

56. The interview has been filmed and figures in the film entitled *The* Tasbirwol *under Attack* (José C. M. van Santen, 2007).

57. Adeline Masquelier, "Debating Muslims, Disputed Practices: Struggles for the Realization of an Alternative Moral Order in Niger," in *Civil Society and the Political Imagination in Africa: Critical Perspectives*, ed. John L. and Jean Comaroff (Chicago: University of Chicago Press, 1999), 219–50.

58. Masquelier further remarks that these confrontations would not have occurred save for an "opening up" of Islamic consciousness that allowed for the emergence of multiple perspectives. It is by contesting a previously unquestioned orthodoxy that Izala can be said to contribute to the emergence of a Nigerian civil society. Y. A. Quadri ("A Study of the Izalah, a Contemporary Anti-Sufi Organization in Nigeria," *Orita* 17, no. 2 (1985): 95–108) examines the views of the Izala in Nigeria and its effects on Nigerian Muslims. Izala has largely failed to achieve its aim of removing what it regards as heretical innovations within the Islamic practices of the Sufis in Nigeria. This is due to its approach to reform, which is violent and puritanical.

59. Schäfer, "The Rosary in Islam," 249.

60. From Saudi Arabia, supposedly, but it is not really clear where they come from. I tried to contact them in 2007, but they refused to receive me.

61. Reinout N. M. van Santen, "Voedsel voor de ziel: Soefi bewegingen in Maleisië," M.A. thesis, Utrecht University, 2007.

62. *Ahz ab* (or *ahzab*) means any single group of liturgical formulas or, simply, prayers. *Awr ad* (or *awrad*) is the term for spiritual practices. See Shua Taji-Farouki, *Ibn 'Arabi: A Prayer for Spiritual Elevation and Protection* (Oxford: Biddles Limited, 2006).

Miniatures and Stones in the Spiritual Economy of the Virgin of Urkupiña in Bolivia, by Sanne Derks, Willy Jansen, and Catrien Notermans

1. The data presented in this chapter were gathered by Sanne Derks during fourteen months of anthropological fieldwork in 2005 and 2007 for her Ph.D. thesis, later published as *Power and Pilgrimage: Dealing with Class, Gender and Ethnic Inequality at a Bolivian Marian Shrine* (Berlin: Lit, 2009). Willy Jansen and Catrien Notermans are researchers in the field of pilgrimage, the anthropology of religion, and gender. All researchers worked together in the project The Power of Marian Pilgrimage: A Comparative Study, which is part of the NWO Program The Future of the Religious Past.

2. L. F. Arnillas, "Ekeko, Alacitas y Calvarios: La fiesta de la Santa Cruz en Juliaca," *Allpanchis* 47 (1996): 119–35.

3. E. Cuentas, "El 'Equeqo' y las 'Alasitas': Manifestaciones de Aculturación Religiosa," *Boletin de Lima* 11, no. 33 (1984): 65–70.

4. C. McDannell, *Material Christianity: Religion and Popular Culture in America* (New Haven, Conn.: Yale University Press, 1995), 6.

5. The term *spiritual economy* was proposed by David Morgan when Derks discussed her work with him (personal communication, April 29, 2007). The term can also be found in the following studies: S. Sweetinburgh, *The Role of the Hospital in Medieval England: Gift-Giving and the Spiritual Economy* (Dublin: Four Courts, 2004); K. Burns, *Convents and the Spiritual Economy of Cuzco, Peru* (Durham, N.C.: Duke University Press, 1999). Sweetinburgh employs the term to describe how

hospitals in medieval England generated gifts, such as money, land, or goods, from rich patrons in exchange for prayers from the poor and sick; Burns uses it to refer to the dense network of interests and investments linking rich Peruvian convents to the material world outside. Like both of these studies in referring to exchange relationships between the spiritual and the material, we use the term to denote the economic symbolism of pilgrims' negotiations with Mary to improve their daily lives.

6. H. van den Berg, *La tierra no da así no mas: Los ritos agrícolas en la religión de los Aymaras-Cristianos* (La Paz: Hisbol UCB, 1990).

7. Pachamama is one of the most important entities in Andean religiosity. The word is a composition of the words *Pacha* and *Mama*. *Pacha* means space, universe as time, and history. *Mama* means "mother" in Quechua and "woman" in Aymara. The name is usually "Mother Earth." See O. Harris, ed., *The Mythological Figure of the Earth Mother* (London: Institute of Latin American Studies, 2000).

8. Ibid., 201–19.

9. J. Estermann, "Filosofía Andina: Elementos para la revindicacion del pensamiento colonizado," *Stromato* 2 (1993): 203–28.

10. O. Harris, "The Sources and Meanings of Money: Beyond the Market Paradigm," in *To Make the Earth Bear Fruit: Essays on Fertility, Work and Gender in Highland Bolivia*, ed. O. Harris (London: Institute of Latin American Studies, 2000).

11. M. T. Taussig, "The Genesis of Capitalism among a South American Peasantry: Devil's Labor and the Baptism of Money," *Comparative Studies in Society and History* 19, no. 2 (1977): 130–55.

12. INE, *Anuario Estadístico 2006* (La Paz: Instituto Nacional de Estadística, 2007), 389.

13. S. W. Derks, "Religious Materialization of Neo-Liberal Politics at the Pilgrimage Site of the Virgin of Urkupiña in Bolivia," in *Moved by Mary: The Power of Pilgrimage in the Modern World*, ed. A. K. Hermkens, C. Notermans, and W. Jansen (Aldershot: Ashgate, 2009). See also Harris, "The Sources and Meanings of Money," 51–57.

14. R. Peredo Antezana, *El milagro de Urcupiña: Antología de las manifestaciones del folklore de Urcupiña* (Cochabamba: Cueto, 1990).

15. W. C. Sanchez, "La fiesta en la entrada de Urkupiña: Música, identidad y conflicto social alrededor de una Virgen," in *Reunión Anual de Etnología* 2 (1992): 141–65.

16. J. Mendoza Flores, "La tradicional entrada folklórica de Urkupiña," *Taquipacha* 1, no. 1 (1996): 31–45.

17. See, e.g., Arjun Appadurai, "Introduction: Commodities and the Politics of Value," in *The Social Life of Things: Commodities in Cultural Perspective*, ed. A. Appadurai (Cambridge: Cambridge University Press, 1986), 3–63.

18. Ibid., 5.

19. I. Kopytoff, "The Cultural Biography of Things: Commoditization as Process," in *The Social Life of Things*, ed. Appadurai, 66.

20. A. K. Hermkens, *Engendering Objects: Barkcloth and the Dynamics of Identity in Papua New Guinea* (Nijmegen: Radboud University Nijmegen, 2005), 10.

21. Appadurai, "Introduction," 5.

22. J. Dubisch, *In a Different Place: Pilgrimage, Gender, and Politics at a Greek Island Shrine* (Princeton, N.J.: Princeton University Press, 1995), 38.

23. McDannell, *Material Christianity*, 4.

24. Los Tiempos, "La fe mueve montañas," *Los Tiempos*, August 17, 2005, A5.

25. Pilgrims do not approach Mary exclusively for material and materialistic requests. Some of them also make spiritual wishes, such as love, harmony, health, and peace. However, the material petitions were salient, and in this paper they are the focus of research.

26. P. F. Aguilo, "La fiesta de Santa Vera Cruz en proceso de cambio," *Nueveamerica* 2, no. 3 (1985): 17–22.

27. Interview with Javier Baptista during fieldwork in Cochabamba, April 7, 2005.

28. D. Freedberg, *The Power of Images: Studies in the History and Theory of Response* (Chicago: University of Chicago Press, 1989), 83–84.

29. Because every year so many pilgrims come to dislodge stones, the back of Calvary Hill has been shrinking. Big holes have arisen, which resemble mines. Over the years, these holes have been cut deeper and deeper by the many pilgrims.

30. M. L. Lagos, " 'We Have to Learn to Ask': Hegemony, Diverse Experiences, and Antagonistic Meanings in Bolivia," *American Ethnologist* 20, no. 1 (1993): 64.

31. K. McCarthy Brown, *Mama Lola: A Vodou Priestess in Brooklyn* (Berkeley: University of California Press, 2001), 254.

32. K. I. Pargament, *The Psychology of Religion and Coping: Theory, Research, Practice* (New York: Guilfort Press, 1997). The term *collaborative approach* is derived from this study of Pargament, a psychologist in the area of religious coping, who developed a classification of religious coping styles.

33. R. A. Orsi, *Thank You, St. Jude* (New Haven, Conn.: Yale University Press, 1996), 136.

Fluid Matters: Gendering Holy Blood and Holy Milk, by Willy Jansen and Grietje Dresen

1. This research is linked to the Program The Power of Pilgrimage: A Comparative Study, funded by the NWO (Netherlands Organisation for Scientific Research), and the Program Gender, Nation, Religious Diversity in Force at European Pilgrimage Sites, funded by NORFACE (New Opportunities for Research Funding Co-operation in Europe).

2. Susan Harding, "Convicted by the Holy Spirit: The Rhetoric of Fundamental Baptist Conversion," *American Ethnologist* 14, no. 1 (1987): 167–81.

3. On blood cults, see Carolyn Walker Bynum, *Wonderful Blood: Theology and Practice in Late Medieval Northern Germany and Beyond* (Philadelphia: University of Pennsylvania Press, 2007).

4. Qur'an, S. 37:107.

5. Judaism shows many similarities to Christianity and Islam in the religious handling of blood and milk. Yet it also diverges from them on so many points that we choose not to include it here, as we would not be able to do full justice to all three religions in such a short article. However, we do refer to some shared sources, such as Leviticus.

6. Marina Warner, *Alone of All Her Sex: The Myth and the Cult of the Virgin Mary* (New York: Vintage, 1983), 192–200.

7. Willy Jansen and Meike Kühl, "Shared Symbols: Muslims, Marian Pilgrimages and Gender," *European Journal of Women's Studies* 15, no. 3 (2008): 295–311.

8. Clifford Geertz, "Religion as a Cultural System," in *Anthropological Approaches to the Study of Religion*, ed. M. Banton (London: Tavistock, 1966), 1–46.

9. Bryan S. Turner, "Social Fluids: Metaphors and Meanings of Society," *Body & Society* 9, no. 1 (2003): 1–2.

10. Mary Douglas, *Natural Symbols* (Harmondsworth: Penguin Books, 1973).

11. Fiona Bowie, *The Anthropology of Religion* (Oxford: Blackwell, 2000), 110–11.

12. Janet Carsten, *After Kinship* (Cambridge: Cambridge University Press, 2004), 109–35.

13. Ibid., 28–29.

14. David Schneider, *American Kinship: A Cultural Account* (Chicago: University of Chicago Press, 1980), 24.

15. Mary Douglas, *Purity and Danger: An Analysis of Concepts of Pollution and Taboo* (London: Routledge & Kegan Paul, 1966), 35–40.

16. Ibid., 7.

17. Ibid., 53.

18. Ibid., 94.

19. Ibid, 39–40.

20. See Qur'an S. 5:3; 6:143; 16:114.

21. For St. Peter, see 1 Peter 1:2 and 19; for St. John, 1 John 1:7, Revelation 1:5, and many other passages; for St. Paul, Romans 3:25, Ephesians 1:7, and Hebrews 9:10. See also *Catholic Encyclopedia*, Precious Blood www.newadvent.org, accessed November 28, 2008.

22. Grietje Dresen, "Heilig bloed, ontheiligend bloed: Over het ritueel van de kerkgang en het offer in de katholieke traditie," *Tijdschrift voor Vrouwenstudies* 14, no. 1 (1993): 25–41, and Grietje Dresen, "The Better Blood: On Sacrifice and the Churching of New Mothers in the Roman Catholic Tradition," in *Wholly Woman, Holy Blood: A Feminist Critique of Purity and Impurity*, ed. K. de Troyer, J. A. Herbert, J. A. Johnson, and A. M. Korte (Harrisburg, Pa.: Trinity Press, 2003), 143–64.

23. Douglas, *Purity and Danger*, 61.

24. Paula M. Rieder, "The Implications of Exclusion: The Regulation of Churching in Medieval Northern France," *Essays in Medieval Studies* 15 (1998): 71–78. See also Paula M. Rieder, *On the Purification of Women: Churching in Northern France, 1100–1500* (New York: Palgrave Macmillan, 2006), in which Rieder shows that churching not only confirmed her relatively inferior role vis-à-vis both men and the Church, who considered her in need of purification, but also allowed legitimately married women public recognition of their respectability and their superiority over "indecent" women.

25. Dresen, "The Better Blood."

26. The churching of women has become rare in Western Christianity, but it is still performed in a number of Eastern Christian churches; see also ibid.

27. Jill Bradley, *You Shall Surely Not Die: The Concepts of Sin and Death as Expressed in the Manuscript Art of Northwestern Europe c. 800–1200* (Leiden: Brill, 2003), 304–12.

28. Willy Jansen, *Women Without Men: Gender and Marginality in an Algerian Town* (Leiden: Brill, 1987), 55–56.

29. Willy Jansen, "Religious Practices: Ablution, Purification, Prayer, Fasting and Piety, North Africa," in *Encyclopedia of Women and Islamic Cultures*, vol. 5, *Practices, Interpretations and Representations*, ed. S. Joseph (Leiden: Brill, 2007), 273–74.

30. Vincent Crapanzano, *The Hamadsha: A Study in Moroccan Ethnopsychiatry* (Berkeley: University of California Press, 1973).

31. Anton Blok, *Honour and Violence* (Cambridge: Polity Press, 2001), 178–83.

32. Qur'an S. 16:66.

33. Qur'an S. 47:15.

34. Warner, *Alone of All Her Sex*, 200 and plate 26. A similar Mary, showing her breast to the crucified Jesus with a similar text, can be found in Anne Margreet W. As-Vijvers, ed., *From the Hand of the Master of the Hours of Catherine of Cleves* (New York: The Morgan Library and Museum, 2009), 130.

35. Augustine, *Confessions* 1.6 and 3.4, and *Patrologia latina* 185, 878. (campus.udayton.edu/mary/questions/yq/yq211.html, accessed July 10, 2007).

36. Cf. the fragment: "The Son is the cup, and the Father is he who was milked; and the Holy Spirit is she who milked him. . . . The Holy Spirit opened her bosom, and mixed the milk of the

two breasts of the Father," quoted by Edward Engelbrecht, "God's Milk: An Orthodox Confession of the Eucharist," *Journal of Early Christian Studies* 7, no. 4 (1999): 509; Gail Paterson Corrington, "The Milk of Salvation: Redemption by the Mother in Late Antiquity and Early Christianity," *The Harvard Theological Review* 82, no. 4 (1989): 408–9. The breasts of Mary are likened to the breasts of Ecclesia (the Church), as depicted in the cathedral at Bourges: Hildreth York and Betty L. Schlossman, "'She Shall Be Called Woman': Ancient Near Eastern Sources of Imagery," *Women's Art Journal* 2, no. 2 (1981–82): 37–41.

37. Margaret R. Miles, "God's Love, Mother's Milk," *The Christian Century*, January 29, 2008, pp. 22–25 (www.religion-online.org accessed December 23, 2008).

38. Warner, *Alone of All Her Sex*, 326, plate 28.

39. Franz Slump (2000), *Gottes Zorn—Marias Schutz: Pestbilder und verwandte Darstellungen als ikonographischer Ausdruck spätmittelalterlicher Frömmigkeit und als theologisches Problem*, p. 17 (www.slump.de/17.htm, accessed July 10, 2007).

40. Susan Starr Sered, "Rachel's Tomb and the Milk Grotto of the Virgin Mary: Two Women's Shrines in Bethlehem," *Journal of Feminist Studies in Religion* 2, no. 2 (1986): 7–22.

41. Quoted by Warner, *Alone of All Her Sex,* plate 30.

42. As Mary does in the altar image *The Holy Bernard and the Wonder of the Lactatio*, by Gottfried Bernhard Göz, 1749.

43. Miles, "God's Love, Mother's Milk," 22–25.

44. Sered, "Rachel's Tomb," 10.

45. Grietje Dresen, "Van Madonna tot Madonna, of: het ideaal van de onbevlekte vrouw," in G. Dresen, *Is dit mijn lichaam? Visioenen van het volmaakte lichaam in katholieke moraal en mystiek* (Nijmegen: Valkhof Pers, 1998), 61–82.

46. Rosan Hollak, "De keutelborst van de Heilige Maagd," *NRC Handelsblad, Cultureel supplement*, April 10, 2009, p. 9.

47. Carolyn Walker Bynum, *Holy Feast and Holy Fast: The Religious Significance of Food to Medieval Women* (Berkeley: University of California Press, 1987), 269–70; Marilyn Yalom, *A History of the Breast* (New York: Random House, 1997), 24.

48. Ibid.

49. Paterson Corrington, "The Milk of Salvation," 410.

50. Ibid., 412.

51. Jansen and Kühl, "Shared Symbols," 295–311; Willy Jansen, "Visions of Mary in the Middle East: Gender and the Power of a Symbol," in *Gender, Religion and Change in the Middle East: Two Hundred Years of History*, ed. I. M. Okkenhaug and I. Flaskerud (Oxford: Berg, 2005), 137–54.

52. Filmed by Nouchka van Brakel in her documentary *Avé Maria: Van dienstmaagd des heren tot koningin van de hemel*, Egmond Film and Television, ABC distribution.

53. Sered, "Rachel's Tomb," 9, 16.

54. W. H. M. Jansen, D. Long, W. B. C. Stevens, and K. Verpaalen, "Moedermelk en zoogverwantschap in de interculturele gezondheidszorg," *Verpleegkunde* 16, no. 2 (2001): 93–100; Willy Jansen, Review of Avner Giladi, *Infants, Parents and Wet Nurses: Medieval Islamic Views on Breastfeeding and Their Social Implications* (Leiden: Brill, 1999), *Bibliotheca Orientalis* 58, no. 3/4 (2001): 499–502.

55. Douglas, *Purity and Danger*, 3.

56. Elizabeth Faithorn, "The Concept of Pollution among the Kafe of Papua New Guinea Highlands," in *Toward an Anthropology of Women*, ed. R. R. Reiter (New York: Monthly Review Press, 1974), 127–40.

57. Thomas Buckley and Alma Gottlieb, eds., *Blood Magic: The Anthropology of Menstruation* (Berkeley: University of California Press, 1988).

58. Anna-Karina Hermkens, Willy Jansen, and Catrien Notermans, *Moved by Mary: The Power of Pilgrimage in the Modern World* (Farnham: Ashgate, 2009).

59. Douglas, *Purity and* Danger, 3–4.

60. See: Hermkens, Jansen, and Notermans, *Moved by Mary*; Sanne Derks, *Power and Pilgrimage: Dealing with Class, Gender and Ethnic Inequality at a Bolivian Marian Shrine* (Berlin: Lit, 2009); Sanne Derks, Willy Jansen, and Catrien Notermans, "Miniatures and Stones in the Spiritual Economy of the Virgin of Urkupiña in Bolivia," this volume; Willy Jansen and Catrien Notermans, eds., *Gender, Nation and Religion in European Pilgrimage* (Farnham: Ashgate, 2012); Catrien Notermans, "The Power of the Less Powerful: Making Memory Through a Pilgrimage to Lourdes," in *Powers: Religion as a Social and Spiritual Force,* ed. Meerten B. ter Borg and Jan Willem van Henten (New York: Fordham University Press, 2010), 181–93.

61. Lena Gemzöe, "Big, Strong and Happy: Reimagining Femininity on the Way to Compostela," and Anna Fedele, "Gender, Sexuality and Religious Critique among Mary Magdalene Pilgrims in Southern France," both in *Gender, Nation and Religion in European Pilgrimage,* ed. Jansen and Notermans.

"When you see blood, it brings truth": Ritual and Resistance in a Time of War, by Elizabeth A. Castelli

NOTE: This essay has had many incarnations and has benefited from generous critique from numerous people. It began as the keynote address at the annual conference of the Center for Religion and Media at New York University in May 2006, which was organized around the theme "Body Counts / Bodies Count." I wish to thank Professors Angela Zito and Faye Ginsberg for the invitation to deliver this lecture and for their ongoing intellectual hospitality. The essay has also benefited from the questions and comments of audiences at many institutions: Pomona College, Grinnell College, Austin College, Mount Holyoke College, Ohio State University, University of Amsterdam, University of California at Davis, Brown University, and Columbia University. Special thanks to Erin Runions, Kathleen Skerrett, Michael Penn, Sarah Iles Johnston, Birgit Meyer, and Mark Elmore for their invitations to speak at their institutions and for their thoughtful feedback on this work. Thanks also to Mary-Jane Rubenstein for her ever-incisive comments and insights. Finally, a special word of gratitude to the St. Patrick's Four and to Bill Quigley, former Legal Director at the Center for Constitutional Rights and legal advisor to the St. Patrick's Four during their federal trial.

1. "Killing Cannot Be with Christ," statement read by the St. Patrick's Four on March 17, 2003, at the Army/Marine Recruiting Station in Lansing, New York: www.stpatricksfour.org/documents/KillingwithChrist.pdf. This statement's opening apology echoes the language used in earlier Catholic antiwar actions, notably the draft-record destruction undertaken by the Catonsville Nine, a group that included the radical priests (and brothers) Philip and Daniel Berrigan. See Daniel Berrigan's poem:

> Our apologies good friends
> for the fracture of good order
> the burning of paper instead of children
> the angering of orderlies in the front parlor of the charnal house
> we could not so help us God do otherwise
> for we are sick at heart
> our hearts give us no rest for thinking of the Land of
>   burning
>   children.

Quoted in Philip Berrigan, *Fighting the Lamb's War: Skirmishes with the American Empire* (Monroe, Maine: Common Courage Press, 1996), 105.

2. Bill Quigley, "The St. Patrick's Four: Jury Votes 9–3 to Acquit Peace Activists Despite Admission They Poured Blood in Military Recruiting Center," *Guild Practitioner* 61 (2004): 110–28. Though the St. Patrick's Four represented themselves in court, they were accompanied by two lawyers who served as advisors; Bill Quigley, a professor of law at Loyola University, New Orleans, was one of those attorneys.

3. Bill Quigley, "Enforcing International Law Through Civil Disobedience: The Trial of the St. Patrick's Four," in *In the Name of Democracy: American War Crimes in Iraq and Beyond*, ed. Jeremy Brecher, Jill Cutler, and Brendan Smith (New York: Macmillan, 2005), 280–85.

4. *U.S. v. Peter De Mott, Clare Grady, Daniel Burns, Teresa Grady*, 05-CR-73, United States District Court, Northern District of New York. September 19–26, 2005. Trial transcript. This transcript is available at http://stpatricksfour.org/?q=node/377. Clare Grady quotation at p. 72, lines 7–14.

5. For a general history of the Catholic Worker movement, see Mel Piehl, *Breaking Bread: The Catholic Worker and the Origin of Catholic Radicalism in America* (Philadelphia: Temple University Press, 1982). See also: Rosalie Riegle Troester, ed., *Voices from the Catholic Worker* (Philadelphia: Temple University Press, 1993); William J. Thorn, Phillip M. Runkel, and Susan Mountin, eds., *Dorothy Day and the Catholic Worker Movement: Centenary Essays* (Milwaukee: Marquette University Press, 2001); Mark and Louise Zwick, *The Catholic Worker Movement: Intellectual and Spiritual Origins* (New York: Paulist Press, 2005); Anne Klejment and Nancy L. Roberts, eds., *American Catholic Pacifism: The Influence of Dorothy Day and the Catholic Worker Movement* (Westport, Conn.: Praeger, 1996). For primary sources derived from *The Catholic Worker* newspaper, see Thomas C. Cornell and James H. Forest, eds., *A Penny a Copy: Readings from "The Catholic Worker"* (New York: Macmillan, 1968). On the more particular question of Catholic Worker involvement in antiwar destruction of property, see Anne Klejment, "War Resistance and Property Destruction: The Catonsville Nine Draft Board and Catholic Worker Pacifism," in *A Revolution of the Heart: Essays on the Catholic Worker*, ed. Patrick G. Coy (Philadelphia: Temple University Press, 1988), 272–309. See also Charles A. Meconis, *With Clumsy Grace: The American Catholic Left, 1961–1975* (New York: Seabury, 1979), and Penelope Adams Moon, "'Peace on Earth—Peace in Vietnam': The Catholic Peace Fellowship and Antiwar Witness, 1964–1976," *Journal of Social History* 36 (2003): 1033–57.

6. Klejment, "War Resistance and Property Destruction," 273.

7. Michael S. Foley, *Confronting the War Machine: Draft Resistance During the Vietnam War* (Chapel Hill: University of North Carolina Press, 2003).

8. Klejment, "War Resistance and Property Destruction," 274.

9. *U.S. v. De Mott et al.*, p. 206, lines 21–25; p. 207, line 1.

10. Tom Cornell, "Nonviolent Napalm in Catonsville," (1968) in *The Universe Bends Toward Justice*, ed. Angie O'Gorman (Philadelphia: New Society Publishers, 1990), 203–8, cited by Sharon Erickson Nepstad, *Religion and War Resistance in the Plowshares Movement* (Cambridge: Cambridge University Press, 2008), 48.

11. Nepstad, *Religion and War Resistance*, 62.

12. For Harriet Tubman and civil rights, see *U.S. v. De Mott et al.*, p. 92, lines 9–16; for Rosa Parks, Susan B. Anthony, and Henry David Thoreau, see ibid., p. 102, lines 6–12; for Martin Luther King, Jr., see ibid., p. 89, lines 9–15 and elsewhere in the transcript.

13. An excellent documentary of this action is *Investigation of a Flame*, directed by Lynne Sachs (First Run/Icarus Films, 2001).

14. See Nepstad, *Religion and War Resistance*, for an in-depth sociological analysis of the Plowshares movement, which includes in its documentation lengthy interviews with its members. See also Fred A. Wilcox, *Uncommon Martyrs: The Berrigans, the Catholic Left, and the Plowshares Movement* (Reading, Mass.: Addison-Wesley, 1991), and Arthur J. Laffin and Anne Montgomery, eds., *Swords into Plowshares: Nonviolent Direct Action for Disarmament* (San Francisco: Harper & Row, 1987).

15. Murray Polner and Jim O'Grady, *Disarmed and Dangerous: The Radical Lives and Times of Daniel and Philip Berrigan* (New York: Basic Books, 1977), 172–73.

16. Quoted in Polner and O'Grady, *Disarmed and Dangerous*, 176.

17. Ibid., 173: "The [Baltimore Customs House] protest's goals were to stall a part of the Pentagon's induction machinery, possibly sparing a few young lives; stimulate debate about the morality of the draft; inspire others to assume greater personal risks in acting against the war; and use the courtroom as a public forum to denounce the war and the injustice of conscription." See also Nepstad, *Religion and War Resistance*, 78–83 ("Tactical Legitimation in Court Trials") for the Plowshares movement's understanding of the courtroom as a site for activism.

18. Nepstad, *Religion and War Resistance*, 56–57.

19. *U.S. v. De Mott et al.*, p. 121, lines 8–13.

20. Ibid., p. 380, lines 15–25; p. 381, lines 1–8, 16–25; p. 382, line 1.

21. Ibid., p. 153, lines 8–11.

22. Ibid., p. 156, lines 2–11, 14–22.

23. The person or people who drew the blood from the bodies of the St. Patrick's Four were never identified at the trial. The practice, over time, seems to have been routinized by activists, but it is interesting to note that, on the first occasion of antiwar blood spilling, at the Baltimore Customs House action in 1967, the activists had considerable difficulty producing enough of their own blood for the action and ultimately resorted to buying duck blood at a local market and mixing it with small amounts of their own blood. See Polner and O'Grady, *Disarmed and Dangerous*, 174.

24. *U.S. v. De Mott et al.*, p. 510, lines 18–20; p. 511, lines 2–19.

25. Ibid., p. 260, lines 16–25; p. 261, lines 1–2.

26. Ibid., p. 312, lines 22–24; p. 313, lines 14–19.

27. Ibid., p. 388, lines 21–25; p. 389, lines 1–7.

28. Ibid., p. 395, lines 16–23.

29. Ibid., p. 714, line 25; p. 715, line 1.

30. Ibid., p. 578, lines 9–18.

31. Ibid., p. 584, lines 22–25; p. 585, lines 1–4.

32. Ibid., p. 519, lines 6–10.

33. Ibid., p. 714, lines 8–11.

34. Ibid., p. 707, lines 13–25; p. 708, line 1.

35. Ibid., p. 713, lines 15–16.

36. Ibid., p. 752, lines 2–25; p. 753, line 1.

37. Ibid., p. 753, lines 11–13.

38. Ibid., p. 701, lines 4–9.

39. Peter DeMott subsequently passed away on February 19, 2009. See his obituary at: http://dccatholicworker.wordpress.com/2009/02/20/in-loving-memory-peter-demott-january-6-1947-february-19-2009/.

40. Penelope Adams Moon, "Loyal Sons and Daughters of God? American Catholics Debate Catholic Antiwar Protest," *Peace and Change* 33, no. 1 (2008): 1–30.

41. Barrie Thorne, "Women in the Draft Resistance Movement: A Case Study of Sex Roles and Social Movements," *Sex Roles* 1 (1975): 179–95, and Marian Mollin, "Communities of Resistance:

Women and the Catholic Left of the Late 1960s," *The Oral History Review* 31, no. 2 (Summer-Autumn 2004): 29–51. But see also the documentary *Conviction*, directed by Brenda Truelson Fox (Zero to Sixty Productions, 2006), concerning the trial of Ardeth Platte, Carol Gilbert, and Jackie Hudson, three Dominican sisters who broke into a missile silo in Colorado in 2002, poured their own blood, and chanted in an effort to draw attention to the proliferation of nuclear weapons.

42. Philip Berrigan, "Letter from a Baltimore Jail," in *Prison Journals of a Priest Revolutionary* (New York: Ballantine Books, 1971), 15–16.

43. Klejment, "War Resistance and Property Destruction," 284–300. For the interview quoted, see Dwight MacDonald, "Revisiting Dorothy Day," *The New York Review of Books* 16, no. 1 (January 28, 1971): http://www.nybooks.com/articles/10685.

44. Nepstad, *Religion and War Resistance*, 160.

45. Ibid., 213.

46. Elizabeth A. Castelli, "Praying for the Persecuted Church: U.S. Christian Activism in the Global Arena," *Journal of Human Rights* 4 (2005): 321–51; Elizabeth A. Castelli, "Théologiser les droits de l'homme: La nouvelle Bible des évangélistes américains," *Vacarme* no. 34 (Winter 2006): 196–200, http://www.vacarme.org/article561.html; Elizabeth A. Castelli, "Theologizing Human Rights: Christian Activism and the Limits of Religious Freedom," in *Non-Governmental Politics*, ed. Michel Feher, with Gaëlle Krikorian and Yates McKee (New York: Zone Books, 2007), 673–87; Elizabeth A. Castelli, "Persecution Complexes: Identity Politics and the 'War on Christians,'" *differences: A Journal of Feminist Cultural Studies* 18, no. 3 (Fall 2007): 152–80.

A Pentecostal Passion Paradigm: The Invisible Framing of Gibson's Christ in a Dutch Pentecostal Church, by Miranda Klaver

NOTE: I would like to thank Birgit Meyer, André Droogers, Linda van de Kamp, Kim Knibbe, Regien Smit, and Peter Versteeg for their feedback on this essay. My epigraph is from David Neff and Jane Johnson Struck, "'Dude, That Was Graphic,' Mel Gibson talks about *The Passion of the Christ*," http://www.christianitytoday.com/movies/interviews/melgibson.html 2/5/2007.

1. The longstanding understanding of Protestantism as an iconoclastic tradition devoid of material history has contributed to a neglect of the material dimension in the study of Christianity. Even when the significance of material culture has been recognized, it has often been subordinated to language. See Matthew Engelke, *A Problem of Presence: Beyond Scripture in an African Church* (Berkeley: University of California Press, 2007), 10.

2. Allan Anderson, *An Introduction to Pentecostalism: Global Charismatic Christianity* (Cambridge: Cambridge University Press, 2004), 188.

3. Karla Poewe, "The Charismatic Movement and Augustine: The Challenge of Symbolic Thought in the Modern World," *Pneuma: The Journal of the Society of Pentecostal Studies* 11, no.1 (Fall 1989): 23.

4. J. Kwabene Asamoah-Gyady, "'Function to Function': Reinventing the Oil of Influence in African Pentecostalism," *Journal of Pentecostal Theology* 13, no. 2 (2005): 232.

5. Huib Zegwaart, "Christian Experience in Community," *Cyberjournal for Pentecostal-Charismatic Research*, February 11, 2002, http://www.pctii.org/cyberj/cyberj11/zagwaart.html.

6. Poewe, "The Charismatic Movement," 34.

7. Colleen McDannell, *Material Christianity: Religion and Popular Culture in America* (New Haven, Conn.: Yale University Press, 1995); Elisabeth Arweck and William J. F. Keenan, "Material

Varieties of Religious Expression," in *Materializing Religion: Expression, Performance and Ritual*, ed. Elisabeth Arweck and William J. F. Keenan (Hampshire: Ashgate Publishing Ltd, 2006); Christopher Tilley, Webb Keane, Suzanne Küchler, et al. eds., *Handbook of Material Culture* (London: Sage Publications, 2006).

8. Webb Keane, "Subjects and Objects," in *Handbook of Material Culture*, ed. C. Tilly et al. (London: Sage Publications, 2006), 200.

9. Simon Coleman, *The Globalisation of Charismatic Christianity* (Cambridge: Cambridge University Press, 2000), 131.

10. Thomas J. Csordas, "Introduction: The Body as Representation and Being-in-the-World," in *Embodiment and Experience: The Existential Ground of Culture and Self*, ed. Thomas J. Csordas (Cambridge: Cambridge University Press, 1994): 12.

11. Webb Keane, *Christian Moderns: Freedom and Fetish in the Mission Encounter* (Berkeley: University of California Press, 2007), 18, 21.

12. The Toronto Blessing refers to a charismatic revival movement that emerged in the Toronto Airport Vineyard Church in Canada during the mid nineties. This movement was characterized by unusual manifestations, including "falling in the Spirit" and "Holy laughter" (Anderson, *An Introduction to Pentecostalism*, 162–64). The leaders of this Dutch Pentecostal church had visited the Toronto church and brought the "blessing" home with them. The Dutch Assemblies of God churches, however, published a position paper in their journal *Parakleet*, no. 57 (1996): 3–4, raising serious doubts whether the Toronto Blessing is the work of God.

13. The New Apostolic Reformation movement was initiated by Peter Wagner; see http://www.-globalharvest.org/index.asp?action = apostolic, 05/08/2008. The concept of the five-fold ministry is based on Ephesians 4:11: "It was he who gave some to be (1) apostles, some to be (2) prophets, some to be (3) evangelists, and some to be (4) pastors and (5) teachers." Biblical church leadership is understood to be a team leadership of five men representing these five gifts.

14. The interim pastor was very inspired by the G12 movement, founded by Cesar Castellanos, from Colombia. Castellanos visited the Netherlands at a national G12 conference for church leaders in 2002. The G12 model was introduced as *the* biblical model for church growth and promised a rapid multiplication of church members. Critics named it a multi-level marketing technique. While plans were made to establish a national G12 network, cultural differences between the Colombians and the Dutch turned out to be unbridgeable—or so the interim pastor commented years later. The official website of the G12 network is at: http://www.visiong12.com/, 05/15/2008.

15. Wilkin van der Kamp, *Het wonder van het kruis: De laatste achttien uur voor Jezus' sterven* (Aalten: Cross Light Media, 2005).

16. Ibid., 54, 55; my translation.

17. Fieldnotes, June 2007.

18. Anne L. Clark, "Venerating the Veronica: Varieties of Passion Piety in the Later Middle Ages," in *Material Religion* 3, no. 2 (2007): 172.

19. The network of biblical narratives is often constructed in a chronological schema of a single overarching biblical history, without taking into account the different genres of text.

20. Wilkin van der Kamp, *Zeven stappen op weg naar vrijheid* (Aalten: Crosslight Media, n.d.).

21. I am aware that focusing on the women's group raises gender issues. But differences in group dynamics between the mixed-couples group and the women's group made me choose the latter. I suspect that personal revelations and intimate conversations were hindered by the presence of partners. Men involved in a men's small group recalled the importance of privacy and the sharing of men's issues in their group. In personal interviews with men, I was told that, although different issues were addressed in their groups ("porn addiction" was often mentioned), the same "spiritual principles" were applied.

22. Ana Mendez Ferell and her husband lead an independent ministry and hold prophetic conferences in several countries. See http://www.voiceofthelight.com/, 05/15/2008.

23. Ana Mendez Ferell, *Eet van Mijn vlees, drink van Mijn bloed* (Vlissingen: Bread of Life, 2006).

24. "Quiet time" refers to the daily practice of a private moment of devotion, with prayer and Bible study.

25. This notion of a legal basis for Satanic visitations is based on a Pentecostal interpretation of Ephesians 4:27, where the apostle Paul admonishes believers not to give the devil a "foothold." "Foothold," a translation of the Greek word *topos*, is interpreted as a license, granting the devil legal access to afflict the believer who has sinned.

26. *The Satanic Bible*, by Anton Lavey, is used in the Church of Satan and is popular among heavy metal fans and gothics. The Pentecostal women associate this book with occult and evil powers.

27. The historical accuracy of the film has been intensely debated, several nonbiblical elements having been drawn from the writings of the Catholic mystics Agrade and Emmerich. See Vincent J. Miller, "Contexts: Theology, Devotion and Culture," in *Mel Gibson's Bible: Religion, Popular Culture, and* The Passion of the Christ, ed. Timothy K. Beal and Tod Linafelt (Chicago: University of Chicago Press, 2006), 49.

28. Coleman, *The Globalisation of Charismatic Christianity*, 131; Susan Harding, *The Book of Jerry Falwell: Fundamentalist Language and Politics* (Princeton, N.J.: Princeton University Press, 2000), 272; Matthew Engelke and Matt Tomlinson, "Meaning, Anthropology, Christianity," in *The Limits of Meaning: Case Studies in the Anthropology of Christianity*, ed. Matthew Engelke and Matt Tomlinson (New York: Berghahn Books, 2006): 22.

29. See: Karla Poewe, "On the Metonymic Structure of Religious Experiences: The Example of Charismatic Christianity," *Cultural Dynamics* 2, no. 4 (1989): 367; Gerard Roelofs, "Charismatic Christian Thought: Experience, Metonymy, and Routinization," in *Charismatic Christianity as a Global Culture*, ed. Karla Poewe (Columbia: University of South Carolina Press, 1994): 217–33.

30. See Keane, *Christian Moderns*, 22, for Peirce's theory of sign relations.

31. Indexical relationships are often connected to claims of power; see Engelke and Tomlinson, "Meaning, Anthropology, Christianity," 16.

32. See Anderson, *An Introduction to Pentecostalism,* 226.

33. Jill Stevenson, "The Material Bodies of Medieval Religious Performance in England," *Material Religion* 2, no. 2 (2006): 206.

34. G. Hughes, *Worship as Meaning: A Liturgical Theology for Late Modernity* (Cambridge: Cambridge University Press, 2003), 298, suggests that religious experiences may be the outcome of boundary or limit experiences. He understands these experiences as expansive intensifications of ordinary things.

35. I am referring here to the desire to become the ideal religious self. A similar argument can be made for the desire to become an ideal cultural self. This is addressed in my *This Is My Desire: A Semiotic Perspective on Conversion in an Evangelical Seeker Church and a Pentecostal Church in the Netherlands* (Amsterdam: VU University, Pallas Publications/Amsterdam University Press, 2011.)

36. See: Saba Mahmood, "Rehearsed Spontaneity and the Conventionality of Ritual: Disciplines of "Ṣalāt," *American Ethnologist* 28, no. 4 (November 2001): 827–53; Birgit Meyer, "Religious Sensations: Why Media, Aesthetics, and Power Matter in the Study of Contemporary Religion," in *Religion: Beyond a Concept*, ed. Hent de Vries (New York: Fordham University Press, 2008), 704–23; Chris Shilling and Philip A. Mellor, "Cultures of Embodied Experience: Technology, Religion and Body Pedagogics," *The Sociological Review* 55, no. 3 (2007): 531–49.

37. Tanya M. Luhrmann, "How Do You Learn to Know That It Is God Who Speaks?" in *Learning Religion: Anthropological Approaches*, ed. David Berliner and Ramon Sarró (New York: Berghahn Books, 2007), 84.

38. For the question of believers' control over material things, see Engelke and Tomlinson, "Meaning, Anthropology, Christianity," 33.

The Structural Transformation of the Coffeehouse: Religion, Language, and the Public Sphere in the Modernizing Muslim World, by Michiel Leezenberg

NOTE: An initial version of this paper was presented at the Conference on Things held in the framework of the NWO Program The Future of the Religious Past. The final version was written during a sojourn at NIAS in Wassenaar. I thank both NWO and NIAS for their financial support, and NIAS for the wonderful environment and facilities it provides.

1. Jürgen Habermas, *Between Naturalism and Religion: Philosophical Essays* (Cambridge: Polity Press, 2008), esp. chaps. 5 and 8. I have discussed Habermas's concept of the post-secular, especially in connection with the modern Islamic world, in "How Ethnocentric Is the Concept of the Postsecular?" in *Exploring the Postsecular: The Religious, the Political, and the Urban*, ed. A. Molendijk and J. Beaumont (Leiden: Brill, 2010).

2. Jürgen Habermas, *The Structural Transformation of the Public Sphere*, trans. Thomas Burger (Cambridge: MIT Press, 1992).

3. Talal Asad, *Genealogies of Religion: Discipline and Reasons of Power in Christianity and Islam* (Baltimore: Johns Hopkins University Press, 1993), and Talal Asad, *Formations of the Secular: Christianity, Islam, Modernity* (Stanford, Calif.: Stanford University Press, 2003); in the former, see esp. "The Construction of Religion as an Anthropological Category" and "Religious Criticism in the Middle East"; in the latter, see esp. "What Might an Anthropology of Secularism Look Like?" and "Reconfigurations of Law in Egypt."

4. Asad, *Genealogies of Religion*, 1.

5. Bruno Latour, *We Have Never Been Modern*, trans. Catherine Porter (Cambridge: Harvard University Press, 1994).

6. Ibid., 15–18, 97–100.

7. Michel Foucault, "La vérité et les formes juridiques," in *Dits et écrits* (Paris: Gallimard, 1994), 2: 631.

8. H. P. Grice, "Logic and Conversation," in *Studies in the Way of Words* (Cambridge: Harvard University Press, 1989). The foundational text in politeness studies is P. Brown and S. C. Levinson, *Politeness: Some Universals of Language Usage* (Cambridge: Cambridge University Press, 1987). Jürgen Habermas's historical analysis of eighteenth-century public reasoning is the basis for his more general theory, elaborated in *Theory of Communicative Action*, vol. 1, *Reason and the Rationalization of Society*, trans. Thomas McCarthy (Boston: Beacon Press, 1984), 273–338. For further elaboration of Habermas's linguistic and pragmatic turn, see esp. Jürgen Habermas, *Wahrheit und Rechtfertigung* (Frankfurt am Main: Suhrkamp, 1999), and Jürgen Habermas, "Communicative Action and the Detranscendentalized 'Use of Reason,'" in *Between Naturalism and Religion* (Cambridge: Polity Press, 2008), 24–76.

9. For an account of the emergence of the coffeehouse in Europe, especially England, see Markman Ellis, *The Coffee-house: A Cultural History* (London: Weidenfeld & Nicholson, 2004), chap. 12; see also L. Klein, "Coffeehouse Civility. 1660–1714," *Huntington Library Quarterly* 59 (1996): 30–51.

10. See, e.g., Sydney Mintz, *Sweetness and Power: The Place of Sugar in Modern History* (New York: Viking, 1985), esp. 141–43.

11. See Richard Bauman and Charles L. Briggs, *Voices of Modernity: Language Ideologies and the Politics of Inequality* (Cambridge: Cambridge University Press, 2003), esp. chap. 2. In their otherwise excellent discussion of the language-ideological consequences of this social unrest, they largely ignore this religious dimension.

12. Immanuel Kant, "What Is Enlightenment?" trans. H. B. Nisbet, in *Kant: Political Writings*, ed. H. Reiss (Cambridge: Cambridge University Press, 1991), 54–60.

13. Ibid., 59.

14. Ibid., 55.

15. Jürgen Villers, *Kant und das Problem der Sprache: Die historischen und systematischen Gründe für die Sprachlosigkeit der Transzendentalphilosophie* (Constance: am Hockgraben, 1997); see also Hans Aarsleff, "Philosophy of Language," in *The Cambridge History of Eighteenth-Century Philosophy*, ed. K. Haakonssen (Cambridge: Cambridge University Press, 2006).

16. Jürgen Habermas, *The Structural Transformation of the Public Sphere*, trans. Thomas Huber, (Cambridge: MIT Press, 1992). See also Habermas's "Further Reflections on the Public Sphere," in *Habermas and the Public Sphere*, ed. C. Calhoun (Cambridge: MIT Press, 1992), 451–95.

17. Some of these, such as Kant's rather idiosyncratic conception of "public"—which displays a tension with the more familiar liberal sense employed by Habermas—contain an elitist bias and a tacit gender asymmetry that have been extensively discussed and do not concern us here. For examples of criticism along these lines, all remaining within Eurocentric confines, see the various contributions to Craig Calhoun, ed., *Habermas and the Public Sphere* (Cambridge: MIT Press, 1992).

18. Webb Keane, *Christian Moderns: Freedom and Fetish in the Mission Encounter* (Berkeley: University of California Press, 2007). See also Bauman and Briggs, *Voices of Modernity*, for an impressive, if still residually Eurocentric, account of the role of changing language ideologies in the political constitution of modernity. The notion of language ideologies is anticipated in the work of, among others, C. S. Peirce and Roman Jakobson, but receives its first full elaboration in Michael Silverstein, "Language Structure and Linguistic Ideology," in *The Elements: A Parasession on Linguistic Units and Levels*, ed. R. Cline, W. Hanks, and C. Hofbauer (Chicago: Chicago Linguistic Society, 1979), 193–247.

19. Ellis, *The Coffee-house*, 26–30, 45.

20. For a historical overview of coffee consumption in the early modern Ottoman empire, primarily from a legal and medical point of view, see Ralph Hattox, *Coffee and Coffeehouses: Origins of a Social Beverage in the Medieval Near East* (Seattle: University of Washington Press, 1985). Another important study, more from the perspective of social history, is Cengiz Kirli, "The Struggle over Space: Coffeehouses of Ottoman Istanbul, 1780—1845" (Ph. D. dissertation, State University of New York at Binghamton, 2000). See also: Cemal Kafadar, *A History of Coffee* (n.d.), available online at http://eh.net/XIIICongress/cd/papers/64Kafadar16.pdf (last accessed April 15, 2010); H. Desmet-Grégoire and F. Georgeon, ed., *Cafés d'orient revisités* (Paris: Éditions CNRS, 1997); S. Akyazici Özkoçak, "Coffeehouses: Rethinking the Public and Private in Early Modern Istanbul," *Journal of Urban History* 33 (2007): 965–86; and the various papers collected in Dana Sajdi, ed., *Ottoman Tulips, Ottoman Coffee: Leisure and Lifestyle in the Eighteenth Century* (London: I. B. Tauris, 2007).

21. Cf. Hattox, *Coffee and Coffeehouses*, 114

22. Kirli, "The Struggle over Space," 49.

23. For more on Janissary coffeehouses, see Ali Çaksu, "Janissary Coffeehouses in Late Eighteenth Century Istanbul," in *Ottoman Tulips, Ottoman Coffee*, ed. Sajdi, 125.

24. Koçu, 1964 *Yeniçeriler*, quoted in ibid., 202n22; Kirli, "The Struggle over Space," 222.

25. See Kirli, "The Struggle over Space," chap. 2; on the importance of networks, see also Karen Barkey, *Empire of Difference: The Ottomans in Comparative Perspective* (Cambridge: Cambridge University Press, 2008).

26. See Dror Ze'evi, *Producing Desire: Changing Sexual Discourse in the Ottoman Middle East, 1500–1900* (Berkeley: University of California Press, 2006), esp. chap. 5, "Boys in the Hood: Shadow Theater as a Sexual Counter-Script."

27. Serif Mardin, "A Note on an Early Phase in the Modernization of Communication Relations in Turkey," *Comparative Studies in Society and History* 3, no. 3 (1961): 250–71.

28. Benedict Anderson, *Imagined Communities: Reflections on the Origin and Spread of Nationalism* (London: Verso Books, 1991).

29. Leslie Peirce, *Imperial Harem* (New York: Oxford University Press, 1993); Alan Mikhail, "The Heart's Desire: Gender, Urban Space and the Ottoman Coffeehouse," in *Ottoman Tulips, Ottoman Coffee*, ed. Sajdi, 133–70.

30. Michel Foucault, "Des espaces autres," in *Dits et écrits* (Paris: Gallimard, 1994), 4:752–62; for an English translation, see "Of Other Spaces," available online at http://foucault.info/documents/ heteroTopia/foucault.heteroTopia.en.html (last accessed October 18, 2009). For a related but different text, see Foucault, *Le corps utopique, suivi de Les hétérotopies* (Paris: Nouvelles editions lignes, 2009).

31. Cf. Özkoçak, "Coffeehouses," 975.

32. Ibrahim Peçevi, *Tarih-i Peçevi*, quoted in Bernard Lewis, *Istanbul and the Civilization of the Ottoman Empire* (Norman: University of Oklahoma Press, 1963), 132–33.

33. Translated into English as G. F. Hourani, *Averroes on the Harmony of Religion and Philosophy* (London: Luzac, 1960).

34. For an analysis of the rise of Ottoman public opinion and the change in governmentality it accompanied, see Kirli, "The Struggle over Space," chaps. 4–5.

35. Abdullah Uçman, ed., *Koca Sekbanbasi risalesi* (Istanbul: Tercüman, 1975). For an English translation, see Appendix 5 to William Wilkinson's 1820 *Account of the Principalities of Wallachia and Moldavia* (London: Longman), esp. 216–21.

36. Ibid., 220.

37. Ibid., 221.

38. See Cengiz Kirli, "Coffeehouses: Public Opinion in the Nineteenth-century Ottoman Empire," in *Public Islam and the Common Good*, ed. A. Salvatore and D. Eickelman (Leiden: Brill, 2004), 75–98. For a more extensive discussion of the same themes, see Kirli, "The Struggle over Space."

39. Talal Asad's fascinating discussion of the genre of *nasiha* or "advice" (which he construes as a nonsecular kind of "criticism") in present-day Saudi Arabia is only a first step in this direction ("The Limits of Religious Criticism in the Middle East: Notes on Islamic Public Argument," in *Genealogies of Religion*, 200–36). It is also incomplete insofar as the Saudi conception of *nasiha* as an individual obligation (*fard 'ayn*) is itself a major conceptual and juridical innovation; moreover, Asad's description implicitly suggests that Saudi Arabia has not had any contact at all with the modernizing Western world (or the Ottoman empire, for that matter). Consequently, the reader may be left with the false impression that Wahhabi conceptions are the predominant, if not the only, option in these matters. To mention only one point, the Wahhabi emphasis on man as God's slave (*'abd*) ignores the influential rival idea, elaborated by authors like Muhammad Iqbal, that man is God's *khalifa*, or "viceregent," and as such also politically sovereign.

40. See the various contributions to M. Hoexter et al., eds., *The Public Sphere in Muslim Societies* (Albany: State University of New York Press, 2002), which tend to lump together historically quite divergent phenomena under a generic and allegedly shared notion of the public sphere.

41. Kirli, "The Struggle over Space," 284–85.

42. See Niyazi Berkes, *The Development of Secularism in Turkey* (Montreal: McGill University Press, 1962), which is still indispensable reading, despite now-outdated secularist and modernization-theoretical assumptions.

43. Asad, *Genealogies of Religion*, 229ff.

44. Ibid., 205.

45. Asad, *Formations of the Secular*, chap. 7.

46. In fact, as Bauman and Briggs, *Voices of Modernity*, 8, observe, the discursive axis is distinctly underdeveloped in Latour's account; as a result, Latour's account of the modern constitution remains undeveloped regarding the dimensions, or spheres, of both language and religion.

47. See the various posts discussing the question "Is critique secular?" on *The Immanent Frame*; available online at http://blogs.ssrc.org/tif/category/is-critique-secular/ and the exchange between Stathis Gourgouris and Saba Mahmood in *Public Culture* 2, no. 3, available online at http://public-culture.org/issues/view/20/3) (last accessed September 11, 2009). See also Talal Asad et al., *Is Critique Secular? Blasphemy, Injury, and Free Speech* (Berkeley: University of California Press, 2009).

48. Kemal Karpat, *The Politicization of Islam* (New York: Oxford University Press, 2001); Tomoko Masuzawa, *The Invention of World Religions: Or, How European Universalism Was Preserved in the Language of Pluralism* (Chicago: University of Chicago Press, 2005).

The Affective Power of the Face Veil: Between Disgust and Fascination, by Annelies Moors

1. This essay builds on Annelies Moors, "The Dutch and the Face-Veil: The Politics of Discomfort," *Social Anthropology* 17, no. 4 (2009): 393–409, which describes and discusses face-veiling cases and debates in the Netherlands in more detail. It is part of a larger, comparative research project entitled "Face Veiling: Public Debates and Everyday Practices." The methods I use are discourse analysis of newspaper articles, official documents, and political talk, as well as ethnographic fieldwork with policy makers, public intellectuals, and face-veiling women, including extensive interviews with twenty women in the Netherlands who wear a face veil, have done so previously, or are considering doing so. The research was partially funded by the Cultural Dynamics Program of the Netherlands Organisation for Scientific Research.

2. For the culturalization of citizenship, see also Peter Geschiere, *The Perils of Belonging: Autochthony, Citizenship, and Exclusion in Africa and Europe* (Chicago: University of Chicago Press, 2009), and Oskar Verkaaik, "The Cachet Dilemma: Ritual and Agency in New Dutch Nationalism," *American Ethnologist* 37, no. 1 (2010): 69–82.

3. Martha Nussbaum, *Hiding from Humanity: Disgust, Shame, and the Law* (Princeton, N.J.: Princeton University Press, 2004): 5.

4. Ibid., 10.

5. William Connolly, "Europe: A Minor Tradition," in *Powers of the Secular Modern: Talal Asad and His Interlocutors*, ed. David Scott and Charles Hirschkind (Stanford, Calif.: Stanford University Press, 2006), 75–92; and Wendy Brown, *Regulating Aversion: Tolerance in the Age of Identity and Empire* (Princeton, N.J.: Princeton University Press, 2006), 150ff.

6. Brian Massumi, *Parables for the Virtual: Movement, Affect, Sensation* (Durham, N.C.: Duke University Press, 2002), 27, points to the need to distinguish between emotions and affect, with the latter referring to the level of the visceral, the less conscious emotional responses.

7. Yael Navaro-Yashin, "Affective Spaces, Melancholic Objects: Ruination and the Production of Anthropological Knowledge," *Journal of the Royal Anthropological Institute*, n.s. 15 (2009): 14.

8. For the different ways in which people relate to clothing, see Daniel Miller, *Stuff* (Cambridge: Polity Press, 2010), 40. He argues that clothing is not simply "a form of representation, a semiotic sign or symbol of the person," but "plays a considerable and active part in constituting the particular experience of the self."

9. See Gillian Vogelsang-Eastwood and Willem Vogelsang, *Covering the Moon: An Introduction to Middle Eastern Face Veils* (Leuven: Peeters, 2008).

10. CGB case no. 2003–40 (see www.cgb.nl). This commission monitors compliance with the Dutch Equal Treatment Act, which prohibits discrimination in education and employment on such grounds as religion, sex, race, and political orientation. It does so by responding to complaints in the format of a nonbinding ruling that is, however, taken seriously in court cases.

11. The women concerned dislike the term *burqa* not only because they consider it a sign of ignorance but also because they recognize the effects of the use of this term.

12. *De Volkskrant, Stijlboek* (The Hague: Sdu, 2006), 34.

13. Ironically, in advertisements for this booklet, the question of when to use *burqa* and when to use *niqab* is provided as a prime example.

14. See Saba Mahmood and Charles Hirschkind, "Feminism, the Taliban, and the Politics of Counter-Insurgency," *Anthropological Quarterly* 75, no. 2 (2002): 339–54; and Lila Abu-Lughod, "Do Muslim Women Really Need Saving? Anthropological Reflections on Cultural Relativism and Its Others," *American Anthropologist* 104, no. 3 (2003): 783–90.

15. Saba Mahmood, *Politics of Piety: The Islamic Revival and the Feminist Subject* (Princeton, N.J.: Princeton University Press, 2005).

16. See also Joan Scott, *The Politics of the Veil* (Princeton, N.J.: Princeton University Press, 2007).

17. *Trouw*, November 21, 2006.

18. *Trouw*, September 28, 2009. In both cases, these intense expressions of dislike were followed by statements that such feelings could not function as a ground for banning face veils from all public space.

19. *Trouw*, February 11, 2008.

20. Parliamentary document TK 2007/08 31 200 VII, Nr. 48. The letter proposed an obligatory ban on face veiling for civil servants and for schools and an inquiry into bans for public transportation. During the consultation, the Cabinet also agreed to look into the need for bans in health care.

21. Peter de Wit, *Burka Babes* (in English; Amsterdam: De Harmonie, 2008). These cartoons were earlier published in the mainstream daily *De Volkskrant*. In December 2006, the newspaper had held a *burka* cartoon contest. The next year De Harmonie published the Dutch-language version of *Burka Babes*; its buyers also received a glossy red bag printed in large white letters with the word *burka*.

22. De Wit, *Burka Babes*, 13.

23. Ibid., 25.

24. See Judith Butler, *Excitable Speech: A Politics of the Performative* (New York: Routledge, 1997).

25. Sara Ahmed, *The Cultural Politics of Emotion* (New York: Routledge, 2004), 93.

26. Face-veiling women stated that when politicians made public statements against face veiling, people generally felt more at liberty to insult them.

27. Ahmed, *The Cultural Politics of Emotion*, 94.

28. Ibid.

29. Julian Sanchez, "Discussing Disgust: On the Folly of Gross-out Public Policy: An Interview with Martha Nussbaum," Reason.com/archives/2004/07/15/discussing-disgust, last accessed April 24, 2010. See also Nussbaum, *Hiding from Humanity*, 14, and Martha Nussbaum, *Liberty of Conscience: In Defense of America's Tradition of Religious Equality* (New York: Basic Books, 2008), chap. 6. There she writes about veiling: "What is going on when people focus on it as a threat to a common culture and seek to ban or limit it? It seems fairly evident that what is really going on is a fear of difference and strangeness, fear of a nonmajoritarian lifestyle that refuses to assimilate."

30. These comments are based on interviews with staff members of Leiden University after the university had imposed a ban on face coverings. See also Linda Herrera and Annelies Moors, "Banning the Face-Veil: The Boundaries of Liberal Education," *ISIM-Newsletter* 13 (2003): 16–27.

31. See Leila Ahmed, *Women and Gender in Islam: Historical Roots of a Modern Debate* (New Haven, Conn.: Yale University Press, 1992).

32. William Miller, *The Anatomy of Disgust* (Cambridge: Harvard University Press, 1997), 81.

33. This to the dismay of the organizers of the event. Barlas then immediately used this picture to discuss stereotypes of Muslim women.

34. This is particularly problematic, as state officials have explicitly been prohibited from wearing face veils since early 2008.

35. Face-veiling women themselves are well aware that face veils can enhance beauty. In Muslim-majority countries where face veils are commonly worn, such as Yemen or Oman, some women say that they like to wear a face veil because it makes them more beautiful. Some also point out that precisely because of this, they also cover their eyes when using eye makeup. For Oman, see Unni Wikan, *Behind the Veil in Arabia: Women in Oman* (Baltimore: Johns Hopkins University Press, 1982); for Yemen, see Annelies Moors, "Fashionable Muslims: Notions of Self, Religion and Society in San'a," *Fashion Theory* 11, no. 2/3 (2007): 319–47.

36. Examples abound. To mention a few: Jean Sasson, *Princess: A True Story of Life Behind the Veil in Saudi Arabia* (Atlanta: Windsor-Brooke Books, 2001); Jean Sasson, *Desert Royal* (New York: Bantam Books, 2004); Jean Sasson, *Mayada, Daughter of Iraq* (New York: Penguin, 2003); Zana Muhsen, *Vechten voor Nadia* (Amsterdam: Maarten Muntinga, 2006); Donya al-Nahi, *Niemand komt aan mijn kinderen* (Amsterdam: Maarten Muntinga, 2007); and Carmen Bin Ladin, *Het gesloten koninkrijk* (Amsterdam: Poema Pocket, 2005). All these books have face-veiled women on the cover, and two of the volumes—*Mayada* and *Vechten voor Nadia*—use the very same picture.

37. Miller, *The Anatomy of Disgust*, x.

38. See Annelies Moors, "Submission," *ISIM Review* 15 (2005): 8–9.

39. See Malek Alloula, *Le harem colonial* (Geneva: Editions Slatkine, 1981), and Meyda Yeğen-oğlu, *Colonial Fantasies: Towards a Feminist Reading of Orientalism* (Cambridge: Cambridge University Press, 1998).

40. De Wit, *Burka Babes*, 47.

41. Ibid., 20.

42. See Pekka Rantanen, "Non-documentary Burqa Pictures on the Internet: Ambivalence and the Politics of Representation," *International Journal of Cultural Studies* 8, no. 3 (2005): 346, 348.

43. Aziz also designed a garment that he called a Lonsdale Burqa for the performance *Extremities*, in which eight gabbers appear in *burqas*.

44. Either particular forms of Islam (such as radical, fundamentalist, etc.) or Islam itself have come to be seen as a threat to Dutch culture, whether defined in terms of a Judeo-Christian heritage, as assertively secular, or as a combination of both.

45. An ability to put up with images one experiences as insulting has become an important means for Muslims to prove that they are well integrated into Dutch society.

"There is a spirit in that image": Mass-Produced Jesus Pictures and Protestant-Pentecostal Animation in Ghana, by Birgit Meyer

NOTE: Earlier versions of this chapter were presented to the Red Lion Seminar, organized by Northwestern University and the University of Chicago, the Institute of Critical International Studies at Emory University, the Department of Anthropology at Brussels University, and the Anthropology Seminar at the London School of Economics. These discussions were fruitful for further developing my argument. Particular thanks go to Martien Brinkman, Marleen de Witte, Matthew Engelke, Miranda Klaver, Harrie Leyten, Roger Sanci Roca, Regien Smit, Bonno Thoden van Velzen, Mattijs van de Port, Jojada Verrips, and three anonymous *Comparative Studies in Society and History* reviewers for stimulating comments. The essay was first published as "'There is a spirit in that image': Mass-Produced Jesus Pictures and Protestant-Pentecostal Animation in Ghana," by Birgit Meyer, *Comparative Studies in Society and History* 52, no. 1 (January 2010): 100–30. Copyright © 2010 Society for the Comparative Study of Society and History. Reprinted with the permission of Cambridge University Press.

1. See Marleen de Witte, "Spirit Media: Charismatic Pentecostalism, African Traditional Religion, and Media Practices in Ghana" (Ph. D. dissertation, University of Amsterdam, 2008); Paul Gifford, *Ghana's New Christianity: Pentecostalism in a Globalising African Economy* (London: Hurst, 2004); Birgit Meyer, "Praise the Lord: Popular Cinema and Pentecostalite Style in Ghana's New Public Sphere," *American Ethnologist* 31, no. 1 (2004): 92–110.

2. Manuel Castells, *The Information Age: Economy, Society and Culture*, 3 vols. (Oxford: Blackwell, 1996–98), 406.

3. Hent de Vries, "In Media Res: Global Religion, Public Spheres, and the Task of Contemporary Religious Studies," in *Religion and Media*, ed. Hent de Vries and Samuel Weber (Stanford, Calif.: Stanford University Press, 2001), 4–42; Birgit Meyer, ed., *Aesthetic Formations: Media, Religion and the Senses* (New York: Palgrave, 2009).

4. Walter Benjamin, "The Work of Art in the Age of Mechanical Reproduction," in *Illuminations*, ed. and introd. Hannah Arendt, trans. Harry Zohn (1936; London: Pimlico, 1978), 211–44. See, e.g., Sudeep Dasgupta, "Gods in the Sacred Marketplace: Hindi Nationalism and the Return of the Aura in the Public Sphere," in *Religion, Media, and the Public Sphere*, ed. Birgit Meyer and Annelies Moors (Bloomington: Indiana University Press, 2006), 251–72.

5. "African indigenous religious traditions" is, admittedly, an awkward expression. In my view, it is nonetheless preferable to the notion of "African Traditional Religion," which is often used in an essentializing manner. That both advocates and critics employ "African Traditional Religion" highlights the extent to which discourses about "traditional religion" are grounded in colonial-historical encounters in which Christianity served as reference point. Acknowledging that "traditional religion" thus usually is framed as Christianity's other implies that, instead of searching for a more suitable neutral term, it is necessary to investigate the politics of use for terms involving "tradition." See Birgit Meyer, "Mediating Tradition: Pentecostal Pastors, African Priests, and Chiefs in Ghanaian Popular Films," in *Christianity and Social Change in Africa: Essays in Honor of J. D. Y. Peel*, ed. Toyin Falola (Durham, N.C.: Carolina Academic Press, 2005), 275–306; see also Marleen de Witte, "The Spectacular and the Spirits: Charismatics and Neo-Traditionalists on Ghanaian

Television," *Material Religion* 1, no. 3 (2005): 314–35, and Marleen de Witte, "Afrikania's Dilemma: Reframing African Authenticity in a Christian Public Sphere," *Etnofoor* 17, no. 1/2 (2005): 133–55. While I take into account that "African Traditional Religion" or "traditional religion" is actually used in local discourse (and hence use quotation marks to indicate this), my choice of "African indigenous religious traditions" indicates a dynamic understanding of tradition as not fixed but subject to transformation.

6. W. J. T. Mitchell, *What Do Pictures Want? The Lives and Loves of Images* (Chicago: University of Chicago Press, 2005), 345.

7. See, e.g.: David Chidester, "Zulu Dreamscapes: Senses, Media, and Authentication in Contemporary Neo-Shamanism," *Material Religion* 4, no. 2 (2008): 136–58; Patrick Eisenlohr, "As Makkah Is Sweet and Beloved, So Is Madina: Islam, Devotional Genres, and Electronic Mediation in Mauritius," *American Ethnologist* 33, no. 2 (2006): 230–45; Charles Hirschkind, *The Ethical Soundscape: Cassette Sermons and the Islamic Counter-Public* (New York: Columbia University Press, 2006); David Morgan, *The Sacred Gaze: Religious Visual Culture in Theory and Practice* (Berkeley: University of California Press, 2005); Christopher Pinney, *"Photos of the Gods": The Printed Image and Political Struggle in India* (London: Reaktion Books, 2004); Patricia Spyer, "Christ at Large: Iconography and Territoriality in Postwar Ambon," in *Religion: Beyond a Concept*, ed. Hent de Vries (New York: Fordham University Press, 2008), 524–49; see also de Vries, "In Media Res," and Meyer, ed., *Aesthetic Formations*.

8. See, e.g.: Arjun Appadurai, ed., *The Social Life of Things: Commodities in Cultural Perspective* (Cambridge: Cambridge University Press, 1988); Alfred Gell, *Art and Agency: An Anthropological Theory* (Oxford: Oxford University Press, 1998); Daniel Miller, "Introduction," in *Materiality*, ed. Daniel Miller (Durham, N.C.: Duke University Press, 2005), 1–50; Jojada Verrips, "The Thing Didn't Do What I Wanted: Some Notes on Modern Forms of Animism in Western Societies," in *Transactions: Essays in Honour of J. Boissevain*, ed. Jojada Verrips (Amsterdam: Het Spinhuis, 1994), 35–52.

9. Peter-Paul Verbeek, *What Things Do: Philosophical Reflections on Technology, Agency, and Design* (University Park: Pennsylvania State University Press, 2005).

10. Bill Brown, "Thing Theory," *Critical Inquiry* 28, no. 1 (2001): 4. See also Bruno Latour, "What Is Iconoclash? Or, Is There a World Beyond the Image Wars?" in *Iconoclash: Beyond the Image Wars in Science, Religion, and Art*, ed. Bruno Latour and Peter Weibel (Karlsruhe: 2km/Center for Art and Media, and Cambridge: MIT Press, 2002), 14–18.

11. Patricia Spyer, "The Body, Materiality, and the Senses," in *Handbook of Material Culture*, ed. C. Tilley et al. (London: Sage, 2006), 126.

12. Marcel Mauss, *The Gift: Forms and Functions of Exchange in Archaic Societies* (1954; London: Routledge, 1970); Marilyn Strathern, *The Gender of the Gift: Problems with Women and Problems with Society in Melanesia* (Berkeley: University of California Press, 1988).

13. As suggested by Amiria Henare, Martin Holbraad, and Sari Wastel in the thought-provoking introduction to their edited volume *Thinking Through Things: Theorising Artefacts Ethnographically* (London: Routledge, 2007), 1–31, such a project moves beyond claiming sheer cultural diversity in subject-object relations. Instead, the very dualism that we call "subject-object relations" may itself be subverted by alternative ontologies, modes of world making in which what things are and what they mean are inextricably intertwined (ibid., 12ff). As Mauss famously showed, this is the case in Maori gift exchange, where valued articles (*taonga*) are identified with the "spirit of the gift" (*hau*), making a strict distinction between gift, giver, and receiver impossible (Mauss, *The Gift*, 8ff).

14. Webb Keane, *Christian Moderns: Freedom and Fetish in the Mission Encounter* (Berkeley: University of California Press, 2007).

15. Tomoko Mazusawa, "Troubles with Materiality: The Ghost of Fetishism in the Nineteenth Century," *Comparative Studies in Society and History* 42, no. 2 (2000): 242–67.

16. William Pietz, "The Problem of the Fetish," part 1, *Res* 9 (1985): 5–17; part 2, *Res* 13 (1987): 23–45 part 3, *Res* 16 (1988): 105–23.

17. Bruno Latour, *We Have Never Been Modern* (Cambridge: Harvard University Press, 1993).

18. Brown, "Thing Theory," 4. See also Mitchell, *What Do Pictures Want?* 145ff.

19. This moment of Westerners' supposed self-recognition in the Orientalist image of the primitive other should not, in my view, result in a sense (celebratory, albeit slightly fatalistic) that the stubborn resilience of the "fetish" expresses a kind of universal primitivism. Instead, we need to ask why the notion of the "fetish" and the readiness to place oneself under the spell of a thing are so appealing, at least for educated Westerners. Is this a way to relativize modern agency and rediscover our long-repressed wildness? My point is not to plea for a rational, modern outlook but rather to warn against an all-too-simple reversal and to place the quest for primitivism in a broader framework. See also Mattijs van de Port, *Ecstatic Encounters: Bahian Candomblé and the Quest for the Really Real* (Amsterdam: Amsterdam University Press, 2011).

20. David Morgan, *Visual Piety: A History and Theory of Popular Religious Images* (Berkeley: University of California Press, 1998).

21. See Martin Jay, *Downcast Eyes: The Denigration of Vision in Twentieth-Century Thought* (Berkeley: University of California Press, 1994).

22. For the argument for merging visual and material culture, see Spyer, "The Body, Materiality, and the Senses." For the materiality of pictures, see, e.g., Elizabeth Edwards, Chris Gosden, and Ruth B. Philipps, eds., *Sensible Objects: Colonialism, Museums and Material Culture* (Oxford: Berg, 2007).

23. Mitchell, *What Do Pictures Want?* 85.

24. See: Chidester, "Zulu Dreamscapes"; de Witte, "Spirit Media"; Birgit Meyer, "Religious Sensations: Why Media, Aesthetics and Power Matter in the Study of Contemporary Religion," in *Religion: Beyond a concept*, ed. Hent de Vries (New York: Fordham University Press, 2008), 704–23; Jojada Verrips, "Offending Art and the Sense of Touch," *Material Religion* 4, no. 2 (2008): 204–25.

25. Hans Belting, "Image, Medium, Body: A New Approach to Iconology," *Critical Inquiry* 31 (2005): 302–19; David Freedberg, *The Power of Images: Studies in the History and Theory of Response* (Chicago: University of Chicago Press, 1989); David Howes, *Sensual Relations: Engaging the Senses in Culture and Social Theory* (Ann Arbor: University of Michigan Press, 2003); Morgan, *The Sacred Gaze*; David Morgan, *The Lure of Images* (London: Routledge, 2007); Laura Marks, *The Skin of the Film: Intercultural Cinema, Embodiment, and the Senses* (Durham, N.C.: Duke University Press, 2000); Bissera V. Pentcheva, "The Performative Icon," *Art Bulletin* 88, no. 4 (2006): 631–55; Vivian Sobchack, *Carnal Thoughts: Embodiment and Moving Image Culture* (Berkeley: University of California Press, 2004); Jojada Verrips, "Haptic Screens and Our Corporeal Eye," *Etnofoor* 15, no. 1/2 (2002): 21–46; Jojada Verrips, "Aesthetics and An-aesthesia," *Ethnologia Europea* 35, no. 1/2 (2006): 27–33.

26. See also van de Port, *The Rest of What Is*.

27. Morgan, *Visual Piety*; see also Birgit Meyer, "Powerful Pictures: Popular Christian Aesthetics in Southern Ghana," *Journal of the American Academy of Religion* 76, no. 1 (2008): 82–110; Pinney, *"Photos of the Gods"*; Allen F. Roberts and Mary Nooter Roberts, *A Saint in the City: Sufi Arts of Modern Senegal* (Seattle: University of Washington Press, 2003); Mattijs van de Port, "Visualizing the Sacred: Video Technology, 'Televisual' Style and the Religious Imagination in Bahian Candomblé," *American Ethnologist* 33, no. 3 (2006): 444–62.

28. Max Weber, *The Protestant Ethic and the Spirit of Capitalism*, ed. and trans. Talcott Parsons (New York: Charles Scribner's Sons, 1920).

29. See Ernst van den Hemel, "Things That Matter," in this volume; Cornelius van der Kooi, *As in a Mirror: John Calvin and Karl Barth on Knowing God* (Leiden: Brill, 2007).

30. Keane, *Christian Moderns*, 17ff, develops the notion of "semiotic ideology" on the basis of the concept of "language ideology," that is, "what one believes about language" or, in the words of Michael Silverstein, "sets of beliefs about language articulated by users as a rationalization or justification of perceived language structure and use" (ibid., 16). "Ideology" is used here not in the sense of a false consciousness but in order to stress "the productive effects of reflexive awareness" (ibid., 17), the point being that such ideologies are not confined to the level of immaterial representation but always require objectification in the material world. Linguistic ideologies, understood in this sense, feature in concrete material settings that are inhabited and embodied by people. Invoking "semiotic" rather than "linguistic" ideology, Keane seeks to encompass semiotic domains other than language alone. The crux of the matter is that semiotic ideologies distinguish significant categories and define their relations in particular ways that organize the material world. See also Webb Keane, "The Evidence of the Senses and the Materiality of Religion," *Journal of the Royal Anthropological Institute*, special issue, *The Objects of Evidence: Anthropological Approaches to the Production of Knowledge*, 14, no. 1 (2008): 110–27.

31. Birgit Meyer, *Translating the Devil: Religion and Modernity among the Ewe in Ghana* (Edinburgh: Edinburgh University Press, 1999).

32. In a similar vein, things would contain characteristics of those using them (not unlike Mauss's notion of the *hau* of the gift, through which a thing embodies its giver). Thus, when people were suspected of having gained wealth through witchcraft, after their death their belongings would be thrown away at a certain place in the bush. Their things were not considered fit for use by others and therefore were left to decay. See also Bonno Thoden van Velzen and Ineke van Wetering, *In the Shadow of the Oracle: Religion as Politics in a Surinamese Maroon Society* (Long Grove, Ill.: Waveland, 2004).

33. Meyer, *Translating the Devil*, 60ff.

34. Jacob Spieth, *Die Religion der Eweer in Süd-Togo* (Göttingen: Vandenhoeck and Ruprecht, 1911), 39, my translation.

35. Note that this is not unlike Mitchell's understanding of the picture as a materialization of an image, without which the latter could not be expressed.

36. Judy Rosenthal, *Possession, Ecstasy, and Law in Ewe Vodoo* (Charlottesville: University Press of Virginia, 1998), 45. Judy Rosenthal quotes a fascinating reflection by the Gorovodu priest Fo Idi: "We Ewe are not like the Christians, who are created by their god. We Ewe create our gods, and we create only the gods that we want to possess us, not any others" (ibid., 45). See also Susan Preston Blier's exploration of the processes through which Ewe and Fon sculptors create so-called *bocio* figures as fearful and awe-inspiring via a process that implies carving as well as a gradual activation and empowerment of these figures with speech and saliva, heat, knotting, and offering (*African Vodun: Art, Psychology, and Power* [Chicago: University of Chicago Press, 1995], 74).

37. When building a new mission post in Amedzofe, for example, the nonlocal workers hired by the mission are reported to have brought a big stone from the bush. This stone turned out to be the dwelling place of a local deity, and local people requested that the stone be taken back to the bush and its spirit appeased. (For a more detailed analysis, see Birgit Meyer, "Christian Mind and Worldly Matters: Religion and Materiality in Nineteenth-Century Gold Coast," *Journal of Material Culture* 2, no. 3 [1997], 319.)

38. See also Jean Comaroff and John Comaroff, "The Colonization of Consciousness," in their *Ethnography and the Historical Imagination* (Boulder, Colo.: Westview Press, 1992), 235–63.

39. The importance of destruction by fire is remarkable, since this not only evokes hellfire but also resonates with local practices of witch burning (after the death of the supposed witch). The

Ewe term *dzo*, usually translated as "magic" or "*juju*," also literally means "fire," thus associating fire with spiritual power. In present-day Pentecostalism, there is much emphasis on the fire of the Holy Spirit, who is supposed to attack evil. This is depicted in the final scene of the Ghanaian-Nigerian movie *Time* (2000), directed by Emmanuel Dugbartey Nanor (Accra and Lagos: Miracle Films and Djoh Mediacraft).

40. During my fieldwork in Peki in the 1990s, I still came across accounts of shrines that had been abandoned or dismantled, rather than being destroyed by fire until only the ashes were left. The priest of the war god Dzebum told me how a Christian member of the household had once thrown Dzebum's paraphernalia into the toilet so as to get rid of him. As one might expect, Dzebum's revenge had resulted in sickness in the family, and their health was restored only after Dzebum had been appeased by a set of purification rituals.

41. Some *dzo* items were not destroyed but were instead sent to the museum in Bremen, where they were categorized as magical objects.

42. Latour, "What is Iconoclash?"

43. For the dialectic of revelation and concealment, see Michael Taussig, "Viscerality, Faith, and Skepticism: Another Theory of Magic," in *Magic and Modernity: Interfaces of Revelation and Concealment*, ed. Birgit Meyer and Peter Pels (Stanford, Calif.: Stanford University Press, 2003), 272–306. In Peki, for instance, I heard many stories about the priest Keteku Kwami from the Tigare cult, who was very powerful in the early twentieth century. My host and key interlocutor, the late Reverend E. Y. Tawia, enjoyed telling me about how the Tigare priest had been unmasked by an evangelist, who found that it was the priest himself who simulated the voices of the spirits by secretly playing a particular drum, thus showing that there was no spiritual power present in the Tigare cave. At the same time, Tawia was adamant that such cults were instances of Devil worship.

44. Meyer, "Christian Mind and Worldly Matters."

45. Meyer, *Translating the Devil.*

46. Ibid.

47. This is markedly different from the Friday Masowe Church analyzed by Matthew Engelke, *A Problem of Presence: Beyond Scripture in an African Church* (Berkeley: University of California Press, 2007), which strongly opposes the "thingliness" of Christianity and for that reason rejects even the use of the Bible.

48. Meyer, *Translating the Devil*, 116.

49. See Kwabena J. Asamoah-Gyadu, "Conquering Satan, Demons, Principalities and Powers: Ghanaian Traditional and Christian Perspectives on Religion, Evil, and Deliverance," in *Coping with Evil in Religion and Culture*, ed. N. van Doorn-Harder and L. Minnema (Amsterdam: Rodopi, 2008), 99ff.

50. I put these terms in quotation marks to underline their groundedness in Pentecostal discourse. The use of "symbol" comes close to Peirce's notion of the "index" (understood as a sign that creates a linkage with the referent, like a trace); the Protestant-Pentecostal use of "idol" brings to mind his notion of the "icon" (understood as a sign that resembles the referent).

51. Morgan, *Visual Piety.*

52. Meyer, "Religious Sensations."

53. See also Birgit Meyer, "Impossible Representations: Pentecostalism, Vision, and Video Technology in Ghana," in *Religion, Media, and the Public Sphere*, ed. Birgit Meyer and Annelies Moors (Bloomington: Indiana University Press, 2006), 290–312; Pinney, *"Photos of the Gods."*

54. Morgan, *Visual Piety*, 2.

55. While the clocks are imported from China, the calendars and posters are produced locally, an example of the endless recycling and remediation of global Christian popular culture. While

there have been such pictures in Ghana at least since I started my research in 1988, their presence and circulation have grown over the past decade, along with a rise in the audiovisual public presence of Pentecostal-charismatic churches.

56. One of the few instances of a black Jesus, a black Last Supper, was photographed by my Ph. D. student Rhoda Woets in Ghana's national museum. Unfortunately, the artist's name is not known.

57. When I asked people about the whiteness of Jesus, I found that, while this whiteness is problematized by critical theologians, many believers did not take it to be an expression of white racial superiority. Pictures of Jesus were rarely read through the lens of racial views, and Christianity is very much appreciated as an African religion.

58. David Morgan, "Rhetoric of the Heart," in this volume. This suggests the existence of a broader Christian popular culture that mobilizes both Catholic and Protestant repertoires and seems to transcend, albeit only partly, the usual cleavages between these two Christianities. I still need to analyze the development of this popular culture in historical perspective, paying particular attention to the appeal to Protestants of typically Catholic pictures. In the relevant literature on Christianity in Ghana, I have found no references to Christian material culture. In my view, this is due to the conceptual bias that has long governed our research and that is only now being sur- mounted through the current "material turn" in the study of religion. Through personal conversa- tions with my former teacher of museum studies, the anthropologist and ex-Catholic priest Harrie Leyten, I came to understand that the Catholic missionaries (many of them Dutch) who were active in Ghana usually were strongly embedded in popular forms of Catholic devotion, which they also brought to Ghana. This means that images of Mary and Jesus played a central role in Catholic piety. This is still the case. During my most recent visit to Ghana, in August 2009, I was able to speak to Father George (Winneba), who pointed out that he found the Protestant-Pentecostal criticism of Catholicism as idol worship hypocritical, since Pentecostals themselves knew that it was not possible to invoke or speak about God without any mediation. In his view, images of Jesus and Mary were not, of course, to be worshipped per se but rather served as points of orientation for personal and communal devotion.

59. In the mid-1980s, a private video-film industry emerged in Ghana and Nigeria. Taking advantage of the availability of the relatively cheap medium of video, untrained producers started to make local movies. This development initiated not only a technological shift from celluloid to video (first tapes, later VCDs—cheap versions of the DVD, using compact disks), but also an ideological shift from a state-run film industry devoted to education to a commercial film industry for the sake of entertainment. Since the latter heavily depends on the support of audiences, the movies mirror popular ideas. An important feature is the visualization of occult forces within a Christian-Pentecostal framework. Because this new industry diverged from the earlier state-governed cinema, it was widely criticized by intellectuals and state officials. See: Meyer, "Praise the Lord"; Meyer, "Christianity in Africa: From African Independent to Pentecostal-Charismatic Churches," *Anthropology* 33 (2004): 447–74; Meyer, "Impossible Representations."

60. Meyer, "Praise the Lord"; Meyer, "Mediating Tradition."

61. *Women in Love I and II*, directed by Socrate Safo (Accra: Movie Africa Productions, 1996).

62. See also Birgit Meyer, "Religious Remediations: Pentecostal Views in Ghanaian Video-Movies," *Postscripts* 1, no. 2/3 (2005): 155–81.

63. In Ghana, as in Africa as a whole, Pentecostal-charismatic churches are very popular. One can distinguish different kinds of churches in the Pentecostal spectrum: preindependence Apostolic churches, which stood close to African Independent Churches; American-derived Pentecostal churches such as the Assemblies of God, which defined themselves against African Independent

Churches; and African-founded charismatic churches, which emphasize the "Prosperity Gospel" and global outreach (Meyer, "Christianity in Africa"). Yet it is important to recognize that these types are not fixed. Certainly, within Ghana's new public sphere, in which media are employed to broadcast messages to the world, Pentecostal-charismatic churches provoke each other, as well as churches in the mainline spectrum, to transform. This gives rise to the broad field of popular Pentecostalism on which I focus here.

64. *The Beast Within*, directed by Nana King (Accra: Astron Productions, 1993). See Meyer, *Translating the Devil*; Meyer, "Praise the Lord."

65. Meyer, "Praise the Lord."

66. Our conversation took place while we waited for a scene to be shot, in Osu cemetery, next to an open grave. The gloomy setting affected the crew, making it difficult to distinguish the plot that required the staging of occult forces from the uncanniness of the actual place. One actress eventually fell into the grave, shrieking with horror.

67. With this understanding, it could even be argued that *The Beast Within* is less scandalous, for it points out exactly the danger imbuing religious pictures and might be interpreted as a warning against their use.

68. Marks, *The Skin of the Film*. See also Sobchack, *Carnal Thoughts*; Verrips, "Haptic Screens."

69. See Marks, *The Skin of the Film*, 162ff.

70. Preston Blier, *African Vodun*, 76.

71. Ibid.

72. Moreover, the moral ambivalence of the local gods, who were held to do both good and evil, informs the fear of the dangerous Jesus picture. Here the ambivalence is played out along the distinction between immaterial and material, the figure behind the picture being the "dear Jesus" and its material manifestation being potentially evil.

73. See James Elkins, "The Object Stares Back: On the Nature of Seeing," reprinted in part in *Religion, Art and Visual Culture*, ed. S. B. Plate (New York: Palgrave, 2002), 40–45; Pentcheva, "The Performative Icon."

74. See also Pinney, *"Photos of the Gods."*

75. Meyer, "Praise the Lord"; Meyer, "Impossible Representations."

76. This pertains to the final product: the VCD. I encountered strong concerns about the excessive potential of things in the process of filmmaking. Making an artificial shrine for the sake of a film would be regarded as potentially dangerous, for instance, because spirits might take over the fake abode, thereby turning it into the real thing. Likewise, it was believed that spiritual forces were prone to impinging on the working of technological devices. Many people found that, since Satan did not like to be exposed via films, he might try to disturb the proper functioning of the camera.

77. Verrips, "Offending Art."

The FedEx Saints: Patrons of Mobility and Speed in a Neoliberal City, by Maria José A. de Abreu

NOTE: This chapter was financed by National Funds through FCT-Fundação para a Ciência e a Tecnologia no âmbito do projecto, *Ref*ª d. Projecto Estratégico—U4038—2011–12.

1. See Eric Kramer, "Law and the Image of a Nation: Religious Conflict and Religious Freedom in a Brazilian Criminal Case," *Law and Social Inquiry* 26, no. 1 (2001): 35–62.

2. Maria José A. de Abreu, "On Charisma, Mediation and Broken Screens," *Etnofoor* 15, no. 1/2 (2002): 240–58.

3. Riolando Azzi, *O Catolicismo Popular no Brasil: Aspectos Históricos* (Petrópolis, Brazil: Vozes, 1978).

4. See Aaron Gurevich, *Medieval Popular Culture: The Problem of Belief and Perception*, trans. Janos M. Bak and Paul A. Hollingsworth (Cambridge: Cambridge University Press, 1990); see also Patrick Geary, "Humiliation of Saints," in *Saints and Their Cults: Studies in Religious Sociology, Folklore and History*, ed. Stephen Wilson (Cambridge: Cambridge University Press, 1983), 123–40. See also Caroline Walker Bynum, "The Female Body and Religious Practice in the Later Middle Ages," in *Fragmentation and Redemption: Essays on Gender and the Human Body in Medieval Religion* (New York: Zone Books, 1991), 161–219.

5. Maria José A. de Abreu, "Breathing into the Heart of the Matter: Why Padre Marcello Needs No Wings," *Postscripts* 1 (2005): 243.

6. For a wonderful and handy description of such examples of religious iconoclasm in the context of colonial Brazil, see the work of historian Laura Mello e Souza, *The Devil and the Land of the Holy Cross: Witchcraft, Slavery, and Popular Religion in Colonial Brazil*, trans. Diane Grosklaus Whitty (Austin: University of Texas Press, 2004).

7. Pedro Oliveira Ribeiro, *Religião e Dominação de Classe: Génese, Estrutura e Função do Catolicismo Romanizado no Brasil* (Petropolis, Brazil: Vozes, 1985).

8. See Peter Brown, "Enjoying Saints in Late Antiquity," *Early Medieval Europe* 9, no. 1 (2000): 1–24.

9. Kenneth L. Woodworth, *The Making of Saints: How the Church Determines Who Becomes a Saint, Who Doesn't, and Why* (New York: Simon & Schuster, 1996).

10. For an account of how the ascendance of electronic media and their impact on existing forms of media, such as print media and their traditionally privileged status as a vehicle to communicate authoritative religious knowledge, see Jeremy Stolow, *Orthodox by Design: Judaism, Print Politics, and the ArtScroll Revolution* (Berkeley: University of California Press, 2009).

11. See, e.g., http://www.santoexpedito.com.br/ (for Portuguese), or http://saintexpedite.org/ (for English).

12. See, e.g., http://www.botanicasanexpedito.com/main/index.php?main_page = page&id = 14& chapter = 0.

13. Maria José A. de Abreu, "Goose Bumps All Over: Breath, Media, Tremor," *Social Text* 96 (2008): 59–78.

14. De Abreu, "On Charisma, Mediation and Broken Screens."

15. Samuel Weber, "Television: Set and Screen," in *Mass Mediauras: Form, Technics, Media* (Stanford, Calif.: Stanford University Press, 1996), 108–28.

16. Ibid., 122.

17. Rafael Sánchez, "Channel-Surfing: Media, Mediumship, and State Authority in the María Lionza Possession Cult (Venezuela)," in *Religion and Media*, ed. Hent de Vries and Samuel Weber (Stanford, Calif.: Stanford University Press, 2001), 423.

18. Ibid., 415.

Enchantment, Inc.: Online Gaming Between Spiritual Experience and Commodity Fetishism, by Stef Aupers

1. James Newman, *Video Games* (London: Routledge, 2004).

2. See: Richard Bartle, *Designing Virtual Worlds* (Berkeley, Calif.: New Riders Publishers, 2004); Edward Castronova, *Synthetic Worlds: The Business and Culture of Online Games* (Chicago: University of Chicago Press, 2005).

3. Johan Huizinga, *Homo Ludens: A Study of the Play Element in Culture* (1938; Boston: Beacon Press, 1950), 10.

4. Bruce Woodcock, *An Analysis of MMOG Subscription Growth: Version 21.0* (2008), http://www.mmogchart.com.

5. Nicholas Yee, "The Demographics, Motivations and Derived Experiences of Users of Massively Multiuser Online Graphical Environments," *PRESENCE: Teleoperators and Virtual Environments*, no. 15 (2006): 309–29.

6. Max Weber, "Science as a Vocation," in *From Max Weber: Essays in Sociology*, ed. Hans H. Gerth and C. Wright Mills (1919; London: Routledge, 1948), 129–56.

7. Simon During, *Modern Enchantments: The Cultural Power of Secular Magic* (Cambridge: Harvard University Press, 2002), 50.

8. Ibid., 49.

9. Weber, "Science as a Vocation," 139.

10. Jan Romein, *Op het breukvlak van twee eeuwen*, 2 vols. (Leiden: Brill, 1967).

11. Weber, "Science as a Vocation," 149, 137.

12. Ibid., 143.

13. Ibid., 149.

14. Ibid., 154–55.

15. Patrick Dassen, *De onttovering van de wereld: Max Weber en het probleem van de moderniteit in Duitsland, 1890–1920* (Amsterdam: Uitgeverij G. A. van Oorschot, 1999), 241.

16. Peter Pels, "Introduction: Magic and Modernity," in *Magic and Modernity: Interfaces of Revelation and Concealment*, ed. Birgit Meyer and Peter Pels (Stanford, Calif.: Stanford University Press, 2003), 17.

17. See, e.g.: Stef Aupers, *In de ban van moderniteit: De sacralisering van het zelf en computertechnologie* (Amsterdam: Aksant, 2004); Lawrence A. Scaff, *Fleeing the Iron Cage: Culture, Politics, and Modernity in the Thought of Max Weber* (Berkeley: University of California Press, 1989); Alan Sica, *Weber, Irrationality, and Social Order* (Berkeley: University of California Press, 1988).

18. Theodore Roszak, *The Making of a Counter Culture: Reflections on the Technocratic Society and Its Youthful Opposition* (Garden City, N.Y.: Doubleday, 1969).

19. Herbert Marcuse, *One-Dimensional Man: Studies in the Ideology of Advanced Industrial Society* (1964; Boston: Beacon Press, 1991).

20. See: Elisabeth Puttick, "Personal Development: The Spiritualisation and Secularisation of the Human Potential Movement," in *Beyond New Age: Exploring Alternative Spirituality*, ed. Steven Sutcliffe and Marion Bowman (Edinburgh: Edinburgh University Press, 2000), 201–19; Roszak, *The Making of a Counter Culture*.

21. Colin Campbell, "The Cult, the Cultic Milieu and Secularization," in *A Sociological Yearbook of Religion in Brittain*, no. 5 (1972): 119–36.

22. Wouter Hanegraaff, *New Age Religion and Western Culture: Esotericism in the Mirror of Secular Thought* (Leiden: Brill, 1996), 17. Hanegraaff argues for a distinction between New Age in a restricted sense and in a general sense: the latter form became dominant starting in the 1980s, as indicated by the publication of New Age bibles such as Marilyn Ferguon, *The Aquarian Conspiracy: Personal and Social Transformation in Our Time* (1980; New York: J. P. Tarcher, 2009).

23. See: Dick Houtman and Stef Aupers, "The Spiritual Turn and the Decline of Tradition: The Spread of Post-Christian Spirituality in Fourteen Western Countries (1981–2000)," *Journal for the Scientific Study of Religion* 46, no. 3 (2007): 305–20; Paul Heelas, Linda Woodhead, et al., *The Spiritual Revolution: Why Religion Is Giving Way to Spirituality* (Oxford: Blackwell, 2005); Dick Houtman and Peter Mascini, "Why Do Churches Become Empty, While New Age Grows? Secularization and Religious Change in the Netherlands," *Journal for the Scientific Study of Religion* 41, no.

3 (2002): 455–73; Miranda Moerland and Anneke Van Otterloo, "New Age: Tegencultuur, paracultuur of kerncultuur?" *Amsterdams Sociologisch Tijdschrift* 23, no. 4 (1996): 682–710.

24. Stef Aupers and Dick Houtman, "Beyond the Spiritual Supermarket: The Social and Public Significance of New Age Spirituality," *Journal of Contemporary Religion* 21, no. 2 (2006): 201–22.

25. Steven Sutcliffe and Marion Bowman, eds., *Beyond New Age: Exploring Alternative Spirituality* (Edinburgh: Edinburgh University Press, 2000), 11.

26. See, e.g.: Aupers and Houtman, "Beyond the Spiritual Supermarket"; Don Grant, Kathleen O'Neil, and Laura Stephens, "Spirituality in the Workplace: New Empirical Directions in the Study of the Sacred," *Sociology of Religion* 65, no. 3 (2004): 265–83; Paul Heelas, *The New Age Movement: The Celebration of the Self and the Sacralisation of Modernity* (Oxford: Blackwell, 1996); Ian Mitroff and Elisabeth A. Denton, *A Spiritual Audit of Corporate America: A Hard Look at Spirituality, Religion, and Values in the Workplace* (San Francisco: Jossey-Bass, 1999); Majia Holmer Nadesan, "The Discourses of Corporate Spiritualism and Evangelical Capitalism," *Management Communication Quarterly* 13, no. 1 (1999): 3–42.

27. See, e.g.: Thomas Frank, *The Conquest of Cool: Business Culture, Counterculture, and the Rise of Hip Consumerism* (Chicago: University of Chicago Press, 1998); David Boyle, *Authenticity: Brands, Fakes, Spin and the Lust for Real Life* (London: Harper Perennial, 2004); Joseph Heath and Andrew Potter, *Nation of Rebels: Why Counterculture Became Consumer Culture* (New York: Harper Collins, 2004).

28. David Lyon, *Jesus in Disneyland: Religion in Postmodern Times* (Cambridge: Polity Press, 2000), 34.

29. For these terms, see, respectively: Cor Baerveldt, "New Age-religiositeit als individueel constructieproces," in *De kool en de geit in de nieuwe tijd: Wetenschappelijke reflecties op New Age*, ed. Miranda Moerland (Utrecht: Jan van Arkel, 1996), 19–31; Malcolm Hamilton, "An Analysis of the Festival for Mind-Body-Spirit, London," in *Beyond New Age*, ed. Sutcliffe and Bowman, 188–200; Adam Possamai, "Alternative Spiritualities and the Cultural Logic of Late Capitalism," *Culture and Religion* 4, no. 1 (2003): 31–45; and Lyon, *Jesus in Disneyland*.

30. Sutcliffe and Bowman, eds., *Beyond New Age*, 1.

31. Thomas Luckmann, *The Invisible Religion: The Problem of Religion in Modern Society* (New York: Macmillan, 1967).

32. Hanegraaff, *New Age Religion*.

33. See, e.g.: Aupers, *In de ban van moderniteit*; Heelas, *The New Age Movement*.

34. Aupers and Houtman, "Beyond the Spiritual Supermarket."

35. Heelas, *The New Age Movement*, 18.

36. Ibid., 19 (italics in original).

37. Emile Durkheim, "Individualism and the Intellectuals," in *Durkheim on Religion: A Selection of Readings with Bibliographies*, ed. W. S. F. Pickering (1898; London: Routledge & Kegan Paul, 1975), 62.

38. Olav Hammer, *Claiming Knowledge: Strategies of Epistemology from Theosophy to the New Age* (Leiden: Brill, 2001).

39. Hanegraaff, *New Age Religion*, 519 (italics in original).

40. Stef Aupers, "'Je hoeft er niet in te geloven: het werkt!': Over de instrumentalisering van New Age-spiritualiteit," *Amsterdams Sociologisch Tijdschrift* 25, no. 2 (1998): 295–321.

41. Zygmunt Bauman, *Postmodernity and Its Discontents* (Cambridge: Polity Press, 1997), 181.

42. Grace Davie, *Believing Without Belonging: Religion in Britain since 1945* (Oxford: Blackwell, 1994).

43. See, e.g., Aupers and Houtman, "Beyond the Spiritual Supermarket"; see also, on the academic dilemmas concerning the "mediated nature of experiences," Birgit Meyer, "Religious Sensations: Why Media, Aesthetics, and Power Matter in the Study of Contemporary Religion," in *Religion: Beyond a Concept*, ed. Hent de Vries (New York: Fordham University Press, 2008), 704–23.

44. Max Weber, *Economy and Society*, 2 vols. (1921; Berkeley: University of California Press, 1978), 506.

45. Fredric Jameson, *Postmodernism; Or, The Cultural Logic of Late Capitalism* (Durham, N.C.: Duke University Press, 1991); Jean Baudrillard, *Simulacra and Simulations* (1981; Ann Arbor: University of Michigan Press, 2000), 161.

46. Annette Markham, *Life Online: Researching Real Experiences in Virtual Space* (Walnut Creek, Calif.: Sage Publications, 1998).

47. Rodney Stark and William S. Bainbridge, *The Future of Religion: Secularization, Revival, and Cult Formation* (Berkeley: University of California Press, 1985).

48. Ibid., 209.

49. Ellen Hijmans, "Televisie en zingeving: Spiritualiteit in de talkshow van Oprah Winfrey," *Sociologische Gids* 47, no. 6 (2000): 443.

50. Heelas, *The New Age Movement*; Bauman, *Postmodernity*.

51. Aupers, *In de ban van moderniteit*.

52. Adam Possamai, *Religion and Popular Culture: A Hyper-Real Testament* (Brussels: Peter Lang, 2005); Partridge, *The Re-Enchantment*.

53. See, e.g.: Margot Adler, *Drawing Down the Moon: Witches, Druids, Goddess-Worshippers, and Other Pagans in America Today* (1979; Boston: Beacon Press, 1986); Erik Davis, *TechGnosis: Myth, Magic and Mysticism in the Age of Information* (1998; London: Serpent's Tail, 1999); Tanya Luhrmann, *Persuasions of the Witch's Craft: Ritual Magic in Contemporary England* (Cambridge: Harvard University Press, 1989).

54. Adler, *Drawing Down the Moon*, 286, 289.

55. See, e.g.: Matt Hills, *Fan Cultures* (London: Routledge, 2002); Henry Jenkins, *Fans, Bloggers, and Gamers: Media Consumers in a Digital Age* (New York: New York University Press, 2006); Christopher Partridge, *The Re-Enchantment*; Possamai, *Religion and Popular Culture*; Glen Yeffeth, ed., *Taking the Red Pill: Science, Philosophy and Religion in the Matrix* (West Sussex: Summersdale, 2003).

56. Hills, *Fan Cultures*, 117–30.

57. Jenkins, *Fans*.

58. Joseph Campbell, *The Hero with a Thousand Faces* (Princeton, N.J.: Princeton University Press, 1949).

59. Possamai, *Religion and Popular Culture*.

60. Pels, "Introduction: Magic and Modernity."

61. Quoted in Partridge, *The Re-Enchantment*, 131.

62. Quoted in Robert Ellwood, *The Sixties Spiritual Awakening: American Religion Moving from the Modern to the Postmodern* (New Brunswick, N.J.: Rutgers University Press, 1994), 201.

63. Patrick Curry, *Defending Middle-Earth: Tolkien, Myth and Modernity* (1997; London: Harper Collins Publishers, 1998), 131.

64. See, e.g.: John Ronald Reuel Tolkien, "On Fairy Stories" (1939), http://brainstorm-services .com/wcu-2004/fairystories-Tolkien.pdf; Stef Aupers, " 'Better than the Real World': On the Reality and Meaning of Online Computer Games," in *Narratives, Roles and Beliefs in the New Age Era: Homo Narrans—Homo Ludens—Homo Religiosus*, ed. Theo Meder, *Fabula* 48, no. 3/4 (2007): 250–69; Michael Saler, "Modernity, Disenchantment, and the Ironic Imagination," *Philosophy and Literature* 28, no. 1 (2004): 137–49.

65. Tolkien, "On Fairy Stories," 12.

66. Aupers, *In de ban van moderniteit*; Aupers, "Better than the Real World."

67. Joseph Pine, II, and James H. Gilmore, *The Experience Economy: Work Is Theatre and Every Business Is a Stage* (Boston: Harvard Business School Press, 1999). See also: Bauman, *Postmodernity*; Jeremy Rifkin, *The Age of Access: The New Culture of Hypercapitalism, Where All of Life Is a Paid-for Experience* (New York: Penguin Putnam Inc., 2000).

68. Ibid., 36.

69. Ibid., 34.

70. Stephen Kline, Nick Dyer-Witheford, and Greig de Peuter, *Digital Play: The Interaction of Technology, Culture, and Marketing* (Montreal: McGill-Queen's University Press, 2003), 20.

71. Aupers, "Better than the Real World."

72. Ibid.; Bartle, *Designing Virtual Worlds*; Brad King and John Borland, *Dungeons and Dreamers: The Rise of Computer Game Culture—From Geek to Chic* (New York: McGraw-Hill, 2003).

73. Sherry Turkle, "Our Split Screens," *Etnofoor* 15, no.1/2 (2002): 18.

74. Bartle, *Designing Virtual Worlds*, 61–62.

75. See, e.g.: Stef Aupers, Dick Houtman, and Peter Pels, "Cybergnosis: Technology, Religion, and the Secular," in *Religion: Beyond a Concept*, ed. Hent de Vries (New York: Fordham University Press, 2008), 687–703; Davis, *TechGnosis*.

76. See, e.g.: Mark Dery, *Escape Velocity: Cyberculture at the End of the Century* (New York: Grove, 1996).

77. See, respectively: R. V. Kelly 2, *Massively Multiplayer Online Role-Playing Games* (Jefferson: McFarland & Company, 2004), 85; John Perry Barlow, *A Declaration of the Independence of Cyber-space* (1993), http://homes.eff.org/~barlow/Declaration-Final.html (20-9-2008) (two quotes); Michael Heim, *The Metaphysics of Virtual Reality* (New York: Oxford University Press, 1993); and Margaret Wertheim, *The Pearly Gates of Cyberspace: A History of Space from Dante to the Internet* (London: Virago Press, 1999).

78. The quote from Moriarty comes from the lecture "The Point Is" (1996; http://ludix.com/moriarty/point.html). The second quote, about magic, comes from the blog Terranova: http://terra nova.blogs.com/terra_nova/2005/09/magic.html.

79. Weber, "Science as a Vocation," 155.

80. See, e.g.: Luckmann, *Invisible Religion*; Possamai, *Religion and Popular Culture*.

81. Anthony Giddens, *The Constitution of Society* (Cambridge: Polity Press, 1984).

82. Luhrmann, *Persuasions*.

83. Huizinga, *Homo Ludens*, 13.

84. Bartle, *Designing Virtual Worlds*, 155–56.

85. Wouter Gomperts, "Herinneringen uit het hiervoormaals: Sociale-erfenisfantasieën van ex-cliënten van reïncarnatietherapie," in *Overdragen en eigenmaken: Over sociale erfenissen*, ed. Christien Brinkgreve, *Amsterdams Sociologisch Tijdschrift* 21 (1994): 197–227.

86. Titus Rivas, "Vroegere levens op de Titanic," *Prana: Tijdschrift voor spiritualiteit en de rand-gebieden der wetenschappen*, no. 107 (June/July 1998): 83–88.

87. Luhrmann, *Persuasions*, 333.

88. Meyer, "Religious Sensations," 712.

89. Klein et al., *Digital Play*, 21.

90. Don Slater, *Consumer Culture and Modernity* (1997; Cambridge: Polity Press, 2008), 111–12.

91. See, e.g.: Bartle, *Designing Virtual Worlds*; Kelly, *Massively Multiplayer Online Role-Playing Games*.

92. David Freeman, *Creating Emotions in Games: The Craft and Art of Emotioneering* (Boston: New Riders, 2004).

93. Robert Marks, *Everquest Companion: The Inside Lore of a Game World* (New York: McGraw-Hill/Osborne, 2003), 76. See also: T. L. Taylor, *Play Between Worlds: Exploring Online Game Culture* (Cambridge: MIT Press, 2006); Jack M. Balkin and Beth Simone Noveck, eds., *The State of Play: Law, Games, and Virtual Worlds* (New York: New York University Press, 2006).

94. Peter van der Veer, "Spirituality in Modern Society," in *Religion: Beyond a Concept*, ed. Hent de Vries (New York: Fordham University Press, 2008), 794.

95. Boyle, *Authenticity*, 104; Frank, *Conquest of Cool*, 31.

96. See, e.g., Aupers, Houtman, and Pels, "Cybergnosis."

97. See, respectively, Theodor W. Adorno and Max Horkheimer, *Dialectic of Enlightenment: Philosophical Fragments*, trans. Edmund Jephcott (1940; Stanford, Calif.: Stanford University Press, 2002); Guy Debord, *Society of the Spectacle* (1967; New York: Zone, 1994); Baudrillard, *Simulations*.

98. Bruno Latour, *We Have Never Been Modern*, trans. Catherine Porter (Cambridge: Harvard University Press, 1993).

99. Danielle Egan and Stephen D. Papson, "'You either get it or you don't': Conversion Experiences and the Dr. Phil Show," *Journal of Religion and Popular Culture* 10 (Summer 2005): 11.

100. Pels, "Introduction: Magic and Modernity," 22–26.

101. Luckmann, *Invisible Religion*.

102. For arguments that it does, see Steve Bruce, *God Is Dead: Secularisation in the West* (Oxford: Blackwell, 2002); for the reverse, see Paul Heelas, *Spiritualities of Life: New Age Romanticism and Consumptive Capitalism* (Oxford: Blackwell, 2008).

103. See, e.g.: Dery, *Escape Velocity*; Steven Levy, *Hackers: Heroes of the Computer Revolution* (1984; New York: Penguin Books, 1994).

104. See, e.g., Kimberly J. Lau, *New Age Capitalism: Making Money East of Eden* (Philadelphia: University of Pennsylvania Press, 2008).

105. Slater, *Consumer Culture*.

106. Lau, *New Age Capitalism*, 9.

Fulfilling the Sacred Potential of Technology: New Edge Technophilia, Consumerism, and Spirituality in Silicon Valley, by Dorien Zandbergen

1. This process can in turn be seen as a continuation of earlier romantic and spiritualist movements. See Wouter Hanegraaff, *New Age Religion and Western Culture: Esotericism in the Mirror of Secular Thought* (Leiden: Brill, 1996); Peter Pels, "Religion, Consumerism, and The Modernity of The New Age," *JASO* 29, no. 3 (1998): 263–72; Stef Aupers, Dick Houtman, and Peter Pels, "Cybergnosis: Technology, Religion, and the Secular," in *Religion: Beyond a Concept*, ed. Hent de Vries (New York: Fordham University Press, 2008), 687–703. While acknowledging that the term *counterculture* is misleading in suggesting a radical difference from a supposedly "mainstream" society, I will nonetheless use it in this chapter to refer to a set of philosophies and ideals that have emerged in most large postwar cities in the Northern and Western hemispheres since the 1960s. For an account of the ways in which the "counterculture" has affected corporate and institutional practice as much as it was a "youth phenomenon," see Thomas Frank, *The Conquest of Cool* (Chicago: University of Chicago Press, 1999).

2. Hanegraaff, *New Age Religion*, 12, 97.

3. Ibid., 97.

4. The New Age emphasis on "naturalness" implies, according to New Age researcher Andrew Ross, a widespread rejection of "external technologies" and an emphasis on "the self-healing capacities inherent in the natural system" (Ross, "New Age Technoculture," in *Cultural Studies*, ed. L. Grossberg, Cary Nelson, and Paula Treichler [New York: Routledge, 1992], 539).

5. Interview by Dorien Zandbergen with Ken Goffman (a.k.a. R. U. Sirius), founder of the New Edge magazine *Mondo 2000*, Mill Valley, Calif., September 2005.

6. For extended discussions of the relationship between religion and media technologies, see, e.g.: Aupers, Houtman, and Pels, "Cybergnosis"; Birgit Meyer, "Religious Remediations: Pentecostal Views in Ghanaian Video-Movies," *Postscripts* 1, no. 2/3 (2005): 155–81; Peter Pels, "The Confessional Ethic and the Spirits of The Screen: Reflections on the Modern Fear of Alienation," *Etnofoor* 15 (2002): 91–119; J. Sconce, *Haunted Media: Electronic Presence from Telegraphy to Television* (Durham, N.C.: Duke University Press, 2000); Hent de Vries and Samuel Weber, eds., *Religion and Media* (Stanford, Calif.: Stanford University Press, 2001); Jeremy Stolow, "Religion and/as Media," *Theory, Culture & Society* 22 (2005): 119–45; D. Noble, *The Religion of Technology: The Divinity of Man and the Spirit of Invention* (Harmondsworth, Middlesex: Penguin, 1999). For thorough discussions of the relationship between religion and consumerism, see, e.g.: R. L. Moore, *Selling God: American Religion in the Marketplace of Culture* (Oxford: Oxford University Press, 1994); C. Campbell, *The Romantic Ethic and the Spirit of Modern Consumerism* (Oxford: Blackwell, 1990); Pels, "Religion, Consumerism and The Modernity of The New Age."

7. Marcel Mauss, *The Gift: The Form and Reason for Exchange in Archaic Societies* (London: Cohen & West, 1990); B. Pfaffenberger, "Fetishised Objects and Humanised Nature: Towards an Anthropology of Technology," *Man*, n.s. 23, no. 2 (1988): 236–52.

8. Many examples can be found in Michael Benedikt's collection *Cyberspace: First Steps* (Cambridge: MIT Press, 1992), in which Benedikt describes cyberspace as the latest stage in an evolutionary movement from matter to spirit, with "the ballast of materiality cast away—cast away . . . perhaps finally" (4). In the same volume, Michael Heim describes cyberspace as a Platonic "home for the mind and the heart," (61), and Nicole Stengers dubs cyberspace a "paradise" (52).

9. Timothy Leary, *Chaos and Cyber Culture* (Berkeley, Calif.: Ronin Publishing, 1994), 5.

10. Pfaffenberger, *Fetishised Objects*, 239.

11. For an overview of the various "generations" of cyber-religion theorists, see M. T. Højsgaard, "Cyber-religion: On the Cutting Edge Between the Virtual and the Real," in *Religion and Cyberspace*, ed. M. T. Højsgaard and M. Warburg (Abingdon, Oxon: Routledge, 2005), 50–63.

12. Hanegraaff, in *New Age Religion*, 33, dubs the New Edge "a trend too recent to put into clear perspective."

13. While I conducted research in Silicon Valley in 2005, *New York Times* journalist John Markoff published a history of the relationship between Silicon Valley and computer culture: Markoff, *What the Dormouse Said: How the Sixties Counterculture Shaped the Personal Computer Industry* (New York: Viking Penguin, 2005). Two years later, Stanford University communication scientist Frederick Turner published a similar account, with different focus, on the same relationship: Turner, *From Counterculture to Cyberculture: Stewart Brand, the Whole Earth Network, and the Rise of Digital Utopianism* (Chicago: University of Chicago Press, 2006).

14. The New Edge has also been produced in an international context. Particularly in the late 1980s and early 1990s, there was much "New Edge traffic" between San Francisco, Amsterdam, and London. Yet it can be said that the cradle of New Edge is the San Francisco Bay Area. For this reason, I will leave the international dimension of New Edge aside in this chapter.

15. http://leda.lycaeum.org/?ID = 2780. Last visited August 10, 2009.

16. For extended descriptions of the rave movements, see, e.g.: G. St. John, ed., *Rave Culture and Religion* (London: Routledge, 2004); M. Collin, *Altered State: The Story of Ecstasy Culture and Acid*

House (London: Serpent's Tail, 1997); M. Dery, *Escape Velocity: Cyberculture at the End of the Century* (New York: Grove Press, 1996).

17. A. M. Butler, *Cyberpunk. Harpenden* (Herts: Pocket Essentials, 2000).

18. Aupers, Houtman, and Pels, in "Cybergnosis," have used the term *cybergnosis* to refer to gnostic awareness induced by digital technologies. In this chapter, however, I also discuss gnostic awareness induced by nondigital technology. I therefore use the more general concept of "gnostic technologies" as a way of describing the various kinds of technical artifacts and concepts that have been embraced for gnostic awareness.

19. Hanegraaff, *New Age Religion*, 519.

20. Paul Heelas, *The New Age Movement: The Celebration of the Self and the Sacralization of Modernity* (Oxford: Blackwell, 1996), 19.

21. Hanegraaff, *New Age Religion*, 516.

22. Heelas, *The New Age* Movement, 19.

23. Tom Wolfe, *The Electric Kool-Acid Acid Test* (New York: Farrar, Straus and Giroux, 1968).

24. Ibid., 44.

25. Aldous Huxley, *The Doors of Perception and Heaven and Hell* (1954; Harmondsworth, Middlesex: Penguin, 1961), 21, 22; mentioned in Wolfe, *Electric Kool-Aid Acid Test*, 44, 45.

26. Ibid.

27. Huxley, *The Doors of Perception*, 24.

28. Ibid., 31.

29. Ibid., 38.

30. Wolfe, *Electric Kool-Aid Acid Test*, 133. In a later book on a new literary style that he labeled New Journalism, Wolfe describes how he did his research for writing the *Electric Kool-Aid Acid Test*. The "new-journalist" method was based on interviews, on the careful observation of nonverbal language, and on what anthropologists would call "participant observation" (Tom Wolfe, *The New Journalism* [New York: Harper & Row, 1973], 32).

31. Wolfe, *Electric Kool-Aid Acid Test*, 133.

32. Ibid., 206.

33. Ibid., 205.

34. Ibid., 150.

35. Ibid., 38.

36. P. Braunstein and M. W. Doyle, eds., *Imagine Nation: The American Counterculture of the 1960s and '70s* (New York: Routledge, 2002).

37. This poem can be found on several places on the Internet. I found it reprinted on the cover of the countercultural computer magazine *People's Computer* 6, no. 4 (January-February 1978).

38. Wolfe, *Electric Kool-Aid Acid Test*, 39.

39. Ibid.

40. Ibid., 103.

41. K. Goffman and D. Joy, *Counterculture Through the Ages: From Abraham to Acid House* (New York: Villard, 2004), 289–93.

42. Braunstein and Doyle, *Imagine Nation*, 35, 36.

43. Interview by Dorien Zandbergen with Stewart Brand, Sausalito Calif., December 2005.

44. Interview, Zandbergen and Brand, December 2005.

45. S. Levy, *Hackers: Heroes of the Computer Revolution* (Garden City, N.Y.: Doubleday, 1984), 130.

46. *People's Computer* 6, no. 3 (November-December 1977): 31.

47. Ibid., 34, 35.

48. T. Nelson, *ComputerLib/Dream Machines* (self-published, 1974), 4.

49. Ibid., section 3, "Dream Machine."

50. Brand and his *Whole Earth Catalog* form the main theme of Turner's *From Counterculture to Cyberculture*. This book gives an excellent account of the relationship between the counterculture and the Silicon Valley computer industry. Turner does not, however, address the spiritual component of this interaction. See also Frederick Turner, "Where the Counterculture Met the New Economy: The WELL and the Origins of Virtual Community," *Technology and Culture* 46 (2005): 485–512.

51. Buckminster Fuller, in *Whole Earth Catalog* (Spring 1969), 4.

52. Ibid., 3.

53. Buckminster Fuller, *No More Secondhand God*, quoted in *Whole Earth Catalog* (Spring 1969), 3.

54. Interviews by Dorien Zandbergen with former Portola volunteers Phillis Cole (Scotts Valley, Calif., November 2005), Joanne Koltnow (Palo Alto, Calif., November 2005), and Bob Albrecht, using Internet conversation program Skype, January 2006.

55. See Barbara B. Brown, *New Mind, New Body* (New York: Harper & Row, 1974), and G. E. Schwartz and J. Beatty, eds., *Biofeedback: Theory and Research* (New York: Academic Press, 1977).

56. The use of biofeedback in extrainstitutional settings is indicated by the concerns, expressed in various manuals and books on biofeedback theory, about its legitimacy. Various practitioners were concerned with situating the practice in the domain of "legitimate science," while trying to keep it from "fad-panacea exploitation," as the editor of one manual formulates it (Hugh Downes, quoted in Barbara Brown, *New Mind New Body*, xi).

57. G. Null and S. Null, *Biofeedback, Fasting and Meditation* (New York: Pyramid Books, 1974), 188. See, for a discussion of the problem of defining these altered states, Schwartz and Beatty, *Biofeedback*, 105. Manuals that are explicitly "New Agey" in their interpretation of biofeedback are: Null and Null, *Biofeedback*; and D. B. Payne and C. T. Reitano, *BioMeditation: The Scientific Way to Use the Energy of the Mind* (Brookline, Mass.: BFI, 1977).

58. Null and Null, *Biofeedback*, 87

59. Ibid., 78, 88.

60. Ibid., 88.

61. Ibid., 17.

62. Payne and Reitano, *BioMeditation*, 17.

63. Interview by Dorien Zandbergen with Phillis Cole, Scotts Valley, Calif., November 2005.

64. See also Levy, *Hackers*, for an account of the disillusionment of Frederick Moore, a frequent Portola visitor.

65. M. W. Krueger, *Artificial Reality* (Reading, Mass.: Addison-Wesley, 1983), xii, xiii.

66. M. W. Krueger, *Artificial Reality*, 2nd ed. (Reading, Mass.: Addison-Wesley, 1991), 261.

67. Krueger, *Artificial Reality* (1983), 3.

68. Interview by Dorien Zandbergen with Galen Brandt, Santa Cruz, Calif., January 2006. See also her website: www.virtualgalen.com.

69. Interview by Dorien Zandbergen with "Verona," Santa Cruz, Calif., January 2006; *Verona* is a pseudonym.

70. Interview, Zandbergen and Brandt, January 2006.

71. T. G. West, *Thinking like Einstein: Returning to Our Visual Roots with the Emerging Revolution in Computer Information Visualization* (New York: Prometheus, 2004), 41.

72. Krueger, *Artificial Reality* (1983), 5.

73. Interview, Zandbergen and Brandt, January 2006.

74. B. Laurel, *Computers as Theatre* (Reading, Mass.: Addison-Wesley, 1991), 200.

75. Ibid., 197.

76. Ibid., 118.

77. Nelson, *ComputerLib*, 10.

78. Krueger, *Artificial Reality* (1983), xii, 261.

79. Ibid., 1.

In Their Own Image? Catholic, Protestant, and Holistic Spiritual Appropriations of the Internet, by Ineke Noomen, Stef Aupers, and Dick Houtman

NOTE: This chapter first appeared as Ineke Noomen, Stef Aupers, and Dick Houtman, "In Their Own Image? Catholic, Protestant, and Holistic Spiritual Appropriations of the Internet," *Information, Communication, and Society* 14 (2011): 1097–117; it has been reprinted courtesy of Taylor & Francis Ltd.

1. Bryan Wilson, *Contemporary Transformations of Religion* (Oxford: Oxford University Press, 1976), 88.

2. See, e.g.: Erik Davis, *TechGnosis: Myth, Magic and Mysticism in the Age of Information* (1998; London: Serpent's Tail, 2004); David Noble, *The Religion of Technology: The Divinity of Man and the Spirit of Invention* (1997; New York: Penguin Books, 1999).

3. Such a study is particularly relevant for debates about the social and cultural shaping of technology in general and the religious shaping of the Internet in particular. For the former, see, e.g., Donald MacKenzie and Judy Wajcman, eds., *The Social Shaping of Technology*, 2nd ed. (1985; Buckingham: Open University Press, 1999); for the latter, see Heidi Campbell, "Spiritualising the Internet: Uncovering Discourses and Narratives of Religious Internet Usage," *Online: Heidelberg Journal of Religions on the Internet* 1, no. 1 (2005).

4. Stef Aupers and Dick Houtman, "'Reality Sucks': On Alienation and Cybergnosis," in *Cyber Space—Cyber Ethics—Cyber Theology*, ed. Erik Borgman, Stephan van Erp, and Hille Haker, special issue *Concilium: International Journal of Theology*, no. 1 (2005): 81–89; Maria Beatrice Bittarello, "Another Time, Another Space: Virtual Worlds, Myths and Imagination," in *Online: Heidelberg Journal of Religions on the Internet* 3, no. 1 (2008); Brenda E. Brasher, *Give Me That Online Religion* (2001; New Brunswick, N.J.: Rutgers University Press, 2004); Davis, *TechGnosis*; Mark Dery, *Escape Velocity: Cyberculture at the End of the Century* (New York: Grove Press, 1996); Anastasia Karaflogka, "Religion on—Religion in Cyberspace," in *Predicting Religion: Christian, Secular and Alternative Futures*, ed. Grace Davie, Paul Heelas, and Linda Woodhead (Burlington, Aldershot: Ashgate 2003), 191–202; Stephen D. O'Leary, "Cyberspace as Sacred Space: Communicating Religion on Computer Networks," in *Religion Online: Finding Faith on the Internet*, ed. Lorne L. Dawson and Douglas E. Cowan (New York: Routledge, 2004), 37–58; Sherry Turkle, *Life on the Screen: Identity in the Age of the Internet* (New York: Simon & Schuster, 1995); Margaret Wertheim, *The Pearly Gates of Cyberspace: A History of Space from Dante to the Internet* (New York: Norton, 1999).

5. For these terms, see, respectively: Nicole Stenger, "Mind Is a Leaking Rainbow," in *Cyberspace: First Steps*, ed. Michael L. Benedikt (1991; Cambridge: MIT Press, 1992), 52; Michael Benedikt, "Introduction," in *Cyberspace*, ed. Benedikt, 14; Michael Heim, *The Metaphysics of Virtual Reality* (Oxford: Oxford University Press, 1993); and Wertheim, *The Pearly Gates of Cyberspace*, 16.

6. Brasher, *Give Me That Online Religion*; O'Leary, "Cyberspace as Sacred Space"; Karaflogka, "Religion on—Religion in Cyberspace."

7. Brasher, *Give Me That Online Religion*, 13.

8. See, e.g.: Lorne L. Dawson and Douglas E. Cowan, "Introduction," in *Religion Online*, ed. Dawson and Cowan, 1–16; Charles Ess, Akira Kawabata, and Hiroyuki Kurosaki, "Cross-Cultural Perspectives on Religion and Computer-Mediated Communication," in *Journal of Computer-Mediated Communication* 12, no. 3 (2007): 939–55; Morten T. Højsgaard and Margit Warburg, "Introduction: Waves of Research," in *Religion and Cyberspace*, ed. Morten T. Højsgaard and Margit Warburg (London: Routledge, 2005), 1–11.

9. Karine Barzilai-Nahon and Gad Barzilai, "Cultured Technology: The Internet and Religious Fundamentalism," *The Information Society* 21, no. 1 (2005): 26.

10. Campbell, "Spiritualising the Internet," and Heidi Campbell, *When Religion Meets New Media* (London: Routledge, 2010).

11. For Islam, see Gary Bunt, *Virtually Islamic: Computer-Mediated Communication and Cyber Islamic Environments* (Cardiff: University of Wales Press, 2000), and Gary Bunt, *Islam in the Digital Age: E-Jihad, Online Fatwas and Cyber Islamic Environments* (London: Pluto Press, 2003); for Christians, see Heidi Campbell, *Exploring Religious Community Online: We Are One in the Network* (New York: Peter Lang, 2005); and for pagans, see Douglas E. Cowan, *Cyberhenge: Modern Pagans on the Internet* (New York: Routledge, 2005).

12. For authority, see, e.g., Eileen Barker, "Crossing the Boundary: New Challenges to Religious Authority and Control as a Consequence of Access to the Internet," in *Religion and Cyberspace*, ed. Højsgaard and Warburg, 67–85. For identity, see, e.g.: Mia Lövheim, "Young People, Religious Identity, and the Internet," in *Religion Online*, ed. Dawson and Cowan, 59–73; Helen A. Berger and Douglas Ezzy, "Mass Media and Religious Identity: A Case Study of Young Witches," *Journal for the Scientific Study of Religion* 48, no. 3 (2009): 501–14.

13. Randolph Kluver and Pauline Hope Cheong, "Technological Modernization, the Internet, and Religion in Singapore," *Journal of Computer-Mediated Communication* 12, no. 3 (2007): 1126.

14. Ibid., 1139.

15. Pauline Hope Cheong and Jessie Poon, "WWW.FAITH.ORG: (Re)structuring Communication and the Social Capital of Religious Organizations," *Information, Communication & Society* 11, no. 1 (2008): 89–110.

16. See, e.g.: Campbell, *When Religions Meet New Media*; Stephen Jacobs, "Virtually Sacred: The Performance of Asynchronous Cyber-Rituals in Online Spaces," *Journal of Computed-Mediated Communication* 12, no. 3 (2007): 1103–21; Campbell, *When Religions Meet New Media*, 6.

17. Campbell, *When Religions Meet New Media*.

18. Paul Dekker and Peter Ester, "Depillarization, Deconfessionalization and Deideologization: Empirical Trends in Dutch Society," *Review of Religious Research* 37, no. 4 (1996): 325–41.

19. Protestantse Kerk in Nederland (PKN), *Leren leven van de verwondering: Visie op het leven en werken van de kerk in haar geheel* (Utrecht: Protestantse Kerk in Nederland, 2005), 7, 6; available online at: http://www.pkn.nl/3/site/uploaded Docs/www51818_PLD_verwondering(1)(1)(1).pdf.

20. Stef Aupers, "'We are all gods': New Age in the Netherlands 1960–2000," in *The Dutch and Their Gods: Secularization and Transformation of Religion in the Netherlands since 1950*, ed. Erik Sengers (Hilversum: Verloren, 2005), 181–201.

21. Wouter J. Hanegraaff, *New Age Religion and Western Culture: Esotericism in the Mirror of Secular Thought* (Leiden: Brill, 1996); Paul Heelas, *The New Age Movement: The Celebration of Self and the Sacralization of Modernity* (Oxford: Blackwell, 1996).

22. Colin Campbell, "The Cult, the Cultic Milieu and Secularization," in *The Cultic Milieu: Oppositional Subcultures in an Age of Globalization*, ed. Jeffrey Kaplan and Heléne Lööw (1972;

Walnut Creek, Calif.: AltaMira Press, 2002), 12–25; Thomas Luckmann, "The Privatization of Religion and Morality," in *Detraditionalization: Critical Reflections on Authority and Identity*, ed. Paul Heelas, Scott Lash, and Paul M. Morris (Oxford: Blackwell, 1996), 73–83.

23. Quirijn Visscher, "Elke Christen z'n eigen zender," *Trouw*, May 6, 2010; http://www .trouw.nl/tr/nl/4324/nieuws/archief/article/detail/1593707/2010/05/06/Elke-christen-z-n-eigen-zen der.dhtml.

24. Ibid.

25. Campbell, "Spiritualising the Internet."

26. Second Vatican Council, "Communio et Progressio" (1971), available online at: http://www .vatican.va/roman_curia/pontifical_councils/pccs/documents/rc_pc_pccs_doc_23051971_commu nio_en.html; see also Pontifical Council for Social Communications, "Ethics in Internet" (2002), online available at: http://www.vatican.va/roman_curia/pontifical_councils/pccs/documents/rc_pc_ pccs_doc_20020228_ethics-Internet_en.html.

27. See, e.g., Christian Smith, with Michael Emerson, Sally Gallagher, Paul Kennedy, and David Sikkink, *American Evangelicalism: Embattled and Thriving* (Chicago: University of Chicago Press, 1998), on American evangelicalism, and Johan Roeland, "Selfation: Dutch Evangelical Youth Between Subjectivization and Subjection" (Ph.D. dissertation, VU Amsterdam, 2009), on evangelicalism in the Netherlands.

28. Campbell, *When Religion Meets New Media*, 26.

29. Respectively, Macha M. Nightmare, *Witchcraft and the Web: Weaving Pagan Traditions Online* (Toronto: ECW Press, 2001), 42; Christopher Penczak, *City Magick: Urban Rituals, Spells, and Shamanism* (York Beach: Weiser Books, 2001), 253; and Phyllis Curott, "Foreword," in: Nightmare, *Witchcraft and the Web*, 17.

30. Maria Bakardjieva, "Virtual Togetherness: An Everyday-Life Perspective," *Media, Culture & Society* 25, no. 3 (2003): 219–313; Willem de Koster, " 'Nowhere I could talk like that': Togetherness and Identity on Online Forums" (Ph.D. dissertation, Erasmus University Rotterdam, 2010); Don Slater, "Social Relationships and Identity Online and Offline," in *Handbook of New Media: Social Shaping and Consequences of ICTs*, ed. Leah Lievrouw and Sonia Livingstone (London: Sage Publications, 2002), 533–46.

31. Barzilai-Nahon and Barzilai, "Cultured Technology"; Campbell, "Spiritualising the Internet."

Contributors

Maria José A. de Abreu has worked on questions of embodiment, technology, and movement in the context of the Charismatic Catholic movement in contemporary Brazil. a religious movement for which notions of breath (as *pneuma*, or spirit, but also as a force of decentered subjectivity) are central. She is currently affiliated with the University of Lisbon and is a visiting scholar at Columbia University, where she is developing a project on identity and substitution at the crossroads of ethnography, history, literature, and urban legends.

Stef Aupers is Associate Professor at Erasmus University Rotterdam and a member of the Center for Rotterdam Cultural Sociology (CROCUS). Most of his research deals with modern spirituality and trends of "re-enchantment" in the modern world. His most recent books are *Religions of Modernity: Relocating the Sacred to the Self and the Digital* (2010; edited with Dick Houtman), *Paradoxes of Individualization* (2011; with Dick Houtman and Willem de Koster) and *Under the Spell of Modernity* (forthcoming). He is currently working on a book about online computer gaming.

Elizabeth A. Castelli is Professor and Chair of the Department of Religion at Barnard College. Her research interests include: bodily pieties in early Christianity, especially martyrdom and asceticism; the afterlives of biblical texts; antiwar religious performances; and, most recently, the theme of confession. She is the author of *Martyrdom and Memory: Early Christian Culture Making* (2004), the coauthor of *The Postmodern Bible* (1995), and the editor of numerous anthologies and special issues of journals, most recently *God and Country*, a special issue of *differences: A Journal of Feminist Cultural Studies* (2007).

Sanne Derks is the author of *Power and Pilgrimage: Dealing with Class, Gender and Ethnic Inequality at a Bolivian Marian Shrine* (2009). Currently she works as a lecturer in Applied Psychology at the Fontys

University of Applied Sciences in Eindhoven. She also directed the documentary *Mary in Times of Crises* (2012), on the intertwinement of religion and economy in the devotion to the Virgin of Urkupiña in Bolivia.

Grietje Dresen works as a senior researcher and lecturer at the Institute for Gender Studies and at the Faculty of Philosophy, Theology and Religious Studies at Radboud University Nijmegen. She is the author of *Onschuldfantasieën: Offerzin en Heilsverlangen in Feminisme en Mystiek* (1990) and *Is dit mijn Lichaam? Visioenen van het Volmaakte Lichaam in Katholieke Moraal en Mystiek* (1998) and has edited or co-edited several volumes covering hermeneutical rereadings and rewritings of topics in the history of moral theology.

Matthew Engelke is Reader in the Department of Anthropology at the London School of Economics. His book *A Problem of Presence: Beyond Scripture in an African Church* (2007) won the 2008 Clifford Geertz Prize and the 2009 Victor Turner Prize. He is the editor of Prickly Paradigm Press and the *Journal of the Royal Anthropological Institute*.

Galit Hasan-Rokem is Max and Margarethe Grunwald Professor of Folklore at the Mandel Institute of Jewish Studies at the Hebrew University of Jerusalem. She has held many visiting appointments, most recently at the Department of Anthropology of the University of California, Berkeley, and at the Divinity School of the University of Chicago. Her books include *Proverbs in Israeli Folk Narratives: A Structural Semantic Analysis* (1982); *Adam Le-Adam Gesher—Proverbs of Georgian Jews in Israel* (1993); *Web of Life: Folklore and Midrash in Rabbinic Literature* (2000); and *Tales of the Neighborhood: Jewish Narrative Dialogues in Late Antiquity* (2003), as well as the co-edited volumes *The Wandering Jew: Interpretations of a Christian Legend* (1986, with A. Dundes); *Untying the Knot: Riddles and Other Enigmatic Modes* (1996, with D. Shulman); *Defiant Muse: Hebrew Feminist Poems from Antiquity to the Present* (1999, with S. Kaufman and T. Hess); *Jewish Women in Pre-state Israel: Life History, Politics and Culture* (2008, with M. Shiloh and R. Kark); *A Companion to Folklore* (Blackwell Companions to Anthropology, 2012, with R. Bendix).

Ernst van den Hemel teaches at Amsterdam University College. He has recently completed his dissertation on the poetics of John Calvin's *Institutes*. In 2009 he published *Calvinisme en Politiek: Tussen Verzet en Berusting*.

Dick Houtman is Professor of Cultural Sociology at Erasmus University Rotterdam and a member of the Center for Rotterdam Cultural Sociology (CROCUS). His principal research interests are the "spiritualization" of religion and the "culturalization" of politics in Western societies since the 1960s. His three most recent books are *Farewell to the Leftist Working Class* (2008; with Peter Achterberg and Anton Derks), *Religions of Modernity*

(2010; co-edited with Stef Aupers), and *Paradoxes of Individualization* (2011; with Stef Aupers and Willem de Koster).

Willy Jansen is Professor of Gender Studies at Radboud University Nijmegen and a member of the Royal Dutch Academy of Arts and Sciences. Her main fields of interest include gender, religion, pilgrimage, sexuality, and education. Her publications include *Women Without Men: Gender and Marginality in an Algerian Town* (1987), *Lokale Islam* (1985; edited), *Islamitische Pelgrimstochten* (1991; co-edited with Huub de Jonge), *Waanzin en Vrouwen* (1991; co-edited with Christien Brinkgreve), and *Gender, Nation and Religion in European Pilgrimage* (2012; co-edited with Catrien Notermans). In the context of the NWO Research Program The Future of the Religious Past, she co-edited, with A. K. Hermkens and C. Notermans, *Moved by Mary: The Power of Pilgrimage in the Modern World* (2009).

Miranda Klaver is affiliated researcher in the Cultural Anthropology Department of the VU University Amsterdam and lecturer in the Theology Department of the Christian University of Applied Sciences Ede. Being an anthropologist as well as a theologian, she researches religious change in Dutch Protestantism and focuses on the rise of Pentecostal and evangelical churches. Her Ph.D. thesis is titled: "This Is My Desire: A Semiotic Perspective on Conversion in an Evangelical Seeker Church and a Pentecostal Church in the Netherlands" (June 2011).

Michiel Leezenberg teaches in the Philosophy Department and in the M.A. program Islam in the Modern World of the University of Amsterdam. Among his publications are *Contexts of Metaphor* (2001), *Wetenschapsfilosofie voor Geesteswetenschappen* (2001, with Gerard de Vries), and various articles in philosophy and intellectual history. His current research interests include the history and philosophy of the human sciences, in particular linguistics, the intellectual history of the modern Muslim world, and the comparative study of orientalisms.

Donald S. Lopez, Jr., is the Arthur E. Link Distinguished University Professor of Buddhist and Tibetan Studies at the University of Michigan. His books include *Elaborations on Emptiness: Uses of the Heart Sutra* (1996); *Prisoners of Shangri-La: Tibetan Buddhism and the West* (1998); *The Story of Buddhism: A Concise Guide to Its History and Teachings* (2001); *The Madman's Middle Way: Reflections on Reality of the Tibetan Monk Gendun Chopel* (2006); *Buddhism and Science: A Guide for the Perplexed* (2008); and *In the Forest of Faded Wisdom: 104 Poems of Gendun Chopel* (2009). His edited volumes include *Buddhist Hermeneutics* (1988); *Buddhism in Practice* (1995); *Religions of Tibet in Practice* (1997); *Curators of the Buddha: The Study of Buddhism under Colonialism* (1995); *Buddhist Scriptures* (2004); and *Critical Terms for the Study of Buddhism* (2005). In 2000 he was elected to the American Academy of Arts and Sciences.

Birgit Meyer is Professor of Religious Studies at Utrecht University. She has conducted research on missions and local appropriations of Christianity, Pentecostalism, popular culture, and video-films in Ghana. Her publications include *Translating the Devil: Religion and Modernity Among the Ewe in Ghana* (1999), *Globalization and Identity: Dialectics of Flow and Closure* (1999; edited with Peter Geschiere), *Magic and Modernity: Interfaces of Revelation and Concealment* (2003; edited with Peter Pels), *Religion, Media, and the Public Sphere* (2006; edited with Annelies Moors), and *Aesthetic Formations: Media, Religion and the Senses* (2009). She is vice-chair of the International African Institute (London), a member of the Royal Dutch Academy of Arts and Sciences, and one of the editors of *Material Religion*.

W. J. T. Mitchell is the Gaylord Donnelley Distinguished Service Professor at the University of Chicago. He is the author of *What Do Pictures Want?* (2005), *The Last Dinosaur Book: The Life and Times of a Cultural Icon* (1998), *Picture Theory* (1994), *Art and the Public Sphere* (1993), *Landscape and Power* (1992), *Iconology* (1987), *The Language of Images* (1980), *On Narrative* (1981), and *The Politics of Interpretation* (1984). His most recent books are *Cloning Terror: The War of Images, 9–11 to the Present* (2011), *Critical Terms for Media Studies* (2010; edited with Mark Hansen), and *Seeing Through Race* (2012). He is the editor of the journal *Critical Inquiry*.

Annelies Moors is an anthropologist at the University of Amsterdam, where she directs a research program entitled Muslim Cultural Politics. She has done fieldwork in Palestine, Yemen, and the Netherlands and has published on Muslim family law, wearing gold, postcards of Palestine, migrant domestic labor, and fashionable and not so fashionable styles of Islamic dress. Her most recent publications include: *Religion, Media, and the Public Sphere* (2006; co-edited with Birgit Meyer), *Narratives of Truth in Islamic Law* (2008; co-edited with Baudouin Dupret and Barbara Drieskens), and *The Colonial and Post-colonial Governance of Islam* (2011; co-edited with Marcel Maussen and Viet Bader). She is currently writing a book on face veiling in the Netherlands and conducting research on informal Islamic marriages.

David Morgan is Professor of Religion at Duke University, with an additional appointment in the Department of Art, Art History, and Visual Studies. Author of *The Lure of Images* (2007), *The Sacred Gaze* (2005), *Protestants and Pictures* (1999), and *Visual Piety* (1998), he is also an editor of the journal *Material Religion* and co-editor of a book series at Routledge entitled Religion, Media, Culture. His latest book is entitled *The Embodied Eye: Religious Visual Culture and the Social Life of Feeling* (2012).

Ineke Noomen studied religion and spirituality on the Internet at the Sociology Department of Erasmus University Rotterdam in the context of the Cyberspace Salvations project of the NWO Research Program The Future of the Religious Past. She now teaches in Erasmus University's Bachelor program in Sociology.

Catrien Notermans works as a senior researcher and lecturer at the Department of Cultural Anthropology and Development Sociology at Radboud University Nijmegen. Her fields of interest include religion, kinship, and gender. She is the co-editor of *Not Just a Victim: The Child as Catalyst and Witness of Contemporary Africa* (2011) and the co-editor of *Moved by Mary: The Power of Pilgrimage* (2009). Her most recent publication is an edited book on pilgrimage with Willy Jansen, entitled *Gender, Nation, and Religion in European Pilgrimage.*

Peter Pels is Professor in the Anthropology of Sub-Saharan Africa in the Institute of Cultural Anthropology and Development Sociology of the University of Leiden. He has published on religion and politics in situations of colonial contact (*A Politics of Presence: Contacts Between Missionaries and Waluguru in Late Colonial Tanganyika*, 1999), the history of anthropology (*Colonial Subjects*, 1999; co-edited with Oscar Salemink), the anthropology of magic (*Magic and Modernity: Interfaces of Revelation and Concealment*, 2003; co-edited with Birgit Meyer), and social science ethics (*Embedding Ethics*, 2005; co-edited with Lynn Meskell). He was the editor-in-chief of *Social Anthropology/Anthropologie sociale*, the journal of the European Association of Social Anthropologists, from 2003 until 2007. He is currently finishing a book entitled *The Spirit of Matter: Religion, Modernity, and the Power of Objects.*

Freddie Rokem is the Emanuel Herzikowitz Professor for Nineteeth- and Twentieth-Century Art and teaches in the Department of Theatre Studies at Tel Aviv University, where he has served as the Dean of the Yolanda and David Katz Faculty of the Arts. He is also a permanent guest professor at Helsinki University and has been a visiting professor at Stanford University, the Free University in Berlin, the University of Munich, the University of Stockholm, and the University of California, Berkeley. Rokem's book *Performing History: Theatrical Representations of the Past in Contemporary Theatre* (2000) received the Association for Theatre in Higher Education (ATHE) Prize for the best theater studies book of 2001. He is also the author of *Strindberg's Secret Codes* (2004) and *Philosophers and Thespians: Thinking Performance* (2010). He is co-editor of *Jews and the Making of Modern German Theatre* (2010; with Jeanette Malkin).

José C. M. van Santen is Senior Lecturer and Researcher at the Institute of Cultural and Social Studies, the University of Leiden, and until recently was a member of the Amsterdam School for Social Science Research (ASSR) in the NWO Research Program Islam in Africa. She is the author of *They leave their jars behind: The Conversion of Mafa Women* *to Islam (Cameroon)* (1993) and the editor of *Development in Place: Perspectives and Challenges* (2008). As a fellow of the Netherlands Institute of Advanced Study in the Humanities and Social Sciences (NIAS), she is finishing a book entitled *Fundamentalism, Islamic Education, and Youth Culture in Cameroon.*

Irene Stengs, a cultural anthropologist, is Senior Researcher at the Meertens Instituut in Amsterdam, where she works on festive culture and ritual in the Netherlands. She is the author of *Worshipping the Great Modernizer: King Chulalongkorn, Patron Saint of the Thai Middle Class* (2009) and the editor of a book on the Dutchness of multicultural ritual in the Netherlands, entitled *Nieuw in Nederland: Feesten en Rituelen in Verandering* (2012).

Dorien Zandbergen is currently a post-doc researcher at the Department of Cultural Anthropology and Development Sociology of the University of Leiden. She conducted research in the context of the Cyberspace Salvations project of the NWO Research Program The Future of the Religious Past and defended her PhD thesis "New Edge: Technology and Spirituality in the San Francisco Bay Area" in May 2011. Her current research is on future forms of technological embodiment.

Index